i

Uncle John's
TRIUMPHANT 20TH ANNIVERSARY
BATHROOM READER®

By the
Bathroom Readers'
Institute

Bathroom Readers' Press
Ashland, Oregon

OUR "REGULAR" READERS RAVE!

"Today my friend was asking me who my best teacher was. I said 'Uncle John.' He was confused and asked me if I was home-schooled. My response? No. I was bathroom-schooled. He went out and bought a copy. Thanks for the education!"

—**Tyler**

"I have taken a few of my *Bathroom Readers* to work at the Post Office, and I can't put them down or someone will pick them up and start reading. My co-workers even go around asking trivia questions on the material they read."

—**Mayra**

"I just wanted to thank you for all your inspiration. I am a singer/songwriter from New Jersey. I've already written three songs based directly on people or events I read about in your books."

—**Eric**

"Just wanted to let you guys know that you are the BEST. I absolutely love your books—I've been reading them since I was ten, and I'm sure I've read all eight or nine in my collection fifteen times each, at least. And thanks to you, I now have an interesting (albeit annoying) tidbit for every conversation! Many kudos."

—**Kristin**

"I just wanted to say how wonderful I have found the *Bathroom Readers*. I have bought several for friends and family, and they are truly addicted now. Everyone seems to spend an extra 10 minutes in the bathroom in order to read."

—**Lisa**

"I have many of your books and enjoy reading them at work. By the way, my job is making toilet paper."

—**Don**

UNCLE JOHN'S
TRIUMPHANT 20TH ANNIVERSARY
BATHROOM READER®

For information, write:
The Bathroom Readers' Institute,
P.O. Box 1117, Ashland, OR 97520
www.bathroomreader.com

Cover design by Michael Brunsfeld,
San Rafael, CA (*Brunsfeldo@comcast.net*)

BRI "technician" on the back cover: Larry Kelp

Uncle John's Triumphant 20th Anniversary Bathroom Reader®
by the Bathroom Readers' Institute

ISBN-13: 978-1-59223-093-8
ISBN-10: 1-59223-093-8

Library of Congress Catalog Card Number:
2007934971

Printed in the United States of America

Fourth Printing: May 2012

4 5 6 7 8   16 15 14 13 12

Hiya, Sophie! Hiya, Jesse!

THANK YOU!

The Bathroom Readers' Institute sincerely thanks the people whose advice and assistance made this book possible.

Gordon Javna	Claudia Bauer
John Dollison	Melinda Allman
Thom Little	Laurel Graziano
Brian Boone	Lisa Meyers
Amy Miller	David Fitzpatrick
Jay Newman	Monica Maestas
Julia Papps	David Calder
Judy Plapinger	Dr. Wendy Schilling
Malcolm Hillgartner	Maggie Javna
Jahnna Beecham	Judy Wicklund
Lorraine Bodger	(Mr.) Mustard Press
Maggie McLaughlin	Steven Style Group
Michael Brunsfeld	Viola Rose
Angela Kern	John Javna
Jeff Altemus	Eddie Deezen
Sydney Stanley	Janet Spencer
JoAnn Padgett	Michelle Sedgwick
Jolly Jeff Cheek	Richard "Noodling" Willis
Scarab Media	Publishers Group West
Jef Fretwell	Raincoast Books
Nancy Toeppler	Porter the Wonder Dog
Karen Malchow	Thomas Crapper

* * *

"A room without a book is like a body without a soul." —**Cicero**

v

CONTENTS

Because the BRI understands your reading needs, we've
divided the contents by length as well as subject.

Short—a quick read
Medium—2 to 3 pages
Long—for those extended visits, when something
a little more involved is required
* Extended—for those leg-numbing experiences

TWENTY YEARS
...AND COUNTING!

Has it really been two whole decades since we first asked, "How come there are no books made especially for the bathroom?" Hard to believe, but that little idea turned into what the industry calls a "publishing phenomenon." (Are we blushing?) Some of you have been with us from the very beginning, and some of you are new friends. Welcome to the family! And don't let the shiny cover fool you, this is still the same great *Bathroom Reader* that you've come to know and love. At 600 pages, it's our biggest all-new edition yet—our anniversary present to the best group of fans any book series could have. We really went all out to bring you a truly special edition. What's in here? Lots!

• **Turning 20.** We tell you what life was like in 1987 (a car phone cost $1,400), plus we have facts about famous "20"s, and some thoughts on what can happen in 20 years.

• **Historical Oddities.** The futuristic world of 1960 (as seen in 1939), a trip to Mars (as seen in 2007), the real Zorro, and the world's first home computer (it had no screen or keyboard).

• **Pop Science.** Eco-friendly used-tire houses, green graveyards, and the greenest nation. Plus how to make your own jello (it isn't pretty), how to build a "memory palace," and everything you always wanted to know about cancer...but were afraid to ask.

• **Life Is Strange.** The guy who almost won a Russian beauty contest (for women), Superman's surreal journey back to the big screen, and a long-lost mom. And from the animal world, obscure marsupials, incredible beetles, killer frogs, and the wild kingdom of farts.

In fact, we found so much great stuff, we couldn't fit it all into this giant book. But have no fear—we're already working on next year's *Bathroom Reader*! Our dedicated in-house Outhouse staff of writers and researchers are committed to bringing you (at least) 20 more years of absorbing reading material! In the meantime...

Keep on going with the Flow!

—**Uncle John, the BRI Staff, and Porter the Wonder Dog**

YOU'RE MY INSPIRATION

It's always interesting to find out where the architects of pop culture get their ideas. These may surprise you.

WILE E. COYOTE AND ROAD RUNNER. Looney Tunes animator Chuck Jones created the pair in 1948. The idea was sparked by a passage from Mark Twain's 1872 book, *Roughing It*, about Twain's travels through the Wild West as a young man. In the passage, Twain noted that the "coyotes are starving and would chase a roadrunner."

WINONA RYDER. Winona Horowitz's first name comes from Winona, Minnesota, the town in which she was born. At age 15, the budding actress and her father chose the stage name Ryder from a Mitch Ryder album that they both liked.

HOUSE, M.D. The popular TV doctor was created by David Shore as an homage to Sherlock Holmes: Both use the same deductive techniques; both have loyal assistants (Dr. Watson and Dr. Wilson); and both live in Apartment 221. Interestingly, Sir Arthur Conan Doyle based the character of Holmes on a real doctor he knew who, like Dr. House, specialized in creative diagnosis.

WONDERLAND. As a young man, Lewis Carroll (real name: Charles Dodgson) lived in Ripon, England. The city is a geological oddity—due to the weak gypsum subsoil that makes up the landscape, deep sinkholes can suddenly appear in the ground. Literary historians believe these strange holes helped inspire Carroll to create *Alice's Adventures in Wonderland*. In fact, the book's original title was *Alice's Adventures Underground*.

ALIEN. Screenwriter Dan O'Bannon read an article about the spider wasp, a bee that reproduces by paralyzing a spider and then laying its eggs on the spider's abdomen. When the bee larvae hatch, they eat right through the still-living spider. This macabre image haunted O'Bannon's dreams for years, but from them he was able to form the basis for the insectlike alien creature that became one of Hollywood's all-time most-feared villains.

You may rely on it: The answer cube inside a Magic 8-Ball is a 20-sided *icosahedron*.

COURT TRANSQUIPS

The verdict is in! Court transquips make for some of the best bathroom reading there is. These were actually spoken, word for word, in a court of law.

Lawyer: All right. I want to take us back to the scene at the bar for a moment again. [*The witness gets up and starts to leave.*] No, you don't have to get up. I just want to take you back there *mentally*.

Q: Now, your complaint alleges that you have had some problems with concentration since the accident. Does that condition continue today?
A: No, not really. I take a stool softener now.

Defendant, acting as his own lawyer: Did you get a good look at my face when I took your purse?

Q: Were you freebasing the cocaine?
A: No. I bought it.

Q: So, besides your wife and children, do you have any other animals or pets?

Q: Meaning no disrespect, sir, but you're 80 years old, wear glasses, and don't see as well as you used to. So, tell me, just how far *can* you see?
A: I can see the moon. How far is that?

Q: And what was he wearing under the mask?
A: Uhh, his face?

Q: Officer, is it true you keep a lock on your locker?
A: Yes, sir.
Q: Do you trust your fellow officers with your life?
A: Above all else, sir.
Q: Now, if you trust your fellow officers with your life, why would you find it necessary to keep a lock on your locker?
A: Well, sir, we share the complex with the courthouse, and sometimes defense lawyers have been known to walk through there.

Q: Ma'am, were you cited in the accident?
A: Yes, sir! I was so 'cited I peed all over myself!

The Air Force uses half of the fuel purchased by the U.S. government.

FOOD ORIGINS

Once again the BRI asks—and answers—the question: Where does all this stuff come from?

SALAD BAR

Rax Restaurants was a fast-food chain that thrived in the Midwest by offering fare not typically served at fast-food restaurants, such as roast beef and baked potatoes. In 1964 Rax added another novelty item: fresh salads. But salads proved to not be very efficient fast food—they took too long to prepare. So, Rax created a "salad bar"—a buffet of lettuces and vegetables where customers assembled their own salads. Only a handful of Rax stores in Ohio had the salad bars, but the concept took off (and was widely copied) after Rax put salad bars in its stores nationwide in the mid-1970s to cash in on the era's health-food fad.

AIRPLANE PEANUTS

Most airlines don't serve meals anymore, but nearly all still hand out free bags of peanuts or pretzels. The tradition began in August 1936, when Colonial Airlines gave away free peanuts to all travelers. Reason: A month earlier, Colonial had become the first carrier to sell beer and cocktails. They decided to give out the peanuts to make people thirsty so they'd buy more liquor.

RICE KRISPIES TREATS

In 1928 Mildred Day graduated from Iowa State University with a degree in home economics. She was hired by Kellogg's to work in their test kitchen to develop an inexpensive baked good (made from Kellogg's products) that Camp Fire Girls could make and sell at fundraisers. She took an old folk recipe for dessert bars—a combination of puffed wheat cereal, vinegar, and molasses—and substituted Rice Krispies cereal for the puffed wheat (and butter and marshmallows for the vinegar and molasses). Kellogg's patented the name and recipe for "Rice Krispies Treats" but didn't introduce the concoction to the general public (aside from the Camp Fire Girls) until 1940, when it started printing the recipe on all packages of Rice Krispies.

There are 7.5 miles of information on a standard DVD.

COIN OF THE REALM

Interesting trivia about American coins.

- The U.S. Mint's first production in 1793 consisted of 11,178 copper cents. Today the Mint produces an average of 14.7 million coins per *day*.

- How many paper bills does the Mint print every year? Not a single note. (That's the job of the Bureau of Engraving and Printing.)

- The first real woman (not a symbolic figure) on an American commemorative coin was also the only *foreign* woman—Queen Isabella of Spain, on an 1893 quarter dollar.

- Why did the Indian Head cent make way for the Lincoln penny in 1909? To commemorate Honest Abe's 100th birthday. The Lincoln Memorial on the back was added for his 150th in 1959.

- That 1909 Lincoln penny was the first circulating (non-commemorative) American coin to depict a real person.

- By law, the design for U.S. coins must feature "an impression emblematic of liberty."

- When the U.S. Mint began in the 1790s, one of the places it bought copper was from a firm owned by Paul Revere.

- First African American to be depicted on an American coin: Booker T. Washington, on a half-dollar coin, 1946–51. (First African American on a U.S. postage stamp: Booker T. Washington, 1940, 10¢.)

- The U.S. Mint has made coins for more than 40 foreign countries. Venezuela was the first, in 1875.

- First commemorative coin in U.S. history: The 1892 Columbian Exposition half-dollar, marking the 400th anniversary of Christopher Columbus's discovery of the Americas.

- From 1873 to 1878, the U.S. Mint produced a silver dollar exclusively for trade with China.

- The 1792 law establishing the U.S. Mint made defacing, counterfeiting, or embezzling of coins by Mint employees punishable by death.

OOPS!

Everyone's amused by tales of outrageous blunders—probably because it's comforting to know that someone else is screwing up even worse than we are. So go ahead and feel superior for a few minutes.

FAIR-WEATHER FRIENDS

"Denver International Airport was reputed to be an 'all-weather' facility that would operate seamlessly in a blizzard, but when it failed during the December 2006 snowstorms (it was closed for 45 hours), an embarrassed airport spokesman, Chuck Cannon, admitted he'd like 'to choke the person who came up with the "all-weather" term for airports.' The Associated Press then discovered a 1992 interview with the same Chuck Cannon, bragging to reporters about his new 'all-weather' airport."

—News of the Weird

PROVING THEIR POINT

"English supermarket chain Somerfield has apologized after it said Easter eggs were to celebrate the 'birth' of Jesus. Ironically, the public relations slip-up came as it sought to publicize a survey suggesting a high level of ignorance about Easter's religious significance."

—BBC News

SPAM FILTER FOOLISHNESS

"Cobb County, Georgia, schools will be paying an extra $250,000 for a phone system from Bell South because the low bidder's e-mail was removed by the school's spam filter. Elite Telecom Systems was asked for additional information on their bid and told they must reply by e-mail. School finance director and computer expert Robert Morales says that Elite Telecom should be smart enough to know how to outwit their spam filter when sending them e-mail and so it's Elite's fault, not the school system's."

—*Atlanta Journal-Constitution*

LIGHTS—CAMERA—YOU'RE UNDER ARREST!

"Several LAPD officers rushed and handcuffed actor Erik Palladino

---

Odds that the turkey you'll eat this Thanksgiving will be a frozen turkey: 75%.

after he was seen brandishing a gun on the streets of Hollywood in February 2007. The only problem: The gun was fake and the only thing Palladino was shooting was a scene for the film, *Hotel California*. Director Geo Santini didn't seem too worried as his star was placed in handcuffs, telling the perplexed actor, 'You gotta be on set tomorrow, that's what the contract says!' Once the crew explained to cops that they were shooting a movie, Palladino was released and filming resumed."

—TMZ.com

PEDAL TO THE METAL

"A valet accidentally drove an amputee's specially equipped car through the Baptist Medical Towers' front entrance, knocking the amputee from his wheelchair. Harold Towne, 52, of Pensacola, was sitting between two sets of automatic glass doors at the hospital when his Chevrolet Cavalier, driven by Adrian Young, hit the wheelchair. Towne was treated and released from the emergency room after the accident. Young, 22, had been returning Towne's car when he apparently confused the car's special gas pedal for the brake. The gas pedal is to the left of the brake. Young pressed the wrong pedal, and the car accelerated. He swerved to avoid a vehicle and went through the outer doors. Willie Sellars, 77, of Pensacola said he and several others were in a waiting area near where the accident happened. 'All of a sudden I heard this noise,' Sellars said. 'I thought it was a tornado.' There was no damage to the car, other than a small dent, but the entrance was heavily damaged, with glass everywhere." (And the wheelchair was totaled.)

—*Pensacola News Journal*

*   *   *

SEE THE LIGHT

The largest statue of Jesus Christ in the United States is "Christ of the Ozarks," located on Magnetic Mountain near Eureka Springs, Arkansas. It's 67 feet tall. Builders wanted to make it taller, but, according to Federal Aviation Association regulations, they would have had to put a blinking red light on top of Christ's head.

IN A PICKLE

Cleopatra is said to have attributed her beauty to eating pickles.
Here are some more fascinating facts about pickles.

First known pickling of a cucumber: in Mesopotamia (Iraq), 2500 B.C.

Cucumbers are native to India, and were spread from there across Western Asia about 5,000 years ago.

East Asians were eating pickled foods as far back as 3,000 years ago—but not cucumbers, which were introduced (to China) about 2,000 years ago.

Pickles are mentioned in the *The Epic of Gilgamesh*, the world's oldest known piece of literature, written by the Sumerians around 4000 B.C.

Christopher Columbus planted cucumbers for pickling in what is now Haiti.

Who wrote: "On a hot day in Virginia, I know nothing more comforting than a fine spiced pickle, brought up trout-like from the sparkling depths of the aromatic jar below the stairs of Aunt Sally's cellar." (Answer: Thomas Jefferson.)

The cucumber is a fruit, so technically the pickle is, too.

The H. J. Heinz Company first sold pickles in 1876. At the 1893 Chicago World's Fair, Heinz gave away "pickle pins" (green pins shaped like pickles with the word "Heinz" on them). Heinz still makes them…and has given away more than 100 million.

Pickles are mentioned in the Bible (in *Numbers* and *Isaiah*.)

Pickle Packers International, the pickle workers union, was founded in 1893 at #1 Pickle and Pepper Plaza, St. Charles, Illinois. (They still represent about 95% of all pickle workers in North America.)

"Pickle" comes from the Middle English *pikel*, meaning "a spicy gravy served with meat."

Different types of pickles are pickled differently. Nearly all start with the *brine fermentation* process—salting and soaking for weeks in brine. They get their different tastes and textures —"bread and butter," "kosher dill," etc.— from what's added to the brine: vinegar, sugar, and spices.

1987: THE YEAR THAT WAS

In celebration of the Bathroom Reader's *20th anniversary,
here's what was going on in the rest of the world in 1987.*

• *The Tracey Ullman Show*, a variety program on the new Fox Network, airs a short cartoon called "The Simpsons."

• **Sen. Gary Hart**, the likely 1988 Democratic presidential nominee, drops out of the race after reports surface of an extramarital affair.

• Scientists spot a naked-eye **supernova**, the first since 1604.

• **Jim Bakker** resigns as head of PTL Ministries after admitting to having an affair with his secretary, Jessica Hahn.

• Surgeons in Baltimore perform the first dual **heart-lung transplant**.

• In July, the **Dow Jones Industrial Average** closes above 2,500 for the first time in history. The market crashes the following October, plunging 800 points.

• **Prozac** is approved for sale in the United States.

• While visiting Berlin in June, President Reagan gives a speech imploring Soviet leader Mikhail Gorbachev to **tear down the Berlin Wall.**

• Nineteen-year-old West German pilot Mathias Rust evades Soviet fighter jets and **lands a plane in Moscow's Red Square**. He's imprisoned for a year.

• **Margaret Thatcher** is elected to her third consecutive term as British prime minister.

• **The Minnesota Twins** beat the St. Louis Cardinals in seven games to win their first World Series championship.

• **World population** reaches 5 billion. (Twenty years later, it's about 6.6 billion.)

• America celebrates the **200th anniversary of the U.S. Constitution**.

• **Born in 1987:** Hilary Duff, Maria Sharapova, Joss Stone, Lil' Bow Wow, Marco Andretti, Elizabeth Smart.

• **Died in 1987:** Danny Kaye, Fred Astaire, Andy Warhol, Woody Hayes, James Baldwin, Maria von Trapp, Rudolf Hess, Andres Segovia, Clare Boothe Luce, Liberace, John Huston, and Joseph Campbell.

Welsh coal miners once believed that washing coal dust from their backs weakened their spines.

A NATION OFF THE GRID

After September 11, 2001, few people in the United States (and maybe in the world) felt good about a trip to the gas station. But is anybody doing anything about it? Yes—Denmark.

INDEPENDENCE

In 1973, in response to the Yom Kippur War between Israel and Egypt, the Organization of Arab Oil Producing Countries began the infamous "Arab oil embargo"—any country that supported Israel in the war would stop receiving shipments of oil. That meant the United States, Japan, and most of Europe. The effect was devastating—soaring oil prices set off a worldwide recession. Most of the affected countries quickly initiated plans to conserve energy: The United States lowered the speed limit to 55 mph and started programs like "turn off the lights at night." But when the crisis ended, most nations dropped those programs and went back to their old ways. Denmark was different: Being 99% dependent on foreign oil, it was particularly badly hit by the embargo. Determined never again to be at the mercy of their oil suppliers, the Danes kept conserving and worked to produce their own energy.

A COMMUNITY EFFORT

In 1976 the Danish public got behind an ambitious (and expensive) program to become entirely energy-independent, and, with the development of new, clean energy systems, to get out of the foreign oil business completely. Some of the steps taken:

• Strict energy-efficiency standards were placed on all buildings.

• Gas and automobiles were heavily taxed. (Today new cars are taxed at more than 105% of the cost of the car.)

• "District heating systems" were implemented throughout the country, reusing normally wasted heat produced by power plants by piping it directly into homes. Today more than 60% of Danish homes are heated this way.

• The government invested heavily in clean and renewable energy systems, especially wind power. Today 21% of Denmark's energy production comes from wind farms. On top of that, they lead the

---

Original name of New York's Park Avenue: 4th Avenue (until they built Central Park).

world in wind-power technology—another product to export. The industry has created more than 20,000 jobs.

• Rebate campaigns helped people buy more energy-efficient—and therefore more expensive—home appliances. Today more than 95% of new appliances bought in Denmark have an "A" efficiency rating ("A" is the best; "G" is the worst.)

• They started drilling for—and finding—more oil and natural gas within their own waters in the North Sea. (Showing that no plan is perfect, these efforts have long been opposed by environmentalists.)

• In 2005 the government committed $1 billion to develop and integrate better solar, tidal, and fuel-cell technology.

RESULTS

Denmark is a small nation geographically—roughly half the size of Maine—with a population of about 5.5 million, so that has to be taken into account when comparing it to larger and more populous countries. Still, the Danes' accomplishments are startling. Remember that in 1973 Denmark was 99% dependent on foreign oil? Today they produce more oil than they use, and have become oil *exporters*. They also produce enough energy to cover all their own needs and sell the extra to other countries, the only European nation to do so. And their energy conservation programs have been so successful that over the last 30 years, even with extensive modernization and a 7% increase in population, their annual energy use has remained basically the same. Still, although Denmark has among the highest taxes in the world, it also has one of the highest standards of living. And polls show that a majority of Danes would pay even higher taxes to remain self-sufficient and live free of fossil-fuel dependence.

In 2007 the Danes set further goals for the country: They hope to be able to provide 75% of all their energy consumption from wind farms by 2025—less than two decades from now. "We aim to make Denmark independent of oil, gas, and coal in the long term," Prime Minister Anders Fogh Rasmussen said, "and strengthen our position as a world leader in clean energy." Svend Auken, a member of the Danish Parliament, added, "It need not be dull, it need not be boring, and we don't have to give up our lifestyle. We just have to be a little bit smarter about how we live."

Movie theater owners' pick for 1926 "Actor of the Year": Rin Tin Tin.

IT'S TAKE ME OUT TO THE MUSTACHE NIGHT!

Minor league baseball teams will do almost anything to get fans to come to the ballpark. It's not just "free hat night" or "nickel beer night" anymore.

Promotion: Second Chance Night
Details: In 2006, the Fresno Grizzlies paid tribute to successful criminal rehabilitation. Probation officers got into the game for free and so did any fans who brought in a traffic ticket to the box office and promised to never do it again.

Promotion: McDreamy Day
Details: On the popular TV show *Grey's Anatomy*, Patrick Dempsey plays a handsome doctor whom female staff members call "Dr. McDreamy." The Hagerstown (Maryland) Suns' "McDreamy Day" included a medical scrubs fashion show and a medical terms spelling bee.

Promotion: Anger Management Night
Details: After a rival team's manager had a meltdown and was thrown out of a game, the Augusta (Georgia) Green Jackets made fun of the event (and the manager) by offering the first 250 fans free "stress balls" and DVDs of the Adam Sandler movie *Anger Management*.

Promotion: Britney Spears Baby Safety Night
Details: After Britney Spears was photographed in 2006 driving with her infant son in her lap instead of in a secure car seat, the Newark (New Jersey) Bears held this promotion. Fans who dressed as a baby, brought a baby toy, or brought an actual baby got in for free. And everybody in the stands received a brochure about baby safety.

Promotion: Kevin Federline Night
Details: The Fresno, California, Grizzlies honored one of Fresno's

The baseball glove was invented in Canada in 1883.

most famous local sons: Kevin Federline, rapper, former backup dancer, and Britney Spears's ex-husband. The first 3,000 fans got free "K-Fed" (temporary) tattoos. The night also included a video montage of Federline's "career highlights" and a dance contest between the Grizzlies' mascot and the local dance troupe to which Federline once belonged. (Federline himself was a no-show).

Promotion: Used Car Night
Details: Usually the giveaways provided by minor league teams are cheap stuff like keychains and bumper stickers. But in 2006 the San Antonio Missions held "Used Car Night." A dozen fans picked at random got used luxury automobiles. Among the prizes were a 1991 Jaguar and a 1990 Cadillac.

Promotion: Jose Canseco Juice Box Night
Details: Jose Canseco ended his steroid-tarnished career in 2006, playing with the Long Beach Armada. To poke fun at Canseco, the rival Fullerton Flyers gave away 500 juice boxes one night when the two teams played. The giveaway mocked both admitted "juicer" Canseco and the release of his steroid-exposé book *Juiced*.

Promotion: College Course Giveaway Night
Details: Fans in attendance at a Southwest Michigan Devil Rays game in 2006 received a certificate for a free three-credit course of their choice at nearby Kellogg Community College.

Promotion: Awful Night
Details: Grossest promotion ever? It might have been this one from the Altoona (Pennsylvania) Curve. Gross competitions and silly events were held all night, including bobbing for onions, a dead-fish-slingshot catch, and autograph sessions with random non-famous people. The first 1,000 fans received a photo of general manager Todd Parnell's gall bladder, which had been recently removed. One "lucky" fan actually won Parnell's gall bladder.

Promotion: Terrell Owens Unappreciation Night
Details: In 2006 the controversial football star Terrell Owens played for the Philadelphia Eagles. The Surf, the minor league baseball team from nearby Atlantic City, New Jersey, held this

promotion, in which fans received whoopee cushions with Owens's picture on them and could also buy 81-cent hot dogs (after Owens's jersey number). Fans who handed in authentic Owens memorabilia got two free seats—in the upper decks. After the game, the memorabilia was set on fire.

Promotion: World Record First Pitch Attempt Day
Details: In April 2007, the Brevard County (Florida) Manatees stadium opened at 6:00 a.m. to accommodate the promotion for a game that wouldn't start until 7:00 in the evening—13 hours away. The team invited fans to stand in line and each throw out a cere-monial first pitch in an attempt to break the record of 5,906 first pitches. (They were short by a few hundred.)

Promotion: *Office Space* Night
Details: The Bowie (Maryland) Baysox honored the 1999 work-place-drudgery comedy *Office Space* with a "flair" contest (one character in the movie works at a chain restaurant where lots of comical buttons—called "flair"—are part of the uniform) and a "Smash Technology for Charity" event. For a $1.00 fee, fans could live out a famous *Office Space* moment and destroy frustrating office equipment (computers, fax machines) with a baseball bat.

Promotion: Mustache Appreciation Night
Details: In May 2007, the Fresno Grizzlies encouraged fans to grow mustaches and solicit donations of friends and families to "sponsor" them. The funds were donated to charity on Mustache Appreciation Night. Fans who'd grown mustaches got in free and were eligible for "awards" in categories such as Best in Show, Best Tom Selleck Look-Alike, and Most Pathetic.

*   *   *

HOLLYWOOD QUIZ

Q: He received no salary for directing a movie that won him an Oscar for Best Director. Name the director.
A: Steven Spielberg. He forfeited his usual salary to make 1993's *Schindler's List.*

Mare mail: In its 19-month run, the Pony Express delivered 34,753 pieces of mail.

ME ME ME ME ME!!!

Why is this Bathroom Reader *so much bigger than any of our past new editions? Because we had to make extra room to fit in all of these giant egos.*

"What's offensive is that I'm portrayed as this prima donna with these sycophants telling me how great I am all the time. Yes, they do work for me, but we're working together for a higher good."
—**Demi Moore**

"Every decade has an iconic blonde—like Marilyn Monroe or Princess Diana—and right now, I'm that icon."
—**Paris Hilton**

"I sell more records than Bruce Springsteen. In the last five years, I've probably sold over 100 million of them. If he got $100 million [for a record deal], I should have got $500 million."
—**Simon Cowell**

"I am one of the greatest entrepreneurs and entertainers the world has ever encountered."
—**Sean (Diddy) Combs**

"I have 20,000 girlfriends, all around the world."
—**Justin Timberlake**

"There are maybe three countries left in the world where I can go and I'm not as well known as I am here. I'm a pretty big star, folks. 'Superstar,' I guess you could say."
—**Bruce Willis**

"All of the women on *The Apprentice* flirted with me—consciously or unconsciously. That's to be expected."
—**Donald Trump**

"My greatest competition is, well, me. I'm the Ali of today. I'm the Marvin Gaye of today. I'm the Bob Marley of today. I'm the Martin Luther King. And a lot of people are starting to realize that now."
—**R. Kelly**

"Beauty is grace and confidence. I've learned to accept and appreciate what nature gave me."
—**Lindsay Lohan**

"I'm one of those people you hate because of genetics."
—**Brad Pitt**

YODELING THE CLASSICS

*If you think the music your kids listen to is garbage, not so fast, Beethoven.
There's been music of questionable taste since the dawn of the record
industry. These bombs might not be musically entertaining,
but they are fun to read about. Here's a sample of
some of the weirdest albums ever made.*

LOU REED—METAL MACHINE MUSIC. In 1975 Reed
released this double LP consisting entirely of guitar feedback
and other ear-piercing electronic noise played back at various speeds. Recorded in his home on a four-track machine, Reed
claims the endless, monotonous noise is an avant-garde symphony.
(*Rolling Stone* called it "the tubular groaning of a galactic refrigerator.") It's rumored that Reed made the album in a hurry to fulfill a
recording contract. He disagrees. "I was serious about it," Reed
later said. "I was also really, really stoned."

JIMMY STURR—POLKA DISCO. In the 1970s, most young
people hated polka music, and their polka-loving grandparents
couldn't stand disco. Sturr, a polka musician, tried to unite the
two camps, but as it turns out, polka accordions and thumping
disco bass guitars don't mix very well.

MARY SCHNEIDER—YODELING THE CLASSICS.
Nicknamed "Australia's Queen of Yodeling," Schneider performs
well-known pieces of classical music, all yodeled. Rossini's "Barber
of Seville." Yodeled. Beethoven's "Minuet for Piano in G Major."
Yodeled. The "William Tell Overture." Yodeled.

HAVING FUN WITH ELVIS ON STAGE. In his later years,
Elvis Presley peppered his concert performances with all kinds of
odd patter—anecdotes and jokes, and the King going off on
bizarre tangents. His manager, Col. Tom Parker, found a loop-
hole in Presley's RCA Records contract that said *he* could keep
all the profits from any Presley album he released, as long as it
didn't contain Presley *singing*. Result: *Having Fun With Elvis on
Stage*—37 minutes of Presley's stage banter spliced together from

dozens of different shows. Parker marketed it as a "live" album, but it's really just Presley making wisecracks and comments, including "Look at all these things in my pants here," "I'm the NBC peacock," "Can I get a glass of water?" and "By the time this show is over, I'll have made a complete, total fool of myself." Presley also demonstrates the 11 different ways to pronounce "Memphis."

URBAN RENEWAL. On this tribute album, rappers and R&B singers perform the hits of one of their most beloved influences. Is it James Brown? George Clinton? Marvin Gaye? No—apparently, the real godfather of soul is soft-rock icon Phil Collins. Especially weird are the rapped versions of Collins's hits "In the Air Tonite" and "Sussudio."

THE TEMPLE CITY KAZOO ORCHESTRA—SOME KAZOOS. Pop and classical songs are played by large numbers of people with kazoos. The kazoo playlist includes "Stayin' Alive" by the Bee Gees, Led Zeppelin's "Whole Lotta Love," and "Also Sprach Zarathustra" (the theme from *2001: A Space Odyssey*).

THE ETHEL MERMAN DISCO ALBUM. Broadway star Merman was retired in 1979. Her show tunes and standards like "Everything's Coming Up Roses" weren't popular anymore, but disco was. Merman hated disco, but the 71-year-old agreed to make a disco album anyway. She knocked out new recordings of seven of her old Broadway classics in one afternoon. Producer Peter Matz then sped them up and added thumping disco beats. The album remains a favorite among kitsch enthusiasts.

FABIO AFTER DARK. In 1993 romance-novel cover model Fabio branched out by writing his own romance novels (*Pirate* and *Viking*), acting in margarine commercials, and recording this album. Interspersed with well-known love songs by the Stylistics, Billy Ocean, and Barry White, Fabio delivers rhyming monologues (backed by super-mellow saxophone music) about love and romance. "It's strange how I feel, everything seems so unreal," Fabio purrs in a very thick Italian accent. "There is no looking back, once you get a love attack."

RANDOM ORIGINS

Once again the BRI asks—and answers—the
question: Where does all this stuff come from?

TELETHONS

After writer Damon Runyon died of cancer in 1946, his friends in the entertainment industry established the Damon Runyon Cancer Research Foundation. The charity held its first big fund-raiser in April 1949—an unprecedented 16-hour television broadcast to solicit donations. This "telethon" ("television" plus "marathon") was the idea of NBC executive Sylvester Weaver, who thought big TV events would entice people to buy television sets. That first telethon wasn't much different from today's telethons: A big star hosted (Milton Berle); an on-screen bank of phone operators accepted call-in donations; and stars of movies, TV, and Broadway performed and pleaded for money. The broadcast raised $100,000 for cancer research.

READER'S DIGEST

In 1914 DeWitt Wallace suffered injuries fighting in World War I and was sent to a French hospital to recover. He and other injured soldiers were incredibly bored and wanted something to read. That gave Wallace an idea: a pocket-size anthology of short articles on a variety of topics including information, entertainment, health, and humor, written in basic, easy-to-understand English. (Sound familiar?) When he got back to the United States after the war, he approached several publishers with his idea. They all rejected it. So in 1922, he printed 5,000 copies of his magazine himself. All 5,000 sold (at 25 cents each), and the popularity of *Reader's Digest* grew quickly. By 1926, just four years after starting, the magazine had a circulation of 40,000. Today *Reader's Digest*'s readership is 38 million people in more than 60 countries.

WORLD CUP SOCCER

Soccer was an Olympic event in the early 20th century, but only amateurs could compete. Professional players wanted to participate, but the Olympics said "no," so FIFA, soccer's governing body, began holding tournaments for professional players in the 1910s, and later organized the Olympic tournaments for amateurs as well. By the late 1920s, FIFA and the International Olympic Committee (IOC) were again in a dispute over whether professionals should be allowed into the Olympics. To make matters worse, the 1932 Olympics were scheduled to be held in Los Angeles, and soccer wasn't popular in the United States. When the IOC announced that it planned to drop soccer from the Olympics, FIFA stepped in and organized its own world championship, open to professionals and amateurs. Dubbed the "World Cup" by FIFA president Jules Rimet, the inaugural 1930 tournament was won by Uruguay, the reigning Olympic champions. The event went on to become the most popular sporting event in the world: More than 1.2 billion people watched the 2006 World Cup final on TV.

TREE-SHAPED AIR FRESHENERS

In 1951 America was obsessed with cars, and many industries sprang up around the craze, from motels to drive-in movie theaters. A New York chemist named Julius Sämann figured that all that time spent in cars made them smell pretty bad, so in his garage-laboratory, he created the world's first air freshener made just for the car. Made of a material similar to a disposable beer coaster, Sämann's prototype was pine-scented, so he cut the freshener into the shape of a tree. Sämann got a patent and opened the Car-Freshener Corporation. Today, Little Trees are the top selling air fresheners in the world. And all of them are tree-shaped, even the top-selling "New Car Scent."

*   *   *

IF THE WORLD'S POPULATION WERE 200 PEOPLE...

...103 would be men, 97 would be women

...34 would be left-handed

...122 would be from Asia

...22 would be homeless

...96 would lack access to proper sanitation

...28 would be malnourished

...1 would eat at McDonald's daily

Lyndon Johnson was the first (and so far the only) U.S. president to be sworn in by a woman.

WINNERS...AND LOSERS

What if you won the lottery and became an instant millionaire? Would you lose your head and burn through the money? Or would you keep your cool and invest? (Tip: Uncle John would invest in toilet futures.)

WHAT ARE THE ODDS?

Your odds of winning the Florida Lotto jackpot are one in 22 million. But don't despair—that's better than your odds of winning the California SuperLotto Plus, which are one in 41 million. According to experts, if one person purchases 50 Lotto tickets each week, he or she *will* win the jackpot...about once every 5,000 years. Still, many people do beat those odds and win. But here's the big question: Do their lotto winnings make them happy?

WINDFALL

• When Juan Rodriguez won $149 million in a New York lottery, his wife of 17 years immediately filed for divorce and claimed half of his winnings.

• Michael Klingebiel was sued by his own mother in 1998 because he failed to share his $2 million jackpot.

• Ken Proxmire, a machinist from Michigan, took his $1 million winnings to California to start a car business with his brothers. Five years later he was bankrupt and back working as a machinist.

• Against all odds, Evelyn Adams won the New Jersey lottery not once, but twice—in 1985 and 1986. Her total winnings: $5.4 million. But she gambled those millions away, and today she lives in a trailer. "Everybody wanted my money," said Adams. "Everybody had their hand out. I never learned one simple word in the English language—'No.'"

LIVING LARGE

It seems like big money just means big trouble. It certainly did for Jack Whittaker of West Virginia. On Christmas 2002, Whittaker won the largest undivided jackpot in United States history—$314 million. Since then he's had hundreds of thousands of dollars in cash stolen from his cars, home, and office. He was arrested twice for drunken driving and pleaded "no contest" to a misdemeanor assault charge against a bar manager. Though Whittaker gave $20 million to churches, charities, and schools, it never seemed to be enough. On a daily basis, strangers rang his doorbell, eager to tell their stories and ask for financial help. The sudden wealth took a toll on his wife and family, too. His 16-year-old granddaughter, Brandi Bragg, who stood beaming by his side at the initial press conference, died of a drug overdose almost two years to the day after the big win. Whittaker's wife told the *Charleston Gazette* that she regrets everything. "I wish all of this never would have happened," said Jewel Whittaker. "I wish I would have torn the ticket up."

CRASH LANDINGS

• Willie Hurt of Belleville, Michigan, won $3.1 million in 1989. He divided his fortune between his ex-wife and cocaine, and by 1991, he was penniless and in jail, charged with murder.

• Victoria Zell, who shared an $11 million Powerball jackpot with her husband in 2001, was broke by 2006 and serving seven years in a Minnesota prison for vehicular manslaughter after killing a friend in a drug-and-alcohol-induced car crash.

• Thomas Strong, winner of $3 million in a Texas lottery in 1993, died in a shootout with police in 2006.

• In 1993 Janite Lee won $18 million in the Missouri Lottery. She spread the wealth around, donating huge sums to schools, political campaigns, community organizations, and charities. But Lee was *too* generous: she filed for bankruptcy in 2001 with just $700 left.

YOU THINK THAT'S BAD?

Jeffrey Dampier won $20 million in the Illinois lottery in 1996. After buying houses and cars for his siblings and parents, and treating 38 of his nearest and dearest friends to a Christmas Caribbean cruise, he was kidnapped and murdered by his own sister-in-law.

WHAT IF YOU WIN?

What if you are one of the rare few struck with "sudden-wealth syndrome"? What should you do with all that money? Enough people have faced this dilemma that organizations like the "Sudden Money Institute" and "The Affluenza Project" have formed to help winners through this life-altering event. Here's some advice from the experts:

1. Don't do anything rash. Don't make any promises to *anyone*.

2. Get out of the house. Better yet, get out of town until the media interest calms down.

3. Get an unlisted phone number.

4. Talk to a tax expert first to find out how much money you'll really get.

5. Talk to two or three financial planners/CPAs before choosing the one that seems like the best fit for you.

6. Take a small percentage of the money, say 5%, and do something just for fun.

7. Create a budget and try to stick with it. Think long-term.

8. Don't invest in anyone's business unless you know something about business.

9. A lot of expenses go along with buying a house (one of the top 10 things winners want to do first). Make a list of those expenses and your monthly payments before you jump into home-owning.

10. Think of yourself as a thousandaire, not a millionaire.

*　　*　　*

BART'S BLACKBOARD

Every episode of The Simpsons *opens with Bart writing something on the blackboard. Some of our favorites:*

"Wedgies are unhealthy for children and other living things."

"I am not certified to remove asbestos."

"Nerve gas is not a toy."

"I will not hang donuts on my person."

"The Pledge of Allegiance does not end with 'Hail Satan'."

"I am not the reincarnation of Sammy Davis Jr."

"My butt does not deserve a Web site."

FLUBBED HEADLINES

We're back with one of our favorite features. We've found that while a lot of flubbed headlines are real goofs, some are written by cheeky copywriters. Either way, they're funny.

Study Reveals Those Without Insurance Die More Often

Man Jumps Off 2nd Street Bridge: Neither Jumper Nor Body Found

WOMAN IMPROVING AFTER FATAL CRASH

Police to probe Barton's backside

COKE HEAD TO SPEAK

TV ads boost eating of obese children by 130%

Men threatened with guns while working on one of them's car

INFLAMMATION LANDS COLON ON THE DL

Global warming rally cut short by cold weather

Butte Blast Blamed on Leaking Gas

CHILDREN LIVING WITHOUT LIMBS LACK SUPPORT

Suicide squirrels driving utilities nuts

Swiss Accidentally Invade Liechtenstein

Dr. Fuchs off to the Antarctic

WOULD SHE CLIMB TO THE TOP OF MR. EVEREST AGAIN? ABSOLUTELY!

Fried Chicken Cooked in Microwave Wins Trip

Soviet virgin lands short of goal again

ANTWERP ZOO ASKS VISITORS NOT TO STARE AT THE CHIMPS

Harrisburg Postal Employees Gun Club Members Meet

LEGISLATOR WANTS TOUGHER DEATH PENALTY

North Korean Leader Names Ancient Frog "Ancient Frog"

Depp's Chocolate Factory Has Tasty Opening

Bon appetit: *Cuisine* is the French word for "kitchen."

BOX-OFFICE BLOOPERS

*Our latest installment of goofs from some
of Hollywood's most popular movies.*

Movie: *The Big Lebowski* (1998)
Scene: In the opening scene, a bowler attempts to convert a 7-10 split.
Blooper: A close-up shows the split being picked up with a different-colored bowling ball.

Movie: *Cast Away* (2000)
Scene: Chuck Noland (Tom Hanks) cuts his hand while trying to build a fire. Angry, he picks up a boxed volleyball with his bloodied hand and throws it.
Blooper: A little later, when Chuck picks up the volleyball and removes it from the box, the handprint is facing upward. This would have been impossible because the box was on the ground when he picked it up—the handprint should be facing down.

Movie: *The Royal Tenenbaums* (2001)
Scene: Chas (Ben Stiller) shows Royal (Gene Hackman) that a BB is still lodged in Chas's hand from years ago when Royal shot him.
Blooper: The close-up shows a watch on Chas's wrist; in the wider shots, he isn't wearing a watch.

Movie: *As Good As It Gets* (1997)
Scene: Carol (Helen Hunt) is riding on a bus.
Blooper: As the camera pans away, it reveals a sign on the side of the bus that says "Subway Shuttle—Not In Service."

Movie: *The Shawshank Redemption* (1994)
Scene: Warden Norton (Bob Gunton) offers Tommy (Gil Bellows) a cigarette.
Blooper: Although the scene takes place in the 1960s, the cigarette pack is clearly marked with the slogan "Marlboro Miles," a campaign that Marlboro ran in the 1990s.

Dustin Hoffman's big break: When Robert Redford turned down the lead role in *The Graduate*.

Movie: *Breakfast at Tiffany's* (1961)
Scene: Every scene with the cat(s).
Blooper: There are two different cats playing the same cat. Not an uncommon practice when filming animals—except in this case one is a yellow mackerel tabby and one is a yellow classic tabby.

Movie: *Star Wars: Episode III–Revenge of the Sith* (2005)
Scene: Anakin (Hayden Christensen) arrives on Mustafar and pulls his hood over his head.
Blooper: The shot clearly reveals Anakin has two normal hands, even though one of his arms was chopped off in the previous film and, up until this point, he had a robotic arm.

Movie: *Batman Begins* (2005)
Scene: The Batmobile is racing across the rooftops of Gotham City while confused cops are trying to figure out what it is.
Blooper: On a rooftop, a police officer yells into his bullhorn, ordering the Batmobile not to move. A bit later, another officer on the street says into his radio: "Can you at least tell me what it *looks* like?" Both cops are played by the same actor.

Movie: *Spider-Man 3* (2007)
Scene: At the very beginning of the movie, Mary Jane (Kirsten Dunst) sings a song on stage at a jazz club.
Blooper: We hear the audience applauding wildly...but we see them sitting completely still.

Movie: *Finding Nemo* (2003)
Scene: In an early scene, Marlin (Albert Brooks) and his wife Coral (Elizabeth Perkins), both clownfish, are about the same size.
Blooper: Female clownfish are actually twice as big as the males.

Movie: *The Fifth Element* (1997)
Scene: Leeloo (Milla Jovovich) is reconstructed from a strand of DNA. She is said to be pure—the "perfect being."
Blooper: Throughout the rest of the movie, Leeloo's "perfect" red hair reveals changing lengths of brown roots.

During Herman Melville's lifetime, *Moby Dick* sold only 3,000 copies.

THE COFFEE LAWSUIT

The "McDonald's coffee case" is frequently cited as the definitive frivolous lawsuit. But it was actually a complex—and legitimate—tale of terrible injury, corporate indifference, personal greed...and millions of dollars.

BACKGROUND

On February 27, 1992, 79-year-old Stella Liebeck was riding in the passenger seat of her Ford Probe in Albuquerque, New Mexico (her grandson, Chris, was driving). The Liebecks went through a McDonald's drive-through and Stella ordered an 8-ounce cup of coffee. Then they parked the car so she could safely add cream and sugar. Liebeck put the cup between her knees and pulled the far side of the lid up to remove it...but she pulled too hard. Liebeck spilled the entire cup of coffee into her lap. She was wearing sweatpants, which quickly absorbed the coffee and held it against her skin, forming a puddle of hot liquid. Frantically, she removed her pants. It took her about 90 seconds, but it was too late: The coffee had already scalded her thighs, buttocks, and groin.

Liebeck was rushed to a hospital, where doctors diagnosed her with third-degree burns (the worst kind) on 6% of her body, and lesser burns on an additional 16% of her body. In total, nearly a quarter of her skin had been burned. Liebeck remained hospitalized for eight days while she underwent skin-graft surgery. She also endured two years of follow-up treatment.

THE CASE

In 1993 Liebeck asked McDonald's for $20,000 to cover her medical bills, blaming the company and its coffee for her injuries. McDonald's made a counteroffer: $800. Liebeck hired attorney Reed Morgan and formally sued McDonald's for $90,000, accusing the company of "gross negligence" for selling "unreasonably dangerous" and "defectively manufactured" coffee. McDonald's still wouldn't settle. Why not? Common sense dictates that a multibillion-dollar corporation would pay out a small amount to make the lawsuit—and the bad publicity—simply go away. But between 1982 and 1992, McDonald's had actually received more than 700 complaints about the temperature of its coffee and had even been sued over it a few times. Every case had been thrown out of court for being frivolous; McDonald's thought Liebeck's suit would be no different.

THE POSITIONS

Liebeck and Morgan used those 700 complaints to argue that McDonald's had consistently sold dangerously hot coffee and "didn't care" about its customers. McDonald's brought in quality-control manager Christopher Appleton, who testified that the rate of complaint amounted to one per 24 million cups of coffee sold—not enough to necessitate a chain-wide change.

So how hot *was* the coffee? McDonald's internal documents—presented by Liebeck's side—showed that individual restaurants were required to serve coffee at 180° to 190°F (water boils at 212°). At 180°, coffee can cause a third-degree burn in only two seconds of contact. Morgan argued that coffee should be served no hotter than 140° and backed it up with evidence showing that other fast-food chains served their coffee at that temperature. McDonald's countered that the reason it served coffee at 180° was because drive-through customers were mostly travelers and commuters who wanted their coffee to remain hot for a long time.

THE FALLOUT

The jury found mostly in Liebeck's favor, but she didn't get millions. They found McDonald's 80% responsible for serving coffee it knew could cause burns and without a decent warning label. Liebeck was held 20% accountable for spilling the cup. She was awarded $160,000 in compensatory damages (80% of the $200,000 she sued for). Morgan suggested that punitive damages should amount to two days' worth of coffee revenues, and the jury agreed, awarding Liebeck that exact amount: $2.7 million. The judge reduced it to $480,000. Both sides appealed the verdict; the parties settled in 1994—nearly three years after the incident—for $600,000.

McDonald's also promised to reduce the temperature of its coffee to about 160°, which it did. But since 1994, McDonald's admits that it has slowly raised it back up to 180°, the same temperature that gave a 79-year-old woman burns on a quarter of her body. So sip carefully.

CURL UP AND DYE

Lots of businesses give themselves punny names, but hair salons are a cut above the rest. Here are the names of some real beauty parlors and barber shops in the United States and Europe.

Headmasters

Director's Cut

Mane Attraction

Barber Blacksheep

Bright N' Bleach

Root 66

Fort Locks

Shear Delight

Fresh Hair

Shear Madness

ExpHAIRtease

Blade Runners

The Best Little Hair House

Do or Dye

In Fringe

Hairloom

It Will Grow Back

Blonde Ambition

The Final Cut

Alive and Klippin'

Hair and Now

Hairoglyphics

Heads of State

Herr Kutz

Curling U Softly

Hair Necessities

Max Headroom

Tortoise & The Hair

Cutting Corner

Headnizm

Talking Heads

The Hairport

Snipping Image

Inhairitance

Permutations

Grateful Heads

Illegally Blonde

Hackers

Cutting Remarks

British Hairways

The Mane Event

Cut 'N' Run

Hair Say

Curl Up and Dye

Judy's Hair-em

Hair On Earth

Lunatic Fringe

Headgames

Crosshairs

Hair Today, Gone Tomorrow

Chop Shop

Hair Raisers

Scissors Palace

Hairanoia

Heads up! More than 700 people are struck and killed by falling objects every year.

HEY! THAT'S MY

_____ ON eBAY!

Ever been looking around on eBay and found something of yours that was being sold by somebody else? Neither have we. (But we're still looking.)

HEY! THAT'S MY GPS!

In December 2006, a man in Long Island, New York, had his global positioning system (GPS) stolen from his car. In January 2007, he called police and told them he'd found the device on the Internet auction site eBay. Officers tracked down the seller's contact information and raided the secondhand shop of 25-year-old Daniel Rangkar in Queens. They found the GPS—along with more than $50,000 in stolen goods. The device's owner, who remained unidentified, said he recognized it on eBay because of its nonstandard power cord.

HEY! THAT'S MY FOOTPRINT!

An anonymous source tipped off Dr. Bill Wimbledon of Wales that some suspicious items were being offered for sale on eBay. The doctor called the police, and they worked together to track the sellers down. In the end, they got the stolen goods back. What were they? 200-million-year-old, fossilized, three-toed dinosaur footprints. (Wimbledon's doctorate is in geology.) They'd been dug up from Bendrick Rock, one of Britain's most important fossil sites, in southeast Wales. Investigators found extensive damage at the site. The footprints were turned over to the Countryside Council for Wales, and a man identified only as an "amateur geologist" was let off with just a warning from police.

HEY! THAT'S MY PARAMOTOR!

Paragliding instructor Geoff Soden of Huntingdon, England, had two specially made "paramotors" stolen during an exhibition in early 2007. The compact engines, which drive small propellers, are strapped onto paragliders' backs to enhance their normally wind-powered flights. Soden had the motors custom made in Italy for about $16,000 each.

During one insanity attack, King George III of England ended every sentence with "peacock."

A month later he found them listed on eBay at a starting price of $2,000. "I don't think the thieves knew how valuable or rare these motors were," Soden said, "or they wouldn't have put them on eBay for all to see." By "rare" he meant that one of the motors was a prototype—the only one like it in the world. Soden contacted the seller and got an e-mail address and phone number, which he then gave to the police, and within five hours the thieves were arrested. Stephen Cresser, 46, and Donald Bennett, 43, who had been employed at the exhibition, pleaded guilty to theft and were fined $1,000.

HEY! THAT'S MY CAMERA

A German businessman was dining at a neighborhood restaurant in Berlin when he set his Samsung GX-1 digital camera down on the table and went to the men's room. When he returned, the camera was gone. A few days later he logged on to eBay to buy a replacement—he wanted the exact same model so his accessories would still work. He quickly found a Samsung GX-1 and was about to buy it...until he noticed that the seller lived near him in the same area of Berlin. Suspicious, he reported it to police, who promptly arrested the seller. Bonus: He got his camera back.

HEY! THAT'S MY ALBUM

In October 2005, the British band The Darkness saw a copy of their second CD, *One Way Ticket to Hell...and Back*, for sale on eBay. Only problem: It hadn't been released yet. Only a handful of people had a copy of the record, all of them record company executives or music journalists. They never found out who the thief was, but they bought the CD—for £350 (about $700).

HEY! THAT'S MY TRAILER!

Carpenter Richard Keen of Barmouth, Wales, was desperate to replace his stolen flatbed trailer, and went on eBay to look for another. He soon became the winning bidder on his own trailer, which he of course recognized. After winning the bid, he got the seller's address. Stefan Rowe, 37, was arrested and pleaded guilty to handling stolen goods, and led police to the man (who was not identified) who had stolen it. "I am glad to have my trailer back," Keen said later, "and I did my bit to help the police."

I WALK THE LAWN

Some facts about America's favorite pastime—lawn care. (And when you're done with this page, get out there and start mowing.)

• An average lawn has six grass plants per square inch. That's 850 per square foot—which can contain as many as 3,000 individual blades of grass.

• There are 50 million lawn mowers in use in the U.S.

• About 65% of all water used in American households goes to watering lawns. (In summer, that's about 238 gallons per person per day.)

• According to the Environmental Protection Agency, as much as 5% of all polluting exhaust in urban areas is from lawn mowers.

• The first lawn-care book: *The Art of Beautifying Suburban Home Grounds*, published in 1870.

• The average lawn absorbs water six times more effectively than a wheat field.

• You can get a degree in lawn maintenance from Penn State University (but they call it "Turf Grass Science").

• The most popular lawn ornament: the pink flamingo (250,000 are sold every year).

• There are about 40 million acres of lawn in the United States—three times the acreage planted with irrigated corn.

• AstroTurf was patented in 1967. It was originally named Chemgrass.

• Before mowers were invented, lawns were cut with scythes (or sheep).

• A lawn absorbs 10 times more water on a hot day than it does on a cloudy day.

• A 150-pound man can burn 380 calories in a half hour of mowing with a push-mower.

• The average lawn grows at a rate of about three inches per month.

• A recent study found that about 65,000 people per year are hospitalized with lawn-mowing-related injuries.

"Regulation" slug races are held on courses one yard long.

MY FIRST JOB

Celebrities, politicians, and captains of industry had to start somewhere. Turns out they pretty much started out with the same lame jobs as the rest of us.

- **Jim Carrey** got a job as a janitor at a tire factory when he was 15.

- **Michael Dell**, founder of Dell computers, washed dishes in a Chinese restaurant.

- **Suze Orman**, financial guru and author of *The Road to Wealth*, trimmed eucalyptus trees with a chainsaw.

- **Steve McQueen** was a towel boy…in a brothel.

- **Johnny Depp** was the lead singer of a Kiss tribute band.

- **Danny DeVito** was a hairdresser at his sister's salon.

- **Chris Rock** was a busboy at a Red Lobster.

- **Madeleine Albright** worked at Jocelyn's, a Denver department store. (She sold bras.)

- **Nancy Grace** (CNN) worked at the candy counter at Sears.

- **Bill Murray** worked at a chestnut stand.

- **Rush Limbaugh** shined shoes.

- **Bill Gates** was a page in the Washington state capitol building.

- **Michael Douglas** pumped gas.

- **Margaret Thatcher** (former British prime minister) was a research chemist for a company called British Xylonite.

- **Quentin Tarantino** was an usher at an adult movie theater.

- **Martha Stewart** worked at the New York Stock Exchange.

- **Michael Jordan** was a bellman.

- **Steve Jobs**, CEO of Apple Computer, was a summer intern at Hewlett-Packard.

- **J. K. Rowling** worked for Amnesty International.

- **Duke Ellington** was a peanut vendor at Washington Senators baseball games.

- **Walt Disney** mashed apples in a jelly factory.

- **Stephen King** was a highschool janitor.

How about you? By age 30, the average American has had 7.5 different jobs.

WATERING HOLES

Thirsty? For most of us, a drink of water is no farther away than the kitchen tap. But animals have to go where the water is…and they never know who they're going to meet.

PETE'S POND
Location: Mashatu Game Reserve in Botswana

History: Named after South African Pete Le Roux, who first visited the area as a zoology student in the 1980s and was shocked to see the lack of game. Agriculture (or failed attempts at it) and rampant poaching had killed or driven away most of the wildlife. Le Roux stayed and eventually became the park's general manager. In 1985 he organized the construction of the huge watering hole as a way to attract animals back to the reserve. The pond plan paid off. Mashatu, Southern Africa's largest private reserve at 75,000 acres, now has the world's largest population of elephants on private land (there are more than 700).

Clientele: Besides elephants, it's home to healthy populations of crocodiles, boars, leopards, aardwolves, honey badgers, baboons, lions, jackals, monkeys, impalas, wildebeest, gazelles, warthogs, zebras, and dozens of bird species, including ostriches. In 2005 the pond received worldwide attention when *National Geographic* set up live 24-hour Web cams, and millions of people around the world logged on to watch the wildlife come for a drink or a swim (or to attack and eat other animals).

ANBANGBANG BILLABONG
Location: Northern Territory, Australia

History: The name "billabong" comes from the indigenous Australian words *billa* (creek) and *bong* (dead), and refers to a pond or stagnant body of water. Anbangbang Billabong is in the Northern Territory's Kakadu National Park, under the imposing Nourlangie Rock, which holds numerous ancient aboriginal rock paintings. Established in 1979, the park lies within an area governed by Aboriginal people. It comprises almost 12,300 square miles of land—roughly the size of the entire nation of Israel.

Clientele: Water buffalo, kangaroos, wallabies, more than 100 species of reptile (including several poisonous snakes), dozens of species of migratory birds, and insects...lots of insects.

One more thing: Huge yellow warning signs can be seen around Anbangbang. Each features a black silhouette of a crocodile's head, mouth agape, closing down on a human form. Like waters all over the NT, Anbangbang Billabong is home to saltwater crocodiles, the largest reptile in the world (they can reach 20 feet long and weigh more than 1,500 pounds)—and one of the most dangerous: Since 2002 there have been dozens of attacks on humans, and at least six deaths.

MANZANITA SPRING

Location: Guadalupe Mountains National Park, Texas

History: The desolate Guadalupes were the site of bloody battles between the Mescalero Apache and the "buffalo soldiers," African-American army regiments sent to fight them in the decades after the Civil War. The park was designated in 1972, and the area remains one of the lower 48's starkest, most remote, and least-visited wildernesses. The mountains themselves are part of a 250-million-year-old fossilized reef from a long-disappeared ocean. That reef remained underground for millions of years, and was later lifted by subterranean forces to form the Guadalupes. Manzanita Spring is an oasis in the brutal desert.

Clientele: Mountain lions (though you'd be lucky to see one of the ultra-wary creatures), coyotes, foxes, bobcats, badgers, mule deer, javelinas, black-tailed jackrabbits, and dozens of reptile species, including diamondback rattlesnakes, black-tailed rattlesnakes, coachwhip snakes, prairie lizards...and scorpions.

YINGXIONGGOU TRIBUTARY

Location: Wolong Nature Reserve, Sichuan Province, China

History: Okay, this one's not exactly a "hole," it's a stream. The Yingxionggou Valley is in China's Himalayan Mountains, and it carries this stream to the Pitiao River. The reserve ranges from 3,000 to higher than 20,000 feet. What's special about this mountain stream is that it runs through the dense bamboo forests of Wolong Nature Reserve, which was established in 1963 and is China's largest giant-panda reserve. Pandas drink a lot of water, so they make several trips a day to the stream. There are more than 100 wild pandas in Wolong, and though that doesn't sound like very many, it's a lot when you consider that there are believed to be no more than 1,500 left in the wild.

Clientele: Giant pandas, red pandas, Tibetan macaques (a monkey species), and birds like the rare Temminck's Tragopan, Bar-Winged Wren-Babbler, and Golden Pheasant. Above 4,000 feet you might see takins (a type of mountain goat). And snow leopards.

THE "YOUTUBE WATERING HOLE"

Location: Kruger National Park, South Africa

History: This world-famous safari park was first established in 1898 to protect the area's wildlife, much of which had been wiped out by a virus in 1896. It became Kruger Park in 1926, taking its name from the Boer revolutionary leader Paul Kruger. The park covers 8,000 square miles—about the size of Wales—and is home to about 147 species of mammals.

Clientele: Elephants, black rhinoceroses, lions, cheetahs, leopards, African buffalo, Nile crocodiles, giraffes, hippopotamuses, impalas, wildebeest, and warthogs, to name a few.

YouTube: In May 2007, a watering hole in Kruger Park became a worldwide sensation when someone posted a video shot there on the Web site YouTube.com. A few lions are seen lying by the water. The camera then pans left to show a herd of very large buffalo approaching the lions; then back to the lions, who go into crouch-and-stalk mode; then back to the buffalo as they scent the lions and run the other way; then a chase; the capture of a young buffalo that then falls into the water with the lions; the lions try to kill the calf and drag it out of the water; a large crocodile suddenly rears out of the water and bites a lion; the lions and the croc play tug-of-war with the calf; the lions win and drag the seemingly dead calf onshore; the herd of buffalo comes back to surround the lions, and charge the cats repeatedly (one buffalo tosses a lion far into the air with its horns); the lions finally flee…and the calf miraculously stands up and totters into the protective herd. (Wow!) More than seven million people have watched the video to date, including, perhaps, you.

FLYIN' FLOPS

Since the dawn of aviation, engineers and hobbyists have been experimenting with new designs. As these failed attempts prove, just because an idea for an airplane looks good on paper doesn't mean it'll ever get off the ground.

THE BEDE BD-10 (1992)

Jim Bede helped successfully launch the build-it-yourself airplane industry when he founded Bede Aviation in 1961. His goal: make civil aviation accessible to average Joes by eliminating labor costs, one of the most expensive parts of building a plane. Thirty years later, in 1991, Bede tried to spark another revolution when he introduced the BD-10, the world's first home-built *supersonic jet*. Bede predicted that the jet, which was about the same size as a Cessna 172, would be able to climb at a rate of 20,000 feet a minute (the Cessna climbs at 720 feet a minute), with a ceiling of 45,000 feet (the Cessna's is 13,500 feet), a top speed of Mach 1.4 (the Cessna's is Mach 0.21) and a range of 2,000 miles (the Cessna's is 790 miles).

The BD-10 suffered from two major problems that doomed it. 1) Overkill: How many people would feel safe smashing through the sound barrier in a plane they built themselves in the garage? 2) *Kill* kill: Of the five BD-10s that were ever built, two crashed and a third disintegrated in mid-air. The pilots of all three planes were killed; the two surviving planes are unflyable.

Bede's home-built jet company declared bankruptcy in 1997.

THE BRISTOL BRABAZON (1949)

One of the challenges facing aviation planners as World War II came to an end was that commercial aviation was still in its infancy. Manufacturers were developing aircraft to serve a market that had yet to materialize. What would air travel look like after the war? How many people would fly, and why?

In 1943 a committee of British aviation planners decided that air travel was likely to remain prohibitively expensive for many years, which meant that flying would be limited to the very rich, and officials on government business. If the U.K.'s state-owned airlines were going to be competitive against ocean liners and rail travel, they were going to have to offer a similar amount of luxury, plus plenty of room to move around. The behemoth that the Bristol Aeroplane Company came up with, the *Brabazon*, made its maiden flight in September 1949. As large as a Boeing 747 (which did not enter service until 1970), it dwarfed every other passenger plane of its day. The *Brabazon* had a bar, a lounge, a movie theater, and seating for 100 people, 80 of whom could be accommodated in sleeping berths. (A 747, by comparison, seats more than 400).

The *Brabazon* was so roomy that every passenger had 200 cubic feet of space to themselves, or about as much room as 12 coach seats take up on a modern airliner. Bristol spent the modern equivalent of about $103 million in taxpayer money developing the *Brabazon*, and for that they got a single, giant plane…that nobody wanted to buy, fearing it would be impossible to operate such a monster at a profit with only 100 paying customers. The *Brabazon* flew less than 400 hours before it was written off as a total loss and sold for scrap.

THE SAUNDERS-ROE PRINCESS (1952)
Another really bad idea from the same committee that cooked up the *Brabazon*, the Saunders-Roe *Princess* was a massive, double-decker "flying boat" nearly as big as the *Brabazon* and designed to carry only 105 passengers. Many seaplanes are referred to as "flying boats," but the *Princess* really *was* one: The fuselage was constructed like an ocean liner; the wings, engine, and other parts were added later.

Making the hull of the *Princess* strong enough to splash down in water added a lot of weight, hurting both performance and fuel economy and making the plane much more expensive to operate than a conventional aircraft. Even worse, as airports were starting to become common all over the world, the only advantage offered by seaplanes was rapidly disappearing. One airline did express interest in buying the *Princess*…but when they saw how under-powered it was, they passed. Three prototypes were built, but only one ever flew, and for only 100 hours. The other two went into storage as soon as they were built and stayed there for 15 years. In 1967 all three planes were broken up for scrap. Estimated cost to British taxpayers: about $120 million in 2007 dollars.

THE SNECMA COLÉOPTERÈ

One of the Holy Grails of aircraft engineering is figuring out how to build a plane that can take off and land in locations too small or too crowded for runways. In 1959 a French company called the Societe National d'Etude et de Construction de Moteurs d'Aviation (SNECMA) came up with the *Coléopterè*, a test plane that could take off and land vertically. One of the strangest-looking jets ever built, the *Coléopterè* had a ring-shaped wing that wrapped all the way around the fuselage, giving the plane the look of a fighter plane stuck in a rain barrel. After takeoff, it was supposed to transition to horizontal flight and then back to vertical for landing, but it was so unstable that after the pilot crashed it during an early test flight, SNECMA never bothered to build another one.

THE VOUGHT XF5U (1947)

The XF5U was called the "Flying Flapjack" because the wings had a disc shape, giving it the appearance of a pancake or a propeller-aided stingray. Although it looked weird, it could fly as fast as 500 mph or as slow as 20 mph, a speed at which normal airplanes fall out of the sky. The design showed promise, but suffered the misfortune of being developed in the mid-1940s, at a time when the United States Navy was switching from propeller planes to jet aircraft. The program was cancelled in March 1947 and the lone XF5U was destroyed. The Flying Flapjack made a bigger impression with conspiracy theorists than it did in aviation circles: Test flights of an earlier prototype spawned rumors that the United States had captured a flying saucer and was conducting experiments to figure out how it worked.

*   *   *

HEART ATTACK HOTEL

In the months before he died, Elvis Presley ate an average of about 65,000 calories each day. That's the equivalent of the maximum recommended daily caloric intake of 26 adult men. (It's also the equivalent of 108 Big Macs.)

BADVERTISING

Companies spend millions on market research before they release ads or begin promotions. Yet despite all that preparation, they can still make colossal goofs.

DIG IT
In 2006 Dr Pepper announced that it had buried a rare coin worth "as much as $1 million" in Boston's 350-year-old Granary Burying Ground, the final resting place for many American founding fathers, including Paul Revere, Samuel Adams, and John Hancock. Dr Pepper encouraged the public to ransack the cemetery to find the coin, but city officials got wind of the promotion and closed off Granary before the desecration could begin. Dr Pepper apologized and took back the coin (actual value: $10,000).

JUICED
In early 1994, Starburst fruit candy unveiled a new campaign featuring the slogan "The juice is loose." Later that year, millions of people watched a two-hour low-speed car chase on live TV as police apprehended O. J. Simpson, also known as "the Juice," for the alleged murder of his ex-wife. Within days, Starburst nixed "The juice is loose" and replaced it with "Turn up the juice."

HOW MUCH DO YOU LOVE CHEESEBURGERS?
In January 2005, McDonald's began a new campaign targeted at college students, focusing on their $1.00 Value Menu. To reach the target audience, they used Internet banner ads, one of which depicted a man eyeing a cheeseburger with the caption: "Double cheeseburger? I'd hit it." The ad was pulled a few days later when the McDonald's marketing department learned that "I'd hit it" is urban slang for "I'd mate with that."

AY CARAMBA
In the early 1980s, Coors introduced its beer to Latin America using a direct translation of its slogan, "Turn it Loose." What they didn't know was that in Spanish "turn it loose" translates to "suffer from diarrhea."

Q & A:
ASK THE EXPERTS

*Everyone's got a question they'd like answered—basic stuff
like "Why is the sky blue?" Here are a few questions,
with answers from the world's top trivia experts.*

A MEATY QUESTION

Q: *What's the difference between white meat and dark meat?*
A: "Chickens and turkeys use their wings for balance and quick escapes, and not much more. The legs and thighs are used far more often. This difference in muscular activity suggests that these muscles have evolved differently. Breasts and wings are dominated by fast-contracting muscle tissue. Thighs and drumsticks are predominantly slow-contracting muscles. Energy for the fast-contracting muscles comes from glycogen, a carbohydrate in the form of glucose. The slow-contracting muscles fuel comes from fat. Dark meat is darker than white because it has more fat." (From *The Accidental Hedonist*, by Kate Hopkins)

SHE LOVES ME, SHE LOVES ME NOT

Q: *Why do teenagers get such powerful crushes?*
A: "It's partly biology. Although teenagers have fewer hormones racing through their bodies, the hormones are a new phenomenon, and the body and mind aren't used to them. Part of it is psychological. Though we hate to quote Sigmund Freud, desire for sexual union is at the core of emotion. When this desire is impeded, or, in the case of teenagers, discouraged by parents and societal norms, we compensate by falling exaggeratedly in love." (From *Why Things Are*, by Joel Achenbach)

FLOORED

Q: *Lots of arenas present basketball games and hockey games. How do they go back and forth between wooden floors and ice?*
A: "The cement floor is riddled with freezer tubes of ethylene glycol (antifreeze). To make the rink, the floor is cooled to zero

---

Air conditioners cause more electrocution deaths per year than hair dryers & power drills combined.

degrees. An eighth of an inch of water is then sprayed on and freezes. The ice is painted white with fine talcum powder and then another half inch of water is sprayed on to freeze. The whole process takes about 12 hours. Removing the ice means heating the tubes until the floor hits about 68 degrees and the sheet of ice pops loose. A tractor with a blade breaks up the sheet and shoves the shards into a pit. The heated tubes dry the floor rapidly and the basketball boards are laid on top." (From *The Slice*, by Katherine Dunn)

A HEAVY QUESTION

Q: *When you lose weight, where does it go?*

A: "Muscles prefer to use sugar for fuel, because it burns easily. Sugar is stored in the muscles, in the liver, and a little circulates in the blood. So muscles burn a mix of sugar and fat. When sugar is completely burned, all that is left is water and carbon dioxide. The carbon dioxide is breathed out. The water is excreted through sweat and urine. Fragments of partially burned fat called *ketones* are left over and processed by the liver. Ketones travel through the blood and get burned in the muscles and the brain for energy." (From *How Come? Planet Earth*, by Kathy Wollard)

ATTENTION STANDUP COMEDIANS

Q: *If the flight data recorder (black box) is indestructible, why don't they make the whole airplane out of the same material?*

A: "Unlike the rest of the aircraft, which is mostly made of light materials such as aluminum and plastic, the cockpit voice recorder and the flight data recorder are encased in stainless steel boxes roughly 10 inches by 10 inches by 5 inches. The steel is about a quarter of an inch thick. A plane built to black box standards would be so heavy you'd have to drive it rather than fly." (From *The Straight Dope Tells All*, by Cecil Adams)

*   *   *

"You do not really understand something unless you can explain it to your grandmother."

—**Albert Einstein**

IF...

"If more people read about the world in the bathroom, the world outside the bathroom would be a better place to live." —Uncle John

"If you don't know where you are going, you will wind up somewhere else."
—Yogi Berra

"If a thing is worth doing, it is worth doing slowly...very slowly."
—Gypsy Rose Lee

"If men have a smell, it's usually an accident."
—Jeff Foxworthy

"If you can't laugh at yourself, make fun of other people."
—Bobby Slayton

"If you can't be kind, at least be vague."
—Judith (Miss) Manners

"If you don't like what you're doing, then don't do it."
—Ray Bradbury

"If your eyes hurt after you drink coffee, you have to take the spoon out of the cup."
—Norm Crosby

"If you don't know to which port you're sailing, no wind is favorable."
—Seneca

"If you cannot feed a hundred people, then feed just one."
—Mother Teresa

"If you have to have a job in this world, high-priced movie star is a pretty good gig."
—Tom Hanks

"If you can convince an American that they are in Canada, you can get more money for a magazine."
—Mitch Hedberg

"If you are not criticized, you may not be doing much."
—Donald Rumsfeld

"If you set out to be liked, you'd better be prepared to compromise at any time...and you would achieve nothing."
—Margaret Thatcher

"If you're going to go through hell, come back having learned something."
—Drew Barrymore

"If you can't explain it simply, you don't understand it well enough."
—Albert Einstein

YOUR GOVERNMENT AT WORK

*Rest easy—we've discovered proof that your
tax dollars are being well spent on...*

NONBINDING RESOLUTIONS
In 2007 the *Tennessean* newspaper discovered that 42%
of all measures filed in the Tennessee state legislature
were nonbinding resolutions with no force of law. Among the
resolutions: one lauding Tennessee native Justin Timberlake and
another celebrating religious freedom in Turkey (the Turkey
measure passed; Timberlake's failed). The paper singled out one
representative, Tom DuBois, who "introduced 167 congratulations, memorials, and proposals to rename stretches of highway."
In all, the resolutions cost Tennessee taxpayers $70,000.

NONEXISTENT ORGANIZATIONS
• Rep. John Murtha (D–Penn.) drafted a bill in 2007 which included
an earmark appropriating $1 million for the "Center for Instru-
mented Critical Infrastructure." According to research by Rep. Jeff
Flake (R–Ariz.), there is no such center. He confronted Democrats
about it on the House floor, but none of them had heard of the
CICI, either. Still, they voted down Flake's measure to strike the
funds. It was later revealed that the $1 million was actually slated
to go to a consulting firm called Concurrent Technologies Corporation, whose CEO had donated $7,000 to Murtha's campaign.

• In 2002 the U.S. Department of Education granted $55,000 in
student loans for three students to attend the "Y'Hica Institute" in
London, England. One problem: Neither the institute nor the students were real. They were created by a congressional investigation team that was testing the DOE's verification policy. It failed.

NONEXISTENT AIRLINE PASSENGERS
A 2005 government audit discovered that between 1997 and 2003,
the Defense Department spent more than $108 million on 270,000

airline tickets…which they never used. In 27,000 instances, they even paid *twice*, by first paying for the unused tickets and then reimbursing the employees who were supposed to have used them. The Government Accountability Office blamed the "glitches" on the failure of department personnel to notify the travel office when tickets weren't used.

JUNK FOOD

Promoting healthy eating is one of the foundations of British Columbia Premier Gordon Campbell's government. It came as a surprise, then, when reports surfaced that Campbell's Liberal MLAs (Members of the Legislative Assembly)—along with the civil servants who work for them—used government-issued credit cards to buy nearly $85,000 worth of pizza in the fiscal year 2005–06. It was also revealed that the Ministry of Children and Families spent $20,000 on doughnuts.

CAR SERVICES

To transport its city engineers to on-site inspections, the New York City government leases 107 SUVs, some of them at a cost of $4,000 per month—the same amount it would cost to rent a luxurious Bentley. An investigation by local news station WCBS discovered that these "Official Use Only" SUVs were rarely put to official use. The news prompted the city comptroller's office to perform an audit, which uncovered even more troubling facts: Many of the city employees who were using the SUVs as personal vehicles had either suspended licenses or DUI convictions…or both. Total annual cost of the cars: $1.4 million.

COMMENCEMENT ADDRESSES

Montana governor Brian Schweitzer gave the graduation address at Froid High School in 2007, which had a graduating class of…one. The governor and his entourage traveled to Froid (pop. 195) to speak to Valedictorian Roxie Britton, the only member of her graduating class. Schweitzer gave a passionate speech to Britton (along with a small, enthusiastic crowd), where he spoke about reducing the need for foreign oil and using more alternative energy. He ended his speech by calling on the Class of 2007 (Britton) to "look toward the future with a positive attitude."

WALKEN TALKIN'

Tim Burton on Christopher Walken: "You look at him and you know there's a lot going on, yet you have no idea what."

"I've always been a character actor, although I'm not quite sure what that means."

"I think I'm strange. I'm happy being strange."

"I don't have a lot of hobbies. I don't play golf. I don't have any children. Things that occupy people's time. I just try to take jobs. I basically work so much because I'm lazy."

"When you're in a scene and you don't know what you're gonna do, don't do anything."

"People are completely mysterious to me. Even in my own family I have no idea what any of them are thinking."

"I don't need to be made to look evil. I can do that on my own."

"I used to be prettier than I am, but I think I look better now. I was a pretty boy. Particularly in my early movies. I don't like looking at them so much. There's a sort of pretty thing about me."

"I think that when I play these villains, maybe what is different is that the audience sees me play these and they know that that's Chris and he's having fun and he knows that and you know that and everybody knows that."

"I make movies that nobody will see. I've made movies that even I have never seen."

"How great would it be if actors had tails because tails are so expressive. I have cats and you can tell if they're annoyed. If they're scared, they bush their tail. If I had to play scared in a movie, all I'd have to do is bush my tail. I think that if actors had tails it would change everything."

"I am a solitary person, as an animal. There are animals who live alone and animals who live in groups, there are aggressive ones and the ones that are like the lilies of the field."

"Bear costumes are funny. Bears as well."

VANISHED!

This stuff used to be a part of everyday life.
Now it's gone. So where did it all go?

PAPERBOYS

The job evolved from *newsies*—boys of the 1920s and 1930s who hawked papers on city street corners. When the population recentralized from cities to suburbs, newsies became paperboys. It's part of an iconic American image: The sun rises, the birds chirp, and the paperboy tosses a newspaper on the porch as he zooms by on his bike. In the mid-20th century, a paper route was often the first paying job for kids as young as nine. But there are still suburbs, and people still read newspapers. So what happened to paperboys? Most daily papers today are morning papers. Few kids are willing to work at 5:00 a.m. (for $5 an hour), and parents won't let them work the streets in the dark (on bikes). The Newspaper Association of America says that 81% of carriers are now adults with cars, who can deliver papers faster anyway.

LOCAL KIDDIE TV SHOWS

From the late 1940s to the early 1970s, nearly every American television market had its own locally produced children's shows. The format was pretty standard: a cowboy/clown/pirate/train engineer/mailman/ringmaster or a guy in an animal suit introduced games, contests, puppet shows, and cartoons. At the height of the era, there were more than 1,400 locally made kids' shows nationwide—the shows were a cheap and easy way for stations to fill time in little-watched early-morning and late-afternoon hours. The advent of PBS's all-educational children's programming killed the cowboys and clowns. Concerned parents urged their kids to watch "educational" shows, such as *Mr. Rogers' Neighborhood*, *Sesame Street*, and *The Electric Company*, instead.

HIT SHOW TUNES

Many of the biggest pop songs of the 1930s, 1940s, and 1950s—including classics like "Some Enchanted Evening" and "You're the Top"—originated in Broadway musicals, such as *South Pacific* and

Anything Goes. Top composers like the Gershwins, Rodgers and Hammerstein, and Cole Porter wrote for Broadway because it was the best-paying venue available to them. Even into the rock 'n' roll era, *The Ed Sullivan Show* still featured performances from a Broadway cast almost every week. And rock music didn't kill show tunes, either—Louis Armstrong's "Hello, Dolly" knocked the Beatles out of the No. 1 spot in 1964. What really killed Broadway was Broadway—show tunes didn't keep up with contemporary musical trends. Major composers gravitated toward movie and TV scores, which are less risky and more lucrative than Broadway. The last hit song from a stage musical: "One Night in Bangkok" by Murray Head, from the 1986 musical *Chess.*

SMOKING

It's difficult today to imagine how prevalent smoking used to be. A common image of the 1950s: adults in suits and party dresses standing around at cocktail parties smoking cigarettes. People smoked in restaurants, airplanes, buses, offices, movie theaters. There was almost no place where smoking *wasn't* allowed (other than hospitals and elementary schools). Then in 1964, surgeon general Luther Terry announced that doctors had linked smoking with lung cancer. The next year, cigarette packs began to carry a health warning. Smoking has been in decline ever since. In 1964, 40% of American adults smoked. By 2006 only 19% did. It's now banned in public places (even bars) in most major cities, including Los Angeles, Houston, and New York City.

VIDEO ARCADES

In the late 1970s and early 1980s, the only place to play video games like Pac-Man and Donkey Kong was at a video arcade. They were popular hangouts for teenagers, which invited criticism from parents' groups—arcades were viewed as poorly lit dens of iniquity where kids could easily skip school and waste money (many arcades had truant officers on the premises). Even when home systems like Atari and Nintendo hit the market, arcade games remained profitable because they had much better graphics than the home versions. But by the mid-1990s, game systems like the Sony PlayStation had graphics equal (or superior) to those of the arcade machines. By then, arcades were on their way out.

RESCUED!

Hair-raising tales of real-life hairy situations...and their happy resolutions. Right hair in the Bathroom Reader.

Rescuee: 11-year-old Hannah Thompson of Australia
Setup: On April 6, 2004, Hannah was swimming with friends in Margaret Bay in northern Queensland when she was bitten on the arm by a crocodile. The 10-foot-long creature immediately pulled her under.

The Rescue: Fifty-seven-year-old Ray Turner was in a small boat nearby when he heard the screams and saw the croc. He quickly dove off the boat, straight onto the crocodile's back. Turner is a former crocodile hunter, so he knew what to do next—he stuck his fingers in the animal's eyes, and the 500-pound croc immediately let go of the girl and fled. "Not many people know to go for their eyes," Turner later told reporters, "but that's what you have to do." Hannah was airlifted to a hospital with deep puncture wounds in her arm, but was soon reported to be in stable condition. Turner said the 11-year-old was incredibly calm and brave during and after the incident. "She made a joke about losing her watch," he said. "She said, 'The alarm's set for five o'clock if you want to go after that crocodile.'"

Rescuee: Mark Orr, 26, of Escatawpa, Mississippi
Setup: In June 2002, Orr and two friends were diving in underwater caves near the Chipola River north of Pensacola, Florida. Deep into the dive the trio became confused in the murky water, but after finally finding their guide lines, they headed back toward the surface. Two of them made it...only to discover that Orr wasn't with them. They contacted authorities and made three attempts to find their friend, but to no avail. Local rescue crews, knowing they were unprepared for such a dangerous search, stayed out of it and called experienced rescue diver Scott Hunsucker.
The Rescue: When Hunsucker arrived on the scene, Orr had been missing for more than five hours. Hunsucker had been on dozens of emergency dives over the years, and he knew that was too long for a diver to survive. But he went down anyway. Half an

---

Myrrh is a resin from the dindin tree.

hour into his search he came to an air pocket in a chamber in the cave…where Mark Orr was just waking up from a nap. "Hey," Orr said, "are you looking for a dead guy?" Hunsucker guided him from the depths, and after being missing for more than six hours, he emerged from the cave alive and well. "I was speechless," Hunsucker said. "I was expecting to be on a body recovery mission. When he asked me if I was looking for a dead guy, I had to say, 'Well, yeah.'" CNN reported that out of the 480 cave divers previously reported missing in United States history, only three had been found alive. Mark Orr was the fourth.

Rescuee: A 2-year-old girl in Kissimmee, Florida

Setup: On March 24, 2004, Alan Burns, 43, was on vacation in the resort town of Kissimmee. He was sitting beside the hotel pool when he heard a woman screaming about a baby. He immediately looked into the pool—but saw no baby. Then he looked up: A toddler dressed in only a diaper was dangling by her hands from a third-floor railing.

The Rescue: He ran to the building toward the child…when it suddenly let go. Burns jumped to where he thought the infant would land and caught her in his arms, and the two of them fell into some bushes. The child survived the three-story fall with a bump on her head. "I just happened to be at the right place at the right time," said Burns, who shared some of the credit with the mysterious woman who screamed for help. "If she hadn't seen the kid," he said, "I wouldn't even have known it."

*   *   *

NAME IS DESTINY?

In 1958 Robert Lane of New York City named his new baby boy Winner, thinking that a person named "Winner Lane" would lead a successful life. In 1961 the Lanes had another boy, and for what they called a "book-end effect," they named him "Loser." Winner Lane, now 49 years old, is a career criminal with 30 arrests for burglary, trespassing, and domestic abuse. Loser Lane went to private school on a scholarship, graduated from college, and rose to the rank of sergeant in the New York Police Department.

Q: Why are canned herring called *sardines*? A: The canning process was developed in Sardinia.

BATHROOM NEWS

*Here are a few choice bits of bathroom
trivia we've flushed out for you.*

UNHAPPY LANDINGS
"Two planes were delayed in the air over Manchester-
Boston Regional Airport in 2007 when the only certified
air traffic controller in the tower had to go to the bathroom. The
flights were forced to circle the airport for 18 minutes before landing. The controller's break also briefly delayed two departing
flights, including one carrying a set of lungs bound for a transplant
in New Jersey. According to FAA spokesman Jim Peters, all procedures were properly followed. 'It is not an unusual circumstance to
put an aircraft into holding,' he said. 'We do it all the time.' Air
traffic controller Regan Mack, 42, said he was five hours into his
shift and had been working more than 2½ hours straight when he
excused himself to go to the bathroom. The break lasted only 12
minutes, according to the FAA. 'In 16 years, this was by far the
most difficult decision I've ever had to make,' said Mack.

'These are human beings,' added FAA spokesman Doug
Church. 'They have to go to the bathroom.'"

—*New Hampshire Union Leader*

BACK TO SQUARE ONE

"Some York County, England, employees rubbed the samples in
their hands to determine which toilet paper they liked better: the
recycled product or the regular one. Which type of toilet paper
ends up in some of the restrooms in county-owned buildings will
actually depend on the price the county receives through bids. But
if the prices are comparable, some officials would like to go with a
recycled product to help the environment. 'I'm not too thrilled
about that,' elections office clerk Neil Manhard said. 'I'm allergic
to a lot of stuff.' Many agreed that they'd like to stay with the
Scott tissue that the county currently provides. 'This just feels
softer to me,' said Pat Ryer, a secretary in the district attorney's
office. Others, though, liked the 'coarser' recycled Bay West toilet
tissue, saying it has more stability. 'It has a thicker feel to it,'

BANG! The groove around the rim of a bullet is called the *cannelure*.

receptionist Jeanne Wilt said. Some took a serious approach to the mini survey. Others burst into laughter, making jokes that were unprintable. Said Commissioner Steve Chronister: 'I hope this is not the biggest decision we make all year.'"

—*The Evening Sun*

DOE!

"Jerry Falkner woke up one morning in June 2006 to the sound of breaking glass. 'I thought someone was breaking in,' he said. 'The next thing I know, a deer is running toward my room.' The deer crashed through one of his apartment windows and then ran into the bathroom, where Falkner locked it inside. Unfortunately, he didn't know his pit bull, Shadow, was in the bathroom with the deer when he closed the door. The frightened deer kicked on the water, flooding the apartment and forcing authorities to shut off power and water to the building. The dog was knocked unconscious for at least 10 minutes. Police arrived and were able to get the dog out of the bathroom, leaving the deer confined. The Wisconsin Department of Natural Resources then tranquilized the one-year-old doe and took it away."

—*Journal Times* (Racine, Wisconsin)

THE PAPER CHASE HAS ENDED

"A serial loo paper thief has been cautioned by police after stealing 10 rolls a day from public toilets for three weeks. The middle-aged woman, who was not named, was caught red-handed by council staff in West Bridgford, Nottingham. 'Ten rolls of paper a day adds up, and we can't allow people to steal public property,' said Bob Alderton, a manager for Rushcliffe Borough Council."

—*The Metro* (U.K.)

SMOKIN' IN THE BOYS' ROOM

"Warning: Smoking in the toilet can be dangerous. A portable toilet exploded after a West Virginia man lit a cigarette. Emergency workers said the man was not severely injured and drove himself to Clay-Battelle Community Health Center. The explosion resulted from a buildup of methane gas inside the portable toilet. The methane did not 'take too kindly' to the lit cigarette, said a spokeswoman for Monongalia Emergency Medical Services."

—**Associated Press**

The NFL buys up to 150 Super Bowl rings per year, at $5,000 per ring. (Losers also get rings.)

WELCOME TO SLAB CITY

Here's a look at one of the most unusual, most unlikely, and, strangely, most beloved campgrounds in the entire United States.

OPEN...AND CLOSED

When the United States entered World War II following the bombing of Pearl Harbor, it was just a matter of time until American soldiers would go into battle against the German and Italian forces occupying North Africa. So in 1942, the Marine Corps opened a base called Camp Dunlap on 630 acres of desert land in southern California, where it trained troops to fight in conditions similar to those in North Africa.

Camp Dunlap wound down after the war and closed for good in 1956. The military stripped the base of everything of value, and after they cleared out, the citizens of nearby Niland, California, tore down the few remaining buildings and used the lumber to build a church. All that was left were the concrete slabs that had served as the floors for dozens of portable buildings and tents. A few ex-marines decided to stay behind, roughing it on campsites they built on the slabs. "The Slabs," or "Slab City," as it's called, has been occupied ever since.

FOR THE BIRDS

Only the toughest and most determined "slabbers" could stand to live at the site year-round; in summer the temperature can climb past 120° in the shade, what little there is. But over the years, the site became a popular wintering spot for RV "snowbirds." By the 1980s, more than 3,000 campers, travel trailers, and motor homes were descending on the site each October and staying until April, when they packed up and headed north again before it got too hot. Slab City had a lot to offer its "citizens," most of whom were on limited or fixed incomes: It was warm in winter but not unbearably hot, and because it was owned by the state (and not private property) it was legal to stay there. It didn't cost a penny in rent, and because it was just 50 miles north of the Mexican border, affordable prescription drugs and medical care weren't far away, either.

What did George Washington and Colonel Sanders have in common? They were Freemasons.

...AND NOW THE FINE PRINT

Before you quit your job and hit the trail for Slab City, there are a few things you need to know. For starters, there's still no water, electricity, or sewage service. There's not much fresh air, either: Slab City is just three miles from the Salton Sea, a dying body of water that's bigger than Lake Tahoe. Fed by salty runoff from the irrigated fields of the Imperial Valley (known as the Valley of the Dead before the irrigation went in), the Salton is already saltier than the Pacific Ocean, and by 2017 it will be so salty that nothing will be able to live in it. The fish die-off is already well under way, and as migratory birds eat the diseased and dying fish they die, too, and end up in the lake. The overpowering stench has been compared to a combination of cow manure, skunk spray, rotten eggs, urine-soaked hallways, and vomit.

And while Camp Dunlap has been closed for more than 60 years, the adjacent Chocolate Mountain Gunnery Range is still open for business. It's attacked day and night by bombers and fighter planes using real ordnance. As if the loud noises and trembling ground weren't enough, some Slab City denizens make extra money sneaking onto the range at night to collect shrapnel that they sell for scrap metal. The military sends out patrols to stop them, but the county sheriff has caught more than one "scrapper" red-handed trying to bring unexploded cluster bombs, anti-tank rockets, and even Sidewinder missiles back to Slab City. A few of the scrappers have been blown to bits by the bombs.

DIFFERENT STROKES FOR DIFFERENT FOLKS

So is Slab City the last bastion of true freedom and independence in America, or is it a stinking, sunbaked, post-apocalyptic ticking-time-bomb vision of hell on Earth? It depends on who you ask. It's certainly not for everyone: A 1989 survey of visitors to the Salton Sea area found that not only did most of them say they'd never want to return, more than half said they were *afraid* to return.

And yet in spite of it all, people keep coming back. They've created quite a thriving community in Slab City, complete with swap meets, a library, a singles club, a Christian center, a church, a pet cemetery, and an outdoor stage where people gather to listen to live music every night. Nearly everyone has a CB, and they're usually tuned to channel 23, the unofficial Slab City channel,

---

Bestselling car of all time: the Toyota Corolla (over 32 million since 1966).

especially for the 6:00 p.m. nightly news bulletins and announcements. Many residents are better known by their CB handles (Stargazer, Brain Dead, Cardboard Johnny) than they are by their real names.

When groups of snowbirds start arriving in October, they tend to cluster their rigs in groups for security. But the various factions at Slab City—snowbirds, year-round slabbers, migrant laborers, the Apple Dumpling Gang (dune buggy enthusiasts), and even the local sheriff's deputies, who patrol the area regularly—manage to interact on a daily basis without much fuss. Many slabbers have built small businesses that provide services to other residents. Does your rig need a new fan belt? Do you need water hauled in, or your garbage hauled out? Is your TV on the fritz? Do you want to replace your electric generator with solar panels? Someone in Slab City can take care of it for you. They even have an Avon Lady.

STAY TUNED

Imperial County isn't crazy about Slab City, and neither is the state of California, which owns the land. But nobody wants the responsibility—or the expense—of closing it down and cleaning it up. Forty years' worth of abandoned cars, burned-out trailers, and other junk would have to be hauled away, and the hundreds of "gopher holes" (makeshift septic tanks) scattered around the site would have to be dealt with. And who knows how many unexploded bombs are still lying around?

On more than one occasion the state has tried to sell Slab City, perhaps to someone who would clean it up, put in utilities and turn it into a for-profit campground. But who would *pay* to camp between the stinky Salton Sea and a live bombing range? And as much as the county must hate to admit it, when all those RVs roll into town each October, they pump a fortune into the economies of Niland and other small towns in the area. Even if the county could get rid of Slab City, would it really want to?

Every year the conversation in Slab City fills with speculation and worry that this season might be the last, and every year the old-timers laugh it off. "Somebody's always got a plan to clean up the Slabs," one resident said in 1994. "I'm 87 now, and if I live to be 100, I'll still be coming here."

Don't believe us? Google it: A *googol* is the mathematical term for 1 followed by 100 zeros.

APRIL FOOLS!

Don't look now, but your fly is open. Ha! Made you look! Here are a few classic April Fools' jokes.

LIGHTS OUT

When Thomas Edison invented the phonograph in 1877, it seemed as if he was capable of anything. When the New York *Graphic* wrote the following year that Edison had invented a machine that could convert dirt into food and water into wine, other newspapers reported the story without bothering to check with Edison if it was true. When the editors of the Buffalo *Commercial Advertiser* praised Edison's genius for ending world hunger, the *Graphic* reprinted the editorial under the headline "They Bite!"

APE VS. NAZI

While Peter Jackson was filming the remake of *King Kong* in 2005, he kept a video diary of the film's progress that was posted daily on his Web site. For the April 1, 2005, entry, he announced plans for two sequels: *Son of Kong* and *King Kong: Into the Wolf's Lair*. Both set during World War II, Jackson said, the films would feature giant apes with giant machine guns mounted on their shoulders and soldiers riding on their backs, fighting the Nazis in Europe. He let the story swirl for about a week before admitting it was a joke. (You can still see the video diary entry online or in the production diaries DVD.)

WHERE THERE'S SMOKE

Early on the morning of April 1, 1974, a prankster named Porky Bicker had a helicopter haul about a hundred old tires up to the top of Mt. Edgecumbe, an old volcano located 13 miles west of Sitka, Alaska. Then he set them on fire. That morning, residents of Sitka awoke to the sight of a smoking volcano and wondered if the end was near…until scientists dispatched to the mountaintop found the words "April Fools!" spray-painted in the snow. When Mount St. Helens erupted in Washington state six years later, someone sent Porky a note that read, "Porky, this time you've gone too far!"

Cost to decorate a Christmas tree with electric lights in 1899: $300.

MOVERS AND SHAKERS

Every year on April Fools' Day, the Web site Howstuffworks.com posts an explanation of how some preposterous, nonexistent product works. Their entry for 2006: "How Animated Tattoos Work." The site claimed that two inventors had come up with a way to implant an ultra-thin LCD screen called a Programmable Subcutaneous Visible Implant (PSVI) just below the surface of the skin. "Animated tattoos are just what they sound like, implanted images that actually move under the skin," the Web site explained. "Because PSVIs are programmable, a person with an animated tattoo can change the image whenever they like by having their tattoo 'reprogrammed.' "

A GLASS HALF FULL

On April 1, 2005, NASA posted a link on its Web site that read "Water on Mars," something that scientists have spent decades hoping to find. Was the search finally over? Not quite—when you clicked on the link you were taken to a photograph of a glass of water...carefully perched atop a Mars candy bar.

GATESGATE

On April 1, 2003, producers at one of South Korea's top three television channels stumbled across an online CNN story that Microsoft chairman Bill Gates had been assassinated in Los Angeles at a charity event, and reported the news on TV. Two other Korean channels quickly picked up the story that Gates, one of the world's leading industrialists, had died, and soon the entire country was buzzing with the news. The Korean stock market dropped 1.5%, losing more than $3 billion in value, before it was discovered that the story was just that—a fake news story cooked up by a gaming Web site...to get a laugh.

*　　*　　*

THREE BAD LITTLE PUNS

- A boiled egg in the morning is hard to beat.
- When a clock is hungry, it goes back four seconds.
- A backward poet writes inverse.

World's largest per-capita consumer of turkey: Israel.

STRANGE LAWSUITS

These days, it seems that people will sue each other over practically anything. Here are some real-life examples of unusual legal battles.

THE PLAINTIFFS: Stephen G. Glover, Alan Smith, and Michael Freeman—prisoners at Walsenburg and Limon prisons, both in Colorado

THE DEFENDANT: Colorado Department of Corrections

THE LAWSUIT: The inmates, all serving life sentences, sued the CDC for the "emotional and mental distress" inflicted upon them by mosquito bites. They claimed they were in mortal danger of contracting West Nile virus and that the prisons were to blame. Acting as their own attorneys, they said in a written statement, "Each mosquito attack constituted bodily injury, which the Department of Corrections had the power to prevent, but consciously elected not to." Prison officials argued that no confirmed cases of the virus have ever been recorded at any Colorado prison, and, besides, they had provided all prisoners with mosquito repellent.

THE VERDICT: Case dismissed. So the prisoners took it to the Colorado Court of Appeals, who also—swat!—dismissed it.

THE PLAINTIFF: Karl Kemp & Associates Antiques

THE DEFENDANTS: Four homeless people, referred to as "John Smith," "John Doe," "Bob Doe," and "Jane Doe"

THE LAWSUIT: Kemp's high-end New York antique store is in a prime location: Madison Avenue on Manhattan's upper east side. Also at that location: several homeless people. Kemp wants them to reimburse him for the $1 million in revenue he claims he's lost because of their presence. According to the lawsuit, they loiter in front of his store, wearing "unsanitary clothing and cardboard boxes...while drinking alcoholic beverages from open bottles, performing various bodily functions on the sidewalk." Kemp maintains that he's tried everything from asking them to move, to asking his landlord to remove the heating duct they huddle around for warmth. Kemp even referred to one of the homeless

---

Ouch! In the U.S., people choke on toothpicks more often than on any other object.

men as a "nice guy." "It's nothing against him," he said. "I want him to be safe and not to be an obstruction to us." No word on how Kemp expects the four homeless people to come up with the $1 million.

THE VERDICT: Pending.

THE PLAINTIFF: William Davis, a Murfreesboro, Tennessee, homeowner

THE DEFENDANT: The Murfreesboro police department

THE LAWSUIT: In December 2003, after Davis's neighbors complained of a horrible smell, police raided his home and found 114 dead cats (and a dead German Shepherd named Snowy), all stored in freezers around his property. On the floor of Davis's home they found "a half-inch deep covering of ground-in feces." The carcasses were removed and destroyed, and Davis was charged with animal cruelty, for which he was given a year's probation. Davis, who is 72, is suing the police department for $1.5 million, claiming that his dead pets not only held "emotional value," but they were also part of a business plan to build a pet cemetery. He also said that one of the dead cats was big enough to have made it into *Guinness World Records*.

THE VERDICT: Pending, but we'll go out on a limb and guess that this one will be dismissed.

THE PLAINTIFF: Timothy Liebaert, a lawyer

THE DEFENDANT: Donovan Judkins, president of Burlington Homes in Bakersfield, California

THE LAWSUIT: In 1999 Liebaert attempted to purchase a home in the Fairway Oaks neighborhood in Bakersfield. On the buyer application, he listed his occupation as "environmental lawyer." When Judkins saw the L-word, he refused the sale. Why? Because, he says, a lawyer is more likely to find miniscule faults in the property and then bog down the developer with litigation, thus lowering profit margins and causing housing prices to rise. Liebaert sued on charges of discrimination, insisting that Burlington Homes had violated his civil rights. "They want to exclude people who have any level of sophistication," Liebaert told *The New York Times*.

"Since I'm an attorney, they think I might try to make them uphold their end of the deal." Judkins claims he was well within the bounds of the law in refusing the sale, pointing out that while California law prohibits housing firms from discriminating based on race, color, national origin, religion, sex, family status, and disability, nowhere does it mention profession. "We do not need to do business with everyone who walks in the door," Judkins said, "just like a lawyer doesn't have to take on everyone who walks in the door as a client."

THE VERDICT: Case dismissed. The judge said that Burlington Homes acted within its rights for refusing to sell a house if it's done "for business reasons." Liebaert appealed, and the case was dismissed again. He is considering another appeal, now claiming that Burlington Homes is discriminating against his *wife* because she is "married to a lawyer." No matter what the outcome, though, Liebaert has probably already cost Burlington Homes more in litigation than he would have if Judkins had simply sold him the home in the first place.

*   *   *

REAL (ODD) BOOK TITLES

- *How Green Were the Nazis?*, by Franz-Josef Bruggemeier
- *The Stray Shopping Carts of Eastern North America: A Guide to Field Identification*, by Julian Montague
- *Tattooed Mountain Women and Spoon Boxes of Daghestan*, by Robert Chenciner
- *Di Mascios Delicious Ice Cream, Di Mascio of Coventry, an Ice Cream Company of Repute, with an Interesting and Varied Fleet of Ice Cream Vans*, by Roger De Boer
- *Proceedings of the Eighteenth International Seaweed Symposium*
- *Better Never to Have Been: The Harm of Coming Into Existence*, by David Benatar
- *People Who Don't Know They're Dead: How They Attach Themselves to Unsuspecting Bystanders and What to Do About It*, by Gary Leon Hill

WHEN YOU GOTTA GO...

Everybody has to die sometime. Some
of us get to go in interesting ways.

UPON FURTHER REFLECTION...

Famous for both his poetry and his love of liquor, Chinese poet Li Po met his end in 762 while riding on a boat at night on the Yangtze River. According to historical reports, Li was very drunk when he saw the Moon's reflection in the water and decided to try to embrace it. He drowned.

SHOCKINGLY INDE-FENCE-ABLE

Yooket Paen, a 57-year-old woman from Thailand, died when she slipped on a pile of cow dung while walking around on her farm. She tried to catch herself on the fence, but accidentally grabbed a live wire running alongside it and was electrocuted. After Paen's funeral, her sister was showing friends where the accident happened...when *she* slipped and suffered the exact same fate.

BUNNY OF DEATH

A woman died while competing in the Chubby Bunny marshmallow-eating contest at the 2006 Western Fair in Ontario, Canada. The rules: Each contestant eats a marshmallow and then says, "Chubby Bunny." The routine repeats until a contestant gags or is unable to say the phrase. The last contestant who doesn't flub "Chubby Bunny" is the winner. Tragically, the 32-year-old woman choked on one of her marshmallows and then collapsed backstage, later dying of a "blockage in the throat." Organizers expressed their deep sympathies and announced that the Chubby Bunny contest will be cancelled from all future Fairs.

NEXT TIME, SKIP THE DESSERT

King Adolf Frederick, who ruled over Sweden in the 18th century, is known today as "the king who ate himself to death." On February 12, 1771, Frederick devoured a feast fit for a *dozen* kings: multiple helpings of lobster, caviar, sauerkraut, cabbage soup, smoked herring, and champagne. Frederick may have survived dinner, but his intestines couldn't take what he ate for dessert: 14 servings of *semla*, a bun filled with hot milk and marzipan, a rich mixture of sugar and ground almonds.

HUMPED

A four-year-old camel named Polo was reportedly "agitated by mating season" when he kicked and then sat on his keeper at the Mini-Akers Exotic Animals park in Florida. The incident occurred while a local television crew was filming a story on the park. Polo's 1,800 pounds were too much for his keeper; she was crushed.

THE REVENGE OF THE CACTUS

In 1982 David Grundman was wandering through the desert with his gun just outside of Lake Pleasant, Arizona. Bored, he started shooting cactuses. After determining that the smaller ones were "too easy," the 27-year-old took aim at a 100-year-old, 26-foot-tall Saguaro cactus. Getting close enough to make sure he didn't miss, he shot off one of the cactus's massive arms. It fell directly on top of Grundman, killing him almost instantly.

GOODIE TO THE LAST DROP

In 1975 a 50-year-old English bricklayer died while watching an episode of a bizarre television show called *The Goodies*. The plot: A Scotsman wearing a kilt demonstrates the martial art of "Hoots Toots Och Aye" by using his bagpipes to fight off a "psychopathic black pudding." Mitchell was so amused that he laughed nonstop for nearly the entire 25-minute run of the show. Then he suddenly stopped laughing and just sat motionless on his sofa. His wife tried to revive him, but Mitchell had died of heart failure.

THE DUMMY DIDN'T USE A DUMMY

In 1912 an Austrian tailor named Franz Reichelt invented an overcoat that was supposed to double as a parachute. He needed to give it a field test, and received permission to try it from the first deck of the Eiffel Tower, almost 200 feet off the ground…as long as he used a dummy. But Reichelt didn't use a dummy. Did he survive? Well, how many overcoat/parachutes are around today?

DO YOU *REALLY* NEED THAT ORGAN?

When a friend told Uncle John that she'd recently had her gallbladder removed, he wondered: What does a gallbladder do, and how can you live without it?

GALLBLADDER

Location: This four-inch pear-shaped sac sits just under the liver, below your ribs on your right side.

What It Does: It's part of the digestive system. The liver produces a substance called *bile*, which gets stored in the gallbladder before moving via a tube called the *duodenum* into the small intestine, where it digests fats.

Get It Out: The liver purifies the blood against toxins. If you eat too much cholesterol, the liver dumps some of it into the bile. During storage in the gallbladder, the cholesterol-bile sometimes hardens into gallstones: greenish, pain-causing lumps that can be as small as a grain of sand or as large as a golf ball. If the gallstones are really big and really hard, a doctor may opt to remove the entire gallbladder. But you can live without it—if you don't have a gallbladder, the liver delivers the bile directly to the duodenum.

TONSILS

Location: The almond-sized lymph nodes found on both sides of the throat.

What They Do: During infancy and childhood, tonsils prevent bacteria and viruses from entering the throat and produce antibodies to counter infections. By adulthood, your body's other defenses have fully developed, and your tonsils—now unnecessary—shrink and stop working.

Get Them Out: If an especially nasty bug goes around, a child's tonsils try to fight it off. They can end up getting so swollen and infected that swallowing becomes difficult, a condition called *tonsillitis*. Decades ago, it was cured by a tonsillectomy—surgical removal of the tonsils. The operation has become increasingly rare—75% fewer tonsillectomies are performed today than in 1970, owing to stronger antibiotics that can cure tonsillitis on their own.

Wheeeee! The first train reached a top speed of only 5 mph.

SPLEEN

Location: This purplish organ (it looks like a relaxed fist) lies under the diaphragm on the left side of your abdomen.

What It Does: As part of the immune and lymph system, the spleen is a blood filter: It produces and regulates the flow of red and white blood cells, which help to fight infectious bacteria and viruses.

Get It Out: If the spleen is ruptured (common in a severe physical trauma such as a car accident) it loses the ability to regulate, so it must be removed. This reduces the body's natural ability to fight infection, so doctors typically prescribe antibiotics, as well as immunization against flu and pneumonia.

THYROID

Location: The butterfly-shaped gland is located at the base of your neck, where it wraps around your windpipe.

What It Does: Part of the endocrine system, the thyroid disperses hormones that help regulate your body's metabolism.

Get It Out: *Hyperthyroidism* is an overactive thyroid and results in an unhealthily low weight. *Hypothyroidism*, an underactive thyroid, lowers the metabolism and, among other symptoms, frequently causes weight gain. Surgical removal of the thyroid is the treatment for the most severe cases of both conditions. Living without the thyroid is possible, but requires a lifetime regimen of oral medication.

APPENDIX

Location: The worm-shaped tube—about three inches long and one inch in diameter—is attached to your large intestine.

What It Does: Nothing—some scientists think it helped early humans digest animal bones, a need we've since evolved away from.

Get It Out: For unknown reasons, in some people the body deposits small amounts of waste in the appendix. Over time, the waste accumulates and causes the appendix to harden and swell (appendicitis) and even burst, an extremely painful and frequently life-threatening situation. The standard treatment is an appendectomy: the removal of the organ as quickly as possible. Life without an appendix proceeds perfectly normally.

A regulation baseball has exactly 108 stitches.

THE WORST CITY
IN AMERICA

Every city has something to be proud of—even the ones listed here. But some cities, despite their beauty, charm, or cultural importance, also have features of which they might be a little less proud. Here are a few cities with dubious distinctions.

• According to a survey by AutoVantage (an auto club like AAA), Miami, Florida, is the city with the rudest drivers.

• A Cornell University study determined that New York City has the lowest quality of housing. (The World Health Organization says that New York is also the noisiest city in the United States.)

• Because of high divorce and unemployment rates and consistently gloomy weather, the city statistics analyzing firm BestPlaces named Tacoma, Washington, the country's most stressful place to live.

• Breathe easy if you don't live in these places: Greenville, South Carolina (where residents suffer the most respiratory tract infections); Scranton, Pennsylvania (the worst city for asthma sufferers); and Tulsa, Oklahoma (the pollen capital of America).

• Based on the number of accidents and fatalities, the International Federation of Bike Messenger Associations named Boston the most dangerous place to ride a bike.

• Zero, a group dedicated to slowing population growth, determined what cities were the best and worst in which to raise children based on the quality of healthcare, education, public safety, transportation, the job market, and the natural environment. The best was Fargo, North Dakota; the worst was Newark, New Jersey.

• According to the National Coalition for the Homeless, Sarasota, Florida, is the city most hostile toward homeless people.

• *Forbes* magazine named Pittsburgh, PA, the worst city for single people. Reasons: expensive beer, few nightclubs, and not enough single people.

Iowa is bigger than Portugal.

- Worst traffic congestion: Los Angeles. (Not coincidentally, it also has the worst air pollution.)

- City with the bumpiest, most pothole-infested roads: Seattle.

- In 2007 *Men's Health* magazine analyzed various cities' obesity rates, eating habits, and other data, including how much time people spend exercising and sitting in traffic. Result: Las Vegas was judged the nation's "fattest city."

- The city with the most suicides per capita is Medford, Oregon.

- Decatur, Illinois, has the highest skin cancer fatality rate.

- America's most rat-infested city is Baltimore.

- New Orleans leads in both gun- and diabetes-related deaths per capita.

- Hallmark Cards calls El Paso, Texas, the city with the worst sense of humor, based on polls in which very few people said they considered themselves funny. (The city also has very low sales of Hallmark's humorous cards.)

- City with the highest percentage of lawyers: Washington, D.C. Nearly 2% of all residents are attorneys.

- According to the book *Cities Ranked and Rated*, the worst overall city in America is Modesto, California. The city scored a 0 on the book's 100-point scale for its high cost of living, high unemployment rate, lack of activities, and the highest car theft rate in the United States.

*　　*　　*

CAN'T WAKE THE DEAD?

"A fake wake organized by Donald Warren for his 80th birthday had to be cancelled...because he died for real the day before. Warren, of Verwood, Dorset, had even rented a coffin in which he was to lie, propped up to watch 'mourners.' But he died from a fatal heart attack. Family members were too upset to comment, but lifelong pal Mike Sharman, 78, said, 'Most of us think the arranging of the party brought on the attack.'"

—*The Sunday Mirror* (U.K.)

MR. MUSIC BOX

Is anybody neutral about karaoke? People either love it or hate it. Some of us (including Uncle John) are too chicken to even try singing in front of other people. Here's a look at the guy who invented it.

SING ALONG

Daisuke Inoue was a nightclub keyboardist in Kobe, Japan, in the early 1970s. He was a terrible singer, and so was everyone else in the band. Not that it mattered—in Japan it's common for people at parties or out on the town to get up and sing a song for their companions, good voice or not. The tradition dates back centuries—even samurai warriors were expected to be able to belt out a song or two when the occasion called for it.

Inoue's band specialized in providing musical accompaniment for these after-hours singers. They had developed a number of tricks for complementing even the most tone-deaf warblers that came into the club: Instead of leading a bad singer, Inoue and his bandmates carefully followed *the singer's* lead, and played their instruments in such a way that they covered the singer's flaws without drowning out their voices.

THE NEXT BEST THING

Inoue's band developed a loyal following among the very worst of Kobe's crooners, and in 1971 one of them, the president of a local steel company, invited Inoue to play for him on a retreat the company was hosting at a hot-springs resort. Inoue wanted to go but he couldn't get off work, so he taped himself playing keyboard to the man's favorite song, "Leaving Haneda Airport on a 7:50 Flight," and gave the man the tape.

The executive was very happy with the result. That made Inoue wonder if other people might enjoy singing to recorded music, too. He installed an eight-track-tape player, a microphone, and an amplifier in a red-and-white painted wooden box, added an echo effect that he thought made singers sound better, and rigged the contraption to accept 100-yen (about 80¢) coins as payment. He named his contraption the 8-Juke. Then he and six of his bandmates formed Crescent, a company that would lease the machines to bars and restaurants in Kobe. Inoue figured that leasing the machines would be more appealing to restaurant owners than buying them, because then he, not they, would be responsible for keeping the music and song sheets current with changing trends in music. Each machine would have a selection of 40 popular songs, carefully chosen to sound good when sung by amateurs.

Inoue's machine was called the 8-Juke, but for the practice of singing along with it he adopted a term that had long been in use by professional singers in Japan. Before they went out on tour, the singers had to decide whether they would bring a live orchestra with them, or sing to recorded music—*karano okesutora* ("hidden" or "empty orchestra") as it was called—*kara oke* for short.

OFF THE CHARTS

Crescent started small. The company made only 11 machines at first, but it quickly found homes for all of them and had to build more. Soon the machines were appearing in bars and restaurants all over Kobe, and then in cities all over Japan. By 1974 the business was so big that other companies jumped in and built their own karaoke machines. It wasn't long before the karaoke craze was spreading all over Asia.

Karaoke machines remained a sideline for existing businesses like restaurants, bars, and hotels until 1985, when a businessman in Okayama divided a shipping container into small cubicles and installed a karaoke machine in each one. From these modest origins, the "karaoke box" became one of the most popular venues for karaoke in Japan—for the first time, teenagers who were too young to hang out in adult establishments (and people who too shy to sing in front of strangers) had an intimate space where they could sing karaoke just to their friends. Where karaoke machines had previously served patrons of restaurants and bars, now restaurants and bars were springing up to serve the karaoke-box trade.

PLENTY TO SING ABOUT

Over the years, karaoke has grown into a $25-billion-a-year business that has reached every part of the globe. The most sophisticated machines hold 30,000 songs or more, and can tell you your horoscope while calculating how many calories you burned whooping out "Mack the Knife," "Love Shack," and "My Heroes Have Always Been Cowboys." Karaoke Web sites let you sing over your Web cam to people who are thousands of miles away; you can even download karaoke tunes and digital song sheets onto your cellphone. Not that you'd want to encounter one on the expressway, but Geely Automobile Company in China has perfected *Car-a-oke*: The company's Beauty Leopard sports cars offer built-in karaoke machines as standard equipment.

MISSED IT BY THAT MUCH

Daisuke Inoue didn't do too badly for himself. Crescent held its own against much larger companies until 1987, when fierce competition and the development of laserdisc technology finally drove it out of the karaoke business. But he didn't do nearly as well as he would have if he'd thought to *patent* his idea. At the time, Inoue didn't think he had anything to patent—after all, all he did was combine an eight-track player, a microphone, and an amplifier in a way that hadn't been done before. By the time he realized he could patent the idea, it was too late. But for a guy who didn't collect one cent of what might have been billions of dollars in royalties, Inoue seems surprisingly unaffected. "I am its natural parent, but having given birth to karaoke, I abandoned it," he joked to *Time* magazine in 1999.

At last report Inoue was still tinkering away. In addition to receiving a patent for plastic-covered songbooks, he has invented a device that automatically kills the cockroaches that crawl inside karaoke machines. "Roaches get inside the machines, build nests and chew wires," he says. "In 80 percent of the cases, karaoke machine breakdown is caused by bugs."

ON-THE-JOB CROONING

In Japan it's common for office workers to hit the karaoke bars after work for obligatory singing sessions with the boss. That could prove fatal to a career, so the Japanese have developed rules of etiquette to help employees survive with their careers intact. Some examples:
• "Listen respectfully to the singing of the boss."
• "Take care not to sing the boss' favorite song as it is likely he will not be able to sing too many different songs."
• "Avoid sexy songs that are likely to offend senior office ladies."

...but among American women, those with the lowest income are most likely to be overweight.

ANIMAL HEROES

Be kind to animals—the life they save may be...yours.

CHAMPION CHIHUAHUA

While one-year-old Booker West was happily splashing his hands in a birdbath in his yard in Masonville, Colorado, Zoey, the family's Chihuahua, was keeping guard. Good thing, too, because a rattlesnake slithered out of the bushes and lunged at Booker. That's when Zoey jumped between snake and baby and took a poisonous bite to her face. Booker's grandfather heard the dog yelp and quickly swooped in to pick the boy up off the ground. Zoey's face swelled up to the "size of a grapefruit," and she nearly died, but veterinarians were able to save her. Denise Long, Booker's grandmother, praised the heroic dog: "These little bitty dogs, they just don't get any credit."

CAPTAIN KANGAROO

In 2003 Leonard Richards, 52, was checking his Tanjil South, Australia, emu farm for storm damage when a tree branch came crashing down on his head and knocked him out. Luckily for Richards, Lulu, his pet kangaroo who "thinks she's a dog," was following him. A short time later, Lynn, Richards's wife, heard furious barking outside. When she opened her door, she instantly knew something was wrong. She followed the barks and found Lulu standing over her unconscious master. Help was called in and Richards was airlifted to a hospital in Melbourne, where he made a full recovery. For her part, Lulu became the first kangaroo to receive the National Animal Valor Award from the RSPCA. "I'd be pushing up daisies if it wasn't for Lulu," said Richards.

SUPER SPIDERS

Danielle Vigue, 18, was awakened in the middle of the night in July 2007...by spiders. Dozens of them. They were crawling all over her and all over her bed. And Danielle *hated* spiders. Freaking out, the Hemlock, Michigan, teenager started killing the arachnids until she noticed even more of them crawling down the

---

The Himalayan Mountains cover one-tenth of the Earth's land mass.

walls. She immediately ran across the hallway to sleep in her 15-year-old sister's room. A little later, their mom woke them up, saying she smelled smoke. Investigating, they slowly opened the door to Danielle's bedroom and…it was on fire! They called the fire department, who rushed in and contained the blaze before it took over the house. But the bedroom was toast—as Danielle would have been, too, if the spiders hadn't made a mass exodus from the attic, where the fire started. After her harrowing experience, Danielle gained a new respect for the creepy-crawlies: "I will never ever kill another spider again," she said.

DILIGENT DOGGY

On the afternoon of January 15, 2007, actress Salma Hayek had a splitting headache. Bad timing: In just a few short hours she was scheduled to attend the Golden Globe Awards, where her TV show, Ugly Betty, was nominated for Best Comedy. But all Hayek could think about was how miserable she felt, so she decided to take a nap. The next thing Hayek knew, her dog Diva was hopping on her bed, barking furiously and tugging at Hayek's arm. Hayek got up and immediately smelled a gas leak. She got out of the house and called in the fire department to turn it off. Crediting her life to her beloved dog, Hayek was able to attend the ceremony that night…where her show won the award.

CLAIRVOYANT KITTY

Oscar isn't exactly a lifesaver, but this unique kitty is credited with predicting when people are about to die. And in doing so, he actually brings comfort to them, and their families. Oscar lives at the Steere House Nursing Center in Providence, Rhode Island, where he roams the halls of the "end-stage dementia unit." Oscar rarely jumps into bed with a patient…except when their passing is within about two hours. After his 13th accurate prediction, the nurses started calling in the families of the soon-to-be-deceased. So far, the two-year-old cat has predicted 26 deaths, and he's seen as a miracle worker at the facility. "Many family members take some solace from it," said Dr. David Dosa of nearby Brown University. "They appreciate the companionship that the cat provides for a dying loved one in their final hours." Dosa added that cat is "not usually friendly to people."

WHY ASK WHY?

Sometimes, the answer is irrelevant—it's the question that counts.

If the doctor always says to take two aspirins, why don't we just double their size?

Why doesn't "Buick" rhyme with "quick"?

Is there ever a day when mattresses are *not* on sale?

Doesn't "expecting the unexpected" make the unexpected expected?

Do bees get wax in their ears?

Why do mirrors reflect backwards, but not upside down?

If Wal-Mart keeps lowering its prices every day, how come nothing in the store is free?

Why is it that no matter what color of bubble bath you use, the bubbles are always white?

Why does it take so little time for a child who is afraid of the dark to become a teenager who wants to stay out all night?

How can traffic come to a standstill? Shouldn't it be a sitstill?

Why do you start slowing down immediately when the sign says "Speed Zone Ahead"?

How much faster would lightning travel if it didn't zigzag?

How do you write zero in Roman numerals?

Why do drugstores make sick people walk to the back to get their prescriptions, while healthy people can buy cigarettes at the front?

Why isn't "palindrome" spelled "palindromeemordnilap"?

How come you have to go to the "Start" menu to shut down your computer?

When the stars are out, you can see them; when the lights are out, you can't. Why?

Can you be a closet claustrophobic?

Why is it that one match can start a forest fire, but it takes a whole box to light a barbecue?

If swimming is such great exercise, how come whales are fat?

Why "milkshake"? Shouldn't it be called a "milkshook"?

Why is it that most nudists are people you would never want to see naked?

"If a word in the dictionary were misspelled, how would we know?" —Steven Wright

DUMB CROOKS

Proof that crime doesn't pay.

BAG MAN

"Clenzo Thompson, 45, was arrested in New York City in January 2007 after allegedly robbing the same Commerce Bank branch twice in three days. The first robbery ended when the chemical dye in the money bag exploded and spooked him. He apparently failed to learn from that, because the dye in the second robbery's money bag also exploded. (And three years earlier, Thompson had been caught after another bank robbery after having accidentally dropped his ID on the bank floor.)"

—**News of the Weird**

WENT TO THE WELL ONCE TOO OFTEN

"A scofflaw who came to be known as the 'gin and tonic bandit' went to the same O'Charley's restaurant in Bloomington, Indiana, every Wednesday for a month, ordered two gin and tonics and a rib-eye steak, then skipped out on his $25.96 bill. At the end of each meal he would excuse himself to use the restroom, then skip out without paying. Amazingly, the man returned a fifth time. This time the restaurant was ready for him. When his server presented the bill, he again claimed he needed to use the bathroom. But when he walked out of the restaurant, four employees were waiting to confront him. He immediately offered to pay the bill...with a check. Told the restaurant didn't accept checks, the man 'got nervous and ran,' according to police. He was quickly caught and arrested."

—**Associated Press**

NO SUCH THING AS A FREE LUNCH

"Richmond Heights police Sgt. Chuck Duffy has long known that Joan Hall is a habitual scammer and thief. After all, he is the detective who spearheaded the case charging the 65-year-old woman with bilking department stores out of millions of dollars through shoplifting and merchandise-return schemes. But even Duffy could hardly believe it when he saw Hall and her co-defendant, Roger

Neff, stealing food from the Justice Center cafeteria during the lunch break from their trial. He reported the incident to cafeteria managers, who summoned sheriff's deputies. Minutes later, they found Hall and Neff lunching at a table—the defense table in Judge Nancy Fuerst's courtroom, where the two are on trial. The judge ordered Hall and Neff to stay out of the cafeteria for the rest of their trial. 'You bring your lunch,' Fuerst told them."

—*Cleveland Plain Dealer*

WILD CARD

"A hapless German thief snapped his credit card in two while prying open his neighbor's lock, inadvertently leaving behind his name and account details. 'He tried to copy what he'd seen them do on television, but the flat-owner woke up and the criminal ran away,' a police spokesman said. 'The victim called up and read us the details off the card. When we got to the burglar's house, the other half of his credit card was sitting on his kitchen table.'"

—**Reuters**

WHO WAS THAT MASKED MORON?

"Daniel Ray Brown, 22, of Decatur, Illinois, is charged with the armed robbery of his 72-year-old grandfather. Hard up for cash, Brown donned a ski mask and jacket, armed himself with a handle from a hydraulic jack, and made the 10-foot hike next door to his grandfather's home, said Detective Kyle Wilson. 'There's a woman that lives there with his grandpa. He says, "Sit down, Bernice." Then he goes to his grandpa's room, who was lying in bed, and he says, "This is a robbery, I need your money, and I mean it, Pa-Paw,"' Wilson said. 'So he grabs Pa-Paw's britches off the chair. The wallet was in there. He got out to the next room, and his Pa-Paw tackled him. There was a scuffle, and he hit his Pa-Paw in the head with the handle,' Wilson said. While his grandfather called 911, Daniel Brown went back to his own home, leaving a trail—the pants, billfold, $5, and the handle—between the two houses. 'That's where he was when I got there,' Wilson said. Brown denied to investigators that he was the man behind the mask."

—*Decatur Daily*

Longest entry in *The American Dictionary of Slang*: "vomit."

WEIRD GAME SHOWS

Here are some of the strangest game shows ever to air on American television.

ACROSS THE BOARD (1959) Concept: Two contestants competed to see who could finish a crossword puzzle first. (Have you ever watched somebody else fill out a crossword puzzle? It's pretty boring.)

LUCKY PARTNERS (1958) Host Carl Cordell read part of the serial number on a dollar bill. Players in the studio—and viewers at home—won prizes if they had a dollar bill with matching numbers. Because of the large number of bills in circulation, there were rarely any winners on *Lucky Partners.*

CELEBRITY BOWLING (1971) That's pretty much it: Celebrities came on and bowled. Frequent guests included Telly Savalas, Roy Rogers, Bobby Darin, Carroll O'Connor, and Sammy Davis Jr. Amazingly, the show ran for seven years and inspired a similar show called *Celebrity Tennis* in 1974.

BALANCE YOUR BUDGET (1952) Between segments by financial experts who provided budgeting techniques and home economics tips, housewives who were in debt competed to win a treasure chest full of cash.

TRASHED (1994) Contestants tried to answer questions correctly. If they didn't, the opposing team got to smash the losing team's prized possessions with a sledgehammer.

THE GRUDGE MATCH (1991) Real people came on to settle a dispute or disagreement in a boxing ring, using "weapons" such as oversized boxing gloves, cream pies, and water balloons. At the end of the show the studio audience voted on a winner.

E.S.P. (1958) Led by host Vincent Price, two contestants were placed in isolation booths, and experiments were conducted to see which person had stronger psychic abilities. After three weeks of shows in which no psychic powers were ever detected, it became a "news" show about E.S.P. (It lasted only a month.)

86ED

If you've ever been in a diner and heard the waitress tell the short-order cook to "86 the onions," you might know that 86 means "remove" or "throw out." But why does 86 mean that? Nobody knows for sure, but there are many theories.

THEORY #1: Delmonico's, a legendary New York City steakhouse (the original restaurant closed in 1926), served dozens of different cuts of steak, and they were all numbered on the menu. Item #86 was the rib-eye, the most popular entree—so popular that Delmonico's frequently ran out of it. The number "86" became staff shorthand for running out of something.

THEORY #2: Another famed 1920s New York establishment, the 21 Club, supposedly had only 85 tables. When the club was full, the host would assign one unlucky customer table #86...and then throw him out.

THEORY #3: Article 86 of an old version of the New York State Liquor Code—adhered to by bars and restaurants—stated that if someone was visibly intoxicated, bartenders were forbidden to serve them any more booze.

THEORY #4: Many soup kitchens in the 1920s and 1930s used huge cauldrons that held exactly 85 bowls of soup. If you were 86th in line, you didn't get any soup.

THEORY #5: British Merchant Marine ships could supposedly carry only 85 sailors. The 86th sailor to report for duty got left ashore.

THEORY #6: Many coffins are eight feet long and buried six feet underground. According to grave-digger slang, when you're buried, you're "86ed."

THEORY #7: One of the observation decks in New York City's Empire State Building is on the 86th floor. The ledges are now fenced off because it used to be a popular suicide jump spot.

THEORY #8: Soda fountain workers in the 1930s used a jargon

---

made up of seemingly random number codes. A "99" was the head soda jerk, a "33" was a cherry Coke, a "55" was a root beer, and an "87½" was a cute female customer. An "86" was anything out of stock.

THEORY #9: It's bartender slang. If a bartender ran out of the high-quality 100-proof whiskey, they'd substitute in the similar (but cheaper) 86 proof.

THEORY #10: By 1886, the Gold Rush in the western United States was over, taken over by mining companies. A single miner looking for a claim was out of luck, or "86ed."

THEORY #11: In the criminal underground of the Cockney parts of London in the 19th century, rhyming slang was used as code. For example, "trouble and strife" meant "wife," "plates of meat" meant "feet," and "bees and honey" meant "money." "86ed" was rhyming slang for "nixed." (For more Cockney, see page 129.)

THEORY #12: Chumley's was a New York speakeasy during Prohibition. The secret alternate entrance was located at 86 Bedford Street. The bar bribed cops to let them know when a raid was coming so their patrons could escape without being arrested. The cops would phone the bar and the bartender would yell "86 everybody!" as a cue to leave via 86 Bedford.

*   *   *

AMERICAN ENGLISH VS. CANADIAN ENGLISH

- In Canada, a studio apartment is a *bachelor.*
- A hooded sweatshirt is called a *bunny hug.*
- A *keener* is another name for a brown-noser.
- A whiny person is called a *suck.*
- Canadian parking garages are *parkades.*
- Whole milk is called *homo* milk (short for homogenized milk).
- Rain gutters are *eavestroughs.*
- A dead-end job in America is a *joe job* in Canada.

7% of Ireland's barley crop is used in the production of Guinness beer.

GNOME GNEWS IS GOOD GNEWS

Garden gnomes do the strangest things.

G NAUGHTY. In April 2007, 26 gnomes were discovered taped to lamp posts around the town of Seaford, England, covered in fake blood, with forks and axes jammed into their heads, and with "gruesome messages" written on them. Police determined the culprits to be "high-spirited youngsters."

UP TO GNO GOOD. The 2007 graduating class of St. Helens High School in Oregon pulled an elaborate senior prank: They stole every garden gnome they could find—more than 60—and placed them around the grounds of the school. Missing gnomes were later claimed by people living as far away as Portland (30 miles away) and Astoria (66 miles).

DO GNOT OPEN. Australian customs officials recently opened a package they suspected of being shipped by a known group of British smugglers. Did they find drugs? Explosives? No, the package contained three garden gnomes. Customs officials then X-rayed the gnomes—standard procedure—and discovered two snakes and three exotic lizards inside. A day later, the same officials analyzed another package of gnomes from Britain, and found five snakes and five lizards. (Bringing animals into Australia without a license is illegal—so smugglers have gotten crafty.)

MAY GNEED SURGERY. In 2006 Michael Naylor of North Yorkshire, England, bought a gnome at a yard sale for £10 ($20). An hour after he bought it (he named it "Stan"), Naylor dropped the gnome on his foot and broke a toe. A month later, Naylor moved Stan from his patio to a flower bed because he was creeped out by the gnome staring at him through a window while he was watching TV. During the move Stan fell on Naylor's hand, tearing a ligament. A few weeks later, Naylor was weeding the flower bed around Stan and the gnome's fishing pole stabbed him in the eye. Naylor said he'd like to get rid of Stan, but he's afraid to go near him again.

PHRASE ORIGINS

Here are the origins of some common phrases.

O N THE LAM
Meaning: To be on the run, especially from the police
Origin: "American slang since the latter part of the 19th century. The root of *lam* is the Old Norse word *lamja*, meaning to 'make lame,' and the original meaning, when it first appeared in English back in the 16th century, was to 'beat soundly.' The change in the meaning from beat to run away probably echoed another slang term for running away—beat it. To beat it or lam it is to rapidly beat the road with one's feet...by running." (From *The Word Detective*, by Evan Morris)

STRAW POLL

Meaning: An unofficial vote indicating the trend of opinion on a candidate or issue
Origin: "The use of the phrase began in America in 1824 when reporters from the *Harrisburg Pennsylvanian* questioned a sample of voters in an attempt to predict the overall result. The findings proved accurate and were considered such a success that the idea caught on and has been used in almost every election ever since. The actual wording of *straw poll* comes from the practice of throwing a handful of straw into the air to determine the direction of the wind." (From *Red Herrings and White Elephants*, by Albert Jack)

THE PITS

Meaning: The worst
Origin: "This disparaging phrase was first linked with Woody Allen in the late 1970s, but was made famous by the 1981 Wimbledon men's singles tennis champion, John McEnroe. The Wimbledon umpire who failed to accept his outbursts in the spirit in which he offered them was compared to that most unsavory location, 'the armpits of the world.'" (From *To Coin a Phrase*, by Edwin Radford and Alan Smith)

The last words Walt Disney wrote were "Kurt Russell."

HOCUS POCUS

Meaning: Expression used by magicians while performing a trick

Origin: "Before performing sleight of hand, conjurors usually mutter the magical words 'hocus pocus.' But they never explain that nonsense phrase. A belief once existed that it came from Latin *hoc est corpus*, meaning 'Here is my body,' used to mock the Roman Church's mass (in which bread is changed into the body of Jesus). Word-followers now believe that the phrase was false or invented Latin, fabricated by magicians to sound impressive as they worked their tricks—but the words had no meaning at all. Although the phrase consists of meaningless rhyming sounds, from *hocus* came the usable words *hoax* and the slang term *hokum*, meaning 'nonsense.'" (From *The Story Behind the Word*, by Morton S. Freeman)

TO SHELL OUT

Meaning: To hand over money or payment of any kind

Origin: "Money was scarce in Colonial America. Not enough coins and bills were in circulation to meet the demands of commerce. As a result of this shortage, Indian corn was used as a medium of exchange. All payments were in the form of shelled corn. Planters usually left it on the cob until the time came to meet an obligation. So when a bill was due, it was time to get the family together for a husking, a 'shelling out.' This practice became so strongly attached to the idea of payment that a person handing over anything of value is said 'to shell out.'" (From *I've Got Goose Pimples*, by Marvin Vanoni)

BATTING YOUR EYELASHES

Meaning: To flutter one's eyelids, usually in a flirtatious manner

Origin: "It has nothing to do with bats flapping in a cave, or someone 'gone batty.' *Batting* in this case comes from falconry in Tudor times. According to a book written in 1615: 'Batting, or to bat, is when a Hawke fluttereth with his wings either from the perch or the man's fist, striving, as it were, to fly away.' The old word had long been used by sportsmen, and some American with a lot of *Sprachgefühl*—'feeling for language'—found a fresh use for it in the 1880s." (From *The Facts on File Encyclopedia of Word and Phrase Origins*, by Robert Hendrickson)

The Sargasso Sea has no coastline. (It's in the middle of the North Atlantic Ocean.)

KING OF THE ONE-LINERS

Henny Youngman (1906–1998) spent 70 years of his life telling jokes. Here are just a few of his thousands of zingers.

"A doctor tells a man, 'You want to improve your love life? Exercise. Run 10 miles a day.' Two weeks later, the man calls the doctor. The doc asks, 'How's your love life?' The man replies, 'How should I know, I'm 140 miles away!'"

"I've got a great doctor. If you can't afford the operation, he touches up your X-rays."

"I said, 'Doctor, it hurts when I do that.' He says, 'Then don't do that!'"

"In high-school football, the coach kept me on the bench all year. On the last game of the season, the crowd was yelling, 'We want Youngman! We want Youngman!' The coach finally says, 'Youngman, go see what they want!'"

"I take my wife everywhere—she always finds her way back."

"I told my wife I was afraid I took too many sleeping pills. She told me to have a few drinks and get some rest."

"My wife has an electric blender, electric toaster, electric bread maker. Then she said, 'There are too many gadgets, and no place to sit down!' So I bought her an electric chair."

"A man calls a lawyer's office. 'Schwartz, Schwartz, Schwartz, and Schwartz,' says the man on the phone. 'Let me talk to Mr. Schwartz.' 'I'm sorry, he's on vacation.' 'Then let me talk to Mr. Schwartz.' 'He's busy with a big case.' 'Then let me talk to Mr. Schwartz.' 'He's playing golf today.' 'Okay, then, let me talk to Mr. Schwartz.' 'Speaking.'"

"I just made a killing on Wall Street. I shot my broker!"

"A woman was taking a shower. There is a knock on the door. 'Who is it?' 'Blind man!' So the woman opens the door. 'Where do you want these blinds, lady?'"

"They certainly are a fastidious couple. She's fast and he's hideous."

Take his wife, please? Henny Youngman was happily married for 59 years.

"My dad was the town drunk. Lots of times that's not so bad...but New York City?"

"My brother-in-law died. He was a karate expert, then joined the army. The first time he saluted, he killed himself."

"My wife was at the beauty shop for two hours yesterday. That was just the estimate."

"My wife and I always hold hands. If I let go, she shops."

"I went to the track. The horse I bet on was so slow, the jockey kept a diary of the trip. The horse was so late getting home, he tiptoed into the stable."

"I know a man who's a diamond cutter. He mows the lawn at Yankee Stadium."

"All men are not homeless, but some men are home less than others."

"I took a trip on an airplane. The food on that plane was fit for a king. 'Here, King!'"

"I told the ticket lady at the airport, 'Send one of my bags to New York, send one to Los Angeles, and send one to Miami.' She said, 'We can't do that!' I told her, 'You did it last week!'"

"A man goes to a psychiatrist and says, 'Nobody listens to me!' The doctor says, 'Next!'"

"The psychiatrist says, 'I think you're crazy.' The man says, 'I want a second opinion.' The psychiatrist says, 'Okay, you're ugly, too!'"

*   *   *

A RANDOM ORIGIN

Hans Riegel, who had worked in candy factories in Bonn, Germany, before World War I, was looking for a way to support his family. He opened his own candy company in 1920 and called it Haribo, an acronym of **Ha**ns **Ri**egel, **Bo**nn. At first he made only hard candy, but in 1922 he mixed gelatin into the recipe. The result: sweet, chewy, semi-transparent candies. He shaped them into bears and named the new candy Gummibäre (German for "rubber bears"). It was an instant success. Today, Gummi Bears are sold in more than 100 countries, making it one of the most popular non-chocolate candies in the world.

SIMPLE MACHINES

Uncle John first learned about simple machines in third grade. Being a fan of anything that's simple, he never forgot them (or his third-grade teacher, Mrs. Sigler). Can these machines actually be the basis for all tools?

TOOLING AROUND

Have you ever tried to lift a 200-pound lawnmower two feet off the ground and put it in the back of a pickup truck? Few people could do it. But from time to time it has to be done, and one way to make the job easier is by using a ramp, or *inclined plane*. An inclined plane is an example of what engineers call a "simple machine," one that requires the application of only a single force—in this case, you pushing the mower—to work.

By pushing the object up the inclined plane instead of lifting it straight up, the amount of strength, or force, required to get the mower into the truck is reduced. But there's a trade-off: You have to apply that reduced force over a greater distance to do the job. If the ramp is 10 feet long, for example, you have to push the mower a distance of 10 feet instead of lifting it straight up just 2 feet onto the truck. This trade-off—applying less force over a greater distance to accomplish tasks that would otherwise be difficult or impossible—is the physical principle behind all simple machines.

The inclined plane is only one type of simple machine—there are five more: the lever, the wedge, the screw, the wheel and axle (which work together), and the pulley. Believe it or not, all complex mechanical machines—bicycles, automobiles, cranes, power drills, toasters, you name it—are nothing more than different combinations of some or all of these six simple machines.

THE WEDGE

A wedge isn't much more than a moving inclined plane—it's so similar, in fact, that some experts consider wedges and inclined planes the same thing. One common example of a wedge is a cutting blade. Take the head of an axe: Its wedge shape converts a small force applied over a long distance—that of the axe head entering the piece of wood—into a force powerful enough to split a piece of wood into two pieces. If the tip of the axe head travels

Largest fruit crop on Earth: grapes. (Bananas are #2.)

half an inch into the wood, its wedge shape drives the wood apart only a fraction of that distance, but it does so with tremendous force, enough to eventually split the wood in two. Try doing that with your bare hands!

The blades of virtually all cutting tools—knives, scissors, can openers, and even electric razors—operate on the same principle, as do zippers, plows, and even the keys to your house. If you examine the serrated edge of your house key, you'll see that it isn't much more than a series of wedges of different heights that lift the pins inside the lock to the precise height needed to turn the lock and open the door. The wedges on the key are double-sided, so that the key can be removed from the lock after it has performed its task.

THE SCREW

A screw may not look much like either a wedge or an inclined plane, but it's pretty much the same thing. It's an inclined plane wrapped in a spiral around a cylinder or shaft. You have to turn a screw several times, using a small amount of force, to drive it a tiny distance into a piece of wood, a task that would otherwise require great force.

THE LEVER

Like the inclined plane, the lever makes it possible to lift things that would otherwise be too heavy for humans to lift. The lever consists of a rod or bar that rests on a point or a supporting object called a *fulcrum*. If you've ever used a claw hammer to pull a nail out of a piece of board, you've used a lever. By applying a small force over a great distance, in this case the distance your hand on the handle travels as you pry the nail out of the wood, the lever converts this into a strong force applied over a short distance. Your hand will travel several inches, but the claw pulls the nail only an inch or so out of the wood. Bottle openers are levers, so are nutcrackers and even wheelbarrows—by lifting the handles of a wheelbarrow a foot or so off the ground, you're able to lift a heavy load near the wheel and push it where you want it to go. The handles of a pair of scissors are levers that magnify the force of the wedge-shaped blades. That's an example of a *complex* machine: a combination of simple machines (levers and wedges) that work together to perform a given task.

Found in a shark's belly in 1941: 3 belts, 9 shoes, 14 stockings, and 43 buttons.

THE WHEEL AND AXLE

One simple example of a wheel and axle is a screwdriver. In this case the handle is the wheel and the shaft is the axle, and, just as with the other machines, it gets its advantage by sacrificing distance for force. When you turn the handle of the screwdriver a full revolution, the shaft has also gone a full revolution—but it's traveled a much shorter distance. And the force it exerts over that distance is several times greater than the force you exerted over the handle's longer distance, allowing you to turn a screw into a wall. Other examples of wheel-and-axle machines that you use commonly: doorknobs, faucets, windmills, and the steering wheel in your car.

THE PULLEY

A single pulley can enable you to change the direction of the force that you use to do work. For example, if you want to lift something off the ground without a pulley, you have to lift upwards. But if you have a pulley attached to the ceiling and a rope running through it that's attached to the object you're trying to lift, by pulling the rope down you can lift the object up.

Using multiple pulleys together in a single device called a *block and tackle* allows you to lift objects heavier than your own weight, something that would be impossible with only one pulley, since you'd lift yourself off the ground instead of lifting the object. The block and tackle does this by distributing the weight of the object over multiple sections of rope—if the block and tackle contains four pulleys, for example, each length of rope will support 1/4 the weight of the object. If the object weighs 200 pounds, each of the four sections of rope is supporting 50 pounds of weight, and you only have to apply 50 pounds of force to lift the object...but you'll have to apply it over a greater distance, by pulling four times as much rope as you would have using only a single pulley. For every foot you want to raise the object off the ground, you will have to pull four feet of rope. As with all the other simple machines, you're applying a smaller force (your own strength) over a greater distance (four feet of rope instead of one) to get the same amount of work done (lifting a heavy object off the ground).

BUZZ BOMB

If, as the Bible says, the first shall be the last and the meek shall inherit the Earth, is it possible that mosquitoes will conquer the universe?

THE STINGING TRUTH

When it comes to mosquitoes—those miniature flying torpedoes—there's good news…and bad news.

Good News: Mosquitoes are tiny. One mosquito weighs only 1/25,000 of an ounce. You can squash it with your thumb.

Bad News: This tiny creature is responsible for more human deaths than any other creature on Earth.

Good News: Male mosquitoes don't bite people; they prefer flower nectar.

Bad News: Female mosquitoes *do* bite people—they need the protein to reproduce.

Good News: A male mosquito's life span is less than three days.

Bad News: Female mosquitoes live for more than three months.

Good News: Mosquitoes don't actually bite.

Bad News: They suck…blood.

Good News: Relax. That welt a mosquito bite raises on your arm is temporary.

Bad News: That welt is your body's allergic reaction to the mosquito's saliva, which it injects into you to prevent your blood from clotting while it drinks.

Good News: Mosquitoes have trouble seeing you.

Bad News: They can smell you. They like carbon dioxide, and use your exhaled breath to track you down. This explains all those welts on your face when you've been out camping.

Good News: At 30 feet, nearsighted mosquitoes can't distinguish you from a tree trunk.

Bad News: At 10 feet, they become heat-seeking missiles, using their antennae's thermal receptors to find you.

Good News: Central America's "Mosquito Coast" is not named after the bug. It's a corruption of Miskito, the name of the indigenous local people.
Bad News: It's still infested with mosquitoes.

Good News: Mosquitoes avoid citronella. It irritates their feet.
Bad News: If you eat bananas, you become a mosquito target.

Good News: You cannot get the HIV virus from a mosquito.
Bad News: You can get malaria, yellow fever, dengue fever, and encephalitis from mosquito bites. They also transmit heartworms to cats and dogs.

Good News: You can take pills to prevent malaria.
Bad News: Not everyone has access to those pills. Mosquito-transmitted malaria kills one million people per year in Africa.

Good News (for Grownups): Mosquitoes prefer children to adults.
Bad News (for Blondes): They prefer blondes to brunettes.

Good News: Mosquitoes rarely travel more than 300 feet from their breeding grounds.
Bad News: One mosquito averages 1,000–3,000 offspring.

Good News: North America has only 170 species of mosquitoes.
Bad News: There are more than 2,500 species in the world.

Good News: Bug zappers kill 3,000 insects a night.
Bad News: Only a handful of them are mosquitoes. The rest are beneficial, like butterflies and moths.

Good News: A mosquito has a built-in mechanism that tells it to stop feeding when it is full.
More Good News: When that chemical signal is disabled, the mosquito eats so much it explodes.

If a tuna stops swimming, it sinks.

GHOST HOSTS

For some reason, Great Britain has more than its share of mansions, estates, and old homes that are reported to be haunted.

Leeds Castle is said to be haunted by a dog. He pays no attention to the people who visit the castle, but he's said to bring bad luck to anyone who spots him.

St. Donat's Castle is a 12th-century Welsh castle that's now a boarding school...and they say a ghost-panther stalks the corridors. In a parlor, a piano plays itself...even when the lid is closed.

Woburn Abbey in Bedfordshire supposedly has a mischievous spirit that loves to fling open doors. Billionaire J. Paul Getty said it once terrified him by barging into his room.

Chatham House is haunted by the ghost of "Hanging Judge" George Jeffreys, the former chief justice of England who liked to hand out death sentences. Jeffreys is said to walk around Chatham House in his black judicial robes, carrying a bloody bone.

East Riddlesden Hall in Yorkshire hosts the "Grey Lady." She reportedly paces up and down the stairs, looking for her lover, who was sealed in a room by her jealous husband and left there to die.

Dover Castle is said to be haunted by a boy murdered during the Napoleonic Wars. The headless ghost stalks the halls, drumming.

Raby Castle near Durham is the home to the "Old Hellcat"—a ghoulish old woman who sits in a chair, knitting. (If you get close enough, you can feel the heat coming off her glowing-red needles.)

The Kylesku Hotel in the Scottish Highlands has a ghost who likes to pop his head through a trapdoor in the ceiling. They say he's friendly—he only does it to startle visitors.

Inverawe House, a hotel in Scotland, has "Green Jean." Instead of trying to scare people, he actually assists the staff, leaving fresh soap and clean towels for the guests.

At **Berry Pomeroy Castle**, the "White Lady" haunts the dungeon and towers. It's supposedly the ghost of Lady Margaret Pomeroy,

---

American police officers were first required to read suspects their Miranda rights in 1966.

who was imprisoned in the dungeon by her sister for 20 years and starved to death. People who see her report feeling a wave of depression and fear.

Rufford Old Hall in Lancashire is haunted by a young woman in a wedding dress who, the legend says, waits for the return of her fiancé, who was killed in battle. The dining room is also reportedly haunted by Queen Elizabeth I.

Netley Abbey, a semi-demolished medieval nunnery in Hampshire, is haunted by the ghost of Walter Taylor, a builder hired to tear it down. A stone from an arch struck him on the head and killed him. The demolition was never completed, and now Taylor's spirit wanders around the ruins accompanied by the sound of falling bricks.

*　　*　　*

CHAMPIONS OF BREAKFAST

Remember Flutie Flakes, *the cereal promoted by NFL quarterback Doug Flutie? Here are some other real athlete cereals. (Most are just Honey Nut Cheerios or Frosted Flakes with flashy packaging.)*

- Slam Duncans (Tim Duncan, basketball)
- Ed's End Zone O's (Ed McCaffrey, football)
- Slammin' Sammy's (Sammy Sosa, baseball)
- Warner's Crunch Time (Kurt Warner, football)
- Lynn Swann's Super 88 (Lynn Swann, football)
- Jeter's (Derek Jeter, baseball)
- MarinO's (Dan Marino, football)
- Hull-O's (Bret Hull, hockey)
- Moss's Magic Crunch (Randy Moss, football)
- EcksO's (David Eckstein, baseball)
- Elway's Comeback Crunch (John Elway, football)
- Zo's O's (Alonzo Mourning, basketball)
- Jake's Flakes (Jake Plummer, football)

Michael Caine's real name: Maurice Mickelwhite. (He took "Caine" from *The Caine Mutiny*.)

POLI-TALKS

Politicians aren't getting much respect these days—but hey, we elected them.

"On behalf of all of you, I want to express my appreciation for this tremendously warm recession."
—**Ron Brown,
former DNC chairman**

"We don't all agree on everything. I don't agree with myself on everything."
—**Rudy Giuliani**

"We are going to take things away from you on behalf of the common good."
—**Hillary Clinton**

"If I tell a lie it's only because I think I'm telling the truth."
—**Phil Gaglardi,
B. C. Minister of Highways**

"My number-one goal is to not go to jail."
—**Rep. Michele Bachmann
(R-MN), during
freshman orientation**

"What we really expect out of the Democrats is for them to treat us as they would have liked to have been treated."
—**Rep. John Boehner**

"A year ago, my approval rating was in the 30s, my nominee for the Supreme Court had just withdrawn, and my vice president had shot someone. Ahhh, those were the good old days."
—**George W. Bush**

"George Bush is a guy who was born on third base and thinks he hit a triple."
—**Ann Richards**

"I inhaled. That was the point."
—**Barack Obama**

"We've got a very strong candidate…I'm trying to think of his name."
—**Christopher Dodd**

"I've been a hunter pretty much all my life."
—**Mitt Romney, who went
hunting twice, once when he
was 15, and again at 59**

"This is still the greatest country in the world if we just steel our wills and lose our minds."
—**Bill Clinton**

UNCLE JOHN'S STALL OF FAME

We're always amazed by the creative ways people get involved with bathrooms, toilets, toilet paper, etc. To honor them, we've created Uncle John's Stall of Fame.

Honoree: The City of Auckland, New Zealand
Notable Achievement: Converting sewage into parkland
True Story: Auckland has figured out a unique way to recycle the 60,000 tons of recycled biosolids (treated human waste) building up in its sewage-treatment facilities. They plan to fill up a 30,000-year-old volcano called Puketutu Island with the human waste and turn it into a regional park. Scheduled to last from 2011 until 2041, the dumping will cost around $25 million (including the price of building the park). Many local residents are understandably apprehensive about a mountain-sized poo park that could potentially erupt, but Ian Smith, an Auckland University volcanologist, assures them that the volcano no longer poses any danger—and that the treated waste doesn't smell bad any more. "I think it is pretty safe," he said.

Honoree: Popular singer Sheryl Crow
Notable Achievement: Using toilet paper to raise awareness of global warming
True Story: When news reports emerged in April 2007 that Crow asked her fans, via her Web site, to curb their use of toilet paper to save valuable eco-resources, no one was sure if she was kidding or not. "Although my ideas are in the earliest stages of development," Crow wrote, "they are, in my mind, worth investigating. One of my favorites is in the area of conserving trees, which we heavily rely on for oxygen. I propose a limitation be put on how many squares of toilet paper can be used in any one sitting. I think we are an industrious enough people that we can make it work with only one square per restroom visit, except, of course, on those pesky occasions where two to three could be required." Environmentalists hailed her idea; skeptics chalked it up as

---

In the 1940s, the Canadian gov't advised moms to begin toilet-training babies at 1 month old.

another example of "left-wing lunacy." Crow claimed the idea was just a lark, but added that she's glad "people are talking about global warming, even if it's brought on by a joke."

Honoree: The Sassy Seaside Belles chapter in Maine
Notable Achievement: Supporting American troops...from the bottom up
True Story: The Sassy Seaside Belles is a chapter of the Red Hat Society, a "social organization where there is fun after 50 for women of all walks of life." In 2006 they turned their attention to more serious matters when one of the Belles received a letter from her daughter, Maj. Sherryl Kempton, serving with the 399th Combat Support Hospital in Iraq. Kempton complained that "Iraqi toilet paper rolls are about two inches wide, and last about an hour." So the Belles asked local residents to donate spare rolls for the war effort. They received hundreds, which they sent over in dozens of care packages. "Every box had toilet paper," Kempton reported happily. "After a while, everywhere you looked, there was toilet paper. It was unbelievable!" And the rolls kept coming—meaning that while the medics still faced their share of wartime problems, being stranded on the toilet wasn't one of them.

Honoree: Simon Norris, a homeless man from England
Notable Achievement: Being the first person in history to have a letter addressed and delivered to him...in a public restroom
True Story: Norris was down on his luck; the recovering alcoholic was jobless and homeless. He requested temporary housing from the city council of Bournemouth, a tourist town in the south of England, but was denied. With seemingly nowhere else to go, in January 2007 Norris, 46, paid £3 for a key deposit to an out-of-commission public restroom (with an ocean view). And there he stayed. A few weeks later, Norris requested assistance from a charity called the Bournemouth Churches Housing Association, giving his address as "The Disabled Toilet, The Lower Pleasure Gardens, Bournemouth." Des Persse, a housing officer, saw Norris's request and wanted to help him, so he wrote him a letter and sent it to the loo. A few days later a postman slipped it under the door. "I was rather surprised when I actually received a letter," said Norris. The association assured him they would try to find temporary

---

To play Mickey Mouse at Disneyland, you must be between 4'6" and 5'2" tall.

housing for him, and also reminded Norris that there is a night shelter located in Bournemouth that would be happy to take him in. But for now, Norris is perfectly happy living in the loo while he awaits further information from the housing board.

Honoree: Joanne Gordon, a playwright
Notable Achievement: Turning a toilet into a stage set
True Story: Charles Bukowski's poetry often used toilet imagery to illustrate the decaying state of Western civilization. So in 2005, more than a decade after the poet's death, Bukowski fan Joanne Gordon wrote and directed a play called *Love, Bukowski*, which featured some of his most poignant words being performed by 10 actors (all in their underwear), sitting on a stage one at a time. The stage featured one prop: a toilet that faces the audience (it actually flushes). Why choose this iconic image? "Everyone uses the toilet," explains Gordon. "It's the great equalizer." *Love, Bukowski* received several nominations by the Los Angeles Drama Critics Circle, including Best Set Design.

*   *   *

STRANGE BREW

Weird beer news.

• In 2007 Gerrie Berendsen, owner of the Dutch brewery Schelde, announced plans to produce Kwispelbier, a beer for dogs. (*Kwispel* means "tail-wagging" in Dutch.) "Once a year we go to Austria to hunt with our dogs," she said. "At the end of the day we sit on the veranda and drink a beer. So we felt the dog earned one, too."

• Abashiri Brewery in Hokkaido, Japan, makes "Bilk"—a beer made from milk. The son of a dairy farmer came up with the idea after local farmers were forced to dump large amounts of surplus milk. Cost: $3.29 per 11-ounce bottle.

• Dusseldorf, Germany's, Uerige beer makes "beer for the blind." All their bottles have braille across the bottom so sight-impaired people know what they're drinking. One blind customer said, "You often have no idea what's about to go in your mouth. But with this bottle you are clearly told what it is—and that's fabulous!"

Gulp! The average person swallows 295 times while eating a meal.

THE COMPANY LINE

How companies got their names.

VERIZON: The name is a combination of *veritas* (Latin for truth) and "horizon."

INTEL: Founders Bob Noyce and Gordon Moore wanted to call their company Moore Noyce Electronics, but it sounded too much like "more noise." Second choice: Integrated Electronics, but the name was already taken, so they used the first syllables of each word instead.

WILLIAMS-SONOMA: In 1956 Chuck Williams opened his first cookware store in Sonoma, California.

VIRGIN: Richard Branson's empire began as a mail-order record business which he named Virgin Records to reflect that the records were in pristine or "virgin" condition.

RAND CORPORATION: The research and development firm's name stands for "**R**esearch **An**d **D**evelopment."

PIXAR: Derived from "pixel art," Pixar was the name of the company's first product, a CAT scan computer.

SHARP: The company's first product was a perpetually sharp pencil.

PEPSI: Soft drinks began as medicinal drinks. Pepsi was named after *pepsin*, a digestive enzyme.

BRIDGESTONE: Founder Shojiro Ishibashi's last name translates as "bridge of stone."

CANON: Precision Optical Instruments Laboratory changed its name to Canon after its first successful product, a camera called the Kwanon. (Kwanon is the name of a Buddhist avatar.)

LYCOS: The Internet search engine gets its name from *lycosidae*, the scientific name for a type of spider. Spiders weave webs, and Lycos searches the Web.

ENRON: Founder Ken Lay originally wanted to use the Greek word *enteron* as the name of his energy company because he liked the way it sounded. He shortened it to "Enron" when he found out *enteron* meant "intestine."

In economics, DINK is an acronym for a married couple with "double income, no kids."

AUNT LENNA THE GREAT

Uncle John's Great Aunt Lenna likes to make people think she has psychic powers, but does she really? See if you can figure out what Aunt Lenna's up to—is she a psychic...or just a trickster?

SEEING IS BELIEVING

"How do you like my new glasses?" Aunt Lenna asked when I arrived for a visit. "It's a pretty strong prescription—so strong, in fact, that I can even see through solid objects."

"No prescription glasses are that strong," I laughed. "That must be your prescription *medicine* talking."

"Okay, Mr. Smarty-pants," Aunt Lenna replied. "Watch this." She went to the kitchen and came back with an empty water glass. Then she rummaged around in her junk drawer and pulled out three old dice. She dropped the dice into the glass and said, "I'll shake the glass, and then you look up through the bottom and add up the numbers you see. Don't tell me what they are. With my new glasses I will look at the *top* of the dice and see right through them to the numbers on the bottom." I knelt down so I could see up through the bottom of the glass. I saw a three, a five, and a two. Three plus five plus two equals 10, I thought to myself. Aunt Lenna remained standing. Peering intently at the tops of the three dice she declared, "The numbers on the bottom of the dice add up to 10." I couldn't believe my ears! After Aunt Lenna repeated the trick four more times, I apologized for the crack about her medicine. How did she do that?

DEAD TO RIGHTS

"These glasses don't just let me see through solid objects, they also let me see dead people, even when blindfolded," Aunt Lenna said. I rolled my eyes. "You doubt me?" she asked.

She pulled a piece of paper out of her desk, then went and got a scarf and a hat out of the closet. "Blindfold me with the scarf," she told me, "but leave my glasses on." I did what she said. Then, still holding the piece of paper, Aunt Lenna tore off the top third, handed it to me, and said, "Write down the name of a living person." I wrote down the name of my next door neighbor, Abe

"Shorty" Rhone. "Put it in the hat," she said. I did. Next, Aunt Lenna tore off the middle third of the paper and handed it to me. "Write down the name of a dead person, and put it in the hat" she said. I wrote "Elvis Presley." Now Lenna handed me the bottom third of the piece of paper and said, "Write the name of another living person on the paper, and drop it into the hat too." I wrote down the name of my ninth-grade teacher, Ms. Luckland, and put it in the hat.

"Finished," I said.

Without removing her blindfold, Aunt Lenna reached into the hat, felt around for a few seconds, and pulled out a piece of paper. "Here's your dead person," she said. I looked at the piece of paper. It read, "Elvis Presley." How did she do that?

RING CYCLE

"Using my psychic powers to collect and transmit information is fun, but what I really like is how I can use them to manipulate physical objects," Aunt Lenna said.

"What do you mean?" I asked.

Aunt Lenna went to the bedroom and got her jewelry box. She pulled out a large yellow bracelet and said, "I can make this bracelet pass through solid objects."

"Mind tricks are one thing, but nobody can mess with molecules. That's a physical impossibility."

"Really?" she asked. "Grab the scarf and tie my hands together." I did as she instructed, tying the toughest knot I knew how to make. "Now hand me the bracelet," she told me. I did. "I'll make it pass through the scarf," she said.

Then Aunt Lenna turned her back to me for just a few seconds. But when she turned back around, the bracelet was around the scarf, and her hands were still tied together. Aunt Lenna didn't have enough time to undo the knot and then tie it again, but I examined it just the same. It was still tied the way I'd tied it—and the only way I could get the bracelet free was to untie the scarf. How did Aunt Lenna do that?

Psychics will know this without being told...but for the rest of us:
The answers to Aunt Lenna's puzzles are on page 592.

The most flowers sold in one day in U.S. history was the day after Elvis Presley died in 1977.

GAMES PEOPLE PLAY

When you think about it, baseball is kind of an absurd game: hit a ball with a stick, and then run around a square as fast as you can. But that's nothing compared to these real games and sports played around the world.

Contest: Vinkenzetting
Played in: Flanders, a region of Belgium
How it's played: In *vinkenzetting*, or "finch-sitting," competitors put a male finch in a box cage. Whoever's bird makes the highest number of complete calls in an hour wins. Winning birds usually make several hundred calls per hour. In one competition, a bird called 1,278 times, inviting doping allegations.

Contest: The Tough Guy
Played in: England
How it's played: This grueling competition begins with a 10-mile cross-country run. It's followed by an obstacle course with an electrified fence, underground tunnels, under*water* tunnels, barbed wire, and waist-deep patches of mud. And it's held in the winter, so the temperature is well below freezing. Around 4,000 people compete every year; their entry fees are donated to charity.

Contest: World Screaming Championships
Played in: Poland
How it's played: The rules are simple: One by one, participants step forward and scream really, really loudly. Loudest scream wins. The record scream was produced in 2000 by Dagmara Stanek, who registered a scream of 126.1 decibels, as loud as a jackhammer.

Contest: Kabaddi
Played in: South Asia
How it's played: Two seven-player teams each occupy half of a court about the size of a soccer field. The teams take turns sending a "raider" into the opposition's territory; the raider tries to tag as many players as possible—without getting blocked or tackled—and then return to his home side...all in one breath. To prove he's not inhaling, the player has to chant "KABADDI" throughout the raid.

No, you're not dreaming: Fantasy sports is a $1.5 billion a year industry in the United States.

Contest: Rootball
Played in: North Carolina
How it's played: Invented by Max Chain, owner of an Asheville bar called the Root, it's a combination of horseshoes and lawn bowling, played outdoors on a court made of sand. Two metal stakes are placed 32 feet apart. The player stands at one stake and tosses a plastic ring at the opposite stake, and then tosses a spiky plastic ball. The closer to the stake, the more points awarded, with bonuses for landing the ball inside the plastic ring, throwing the ball through the ring, leaning the ring against the stake, etc. (It's patented, by the way.)

Contest: Unicycle Hockey
Played in: England and Germany
How it's played: It's actually been played since 1925, when European unicycle manufacturers first suggested it as a new use for the one-wheeled contraptions. No skates are used, and it's played on flat pavement, not ice. Ice hockey may be hard, but balancing on a unicycle while reaching out with a stick to hit a plastic ball is even harder. It's actually more like polo than hockey…if polo were played on wobbly horses.

Contest: Noodling
Played in: The American South and Southwest
How it's played: It's not exactly a sport. A 200-year-old tradition along the Mississippi River, it's catfish fishing without a pole, without a net, without even bait. Noodlers stick their arms (called "noodles") into stagnant river water where catfish are usually found, often behind or inside of large logs. When they find a catfish, they splash in the water to get the fish's attention, then plunge their arms directly into the throat of the fish, which may weigh as much as 50 pounds. The fish—who are often guarding eggs—respond to the attack by clamping down on the angler's arm. It's so dangerous—hazards can include drowning or being bitten by snapping turtles and water snakes—that it's illegal in 11 states. It's popular (and legal) in Louisiana, Mississippi, Oklahoma, Tennessee, Kansas, and Missouri.

GIVE US OUR ROSES!

*This quaint piece of American history may make you
want to stand up and say, "It's a bloomin' crime!"*

PAY THE RENT!

In 1768 Benjamin Chambers, founder of Chambersburg, Pennsylvania, offered a piece of land to the local Presbyterian congregation so that they could build a church. It wasn't free—he demanded an annual rent, to be paid on the first day of every June. The rent: a single rose. In 1780 two more churches were given land under the same terms. The three became known as Chambersburg's "Rose Rent Churches."

The tradition stems back to 14th-century England, when a military commander was sanctioned for building a foot bridge in London without proper authorization. Out of respect for his military service, the "fine" was a single rose from his garden, to be paid to London's Lord Mayor every year on Midsummer Day. (The tradition is still carried out today.) The custom spread and became fairly common, especially regarding land deals for churches.

LOST FLOWER

The Rose Rent Churches happily paid their yearly roses to the descendants of the Chambers family for more than two centuries. Then in the late 1990s, John George, a sixth-generation descendant and the current recipient of the "rose rent," found he was owed additional roses: He discovered a deed dated from 1784 showing that the local courthouse sat on land leased to the county under the same terms...but the roses had never been paid.

George bugged the county about the "back rent" for years, but he was never taken seriously. When he died in July 2007, the roses were still unpaid. But family members fought on, calling on county officials to pay up. The story, until then only a local news oddity, was picked up by the wire services and reported in newspapers and on TV nationwide. "He's probably up there laughing," George's widow, June, told reporters, "and saying, 'It's about time!'"

The county still has not paid the overdue rent, which as of June 1, 2007, stood at 221 roses.

The 2½ bucks stop here: Original U.S. gold coinage included $10, $5, and $2.50 coins.

ROBOTS IN THE NEWS

Once they rise up and take over, you'll be reading about them everywhere.
Until then, Uncle John is your top source for news about robots.

THRILLER-BOT

In 2007 Michael Jackson was planning a comeback. He was considering a deal to become a permanent performer in Las Vegas, like Elvis Presley or Celine Dion. His idea for how to attract people to his shows: a 50-foot-tall robotic Michael Jackson erected in the Nevada desert just outside the city. "Laser beams would shoot out of it," said Mike Luckman, Jackson's publicist, "so it would be the first thing people flying in would see."

METRO-BOT

In 2009 the South Korean government plans to spend $530 million to construct "Robot Land," a city dedicated to robotics. The ultra-modern complex will include robot research laboratories, robot development plants, and robot factories as well as an exhibition hall for performing robots and a stadium for robot-vs.-robot sporting events.

SNOT-BOT

Scientists at Warwick and Leicester Universities in England developed a robotic nose they hoped would be able to identify smells. It began working properly in 2006 only after the scientists developed artificial snot for its robotic "nostrils"—they coated one of the nose's sensors with a substance that mimics human mucus. The robot can now differentiate between the smells of milk and bananas.

GASTRO-BOT

One of the more invasive medical procedures is the colonoscopy, in which a small camera on a flexible tube is inserted through the rectum into the intestine to look for cancer cells. Dutch scientists say they've developed a way to make colonoscopies less stressful—a camera attached to a tiny robot that propels itself through the colon. Doctors say the robot moves in a way similar to a snail,

---

Q: What is a *bladderpipe*? A: A bagpipe that includes a hedgehog bladder.

which moves itself by attaching part of its body onto something while the rest of it glides forward on a pile of its own slime. The only difference is that the robot doesn't make its own slime—it attaches itself to tissue and moves along on the naturally occurring mucus inside the human intestine.

ILL-BOT

Robots are supposed to be immune to the things that slow humans down. They're not supposed to get sick...unless that's what they're programmed to do. Researchers at Japan's Gifu University have created a "female," humanoid robot that mimics the symptoms of several diseases. She's a training tool for medical students—the robot even answers questions about how she feels. For example, when she's programmed to have *myasthenia gravis*, a muscle disease, the robot tells doctors her eyelids are heavy and she hunches forward, both telltale symptoms of the condition.

THINK-BOT

Computer scientists at the University of Washington have figured out a way to control a robot's actions. What's so unique about this new programming technique? The scientists control the robots *with their minds*. They gave a humanoid robot a special cap outfitted with 32 electrodes. On the other end of the electrode cap was a human subject in a similar cap who, just by thinking about telling the robot to move forward or grab an object, was able to do so via the power of brain waves.

VOTE-BOT

In 2006 the British government released a report called *Robo-rights: Utopian Dream or Rise of the Machines?* It outlined possible major social problems that could result in England one day should robots develop artificial intelligence and become independent. The report says the government may have to provide robots with housing, health care, and the right to vote. Robots, meanwhile, would be expected to pay taxes and serve in the military.

*   *   *

"If you believe you have a foolproof system, you've failed to take into consideration the creativity of fools."   —**Frank Abagnale**

75% of wild birds die before they are 6 months old.

GRANDFATHERED IN

*Or grand*mother*ed, in some cases.*

GRANDPA CLAUSE

Most people are familiar with the "grandfather clause"—a clause that exempts some people from a new rule or a new law that would otherwise affect rights or privileges they had before the law was enacted. Example: In 1979 the National Hockey League made wearing helmets mandatory, but the new rule permitted any players who were already in the league to continue playing without helmets if they didn't want to wear them. They were "grandfathered in."

But if most people are familiar with the concept, a lot fewer are familiar with where it came from.

The original case of a grandfather clause in law goes back to the Jim Crow era of the late 19th and early 20th centuries in America. After the 15th Amendment to the U.S. Constitution was passed in 1870, allowing men (but not women) of all races to vote in elections, many states enacted laws requiring potential voters to pay poll taxes or pass literacy tests as a way to suppress the minority vote. But because the law would have disqualified many whites from voting (there were plenty of poor, illiterate whites, too), they put in a "compromise" clause: A man could skip the test or the tax if his father—or grandfather—had voted before slavery was abolished. Hence, whites, but not blacks (or Native Americans), could vote. The grandfather clause was found unconstitutional in 1915, but it wasn't until the 24th Amendment, the Voting Rights Act of 1965, that poll taxes and literacy tests were officially outlawed in the United States. (Five states—Virginia, Alabama, Texas, Arkansas, and Mississippi—still had poll taxes in 1965, and Alabama still had a literacy test: See page 324.)

GRANDFATHERING ON

Fortunately, the Jim Crow laws are gone, but the grandfather clause lives on, and most often for much more benign applications. Some examples:

Downsizing? Americans spend about $30 billion per year trying to lose weight.

The Last Spitballer. In 1920 Major League Baseball outlawed the "spitball," a pitch wherein the pitcher applies spit—or some other substance—to a baseball in order to make it sink...and much harder to hit. But because many of the best pitchers of the day threw little else, the league decided on 17 pitchers who would be exempt from the new rule. The last major leaguer to legally use the spitball: Hall of Famer Burleigh "Ol' Stubblebeard" Grimes, who finished his career with the New York Yankees in 1934.

The Last Lay Midwife. In 1983 North Carolina outlawed the practice of "lay midwifery"—non-nurses attending to the births of children in homes. But State Representative Robert C. Hunter wrote an amendment to the bill, creating an exception for midwives who had been practicing in the state for more than 10 years. That allowed Lisa Goldstein—and only Lisa Goldstein—who'd been bringing children into the world since 1958, to be "grandmothered in," and to continue her practice. ("Some people do drugs," Goldstein said of her passion for childbirth. "I do babies.")

The Last Machine Gunners. A 1986 federal law made owning a machine gun illegal...unless you already owned one legally. And a gun owner can still legally transfer a pre-1986 machine gun and registration to another person, which means, according to government reports, that there are more than 250,000 "grandfathered-in" machine guns in the United States today. About half are owned by law enforcement agencies; the other half are owned by civilians.

The Last Guy Without "Helmet Hair." In 1997 Craig MacTavish, center for the St. Louis Blues NHL hockey team, announced his retirement. Hockey fans called it the end of an era because MacTavish was the last player to play without a helmet. He had joined the league in 1978, the year before they made the use of helmets mandatory, so he got to decide for himself whether or not to wear one. He chose not to, calling it "a comfort thing," and for the next 18 years played helmetless (and was never seriously hurt).

The Last Number 42. In 1997 Major League Baseball Commissioner Bud Selig announced that the number 42 would be universally retired and no longer available to be used by any player. It was done to honor baseball's first black Major Leaguer, Jackie Robinson, who'd begun his career 50 years earlier in 1947, when he wore number 42 with the Brooklyn Dodgers. But Mariano Rivera, star relief pitcher for the New York Yankees, had worn "42" since he joined the team in 1995, so he was allowed to keep it, making him the last baseball player with a 42 on his jersey. "As a minority, I feel honored wearing the No. 42 and carrying the legacy that Jackie Robinson left," Rivera told reporters. "I wear it with good pride."

The Old Runway. In December 2005, a Southwest Airlines flight skidded off the end of a runway in a snowstorm at Midway Airport in Chicago. The plane then crashed through a barrier fence and onto a road, causing several accidents and injuries, and the death of a six-year-old boy. Federal investigators said the crash was caused by the snow, a tailwind that was pushing the plane—and the length of the runway's "safety area." Federal standards mandate a zone of at least 1,000 feet after the end of a runway. Midway's is only 82 feet long. The airport was commissioned in 1927 and a grandfather clause allows them (still) to bypass the federal standards.

The Last Planet (Maybe). In 2006 the International Astronomical Union officially demoted Pluto off its list of planets in our solar system, giving it a new "dwarf planet" designation. That created a controversy among astronomers. It also created a problem for science teachers. For more than 70 years, schoolchildren had learned the names of the planets through a mnemonic phrase: "My Very Educated Mother Just Served Us Nine Pizzas." (Mercury, Venus, Earth, Mars, Jupiter, Saturn, Uranus, Neptune, Pluto.) Becky Peltonen, an elementary school teacher in Panama City, Florida, said that Pluto, the last of the nine planets to be discovered, should be grandfathered into the club. "I'm going to have to write a new song," she told CNN.

The Last Free Driver in Scotland. In April 2007, Sheila Thompson of Broughty Ferry, Scotland, turned 105 years old. And she is, by far, the UK's oldest driver. She drives her Peugeot 106 to church every Sunday, a 15-mile round trip—and she's so old that she doesn't need a driver's license. There was no such thing as a driver's test in Scotland when she started driving in 1935, so she doesn't have to take one. And she says she has no problem getting behind the wheel. "I don't get nervous," Thompson told the BBC. "I just take it as I find it." She added that she has no plans to give up driving. (And in 2008, she'll match the "106" on her Peugeot.)

Butterflies hold their wings upright when they rest; moths keep their wings spread.

YOU CALL THAT ART?

If you were to see some of the tacky stuff that adorns the walls here at the BRI, you may not think we're qualified to comment on what anyone else considers art. Well, we say: If dogs can play poker, anything is possible.

ARTIST: Rebecca O'Flaherty, the Monet of Maggots

THIS IS ART? When making her paintings, O'Flaherty kind of cheats—she lets the maggots do the work for her. An entomology doctoral student at the University of California at Davis, O'Flaherty is fascinated with the larvae of flies. She dips the maggots in nontoxic paint, then lets them writhe around on the canvas (a piece of white copier paper). Result: unique trails of color and form. O'Flaherty displays her maggot paintings at gallery exhibits and even holds maggot-art workshops for kids. She also teaches forensic officers how to collect maggots at a crime scene for evidence and uses the maggot art as an "icebreaker" to get them used to dealing with the squirmy creatures.

ARTIST STATEMENT: "The activity usually begins with some measure of skepticism or disdain, but the maggots are quick to win over the critics."

ARTIST: Jessica May, the Rembrandt of Roadkill

THIS IS ART? May, a 24-year-old graduate art student at Southern Illinois University–Edwardsville, decided that the roadkill lying on the roadsides in and around her Midwestern town needed a little sprucing up. So she dressed dead raccoons in baby clothes, put nail polish on the claws of dead possums, and gave a deer carcass a coat of gold spray paint. May wears gloves when she works on her art, because when she finds the animals, they're "pretty far gone."

ARTIST STATEMENT: "I think of this as my way of paying homage to these animals."

ARTIST: Colin Douglas Barnett, the Picasso of Publicity

THIS IS ART? Frustrated that his art wasn't getting the attention he thought it deserved, Barnett, 46, decided to scare up some publicity in Melbourne, Australia. In October 2005, he sculpted a

---

The world's first skateboard park was built in Port Orange, Florida, in 1976.

vase out of clay and placed it on the sidewalk in front of the National Gallery of Victoria. Labeling it the "Peace Bomb," he called police and reported a suspicious package outside of the building. The gallery was evacuated, the surrounding roads closed, and the bomb squad was called in. Barnett received the press he was looking for, but it came in the form of news stories reporting his arrest. The artist was ordered to pay for the police investigation and sentenced to three months in jail.

ARTIST STATEMENT: "I'm totally embarrassed."

ARTIST: Wenda Gu, the Kandisnky of Coiffure

THIS IS ART? The Chinese artist was commissioned by Dartmouth College in Hanover, New Hampshire, to create two installation on their campus. First project: "The Green House," an 80-foot banner made from 420 pounds of human hair. All that hair came from Hanover barbershops, who collected the clippings from 42,000 haircuts and shipped it to Wenda's Shanghai studio, where his workers dyed it bright colors. Wenda then wove the strands together, creating the colorful banner that now hangs in the college library. Second project: "United Nations, United Colors," a seven-and-a-half-mile-long braid (begun in 1993) made from leftover hair donated by wig factories in China and India.

ARTIST STATEMENT: "The banner is a comment on education and capitalism, and the braid represents a utopian vision of unity among nations."

ARTIST: Ian Thorley, the Degas of Doormats

THIS IS ART? In October 2006, Thorley, a British performance artist, received a £1,600 grant ($3,176) from the Wansbeck and Blyth Valley town councils for his weeklong art project "Utilitarian Utopia." The project: Thorley wore a badge that said "Government Doormat Tester" and stood on a doormat in the middle of a sidewalk for a week. The councils were widely criticized for spending taxpayer money on the art. But they defended their actions, saying that Thorley "provides viewers with a thought-provoking experience."

ARTIST STATEMENT: "It's about drawing attention to, and invoking some sense of, the absurdity of existence and the things that we do."

UNCLE JOHN'S PAGE OF LISTS

Random bits of information from the BRI files.

4 Classic Toys That Hit Stores in November 1983
1. Cabbage Patch Kids
2. My Little Pony
3. Care Bears
4. Trivial Pursuit

6 Biblical Phrases
1. The handwriting is on the wall
2. A wolf in sheep's clothing
3. The blind leading the blind
4. Your days are numbered
5. The four corners of the Earth
6. The powers that be

7 Women whose real first name is "Mary"
1. Meryl Streep
2. Tipper Gore
3. Barbara Cartland
4. Lily Tomlin
5. Dusty Springfield
6. Sissy Spacek
7. Debra Winger

The Only 3 Trademarked Sounds
1. Harley Davidson's V-twin engine roar
2. NBC's three chimes
3. MGM's lion roar

The 8 Cuts of Beef
1. Chuck
2. Rib
3. Short loin
4. Sirloin
5. Round
6. Brisket and shank
7. Short plate
8. Flank

11 Vowel-less Words Accepted in Scrabble
1. Nth
2. Sh
3. Shh
4. Cwm
5. Pht
6. Tsk
7. Pfft
8. Brrr
9. Phpht
10. Crwth
11. Tsktsk

6 Bestselling Video Games of All Time
1. Super Mario Brothers
2. Tetris
3. Pokemon Red and Blue
4. Super Mario Brothers 3
5. Super Mario World
6. The Sims

4 Sports You Can Only Win by Going Backwards
1. Rappelling
2. Rowing
3. Tug-of-war
4. High jump

4 Names of Cartoons in Spain
1. *Los Supersonicos* (*The Jetsons*)
2. *Bob Esponja* (*Spongebob Squarepants*)
3. *Las Tortugas Ninja* (*Teenage Mutant Ninja Turtles*)
4. *Futurama* (*Futurama*)

HOW SWEET® IT IS

Sugar is sweet, but sugar substitutes like saccharin, NutraSweet, and Splenda are even sweeter. Here's how they were discovered.

SACCHARIN

In 1879 Ira Remsen and Constantin Fahlberg, chemists at Johns Hopkins University in Baltimore, were working with a coal tar derivative called *orthobenzoyl sulfmide*. Without knowing it, Remsen accidentally spilled some on his hands in the lab one day. At dinner that night he noticed that the roll he was eating tasted sweet, and then suddenly bitter. His wife didn't taste anything odd in her food, so Remsen retraced his steps and determined that the sweet flavor and bitter aftertaste must have come from the coal tar derivative. Subsequent testing revealed that the substance was technically hundreds of times sweeter than sugar *without* the calories of sugar, but *with* that terrible aftertaste. In 1880, Remsen and Fahlberg published their discovery—the world's first synthetic sweetener—in a medical journal, calling the new substance *saccharin*, a pun on "saccharine," which refers to something overly sweet or sappy.

Saccharin was soon commercially available, but it wasn't widely used until World War I, when a sugar shortage forced substitutions. Saccharin's popularity exploded in the 1960s, especially when it was used to sweeten Tab, Coca-Cola's first sugar-free soft drink. But after some 1970s tests that suggested it caused bladder cancer in laboratory mice (the tests have since been discredited), and a proposed ban in the United States (the ban was ultimately rejected in favor of a warning label), use of Saccharin declined sharply. Primary use today: It's the main ingredient in Sweet'N Low.

NUTRASWEET

James Schlatter, a chemist working for the pharmaceutical company G. D. Searle, was trying to perfect an anti-ulcer drug called *aspartame* in 1965. One day he got some of it on his fingers and later noticed a sweet taste when he licked his finger to grab a piece of paper. Ruling out the donut he'd eaten (he remembered washing his hands *after* the donut, but *before* handling the aspartame), he figured out that the sweetness must have come from the ulcer drug. Schlatter took his discovery to his bosses at Searle. This was around the same time that a possible link between saccharin and cancer was being studied, so the market for a better artificial sweetener—and aspartame didn't even have a bitter aftertaste—was very lucrative. Searle decided to market the anti-ulcer drug as an artificial sweetener instead. But fears surrounding saccharin (and an earlier sweetener, cyclamate) were so intense that aspartame didn't receive full FDA approval until nearly two decades later, in 1983. It first appeared in Diet Coke, Diet Pepsi, and a sugarlike sweetener called Equal. Today, under the brand name NutraSweet, it's used to flavor more than 1,200 products.

SPLENDA

Like saccharin and aspartame, *sucralose*, the chemical that goes by the brand name Splenda, was discovered by accident (one would think scientists would be more careful when handling chemicals). In 1976 the British agricultural chemical company Tate & Lyle hired chemists at Queen Elizabeth College to test the industrial uses of chlorinated sugars—sugar molecules that had had some atoms removed and replaced with chlorine. Lead chemist Leslie Hough asked his assistant Shashikant Phadnis to *test* one powdered compound. But Phadnis, an Indian native new to England and the English language, thought Hough had told him to *taste* it. So he tasted it. Luckily, it was not poisonous, and it tasted exceptionally sweet. After a year of testing and tweaking the chemically altered sugar (it was determined to be 600 *times* as sweet as real sugar), a final formula for sucralose offered the taste of sugar with no aftertaste and virtually no calories. And unlike other sugar substitutes, sucralose could stand up to heat and freezing, making it suitable for cooking and baking.

But the controversy over saccharin and other artificial sweeteners was still fresh on people's minds in 1977, and it would be a long time before sucralose was made available to the public. Marketed as Splenda by Johnson & Johnson, it hit the market in Canada in 1991 and the United States in 1998 (primarily in packets to compete with Sweet'N Low and Equal). Interestingly, Splenda was unavailable in Britain, where it originated, until 2004. It's now the sweetener in 4,000 products worldwide.

The Amazon River is visible from space. (Amazon.com is not.)

TOP 10 OF 1987

Uncle John started making Bathroom Readers *in 1987. But what else was going on that year? In honor of our 20th anniversary, here are the biggest movies, TV shows, songs, and people from 20 years ago.*

PEOPLE MAGAZINE'S "MOST INTRIGUING PEOPLE"
1. Donald Trump
2. Donna Rice
3. Fawn Hall
4. Oprah Winfrey
5. Jessica Hahn
6. Gary Hart
7. Garrison Keillor
8. Brigitte Nielsen
9. Dana Carvey
10. William Casey

HIGHEST-GROSSING MOVIES
1. *Three Men and a Baby*
2. *Fatal Attraction*
3. *Beverly Hills Cop II*
4. *Good Morning, Vietnam*
5. *Moonstruck*
6. *The Untouchables*
7. *The Secret of My Success*
8. *Stakeout*
9. *Lethal Weapon*
10. *The Witches of Eastwick*

• The average price of a movie ticket in 1987: $3.90
• 1987's Oscar winners: Best Picture: *The Last Emperor.*

Best Actress: Cher (*Moonstruck*). Best Actor: Michael Douglas (*Wall Street*).
• The biggest flop of 1987: *Ishtar,* starring Dustin Hoffman and Warren Beatty. It had a budget of $55 million, made $14 million, and received some of the worst reviews of any movie ever.

BILLBOARD'S BIGGEST SINGLES
1. "Faith," George Michael
2. "Alone," Heart
3. "I Wanna Dance With Somebody," Whitney Houston
4. "C'est La Vie," Robbie Nevil
5. "Shake You Down," Gregory Abbot
6. "La Bamba," Los Lobos
7. "Livin' on a Prayer," Bon Jovi
8. "Here I Go Again," Whitesnake
9. "Heaven is a Place on Earth," Belinda Carlisle
10. "The Time of My Life," Bill Medley and Jennifer Warnes

- 1987's Grammy winners included Paul Simon's "Graceland" (Record of the Year), U2's *The Joshua Tree* (Album of the Year), and Jody Watley (Best New Artist).
- Bestselling albums of the year: Bon Jovi's *Slippery When Wet*, The Beastie Boys' *License to Ill*, Bruce Hornsby and the Range's *The Way It Is*, and Janet Jackson's *Control*.

MOST-WATCHED TV SHOWS

1. *The Cosby Show*
2. *A Different World*
3. *Cheers*
4. *The Golden Girls*
5. *Growing Pains*
6. *Who's the Boss*
7. *Night Court*
8. *60 Minutes*
9. *Murder, She Wrote*
10. *Alf*

- Eight of the top 10 were sitcoms. The sitcom isn't as popular in 2007—only one comedy is in the top 20: *Two and a Half Men*.
- *The Golden Girls* won the Emmy for Best Comedy.
- Only show from the list still on the air today: *60 Minutes*.
- *The A-Team, Remington Steele,* and *Hill Street Blues* ended after long runs.

TOP 10 BESTSELLING NOVELS OF 1987

1. *The Tommyknockers* (Stephen King)
2. *Patriot Games* (Tom Clancy)
3. *Kaleidoscope* (Danielle Steel)
4. *Misery* (Stephen King)
5. *Leaving Home* (Garrison Keillor)
6. *Windmills of the Gods* (Sidney Sheldon)
7. *Presumed Innocent* (Scott Turow)
8. *Fine Things* (Danielle Steel)
9. *Heaven and Hell* (John Jakes)
10. *The Eyes of the Dragon* (Stephen King)

- Pulitzer Prize for fiction: *Beloved* by Toni Morrison
- Nobel Prize for literature: Russian author Joseph Brodsky

10 SPORTS WINNERS

Super Bowl: Washington Redskins
Stanley Cup: Edmonton Oilers
NBA Finals: L.A. Lakers
Kentucky Derby: Alysheba
Indianapolis 500: Al Unser, Sr.
NCAA Basketball: Indiana
PGA Championship: Larry Nelson
Wimbledon (Men's): Pat Cash
Iditarod: Susan Butcher
World Series: Minnesota Twins

RETURN TO THE MOON, PART I

Anyone who witnessed the first Apollo Moon landing in 1969 probably remembers it as moment of exultation, full of hope for the future. Well, just because NASA hasn't landed astronauts on the Moon since 1972 doesn't mean they haven't been thinking about how to do it again when the time comes. And the planning is further along than you might think.

GET BACK

For more than 30 years after *Apollo 17* returned from the Moon in December 1972, the question of whether the United States (or anyone else) would ever go back remained open. The Soviet Union had secretly tried to land cosmonauts on the Moon...and failed. The few other countries that could afford to go—Japan, England, and France—were not interested. And neither was NASA: After six successful Apollo Moon missions (plus one failed attempt, *Apollo 13*), the space agency redirected its resources toward the Space Shuttle, unmanned missions around the solar system, and the International Space Station.

That all changed in 2004, when President George W. Bush recast NASA's priorities and put the United States back on a course to the Moon. According to Bush's roadmap for the space agency, the Vision for Space Exploration, manned lunar missions will be the first step in a decades-long effort to build a permanent Moon base and send astronauts to Mars and beyond. The entire effort is known as Project Constellation.

ON A DIME

One thing the Vision for Space Exploration lacks is a Vision for How All of This Stuff Is Going to Be Paid For. After the report was published, NASA's annual budget was increased...by only a couple of percentage points per year—and even that was for only a few years. More funds may be freed up when the Space Shuttle is retired after 2010, but even then money will be tight. That makes expensive options, like engineering an entirely new spacecraft from scratch, out of the question. Instead, NASA hopes to borrow existing technologies from the Space Shuttle and the Apollo pro-grams for its next Moon landing, tentatively planned for 2019. The spacecraft are still in the very early planning stages, but a picture of what they'll look like is beginning to emerge.

BLAST FROM THE PAST

Are you old enough to remember the Apollo program? Since the next lunar program is going to look a lot like the first one, here's a quick refresher. The spacecraft that went to the Moon aboard the giant Saturn V rocket comprised three major components:

1) The Hershey's Kiss-shaped Command Module, where the astronauts spent most of their time during the mission.

2) The cylinder-shaped Service Module, which housed oxygen tanks, fuel tanks, life-support equipment, and the rocket motor that would take the spacecraft out of lunar orbit and back to Earth at the end of the mission. The Command Module attached to the Service Module, as below, were referred to together as the Command Service Module (CSM):

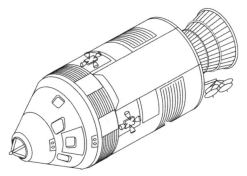

The Command Service Module (CSM)

3) The bug-shaped Lunar Excursion Module (LEM), the vehicle that the astronauts used to land on the lunar surface, which was attached to the nose of the CSM. The LEM was comprised of a *descent stage*, which contained the landing gear, a *descent engine* and fuel tanks; and an *ascent stage*, consisting of the *crew module* and *main engine*. When the astronauts were ready to lift off from the lunar surface, the descent stage served as the launchpad for the ascent stage and never left the Moon.

...from the Rockefeller Foundation as a bookmark, and then lost the book.

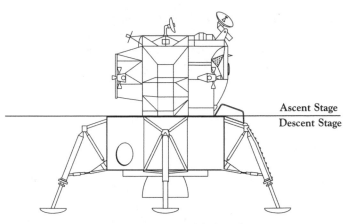

Ascent Stage
Descent Stage

Lunar Excursion Module (LEM)

STEP BY STEP

Each of the six successful Apollo missions followed the same
sequence of events. The three-stage Saturn V rocket, which was
effectively three rockets stacked into one, lifted the CSM and
LEM off the launchpad, jettisoning its first and second stages and
firing the third stage to get into Earth orbit. Then, after the astronauts completed preparations for "translunar injection," the Saturn V's third-stage engine fired a second time, launching them on
a course to the Moon. When the spacecraft neared the Moon, the
CSM's engine fired to slow it down and get it into lunar orbit.
Two of the astronauts then transferred into the LEM, and headed
down to the surface of the Moon. (The third crew member had to
remain aboard the CSM and never got to set foot on the Moon.)

When the two astronauts on the Moon's surface completed their
assigned tasks, they climbed back into the LEM, fired the main
engine and returned to the CSM, which was still in lunar orbit. The
LEM was jettisoned and allowed to crash back onto the lunar surface. The CSM's engine was fired for *transearth injection* (NASA-
speak for "heading back to Earth.") When they got close to Earth,
the astronauts jettisoned the Service Module, re-entered Earth's
atmosphere aboard the Command Module, and splashed down in
the ocean, where they were recovered by waiting Navy ships.

That's what the last *Moon ship looked like. What will the*
next one be? For Part II of the story, *turn to page 305.*

Get out of the way! A typical American driver will honk the horn 15,250 times in their life.

NEWS CORRECSHIONS

Each year a media watchdog site called "Regret the Error" releases its "Crunks" awards, which highlight the funniest news flubs. Here are some of our favorites from the past few years.

"Because of an editing error, a recipe last Wednesday for meatballs with an article about foods to serve during the Super Bowl misstated the amount of chipotle chilies to be used. It is one or two canned chilies, not one or two cans."

—*The New York Times*

"An editorial in Friday's paper incorrectly stated that Florida Cresswell, a candidate for state representative in the 28th District, was convicted in 1999 of battery and stealing Tupperware. In fact he was convicted of stealing a battery from a van as well as Tupperware that was inside the van."

—*Chicago Tribune*

"The problem arose when the computer spell checker did not recognise the term 'WNO' (Welsh National Opera). A slip of the finger caused it to be replaced with the word 'winos.' It just goes to show that it's hard to beat the good, old-fashioned dictionary."

—*Liverpool Daily Post*

"In our cover story about Hunter S. Thompson yesterday we mistakenly attributed to Richard Nixon the view that Thompson represented 'that dark, venal and incurably violent side of the American character.' On the contrary, it was what Thompson said of Nixon."

—*The Guardian* (U.K.)

"An Oct. 19 article on songwriter John Bucchino incorrectly stated that he doesn't read. It should have said he doesn't read music."

—*Dallas Morning News*

"MAPLE leaves, not cannabis, were the adornment on Britney Spears' coat sleeves in our picture."

—*The Mirror* (U.K.)

"A headline on Page One on Saturday should have made clear that Oregon Health & Sciences University will be studying the effects of meth, not cooking it."

—*The Oregonian*

It took 20,000 people 22 years to build the Taj Mahal.

"An article in Tuesday's Calendar section on British singer Joss Stone referred to musician Johnny Otis as 'the late bandleader.' Otis is 85 and living in northern California. The article also described songwriter-producer Lamont Dozier as a 'Philly soul icon.' Dozier was a key member of the Motown Records hit-making team in Detroit."

—*Los Angeles Times*

"It has come to the editor's attention that the *Herald-Leader* neglected to cover the civil rights movement. We regret the omission."

—*Lexington Herald-Leader* (Kentucky)

"Norma Adams-Wade's June 15 column incorrectly called Mary Ann Thompson-Frenk a socialist. She is a socialite."

—*Dallas Morning News*

"In Wednesday's Taste section, a *Washington Post* recipe on Page F7 included an incorrect cooking time for carbonada (braised beef with onions and red wine). The dish should be cooked for 2 1/2 hours, not 10 to 20 minutes."

—*The Sacramento Bee*

"A map Tuesday showing the locations of Tribune Co. properties erroneously depicted Denver as being in Wyoming. It is, of course, one state to the south, in Colorado."

—*USA Today*

"A story in the July 24 edition of the *Sentinel & Enterprise* incorrectly spelled Sheri Normandin's name. Also, Bobby Kincaid is not a quadriplegic. We regret the errors."

—*Sentinel & Enterprise* (Fitchburg, Massachusetts)

"In the 'Summertime' feature on page 114, we say that before you use the Schick Intuition razor you should lather on cream or gel. But the beauty of Intuition is its simplicity—no need for shave gel, soap, or body wash! Intuition's All-in-One cartridge contains pivoting triple blades surrounded by a Skin Conditioning Solid that has a blend of sheer fruity notes of melon and fresh cucumber for normal to dry skin types. You can find the Schick Intuition Cucumber Melon at your local drug and grocery stores for $7.99."

—*Woman's Day* magazine

A "gut feeling" is also called a *splanchnic,* relating to the splanchnic nerves of the intestinal area.

ALL BROKEN UP

Whenever Uncle John has a question about failed relationships, he consults his love guru, Neil Sedaka. What does Neil always say? "Breakin' up is hard to do." In the case of these stories, Neil's right.

THE KING SOLOMON SOLUTION

A married couple in Germany were mired in a bitter divorce. At the center of their dispute: who would get the summer home they owned in Sonneburg. The 43-year-old husband (unnamed in press reports) decided to put an end to negotiations by cutting the house in half. He used a chainsaw to saw through the middle of the 24-by-18-foot structure, and then loaded his half onto a forklift, which he drove to his brother's house. According to a police spokesman, the man said he was just "taking his due."

DUMPED

Emma Thomason, a 24-year-old woman from Whitehaven, England, had been engaged to Jason Wilson, also 24, until the two had a fight in May 2007. Their seven-year relationship ended for good when Thomason put all of Wilson's clothes, DVDs, and CDs into his van, drove it to a nearby harbor, jumped out of the moving vehicle, and let it coast into the water. Thomason was arrested for "aggravated vehicle-taking without consent" and is facing jail time. The authorities were particularly upset because part of the harbor had to be drained to retrieve the van. A despondent Wilson told reporters, "I haven't told her yet that the wedding is off, but I think she can put two and two together."

TAKE MY WIFE, PLEASE!

When a Romanian man named Emil Iancu couldn't come up with the money he needed to pay back his creditor (who was inside his home, demanding payment), he offered his wife instead. Incredibly, Iancu's creditor, 72-year-old Jozef Justien Lostrie, accepted the deal. How did Iancu's wife, Daniela, feel about it? Happy. "Before, I had to clean the house and look after our three children on my own, while Emil did nothing," she said. "Now I am treated like a guest and hardly have to raise a finger!"

GAVE HER THE FINGER

A bitter ex-husband (name not released) from Vienna, Austria, was so intent on sending his ex-wife the message that he was over her that he sent her his wedding ring...with his ring finger still attached. After receiving the severed digit, the ex-wife called police, who charged the man with harassment and assault. He was remorseless when he told the judge that it was an "act of breaking free"—not just from this marriage, but from the concept of marriage, which the nine-fingered man has sworn off for the rest of his life.

ANOTHER BRICK IN THE WALL

By August 2005, Simon and Chana Taub's rocky marriage was over—they wanted nothing more to do with each other. They wanted a divorce from each other, but not from their luxurious three-story house in Brooklyn, New York. Neither would agree to leave (even though they co-owned another house two doors down that either could have moved into). Solution: The judge ordered that a drywall partition be erected to divide the residence in two. That worked until Mr. Taub let his toilet back up—stinking up the *entire* house. At last report, the two are battling it out in court...again.

TUNNEL OF LOVE

Resident priests at the 800-year-old Yasui Konpiragu Shrine in Kyoto, Japan, offer a variety of services to the more than 40,000 lovesick people who visit there every year: counseling and match-making services, consolation prayers, or the most popular—a crawl through the "Wish Tunnel," where they can pray for the strength to end a troubled relationship...either theirs or someone else's.

THE BREAKUP MAN

In Germany, people who don't have the guts to end their relationship themselves can hire Bernd Dressler to do it for them. Charging clients 50 euros ($68), the former economist goes to the soon-to-be-dumped's home and delivers the bad news. In his first year of business, Dressler facilitated more than 200 breakups. The session usually lasts about three minutes, and the recipients are left in a state of shock. "I almost never get invited in for a coffee," he says.

Rabbits love licorice.

COCKNEY SLANG

*In keeping with our love of strange lingo and odd English
dialects, here's a look at a sometimes perplexing,
but always rhyming, form of British slang.*

BACKGROUND

Cockney is the name given to London's blue collar working classes who reside in the east end of the city. You're probably familiar with the Cockney accent—remember Bert, the chimney sweep (Dick Van Dyke) in *Mary Poppins?* That's the Cockney dialect. Along with that distinctive accent ("allo, gov'-nah!"), Cockney speakers have another linguistic tradition, dating back to the 1850s: their own brand of rhyming slang. Here's how it works: They take a word, replace it with a phrase that rhymes with the original word, and then, if the replacement's too long, they shorten it to create an entirely new expression.

• For example, instead of saying "my feet hurt," you'd say "my plates hurt." Why? Because "Plates of meat, that's your feet." And "plates of meat" gets shortened to just "plates."

• Here's another: "Give us a broken" means "give us a hug." Because "broken mug, that's a hug." "Broken mug" is shortened to "broken."

• One more: "Tell me a weep" means "tell me a tale," because "weep and wail, that's a tale," and the "wail" gets dropped.

Got it? Here are some more classic Cockney slang terms.

Ancient: freak (short for "Ancient Greek")

Iron: the bank (short for "iron tank")

Ari: bottle (short for "Aristotle")

Bacons: legs (short for "bacon and eggs")

Moby Dick: sick

Bag: priest (short for "bag of yeast")

Trouble and strife: wife

Minces: eyes (short for "mince pies")

Barbed: tired (short for "barb wired")

Upper: neck (short for "upper deck")

All the better to see you with: Women have wider peripheral vision than men.

Bunnies: tears (short for "bunny ears")

Bathtub: a pub

Daft: the army (short for "daft and barmy")

Candle: tax (short for "candle wax")

Bees: keys

Porkies: lies (short for "pork pies")

Almonds: socks (short for "almond rocks")

Mother Hubbard: a cupboard

Taters: see you later (from "fish and taters")

Mutt and Jeff: deaf

Oxford: a dollar (short for "Oxford scholar")

Bangers: trash (short for "bangers and mash")

Loaf: your head (short for "loaf of bread")

Morning: a story (short for "morning glory")

Toes: your nose (short for "hairy toes")

Whistle: a suit (short for "whistle and flute")

Pearl: a girl

Supersonic: a gin and tonic

Dancing bears: stairs

Bucket: jail (short for "bucket and pail")

Auntie Ella: an umbrella

Buckle: chuckle

Germans: hands (short for "German bands")

Metrics: piles, the English term for hemorrhoids (short for "metric miles")

Baked bean: the Queen

Daisies: boots (short for "daisy roots")

Irish jig: a wig

Romans: sandals (short for "Roman candles")

Poor Man's Gruel: Liverpool

Hairy: your "mum" (short for "hairy bum")

Aprils: flowers (short for "April showers")

Egg: a joke (short for "egg yolk")

Corn: a job (short for "corn on the cob")

For some modern examples of Cockney slang, turn to page 424.

Got a quarter? There are more than 16,400 parking meters in Manhattan.

FUTURAMA!

"Come tour America of 1960 with General Motors! See a view of tomorrow's cities, a panorama of tomorrow's countryside, on moving sound-chairs while the friendly voice of an unseen guide describes the wonders that can happen here!" —World's Fair brochure, 1939

BEHOLD THE FUTURE

One of the most popular exhibits at the 1939–1940 New York World's Fair was the "Highways and Horizons" pavilion, part of General Motors' "Futurama" exhibit. Via a 15-minute journey across an extremely intricate, 36,000-square-foot diorama depicting the countryside and city, visitors got to see GM's vision of the future in the far-off year of 1960. Every day, more than 28,000 people lined up to take the ride that featured 322 easy chairs fitted onto a slow-moving conveyor belt. While a narrator detailed the world of tomorrow, visitors soared over realistic miniatures of farms, orchards, dams, power plants, amusement parks, suburbs, and a huge city full of towers made of steel and glass. The exhibit incorporated 500,000 miniature houses, a million tiny trees of 18 different species, and 50,000 miniature cars, 10,000 of which actually moved. At the end of the ride, fair patrons got a lapel pin that said, "I have seen the future," and disembarked onto a glistening, life-size street from the city-of-the-future that they'd just seen in miniature form.

THE WORLD OF TOMORROW

The ride provided a fascinating glimpse at what developments in society and technology might be possible just 20 years down the line. It also provided a rosy outlook that served as escapism from the Great Depression, as well as World War II, already under way in Europe and just around the corner for the United States.

Here's what "Futurama" predicted 1960 would be like:

• All fruit diseases and all insects that feed on fruit will have been identified, allowing scientists to develop technology to keep orchards free of disease and insects. It helps that all fruit and vegetable farming is done under glass domes.

Raising the dead: In WWII, Japanese officers killed in battle were promoted to a higher rank.

- The food supply will be endless, as scientists have developed methods to artificially pollinate plants and flowers.

- All American homes will have electricity. (In 1939, 70% of homes did.)

- The principal source of power will be hydroelectric plants situated in mountainous, lake- and river-filled areas, providing electricity for cities up to several hundred miles away.

- In 1960 nobody lives in the city anymore. Everybody lives in suburbs or the country. Cities are devoted to industry, business, and cultural pursuits.

- Those who don't work in the city or live in the suburbs reside in small villages. Each such village is home to one factory that produces one industrial item.

- The average highway will be 14 lanes wide—7 in each direction. But all the lanes don't have the same speed limit: Four lanes are for driving at 50 mph, two are for 75 mph, and one is for 100 mph. And the road isn't flat—the edges of the road curve up to create barriers on each side so each lane remains separate and the fast-moving cars don't veer into each other.

- To prevent accidents, radio waves ensure that cars travel at equal distances from each other, never getting too close.

- These superfast highways will enable coast-to-coast travel in about 24 hours, allowing Americans to spend their two-month compulsory vacation virtually anywhere they please.

- At night, the highway surface is automatically lighted by fluorescent tubing in the road.

- All skyscrapers are outfitted with landing decks for helicopters and "autogyros."

- Airports are hubs for car, rail, and air travel. They're also round and built on rivers in the middle of cities. The water makes it easier for a dirigible (blimp) to turn around in the airport's large underwater hangar.

These predictions for 1960 didn't all pan out, so General Motors staged another "Futurama" for the 1964 World's Fair to show once again what the future would be like.
To read about it, turn to page 366.

1st man to walk around the world: Dave Kunste, in 1970. It took 4 years, 3 months, 16 days.

UNDERWEAR STORIES

Fascinating origins that answer the question: What lies beneath?

CORSET

Meaning: A stiffened undergarment extending from a woman's hips to below her chest, to support and shape the torso

Origin: *Corset* is Old French for "little body," from the Latin *corpus*, or "body." (*Body*—later *bodice*—was used to refer to the part of a dress that covers the torso.) The garment has its origins in ancient Greece and Rome, where women sometimes wrapped broad bands around their bodies. By the 17th century, it had evolved into a tight inner bodice, sometimes of leather, stiffened with whale-bone, wooden splints, or steel, and worn by both men and women. By 1900 the corset was again primarily a female garment, and was modified to conform to the natural lines of a woman's body.

GARTER

Meaning: An elastic or cloth band worn around the leg to keep up a stocking or sock

Origin: The word derives from the Old French *gartier*, meaning "bend of the knee." According to popular legend, in 1348 Joan, Countess of Salisbury, accidentally lost her garter while dancing at a court ball. It was picked up by her partner, King Edward III, who gallantly diverted attention away from her bare leg by placing the blue band on his own, saying (in French), "Shame on those who think ill of this." With that he formed the Order of the Garter, the highest grade of knighthood in England.

TANK TOP

Meaning: A sleeveless, tight-fitting shirt with wide shoulder straps and no front opening, often worn under a shirt

Origin: The term became popular around 1968, deriving from *tank suit*, a one-piece "bathing costume" for men (and later, women) in the 1920s. The tank suit was so called because it was worn in a pool, or "swimming tank." The tank top became a fashion staple (on the outside) in the 1970s and 1980s.

Got a sweater? During a total solar eclipse the temperature can drop by as much as 20°F.

CAMISOLE

Meaning: A women's sleeveless top, often worn under a sheer blouse

Origin: The word is French, from the Latin *camsa*, or "shirt." The camisole evolved from a simple corset cover in the mid-19th century. Designed to protect the dress from the corset, it was often decorated with embroidered flowers. The camisole itself evolved into two other undergarments: combined with knickers, it became the teddy, and joined with the petticoat, it became the slip.

NEGLIGEE

Meaning: A light dress or gown, frequently of a delicate, filmy fabric; often comes with a matching robe.

Origin: From the French *négliger*, "to neglect," although in this case the meaning is closer to "to let go." This sense originates with 18th-century women who, during rest periods after lunch, put on a lightweight, loose-fitting garment that released them temporarily from the tight-fitting dresses of the time. The modern, sexier negligee was popularized by a 1941 photo of Rita Hayworth in *Life* magazine; after World War II, it became a sought-after item of lingerie.

DRAWERS

Meaning: An old-fashioned term for underpants

Origin: Originally a men's garment, adopted by 18th-century women to wear under hoopskirts. Before the Civil War, American men's underwear were usually made of wool flannel. Most were knee-length with a simple button overlap in front and a drawstring at the waist. The word *drawers* dates from 1567 and indicates a garment that is pulled or "drawn" on, from the Norse *draga*, "to draw."

MERRY WIDOW

Meaning: A strapless corset with attached garters

Origin: Introduced in 1951 by Warners, but popularized by Maidenform in 1952 for the film *The Merry Widow*, starring Lana Turner. The movie version of the merry widow was an elaborate contraption with panels of black and white lace, black elastic netting, a heavy zipper behind a velvet-backed hook-and-eye, and nine long spiral "shaping" wires encased in black satin. Turner reportedly said of it, "I tell you, the merry widow was designed by a man. A woman would never do that to another woman."

THE IG NOBEL PRIZES

Here's a look at one of our favorite annual awards, the
Ig Nobel Prizes, which are given out each year at
about the same time as the real Nobel Prizes.

DUBIOUS ACHIEVERS
In 1991 the scientific humor magazine *Annals of Improbable Research* created the Ig Nobel Prizes to honor discoveries "that cannot, or should not, be reproduced." The mission has changed somewhat since then; today the prizes are awarded for achievements that "first make people laugh, and then make them think." Actual Nobel Prize winners are on hand each year when the Ig Nobel Prizes are handed out at Harvard University's Sanders Theater. The presentation ceremony is broadcast on the Friday after Thanksgiving on National Public Radio's *Science Friday*, hosted by Ira Flatow. Here's a look at some recent winners.

Ig Nobel Prize: Physics (2003)
Award-Winning Topic: "An Analysis of the Forces Required to Drag Sheep Over Various Surfaces," by Jack Harvey of the University of Ballarat, Australia, et al.

• "Sheep shearing is an arduous occupation involving a range of physically demanding tasks.... Many shearers suffer back injuries during sheep dragging."

• "The texture with the lowest mean dragging force was wooden boards laid parallel to the drag.... This orientation is also favored by shearers for another reason. Sheep catch their toes much less in the 'parallel' floor than they do with steel mesh or with boards at right angles to the drag, resulting in a reduction in the effort expended in tipping sheep over."

Ig Nobel Prize: Medicine (2004)
Award-Winning Topic: "The Effect of Country Music on Suicide," by Steven Stack of Wayne State University, et al.
• "Country music is hypothesized to nurture a suicidal mood

through its concerns with problems common in the suicidal population, such as marital discord, alcohol abuse, and alienation from work."

• "The results of a multiple regression analysis of 49 metropolitan areas show that the greater the airtime devoted to country music, the greater the whole suicide rate. The effect is independent of divorce, southernness, poverty, and gun availability."

Ig Nobel Prize: Chemistry (2002)

Award-Winning Topic: The Periodic Table Table. Theodore Gray of Champaign, Illinois, built a Periodic Table of the Elements that doubles as a conference table, and stuffed it with samples of as many real elements as he could get ahold of.

• "One evening while reading *Uncle Tungsten* by Oliver Sacks, I became momentarily confused. He begins a chapter with a description of a periodic table display he loved to visit in the Kensington Science Museum, and in misreading the paragraph, I thought it was a *table*, not the wall display it actually is. When I found out there wasn't a Periodic Table in the British Museum, it left a hole I felt I had to fill."

• "Each element group (e.g., alkali metals, noble gases, etc.) is represented by a different type of wood. Then of course there's the whole question of collecting elements! You'd be surprised how many are available at Wal-Mart."

Ig Nobel Prize: Biology (2004)

Award-Winning Topic: "Sounds Produced by Herring Bubble Release," by Ben Wilson of the University of British Columbia

• "Herring apparently communicate by farting."

Ig Nobel Prize: Engineering (2004)

Award-Winning Topic: The comb-over. In 1975 Donald J. Smith and Frank J. Smith of Orlando, Florida, applied for a patent on the comb-over and were actually *granted* it two years later.

• "The hair is folded over the bald area beginning with the hair from the back of the head, and then from first one side and then the other. Hair spray is applied after the hair from said first side is folded into place and again after said second side being folded into place. The uppermost section can then be styled to the person's personal taste."

OTHER WINNERS

• **Ornithology** (2006): "Woodpeckers and Head Injury" (a study of why woodpeckers don't get headaches)

• **Interdisciplinary Research** (2003): "Chickens Prefer Beautiful Humans"

• **Agricultural History** (2005): "The Significance of Mr. Richard Buckley's Exploding Trousers"

• **Physics** (2004): "Coordination Modes in the Multisegmental Dynamics of Hula Hooping"

• **Biology** (2003): "The First Case of Homosexual Necrophilia in the Mallard"

• **Medicine** (1994): Awarded in two parts to 1) "Patient X," who was bitten by his pet rattlesnake and tried to treat himself with electroshock therapy by applying sparkplug wires to his lips for five minutes while a friend revved his car up to 3,000 rpm; and 2) Dr. Richard C. Dart and Dr. Richard A. Gustafson, authors of the medical paper "Failure of Electric Shock Treatment for Rattlesnake Envenomation."

• **Medicine** (2006): "Termination of Intractable Hiccups with Digital Rectal Massage"

* * *

FIVE FACTS ABOUT INDIA

1. India's national bird is the peacock.

2. The national sport is field hockey; the most popular is cricket.

3. The world's highest cricket pitch (playing field) is in Chail, Himachal Pradesh. It was built in 1893 and sits 2,250 meters— about 7,382 feet—above sea level.

4. The Indian railway system is the world's largest commercial employer, with more than 1.6 million workers.

5. India has two national languages: Hindi and English (it has 22 other officially recognized languages).

Pepper was so valuable during Elizabethan times that it was sold by the individual grain.

"I'M IN THE SEDIMENT"

Every language has its own unique idioms and expressions. They may sound perfectly normal to a person who uses them every day, but translated into other languages, they can seem pretty funny. Here are some common Russian slang terms and how they translate into English.

Ni khrená! (nee crenna)
Literally: "Not a horseradish!"
Meaning: "Nothing of the kind!"

Blin! (blin)
Literally: "Pancake!"
Meaning: "Ah, shoot!"

Bábki (bobki)
Literally: "little cakes"
Meaning: "money"

Bardák (bar-doke)
Literally: "a brothel"
Meaning: "It's a mess."

Krúto! (kroo-toe)
Literally: "Sharp!"
Meaning: "Cool!"

Lípa (lee-pah)
Literally: "a lime tree"
Meaning: "a phony"

Mézhdu nám... (mezh-doo nahm)
Literally: "Between us girls..."
Meaning: "Frankly speaking..."

Na ushákh (nah oosh-awk)
Literally: "on his ears"
Meaning: "drunk"

Ne goní purgú! (nay go-nee purr-goo)
Literally: "Don't chase away the snowstorm!"
Meaning: "Be honest!"

Gemorróy (gehm-err-oy)
Literally: "hemorrhoids"
Meaning: "a huge problem"

Kozël (koe-zull)
Literally: "a billy goat"
Meaning: "a loser"

Táchka (tash-kuh)
Literally: "a wheelbarrow"
Meaning: "a car"

Tórmoz (torr-moes)
Literally: "an obstacle"
Meaning: "a dumb person"

Fonár (phone-arr)
Literally: "a lamp"
Meaning: "a black eye"

Yáscik (yash-ick)
Literally: "a garbage can"
Meaning: "a TV set"

Ni figá sebé! (nee fegg-uh suh-bay)
Literally: "Not a fig to itself!"
Meaning: "Golly!"

Pértsy (purt-see)
Literally: "peppers"
Meaning: "the cool kids"

Porót chush (poor-oat choosh)
Literally: "to pick apart the garbage"
Meaning: "to chitchat"

Rubít kapústu (roob-it kup-oose-too)
Literally: "chop the cabbage"
Meaning: "make some quick cash"

Pervodít strélki (pare-vood-eet strell-kee)
Literally: "transfer the needle"
Meaning: "blame somebody else"

Cháynik (shay-nik)
Literally: "a teapot"
Meaning: "a novice"

Shíshka (shish-kuh)
Literally: "pinecone"
Meaning: "important person"

M˘lo (mm-loe)
Literally: "soap"
Meaning: "an e-mail message"

Ya v osádke! (ya vuh ose-odd-kuh)
Literally: "I'm in the sediment!"
Meaning: "I'm surprised!"

Stvol (stvole)
Literally: "a tree trunk"
Meaning: "a gun"

Kr˘sha poékhala! (kurr-shuh poke-uh-lah)
Literally: "The roof is gone!"
Meaning: "I'm so angry!"

Ljubop˘tnaya Varvára (ludge-bop-tuh-nay-uh var-vur-uh)
Literally: "a curious Barbara"
Meaning: "a nosy person"

Mne do lámpochki! (nay doe lam-poach-kee)
Literally: "It's up to the lightbulb!"
Meaning: "I don't care!"

*   *   *

WE WIN!

A car dealership in Roswell, New Mexico, ran a promotional contest in 2007. They mailed out 50,000 scratch-off tickets to local residents, one of which was supposed to win a grand prize of $1,000. But because of a printing goof, *every* ticket was a $1,000 winner. When the throngs of "winners" showed up to claim their prize, the embarrassed dealership tried to settle the $50-million mistake by giving each of them a $5 Wal-Mart gift card.

THE "SUE ME, SUE YOU BLUES," PART I

The business side of music can be a world of cutthroat legal practices and endless litigation. Here's Part I of the story of one of the biggest music legal battles of all time.

SOLO FLIGHT

In 1969 George Harrison was on a break from the Beatles and was doing some concerts in Copenhagen, Denmark, with the group Delaney and Bonnie and Friends. One day he slipped out of a press conference, grabbed his guitar, and started playing some guitar chords that were in his head. Then he added in two religious chants: the Christian "hallelujah" and the Hindu "hare krishna." Later he played it for the band, who joined in with four-part vocal harmony. Harrison fleshed out some verses about yearning to be closer to God, and titled it "My Sweet Lord."

A week later, Harrison flew to London to help produce an album by singer/keyboardist Billy Preston and gave him "My Sweet Lord" to record. The song went nowhere, but Harrison decided to record it himself for his first post-Beatles album, *All Things Must Pass*. Released as a single, "My Sweet Lord" became a number-one hit in January 1971.

At the time of the song's birth, Harrison thought elements of the song just popped into his head. He later figured out that subconsciously he'd been inspired by an old gospel song called "Oh Happy Day." Harrison insisted he hadn't "stolen" the song, he just used it as a starting point. And even if he had copied it directly, there were no legal ramifications—"Oh Happy Day" was in the public domain.

But as it would later turn out, another song did "pop" into Harrison's head and subconsciously inspire him. And that one had *serious* legal ramifications.

COVER ME

As "My Sweet Lord" rose up the charts, a cover version was released by a group called the Belmonts (formerly Dion and the Belmonts,

---

The Emmy award was originally called the Immy. It's named after TV camera "imaging" tubes.

best known for the 1959 hit "A Teenager in Love"). But instead of a straight cover of Harrison's song, the Belmonts' version interspersed lyrics from "He's So Fine," a 1963 hit by the girl group the Chiffons. It was uncanny: The songs meshed together perfectly, with nearly the exact same chord structure and many of the same notes.

The Belmonts' version was only a minor novelty hit. But it caught the attention of executives at Bright Tunes, the music publishing company that owned the copyright to "He's So Fine." In 1971 they sued Harrison, his label (Apple Records), and his publisher (Harrisongs Music Limited), claiming that Harrison had plagiarized "He's So Fine" and turned it into "My Sweet Lord," and was now profiting from it.

YOU NEVER GIVE ME YOUR MONEY

Guiding Harrison in the lawsuit was his business manager, Allen Klein. They'd worked together since early 1969, when Klein became the Beatles' business manager. Klein handled the Beatles' financial affairs shrewdly, saving Apple Records from bankruptcy, negotiating a new royalty rate ($.69 per album—the highest ever, at the time), and working for only a percentage of increased business. Nevertheless, Paul McCartney didn't trust Klein (he had an abrasive demeanor and was rumored to engage in shady business practices), and never actually signed the contract authorizing Klein to make decisions for him—one of the many disagreements that led to the Beatles' breakup in 1970.

Harrison tried to settle the suit quickly by offering to purchase the copyright to "He's So Fine" (for an undisclosed sum, probably less than $100,000), but despite being on the verge of bankruptcy, Bright Tunes declined. Reason: Klein had secretly met with Bright Tunes execs and told them they'd get more money by suing Harrison than by settling. He produced documents showing that Harrison stood to make more than $400,000 from "My Sweet Lord," to which Klein told Bright Tunes that they had a right—and a shot in court—at ownership.

SOMETHING IN THE WAY HE SUES

Bright Tunes was in deep financial trouble at the time, and Klein likely knew it. A lengthy court battle would further deplete their funds, making Bright Tunes far more likely to settle for an offer—

Kids, don't try this at home: If you hit it hard enough with a hammer, a diamond will shatter.

any offer—made for their back catalog. By encouraging Bright Tunes to sue Harrison, Klein was actually hoping to bring down the price on "He's So Fine" so that *he* could buy the rights and sue Harrison for copyright infringement himself.

Unaware of Klein's duplicity, Harrison was baffled when Bright Tunes declined his offer. Instead, they amended their lawsuit to request ownership of "My Sweet Lord" and half of all songwriting royalties earned by Harrison on the song, past and future. Harrison said no and the matter was headed for court.

I, ME, KLEIN

But in late 1971, before the case could be heard, Bright Tunes filed for bankruptcy (after they turned down *another* offer from Harrison—this time to buy their entire catalog). All legal matters would be delayed until the company was financially stable again.

Harrison's camp was also in chaos. Earlier in 1971, Harrison had organized the Concert for Bangladesh. From the proceeds of the concert and album sales, nearly $10 million was raised for UNICEF to help refugees in the war-torn Asian nation. But little of it actually went to those in need. Klein, acting as Harrison's business manager, should have arranged the donation with UNICEF prior to the concert or the album's release, but he didn't. Because of this, a hefty portion of the proceeds was taken out for taxes. And because it was reported after the fact, the IRS—and Harrison—suspected that Klein had embezzled some of the money. When Klein's contract with Harrison expired in 1973, it wasn't renewed.

In January 1976, nearly five years after the lawsuit was first initiated, Bright Tunes finally pulled itself out of bankruptcy. At that point Harrison offered Bright Tunes another deal: He would pay them $148,000 (40% of estimated royalties for "My Sweet Lord") to settle the suit, but he would get to keep the copyright. Again— on the advice of secret collaborator Allen Klein—Bright Tunes turned it down and went to court in the hopes of more money. In the summer of 1976, the case finally went to trial.

The stage for one of the most famous show-biz trials of all time is set, and you may think you know the good guys from the bad guys, but you might be surprised at how this saga ends. For Part II of our story, turn to page 351.

FARTS IN THE NEWS

You can't see them, but you know they're there.

JAIL FARTS

Two inmates in a Nebraska prison got into a squabble about farting, which led to one of them getting charged with assault. The alleged farter, 38-year-old Brian Bruggeman, was accused of "passing gas repeatedly in front of his cellmate." The fartee, Jesse Dorris, claims that Bruggeman repeatedly—and intentionally—farted at him not only in their cell, but also outside in the yard and even while the two were waiting in the lunch line. After the tension built up to a bursting point, the two prisoners started throwing punches, and Bruggeman was charged with assault.

JAR FARTS

The "Fart in a Jar" is a new fad on eBay, and people are buying. One such Fart in a Jar—reportedly the gas of an actual fart that was deposited there by a "hot girl"—sold for $71 after 24 bids. The ad even featured an audio file to prove the fart's authenticity.

STAR FARTS

While filming a love scene for the 2002 movie *The Heart of Me*, actor Paul Bettany was horrified by a loud emission from co-star Helena Bonham Carter. "She farted on me, announced the fact to the cast and crew, and I was the one who ended up feeling embarrassed," said Bettany. But he was also impressed by the movie beauty's candor. "She's barking mad and keen as mustard," he said.

PUB FARTS

Thirsty Kirsty's Pub, located in Dunfermline, Scotland, enforced an anti-smoking ban in 2006. One unforeseen consequence of the ban is that other odors, previously overpowered by the smoke, are now wafting their way to customers' noses. And it led to the banning-for-life of Stewart Laidlaw, a pub patron who was passing gas for his amusement...much to the dismay of the pub's other customers. According to owner John Thow, "It is just disgusting. He revels in this and does it all the time and it's absolutely foul." The 35-year-old Laidlaw is fighting the ban, claiming that his wind is far less toxic than the smoke that preceded it. Thow isn't budging, though, insisting that the ban will stay in place. "He has been warned and asked politely to stop on many occasions. Anybody can pass wind, but when you make a hobby of it, that's going too far."

BOX FARTS

Early one February morning in 2007, a post office in New Zealand was evacuated when a "fart bomb" detonated inside its box while being weighed on the postal scales. The foul-smelling prank device, designed to remain closed until switched on, was being mailed by an Internet magazine to the lucky subscriber who won it in a contest. But it never made it there. Local fire chief Mike McEnaney defended the decision to evacuate the post office and all the other businesses on the street, telling reporters: "Until you can identify what the substance is, you have got the potential there for a hazardous chemical incident." Once the contents were determined to be noxious but not hazardous, the post office reopened. (They also sent the Internet company detailed information about the proper way to pack and ship potentially hazardous materials.)

BUSH FARTS

An anonymous aide to President George W. Bush reported to *U.S. News & World Report* that the commander in chief "can't get enough of fart jokes." And not only that, Bush has often greeted young aides with a "21-trumpet salute," just to alleviate some of the stress they may be feeling about meeting the president of the United States.

UNPATRIOTIC FARTS

In a routine police stop in a Warsaw, Poland, train station in 2006, cops asked Hubert Hoffman what he thought about Polish president Lech Kaczynski. After complaining that Kaczynski was leading Poland back to a Communist-style government, Hoffman summed up his feelings for the head of state with a loud fart. Hoffman was arrested on charges of contempt and released on bail but failed to report to his trial, launching a nationwide manhunt for the flatulent offender.

Eeew! In an average year, 311 New York City residents report being bitten by a rat.

DOUBLE TROUBLE

*Just about everyone has wondered what it would be like to
have an identical twin—someone you could switch places
with in school, on dates, on the job, etc. It would be
great! No one would ever know...or would they?*

TWINS: Tanya and Tamara Smith, 24

BACKGROUND: In 1984 Tanya Smith was arrested and charged with bank fraud after someone matching her description used a phony wire transfer to steal $4,000 from the American National Bank in St. Paul, Minnesota. She was also charged with attempting the same scam in three other banks in the state.

DOUBLE TROUBLE: At her weeklong trial, Tanya testified that she was innocent and that her twin sister, Tamara, was the real culprit. Tamara was a cocaine addict and stole the money to support her habit, Tanya told the court. "I don't like drugs. They make Tamara do things she shouldn't do." Tamara, who was on the run from the law after being convicted of forgery in another case, was not available to testify at the trial.

WHAT HAPPENED: Tanya was found not guilty...but prosecutors never really bought her "Tamara did it" defense. For one thing, eyewitnesses said the person committing the bank fraud had a facial scar, and Tanya was the only twin who had one. For another thing, Tanya wrote letters to the cops bragging that they weren't smart enough to catch her. Unfortunately for Tanya, they were. The FBI stayed on the case, and in 1986 arrested *both* sisters, who had both been in on the crime from the beginning. They were found guilty of stealing nearly $400,000 from banks in 10 different states. Tamara got 8 years in prison; Tanya got 13.

TWINS: Leonard and Lamont Hough, 23

BACKGROUND: One evening in March 1993, Lamont dropped by the apartment that Leonard shared with his girlfriend in Hempstead, New York, to see if Leonard was home. The girlfriend told him no, so Lamont left.

DOUBLE TROUBLE: Two hours later, "Leonard" came home

Did you get one? Approximately 165 million Easter cards are purchased each year in the U.S.

and spent the night with his girlfriend. The next morning when the man in her bed asked her, "What are you going to tell Lenny?" the girlfriend realized she'd been sleeping with her boyfriend's identical twin brother.

WHAT HAPPENED: The girlfriend called the police and Lamont was taken into custody. Lamont was originally charged with sexual misconduct, but a judge threw that out, ruling that since the affair was consensual, no misconduct had occurred even if the consent was obtained through fraud. So prosecutors charged Lamont with criminal impersonation instead. His attorneys argued that since he'd done nothing to impersonate his brother, it wasn't his fault that the girlfriend had mistaken him for Leonard.

The jury deliberated for five minutes…and found Lamont not guilty.

TWINS: Emma and Laura Brodie, 20, of Great Britain
BACKGROUND: Emma was engaged to 32-year-old Gary Eales, and the wedding was set for October 1995. But less than two months before the wedding, Gary called it off. A few days later he changed his mind and the wedding was back on again. Ultimately, the wedding went off without a hitch—but the marriage was another story.

DOUBLE TROUBLE: Why had Gary wanted to call the wedding off? Emma stumbled onto the answer just four weeks into the marriage, when she caught Gary and Laura smooching at the local pub. Caught red-handed, Gary admitted he'd fallen *out* of love with Emma months before the wedding…and had fallen *in* love with her twin, Laura.

WHAT HAPPENED: Emma was furious, but somehow she made peace with the situation and agreed to a divorce so that Gary could marry Laura. Emma even agreed to be her sister's bridesmaid. "I'm just glad Emma and Laura can both laugh now about what's happened between us," Gary says.

*   *   *

FOREIGN EXCHANGE

Percentage of the American population that's British-born: 0.41.
Percentage of the British population that's American-born: 0.42.

WEIRD CANADA

Canada: land of beautiful mountains,
clear lakes...and some really weird news.

SUITING UP

In January 2007, Canadian inventor Troy Hurtubise announced that he'd spent $15,000 developing a high-tech suit of armor for Canadian soldiers. Hurtubise took up the cause after spending four years designing an indestructible suit for fighting grizzly bears. (It didn't work.) He calls the military suit "the first ballistic, full exoskeleton body suit of armor" and claims it can withstand rifle fire. But just in case, it also carries an emergency syringe full of morphine.

WEATHERING CHANGE

Dexter Manley played defensive end in the NFL for 10 seasons until he failed his fourth drug test in 1991. The following year, he resumed his career by playing for the Ottawa Rough Riders of the Canadian Football League. That appears to be when he got in touch with his "inner Canadian." In 1994 Manley claimed he was visited by the ghost of deceased Canadian prime minister William Lyon Mackenzie King. "We talked about thunder and lightning," Manley said.

POLKA DON'T

In July 2005, 644 people gathered in Kimberley, British Columbia, and set a world record when they simultaneously played accordions for half an hour. If that isn't scary enough, just a month later at a folk music festival in St. John's, Newfoundland, that record was broken by 989 accordion players.

BOOKED

While serving a prison sentence in Winnipeg, James Skinner asked the warden's office for a copy of *Funk and Wagnall's Canadian College Dictionary* to keep in his cell. The officials turned him down, saying that the book was so large it could be used as a weapon.

LEGAL BRIEFS

The Canadian Defence Department has 17 pages of guidelines for manufacturers who want to supply underwear to the Canadian military. According to the document, the underwear must be durable enough to be worn for up to six months without being changed. (It must also be invisible to the enemy's night-vision goggles.)

POOPUS INTERRUPTUS

In May 2006, Guy Fournier, chairman of the state-run Canadian Broadcasting Corporation, appeared on the TV talk show *Tout le Monde en Parle* ("Everyone's Talking About It"). Fournier commented on the air that at his age (74) he enjoyed defecation more than lovemaking. The remark created such a public outcry that he had to resign his job.

ANIMAL ACT

In 2007 Mike Lake, a Member of Parliament from Edmonton, Alberta, presented a petition from 500 of his constituents to the House of Commons to "establish legislation to effect immediate protection" of Bigfoot. Lake essentially asked the Canadian government to put Bigfoot—nearly universally believed to be a myth or a hoax—on the endangered species list. The House of Commons declined.

ODOR IN THE COURT

In 1994 Ontario judge Lee Ferrier found for the defendant, Calvin Klein Canada, in a wrongful termination suit brought by former cologne demonstrator Sharon Bagnall. Judge Ferrier found that Bagnall had been ineffective at her job based on testimony from witnesses that she "had a personal hygiene problem" and smelled "like an armpit."

*   *   *

CRAZY CLASSIFIED

"We seek a journalist based in India to report on the city government and political scene of Pasadena, California, USA."

—**Job announcement from PasadenaNow.com**

Most common surname on Long Island, Nova Scotia: Outhouse.

LIBERTY...OR DEATH!

One of the most famous cries in American history.

VIRGINIA REAL
Unlike America's other Founding Fathers, who were classically educated and high-born, Patrick Henry was more a man of the people—an unsuccessful farmer and shopkeeper before becoming a self-taught lawyer. A passionate voice against taxation without representation, he argued in court against the imposition of unfair British taxes. In 1765 he was elected to the legislature of the Virginia Commonwealth, where his anti-British advocacy was considered treasonous. On March 23, 1775, he rose to address the Virginia legislative convention, giving a speech that inspired many delegates to take up arms in the Revolutionary War.

According to most accounts, Patrick Henry was a firebrand as a speaker, using language designed to incite the emotions of his audience. He left few papers of any kind after his death; there are no written copies of his speech and no official transcript of the convention. The first written version of Henry's "Give me liberty" speech appeared in William Wirt's 1817 book, *Sketches in the Life and Character of Patrick Henry*. Wirt used the reminiscences of people who were actually at the convention, plus other contemporary sources, to reconstruct it. Though it's certain that many of the embellishments are Wirt's—possibly including the famous last line—it matches Henry's evangelical style and includes phrases he was known to use. Regardless of his exact words, Patrick Henry was responsible for propelling the Virginians into the Revolution. And regardless of who wrote what, the speech we've been reading for almost 200 years is still a great one.

THE SPEECH

Mr. President, it is natural to Man to indulge in the illusions of hope. We are apt to shut our eyes against a painful truth, and listen to the song of that siren, till she transforms us into beasts. Is this the part of wise men, engaged in a great and arduous struggle for liberty? Are we disposed to be of the number of those who, having eyes, see not, and having ears, hear not, the things which so nearly

Potatoes, sweet potatoes, and yams are botanically unrelated.

concern their temporal salvation? For my part, whatever anguish of spirit it may cost, I am willing to know the whole truth, to know the worst and to provide for it.

I have but one lamp by which my feet are guided, and that is the lamp of experience. I know of no way of judging of the future but by the past. And judging by the past, I wish to know what there has been in the conduct of the British ministry for the last ten years, to justify those hopes with which gentlemen have been pleased to solace themselves. Is it that insidious smile with which our petition has been lately received? Trust it not, sir; it will prove a snare to your feet. Suffer not yourselves to be betrayed with a kiss. Ask yourselves how this gracious reception of our petition comports with these warlike preparations which cover our waters and darken our land. Are fleets and armies necessary to a work of love and reconciliation? Have we shown ourselves so unwilling to be reconciled that force must be called in to win back our love? Let us not deceive ourselves, sir. These are the implements of war and subjugation, the last arguments to which kings resort.

Sir, we have done everything that could be done to avert the storm which is now coming on. We have petitioned; we have remonstrated; we have supplicated; we have prostrated ourselves before the throne. Our petitions have been slighted; our remonstrances have produced additional violence and insult; our supplications have been disregarded; and we have been spurned, with contempt, from the foot of the throne. In vain, after these things, may we indulge the fond hope of peace and reconciliation. There is no longer any room for hope. If we wish to be free—if we mean to preserve inviolate those inestimable privileges for which we have been so long contending—if we mean not basely to abandon the noble struggle in which we have been so long engaged, and which we have pledged ourselves never to abandon until the glorious object of our contest shall be obtained, we must fight! I repeat it, sir, we must fight! An appeal to arms and to the God of Hosts is all that is left us!

They tell us, sir, that we are weak, unable to cope with so formidable an adversary. But when shall we be stronger? Will it be the next week, or the next year? Will it be when we are totally disarmed, and when a British guard shall be stationed in every house? Shall we gather strength by irresolution and inaction? Shall we acquire the means of effectual resistance, by lying supinely on our backs, and hugging the delusive phantom of hope, until our enemies shall have bound us hand and foot? Sir, we are not weak, if we make a proper use of the means which the God of nature hath placed in our power. Three millions of people, armed in the holy cause of liberty, and in such a country as that which we possess, are invincible by any force which our enemy can send against us. Besides, sir, we shall not fight our battles alone. There is a just God who presides over the destinies of nations, and who will raise up friends to fight our battles for us. The battle, sir, is not to the strong alone; it is to the vigilant, the active, the brave. Besides, sir, we have no election. If we were base enough to desire it, it is now too late to retire from the contest. There is no retreat but in submission and slavery! Our chains are forged! Their clanking may be heard on the plains of Boston! The war is inevitable—and let it come! I repeat it, sir, let it come!

It is in vain, sir, to extenuate the matter. Gentlemen may cry, "Peace! Peace!"—but there is no peace. The war is actually begun! The next gale that sweeps from the north will bring to our ears the clash of resounding arms! Our brethren are already in the field! Why stand we here idle? What is it that gentlemen wish? What would they have? Is life so dear, or peace so sweet, as to be purchased at the price of chains and slavery? Forbid it, Almighty God! I know not what course others may take; but as for me, give me liberty, or give me death!

*   *   *

A VISION OF THE FUTURE

• In a 1987 *Omni* reader poll, 41% of respondents predicted that in 2007 "computers will supplement human teachers in nearly every classroom, and software will replace textbooks as the primary source of teaching material."

• Richard Selzer of Yale Medical School predicted that the biggest major medical problem of the future would be boredom.

• Isaac Asimov predicted that by 2007 there would already be a fully operational mining station on the Moon.

He said, he said? Before the year 1000, the word "she" didn't exist in the English language.

TO WIT

Clever quotes from clever folks.

"The shortest distance between two points is under construction."
—**Noelie Altito**

"I might be in the basement. I'll go upstairs and check."
—**M. C. Escher**

"There are only two rules for success: 1) Never tell everything you know."
—**Roger H. Lincoln**

"All generalizations are false."
—**R. H. Grenier**

"Summer bachelors, like summer breezes, are never as cool as they pretend to be."
—**Nora Ephron**

"The four most beautiful words in our common language: I told you so."
—**Gore Vidal**

"Housework, if you do it right, will kill you."
—**Erma Bombeck**

"All it takes to fly is to hurl yourself at the ground…and miss."
—**Douglas Adams**

"I'm all in favor of keeping dangerous weapons out of the hands of fools. Let's start with typewriters."
—**Frank Lloyd Wright**

"Life is like an onion. You peel it off one layer at a time, and sometimes you weep."
—**Carl Sandburg**

"Research is what I'm doing when I don't know what I'm doing."
—**Wernher von Braun**

"There is a remote tribe that worships the number zero. Is nothing sacred?"
—**Les Dawson**

"In a world where everything is ridiculous, nothing can be ridiculed. You cannot unmask a mask."
—**G. K. Chesterton**

"I hope life isn't a big joke, because I don't get it."
—**Jack Handey**

"And that's the world in a nutshell—an appropriate receptacle."
—**Stan Dunn**

Diameter of the wire in a standard paper clip: about 4 hundredths of an inch.

ORIGINAL ZIN

White zinfandel is one of America's most popular (and affordable) wines. But unlike other wines, it doesn't have a long history and it's not an old European style. White zinfandel was invented in the United States...by a series of accidents.

R ED RED WINE
The zinfandel grape has been grown in the United States since the 1820s. It came to North America from Austria in 1829, when a Long Island plant nursery owner named George Gibbs brought home some grapevine cuttings from the Austro-Hungarian Imperial Nursery in Vienna. But during the ship voyage back, the labels on the cuttings got mixed up. Gibbs sorted it out...or at least he thought he did. Gibbs actually mislabeled the *primitivo* vine sample as *zierfandler*. In 1851 a California wine grower named Agoston Haraszthy (often called the father of the California wine industry) bought a sample of Gibbs's "zierfandler," Americanized the name to *zinfandel*, and planted the grape in California.

Zinfandel arrived in California at the perfect time. The California Gold Rush brought hordes of people to the West Coast for the first time. Settlers also discovered that California's climate and soil made it the perfect place to grow wine grapes. Zinfandel, especially, thrived—it can grow in many different kinds of soils and climates and, on average, produces twice as many grapes as other kinds of vines. Haraszthy sold cuttings to numerous other winegrowers and zinfandel quickly became the most produced grape in California. The wine made out of it was red, hearty, and had a high alcohol content. From the 1850s to the turn of the century, zinfandel was the most planted grape and bestselling wine in the United States.

GRAPE EXPECTATIONS
The zinfandel grape wasn't just being used for a red wine called "zinfandel." It was—and still is—a source for many different kinds of wines, including claret, port, and cabernet. In 1869 winemakers at the El Pinal Winery in Lodi, California, were experimenting with ways to expand zinfandel's versatility even further. Part of why red wines have a rich and slightly bitter taste is because of

tannins that are found in grape skins. El Pinal wondered what would happen if they peeled the grapes before they fermented into wine. The result was a new kind of wine. It had most of the flavor of red wine, but it was pink. El Pinal abandoned the wine, and "white zinfandel," as they called it, became a footnote in the history of winemaking. Red zinfandel wine remained America's bestseller for another hundred years.

RED, WHITE, AND PINK
By the end of the 1960s, white wines (including chardonnay) began to outsell red wines. Sales of zinfandel, in particular, plummeted. It got so bad that many of California's Napa Valley wineries—which had been producing zinfandel for nearly a century—stopped growing zinfandel grapes altogether and replanted their vineyards with more popular and profitable grapes, like sauvignon blanc.

But not all of them stopped. Zinfandel still had a modest fan base, so one winery, Sutter Home, decided to continue making zinfandel and go after that niche market. In fact, Sutter Home experimented with ways to make the traditional red zinfandel even stronger, richer, and more bitter—going against the mainstream market, which was demanding lighter-tasting white wines.

A CASE OF MISTAKEN IDENTITY
In 1972 Bob Trinchero, chief winemaker at Sutter Home, had an idea. He theorized that the zinfandel wine might be thicker and richer if he squeezed some of the juice out of the grape skins just before they fermented into wine. He was right: The resulting zinfandel was concentrated, and so rich and bitter that it was almost lip-puckering. But Trinchero had a problem: what to do with all the leftover grape-skin juice he'd removed. That juice had also fermented into wine, but it was like nothing he'd seen or tasted—it was pink and dry and had a very "light" taste, but not as light as a regular white wine.

Trinchero didn't think the pink wine had much appeal, but, since he had 550 gallons of the stuff, he had to do something with it. He talked the Corti Brothers grocery chain into buying half of the yield. The rest he'd sample off in the Sutter Home tasting room. He needed a name for the wine, something that sounded French and classy to legitimize the pink "garbage" wine to customers. He settled on *Oeil de Perdix*, which translates to "eye of the partridge," which sounded good even though it didn't mean anything. But the Bureau of Alcohol, Tobacco, and Firearms rejected the name, unless Trinchero put an English translation on the label. "Eye of the Partridge" was nonsense, so Trinchero borrowed a name for the new pink wine from an old pink wine he'd once read about: *white zinfandel*.

FIRST THE COLOR, NOW THE FLAVOR

The wine sold surprisingly well at Corti Brothers and in the tasting room, so Sutter Home kept making it...until 1975. That year the entire production run of white zinfandel was ruined by "stuck fermentation." Ordinarily, the sugars in grapes ferment into alcohol when yeast is added. When stuck fermentation occurs, the yeast dies before the fermentation is complete. Result: lots of sugar remains unfermented, creating a very sweet wine. But white zinfandel wasn't supposed to be sweet...or was it?

Trinchero figured the run of white zinfandel (and a lot of money) was lost. Then he tasted the wine. It was sweet, but still tasted light and airy—much lighter than the usual batches of white zinfandel. Trinchero quickly realized that this new wine had the potential to be hugely successful. It was a wine for people who didn't like the taste of regular red or white wines.

WINE AND DANDY

Trinchero began bottling the new, sweeter wine under the name white zinfandel, and it *was* huge. From 1980 until 1998, it was the bestselling variety of wine in the United States. The popularity of the white zinfandel also led Sutter Home to shift from producing mostly premium red wines to inexpensive, sweet white wines with broad appeal (most Sutter Home wines cost under $7.00). Sutter Home—where Trinchero is now chairman—sells 42 million bottles of white zin each year.

*　　*　　*

"Milk is the drink of babies, tea the drink of women, water the drink of beasts, and Wine is the drink of the gods."

—John Stuart Blackie

NUDES & PRUDES

Nudity can be shocking—and so can prudery.
Which side of the fence do you fall on?

NUDE: Jesse Hale is a music major at Austin Peay State University in Clarksville, Tennessee. Her passion is playing the cello...naked. She's preferred playing in the buff since she was a child, because, as she puts it, "cellists make full body contact with their instrument...it just feels natural." (Hale isn't the only one—she's a member of the CJ Boyd Sexxxtet, a group of musicians who travel the world playing "experimental chant-like" songs in their birthday suits.)

PRUDE: While campaigning for the presidency in 2007, Senator Barack Obama made a fundraising stop at the Planet Zero Art Gallery in Richmond, Virginia. And although he's campaigning on a progressive platform, one of the artworks on display was too risqué for the senator. It was a 6-by-10-foot oil painting called "Snake Charmer," which features Britney Spears (sans underwear) getting out of Paris Hilton's limo. "I wished we could have had a good dialogue about freedom of speech," said the artist, Jamie Boling, "but I understand that a politician might want to avoid being photographed in front of Britney Spears' crotch."

NUDE: In 2006 Polish artist Pawel Althamer created a controversial self-portrait: a 70-foot-long anatomically correct helium-filled balloon sculpture of himself—naked—that hovered above the Palazzina Appiani in Milan, Italy. Oddly, it didn't create much controversy. The display garnered only a few complaints from the 3,000 park visitors who saw it. Said the mother of a three-year-old boy who lives nearby: "To be honest with you, it's nothing new. He sees his father naked all the time."

PRUDE: In 2007 Jason Brenner, a high-school teacher from Englewood, Florida, starred in a small stage production of *The Full Monty*, a story about some friends who try to raise money by dancing nude on stage. At the end of the play, Brenner bared it all, but used a lighting scheme that made sure nothing was revealed. Even so, school officials sent him a letter: "Either stop doing the show; continue the show but take yourself out of the last scene, or continue doing the show at full capacity but hand in a letter of resignation." Brenner chose the third option and quit. Even though he revealed nothing, he said, he "didn't want to compromise his art."

NUDE: Realizing that having an average age of 55 might deter young people from joining their ranks, directors of the Solair Recreation League nudist camp in Connecticut decided to lift their sagging image by offering age-related discounts to new members. The price breakdown: $400 per year for nudists over 55; $300 for middle-aged nudists; and only $150 for college-aged nudists.

PRUDE: *The Higher Power of Lucky*, a Newberry Medal-winning children's book by Susan Patron, covers some weighty subject matter—religion, drug addiction, and parental abandonment. But that wasn't the reason that several U.S. libraries took it off their shelves in 2007. The culprit was a word that appeared on page one: "scrotum." (The main character overhears some adults talking about a dog whose aforementioned body part was bitten by a rattlesnake.) Patron argues that banning the book only calls more attention to the word. "There's a direct correlation between fear of naming body parts and kids' interest in finding out about them," she said.

NUDE: A gym in Amsterdam announced a "Naked Sundays" promotion in 2007. "I heard that some other gyms are offering courses on 'pole-dancing' as a sport," explained owner Patrick de Man, "so I thought, why not bring something new to the market?" The main question his customers ask is not whether the promotion is in good or bad taste, but if it is sanitary. Yes, says de Man. A towel must be placed on a piece of equipment before any bare skin touches it.

PRUDE: When George Lucas was making the first *Star Wars* movie in 1976, executives at 20th Century-Fox reviewed the script and were especially concerned with the character of Chewbacca. Their problem: The Wookie wore no pants. When Lucas received a memo suggesting that they give Chewbacca a pair of trousers, he ignored it. The Wookie remained naked (except for his munitions belt, of course).

...beauty. (They paint black lines down the center of their noses to make them appear longer.)

SAY IT WITH ROSES

You probably know that red roses symbolize love and passion, but you may not know that the color, number, and how roses are combined have coded meanings dating to the Victorian era. Here's a guide to sending the perfect bouquet.

1 red rose: "I like you."

6 red roses: "I adore you."

A dozen red roses: "It's true love."

15 red roses: "I'm sorry."

25 red roses: "Congratulations!"

50 red roses: "I love you, no matter what."

100 red roses: "I'm devoted to you."

108 red roses: "Will you marry me?"

Yellow: "Let's just be friends."

Red, white, and pink mixed: "May God bless you." (The three colors symbolize the Holy Trinity.)

Red and white mixed: "We belong together."

Two intertwined red roses: "I have something to ask you." (A marriage proposal is imminent.)

Red and white with ivy: "We will be together forever."

White: symbolizes innocence and purity.

White buds: "I'm too young for love."

Red and yellow: "Let's celebrate."

Light pink: "You make me happy."

Dark pink: "Thank you."

Blue: "You're mysterious."

Lavender: "It was love at first sight."

Coral: "I want you."

Burgundy: "You're beautiful."

Orange: "You fascinate me."

White tea roses with pink borders: "I must confess— I'm still in love with you."

Very dark red (almost black): "My condolences."

Sample from Uncle John's rose code. Dead roses: "I meant to give you these sooner."

GOOD GRIEF: THE *PEANUTS* STORY

Here's an inside look at the world's most popular comic strip and the man who created it.

BACKGROUND
To say that *Peanuts* is the most famous daily comic strip in the history of the art form is an understatement. Like Superman and Mickey Mouse, *Peanuts* transcended its medium and became woven into the fabric of society. Readers of all ages found something to connect with—Charlie Brown's perseverance in the face of one disappointment after another, Snoopy's cool, Lucy's crabbiness, or Linus's innocent wisdom. The sheer numbers *Peanuts* generated are still unmatched, nearly a decade after the strip came to an end: From 1950 to 1999, Charles Schulz wrote and drew 18,250 daily *Peanuts* strips. They appeared in 2,600 newspapers, reaching 355 million readers in 75 countries, and were translated into 21 different languages. Between the daily strips, the merchandising tie-ins, and the television specials, *Peanuts* is also a phenomenal moneymaker—at its peak, it earned more than $1 billion per year and made its creator, Charles M. Schulz, one of the richest entertainers in the world.

CRACKS IN THE ARMOR

So what *was* the appeal? For one, *Peanuts* was ahead of its time. *Doonesbury* creator Garry Trudeau, who grew up reading the strip, said, "*Peanuts* vibrated with '50s alienation. Everything about it was different. Edgy, unpredictable—it was the first Beat strip."

Early-1950s America was a time of prosperity: World War II had been won, the economy was strong, President Eisenhower encouraged good old American know-how for the construction of interstate highways and pristine neighborhoods. This optimism played out in popular movies, on television, and even in the comics. The few comic strips that featured children, like Ernie Bushmiller's *Nancy*, portrayed kids as innocent and…well, kidlike. In the movies, children routinely got into and out of cute adven-

---

A coffee tree yields only about a pound of coffee each year.

tures, never offering any great philosophical truths. And no one expected them to. Then, all of a sudden, here was a comic strip with a strange round-headed boy saying, "I don't feel the way I'm supposed to feel."

Statements like that reflected the painful truth that a lot of people *weren't* content. Treading a thin line between wholesome and subversive, Charlie Brown and his friends jumped off the page and connected with readers. Schulz tapped into something that kept people glued to *Peanuts'* extended storylines (something new to kid-oriented strips): they dealt more with pain than triumph.

The pain that emanated from the strip came straight from Schulz's own life. He once admitted, "I worry about almost all there is in life to worry about. And because I worry, Charlie Brown has to worry." Schulz also pointed to the strip's recurring themes: "All the loves are unrequited; all the baseball games are lost; all the test scores are D-minuses; the Great Pumpkin never comes; and the football is always pulled away." Schulz knew that for every winner out there, there were 10 more losers. They all want to win—to fit in—but most have to make do with what they end up with. The struggle to fit in had been a part of Schulz's life for as long as he could remember.

A BOY AND HIS DOG

Charles Monroe Schulz was born in Minneapolis, Minnesota, on November 26, 1922, to parents of German and Norwegian descent, and the family soon moved to nearby St. Paul. Daily newspaper comic strips were always a big part of his life (when he was two days old, an uncle gave him the nickname he carried for the rest of his life, "Sparky," after a horse called Sparkplug from the comic strip *Barney Google*).

In a way, reading *Peanuts* is like reading about Schulz's childhood. He owned a black-and-white dog named Spike that followed him around the neighborhood and ran onto the field during his baseball games. Just like Charlie Brown, Schulz flew his kites into the trees, liked to ice skate, went to summer camp reluctantly, and had a father who was a barber.

Also like Charlie Brown, Schulz was often teased by his friends, which led to a lifelong inferiority complex. Schulz's high marks in grammar school led to his being promoted from the third grade to the fifth grade, putting him in a classroom full of kids who were bigger, older, and more streetwise than he was. By the time he got to high school, Schulz suffered from bouts of depression.

But when he was alone, he found solace in reading and drawing comic strips. His first published drawing—at age 15—was a picture of Spike that he submitted to *Ripley's Believe It or Not!* Yet the drawings that Schulz submitted to his high-school yearbook were rejected. "I was a bland, stupid-looking kid who started off badly and failed at everything," he once said in an interview. Schulz never stopped drawing, though, and filled sketchbook after sketchbook with depictions of Popeye, Mickey Mouse, Donald Duck, and dozens more of his comic-strip heroes.

OFF TO WAR

After high school finally ended, Schulz dove straight into his dream. With his parents' support, he took a correspondence course at the St. Paul Art Instruction School. But his dreams were put on hold when he was drafted into the army and sent to Europe as a machine-gun squad leader. (On his only opportunity to shoot someone, his gun wasn't loaded. Fortunately, the German soldier surrendered.) Schulz's feelings of isolation only grew more intense during the war. He was still grieving for his mother, who had died in 1943, and he never really fit in with the other guys. Just as he had in high school, Schulz lost himself in his sketchbook. "The army taught me all I needed to know about loneliness," he said.

BACK TO THE DRAWING BOARD

Schulz returned to St. Paul in 1945 even more disillusioned, but he knew his path: cartooning. He went back to the Art Instruction School and asked them for a job as a correspondence-course instructor. They hired him. He soon landed a second job at a Catholic comic magazine called *Timeless Topix*, lettering their comics pages. While there, Schulz met a comic-strip artist named Frank Wing, who would become his mentor. Soon Schulz was drawing his own cartoons at *Timeless Topix*. His first: a single-panel cartoon with two kids sitting on a curb. "One kid," Schulz wrote, "is sitting on the curb with a baseball bat in his hands talking to a little girl, saying, 'I think I could learn to love you, Judy, if your batting average was a little higher.'" Wing saw the cartoon and told Schulz, "Sparky, I think you should draw more of those little kids. They're pretty good."

Around this time, Schulz discovered a classic comic strip called *Krazy Kat*, drawn by George Herriman. Without *Krazy Kat*, *Peanuts* might have been just another comic where the kids did kidlike things. But *Krazy Kat* was surreal—a cat, a mouse, and a dog living in a dreamlike world. They had childlike qualities countered by very advanced vocabularies. *Krazy Kat* demonstrated to Schulz that fantasy and grown-up language could be effective tools to describe not only the everyday lives of children, but of people in general. Even though he drew only kids from then on, Schulz's comic strips would be primarily targeted toward adults.

LI'L FOLKS

In 1947 Schulz sold his first newspaper cartoons—single-panel gags—to his hometown paper, the *St. Paul Pioneer Press*. Called *Li'l Folks*, it had no set cast of characters, but there was a kid he called Charlie Brown (borrowed from the name of an artist friend) and a dog that resembled Snoopy. While writing *Li'l Folks*, Schulz also sold 17 cartoons to the *Saturday Evening Post* from 1947 to 1950. Bolstered by these successes, he attempted to syndicate *Li'l Folks* in other newspapers, but couldn't get it picked up. Then in 1949 the *Pioneer Press* dropped *Li'l Folks*.

Rather than admit defeat, in 1950 Schulz shopped his best single-panel gag cartoons to United Features Syndicate in New York. They liked them…but thought they weren't original enough to stand out. So Schulz showed them a few four-panel comic strips he'd been working on. The syndicate loved them and asked Schulz to create "some definite characters." Energized, Schulz returned to St. Paul and started forming the characters that he would draw for the rest of his life.

For Part II of the Peanuts story, go to page 295.

For Part II of the Peanuts story, go to page 295.

*   *   *

There is only one beautiful child in the world, and
every mother has it.   —**Chinese proverb**

Read 'em and weep: More than 100 romance novels are published every month.

ALASKA: IT'S DIFFERENT UP HERE

And by different, we mean "Different like an Arctic fox!"

IT'S A BIRD! IT'S A DEER HEAD!

"About 10,000 Juneau residents briefly lost power after a bald eagle lugging a deer head crashed into transmission lines. 'This is the story of the overly ambitious eagle, who evidently found a deer's head in the landfill,' said Alaska Electric Light & Power spokeswoman Gayle Wood. The bird, weighed down by the deer head, apparently failed to clear the transmission lines. A repair crew found the eagle dead, the deer head nearby. 'You have to live in Alaska to have this kind of outage scenario,' Wood said."

—Associated Press

THE MONEY, OR THE SCARECROW GETS IT

"Authorities were looking for a man who robbed a bank in Anchorage while swinging a flaming torch fashioned from a burning T-shirt and a yard-long metal pole. The masked robber threatened to set fire to people, including the teller, and burn down the bank building in Fairview if his demands weren't met. He stormed the Alaska USA Federal Credit Union branch at about 3:45 p.m., said FBI spokesman Eric Gonzalez. He fled on foot with an undisclosed amount of money. Gonzalez said that in his more than 15 years at the FBI he could not recall a robber using a torch as a weapon."

—*Canoe News* (Canada)

WALK OF LIFE

"You can lead an elephant to a treadmill, but you can't make her walk. That's the lesson zookeepers are learning in Anchorage, where they have been struggling to get the zoo's resident elephant to exercise. Maggie, a 23-year-old African elephant, is the only pachyderm at the Alaska Zoo, where she is kept indoors much of the time to protect her from the cold. Critics say Maggie should be moved to a zoo in a warmer climate, where she can enjoy the outdoors and the company of other elephants. But rather than

---

Family values: According to Walt Disney, Mickey and Minnie Mouse are married.

give her up, Alaska Zoo officials decided to build her the world's first elephant treadmill. The 25-foot-long apparatus was custom-made by an Idaho firm that constructs conveyor belts. But building it turned out to be the easy part. Zookeepers have used apples, carrots, birch-tree branches—and, yes, peanuts—to try to coax her onto the contraption. So far she's gotten just three of her feet on the belt before backing off. 'We have to be patient,' trainer Beth Foglesong told the Anchorage *Daily News*. 'Nobody has ever done this before.'"

—**National Geographic**

NO MULLIGAN, MULLIGAN

"Freedom didn't last long for David Mulligan. Police in Juneau, Alaska, report that Mulligan stole a van just three minutes after he was released from jail. He had served 25 days for drunken driving. A man who lives a block from the jail had left his 1997 Dodge van running to warm up. When he came out of his house, it was gone. Two hours later, the owner called police on a cell phone, saying he was following his stolen van in traffic. Police busted Mulligan, who now faces up to five years in prison."

—**The Anchorage Press**

STILL THE LAST FRONTIER

"Anderson, a little town in Alaska's interior, has no gas station, no grocery store, and no traffic lights, but it does have plenty of woodsy land—and it's free to anyone willing to put down roots in the often-frozen ground. In a modern twist on the homesteading movement that populated the Plains in the 1800s, the community of 300 people is offering 26 large lots on spruce-covered land in a part of Alaska that has spectacular views of the Northern Lights and Mount McKinley, North America's highest peak. And what's an occasional day of 60-below cold in a town removed from big-city ills? 'It's Mayberry,' said Anderson high-school teacher Daryl Frisbie, whose social studies class developed a Web site to boost the town's dwindling population. 'Are you tired of the hustle and bustle of the Lower 48, crime, poor schools, and the high cost of living?' the Web site asks. 'Make your new home in the Last Frontier!'"

—**Fox News**

Electronic equipment gets dusty faster than furniture.

THE LAKE THAT WOULDN'T FREEZE

Lake Tazawa is situated in Akita Prefecture in the far north of Japan's Honshu island. Surrounded by snow-packed mountains, the 1,400-foot-deep lake—the deepest in Japan—endures bitter winters, but its surface never freezes over. Some say it's because the lake is fed by warm springs. But an ancient folk legend from our Japanese history correspondent, Jeff "Ninja" Cheek, offers a much more colorful answer.

HOT-BLOODED

A long time ago, a boy named Hachirotaro was in the mountains gathering wood to make crafts for his family when he stopped to camp by a stream. He caught three fish, cooked them up, and ate them…but then something very strange happened. Hachirotaro became very thirsty, and he drank a pail of water, but his thirst was not quenched. He went to the stream and crouched down and drank deeply from it, but no matter how much he drank, he became thirstier and thirstier. Hachirotaro drank from the stream for 33 straight days, and when he stopped his body felt very strange—bloated and swollen and dried out like leather. He peered at his reflection in the water: Hachi-rotaro had been transformed into a water dragon.

He could not return to his family's home as a dragon, so Hachirotaro dammed up the stream and created a lake in which to dwell, soon to be known as Lake Towada. But it was not to be his home for long: A local sorcerer wanted the lake for himself, and he chased Hachirotaro away. He was forced to make a new home in nearby Lake Hachiro.

BEAUTY QUEEN

Meanwhile, in a small nearby village lived a beautiful young girl named Takko Hime. The area was already famous for its lovely, ivory-skinned maidens, but Takko Hime's beauty surpassed any that had ever been seen. One day, to her dismay, Takko Hime learned that like everyone else, she would eventually grow old and die, and that her beauty would be lost. In despair she went to a mountaintop and prayed to the Japanese Buddhist goddess of mercy, Ryuzu Kannon, for 100 days and nights, asking that she—and her beauty—be allowed to live forever.

WISH GRANTED...

On the final day of her vigil, the goddess told Takko Hime to drink from a nearby spring and her wish would be granted. She obeyed, and as soon as she took her first sip the Earth shook and lightning flashed and a huge storm erupted. When it was over, Takko Hime found herself hovering above a newly formed lake—today known as Lake Tazawa—and that she, like Hachirotaro, had been transformed into a water dragon.

Both the sorcerer and Hachirotaro saw Takko Hime and immediately fell in love with her. They fought an epic battle for her hand, but this time, fueled by love, Hachirotaro defeated the sorcerer and drove him back to Lake Towada. Takko Hime happily accepted Hachirotaro's invitation to live with

her in Lake Tazawa, and the two water dragons prepared to live happily ever after...but the evil sorcerer had one last trick to play.

DRAGON OF WINTER

He cast a spell on Hachirotaro, requiring the dragon to spend exactly half of each year—from spring until the autumnal equinox—in his old home of Lake Hachiro. Ever since then, every spring Hachirotaro bids Takko Hime goodbye, promising to return and comfort her during the long, cold, and gloomy winters, and every autumn he leaves the lagoon and rushes to join his waiting bride in the depths of Lake Tazawa.

BLINDED BY SCIENCE

Scientists will tell you that Lake Tawaza does not freeze because there are scores of subterranean springs pouring warm water into the lake, so the surface temperature never falls below freezing. But the legend knows better: Lake Tawaza does not freeze because of the heat generated by Hachirotaro and Takko Hime—its guardian water dragons—and their deep underwater passions.

What about the rest? 85% of all Canadian brides receive a diamond engagement ring.

THE SOUND OF MOVIES

*In modern movies, nearly every sound effect you hear was created in
postproduction. Footsteps, gunshots, kisses—they're all recorded by "Foley
artists," named for movie sound pioneer Jack Foley (1891–1967).
These highly specialized technicians often have to improvise...
and some of their creative solutions may surprise you.*

R AIDERS OF THE LOST ARK (1981)
We Hear: A giant stone ball rolling out of a cave, chasing
Indiana Jones (Harrison Ford) at the beginning of the film
Actual Sound: A Honda Civic coasting on a gravel road

MEN IN BLACK (1997)
We Hear: The beating of a dragonfly's wings as it is flies down the
road during the opening credits
Actual Sound: "We ended up using a little toy fan that I found in
Toys 'R' Us," said Foley artist Dustin DuPilka. "We wrapped the
handle in cloth to muffle the motor, then snipped off the fins and
replaced them with duct tape. We put three full days of work into
[the two-minute scene] and it came out pretty nice." (They first
tried recording a real dragonfly, but director Barry Sonnenfeld
thought it didn't sound "real enough.")

NOTTING HILL (1999)
We Hear: William (Hugh Grant) kissing Anna (Julia Roberts)
Actual Sound: The Foley artist slobbering on his forearm. (The
sounds of many famous movie kisses were also achieved in this
manner.)

THE PERFECT STORM (2000)
We Hear: A faint thumping sound as Linda (Mary Elizabeth
Mastrantonio) gives the eulogy for the fallen fishermen
Actual Sound: Mastrantonio's heartbeat. Because there were so
many extras involved (as well as other unwanted noises), her
microphone needed to be placed very close to her. It was *so* close
that the sensitive mic accidentally picked up her heartbeat. When
director Wolfgang Petersen reviewed the dailies, at first he couldn't

---

Fone tone: The dial tone of a normal telephone is in the key of "F".

figure out where the low thumping sound was coming from. When he did, he loved it, and he kept it in the final mix.

E.T. THE EXTRA-TERRESTRIAL (1982)

We Hear: The squishy sound of E.T.'s feet as he walks
Actual Sound: Foley artist John Roesch squishing a wet T-shirt stuffed with Jell-O

THE LORD OF THE RINGS: THE TWO TOWERS (2002)

We Hear: The massive Uruk-hai army yelling war chants and banging on their chests just before they attack Helm's Deep
Actual Sound: 25,000 cricket fans during a match between New Zealand and England. Director Peter Jackson walked onto the field at halftime and prompted the crowd to speak the Uruk-hai words when they appeared phonetically on the Diamond Vision screen. Sound engineers then recorded the enthusiastic fans beating their chests and stomping their feet in unison.

THE EXORCIST (1973)

We Hear: A crackling sound when Regan (Linda Blair) spins her head all the way around
Actual Sound: A cracked leather wallet with old credit cards still inside it. After trying many different tactics to create the effect, sound designer Gonzalo Gavira borrowed a crew member's aging wallet and twisted it until it made the desired crackling sound.

ICE AGE (2002)

We Hear: The mammoth walking through the snow
Actual Sound: A log dropping into a pit full of dirt and pebbles

THE STAR WARS TRILOGY (1977–83)

We Hear: R2-D2 "talking"
Actual Sound: A recording of sound designer Ben Burtt making baby sounds, run through a synthesizer

We Hear: The sound of a blaster (laser gun) being fired
Actual Sound: A small hammer hitting a guy wire—a tightly pulled metal wire that's holding up a radio tower

A typical American kid spends 68 days—18% of the year—in front of a TV or computer screen.

We Hear: Darth Vader's menacing breath
Actual Sound: Burtt again. This time he put a small microphone inside an old SCUBA regulator and recorded himself breathing.

We Hear: TIE fighters whizzing through space
Actual Sound: The sound of a car driving on a rain-slicked road…combined with the squeal of a young elephant

AIRPLANE! (1980)

We Hear: A propeller (but we see a jet plane)
Actual Sound: A propeller plane. Writers Jim Abrahams, David Zucker, and Jerry Zucker wanted to use footage of a propeller plane for the exterior shots, but the studio balked because the inside of the plane was obviously a passenger jet (the studio was afraid viewers would be confused by the joke). Reluctantly, the writers relented and used a model jet for the exteriors, but they did keep the humming noise of a prop plane in the final mix whenever the jet is seen flying (mostly to amuse themselves).

TITANIC (1997)

We Hear: Very little. After the ship sinks, Jack (Leonardo DiCaprio) and Rose (Kate Winslet) are clinging to life on a makeshift raft in the ice-cold water.
Actual Sound: Water and celery. The quietest scene of the film was one of the most challenging to provide sound for. Other than the voices of the actors, director James Cameron wanted only two noises: 1) "surrounded by water" and 2) the sound of Rose's hair as it freezes. Sound designer Chris Boyes couldn't find any place in or near the recording studio quiet enough to get the first sound, so he took a camping trip during a break from production and brought his recording equipment. At 2:30 a.m. he recorded the calm water of a lake at night with his most sensitive microphone. That was the mood Cameron was looking for.

For the sound of Rose's hair freezing, the Foley artists froze some celery stalks and then recorded the ice crystals popping on them. "Between the frozen hair and the presence of water," said Boyes, "I think we leave the audience with an absolutely chilling emotional moment. And it worked out magically."

When the Pony Express went out of business, it was $200,000 in debt.

"MADMAN" NEWMAN'S BRAINTEASERS

Every summer, Uncle John makes a pilgrimage to the Siskiyou Mountains to confer with his puzzle guru, crazy Ol' Man Newman. As always, this year he came back with another collection of mind-bending logic puzzles. The answers (should you need them) are on page 592.

1. RAPID AGING?

The day before yesterday, Johnny was 9 years old. Next year he'll be 12. How is this possible?

2. TIME AFTER TIME

After a power surge disrupted all the electronic devices in Brian's house, he had to go over to Amy's to find out what time it was. After she told him, Brian walked home and set all of his clocks. Even though Brian didn't know how long it had taken him to get home, he was able to set his clocks to exactly the right time. How?

3. A BAD FLIGHT PLAN

Uncle John was about to leave on a morning flight to the World Toilet Summit when he realized he left his *Bathroom Readers* at the BRI office. He rushed back to get them, but the night watchman said, "Do not get on that plane! I had a dream last night that it's gonna crash!" Not wanting to tempt fate, Uncle John followed the watchman's advice. Sure enough, the plane crashed. That evening, Uncle John thanked the man for saving his life, then fired him. Why?

4. STORMY WEATHER

Five men were leaving church together when it started to rain. The four who ran got wet; the fifth, who didn't move, stayed dry. How?

5. A CLOWN-UNDRUM

Plungy the Clown had just earned three gold bricks after working a kids' party. While walking home, he came to an old foot bridge. The sign said, "Weight Capacity: 150 pounds." Plungy weighs 148 pounds; the three bricks weigh one pound each. How did Plungy make it across safely in one trip with all of his gold?

Q: Why were they called the Dark Ages?...

6. PUZZLING BUS TRIP

A bus full of people is travelling over a bridge on its way to Las Vegas. No one gets on or off, but when the bus reaches the other side, there's not a single person on the bus. How can this be possible?

7. COUNT DUCKULA

Julia and Viola were comparing their rubber-ducky collections. Julia said, "If you give me one of your ducks, I will have double of what you have remaining."

Viola replied, "Oh, yeah? Well, if you give me one of your ducks, then we'll both have the same amount."

How many duckies does each girl have?

8. MARITIME QUERY

Gordon sailed his sailboat, the *Uncle John*, across the Pacific Ocean. When he reached the coast, he asked me, "Which part of my boat traveled the longest distance?"

9. BRIGHT THINKING

One day, Thom found himself trapped in a room with two doors. Behind the first door was a room made of thick glass that would magnify the Sun's heat to fry whoever went in. Behind the second door was a fire-breathing dragon that would do the same. How did Thom escape unscathed?

10. RELATIVITY

Some people are riding in a car. They consist of a mother, father, brother, sister, son, daughter, niece, nephew, aunt, uncle, and two cousins. What is the minimum number of people that can be in the car?

11. AND THEY'RE OFF!

Malcolm and Jahnna competed in a strange horse race: Whoever's horse reaches the finish line *last* is the winner. After we waited four hours for them to go a few feet, Uncle John walked out, called them off their horses, and told them something. Immediately, Malcolm and Jahnna jumped up on the horses and rode them as fast as they could to the finish line. Uncle John swears he didn't call off the race or change the rules, so what did he tell them?

*   *   *

"There is much pleasure to be gained from useless knowledge."

—**Bertrand Russell**

...A: There were lots of knights. (The joke wasn't funny then, either.)

GOT WORM?

Wormy news from the worm world. Worm out, worms.

THAR' SHE WORMS!

Marine biologists in California discovered a new (and bizarre) species of sea worm in 2002. The two-inch-long red worms were discovered near Monterey Bay at a depth of about 9,000 feet, and they had no eyes, no mouths, and no stomachs. They eat, it was discovered, by growing green "roots" down into the bones of dead whales. The worms' digestive juices dissolve the bones, allowing them to live off the fats contained therein. They're the only animal known to eat in such a way. The worms, named *Osedax*, Latin for "bone eater," have another interesting characteristic. "Initially we were puzzled," said Robert Vrijenhoek of the Monterey Bay Aquarium Research Institute, "why every worm was a female." Then they looked closer: Each female had 50 to 100 microscopic males living *inside* them. The males barely develop, it seems, beyond their ability to produce sperm. All of the females' eggs were in sacs located inside the whale bones.

INVASION OF THE BODY SNATCHERS

In 2005 French researchers set out to resolve a simple question—why do parasite-infected animals often behave strangely?—and discovered something truly bizarre. Tests on grasshoppers that had contracted hairworms by drinking water containing hairworm larvae revealed that the larvae feed off the grasshopper's insides and grow until one of them takes up most of the insect's body cavity. When the worm is ready to reproduce, it secretes a protein that affects the grasshopper's central nervous system, mimicking messages to its brain. The messages drive the grasshopper to water, where it doesn't stop for a drink…it jumps in and drowns. It is effectively induced to commit suicide. The worm, which by this time can be three times the length of the grasshopper, then crawls out of the carcass and swims off to find a mate. The next round of larvae wait for another unlucky grasshopper to come along. "It's one of the most horrific things I've ever seen," said researcher Hugh Loxdale. "It makes the film *Alien* look pretty tame in comparison."

First company to earn $1 billion in one year: General Motors, in 1955.

DR. WORM

In 2002 Dr. Joel Weinstock of the University of Iowa performed some tests in which he had people drink a concoction containing thousands of whipworm eggs. (Eeeww!) Weinstock had noticed a correlation between the prevalence of inflammatory bowel diseases (IBD), such as colitis and Crohn's disease, and a drop in the incidence of infection by parasitic worms. That kind of infection is still common in the developing world, where inflammatory bowel disease is rare. He surmised that parasite infection was normal for most of human history, and the body had developed immune responses to fight it. When Western medicine largely eradicated such infections, the immune system turned on the intestine itself. Weinstock tested 200 people with IBD, and, sure enough, most of their symptoms, such as pain, bleeding, and diarrhea, completely disappeared, in some cases for years. He hopes the research will lead to effective treatment of IBD, but understands the difficulty of getting people behind the idea. "People have an irrational fear of worms," he told the BBC. "Nobody wants to look into the toilet and see something wiggle."

ALL-YOU-CAN-EAT WORM FESTIVAL

The palolo worm is a small marine worm that makes its home in shallow coral reefs around the tropics, including those around the Samoan islands. Every October, island natives wait for the moment when the six-inch-long, blue-and-pink palolos come to the surface —for just a few hours every year—and engage in a gooey mating frenzy. Word spreads quickly and people show up with nets and boats to scoop up the wiggling worms. The following day, the annual "palolo festival" takes place all over the islands, with the worms cooked in a variety of recipes and eaten. And if that's not weird enough, everybody always thought they were eating worms, until a 19th-century biologist noticed that the "worms" had no heads; they were only worm *parts*. Every spawning season the organs in the posterior section of the palolo shrink and disappear and are replaced by either sperm or eggs. Then, at virtually the same moment for thousands and thousands of worms in a colony, the posterior breaks off the worm and rises to the surface. After about an hour of wriggling there it finally bursts. This allows the sperm and eggs to mix and do their business, and according to Samoans, they're delicious. (They're said to taste like caviar.)

UNCLE JOHN'S TOY BOX

You can find some of the oddest things to play with in the BRI's toy box!

THE LIBRARIAN ACTION FIGURE—*With amazing push-button shooshing action!* This five-inch doll is based on a real librarian named Nancy Pearl. And she loves it. "It's a lovely idea and a lovely tribute to my chosen profession." But some librarians are less than thrilled with the "push-button shooshing action." Says one: "It's so stereotypical I could scream!"

BENIGN GIRL. Made in Taiwan, this hot-pink toy cell phone comes with a picture of a Barbie-esque doll on the "screen." Benign Girl's features are printed on the box: • BATTERY • OPERATED • CREATIVE • VARIOUS MUSIC. The instructions: "Beautiful girl, press any button!"

THE HORRIFIED B-MOVIE VICTIMS PLAYSET. Includes nine "victims," each about three inches tall. They come in various poses reacting to the horror of whatever monster is chasing them. (Monster not included.) *But the good news:* Any standard household item can be used as a substitute monster—a Chia pet, Mr. Potato Head, the cat, a vacuum cleaner...

JOHNNY REB CANNON. This early-1960s toy could never be released today. Not only did it feature a Confederate flag, the 30-inch cannon came with a ramrod and fired hard plastic cannonballs up to 35 feet. And then there's the jingle: "We'll all be gay when Johnny comes marching home!"

FLYING WITCH 2000 B.C. It looks like the makers of this toy confused B.C. with A.D. Why? Because this little green witch rides a big yellow rocket. Hung on a string and powered by a tiny propeller, the witch is supposed to fly in circles...on her rocket.

REMOTE-CONTROL FARTING BEAR. "He's cute, he's cuddly, and he's flatulent. There's nothing he likes more than to be in the arms of some poor, unsuspecting victim so he can let out a big, juicy one when you press the remote control!"

Little things mean a lot: 200 million atoms placed in a row would measure one inch.

MISSED IT
BY THAT MU...

*How frustrating is it to work for so long on something only
to see it fail right before the payoff? These people know.*

THE GRAND SCHEME: A group of inmates at Kinross Correctional Facility in Michigan spent three months planning and implementing a daring escape. Because the prison was originally built as an Air Force barracks, the walls weren't fortified the way most modern prison walls are. All the cons had to do was break through eight inches of unreinforced concrete and then dig out about 50 feet of soft dirt. To start, one of the prisoners made a small hole in the back corner of his cell, where guards routinely look but seldom touch. (Authorities believe he may have used a dumbbell from the gym as a hammer.) Then each night he would dig a little more, keeping some of the dirt in the crescent-shaped tunnel and flushing the rest down the cell toilet (which caused clogs in the system that baffled prison administrators). By March 2007, the tunnel extended several feet beyond the outside fence. All they had left to do was dig "up" to freedom.

FOILED: During a routine check of the cell, one of the guards noticed something odd on the wall; he touched it and found the soft spot, prompting an immediate investigation...and the end of the escape plan. Although little information about the case was given to the press, one thing is known: Only one more night of digging and the prisoners would have made it.

THE GRAND SCHEME: For more than two years, John and Penny Adie, organizers of an annual classical music festival in England, had been working tirelessly to raise enough money to buy a Bösendorfer grand piano. Valued at £45,000 ($89,000) and made exclusively in Austria, Bösendorfers are the preferred piano of many of the world's greatest players. "They're the Stradivarius of the piano world," said John Adie. By April 2007, they had finally raised all the money they needed and they purchased the piano at a London auction. The only thing left to make their dream a reality was to deliver the Bösendorfer to the concert hall.

Silly rabbit! Trix are for dentists! When Trix cereal was introduced in 1954, it was 46.6% sugar.

FOILED: As the delivery workers were hauling "the Stradivarius of the piano world" up the walkway, 20 feet from their destination they lost control of the dolly…and John and Penny watched in horror as their prized piano fell eight feet off of a ledge and smashed discordantly onto the ground below. "It was a total loss," said John, noting that insurance would probably cover only half of what the piano is worth. "It's more than money that is the issue here," said John. "It was like seeing a priceless painting torn to shreds," Penny added.

GRAND SCHEME: Charles McKinley, a 25-year-old shipping clerk from Brooklyn, New York, wanted to fly home to see his parents in DeSoto, Texas, in 2003—but he couldn't afford a plane ticket. So he decided to use one of the big boxes from his workplace and ship *himself* home (with his employer unknowingly footing the bill). McKinley poked some holes in the box, then packed himself, some clothes, food, and his computer inside. An accomplice sealed the box and marked it "Computer Equipment." McKinley's two-day wild ride in a box took him on a shipping truck from Brooklyn to New Jersey, then on a plane to Buffalo, New York, which then flew him to Fort Wayne, Indiana, then (after changing planes) to Fort Worth, Texas, and finally on a truck to DeSoto, about 14 miles south of Dallas.

FOILED: As the driver was retrieving the "package" from the back of the delivery truck to bring it to McKinley's dad's house, he noticed a little slit in the top, and peeking through the slit was an eye looking up at him. The driver gasped. McKinley kicked open the side of the box, picked up all of his stuff, and calmly walked into the house. The driver called his boss, who then called the Feds, who came and arrested McKinley. He was charged as a stowaway, which is a federal offense. McKinley later revealed that just before the driver went to retrieve the box, he moved a piece of clothing that had been covering him so he could get a peek at the man. If McKinley had only waited one more minute for the driver to leave, he would have been home free.

*　　*　　*

Q: What time of day was Adam born?
A: A little before Eve.

Losing face: In ancient China, criminals caught robbing travelers had their noses cut off.

PHRASED BY THE BARD

"If you know Shakespeare, you'll always have an exit line." Uncle John heard that in a movie once and was pretty impressed. But it turns out we all know a lot more Shakespeare than we thought.

THERE'S THE RUB

Meaning: "That's the problem."

Origin: *Hamlet*, Act 3, Scene 1: "To sleep, perchance to dream. Ay, there's the rub; / For in that sleep of death what dreams may come, / When we have shuffled off this mortal coil, / Must give us pause."

THE UNKINDEST CUT

Meaning: A devastating insult, often inflicted by someone previously considered a friend

Origin: *Julius Caesar,* Act 3, Scene 2. Mark Antony stands over Caesar's body and orates: "For Brutus, as you know, was Caesar's angel. / Judge, O you gods, how dearly Caesar lov'd him! / This was the most unkindest cut of all; / For when the noble Caesar saw him stab, / Ingratitude, more strong than traitors' arms, / Quite vanquished him."

SOUND AND FURY

Meaning: Meaningless noise and commotion

Origin: *Macbeth*, Act 5, Scene 5: "Life's but a walking shadow, a poor player, / That struts and frets his hour upon the stage, / And then is heard no more; it is a tale / Told by an idiot, full of sound and fury, / Signifying nothing." (William Faulkner used the phrase for the title of his 1929 novel, *The Sound and the Fury*.)

THE PRIMROSE PATH

Meaning: The path of pleasure and ease, which inevitably leads to ruin

Origin: *Hamlet*, Act 1, Scene 3, in which Laertes warns his sister Ophelia to be wary of Hamlet's attentions. She responds: "Do not, as some ungracious pastors do, / Show me the steep and thorny

---

Egad! Although it is widely attributed to him, Shakespeare never used the word "gadzooks."

way to heaven, / Whiles, like a puffed and reckless libertine, / Himself the primrose path of dalliance treads."

A LEAN AND HUNGRY LOOK

Meaning: Readiness to fight or act; ambitious, usually overly so

Origin: *Julius Caesar*, Act 1, Scene 2. Caesar says to Antony: "Let me have men about me that are fat; / Sleek-headed men, and such as sleep o'nights. / Yond Cassius has a lean and hungry look; / He thinks too much. / Such men are dangerous."

HOISTED ON ONE'S OWN PETARD

Meaning: Destroyed by one's own weapon, or caught in one's own trap

Origin: *Hamlet*, Act 3, Scene 4: "For 'tis the sport to have the engineer / Hoist with his own petard and it shall go hard / But I will delve one yard below their mines, / And blow them at the moon." (In French, a *petard* was a mine-like explosive device used in medieval warfare. To be hoisted, or lifted, by a petard literally means to be blown up. It's often used nowadays to refer to hypocritical politicians.)

THE BEAST WITH TWO BACKS

Meaning: A euphemism for, er, uh…the sexual act

Origin: *Othello*, Act 1, Scene 1, in which Iago cruelly tells Desdemona's father: "I am one, sire, that comes to tell you your daughter and the Moor [Othello] are now making the beast with two backs."

GILD THE LILY

Meaning: To add unnecessary ornamentation to something already beautiful, and thus cheapen or spoil it

Origin: *King John*, Act 4, Scene 2. Lord Salisbury admonishes the king for holding a second coronation: "Therefore, to be possess'd with double pomp, / To guard a title that was rich before, / To gild refined gold, to paint the lily, / To throw perfume on the violet… / To seek the beauteous eye of heaven to garnish, / Is wasteful, and ridiculous excess."

STRANGENESS ON A TRAIN

*Lots of people still travel by rail. And where
there are people, there's weirdness.*

BLACK-TIE AFFAIR
Just outside of Neuwid, Germany, in 2007, passengers were
stranded for hours after their train made an emergency stop
when conductor Udo Vergens spotted a dead or sleeping man
lying face down on the tracks, wearing a tuxedo. At least that's
what he thought he saw. Upon closer inspection, the formally
dressed corpse turned out be a large stuffed penguin doll.

GET A LEG UP
In 1986 in Littleville, Alabama, Terry Mills, lying on a railroad
track for unknown reasons, was struck by a train, resulting in the
amputation of his right leg. Tragic? Yes, but it's also weird. Eight
years later, in 1994, Mills was lying on the same railroad track just
a few feet away from the site of his earlier accident, and was struck
by another train, resulting in the amputation of his *left* leg.

NUMBER-ONE SOLUTION
KNSB, the union for Bulgarian train drivers, complained to rail
companies that tight schedules (and the fact that many trains lack
bathrooms) forced drivers to urinate out train windows while they
drove. One railway company's unique response: They installed
rotating seats for the drivers, so they could pee out the window
without having to leave the controls.

THE DIGITAL AGE
In 2007 a 34-year-old man tried to board a train as it was pulling
away from a station in Cologne, Germany. He stuck his hand in
the door as it was closing, but didn't make it. The train pulled away,
taking one of the man's fingers with it. The finger was located
when a horrified passenger discovered it on the ground more than
40 miles away. Doctors successfully reattached the man's digit.

"A fanatic is one who can't change his mind and won't change the subject." —Winston Churchill

GOTTA GO

Berlin, Germany, is one of the busiest railway hubs in Europe. To deal with the traffic, the city built a brand-new state-of-the-art train station at a cost of 700 million Euros ($950 million). But despite the huge budget and months of planning, engineers somehow underestimated the number of bathrooms the station would need. The station's 30,000 daily travelers have access to just two restrooms. "We realize there is a problem and are now planning to build a second set as quickly as possible," station spokesman Holger Auferkamp told reporters.

RUNNING AWAY FROM HOME(WORK)

Police at a train station in Guangzhou, China, found a 10-year-old boy, Xu Zhiqiang, who seemed to be lost. The boy, who had been reported missing from Cili, thousands of miles away, admitted that he ran away from home, snuck onto a train, and hid under a seat for an entire day and night. His reason: He couldn't cope with the amount of homework he'd been assigned over winter vacation. "Take the mathematics homework as an example," Xu said. "It's 100 pages!"

THAT'S WHAT YOU GET

In November 1994, a black man was waiting for a train at a station in Vienna, Austria, when an elderly white woman approached him and began making "racist remarks," which she continued when they both boarded the same train. After enduring the verbal abuse for a while, the man finally grabbed the woman's train ticket out of her hand...and ate it. When the conductor came by, the woman was fined and ejected from the train at the next stop, not for what she'd said to the man, but because she didn't have a ticket.

A LITTLE HELP?

In May 2007, an electric commuter train stalled outside the city of Patna, India. In order to get going again, the train had to move forward just 12 feet so that it could come in contact with overhead electrical wires and restore power to its motor. So, the conductor told his passengers to get out and push. It took a few hundred people, but 30 minutes later the train had moved the 12 feet, reconnected to the power grid, and resumed service.

Nowhere in the Bible does it say there were three wise men.

...NEWS FLUSH...

*We admit it: We selected these actual lines from recent
news stories because they all had the word "toilet"
in them. But they're pretty funny, too.*

- "...the next, she was wrestling with getting a toilet seat off her son's head. She didn't make it to work."

  —*Savage Pacer* (Minnesota)

- "...Meanwhile, he tied his shirt to a stick and spread toilet paper in the branches, in the hope of attracting rescue crews."

  —The *Independent* (U.K.)

- "...Mr. Thorne grins as he waves his hand under a toilet paper dispenser in a women's restroom."

  —Associated Press

- "...Would Mr. Mittiga suggest that we not flush the toilet? I think not. My large family is not a luxury, like a car or a house."

  —letter to the editor, *The Free Lance-Star* (Virginia)

- "...Toilet paper covered the road to the Cathedral High School in Indianapolis. Provided by: NBC"

  —MyATL-TV (Atlanta)

- "...try to play this horn, and 'urine' for a shock—because it's been turned into a toilet."

  —The *Sun* (UK)

- "...Police say Delgado also tried to flush so much fudge down the toilet, she clogged it up."

  —KTVO (Missouri)

- "...We are spreading toilet culture. People can listen to gentle music and watch TV. After they use the bathroom they will be very, very happy."

  —The *Denver Post,* quoting a Chinese official, on the opening of a 1,000-seat public toilet in Beijing

---

Learning the hard way: In Bangladesh, kids as young as 15 can be jailed for cheating on final exams.

THE MORE THINGS CHANGE...

"Modern" society is older than you think. Here are some quotes from thousands of years ago that could have been said today.

THESE KIDS TODAY...

"What is happening to our young people? They disrespect their elders. They disobey their parents. They ignore the law. They riot in the streets inflamed with wild notions. What is to become of them?"

—Plato, 427–347 B.C.

"The young people of today think of nothing but themselves. They have no reverence for parents or old age. They are impatient of all restraint. They talk as if they knew everything, and what passes for wisdom with us is foolishness with them. As for the girls, they are forward, immodest and unladylike in speech, behavior, and dress."

—Peter the Hermit, 1050–1115 A.D.

PUBLIC WORKS

"No job worth doing was ever done on time or under budget."

—Khufu, Egyptian Pharaoh, c. 2560 B.C., on building the Great Pyramid

SLEAZY POLITICS

"Nothing is more unpredictable than the mob, nothing more obscure than public opinion, nothing more deceptive than the whole political system."

—Cicero, 106–43 B.C.

PARTY ANIMAL

"Quickly, bring me a beaker of wine, so that I may wet my mind and say something clever."

—Aristophanes, the "Father of Comedy," 456–386 B.C.

THE CLASSIFIEDS

"The Arrius Pollio Apartment Complex owned by Gnaeus Allius Nigidius Maius FOR RENT from July 1st. Street-front shops with counter space, luxurious second-story apartments, and a townhouse. Prospective renters, please make arrangements with Primus, slave of Gnaeus Allius Nigidius Maius."

—Roman rental notice from Pompeii, 1st century A.D.

If you are right-handed, you will tend to chew your food on the right side of the mouth.

HOW TO SPEND A MILLION

Just won the lottery? Congratulations! You don't want to end up like the winners on page 31, but you'd like to do a little shopping. So Uncle John put together these fantasy packages to show you what a million dollars buys these days.

THE "RANCH" PACKAGE

60-acre horse ranch with geothermal-heated home (Sikeston, Missouri)	$685,000
Two Thoroughbred horses	$120,000
4-horse trailer with living quarters	$40,200
Thoroughbred stud fees	$1,500
Ford F-450 Super Duty Lariat pickup	$47,660
John Deere 4720 tractor	$26,609
Deluxe ATV	$18,095
Viking Ultra-Premium Gas Barbecue Grill	$4,429
Scrimshaw "Howling Wolf" bolo tie	$65
Classic Sterling Star belt buckle	$275
Four-year degree in Animal Sciences from Missouri State University	$48,816
Vacation: 7-day Maui getaway for two, with convertible	<u>$5,192</u>
Grand Total	**$997,841**

THE "CALIFORNIA" PACKAGE

2-bedroom, 2-bath condo at Lake Tahoe	$749,000
Hammacher Schlemmer 2-seat electric car	$108,000
Audi A8 Sedan	$68,900
Bayliner 197 Ski Boat	$22,750
Skis, boots, and bindings for two	$3,500
Commercial-grade multi-station home gym	$6,095
Elliptical trainer	$1,700
For him: Facelift	$9,000
For her: Breast augmentation (silicone)	$8,000
Vacation: 105-day world cruise on the *Queen Victoria*	<u>$22,251</u>
Grand Total	**$999,196**

Bears live in *dens*, badgers live in *setts*, and squirrels live in *dreys*.

THE "ADVENTURE" PACKAGE

Mountaineering course, 6 days (for two)	$2,000
Rafting the Grand Canyon, 15 days (for two)	$6,690
Greenland ski & dogsled expedition, 21 days (for two)	$11,106
African safari, 16 days (for two)	$33,960
North Pole skiing expedition, 14 days, plus 5 days of training (for two)	$60,000
Mt. Everest climb (for two)	$130,000
South Pole kiting expedition, 45 days, equipment included (for two)	$140,000
Bring a private doctor along with you (3 months)	$30,000
Send two kids to four years of "Adventure Training" at Prescott College, Arizona…	$236,080
…while you sail around the world in your 50' Van der Laan-50 3-cabin sailboat	$350,000
Grand Total	**$999,836**

THE "TRAILER" PACKAGE

3-bedroom, 2-bath 2,300-sq.-ft. triple-wide in Ocala, FL	$169,000
His-and-hers Hogs (Harley-Davidson Electra Glide Classics)	$36,190
Used 2005 Ford F-150 Monster Truck with 37" radial Nitto tires, rear camera, 2 DVD players, three screens, phone system, heated seats, tinted windows	$35,000
Restored 1967 Chevy Camaro convertible	$31,000
Hummer H2	$54,115
Bearcat Police Scanner	$150
73" rear-projection HD TV	$4,845
Satellite dish: 2.4m Dual Optics	$4,800
Lucchese Hornback Caiman cowboy boots	$1,854
Diamond-studded pedicure	$60
Daytona 500 start/finish area 4-day package seat	$3,590
Racetrack scanner (hear the drivers, pit crew, security)	$200
Vacation: Alligator trophy hunt (guaranteed 12' gator)	$5,000
Two Miami Dolphins "Big Daddy" recliners	$1,378
Florida Gators sofa	$839
Used shrimp boat, the *Freedom*	$538,000
Grand Total	**$886,021**

(That's less than a million, but you'll need the rest to pay for gas.)

THE "HIPPIE" PACKAGE

Rock River Organic Farm, Virginia: 66 acres, 2 houses, 3 cabins, 1 studio/barn, two wells, compost toilet, greenhouse, pyramid meditation room, loft, and Holland hydrostatic tractor	$725,000
Freedom Fueler Deluxe Biodiesel Kit: Make your own biofuel out of vegetable oil	$4,529
1983 Westphalia camper van from U.K., diesel	$5,458
VW Beetle, diesel	$20,835
Lifetime family membership at Food Co-op	$125
Retreat: 2-bedroom, 1-bath Earthship house in Taos, New Mexico (off the grid)	$220,000
Grand Total	**$975,947**

THE "NEW YORK" PACKAGE

One-bedroom Wall Street condo (908 sq. ft.)	$1,499,999
Dinner for one at McDonald's (Dollar Menu: cheeseburger, fries, and soda)	$3
Grand Total:	**Whoops! Too much**

ULTIMATE JACKPOT!

You won more than a million? Way more? Here are a few more baubles to put in your shopping cart.

• 5-bedroom, 6-bath home in Pacific Heights, San Francisco (7,800 sq. ft.)	$9,850,000
• Personal submarine: Seattle Luxury Sub 1000 (213')	$19,700,000
• 8-bedroom, 9.5-bath oceanfront home on 1 acre in Kaanapali, Maui (11,076 sq. ft.)	$23,800,000
• Round-trip ticket to the International Space Station	$25,000,000
• Boeing 767	$118,000,000
• Yacht just like the *Octopus*, owned by Microsoft billionaire Paul Allen (414' long, comes with mini-sub, 3 helicopters, and 60' tender boat)	$200,000,000

*   *   *

"Everyone's a millionaire where promises are concerned."   —Ovid

...Present-day value for a copy in mint condition: $600,000.

POLICE BLOTTERS

Don't have a lot of time but still want to read interesting little stories?
Just check out the police blotter of your local paper.

- "A man reported a burglary around 10 p.m. Thursday after he returned home and found his 36-inch Samsung TV missing. It had been replaced with an RCA TV. Decorative items were placed around the new TV in an apparent attempt to fool him."

- "A green and gold colored bird on Southwood Drive appeared injured. It ran into the bushes when questioned by police."

- "A male was yelling and screaming obscenities in his Randolph Avenue driveway. Police reported he actually was trying to rap."

- "The glass to a snack machine in the Knott Hall commuter lounge was reported to be broken. Campus Police responded and removed all remaining snacks."

- "A 22-year-old man was arrested after allegedly ordering a stranger to fix his truck at gunpoint."

- "The mother of an adult man called police, concerned he was running with the wrong crowd."

- "Clinton Police responded quickly to an accident in the parking lot of a Dunkin' Donuts. The prompt response time is accredited to there being a squad car waiting in line at the drive-up window."

- "A woman reported that someone entered her condo, tied her shoelaces together, tilted pictures on the walls, and removed the snaps from her clothing."

- "At 11:50 p.m. police talked to four nude people seen running down Lincoln Street, and advised them not to be nude in public again."

- "A woman said she suspected someone had sabotaged her washing machine. A police investigation concluded that an unbalanced laundry load had caused the shaking."

- "Teens who dialed 9-1-1 to report that 'everything is fine' were checked on and found to be in possession of alcohol."

- "A resident called police after finding a 12-pack of toilet paper on her doorstep on Greenridge Drive, not for the first time."

World's longest mountain range: The Andes, stretching more than 4,000 miles through 7 nations.

HUMAN OIL (AND OTHER HOAXES)

These hoaxes are so absurd, it's hard to believe that
anybody was fooled…but lots of people were.

WHAT A HELLHOLE

The Story: In early 1990, the Trinity Broadcasting Network reported that Russian geologists on Siberia's Kola Peninsula had discovered Hell. They were using a giant drill, said TBN, to test how deep into the Earth they could reach. In November 1989, nine miles into the ground, the drill suddenly stopped spinning—it had hit air. The team lowered a thermometer into the hole. The temperature inside was 2,200°F—five times as hot as it should have been at that depth. They lowered a microphone down to record the sounds of shifting plates, and heard human screams. Then a black, spectral figure in the shape of a bat screeched and flew out of the hole.

The Hoax: TBN claimed (on the air) that its source for the story was *Ammennusatia*, "Finland's most respected newspaper." They'd gotten the article from a Texas minister who sent it in, claiming it was from Finland's top scientific journal. Actually, *Ammennusatia* is a paranormal newsletter (it *is* from Finland). *They* got the story from a staffer who wrote it from memory after having read it in *Etela Soumen*, another Finnish newspaper, which ran the piece in a section where readers were invited to publish anything they liked—including fiction. Someone had sent the story to *Etela Soumen* after reading it in *another* weird Finnish newsletter called *Vaeltajat*. That paper got it from an obscure American religious newsletter called *Jewels of Jericho*, which had completely made it up. TBN reported the story without bothering to find out if it was true. A few months later, they announced that because of the story, 3,000 people had converted to Christianity. Ironically, the story is rooted in fact: From 1970 to 1989, Soviet scientists *were* involved in a project called the Kola Superdeep Borehole. The point *was* to drill as deep into the Earth as possible. They got about 7.6 miles in, but never encountered any fiery air holes, human screams, or ghostly bats.

Hey, shorty! The length of a single human DNA molecule, when extended, is 5'5".

VIVOLEUM FOR EVERYONE!

The Story: At the 2007 Gas and Oil Exposition, Canada's largest annual oil-industry convention, a National Petroleum Council representative named Shepard Wolff and an Exxon Mobil executive, Florian Osenberg, unveiled "Vivoleum"—a revolutionary process that turned human flesh into gasoline (very handy, should oil reserves ever dry up). The executives then played a film about a deceased Exxon janitor who had volunteered to be turned into Vivoleum, and passed out candles to be lit in the janitor's memory. That's when they announced that the candles *were* the janitor—transformed by Vivoleum.

The Hoax: After the two men passed out the "human candles," the event's organizers realized "Wolff" and "Osenberg" were phonies. They were really Andy Bichlbaum and Mike Bonanno, two members of the Yes Men, an anti-consumerism group that stages high-profile stunts to embarrass corporations with poor environmental or human rights records. Bichlbaum and Bonanno had set up a fake Exxon Web site (vivoleum.com), through which they got themselves invited to the Oil Exposition. Convention organizers threw them out and threatened to have them arrested. A few days later, Exxon demanded they shut down the Vivoleum site. They declined, saying it was parody and thus protected under the First Amendment. (The Web site has since shut down.)

MOSTLY CLOUDY

The Story: On a Sunday morning in June 2007, CT2, a television station in the Czech Republic, was airing a weather update. As weather stats scrolled along the bottom of the screen, the camera panned the country's scenic Krkonose Mountains. Suddenly, off in the distance, a fiery mushroom cloud filled the sky. The screen went black—the Czech Republic had just been nuked.

The Hoax: A Czech performance art group called Initiative Ztohoven had hacked into CT2's feed and replaced it with its own footage—undetectably similar...up until the bomb part. The mushroom cloud was just simple video editing done on a computer. After the initial blackout, CT2 came back on the air to reassure viewers that they weren't under attack. Members of Initiative Ztohoven are under investigation by the Czech government and may face terrorism charges.

SONS OF GUNS

We aimed for this page to be a high-caliber bulletin loaded with surefire origins of some famous "peacemakers." Bull's-eye!

ELIPHALET REMINGTON II (1793–1861)

The story goes that in 1816 young Remington needed a new rifle—so he made one at his father's forge at Ilion Gulch, in upstate New York. That fall he entered a shooting contest with his new flintlock. He won only second place, but the gun was so good (and so good-looking) that before the day was over, Remington had taken orders for several more rifles. Suddenly he was in the gun business. By 1839 E. Remington & Sons was a booming company in Ilion. Though it's no longer a family business, Remington still manufactures world-renowned rifles on the same site. (They also made typewriters and electric shavers.)

SAMUEL COLT (1814–1862)

At age 15, Colt left his father's textile mill in Connecticut for a sailor's life. Legend says he was at the ship's wheel when he got his big idea—a pistol with a revolving cylinder. Colt received a European patent for the invention in 1835 and took it to the United States the following year. His fortune was assured when the U.S. army began supplying its officers with Colt revolvers during the Mexican War from 1846 to 1848. The Colt .45 Peacemaker became—and still is—a symbol of the American West.

GEORG LUGER (1849–1923)

The real name of Luger's gun is "Pistole Parabellum." Americans know it as the "Luger" because the U.S. importer in the 1920s, AF Stoeger & Co., marketed it under the German gun designer's name. Georg Luger made the first Luger-type pistol for a German weapons manufacturer in 1898. The German military started buying them in the early 1900s; during World War II they were the official sidearm of the Nazis. The sleekly designed guns are prized by collectors today and are still used in competitions because of their accuracy. Why "Parabellum"? It comes from the Latin phrase *Si vis pacem, para bellum*—"If you want peace, prepare for war."

Can you spot him? Wesley Snipes was in Michael Jackson's "Bad" music video.

HORACE SMITH (1808–93) & DANIEL WESSON (1825–1906)

Smith was a Springfield, Massachusetts, toolmaker; Wesson was a gunsmith from nearby Northborough. They joined forces in 1852, introducing a groundbreaking invention: the self-contained, waterproof "cartridge," or bullet. Before that, all the ingredients—gunpowder, ball, and primer—had to be mixed by hand. In 1869 they introduced the Smith & Wesson "Model 3 American" pistol. Customers ranging from the Russian army to Annie Oakley helped make it one of the most popular handguns in the world. Other Smith & Wesson notables: the .357 Magnum and the .44 Magnum, made famous by Clint Eastwood in the *Dirty Harry* movies.

DR. RICHARD J. GATLING (1818–1903)

Gatling was an inventor during the mid-1800s. Most of his inventions were agriculture-based, but in 1861 he came up with the fearsome Gatling Gun, a hand-cranked machine gun that fired 200 bullets a minute. A medical doctor, Gatling thought his gun's super firepower would require fewer soldiers on the battlefield, resulting in fewer casualties. He was wrong; it just made soldiers more effective killing machines. After improvements were made in 1866, it became a weapon of choice for armies worldwide for the next 40 years.

HIRAM MAXIM (1840–1916)

Legend has it that Maxim, an American expatriate, visited the 1881 Paris Electrical Exhibition, where he heard someone say, "If you want to make a lot of money, invent something that will enable Europeans to cut each other's throats with greater facility." Shortly thereafter, Maxim invented the first "automatic" machine gun—it reloaded itself automatically, firing more than 500 bullets per minute. The British bought it in 1889 (the United States turned it down), and by 1905 more than 20 armies and navies around the world were using the Maxim Machine Gun. Other Maxim inventions: the gun silencer and cordite (smokeless gunpowder). Knighted by the British in 1901, Sir Hiram died in 1916.

JOHN CANTIUS GARAND (1888–1974)

In 1934 Garand, a Canadian-born employee of the United States Armory in Springfield, Massachusetts, designed what would

---

There are more insects in 10 square feet of a rain forest than there are people in Manhattan.

become the mainstay of the American military, the M-1 Garand rifle. It was "gas operated," meaning that gas buildup behind an exiting bullet was routed to drive a piston that put the next bullet into place—very quickly. That made it semiautomatic, a huge advantage over Japanese and German rifles, which were still bolt-action at the start of World War II. Almost four million M-1 rifles were made during the war, and Garand didn't make a cent off them—he worked for the Armory for 36 years and never received more than his standard pay.

MIKHAIL TIMOFEEVICH KALASHNIKOV (B. 1919)
Kalashnikov was a Russian tank driver during World War II. After being badly injured in 1941, he turned to weapon design and produced the light, inexpensive, and extremely durable AK-47. The "AK" stands for Automatic Kalashnikov; the "47" comes from 1947, the year the new rifle was introduced. The gun became standard issue for the Soviet army in 1949 and was soon being used by communist armies and insurgents all over the world. It's estimated that there are more Kalashnikovs worldwide—perhaps as many as 100 million—than any other gun in use today.

UZIEL GAL (1923–2002)
Gal was a young Israeli army officer who submitted a design for a new submachine gun to the military in 1951, shortly after the founding of Israel. The "Uzi," as it came to be known, was small, powerful, cheap to manufacture, and easy to maintain. The most innovative part of Gal's design: putting the magazine inside the pistol grip, making it easy for soldiers to reload in the dark. Today Uzis are used by military and police in more than 90 countries; the gun has made the Israeli munitions industry more than $2 billion. Gal died in 2002, and the Israeli military officially stopped using the Uzi a year later. Ironically, he asked that his name not be used for the gun. (The request was ignored.)

*   *   *

YOUR TAX DOLLARS AT WORK
In 1996 Redwood City, California, installed eight microphones around town to identify possible drive-by-shootings. Number of Redwood City drive-bys before the installation: 0. Number after: 0.

Donald Rumsfeld was the youngest, and oldest, defense secretary in US history. (He served twice.)

IT'S A BOY!

Preferences for baby names change dramatically from year to year.
Here are lists of the most popular names from 1907—and now.

1907	2007
1. John	1. Jacob
2. William	2. Michael
3. James	3. Joshua
4. George	4. Ethan
5. Robert	5. Matthew
6. Charles	6. Daniel
7. Joseph	7. Christopher
8. Frank	8. Andrew
9. Edward	9. Anthony
10. Henry	10. William
11. Thomas	11. Joseph
12. Walter	12. Alexander
13. Willie	13. David
14. Harry	14. Ryan
15. Albert	15. Noah
16. Arthur	16. James
17. Harold	17. Nicholas
18. Clarence	18. Tyler
19. Fred	19. Logan
20. Paul	20. John

• Jacob has been the most popular boy's name since 1999. Before that, it was Michael, which had been the most popular name for the previous 35 years.

• Biblical names aren't "old-fashioned"—they're extremely popular today. Thirteen of the top 20 boys' names are from the Bible. In 1907, only five were—John, Joseph, Thomas, James, and Paul.

It was once a custom in England to pass a newly born baby through the rind of a cheese.

IT'S A GIRL!

What would you have named your daughter if she were born in 1907?
Here are that year's most popular names for baby girls, and 2007's.

1907	2007
1. Mary	1. Emily
2. Helen	2. Emma
3. Margaret	3. Madison
4. Anna	4. Isabella
5. Ruth	5. Ava
6. Dorothy	6. Abigail
7. Elizabeth	7. Olivia
8. Mildred	8. Hannah
9. Alice	9. Sophia
10. Marie	10. Samantha
11. Florence	11. Elizabeth
12. Ethel	12. Ashley
13. Lillian	13. Mia
14. Gladys	14. Alexis
15. Edna	15. Sarah
16. Frances	16. Natalie
17. Rose	17. Grace
18. Evelyn	18. Chloe
19. Annie	19. Alyssa
20. Grace	20. Brianna

• Experts attribute the sudden popularity of the name Emma in the 2000s to the TV show *Friends*. That's what Jennifer Aniston's character named her baby. According to the Social Security Administration, Emma hadn't been a popular name in the U.S. since the 1880s.

• Similarly, Ava was out of favor until shortly after actress Reese Witherspoon gave her daughter the name in 1999.

Population explosion: From fertilization to birth, a baby's weight increases by 5 billion times.

HEY! THAT'S MY _____ ON eBAY!

Here are some more folks who found their stolen items on eBay.

HEY! THAT'S MY DAUGHTER'S COAT!

In January 2007, the mother of a third-grade student at Jackson Elementary School in Hillsboro, Oregon, searched eBay to find a new winter coat for her daughter to replace the one that had disappeared at school the previous week. The mother found a similar coat, an expensive Columbia Sportswear ski jacket, on the site, and then noticed that the seller was in her hometown…and that the coat went up for sale the day after her daughter's disappeared. She contacted another bidder to warn her that she thought the coat was stolen, but that bidder tipped off the thief. A short time later the coat, now damaged (supposedly by a dog), turned up in the school playground. The mother called the cops, who made an interesting discovery when they tracked down the seller through eBay records: It was 41-year-old Elizabeth Logan—a first-grade teacher at Jackson Elementary who had been highly respected in the area for 20 years. Police reported that Logan had an extensive selling record on eBay, and that they'd be going through those records to see if any other items were stolen. Logan was charged with two felonies.

HEY! THAT'S MY WALL!

British graffiti artist "Banksy" has become internationally famous for the evocative public paintings he has created across London and in cities around the world. Some of his framed original works of art now sell for hundreds of thousands of dollars at the world's most prestigious auction houses. But Banksy's fame has had its downside. In 2007 a painting he did on a park wall in the town of Paddington—an image of a rat bouncing a ball below a city sign that reads "No Ball Games"—was stolen. Thieves used a stone cutter to chop through the brick and concrete, then hauled away the painting and the piece of wall. It later showed up on eBay with an opening price of $20,000. Complaints from representa-

---

When Harper Lee won the 1961 Pulitzer Prize for *To Kill a Mockingbird*, she broke out in hives.

tives for the artist to eBay officials prompted the painting's removal from the site. "This is an increasingly common problem for Banksy," said a spokesman for the artist. "When people see his work sells for tens of thousands of pounds, greed takes over." The wall-cutting thieves were never apprehended.

HEY! THAT'S MY iPOD!

On April 7, 2005, the home of Karen Todd of Bowie, Maryland, was burglarized. Police told her it was one of several thefts in the area in the past few months. The burglars made off with a ring she inherited from her grandmother, a laptop computer, and a digital camera. But the biggest loss was her husband's iPod. She had given it to him as a gift and had had it specially inscribed with a lyric from her husband's favorite song, "Have a Little Faith in Me," by John Hiatt. "It read, 'When your back is against the wall, turn around and see,'" she told the *Washington Post*. "I thought it was kind of silly, because if your back is against the wall and you turn around, you'll see the wall, but my husband appreciates lyrics like that." Todd was so upset that she decided to try and find the iPod on eBay. And she did. "I was like, 'That's mine! That's mine!'" she said. "When I found it, I clicked on 'See Seller's Other Items,' and lo and behold, there was my laptop." Police tracked the goods to J&K Sports Cards and Memorabilia in the nearby town of Beltsville. Owner Joseph Stratton directed them to 21-year-old Ibrahima Kalil Toure, the man who'd sold the items to him. And a search at Toure's house linked the young man to 10 burglaries in the area. Police were so impressed with Todd's eBay detective work that they presented her with a special commendation and a $100 gift certificate to a local electronics store. "She cracked the case," said Detective Ray Gignac. "It's pretty amazing."

*　　*　　*

OSCAR TRIVIA

Until 1989, Academy Award presenters said, "And the winner is..." But when some people complained that the word "winner" implied the four who didn't win were losers, the announcement was changed to "And the Oscar goes to..."

HELLO, JUNG LOVERS

Wise words from one of the founders of modern psychology, Carl Jung (1875–1961).

"The shoe that fits one person pinches another; there is no recipe for living that suits all cases."

"We cannot change anything unless we accept it. Condemnation does not liberate, it oppresses."

"If there is anything that we wish to change in the child, we should first examine it and see whether it is not something that could better be changed in ourselves."

"In all chaos there is a cosmos, in all disorder a secret order."

"Mistakes are the foundations of truth, and if a man does not know what a thing is, it is at least an increase in knowledge if he knows what it is not."

"The greatest and most important problems of life are all fundamentally insoluble. They can never be solved—only outgrown."

"People will do anything, no matter how absurd, in order to avoid facing their own soul."

"Sometimes there is such a discrepancy between the genius and his human qualities that one has to ask oneself whether a little less talent might not have been better."

"People cannot stand too much reality."

"Your vision will become clear only when you can look into your own heart. Who looks outside, dreams; who looks inside, awakes."

"To be normal is the ideal aim of the unsuccessful."

"The more one sees of human fate and the more one examines its secret springs of action, the more one is impressed by the strength of unconscious motives and by the limitations of free choice."

"You can exert no influence if you are not susceptible to influence."

"Shrinking away from death is something unhealthy and abnormal which robs the second half of life of its purpose."

ODD BUILDINGS

*We're used to thinking of buildings as pretty sober affairs—steel and glass,
bricks and mortar, right angles and straight lines...but every once in
a while somebody decides to do something a little different.*

BUILDING: The Corn Palace, Mitchell, South Dakota
DETAILS: This auditorium is covered from top to bottom
in elaborate murals made out of thousands of ears of yellow,
red, brown, blue, speckled, and white corn, plus additional tons of
oats, barley, and other grains. It was built by local farmers in 1892
in an attempt to attract more settlers to the area. It must have
worked (although a parallel attempt to move the state capital from
Pierre to Mitchell failed miserably), because they've rebuilt the
Corn Palace three times since then, and they replace the murals
outside the building every year. Not that they have a choice—in
addition to attracting 50,000 visitors to the town each year, the
edible murals attract so many ravenous, pecking pigeons and other
fowl that locals call the building the World's Largest Bird Feeder.

BUILDINGS: Ice Hotels
DETAILS: People have been building "palaces" out of giant blocks
of ice and staging winter exhibits of one kind or another in them
for centuries. As early as 1739–40, the Russian empress Anna had
one built to celebrate a military victory over the Ottoman Empire.
Ice *hotels* aren't nearly as old. They were invented by accident in
Jukkasjarvi, Sweden, in 1990. That year an ice palace art exhibit
was so well attended that there weren't enough hotel rooms for
all the visitors, so a few of them had to sleep in the ice palace.
Jukkasjarvi has been building ice hotels every winter since then.

If you want to spend a night in an ice hotel, you don't have to
go to Europe: the Ice Hotel Quebec outside of Quebec City,
Canada, has been opening its frozen doors every winter since 2000.
Everything—the 80+ hotel rooms, the furniture, the movie theater, the wedding chapel, even the dinner plates and drink glasses—
are all made of ice and snow, more than 15,000 tons in all. (The
bathrooms are a happy exception: They're in a separate, *heated*
wing of the building.) Should you decide to book a room in the

Ice Hotel, plan on sleeping in head-to-toe undergarments (socks and a hat that covers both ears and neck) in a sleeping bag placed on top of wool blankets and deer pelts over a bed made of a giant slab of ice. You're going to need all the insulation you can get— on a good night, the temperature in your hotel room will range between 4° and 9° *below* freezing. Bonus: "To keep your belongings safe from low temperatures, all luggage can be stored in lockers in a heated room."

BUILDING: The 747 Wing House, Malibu, California
DETAILS: When retiree Francie Rehwald, 60, went looking for an architect to design a house for her 55-acre parcel in the Malibu mountains in southern California, she wanted it to be environmentally friendly, and she also wanted it to have a "feminine" shape. Her architect, David Hertz, suggested building the house out of parts from an old Boeing 747. Rehwald was ecstatic. "It's 100% post-consumer waste," she told *The Wall Street Journal* in 2005. "Isn't that the coolest?"

It's a good thing she's a member of the family that founded southern California's oldest Mercedes-Benz dealership, because it's going to take a lot of post-consumer car payments to get the thing built. The junked plane alone cost $100,000, plus $80,000 to helicopter the pieces up to the building site. Another $200,000 went to consultants, and because the house lies along a flight path into Los Angeles International Airport, more money will have to be spent to honor the FAA's request that the roof be specially painted to prevent airline pilots from mistaking the house for a crash site.

The 747's wings will serve as the roof for the main house; the two horizontal stabilizers from the tail will shelter the master bedroom suite. Part of the upper fuselage will be used to make an art studio, and the first-class cabin will be converted into a guest house. The cockpit? That's going to be pointed nose-up at the sky and converted into a "meditation pavilion." (Did we mention that Rehwald lives in L.A.?) "Several other components are contemplated for use in a sublime manner, which include an animal barn and sauna structure," Hertz says on his Web site. "We're trying to use as many of the components as possible, like the Native American Indians used every part of the buffalo." Rehwald hopes to be living in her finished home by the end of 2007.

WEIRD WRESTLERS

Professional wrestling is already pretty silly, with good guys and bad guys, over-the-top acting, and rigged matches. But the "sport" outdid itself when it introduced these really silly wrestling characters.

THE GOBBLEDY GOOKER. He was a giant turkey, complete with feathers, a beak, and wings. When the character debuted, he popped out of a huge egg.

SERGEANT SLAUGHTER. At the peak of the first Gulf War in 1991, the WWF brought in this villain, an Iraqi-flag-waving Saddam Hussein sympathizer.

GIANT GONZALES. A failed NBA basketball player, Gonzales was a lanky 7'7" and not muscular enough to wrestle. Solution: He wore a rubber suit covered with fake hair and painted muscles.

DOINK THE CLOWN. Since 1993 "Doink" has wrestled in a full clown costume, with face makeup and bright green hair. (In tag-team matches he's assisted by "Dink the Clown," an identically dressed dwarf clown.)

THE JUICER. A steroid addict? No—the Juicer was introduced in 1989 to capitalize on the movie *Beetlejuice*. Like the movie's title character, the wrestler sprayed "death breath" (green mist) and attacked with Silly String.

RED ROOSTER. A guy with dyed scarlet hair who flapped his arms like wings and chicken-danced around the ring, screaming "cock-a-doodle-doo!"

THE GENIUS. Coming to the ring wearing a graduation cap and gown, the Genius appeared to be highly intelligent, speaking in a haughty accent and peppering his sentences with big words...and then he beat people up.

ISAAC YANKEM, DDS. An evil dentist, dressed in a white smock and face mask, who threatens to remove his opponents' teeth.

The 40-day pre-Easter period of Lent is actually 46 days long (Sundays aren't counted).

IRWIN R. SCHEISTER. Somebody everybody could fear: an IRS agent. He wore glasses, a shirt, and a skinny tie, and hit people with his briefcase. As sportswriter Mike Stokes put it, the tax collector came across as "a cranky math teacher."

THE POET. He read poetry at the beginning of fights…and then he beat people up.

AKEEM THE AFRICAN DREAM. Akeem dressed, talked, and acted "black." He wore a traditional African dashiki, spoke in 1970s jive, and had a street pimp named Slick as a sidekick. And he was portrayed by a white guy.

ROADBLOCK. He looked like a road. He had a yellow "dead end" sign painted on his stomach, hit opponents with a barricade, and dressed in a black bodysuit (to look like pavement).

GOLDUST. He wore a sparkly robe and a long blond wig and intimidated opponents by licking their faces. His skin was spray-painted gold and he'd stop matches to cry about how his father didn't love him enough.

BROTHER LOVE. A stereotypical Southern evangelist who preached "the word of love"…and then beat people up.

SEXUAL CHOCOLATE. A deep-voiced, smooth-talking ladies' man, like 1970s soul singer Barry White. The character was based on *South Park*'s Chef—a parody of deep-voiced, smooth-talking 1970s soul singers.

THE BOOTY MAN. On his way into the ring, he dropped his pants and shook his bare buttocks. (He was actually wearing a flesh-colored prosthesis.)

AMISH ROADKILL. Inspired by the 1996 Amish-themed movie *Kingpin*, Amish Roadkill wore plain black Amish clothing, a black hat, and a long beard. He usually lost matches, because the Amish don't believe in fighting.

*   *   *

"Win if you can, lose if you must, but always cheat!"

—Jesse "The Body" Ventura

The other *Gong Show:* People who once cleaned out cesspits were known as *gongfermers*.

PROJECT GREEK ISLAND, PART I

Here's Part I of our look at one of the best-kept secrets of the Cold War...or was it? It depends on how you look at it.

COOKING THE BOOKS

In 1980 a hotel executive named Ted Kleisner landed a job as the general manager of the Greenbrier, a five-star luxury resort in the Allegheny Mountains of West Virginia. The resort sprawls over 6,500 acres and includes hiking and biking trails, three championship golf courses, a hotel with over 600 rooms, more than 90 guest houses, and its own private train station. Learning to run such a large facility would have been a big job for anyone. Even so, it only took a few days for Kleisner to notice that there were some serious discrepancies in the company's books. For example:

• The resort was spending a fortune on "maintenance" of equipment that it didn't own.

• It had ordered thousands of gallons of diesel fuel that it had no need for. The fuel had disappeared without a trace.

• Every payday, dozens of paychecks were being mailed out to people whose names did not appear on the employee roster.

The deeper Kleisner dug, the more problems he found.

BENEATH THE SURFACE

Strangely, when Kleisner took his concerns to his superiors, they didn't seem that concerned...until he talked about turning the matter over to the police.

That got their attention. Not long afterward, Kleisner was instructed to report to a building in a remote section of the grounds, where a man identifying himself as a senior Pentagon official invited him into an office. "He turned up a radio very loud and shut the blinds," Kleisner recalled in a 1995 interview with

A pelican can hold about 25 pounds of fish in its pouch.

the London *Times*. "Then he said, 'You are about to be briefed on a top-secret government project that is part of the Greenbrier.' " After Kleisner signed a pledge of secrecy, the official let him in on one of the most sensitive secrets of the Cold War era: 65 feet beneath the West Virginia wing of the Greenbrier was a fully staffed, fully operational bomb shelter large enough to accommodate both houses of the United States Congress, plus family members and key aides, for up to 60 days in the event of nuclear war.

SHELTER SHOCK

The shelter dated back to the late 1950s and was the brainchild of President Dwight D. Eisenhower. A former five-star general, Ike knew that the Pentagon was building numerous "emergency command relocation centers" for top military leaders (including himself), to ensure that they would survive a nuclear attack by the Soviet Union and would be able to continue to oversee the defense of whatever was left of the country.

But what would happen if the military leaders were the *only* top officials to survive a nuclear war? Eisenhower worried that America might slide into dictatorship. He believed that the United States had to put as much effort into building shelters for the legislative and judicial branches of the government as it did for the military and the commander-in-chief.

HIDE AND SEEK

One of the tricks to building an effective bomb shelter, especially one designed to house top government officials, is doing it in complete secrecy—the enemy can't bomb it if they can't even find it. But how do you hide a bomb shelter large enough to accommodate more than 1,000 people, plus all the food, supplies, machinery, and equipment necessary to keep them alive for 60 days?

Eisenhower himself has been credited with being the one who came up with the idea of burying it beneath the Greenbrier resort. He had visited it a number of times over the years and liked to play golf there. The place had a lot going for it as the potential site for an important bomb shelter: It was 250 miles southwest of Washington, D.C., close enough to be accessible but far enough away to survive a nuclear strike against the city. Since it had its own train station, large numbers of people would be able to evacuate there in an emergency. Best of all, as Eisenhower learned, the Greenbrier was planning to add a giant new wing to the hotel.

At Eisenhower's request, the Architect of the Capitol approached the owners of the resort with a deal: In exchange for allowing the government to build the bomb shelter underneath the new wing *as* it was being constructed, the government would pay for the wing as well as for the bunker. Because both would be built at the same time, the thinking went, the shelter wouldn't attract much attention. Anyone who saw the work under way would naturally assume that it was all part of the hotel.

Who could pass up an offer like that? The Greenbrier's owners took the deal and work on "Project Greek Island," as the bomb shelter was code-named, began in 1958.

YOUR TAX DOLLARS AT WORK

What kind of a bomb shelter would you build if you had the unlimited resources of the federal government behind you, and no public oversight thanks to the fact that the project was a secret? The bomb shelter built underneath the Greenbrier was enormous and had everything. The size of two football fields stacked one atop the other, it was more than 60 feet underground and protected by concrete walls and ceilings 5 feet thick. It had 153 rooms, including 18 dormitories that slept 60 people each; a kitchen and a cafeteria large enough to feed 400 people at a sitting, and a full hospital suite complete with two operating rooms, an intensive-care unit, a 12-bed ward, and a "pathological-waste incinerator" large enough to serve as a crematorium if the need arose. Thirty-five doctors and nurses would have staffed the hospital if it were ever activated.

The shelter also had its own air and water decontamination facilities and a power station stocked with 42,000 gallons of fuel, enough to keep the shelter's giant diesel generators running for months on end. Giant steel and concrete blast doors protected the shelter's four hidden entrances. The largest door, which protected a tunnel large enough to drive trucks into, weighed 40 tons.

HANG IN THERE

Maintaining contact with government and military officials in other secret bunkers during a nuclear war was a top priority, as was

---

Although Morse Code is named for Samuel Morse, it was invented by Alfred Vail.

broadcasting messages of hope and encouragement to any survivors fending for themselves in post-nuclear-war America. To this end the shelter was also equipped with a sophisticated communications area, complete with telephone equipment and TV and radio broadcasting studios. Who knew when nuclear war might come? The TV studio had four different pull-down backdrops of the Capitol dome, one for each season of the year, so that elected officials would look in season when speaking to their constituents back home.

AN OPEN SECRET

The bomb shelter also contained two rooms large enough to serve as House and Senate chambers. A third, even larger room, would have served as office space for the officials and their aides, and was also large enough to host joint sessions of Congress if the need ever arose.

Unlike the rest of the bomb shelter, which was concealed behind a locked and carefully guarded door marked "Danger: High Voltage–Keep Out," these large rooms were hidden in plain sight —they were open to the public and used by the Greenbrier as a basement exhibition hall. The only hint of the room's true purpose was a movable, wallpapered panel next to the corridor leading to the hotel. The panel concealed a 25-ton blast door that was normally kept open to allow access to the hall. But if a crisis ever erupted, the public would have been hustled out of the exhibition hall (the shelter was stocked with firearms and riot gear for just such an occasion); then the blast door would have been closed and locked from inside the shelter, sealing its occupants off from Armageddon and abandoning the Greenbrier and its guests and staff to their fate.

Did you ever attend an exhibit or trade show in the basement of the Greenbrier? Or maybe you saw a movie in the Governor's Hall? (The House chamber was disguised as a theater, and movies really were shown there.) If so, you were in one of the most secret bomb shelters in the world, and you didn't even know it.

What else didn't you know about the Congressional bomb shelter? For Part II of the story, turn to page 392.

In Germany, frogs say *quaak-quaak*.

FACT-A-RONI

We hope you don't find this page of macaroni trivia too cheesy.

• *Macaroni* is a corruption of the Italian *maccheroni*, which comes from the Latin *macer-are*. The word means to bruise or crush; crushing wheat is how pasta is made.

• In the United States and England, they call it macaroni and cheese. In Canada it's Kraft Dinner.

• Kraft sells about a million boxes of macaroni and cheese per day. All-time bestselling non-elbow shape: SpongeBob SquarePants.

• Why did Yankee Doodle stick a feather in his cap and call it macaroni? In the 1700s, fashionable men who wore expensive Italian clothes were called *macaroni*, another word for "dandies." The patriotic song is a jab at Americans who were so boorish that they thought a feather would make them fashionable.

• The macaroni penguin, with black and yellow plumes on its head, is named after those very same dandies from "Yankee Doodle."

• Emergency tip: You can cook pasta in a coffee pot. Just put the noodles in the filter basket and fill the tank with water. The hot water cooks them.

• The average American eats 19.8 pounds of pasta each year. The average Italian eats 62 pounds.

• In Hong Kong, macaroni is traditionally a breakfast food, cooked with mushrooms, peas, ham, eggs, and chicken stock.

• Thomas Jefferson introduced macaroni to the United States in 1789. He brought back a macaroni shaping machine after eating the dish in Naples, Italy.

• There are about 350 different "authentic" shapes of pasta—meaning ones that originated in Italy.

• Coincidence? According to a study by the Animal Behavior Society, the favorite food of city-dwelling rats is macaroni and cheese. It's also the most requested food in college dorm cafeterias.

LOCAL HEROES

*How quickly could you react when disaster strikes? Let these folks be
a reminder that ordinary people can do extraordinary things.*

LEAVE THE DRIVING TO HER

Local Hero: Laura Simpson, a 16-year-old girl from Queensland, Australia

Heroic Deed: While being bused home from a private school in
March 2007, Laura was sitting in the third row on the all-night
trip. Most of the other passengers—kids aged 6 to 12—were sleeping. At around 3:00 a.m., on a desolate road, the bus suddenly
veered out of control, smashing through a sign and swerving into a
dry creek bed…and it wasn't slowing down. Laura jumped out of
her seat and saw that the driver was having some sort of seizure—
his body was stiff, his eyes were rolled back in his head, and his
foot was pressed hard against the accelerator. Straight ahead was a
river. Thinking quickly, Laura grabbed the wheel and steered the
bus back toward the road, yelling at the driver to wake up. He did,
stopped the bus on the side of the road, and then fell back unconscious. Then the teenager called the paramedics (and the bus
company) on her cell phone. Four hours later, help arrived and
the children were taken home.

Simpson got a hero's welcome in her hometown of Longreach.
She said she's just glad she was able to help, adding "I'm kind of
glad my parents taught me how to drive early."

TANKS A LOT

Local Hero: Michael Drozdo, a 31-year-old furniture delivery
salesman from Holly Township, Michigan

Heroic Deed: On the morning of April 3, 2006, Drozdo was driving home when he noticed flames engulfing a house across the
street from his. Without hesitating, Drozdo stopped his truck,
jumped out, and ran up to the house. Forcing his way in through a
locked door, Drozdo found his neighbor, 48-year-old Diana Bowman, unconscious on the floor, badly burned but alive. Adding to
the danger were the presence of several medical oxygen containers. With the flames spreading, Drozdo picked up Bowman and

Evangelist Aimee McPherson was buried with a working telephone so she could contact…

headed toward the front door. That's when the oxygen tanks began exploding. As they were whizzing through the room like missiles, Drozdo carried Bowman out as fast as he could, and neither victim nor rescuer were hit by the tanks.

Update: Drozdo later received the Carnegie Hero Fund Commission Medal, a national award that celebrates people who risk their own lives to save others. And in true hero fashion Drozdo downplayed his feat and asked that there be no big ceremony. There wasn't. Drozdo used most of the $5,000 prize money to pay bills and the rest to buy a rowboat.

CIVILITY IN A CIVIL SUIT

Local Hero: La Tina Osborne, a 32-year-old pediatric nurse from Folcroft, Pennsylvania

Heroic Deed: In 2007 Osborne was representing herself in a court case brought by her landlord, Genevieve Zumuda. While Osborne was in the middle of pleading her case, Zumuda, 77, "started shaking and her eyes rolled back into her head." Without hesitating, Osborne rushed over to the woman who was suing her, and found that Zumuda wasn't breathing. Osborne quickly placed Zumuda on the courtroom floor and kept her alive by performing CPR until the paramedics arrived. Zumuda was rushed to the hospital and is expected to make a full recovery. (No word on the fate of the lawsuit.) Osborne said that she is not a hero, saying simply, "When people are down, if you can help them, you help them."

HEAR THAT TRAIN A-COMIN'

Local Hero: Wesley Autrey, a 50-year-old construction worker and U.S. Navy veteran from New York City

Heroic Deed: At a Manhattan subway station in January 2007, Autrey and his two daughters were waiting on the platform for their train to come. Autrey saw a man a few feet away collapse and start convulsing on the concrete floor. He helped the 20-year-old film student, Cameron Hollopeter, back onto his feet. But then Hollopeter started shaking, and fell again…this time onto the tracks below. Autrey looked down the tunnel and saw the lights of the oncoming train. Then he looked down at the tracks and saw the man writhing and convulsing. "I had to make a split-second decision," said Autrey. He jumped down, knowing there was no time to lift Hollopeter off the track. So instead, Autrey lay down on top of him and pressed him into the small space between the tracks, which is only about a foot deep. As the train approached, its horn blew and brakes screeched, but there was no way it could stop in time. There was nothing else for Autrey to do except put his head down as low as possible and hope for the best. The train finally stopped, right on top of the two men. As witnesses on the platform screamed, Autrey reassured them: "We're okay down here, but I've got two daughters up there. Let them know their father's okay!" Rescuers cut the power to the station and freed Autrey and Hollopeter—to thunderous applause. After he was safe, Autrey realized how close to death he came when he noticed the oily marks on his knit cap—the train had passed barely an inch over his head. "I don't feel like I did something spectacular," he told *The New York Times*. "I just saw someone who needed help. I did what I felt was right."

*　　*　　*

LOVE, ELIZABETH TAYLOR STYLE

- "I love him better every day." (*On her marriage to her first husband, Conrad Hilton, in 1950. They were divorced in 1951.*)

- "I just want to be with him, to be his wife." (*On her marriage to second husband Michael Wilding in 1952. They divorced in 1957.*)

- "Thirty or forty years." (*Predicting the length of her marriage to fourth husband Eddie Fisher, 1959. It lasted five years.*)

- "This marriage will last forever." (*On her marriage to fifth husband Richard Burton in 1964. They were divorced in 1974.*)

- "We are stuck together like chicken feathers to tar." (*On her remarriage to Burton in 1975. It lasted less than a year.*)

- "I have never been so happy." (*After marrying Sen. John Warner in 1976. They divorced in 1982.*)

- "This is it, forever." (*Announcing her marriage to Larry Fortensky in 1991. The marriage lasted five years.*)

BUTT FACIALS

*Beauty is in the eye of the person with
the weirdest beauty treatment.*

HERE'S EGG ON YOUR FOOT. The Spa-Newbery in
Boston offers foot massages with a concoction that
includes…caviar. The spa's owner, Selena Belise, says the
fish-roe lotion is "similar to the skin's own chemistry, so it binds
the skin and brings nutrients." The treatment costs $100. (Sounds
fishy, though.)

NON-LIFTS. Platinum Skin Care & Medi Spa of Chesterfield,
Michigan, offers "Non-Surgical Face Lifts." How do they do it?
The technician massages your face while wearing "electric gloves,"
giving it a "low-frequency treatment to re-educate the muscles."
Cost of the re-education? About $100.

CAN YOU FEED ME NOW? Here's a new alternative to dieting:
weight-loss ear staples—tiny pieces of metal that are stapled into
your ear cartilage, near the traditional "stomach" acupuncture
point. A good stapling purportedly causes a decrease in appetite.
It's become so prevalent that several states around the U.S. have
begun to regulate the practice, citing the fact that many people
have developed dangerous infections after the procedure. Cost:
$50 to $125.

FACE TO FACE. Getting ready for bikini season? Well, don't
forget the latest skincare craze: a butt facial. Just like a face facial,
exfoliants are applied to "detoxify" your skin, but it's not done to
your face—it's done to your butt. (That's probably why it's called a
butt facial.) Cost: around $75.

JUST STAND UNDER THE BIRDCAGE. Nightingales are
famous for their beautiful songs, and, according to Diamond
Hawaii Resort & Spa in Maui, their poop makes your face softer.
They say that Japanese geisha and Kabuki actors have used it for
centuries to remove their makeup and refresh their skin. Cost: It's
a secret, but judging by the prices of their other products—a lot.

In ancient Egypt, warm donkey droppings were prescribed to alleviate sore eyes.

ESCAR-GROSS. Do you have acne, sun spots, freckles, or wrinkles? Get some Elicina cream. It's made from 80% snail extract. How was it discovered? "Snail handlers noticed how quickly minor cuts healed without infections or scars, as well as the unusual softness of their hands." Somehow they get the "extract" without hurting the snails. Cost: $25 a jar. (They make snail-extract aftershave, too.)

HIGHBROW. What's the latest craze in Singapore? "Eyebrow embroidery." Many women are getting all their eyebrow hairs plucked, then having the appearance of eyebrows reapplied with tattoos. It's become a huge industry in Singapore, generating more than $3 million a year.

FARM FRESH! Hari's Salon in Cheshire, England, offers 45-minute bull-sperm hair treatments. "We chose to use bull semen in our latest 'Aberdeen Organic Hair' treatment," a spokesman said, "after we discovered the rich proteins it contains gives a shine to the hair that other treatments could not." Cost: about $110.

MMMM, SPA. At the Chodovar Family Brewery in the Czech Republic, you can take a beauty bath in beer. According to the Chodovars, "beer yeast provides the skin with a wide range of vitamins, proteins, and saccharides—and contributes to overall softening and regeneration of the cuticle." They also offer beer massages, beer wraps, and beer cosmetics. And you can have a beer while you're having a bath…in beer. Cost: Who cares?

TAJ MAH-UD. In May 2007, officials in India announced that they had endorsed a mud-pack beauty treatment…for the Taj Mahal. The 359-year-old white-marble masterpiece has been turning yellow because of pollution. Officials say attempts to clean the structure with modern chemicals could harm it, so they've agreed to treat it with non-corrosive clay packs. The process, which will use mud similar to those used in face (and butt) treatments, will take between two and three months.

*   *   *

Knowledge that is not used is abused. **—Cree proverb**

Michael Jordan shaves his head twice a week.

KNOW YOUR GEOGRAPHY

There are certain places you hear mentioned on the news or read about in magazines that aren't exactly countries—they're more like regions or "geographic distinctions." But where are they? (Here they are.)

IBERIA. The peninsula at the far west of Europe occupied by Spain and Portugal. The name was derived from *Iber*, the Greek name for the river that flows across the peninsula.

THE FERTILE CRESCENT. Coined around 1900 by American archaeologist James Henry Breasted, the term refers to the crescent-shaped area that ranges across Syria, Israel, Jordan, Lebanon, and Iraq. It encompasses ancient Mesopotamia, between the Tigris and Euphrates Rivers, known as "the birthplace of civilization."

THE GREAT STEPPE. A *steppe* is a grassy plain that can be flat or hilly. The Great Steppe in Europe and Asia is a vast expanse bordered by the Black Sea that extends over Russia, eastern Europe, and former Soviet republics Turkmenistan and Kazakhstan. Historically, it was home to nomadic tribes and conquering hordes on horseback.

THE CAUCASUS. This mountain range divides Europe from Asia. It's nestled between the Black and Caspian seas, and bordered by Ukraine and Turkey. The region includes southwest Russia, Azerbaijan, and Armenia. The name comes from the ancient Greek word *kau*, meaning "mountain."

TORA BORA. A cave complex situated at nearly 13,000 feet in the Safed Koh mountain range on the Pakistan-Afghanistan border. *Tora bora* is the local Iranian dialect's term for "black dust." After the 2001 U.S.-led invasion against the Taliban, Tora Bora was the suspected hideout of al-Qaeda leader Osama bin Laden.

BALKANS. Comprising a mostly mountainous region in southeastern Europe, the Balkan Peninsula is bordered by the Adriatic Sea on the west and the Aegean and Black Seas on the east. Countries making up the Balkan states: Albania, Bosnia and

---

What do you call the saddle on an elephant (besides "elephant saddle")? A *howdah*.

Herzegovina, Bulgaria, Croatia, Greece, Macedonia, Romania, Serbia and Montenegro, Slovenia, and the European tip of Turkey. *Balkan* is the Turkish word for "mountain."

PATAGONIA. A desert in the southernmost parts of Argentina and Chile that extends almost to Antarctica. The name comes from *pata*, Spanish for "paw." According to legend, when Magellan explored the area in 1520, he was impressed by the gigantic tracks he found in the snow and thought they must belong to a race of giants. In truth, the marks were probably left by the oversize llama-skin shoes worn by the indigenous Tehuelches people.

THE BALTICS. The three westernmost former Soviet republics Latvia, Lithuania, and Estonia. These eastern European nations are bordered by the Baltic Sea, and other than geographic proximity they have little in common. Latvians and Lithuanians speak related languages, but Estonians use a language similar to Finnish.

ASIA MINOR. A peninsula in western Asia, bounded by the Black Sea on the north and the Mediterranean Sea on the south. The entire landmass is occupied by Turkey. It gets its name from the fact that it's a small part of Asia that connects the continent to Europe.

THE TROPICS. The Tropics is a band between two imaginary lines that circle the Earth, parallel to the equator. The Tropic of Capricorn is 23° south of the equator, and the Tropic of Cancer is 23° north of it. The distinguishing characteristic of the region is that the Sun is directly overhead at least once a year. This makes for very warm climates in locales like Brazil, Polynesia, and northern Australia. The two Tropics are named after the constellations where the Sun was positioned, in ancient times, during the summer solstice.

SUB-SAHARAN AFRICA. The Sahara Desert stretches across the northern third of Africa through Algeria, Libya, Egypt, Sudan, Niger, Chad, Mauritania, Mali, Morocco, and Tunisia. These nations, some of which have oil-based economies, are largely made up of Muslim Arabic peoples. Nations south of the desert, in sub-Saharan Africa ("below the Sahara"), are inhabited mostly by non-Arabic people. The climate is much hotter and there's little oil.

DUSTBIN OF HISTORY: BERNARR MACFADDEN

He was a founder of the fitness movement in America and the most successful publisher of the early 1900s. He even hobnobbed with national politicians and Hollywood stars. Yet hardly anyone today has heard of him.

THE WEAKLING

Bernard McFadden was born into an impoverished family in Mill Spring, Missouri, in 1868. Both his father and mother died by the time he was 11, and after he was orphaned he was placed with a farmer in Illinois and put to work.

Bernard had been frail and sickly his entire life, but the fresh air, hard work, and wholesome foods on the farm turned him into a strong, healthy boy for the first time. Then when he was 13, he moved to St. Louis and found work in an office, where the sedentary lifestyle and bad eating habits quickly caught up with him, and soon he was as sick as he'd been before he got to the farm. "By the age of 16 I was a physical wreck," he wrote in his memoir. "I had the hacking cough of a consumptive, my muscular system had so wasted that I resembled a skeleton; my digestive organs were in a deplorable condition."

BACK TO BASICS

Even at that early age McFadden didn't trust doctors—he had nearly died in childhood after receiving a "vaccination" from a quack—so he put himself in charge of regaining his health. He began working out with a dumbbell and walking as many as six miles a day. He also became a vegetarian.

McFadden's reformed lifestyle produced quick results. His health returned and he developed a strong physique, which prompted him to take up gymnastics and later wrestling. He excelled at both, and in the process he discovered that he loved performing in front of the public. In 1887 he became what today would be called a personal fitness trainer (McFadden called himself a "kinestherapist" and practitioner of "higher physical culture"); then in 1889 he signed on as an athletic coach at an Illinois military academy.

How many—*hic!*—have you tried? There are more than 20,000—*burp!*—brands of beer worldwide.

WHAT'S IN A NAME

Working with the athletes gave McFadden a chance to develop his ideas on nutrition, fitness, and exercise, and over the next few years he formed detailed theories on how to live a healthy life. By 1894 he was ready to share them with a larger audience, so he quit his job, moved to New York City, and converted his two-room apartment into a fitness studio. It was at this time that he also changed the spelling of his name to Bernarr Macfadden—"Bernarr" sounded like the roar of a lion, he thought, and Macfadden seemed a more masculine spelling than McFadden did.

In the mid-1890s, he patented an exercise machine made with ropes and pulleys. It made him a lot of money, but in the end it was the instruction booklet that came with it that became the foundation for his fortune: Included along with the instructions were so many health and diet tips that many customers mistook the booklet for a magazine and asked Macfadden for a subscription.

PAPER PULPIT

Macfadden decided that if his customers wanted a magazine, he would give them one: Working from a desk he rented in a real-estate office, he began work on a magazine he called *Physical Culture*. The first issue hit newsstands in March 1899.

Physical Culture was one of the very first fitness magazines in the United States, and it was completely unlike the ones that had come before it. The magazine was packed with photos of scantily clad, muscular young men and women—which no doubt broadened the magazine's appeal—at a time when other magazines had only a few photographs or none at all. Like the instruction booklet that inspired it, *Physical Culture* was overflowing with Macfadden's maxims on healthy living: Vegetables, fresh air, and exercise were good; white bread (the "staff of death," he called it), alcohol, tobacco, and caffeine were bad. The healthy human body was an object of beauty. Sexual desire was normal and healthy; sex itself was meant to be enjoyable. Doctors were pill-pushing frauds, and most diseases could be cured with fasting and hot baths. *Really* bad diseases like cancer, syphilis, and gout could be cured with an all-milk diet. Macfadden had opinions on everything, and they all ended up in the pages of *Physical Culture*.

The secret to his success? Napoleon carried chocolate with him on all of his military campaigns.

By 1903 *Physical Culture* had a circulation of more than 100,000, making it one of the bestselling magazines in the country. And yet as popular as the magazine was, it attracted few advertisers—not many businesses wanted to be associated with Macfadden's risqué photographs and kooky medical advice.

Macfadden managed to turn this to his benefit by filling the magazine's pages with his *own* ads for his books (he wrote 79 in all), health products, and other business ventures. In the years to come, he expanded his empire with Bernarr Macfadden bodybuilding contests, Bernarr Macfadden sanitariums, Bernarr Macfadden health food restaurants, and the Bernarr Macfadden Institute, which schooled coaches, trainers, and physical therapists in his theories and methods. The name "Bernarr Macfadden" was as well known in his day as Martha Stewart's and Donald Trump's are today.

TAKE IT FROM ME

For all his accomplishments in the fitness and health arena, Macfadden's most lasting contribution (not to mention his fortune) came from the fact that he also helped usher in America's "confessional culture." Over and over again in the pages of *Physical Culture*, he recounted the story of how he'd transformed himself from a scrawny weakling into America's greatest he-man through clean living, vigorous exercise, and sheer force of will. His openness and honesty about his own failings (long since corrected, of course) prompted readers to write in asking for help with their own problems; others wrote in with tales of their triumphs over adversity.

Broken hearts, unrequited love, marital problems, out-of-wedlock pregnancies, things that weren't even discussed *in private*, let alone in the pages of a national magazine—these were the things that Macfadden's readers shared with him. He established such a powerful bond with them that they wrote to him about anything and everything, and with their permission he published it all.

UP, UP, AND AWAY

By 1919 interest in *Physical Culture*'s confessional stories had grown so much that Macfadden spun them off into a magazine of their own called *True Story*. It was a hit from the first issue and soon shot past *Physical Culture* to reach a circulation of two mil-

First bird mentioned in the Bible: a raven, in Genesis 8:7. Second bird: a dove, in verse 8.

lion. *True Story's* success prompted Macfadden to launch scads of other magazines, including *True Romances, Dream World, True Detective Stories, True Ghost Stories,* and *Photoplay.* By the mid-1920s, America's biggest fitness guru was also the country's most successful magazine publisher and a multimillionaire.

AND THEN THE FALL...

Even as he was reaching his greatest heights, Macfadden was also laying the groundwork for his eventual demise. In 1924 he took his publishing company public, which gained him access to outside investors but also put him under their thumb. Not that Macfadden saw it that way: He continued to spend company funds as if they were his own until 1940, when the investors sued to get the money back. Macfadden eventually had to settle the case by selling his stock, resigning as president, and repaying his investors $300,000.

And then there were the women. Macfadden was a man who practiced what he preached, and enjoying sex was no exception. He was a notorious philanderer, and that, combined with his iron will and his conviction that he was right all the time, made him difficult to live with. He married and divorced four times, his last marriage ending when his 44-year-old wife caught him in bed with another woman. (He was 82.)

Macfadden learned the hard way that big businesses can lose money as fast as they make it. One by one, his remaining enterprises shut their doors. By the early 1950s, he was so short on cash that he was jailed for nonpayment of alimony. Twice.

...INTO THE DUSTBIN

In the fall of 1955 Macfadden, nearly broke, was living in a run-down hotel in New Jersey. As confident as ever in his own medical theories, when he started having abdominal pains he tried to treat his condition with fasting and hot baths. By the time his landlord found him comatose on the floor of his hotel room, it was too late to save him. He died on October 12, 1955, at the age of 87. Cause of death: "Jaundice, aggravated by fasting." Killed by the same theories that turned him into a household name, he left his nine surviving children an estate valued at $5,000.

As of the summer of 2007, *True Story* magazine is still in print.

WHAT'S WRONG WITH THIS PICTURE?

Uncle John has given you pages of irony, pages of "oops," and pages of weird world news. Somewhere in the middle of all that sit these stories, in which somebody clearly missed the point, dropped the ball, or just didn't "get it."

STOP WINING

The Story: In 2006 HBO sent 11,460 bottles of a specially made wine called "Rome" to expensive Italian restaurants in Los Angeles, Chicago, and New York to promote its series *Rome*. Lucky patrons had a free bottle waiting at their tables with a note that read "A Taste of Rome awaits you."

What's Wrong With This Picture? The Italian-style red wine was bottled in...California.

GASSY FEELING

The Story: *Judgment at Nuremberg*, the classic film about the war-crimes trials of Nazi officers, was first shown on American television in 1959.

What's Wrong With This Picture? All references to the Nazi gas chambers were removed at the request of the broadcast's sponsor, the American Gas Association.

FAT CHANCE

The Story: In 2005 the Girl Scouts introduced a new, healthier version of their Thin Mints cookies, free of unhealthy trans fats.

What's Wrong With This Picture? The cookies contained more sugar and saturated fat than the old version, making the new "healthy" cookies actually less healthy than the original "unhealthy" cookies.

THE TIMES THEY ARE A-CHANGIN'

The Story: Before its sketch comedy show *The State* premiered in 1993, MTV told the show's writers that they couldn't do a planned sketch about Bob Dylan because their audience—mostly teenagers—"didn't know who Bob Dylan was" and to instead focus on current stars like Kurt Cobain of the band Nirvana.

What's Wrong With This Picture? In 2007 MTV aired another sketch show, called *Human Giant*. The cast told an interviewer (coincidentally, a former cast member on *The State*) that MTV prevented them from doing a Kurt Cobain sketch because MTV's teenage audience "wouldn't know who that was."

OGRES WILL EAT ANYTHING

The Story: In April 2007, the U.S. Health and Human Services Department ran an ad campaign aimed at getting kids to exercise and eat better. They licensed characters from the Shrek movies for the campaign, which they called "Get Healthier."

What's Wrong With This Picture? Around the same time, a promotional blitz for *Shrek the Third* began, with the same Shrek characters appearing on Happy Meals, Snickers Bars, Sierra Mist, Froot Loops, and Pop-Tarts.

BUSHWHACKED

The Story: In response to the Valerie Plame scandal in 2003, in which a presidential staff member leaked the name of a CIA operative to the media, President George W. Bush demanded an end to leaks of sensitive information by unnamed members of his administration.

What's Wrong With This Picture? Bush's demand was actually made to his staff in secret—the news was leaked to the media by an unnamed member of his administration.

THERE'S AN EASIER WAY

The Story: Marilee Jones, dean of admissions at the prestigious Massachusetts Institute of Technology, was an outspoken opponent of the practice of high school students working themselves too hard building up their resumes so they could get into elite colleges (like MIT).

What's Wrong With This Picture? After 20 years on the job, Jones had to resign her position after MIT officials discovered that she'd lied about her academic credentials on her resume.

THE PROVERBIAL TRUTH

You know that "all that glitters isn't gold," but there are countless other proverbs that you may never have heard. Here are some of the BRI's favorites from around the world.

To forgive the unrepentant is like making pictures on water.
Japanese

The man with a big nose thinks everyone speaks of it.
Scottish

Love your neighbor, but don't pull down the hedge.
German

Though the emperor is rich, he cannot buy an extra year.
Chinese

When children are little, they make our heads ache; when they're grown, our hearts.
Italian

A man isn't honest simply because he's never had a chance to steal.
Yiddish

Flowers fade fast. Weeds last the season.
Swedish

Night rinses what the day has soaped.
Swiss

It's not the fault of the post that the blind man can't see it.
Sanskrit

God deliver me from a man of one book.
English

Old age does not announce itself.
Zulu

Put a snake in a bamboo tube, but that won't change its wriggling disposition.
Japanese

Facts, not speech, convince.
Greek

A tree tends to fall the way it leans.
Bulgarian

A little help is better than a lot of pity.
Celtic

The rain doesn't fall on one roof alone.
Cameroonian

Nobody will give a pauper bread, but everybody will give him advice.
Armenian

The thief is sorry that he is going to be hanged, not that he was a thief.
English

They are free with their horse who have none.
Scottish

If I die, I forgive you; if I recover, we'll see.
Spanish

Most popular TV show in the world in 2007—*CSI: Miami.*

20 TWENTIES

We thought it would be fun to celebrate our 20th year by telling you about some of the most famous (and not-so-famous) references to this number from history, entertainment, sports, and pop culture.

1. THE ROARING TWENTIES. The 1920s. Jazz and flappers, Al Capone and bootleg whiskey served in speakeasies—a decade of great societal and cultural upheaval. Like a lot of wild parties, this one came to a spectacular end: the stock market crash of 1929.

2. THE TWENTY. You know all those pre-movie ads, announcements, and trailers you see in a theater before the feature film is shown? They're called the TWENTY...because they run about 20 minutes long.

3. WHAT'S YOUR 20? Popularized by the CB lingo that commercial truckers used in the 1970s, this phrase is one of many law-enforcement "10-codes" created to improve radio communications in the 1930s. Meaning: "What's your location?"

4. MATCHBOX TWENTY: Popular Orlando, Florida rock band best known for collaborating on the 1999 megahit "Smooth" by Carlos Santana. Matchbox Twenty's Rob Thomas sang the lead.

5. 20 QUESTIONS: How long has it been since you last played? You pick an object; your opponents have 20 questions to guess what it is. Typical questions: "Is it bigger than a breadbox?" or "Is it animal, vegetable, or mineral?" Fun on long car trips. (It was also the name of a popular game show in the 1940s and '50s.)

6. TWENTY, ENGLAND. A tiny town in the county of Lincolnshire on the southeast English coast. It's believed to be named after the nearby Twenty Foot Drain, a land drainage system completed in the area in the 17th century.

7. 20/20 VISION. Doctors evaluate your eyesight against what a person with "normal" vision sees on an eye chart from a distance of 20 feet. If that's you, you have 20/20 vision. If what you see from 20 feet is what they can see from 100 feet, you have 20/100 vision, and so on. (The cutoff for legal blindness: 20/200.)

---

8. 20/20. One of TV's pioneering "infotainment" shows, ABC's *20/20* has been airing hard-hitting news segments alongside powder-puff celebrity interviews and human-interest stories since 1978. Hugh Downs, Barbara Walters, Diane Sawyer, Sam Donaldson, and Connie Chung have all hosted over the years.

9. MD 20/20: Also called "Mad Dog 20/20," it's a fortified wine that comes in fruit flavors like Orange Jubilee and Tangerine Dream. Cheap and strong, it has long been associated with hard-drinking "bum" types. No doctors here—the "MD" stands for "Mogen David," the Westfield, New York, company that makes it.

10. TWENTY: There at least two music albums that go by this name: It's a 2005 album by five-time Grammy-winning bluesman Robert Cray (the music video of the title track, a song about a young soldier who questions his role in the war, became an Internet hit in 2006). It's also the title of a 1997 Lynyrd Skynyrd album that commemorates the 20th anniversary of the plane crash that decimated the band.

11. 4:20: Among the marijuana-smoking community in the United States, 4:20 (or 4/20, or just 420) is code for "getting high." Its origins are unknown, but many people believe it came from a group of San Rafael, California, high-school students who, in 1971, would meet after school (at 4:20) under a statue of Louis Pasteur to "partake." Their secret code was "420 Louis." Today, it's also the name of a movement to educate people about the benefits of marijuana. (Their annual holiday takes place on April 20th.)

12. THE 20 GAUGE: Shotgun of choice for bird hunters, the 20 Gauge gets its name from the odd way it is measured: A lead shot just large enough to fit inside the barrel of this gun weighs 1/20th of one pound.

13. 20-GAME WINNER. In a 162-game baseball season, a starting pitcher plays only in every fifth or sixth game. Between the inevitable losses and no-decisions, reaching 20 wins is very difficult, and increasingly rare: While 96 pitchers won 20 games in a season in the 1970s, only 37 pitchers accomplished the feat in the 1990s. And 2006 was the first full year in Major League Baseball's 130-year history in which there were no 20-game winners.

14. THE RALEIGH TWENTY. Also called the "R20," this was a bicycle launched in 1968 by the British Raleigh Bicycle Company, one of the oldest and most respected bike makers in the world. Named for its 20-inch tires, the R20 was the company's most popular model of the 1970s, and is now considered a collector's item.

15. THE "TWENTY-YEAR CURSE." For some reason, the man elected U.S. president in the years 1840, 1860, 1880, 1900, 1920, 1940, and 1960 died while in office. President Reagan, elected in 1980, "broke" the curse by serving two full terms.

16. 20TH CENTURY FOX. The movie studio formed in 1935 when 20th Century Pictures merged with the Fox Film Corporation. It's also the name of a 1967 song by the Doors. Jim Morrison sings about a typical modern woman who "won't waste time on elementary talk, 'cause she's a [dunh-dunh] 20th-century fox."

17. FOUR AND TWENTY BLACKBIRDS. This phrase comes from an old English nursery rhyme: "Sing a song of sixpence, a pocket full of rye / Four and twenty blackbirds, baked in a pie." It also inspired Australia's bestselling Four'N Twenty Meat Pie, traditionally eaten during Australian-rules football matches.

18. *TWENTY BUCKS.* A quirky 1993 film that follows a $20 bill as it goes from person to person, sometimes for a brief moment, sometimes taking a couple of days to move on. Along the way, the audience sees a snippet of each of the characters' lives.

19. COMMODORE VIC-20. The first inexpensive color computer, and the first computer ever to sell more than a million units. Priced at $299 in 1980, it didn't have a lot of business applications, but buyers loved it for games. The "VIC" in VIC-20 stands for **V**ideo **I**nterface **C**hip; the 20 "just sounded good."

20. *20,000 LEAGUES UNDER THE SEA.* So you think you've read this 1870 science fiction classic, starring Captain Nemo and his fantastic submarine, the *Nautilus*, as they do battle against warships, giant squids, and other mysteries of the deep? Think again: The first English translation of the book, done in 1873, cut out large sections of French novelist Jules Verne's original 1870 text and mistranslated much of the rest. This version remained the standard English translation for more than a century.

BEASTLY APPETITES

Some animals will eat anything. We know a black Lab that once ate an entire box of chocolates—including the cardboard and foil they were wrapped in. (He survived.) Here are a few more animals with bizarre appetites.

CHICKEN-EATING CALF

Ajit Ghosh, a farmer in Kolkata, India, couldn't figure out why his chickens kept disappearing at night. At first he blamed his dogs, so he kept them inside. But the chickens kept disappearing—48 gone in a single month. Finally the Ghosh family decided to stake out the coop. "We watched in horror," said Ajit's brother Gour, "as a calf, whom we had fondly named Lal, snuck into the coop and grabbed the little ones with the precision of a jungle cat." This caused quite a stir—not only because cows are sacred in India, but also because they are herbivores. A local veterinarian attributes the calf's strange behavior to a lack of minerals, but villagers believe that Lal likes eating chickens because in a previous life he was a tiger. Meanwhile, Lal has become a local celebrity, entertaining dozens of visitors a day—but they only get to see him eating grass. The chicken coop is now locked.

DENTURE-EATING DOG

Like many puppies, Desmond, a one-year-old Jack Russell terrier, has an appetite that includes shoes, newspapers, and power cables. But Desmond made the news when he found something unusual to chomp on. It happened while his owner, Marjorie Johnson, was in the bathroom. When she got out, Johnson noticed that her dog was sick...and her dentures were missing. She rushed Desmond to the vet, where X-rays clearly showed the false teeth lodged in the puppy's stomach. After a costly operation, Desmond is recovering in his South Shields, England, home. "He's mischievous," said Johnson. "He ate them for the fun of it."

FROG-EATING FROGS

The Lily Pond in San Francisco's Golden Gate Park was a peaceful little spot...until somebody secretly introduced vicious African clawed frogs there in 2006. Now they're terrorizing not only the other animals, but also visitors to the famous pond. "They've eaten everything they can get their mouths around," said Eric Mills, a spokesman for the animal rights group Action for Animals. That includes turtles, fish, birds, small snakes—and now, says Mills, "they're eating each other." Will the invasive amphibians venture out of the Lily Pond and wreak havoc on the rest of San Francisco? Probably not: A plan is currently under way to drain the pond and eliminate the killer frogs.

CASH-EATING MOUSE

An ATM machine in Estonia seemed to be malfunctioning over a weekend in March 2007. Some customers received nothing at all from the machine; others received their *kroon* (Estonian currency) in shreds. When technicians opened the machine, they found a mouse. It had eaten thousands of pounds of kroon, and what it didn't eat, it shredded up into a nest. (The mouse was relocated.)

CAR-EATING RATS

When Beth Thomas's 1999 Chrysler Concord wouldn't start in front of her Boston apartment in October 2006, she had it towed to her mechanic, Bill Doherty. Noticing that the "check engine" light was on, he hoped the car just needed a tune-up but feared it was something worse. Sure enough, when he opened the hood, there was a big rat's nest right on top of the engine block. Further investigation revealed that the rats had been chewing on the car's wires. And this wasn't the first time Doherty had heard of rats eating cars. In fact, one once jumped out of an engine hood at him. Engines, explained Doherty, provide the rats with warmth (and stuff to chew on). City officials are trying to eradicate the rats, but so far the vermin are winning.

DIAMOND-EATING DOG

Missy the pit bull likes to eat precious gems. That's why Tina Burlett's grandmother suggested checking the dog's insides when Burlett's $5,000 diamond wedding ring went missing. The pit bull, noted Grandma, had already been scolded once for chewing on Tina's diamond earrings. Sure enough, the ring showed up in an X-ray of Missy's stomach. Instead of surgery, the vet gave Missy some peroxide, and the dog barfed up the diamond ring. "I didn't think so at the time," said Burlett, "but it's funny now."

The first Santa Claus School opened in September 1937 in Albion, New York.

POLITICAL SQUIRMING

Few people have mastered the fine art of the excuse/apology as well as
seasoned politicians have. Let's all watch as they try to squirm
their way out of some embarrassing political predicaments.

POLITICIAN: Rep. Frank Chopp (D-Wash.)
OFFENSE: In 2007, during debates over whether a taxpayer-
funded NASCAR raceway should be built near Seattle, a
reporter asked Chopp, who opposed the raceway, if he was aware
that racing legend Richard Petty was currently in town to promote
it. Chopp's response: "You mean that guy who got a DUI?" Realizing his mistake, Chopp quickly started backtracking.

SQUIRM: "By the way, on that last point, I was told that—so I'm
not sure. You better check to make sure it's accurate."

AFTERMATH: Not only was it inaccurate, but Petty has long
advocated *against* drunk driving—he even refuses sponsorship from
any company that sells alcohol. The next day, Chopp invited
Petty to his office to apologize personally. Petty hadn't heard what
Chopp had said; he figured the congressman was simply apologizing for his opposition. But when Petty found out later, he said,
"I'm glad you didn't tell me that before because I might have went
off on him. I don't drink, okay?" He then joked, "I'm not saying I
don't run over people when I'm sober, though."

POLITICIAN: California Governor Arnold Schwarzenegger
OFFENSE: During a closed-door policy meeting in 2006, the
Governator made a few racy statements about Assemblywoman
Bonnie Garcia. He joked to an aide that Garcia's "black blood" and
"Latino blood" made her "very hot." A few months later the tape
was leaked to the press—Schwarzenegger's comments were printed
in newspapers all over the United States, prompting this apology.
SQUIRM: "Anyone out there that feels offended by these com-
ments, I just want to say I'm sorry. The fact is that if I would hear
these kinds of comments in my house, by my kids, I would be
upset, and today, when I read it in the papers, it made me cringe."
AFTERMATH: The person least upset by the comments was
Garcia herself. In fact, she saw it as a compliment. "I love the

---

In Rochester, MI, anyone swimming in public must have their suit inspected by a police officer.

governor because he is a straight talker, just like I am," she said. "Very often I tell him, 'Look, I am a hot-blooded Latina.' I label myself a hot-blooded Latina that is very passionate about the issues, and this is kind of an inside joke that I have with him.'"

POLITICIAN: Cynthia Hedge-Morrell (D), New Orleans city councilwoman

OFFENSE: Late for a meeting with FEMA officials in February 2007, Hedge-Morrell checked out a government-issued SUV and sped down the highway at nearly 100 mph with the vehicle's blue lights flashing, weaving in and out of cars and driving on the shoulder. When a state trooper pulled her over, Hedge-Morrell refused to exit the vehicle, yelling, "Do you know who I am? What the hell are you stopping me for?" After waiting a few minutes for a police supervisor to show up, Hedge-Morrell was released without a speeding ticket. New Orleans citizens, still weary of their elected officials' bungled response to Hurricane Katrina, demanded that Hedge-Morrell not be given special treatment just because she's on the city council. Said Gary Russo, the driver who called 911 on the former elementary school principal, "We all have to deal with traffic, simple as that. She ain't the president."

SQUIRM: "I deeply regret the incident, and I will be a more careful driver in the future. I take responsibility for my actions, because when I taught children, I always told them to step up and take responsibility when you make a mistake. Admit what you did wrong, and only use the word 'I.'"

AFTERMATH: Hedge-Morrell was never issued a ticket, remained on the city council, and continues to use the taxpayer-funded SUV…along with a driver to take her to meetings.

POLITICIAN: Tom DeLay (R-Tex.), House majority leader

OFFENSE: In 2005 DeLay commented on the controversial rulings of the federal judges in the case of Terri Schiavo, the brain-damaged Florida woman who spent 15 years in a persistent vegetative state and was at the center of a battle between family members over whether to maintain her life support. "We will look at an arrogant, out-of-control, unaccountable judiciary that thumbed their nose at the Congress and the president," said

The world's first airline, DELAG (Germany, 1909), used zeppelins, not airplanes.

DeLay, who then bitterly added, "The time will come for the men responsible for this to answer for their behavior." Almost immediately, critics on both sides accused DeLay of advocating violence against the judges, prompting him to elaborate...more on the wording itself than the implications it suggested.

SQUIRM: "I said something in an inartful way. I shouldn't have said it that way, and I apologize for saying it that way. It was taken wrong. I didn't explain it or clarify my remarks, as I'm clarifying them here. I am sorry that I said it that way, and I shouldn't have."

AFTERMATH: DeLay weathered that storm, but soon found himself at the heart of another scandal—receiving gifts from a lobbyist in exchange for favorable legislation. In January 2006, he resigned from his post as House majority leader, and in April resigned from his seat in congress.

POLITICIAN: Ray Nagin, mayor of New Orleans

OFFENSE: During the aftermath of Hurricane Katrina, the African-American mayor spoke in January 2006 of his plans for rebuilding his home town. "This city will be chocolate at the end of the day," he proudly announced. "You can't have New Orleans no other way—it wouldn't be New Orleans." The remark "chocolate city" outraged not only his fellow politicians, but also many New Orleans citizens who felt it was a limited and racist portrayal. Nagin needed to save face, and quick, as he was up for reelection.

SQUIRM: "How do you make chocolate? You take dark chocolate, you mix it with white milk, and it becomes a delicious drink. That is the chocolate I am talking about. New Orleans was a chocolate city before Katrina. It is going to be a chocolate city after. How is that divisive? It is white and black working together, coming together and making something special."

AFTERMATH: Nagin won reelection.

* * *

"You have a cough? Go home tonight, eat a whole box of Ex-Lax. Tomorrow you'll be afraid to cough."

—**Pearl Williams**

Grape-Nuts cereal was once advertised as an aid to sobriety.

OOPS!

*More tales of outrageous blunders to let us know that
someone's screwing up even worse than we are. So
go ahead and feel superior for a few minutes.*

COVER UP

"Bungling workmen painted over a mural worth £100,000 by famed British street artist Banksy. The graffiti removal team mistook the 25-by-4-foot artwork for vandalism and coated it in black paint. Locals in Banksy's home city of Bristol, England, are furious that the series of blue shapes—the earliest surviving mural by the artist—is gone forever. The same workmen tried to remove another Banksy work but were stopped by angry residents. The Bristol City Council launched a full investigation. Apparently the contractors had been told NOT to remove the Banksy art."

—*The Sun* (U.K.)

WHITE POWDER FEVER

"Merv Bontrager had his eyes on his donuts when he should have had them on the road. The truck driver says he flipped his semi in North Dakota because he looked to see where his bag of donuts had gone. 'I just looked down briefly on the floor where I had thrown a couple of donuts I was going to eat later,' he said. 'That's all it took.'"

—*New York Post*

ODIE'S REVENGE

"Joseph Savarino, 23, was given a suspended sentence after pleading guilty to misdemeanor charges of criminal mischief, saying he panicked after the statue of Garfield's head came off when he hugged it. 'I'm very sorry that I did it,' he said. 'It was not on purpose.' In Marion, Indiana, the fiberglass head of Garfield, the cartoon cat, was missing for three days in December 2006. Placed there to honor Jim Davis, who grew up on a farm near there, the broken head was found along the side of a country road near the Mississinewa Reservoir, where Savarino had hidden it."

—**Associated Press**

Sunlight can penetrate clean ocean water to a depth of 240 feet.

SOCIOLOGY TEST OF HORROR

"A Massachusetts teen's frightful homework stunt has landed him in court and apologizing to his terrified elderly victim. David Goodhue, 18, is facing disorderly conduct charges. Police say the teen knocked on an 85-year-old woman's door dressed in all black and wearing a ghoulish mask. 'What if this woman had a heart attack?' said police spokesman Lt. Paul Shastany. The teen had told his teacher he was going to dress up as Spider-Man and go trick-or-treating as part of a sociology assignment to record reactions. Goodhue has been ordered to write a letter of apology to both the elderly woman whom he scared and his teacher, for what he put her through by making her go to the police station."

—*MetroWest Daily News*

AT LEAST HE'S BOOK SMART

"An acclaimed novelist lost his office in Carson City in January 2007 when he threw a lit piece of paper into gasoline. Fantasy writer David Eddings, 75 (and author of 27 novels), said he was using water to flush out the gas tank of his broken-down Excalibur sports car, when some fluid leaked. In a lapse of judgment, Eddings lit a piece of paper and threw it into the puddle to test if it was still flammable. The answer came in an orange torrent. The fire raged through the garage and into the office next door to his home. Eddings said his intention was to prevent a fire—he was afraid to leave a tank full of gasoline in a car that had gone kaput—but instead he did the opposite. 'One word comes to mind,' the wordsmith said as he stood in a pajama shirt and slippers. 'Dumb.'"

—*Nevada Appeal*

THAT'S THE WAY THE COOKIE CRUMBLES

"A New York state woman who was holding a rummage sale mistakenly accepted 50¢ for a ceramic turtle with the ashes of her husband's previous wife inside. Now Anita Lewis is desperately searching for the buyer, who planned to use the urn as a cookie jar. Lewis said she hauled items into her yard early Saturday while her husband slept. The buyer quickly selected the large turtle container, despite being unable to get the lid open. Lewis's husband's previous wife collected turtles."

—**United Press International**

LANDLORDS FROM HELL

Some great reasons to buy, not rent.

VICTIM EVICTION. Dorothea Thomas of Jacksonville, North Carolina, was attacked in her apartment by an ex-boyfriend. Thomas, a police officer and former Marine, suffered six gunshot wounds but was able to escape by jumping out of a second-story window. When she was released from the hospital a week later, she found an eviction notice on her front door: Her landlord said the attack violated a "no-disruptive-activity clause" on her lease.

GAS ATTACK. Landlord Joseph Hammock evicted the tenant from a house he owned in Lanett, Alabama. When the tenant refused to vacate the premises, Hammock tossed a tear-gas grenade into the house. No one was injured; Hammock was arrested.

DUEL PERSONALITY. Christina Tuzzolino and Clyde Davis of Lakeland, Florida, got behind on the rent. Bad idea. Their landlord, Harland Pollard, showed up to collect his money…with a sword. He chased the tenants into a bedroom, then locked them in by nailing plywood over the door. Tuzzolino and Davis called police, who helped them escape through a window. Pollard was arrested on charges of aggravated assault and false imprisonment.

CRAZY HOUSE. Seventy-year-old Rebecca Neely was surprised to see an ambulance pull up to her Chicago doorstep one day. Even more surprising: The paramedics had a court order declaring her mentally ill and committing her to a mental hospital. Who had signed the order? Carla Baity, the property manager of Neely's apartment building; the two were in an ongoing dispute about the apartment. But since Neely was *not* mentally ill, police called it an "unauthorized removal" and launched an investigation of Baity and her property management company.

FAMILY FEUD. When Damon Hopkins's landlord raised the rent on his Philadelphia apartment by $100 in 2001, Hopkins saw it as an attempt to get him to leave…so he refused to pay the increase. Then he was evicted—and he refused to go. Then his landlord shot him. The landlord, Laverne Hopkins (she claimed the shooting was self-defense), is also Damon Hopkins's mother.

In early Colonial times, pumpkins were used for the crust of pies, not the filling.

IT'S OXYMORONIC

An oxymoron is a phrase in which contradictory terms are combined for effect. Examples: "a deafening silence" or "poor little rich girl." Here are some oxymoronic quotes that, though contradictory, make a lot of sense.

"Melancholy is the pleasure of being sad."
—**Victor Hugo**

"Lying is the strongest acknowledgment of the force of truth."
—**William Hazlitt**

"Under Richard Nixon, 'launder' became a dirty word."
—**William Zinsser**

"I must follow the people. Am I not their leader?"
—**Benjamin Disraeli**

"I hate intolerant people."
—**Gloria Steinem**

"People have one thing in common—they are all different."
—**Robert Zend**

"Unpredictability can become monotonous."
—**Eric Hoffer**

"There must be more to life than having everything."
—**Maurice Sendak**

"I find nothing more depressing than optimism."
—**Paul Fussell**

"It is fatal to live too long."
—**Racine**

"A man's memory is what he forgets with."
—**Odell Shepard**

"I'm in favor of free expression provided it's kept rigidly under control."
—**Alan Bennett**

"Why do you have to be a nonconformist like everybody else?"
—**James Thurber**

"There is no more expensive thing than a free gift."
—**Michel de Montaigne**

"I always advise people never to give advice."
—**P. G. Wodehouse**

"The only certainty is that nothing is certain."
—**Pliny the Elder**

The only formal qualification to be appointed a Florida executioner is to be at least 18 years old.

LET'S PLAY BATHROOM BLACKJACK!

Tired of reading in the bathroom? Can't afford a trip to Las Vegas? Kill two birds with one stone—turn your commode into a casino. (Gives new meaning to the term "ace in the hole.")

WHAT YOU NEED: A 12-cup muffin pan, 10 nickels (which represent your cards), and 10 dimes (which represent the dealer's cards)

SETTING UP: Mark the cups in the muffin pan so that each one represents a different card. You can do this by writing the card names (Ace, King, etc.) on strips of paper and putting one in each cup. Arrange them in order or at random; it doesn't matter.

• Since there are 13 cards in a suit but only 12 cups in the pan, the rim of the pan will represent the 13th card.

• Place the pan on the bathroom floor a few feet from the toilet.

HOW TO PLAY: "Deal" two cards to yourself by throwing two nickels into the pan. Where they land is what you get.

• Since in blackjack the dealer gets one face-up card and one face-down card, you're going to throw only one dime for the dealer right now. The dealer's other card will remain hidden.

• Compare your cards to the dealer's one card and decide if you want to hold or want another card. If you want more cards, throw more nickels. (Careful! If you go over 21, you lose.)

• Now throw a dime at the pan to find out what the dealer's second card is. In blackjack, if the dealer gets 17 or more, they must stay. If they get 16 or less, they must deal themselves another card. So if the value of the dealer's cards is 16 or less, throw another dime to get a third card. The person closest to 21 wins; if you both get 21, the dealer wins. If the dealer goes over 21, they lose.

• Use the remaining coins to play additional hands. If you're still playing when your legs go numb from sitting too long on the pot, it's time to admit you have a problem. Get help—join Bathroom Gamblers Anonymous.

Enough beer is poured every Saturday across America to—*burp!*—fill the Orange Bowl.

FOUNDING FATHERS

You know the names. Here's a look at the people behind them.

JOHN MOLSON

In 1782 Molson left England and arrived in Montreal, at the time a small British colony. He formed a partnership with fellow English immigrant Thomas Lloyd and started a brewery together. Their first year was a disaster: the beer didn't sell well. Lloyd wanted to quit the business, so Molson bought him out. Good timing for Molson: After the American Revolution, thousands of British loyalists moved to Montreal and brought their thirst for beer with them. The 22-year-old Molson made 4,000 gallons of beer that year and sold it all. With the profits he expanded the brewery, and by 1791 Molson Brewery was turning out 30,000 gallons a year. Molson himself became one of early Canada's wealthiest men, investing in steamships, railroads, and banks. But today he's best known for the beer that still bears his name. It's one of Canada's bestselling beers and North America's oldest brand, with annual sales exceeding $7 billion.

ARTHUR FROMMER

Frommer graduated from Yale Law School in 1950, where he'd served as editor of the *Yale Law Journal*. Drafted into the army in 1951 and assigned to a base in Germany, Frommer wasn't serving combat duty, so he had a lot of furlough time, which he used to travel around western and central Europe. He discovered that he could do it cheaply, staying in small hotels or hostels, and visiting out-of-the-way sights. Upon his discharge and return to the United States, Frommer compiled a book of travel advice based on his experiences, and self-published *The G.I.'s Guide to Traveling Europe* in 1957. It sold well for a travel book—about 10,000 copies—so Frommer took the money he earned from it and expanded the book into a civilian version called *Europe on 5 Dollars a Day*. It was a bestseller. But more importantly, it revolutionized the travel industry, launching Europe as a tourist destination for middle-class Americans. Frommer's book was one of the first major travel guides, and it showed Americans that travel wasn't necessarily

---

An athletic shoe can stay afloat in the ocean for 10 years. (It's still wearable after 3.)

expensive or scary. He went on to write more than 350 *Frommer's Guides* for destinations all over the world.

JOE VLASIC

A Croatian immigrant named Frank Vlasic came to America in 1912 and started a small dairy processing company in Detroit that eventually grew to become one of the midwest's largest cheese makers. In 1920 Vlasic turned the business over to his son, Joe. But by that time, there was so much competition in the dairy industry that Joe Vlasic felt the company had to diversify if it wanted to stay afloat. His solution: pickles. In eastern Europe pungent garlic and dill pickles were common, but in the United States they were just starting to catch on. For the next two decades, barrels of pickles sold to delis in Detroit kept Vlasic's company in business. When World War II started, Vlasic came up with an idea that would prove successful and profitable: Demand for pickles remained high (they were cheap), but because of rationing, supply was unreliable. Vlasic figured that if he packaged pickles in glass jars, they'd keep longer and he could ship them farther. It worked. After the war, Vlasic dropped dairy products entirely and made pickles exclusively, becoming America's number-one pickle producer.

FREDERICK MAYTAG

In 1893 Maytag moved from his family's farm in Illinois to Laurel, Iowa, to start a farm-tool business. He and three business partners, including inventor George Parsons, pooled $2,400 to establish Parsons Band-Cutter and Self-Feeder Company, selling Parsons's inventions—safety attachments for threshers (notorious for maiming farmworkers). In 1900 Maytag bought out his partners and took control of the business, renaming it the Maytag Company. In 1910 he left day-to-day operations to his sons so he could work on his pet project: improving the electric washing machine. Maytag introduced a new agitator that cleaned clothes while tearing them less often than previous models, and an aluminum washtub inside the machine to eliminate rust and leakage. Maytag was so successful that in 1922 the company switched completely to washers. By 1924, 20 percent of all washing machines in the world were Maytags. The company made its one-millionth washer in 1927 before moving on to make dryers, dishwashers, ranges, and refrigerators.

BANNED IN BOSTON

*It's hard to believe, but Boston—in many ways, one of the most liberal
cities in the nation—once led the country in suppression. Here's
how the phrase "banned in Boston" became synonymous
with anything tawdry and controversial.*

CHRISTMAS GETS BANNED

In 1659, just a few decades after they had arrived in the
New World, the Puritans banned the celebration of
Christmas (as well as gambling and congregation for non-religious
purposes). The holiday reminded them of Old World customs
from England (the nation from which they'd fled to escape religious persecution). In fact, they refused to consider December 25th
a holy day at all—the Catholic Church had selected the date as
the day to celebrate Christ's birthday because it coincided with an
ancient, popular *pagan* festival. Anybody in Boston caught singing,
drinking, playing games, or having a feast on Christmas was fined
five shillings. The bans were later revoked, but it wouldn't be the
last time a moral outcry deprived Bostonians of diversions that
seem relatively harmless today.

BOOKS GET BANNED

In 1878 a Methodist minister from Boston named J. Frank Chase
formed the Watch and Ward Society, dedicated to banning all
books he considered indecent or obscene (which meant books
that had any sexual content). Boston's population, especially
conservative Irish Catholic immigrants, supported Chase's crusade against "filth." The Society even had an agreement with
police—all complaints about indecent books were sent directly
to the Society. If the Society thought the book was indecent, it
notified Boston booksellers that they had three days to remove
the book from their shelves or they could be arrested on obscenity charges. The Watch and Ward Society held power in Boston
for over half a century.

• They banned Walt Whitman's *Leaves of Grass* in 1882, Thomas
Hardy's *Tess of the D'Urbervilles* in 1891, and Elinor Glyn's 1907
bestseller *Three Weeks*. They all depicted premarital sex.

Wide load: The average iceberg weighs 20 million tons.

• In 1926 author and editor H. L. Mencken directly challenged the Society's authority. He went to Boston and publicly sold an issue of his literary magazine, *American Mercury*, which featured a short story entitled "Hatrack." The plot: A prostitute goes to a Methodist church to seek forgiveness, is shunned, and returns to prostitution. The Methodist-based Watch and Ward Society called the story both obscene and personally offensive and took Mencken to court on obscenity charges. Mencken won.

• In 1928 the Society tried to ban *Candide*, Voltaire's 1759 satire, for blasphemy and sex, and Aldous Huxley's *Point Counter Point* for depicting a man who *considers* cheating on his wife. Neither attempt was successful, although they were able to remove Erich Maria Remarque's *All Quiet on the Western Front* in 1929 because of vulgar language.

The Watch and Ward Society's reign over Boston ended for good in 1948. The new director, Dwight Strong, changed the organization's name to the New England Citizens Crime Commission and focused on gambling, not books. They would have been powerless in just a few years, anyway: Several Supreme Court rulings denied a city's legal ability to regulate books.

MUSIC AND THEATER GET BANNED

From 1955 to 1982, Richard Sinnott (pronounced "sin-not") served as chief of Boston's licensing division, which oversaw health and safety at entertainment venues. That allowed Sinnott to ban or change any performance he deemed "morally unhealthy."

• **"Louie, Louie."** In 1955 many people thought the nearly incomprehensible lyrics *had* to be obscene. Sinnott investigated, but a proposal to prevent bands from performing the song had to be dropped because Sinnott couldn't understand the lyrics, either.

• *Who's Afraid of Virginia Woolf?* In 1963 Sinnott threatened to cancel performances of Edward Albee's Tony Award-winning play. Reason: Some dialogue "took the name of the Lord in vain." To avoid the cancellation, producers agreed to change any references to Jesus to "Mary Magdalene."

• **The Jackson Five.** The pop group was banned from performing in 1970 because Sinnott thought they had violent fans.

• **Marvin Gaye.** In 1975 a federal judge ordered Boston to integrate its public schools, leading to the busing of inner-city minority kids to mostly white schools. Racially motivated violence and rioting ensued. Sinnott banned Marvin Gaye from performing in Boston because "we didn't want black and white together so they wouldn't kill each other."

• **Ozzy Osbourne.** In one of Sinnott's last acts on the job (his position was eliminated in 1982), Osbourne was banned from performing in Boston shortly after he was arrested in San Antonio for urinating on the Alamo.

Surprisingly, in 1960 Sinnott *didn't* ban a ballet that featured topless women. Because the show was about Africa and featured African choreography, Sinnott reasoned that the topless dancing made sense and was essential to the ballet.

MORE BANS

Many other groups and individuals have taken it upon themselves to protect Bostonians—even recently.

• *Welcome Back, Kotter.* In 1975 Boston's ABC affiliate WCVB-TV refused to air the new sitcom *Welcome Back, Kotter*. Because it was about juvenile delinquents? No—because they thought it was about school busing and desegregation. After blacking out the first eight episodes, the station aired the show to no complaint.

• *The Warriors.* When the ultra-violent movie about street gangs was released in 1979, two teenagers in New York City died as a result of copycat violence. A few members of the Massachusetts legislature (from Boston) introduced a bill to ban the movie in Beantown. The bill failed.

• **Video-game ads.** In 2006 a Boston advocacy group called the Campaign for a Commercial-Free Childhood asked the city to remove ads for the violent video game Grand Theft Auto from subway cars. The Massachusetts Bus and Transit Authority refused.

*   *   *

"I believe in censorship. I made a fortune out of it."

—Mae West

HAPPY CHICKEN WINGS DAY!

...and other weird—but real—"holidays."

JANUARY: Oatmeal Month
Jan. 6: Fruitcake Toss Day
Jan. 29: Bubble Wrap Appreciation Day
Jan. 30: Inane Answering Message Day

FEBRUARY: Return Shopping Carts to the Supermarket Month
Feb. 4: Dump Your Significant Jerk Day
Feb. 11: White Shirt Day
Feb. 28: National Tooth Fairy Day

MARCH: International Mirth Month
Mar. 13: National Open an Umbrella Indoors Day
Mar. 18: Awkward Moments Day
Mar. 26: Make Up Your Own Holiday Day
Mar. 31: Bunsen Burner Day

APRIL: Straw Hat Month
(*Sponsor: Headwear Information Bureau*)
Apr. 7: No Housework Day
Apr. 11: Barbershop Quartet Day
Apr. 17: Blah! Blah! Blah! Day
Apr. 21: World Cow Chip Day

MAY: National Correct Posture Month (*Sponsor: American Chiropractic Association*)
May 2: No Pants Day
May 11: Eat Whatever You Want Day
May 16: National Sea-Monkey Day
May 24: Tiara Day

JUNE: Potty Training Awareness Month
June 21: Pee on Earth Day
June 25: Please Take My Children to Work Day
June 29: Chicken Wings Day

JULY: Baked Bean Month
July 6: Take Your Webmaster to Lunch Day
July 15: Be a Dork Day
July 23: Gorgeous Grandma Day
July 27: Walk on Stilts Day

AUGUST: Get Ready for Kindergarten Month
Aug. 8: National Underwear Day
Aug. 10: Duran Duran Appreciation Day
Aug. 17: Men's Grooming Day
Aug. 31: Love Litigating Lawyers Day

That swollen, light-colored section seen on earthworms has a name: the *clitellum*.

SEPTEMBER: National Coupon Month

Sept. 8: Bald Is Beautiful Day

Sept. 9: Wonderful Weirdos Day

Sept. 22: Hobbit Day

OCTOBER: National Pajama Month

Oct. 10: National Bring Your Teddy Bear to Work Day

Oct. 12: International Moment of Frustration Scream Day

Oct. 23: TV Talk Show Host Day

NOVEMBER: Celebrate Empty Nester Month

Nov. 3: Cliché Day

Nov. 15: National Bundt Pan Day

Nov. 25: Blasé Day

DECEMBER: National Women's Volleyball Month

Dec. 15: Cat Herders Day

Dec. 16: Barbie Backlash Day

Dec. 25: A'phabet Day (It's "No 'L' Day." Get it? "Noel"—it's Christmas.)

*   *   *

SAVED BY THE CELL

While Esther Green was waiting for a friend outside a store in an Atlanta suburb, she climbed into the back seat of her Mercedes to sit with her 10-month-old daughter. At the same time, two car-jackers jumped into the front seat and started driving the car away—with Green and her baby still in the back seat. Very discreetly, Green reached into the baby's diaper bag and dialed 911 on her cell phone. She immediately started dropping clues to the dispatcher. First, she established what was happening: "Please stop the car....Please let me get my baby out of the car. Please. Please." Then she started giving road names, such as, "Why are we on Highway 314?" and "This is Belles and Beaus. Why don't y'all let us out?" Green also gave clues as to the make and color of the car, as well where they were headed: "You're going toward Riverdale." She didn't even know if anyone was listening on the other end, but kept the act going just in case. Luckily, Holly Eason, the 911 dispatcher, understood exactly what Green was doing and relayed all of the information to the police. After a scary 16-minute car ride, the carjackers were captured without a fight, and Green and her daughter emerged unharmed.

Princess Diana was 1/64 Armenian.

MARTIAL ARTS

There are numerous different forms of martial arts, and they come from all over Asia, including Japan, China, and Korea. Some, like karate and jujitsu, are on the martial end of the spectrum; others, like T'ai Chi, are more, well, arty. Here's a look at some of the most popular forms.

JUJITSU. "Yielding or compliant art," in Japanese. Jujitsu emphasizes yielding to your opponent's force and using it against him. Developed at a time when samurai wore body armor, it also incorporates blows to the face and other unprotected parts of the body.

AIKIDO. A martial art with spiritual and even pacifist origins, this "Way of Harmonious Spirit" idealizes defending yourself from attackers without harming them, largely by locking up their joints and tossing them aside.

JUDO. Translates as "gentle way" in Japanese. Gentle? It turns out that in judo, "gentle" means grabbing your opponents and throwing them to the ground…but without kicking or punching them.

KARATE. "Empty Hand" emphasizes fierce blows to vulnerable parts of the body (throat, stomach, etc.) using hands, feet, elbows, and knees.

TAE KWON DO. Translates as "kick punch art" from Korean. Like karate, tae kwon do features sharp blows with bare hands and feet.

KUNG FU. A Chinese form of karate, practiced for more than 1,000 years. Kung fu favors flowing, circular movements over the sharp kicks, punches, and jabs found in other popular forms of karate.

JEET KUNE DO. "The Way of the Intercepting Fist." A style of kung fu formulated by Bruce Lee, Jeet Kune Do abandons the rigid stances found in many martial arts in favor of more fluid movements Lee had observed in boxing and fencing competitions.

T'AI CHI CH'UAN. Translates as "supreme ultimate boxing," but it's actually a Chinese method of stress relief and relaxation through stretching, correct posture, and slow movements timed with breathing exercises.

DUMB CROOKS

Here's more proof that crime doesn't pay.

PHONE-Y ARREST

Justin Graci mugged two Rutgers University students in May 2003. After he punched one of them in the stomach, he got away with $20. But Graci dropped his cell phone at the scene. Police officer James Bobadilla found it while interviewing the victims and answered it when it rang. It was Graci. Not knowing he was talking to a cop, he offered Bobadilla a bag of marijuana for the phone's return. Bobadilla agreed to meet Graci at a nearby motel. The victims came along and identified Graci as their attacker, and he was immediately arrested for robbery (and drug possession).

GETTING THE JOB DONE

Twenty-year-old Anthony Kaleb Phillips went to a construction site in Stillwater, Oklahoma, in June 2003 to apply for a job. There was nobody around, so instead of leaving an application, he stole $1,000 worth of power tools and other items from an employee's car. Amazingly, Phillips returned to the site the next day to apply for the job again, but employees recognized him as the thief from surveillance video and called the police.

LIAR, LIAR...

Tallahassee, Florida, police spotted Carl Franklin standing beside a fence with his pants down, about to relieve himself. The cops shouted at him to stop, so he ran. Apparently he'd been smoking before peeing and put the lit cigarette in his pants pocket for safekeeping. The cops quickly caught up with the man, whose pants were on fire.

DON'T BE SO HASTY

In August 1992, Donald Murray was on trial in Gastonia, North Carolina. When the jury retired to the deliberation room to decide his fate, he got so scared they would return with a guilty verdict that he jumped up and ran out of the courtroom, successfully escaping. A few moments later, the jury returned with its decision: not guilty. An arrest warrant was issued for Murray.

NO-GOOD ALIEN PUNKS

A Pennsylvania man came home one night in 2003 to find his window broken and a man bleeding profusely, lying on the couch. It was obvious that the bleeding man, Brian Waddington, had tried to burglarize the home. But he claimed aliens had kidnapped him, flew him 170 miles, and randomly dropped him off at the house. Police weren't amused; they arrested Waddington for burglary. "I assure you that if our detectives find any aliens," a police spokesman said, "we'll drop the charges."

GREAT EXCUSE

A man on trial for murder in Nashua, New Hampshire, in 2004 pled not guilty to the charge and took the stand in his own defense. His alibi: He couldn't have committed the murder because at the time of the crime, he was trying to kill a man in Lowell, Massachusetts.

THIS IS YOUR BRAIN ON DRUGS

Simon McDermott, a police officer in Visalia, California, brought a search warrant to the home of a suspected marijuana grower. He found the drugs, so he arrested the suspect. While the suspect called his lawyer, McDermott found the man's diary, which detailed his drug-growing operation. This conversation followed:

Suspect: Do you want me to explain that to you?
McDermott: Didn't you just talk to a lawyer?
Suspect: Yes.
McDermott: What did he tell you?
Suspect: I don't remember.
McDermott: Didn't he just tell you not to speak to me?
Suspect: Oh, yeah.
McDermott: Then you probably shouldn't explain it.
Suspect: Oh, yeah. Thanks, man.

EVEN BURGLARS GET SLEEPY

Daniel Wootton, 21, broke into a Bartlett, New Hampshire, house, ransacked it, and put his plunder in a bag by the front door. Then he decided to take a nap. In the house. A neighbor spotted Wootton's suspicious car in the driveway and called police, who had to wake up Wootton so they could arrest him.

Li'l fascist: Benito Mussolini was expelled from school for stabbing another kid in the buttocks.

TV NEWS UNFILTERED

Next time you think there's nothing on TV, remember Brian Lamb's story and spend a few minutes watching his channel. What channel? Read on.

MR. LAMB GOES TO WASHINGTON

During the Vietnam War, a young navy lieutenant from Indiana named Brian Lamb was assigned to the Pentagon press office to report troop deaths to the media. The amount of information either omitted or censored in order to paint a rosier picture of the war appalled him. "The government lied to us," he later recalled. "We just weren't getting the straight scoop."

During that time, Lamb also served as an aide in the Johnson White House. Once again he saw a huge gap between what the American people knew and what was really happening. "I got a firsthand education about how the media interacts with the government, and it led me to think that there could be a better way."

That better way was a news outlet that would report what was happening in politics—with two major differences: 1) no censorship from government; and 2) no commentary from media pundits.

FINDING AN IN

Over the next decade, as Lamb worked in various television and political jobs, he tried to drum up support for a news channel that showed gavel-to-gavel coverage of Congress. Although many people agreed that it was a good idea, it wasn't feasible. Why? The Big Three networks had cornered the market on delivering the news to the masses. And besides, all-day congressional debate wasn't exactly something the public was clamoring for. But then in the late 1970s, cable TV hit the scene. That changed everything.

Cable meant more channels, which meant Lamb now had a place to put his network. But he still needed money and—more importantly—he needed the government's permission.

• Government approval was the easy part. In 1977 Lamb met with House Speaker Tip O'Neill and learned that Congress had been thinking the same thing—they'd recently passed House Resolution 866, permitting broadcast coverage of House proceedings.

Producer Robert Stigwood came up with "The Bee Gees." The band preferred "Rupert's World."

• Finding the money took a little longer. Lamb knew that trying to convince taxpayers to pay for a free government-access channel would be a tough sell, so instead he went to the CEOs of emerging cable companies around the country and asked *them* to finance the channel by setting aside a small percentage of their revenue. The response was slow at first, but after Bob Rosencrans, the CEO of Columbia Cablevision, wrote a check for $25,000, others chipped in, and Lamb found himself with $400,000.

AMERICA'S NETWORK OF RECORD

On March 19, 1979, the Cable-Satellite Public Affairs Network, or C-SPAN, with a staff of four, began cablecasting the United States House of Representatives daily proceedings (gavel-to-gavel and without commentary) to 3.5 million households. At first it only aired from 8:00 a.m. to 5:00 p.m. on weekdays, but soon switched to 24-hour coverage, replaying the day's events in prime-time. In 1980 C-SPAN added a call-in feature to give people the opportunity to ask politicians direct questions. This was the first large-scale avenue for regular citizens to speak directly to their political representatives. That year C-SPAN also received its first of many Cable Ace Awards. By 1984 it was covering every political event to which it had access, and really made its mark during the presidential campaign. While the Big Three covered the highlights, C-SPAN broadcast every minute of the Iowa caucus and both the Republican and Democratic national conventions.

THIS LAMB AIN'T NO SHEEP

Over the years, Lamb has had to remain diligent to ensure that the network's coverage remains both complete and objective. C-SPAN has never received a cent from either political party (not that they haven't offered). Corporations have also offered to pay the network substantial fees in return for displaying their logos onscreen. And on a few occasions C-SPAN has been asked to omit or edit certain sections of congressional debates that got out of hand. Lamb's response is always the same: No.

Yet while C-SPAN strives to be nonpartisan, both sides have accused the network of bias: In March 2007, conservatives accused it of catering to the left by broadcasting coverage of an anti-Iraq War march, but staying away from a smaller march in favor of the

Oops! Cover of *Time* magazine on March 21, 1983: "New Plan for Arms Contol."

war. On the other side, liberals point to reports that C-SPAN's morning call-in show, *Washington Journal*, features nearly twice as many Republicans as Democrats. So does Lamb have a political bias? He won't say. "I vote in every general election, but I'm not a party member—I've never told anyone who I've voted for."

RATINGS, SHMATINGS

One way Lamb curtails the criticism is to completely ignore C-SPAN's numbers. "We don't know whether we have three viewers or three hundred thousand," he says. "It's probably a good thing, too, because then someone might be on our backs to increase the numbers, or worse, we'd stop broadcasting what deserves to be on." What is known is this: 85 million homes receive C-SPAN; 52 million people admit to being "sometime" or "regular" viewers.

And they have a lot to tune in to. Today C-SPAN consists of three separate networks, a radio station, and 17 Web sites. In 1996 the network added *About Books*, which gives authors exposure they couldn't get anywhere else. And even though C-SPAN is now a multimedia juggernaut, it's still a nonprofit organization and still receives its money solely from cable companies. "C-SPAN," says Lamb, "is the voice of America, with all its flaws."

WHAT'S ON C-SPAN?

Think it's just long-winded politicians speaking into microphones on the House floor? Well, most of it is, but you can also find:

• **International flair:** The often-lively proceedings of the Parliaments of the United Kingdom and Canada.

• **State funerals:** Every big funeral from Richard Nixon to Rosa Parks. "Our coverage of funerals is very popular," boasts Lamb.

• **Political goofs:** Regular C-SPAN viewers see their fair share of questionable political gestures and slips of the tongue. For example, in July 2006, Senator Joe Biden of Delaware said on camera that "you cannot go into a Dunkin' Donuts or a 7-Eleven unless you have a slight Indian accent." (He later said it was a compliment.) And in July 2007, Senator Bill Nelson of Florida said on the Senate floor, "Certainly, all the intercourse that I had as a military officer was the best. But that was not the case for a lot of our returning soldiers." (He was talking about how he was treated by the public after returning home from Vietnam. We think.)

DIAPER SIN
IS REPAID

A palindrome is a word or phrase that reads the same backward as it does forward. Some classic examples: "Madam, I'm Adam," or "race car." Here are a few more we've collected.

Lager, Sir, is regal.

A nut for a jar of tuna.

I roamed under it as a tired, nude Maori.

Lived on decaf, faced no devil.

I did roll. Or did I?

Too hot to hoot.

Darn ocelots stole Conrad.

Straw warts.

Feeble Tom's motel beef.

Did I draw Della too tall, Edward? I did!

He won a Toyota now, eh?

Step on no pets.

Dr. Awkward.

Never odd or even.

Draw putrid dirt upward.

Young Ada had a gnu. Oy!

Reviled, I wonder if I fired. Now, I deliver!

Zeus sees Suez.

E.T. is opposite.

Mom's Dad? Dad's Mom?

Stop! Murder us not, tonsured rumpots!

Cigar? Toss it in a can. It is so tragic.

Lisa Bonet ate no basil.

Egad, a base life defiles a bad age.

"Bed stress!" asserts Deb.

Gary knits a stinky rag.

Did I strap red nude, red rump, also slap murdered underparts? I did!

Eh, Canada had an ache?

Gabe's on a nosebag.

Oh, cameras are macho.

Diaper sin is repaid.

Emil's slime.

Am I loco, Lima?

Shaquille O'Neal was sworn in as a Miami Beach reserve police officer on December 8, 2005.

LUCKY FINDS

*Ever find something valuable? It's one of the best feelings
in the world. Here's another installment of one
of our favorite* Bathroom Reader *topics.*

GOOD LOVE, BAD MEMORY
The Find: A wallet
Where It Was Found: In a car
The Story: In 1952, while Glenn Goodlove was home in western
Washington on leave from the navy, he met a young lady and the
two spent some time necking in the backseat of his grandfather's
1946 Hudson. More than 50 years later, Goodlove received a telephone call at his San Diego, California, home. The caller said that
he'd found a wallet in the back of a car he was restoring and
thought it might be Goodlove's. Then Goodlove remembered the
car, and the girl, and how he'd lost his wallet. "If it was in my
sailor mentality," he later told reporters, "I might have attempted
to, as we said back then, 'make out.'"

Jon Beck, 61, and Chuck Merrill, 72, had been restoring the
out-of-commission Hudson in Twin Falls, Idaho, when Merrill
"saw something about to fall out." Seeing it was a wallet, they
were hoping there was a bunch of money inside it. The final tally
was only $11, but they also found Goodlove's first driver's license
(it was handwritten), his military ID, a $1 silver certificate, and
some jewelry receipts (most likely for the girl he was wooing).
Said the 76-year-old Goodlove, "It's a miracle."

WORTH A THOUSAND WORDS
The Find: A camera
Where it was: In a vacant lot
The Story: Leslie Mason owns some property in Menasha, Wisconsin. In March 2007, her son was cutting down some trees along the
border of the vacant lakeside lot when he spotted an expensive-
looking digital camera in the bushes. Mason checked the camera
and found the contact info for a professional photographer named
Charles Boesen on it. She called Boesen and told him she'd found
his camera. He was surprised—it had been stolen a year earlier,

right after he photographed a wedding but before he made prints for the newlyweds, Karen and Tory Nordlinder. Amazingly, when Boesen checked the camera, the memory card was still intact. Could the digital information have survived a rough Wisconsin winter? He put the card into his computer and—there were the pictures. "I almost cried," said the relieved photographer. "I'm thinking, this bride is going to be so overjoyed when she finds out." And she was, saying, "This is just something I never thought we'd see. Ever!"

MUGGED

The Find: A wallet

Where It Was Found: Behind the wall of an old theater

The Story: On April 11, 1951, Val Gregoire was mugged on his way back to Boston Harbor to report to his ship, the USS *Macon*. The thief punched him and then stole his wallet and pants. (Without his wallet, the 18-year-old sailor couldn't prove his identity to the guards and ended up spending a night in the brig.) On April 11, 2007—56 years to the day after the wallet went missing—a demolition worker named Richard Bagen found the old, partially disintegrated wallet behind a wall at the Paramount Theater in Boston. The wallet was falling apart, but the items inside were perfectly preserved (minus the money). There were photos, Gregoire's birth certificate, and the ID card that would have kept him from spending that night in the brig. Bagen's wife, Kathy, was so amazed that the date on the weekend pass was exactly 56 years earlier that she decided to track down the owner of the wallet. She searched for the name "Gregoire" on the Internet, and after a few tries reached Val's widow, Jeannette, in Lewiston, Maine. "At first I thought she was a solicitor," she said. But then she remembered the mugging story—she'd actually been with Val earlier that day and had heard him tell the story of losing his wallet and pants many times over the next 50 years. "I was stunned," she said. "How could this have survived?" (No word on the whereabouts of the pants.)

"SQUAWWWK! DUSTY WANTS A RIDE HOME!"

The Find: A parrot

Where It Was Found: In Las Vegas

The Story: After Dusty, a Congo African Grey parrot, flew out of

---

Q: What's an *olf*? A: A unit of indoor odor equal to one day's effluence from a sedentary human.

the window of his New Boston, Michigan, home in late 2006, his owner, April Konopka, was forlorn. "I tried to run after him but I have a prosthetic knee," she lamented. "I fell, and I cried because he just kept going higher and higher." Konopka began an intense search, utilizing Web sites that help people find lost pets. But as autumn turned to winter, and winter to spring, Konopka's hope faded. In nearly all cases, if a bird that flies the coop isn't found within a week or two, it won't be recovered at all. But then one day in May 2007, a truck driver called her from Las Vegas—2,000 miles away. He had found a bird that matched her pet's description, he told her. Was it Dusty? Konopka asked to speak to it. "As soon as Dusty heard my voice," she said, "he went right for the phone and started saying, 'Hello!'" Konopka had no doubt it was Dusty. The bird was trucked back home to Michigan, and the happy couple was reunited. Konopka now keeps the windows closed when Dusty is out of his cage.

*　　*　　*

ELVIS IN THE HEADLINES

The King died in 1977, but he's still in the news on a regular basis. Here are a few headlines we found recently.

Kanye West and Elvis Top U.K. Charts
(*I Like Music*, U.K.)

eBay Steal of the Week: Elvis-Chewed Gum
(*Washington Post*)

County Attorney "All Shook Up" as Elvis
(*Minnesota This Week*)

Elvis Straightened my Eyelashes
(*Niagara Gazette*, New York)

Dentist Buys Elvis Presley's Crown
(FOX News)

"I Saw Elvis in a Cloud"
(*I-C-Wales*, U.K.)

Tiny Elvis
(AOL News)

Earnhardt Jr. Pays Tribute to Elvis
(*Kansas City Star*)

Elvis Re-appears to the Delight of Fountain Lake Rehab fans
(*Hot Springs Village Voice*, Arkansas)

Elvis Who?
(*Manila Standard Today*, Philippines)

Because of Saturn's tilt and the thinness of its rings, every 14 years the rings seem to disappear.

KIMI GAYO

*Ladies and gentleman, please sit down for the story
of the national anthem of Japan. (But stand
up when the anthem is actually played.)*

GREAT WALL OF JAPAN

In 1853 the American naval fleet, under the command of Commodore Matthew Perry, sailed into Tokyo Bay, forcing an end to Japan's 200-year, self-imposed isolation. As trade with the West began, it ushered in an era of rapid modernization, both politically and technologically.

The Japanese soon recognized that they didn't have the kind of national symbols used by countries in the Western world, and decided they wanted their own. They adopted the Rising Sun banner as their flag, since their name for their nation, Nippon, means "the place where the sun rises." But they still needed a national anthem.

GOD SAVE THE EMPEROR!

In 1869 the royal court of Japan commissioned an Irish military band leader in Yokohama, John William Fenton, to compose music for "Kimi Gayo," a beloved Japanese poem written hundreds of years earlier by an unknown poet. The 31-syllable poem (called a *tanka*) is a paean to the emperor meaning "May 1,000 Years of Happy Reign Be Yours." Fenton's music sounded a lot like the British national anthem, "God Save the King," but used the traditional lyrics the Japanese people loved.

The song remained Japan's national anthem for 11 years, until the imperial household decided they wanted a more Japanese-sounding hymn. In 1880 Hiromori Hayashi, the leader of the royal court musicians, was directed to write new, traditional Japanese music for the old poem. His new arrangement was first played for Emperor Mutsuhito on his birthday, November 3, 1880. And in 1903 the song became the pride of the nation when, at the International National Anthem Contest held in Berlin, Germany, "Kimi Gayo" won first prize for the most beautiful anthem in the world.

Bet you can't try them all: The United States has 300 different types of fast-food chains.

THE HISTORY OF BREAD, PART I

We hope you get a rise out of this story—it cost us a lot of dough to put it together, but it was the yeast we could do!

RISE AND SHINE

Did you eat a sandwich today? Did you have an English muffin this morning or a slice of pizza last night? Americans eat 34 million loaves of bread per day, not to mention rolls, baguettes, bagels, croissants, pitas, doughnuts, and dozens of other kinds of bread. Bread was the first processed food in human history, and it's still the world's largest single food category—more people eat some form of bread on a daily basis than any other food product.

Most bread falls into one of two groups: *leavened*, which rises with the help of an ingredient (yeast is the most common leavening agent) and *unleavened*, which is basically flat. Many flat varieties—for example, Mexican tortillas, Jewish matzo, Norwegian flatbrød, or Indian chapati—have remained virtually unchanged for thousands of years. But the history of bread is really about the flatbreads that *did* change—and evolved into the leavened loaves we know today.

TIMELINE

• The history of bread begins with wild grain. According to historians, around 11000 B.C. huge fields of grain appeared in southwest Asia as the glaciers began to retreat. Nomadic people ate the raw seeds (in addition to whatever else they could gather).

• By about 8000 B.C., people had learned that the seeds could be planted and cultivated, that they would yield reliable crops, and that families could be fed from those crops. It was the beginning of agriculture; traditional nomadic life evolved into settlements (after all, if you're going to raise crops like wheat, barley, spelt, rye, and oats, you've got to stay put). And with the introduction of the mortar and pestle for grinding the grain into flour, most of these early agrarian cultures invented some kind of bread—flat, coarse, and probably not very tasty, but they were sustaining and they lasted longer than foods that had to be hunted or gathered daily.

The walrus has only one known natural predator—the orca.

• The next few thousand years saw all kinds of agricultural developments that helped make bread a staple food: Farmers along the Euphrates River in the Middle East invented plows and irrigated fields around 4000 B.C.; the Sumerians invented a sickle for harvesting grain; farmers in northern China learned to cultivate wheat and barley strains that tolerated low rainfall; and in eastern Europe, where the growing season is too short for wheat, rye became a major crop.

CIVILIZATION ON THE RISE

• Around 2000 B.C., the Egyptians hit the jackpot: They discovered leavening, the ingredient that makes bread rise. The discovery probably came about by accident, when airborne wild yeast spores got into some bread dough. Yeast is a living microorganism that occurs naturally in the environment—on plants, in the soil, and on animals. And under the right conditions (warm liquid, and sugar or starch to feed on), it will grow and produce carbon dioxide, which, in the case of bread, bubbles through the dough and makes it rise. And that's what makes bread light and fluffy. (Wild yeast was also noted for its ability to *ferment* the sugars in grain. The by-product of fermentation is alcohol, which made another food possible—beer, which the Egyptians valued highly.)

• The Egyptians also figured out how to use two stones for grinding grain to make flour with a much finer texture than the old mortar and pestle had yielded. Egyptians were expert wheat growers, but it was a labor-intensive crop, which made wheat flour expensive to produce. Result: Common people ate cheaper, coarser, darker, flatter barley bread; the wealthy ate finer, whiter, fluffier wheat bread.

• One more Egyptian innovation: Flat stones or griddles were used for baking flatbreads, but the Egyptians had a class of professional bakers who used cone-shaped clay ovens, with which they could control the heat for making leavened bread.

SAIL AWAY

• Around 600 B.C., Phoenician sailors brought Egyptian flour and bread technology to Greece. The Greeks already had a bread-baking culture, but they quickly adopted the Egyptian improvements and soon Greek states vied with each other in bread-making skill

---

Technically speaking, "midday" is the exact moment the Sun crosses the local meridian.

(Athens claimed to be the best). They further advanced the development of bread through the use of a Greek invention: the front-loading oven, an improvement over the Egyptians' top-opening version.

• From Greece, bread know-how spread west to Rome. The Romans considered bread even more important than meat, and it was a stabilizing factor in the smooth running of the Roman welfare state: Grain was distributed to the populace of Rome (later the government even baked the bread), and Roman soldiers were adamant about receiving their full allotment of bread.

MIDDLE-AGE SPREAD

• The expansion of the Roman Empire northward took Greek bread-baking techniques throughout Europe. But with the decline of the Empire around 400 A.D., the quality of bread-making skills declined, too, and unleavened bread became the norm again. During the first half of the Middle Ages (400–1000 A.D.) bread history gets a little hazy, but the Normans are believed to have reintroduced leavened bread to England in the 12th century, and by the 13th century all of Europe again had better flour, better bakers, and better bread.

• Milling and baking soon became highly skilled professions, making millers and bakers influential and rich. *Bakehouses* (the medieval term for "bakeries"), with their large ovens, were serious fire hazards, so they were built far from the shops where the bread was sold. The bakehouses usually belonged to feudal lords, who allowed bakers to use the ovens for a fee or in exchange for bread. Gradually bakers began setting up their own bakehouses (sometimes communally owned), and forming guilds to protect themselves from the lords and to regulate bread production.

THE ROLL OF LAW

• In 1266 England established the "Assize of Bread," a set of laws regulating the weight and price of bread. Because bread was such an important staple, bakers were in a position to take advantage of consumers by price gouging. These laws regulated bread prices in relation to the price of grain. If a baker broke those laws (they were in force until the 19th century), he could be punished severely, even banned from baking for life. The penalties were so severe that bakers got into the habit of giving an extra measure of bread (13 instead of 12) so they couldn't be accused of short-changing customers, which is the origin of the term "baker's dozen."

RYE COMMENTS

• During the next few centuries, bread continued to be the staple food of most people's diets, and since the majority of people were poor, it was a heavy brown bread made from the cheaper grains—barley, oats, or rye. But because people had become so dependent on bread, governments and rulers survived and flourished *only* if they could supply enough bread to their people...or control the rebellions that broke out when they couldn't. Example: The storming of the Bastille in Paris, which set off the French Revolution in 1789, began with a bread riot.

• In the 1800s, most bread was still baked with homegrown (or brewery-grown) yeast. It was time-consuming to nurture, and performed unpredictably. In 1825 German bakers introduced packaged cake yeast that made home baking easier, and made the results more consistent (and tastier). Two Austrian brothers, Charles and Max Fleischmann, brought the innovation to America. In 1868 they opened a factory for the commercial production of compressed yeast in Cincinnati. (Fleischmann's is still the biggest producer of yeast for home baking, but home baking isn't what it used to be—by the 1960s almost *all* of America's bread was made commercially.)

• By the late 19th century, the Industrial Revolution was in full swing, and gas-fueled ovens had replaced wood- and coal-burners. With the European invention of more efficient steam-powered flour mills, it became possible to produce enough wheat flour so that for the first time, white bread was affordable to most people. At the same time, the newly developing heartland of America was producing so much wheat that huge amounts of bread could now be turned out efficiently in industrial-scale bakeries. By the early 1900s, factory-made white bread was available all across Europe and North America.

How did mass production turn bread into the pre-sliced loaf that's in almost every kitchen today?
For Part II of the story, turn to page 415.

SMILE: YOU'RE ON DUMB#*% CAMERA!

No, really—you are. Right now. Look out the window.

HI, HONEY!
In May 2007, a TV crew in a helicopter was shooting scenes of the Giro d'Italia bicycle race (similar to the Tour de France) in northern Italy. As the camera panned over from the race to a man and a woman on the beach, the man looked up, smiled, and waved. The shot went out on live television, where the man's brother-in-law saw it, recognized him, and excitedly called his sister's cell phone to tell her he'd seen them on TV. Only problem: His sister wasn't at the bicycle race—she was home alone, and her husband was away on business. The woman in the shot turned out to be his mistress. (No word on whether he's still married.)

I DON'T NEED NO STINKIN' PANTSES!

In February 2003, police in Cardiff, Wales, arrested a man walking down the town's main street in his underpants—only his underpants—carrying a shovel, which he had used to smash 43 shop windows. The primary evidence against Andrew Roxberry, 30, was video surveillance footage taken the night of the window-smashing spree. After his first court appearance (he pled guilty), police released the video to the press. The police didn't say why they released the video, which was shown on all of the U.K.'s major TV news broadcasts, but one can only assume it was for the entertainment value.

NAKED AMBITION

A man walked into the Kwik Fill convenience store in Menallen Township, Pennsylvania, in October 2006, and, as the store's video *clearly* showed, took off all his clothes and tried to seduce the clerk. All romantic activities came to an abrupt halt when his girlfriend walked in and saw what he was doing. The 25-year-old

---

The English horn was invented in France.

man was arrested a week later and charged with indecent expo-sure. (That was probably the least of his worries.)

DID HE SMELL GOOD?

A man held up a bank in Orlando, Florida, in November 1995, but even though he was caught on video doing it, police couldn't identify the burglar because he was wearing a disguise—fake glasses with a large plastic nose. Hoping for some tips, they gave a photo of the man to the *Orlando Sentinel*. Numerous people called to identify the man as Charles Newman. How did they recognize him? By the nose: It turned out it wasn't fake—he just has a really huge nose.

MOORE SMARTER

Craig Moore of Doncaster, England, was speeding down a road near his home when he saw the telltale flash of a speed camera. He returned to the scene of the crime a short while later with a cache of explosives…and blew up the camera. That, he thought, would get him out of a ticket. But the speed trap pictures weren't in the camera—they were safely stored (digitally) in a remote location. Not only that, but the blast from the explosives, which Moore had stolen from his workplace (he's a railway welder), caused the camera to take one last photograph before it was destroyed. It was of Moore. The explosion caused more than $23,000 worth of damage, earning Moore a hefty fine and four months in prison.

*   *   *

BAD NEWS BEAR

"Christmas shopper Roy Edensor was stunned when a teddy bear he had bought for his son shouted 'PR*CK!' when he took it out of the box. The talking toy is a copy of Nev the Bear—star of CBBC's *Smile* show. It should say 'I love you,' 'Fwightened' and 'Yum Yum.' Edensor bought the toy at a local shop. He said: 'I could not believe my ears.' Store managers say they have removed a batch of the bears and are investigating."

—*The Sun* (U.K.)

Flying fish can swim—and glide through the air—as fast as 45 mph.

TEST YOUR MOVIE IQ

Like it or not, movies are ingrained in American culture. Don't believe it? Take this quiz and see if you can identify the classic Hollywood films these famous lines come from. You may be surprised at how quickly each movie comes back to you from just a single line. (But before you start, ask yourself one question: "Do I feel lucky?" Well, do ya, punk?)

1. "Well, here's another nice mess you've gotten me into!"

2. "Oh, no, it wasn't the airplanes. 'Twas Beauty killed the Beast."

3. "Plastics."

4. "I *am* big! It's the pictures that got small."

5. "You talkin' to me?"

6. "I'm mad as hell, and I'm not going to take this anymore!"

7. "Snap out of it!"

8. "You know how to whistle, don't you, Steve? You just put your lips together and blow."

9. "We rob banks."

10. "Made it, Ma! Top of the world!"

11. "I'll have what she's having."

12. "They're here!"

13. "Gentlemen, you can't fight in here! This is the War Room!"

14. "I see dead people."

15. "You're gonna need a bigger boat."

16. "Surely you can't be serious!" "I am serious...and don't call me Shirley."

17. "Get your stinking paws off me, you damned dirty ape!"

18. "I'm the king of the world!"

19. "Fasten your seatbelts. It's going to be a bumpy night."

20. "You can't handle the truth!"

21. "Cinderella story. Outta nowhere. A former greenskeeper, now, about to become the Masters champion. It looks like a mirac...It's in the hole! It's in the hole! It's in the hole!"

Fewer than 100 major Hollywood movies have been directed by women.

22. "A boy's best friend is his mother."

23. "I love the smell of napalm in the morning."

24. "No wire hangers, ever!"

25. "There's no crying in baseball!"

26. "What we've got here is a failure to communicate."

27. "Nobody puts Baby in a corner."

28. "Show me the money!"

29. "Love means never having to say you're sorry."

30. "Greed, for lack of a better word, is good."

31. "I'll get you, my pretty, and your little dog, too!"

32. "It's alive! It's alive!"

33. "Mother of mercy, is this the end of Rico?"

34. "One morning I shot an elephant in my pajamas. How he got in my pajamas, I don't know."

35. "Keep your friends close, but your enemies closer."

36. "Carpe diem. Seize the day, boys. Make your lives extraordinary."

37. "Listen to them. Children of the night. What music they make."

38. "I'm walking here! I'm walking here!"

39. "After all, tomorrow is another day!"

40. "Wait a minute, wait a minute. You ain't heard nothin' yet!"

For the answers, turn to page 593.

*   *   *

HADAGREATSHOWERREALLYAWAKENOW!!!!!

If your morning latte isn't doing the trick, now there's "Shower Shock," the world's first caffeinated soap. This vegetable-based glycerin soap releases 200 milligrams of caffeine into your system directly through your pores, providing the same pep as about three normal-sized cups of coffee. (Shower Shock is scented with peppermint oil, so you don't *smell* like a cup of coffee.)

Somebody's gotta do it: Verminus was the Roman god who protects cows against worms.

VAMPIRES PICKET BLOOD BANK!

...and other great (and real) tabloid newspaper headlines.

Researcher Calculates A Snowball's Chance In Hell To Be .000000000134%

MISSING BABY FOUND INSIDE WATERMELON! HE'S ALIVE!

SCIENTIST PROVES EARTH IS GOING THROUGH MENOPAUSE! Global Warming Is Earth's Hot Flashes!

Flea circus goes wild with hunger and attacks trainer!

Researcher finds more than 100 businesses that are like show business!

PROM KING AND QUEEN SEEK U.N. RECOGNITION OF THEIR OWN COUNTRY ...PROMVANIA!

Veggie-Eating Mother Has Green Baby!

MEEK SUE TO INHERIT THE EARTH!

Satan Hires Publicist To Improve His Image!

Firefighter Fired For Fighting Fire With Fire!

Adam and Eve Found in Asia

BIGFOOT CURED MY ARTHRITIS!

Bin Laden Wants To Join ZZ Top!

MOON RAYS TURNED APOLLO ASTRONAUTS INTO WEREWOLVES

Germany invaded—by Nazi raccoons!

Toads explode in "Pond of Death"

2,000-Year-Old Man Found In Tree...Wearing Watch That Still Ticks!

Vampires Picket Blood Bank

SEVEN-YEAR-OLD GANG MEMBER HIJACKS UFO!

Dog lands plane after pilot has heart attack

Night Watchman Sues Over Working Nights

Kenny G.'s real last name is Gorelick.

SONGS THAT CHANGED THE WORLD

Songs that made the whole world sing...or at least sit up and take notice.

The Song: "Do They Know It's Christmas?"
Recorded by: Band Aid
Story: In November 1984, Irish rock musician Bob Geldof of the Boomtown Rats saw a TV news report about the millions of people suffering from a famine in Ethiopia. He wanted to do something about it—fast. With Midge Ure of the band Ultravox, Geldof wrote "Do They Know It's Christmas?," depicting the stark contrast between the "first world" and the "third world." Then he recruited more than 30 British pop stars (including members of U2, Culture Club, and Duran Duran), and recorded and released the song before the end of November, just in time for Christmas. In just a month, the song (credited to "Band Aid") raised over $3 million.

The Song: "Happy Birthday"
Recorded by: Stevie Wonder
Story: After Martin Luther King, Jr. was assassinated in 1968, Michigan congressman John Conyers introduced a bill to make King's birthday a national holiday. It failed. Labor unions continued to promote the idea throughout the 1970s, but it didn't gain mainstream support until Stevie Wonder released "Happy Birthday" in 1980. Wonder dedicated the song to King, with lyrics explicitly advocating a formal holiday in his honor. The hit record generated new interest, which led to a petition signed by six million Americans, which in turn led to new legislation. On November 2, 1983, President Ronald Reagan signed the bill, making Martin Luther King, Jr. Day a federal holiday.

The Song: "We Are the World"
Recorded by: USA for Africa
Story: Like Bob Geldof, Harry Belafonte wanted to do something for Ethiopia. He started organizing a charity concert, but his manag-

er, Ken Kragen, believed a charity record would generate more money. So Kragen persuaded Lionel Richie and Michael Jackson to write "We Are the World," a song about how America, as the wealthiest country on Earth, has both the power and the responsibility to effect change. Quincy Jones, Stevie Wonder, Bruce Springsteen, Ray Charles, Bob Dylan, Tina Turner, and 40 other stars participated in the recording session. Columbia Records distributed the record for free. Released in March 1985, it became the #1 song in the United States and England within two weeks. It ultimately sold over 10 million copies and raised $50 million for famine relief.

The Song: "Helter Skelter"
Recorded by: The Beatles
Story: This song changed the world for the worse. Paul McCartney wrote "Helter Skelter" in 1967 after challenging himself to write something louder and noisier than the Who's "I Can See for Miles." According to McCartney, the song is about an amusement park ride. But mass murderer Charles Manson believed it contained secret messages about an upcoming race war, in the aftermath of which Manson would become the ruler of the world because he'd be the only white man left. Led by this delusion, Manson sent his followers on a killing spree in 1969. They brutally murdered seven people in Los Angeles and left the words "healter skelter" crudely scrawled (and misspelled) on one of the victims' refrigerators.

The Song: "Strange Fruit"
Recorded by: Billie Holiday
Story: "Strange Fruit" is a stark condemnation of lynching written in 1937 by Abel Meeropol, a Bronx schoolteacher and social activist. Lyrics include "Southern trees bear a strange fruit / Blood on the leaves and blood at the root / Black bodies swinging in the southern breeze / Strange fruit hanging from the poplar trees." Meeropol played the song at a 1939 union rally where it was heard by Barney Josephson, owner of Café Society, a New York night club, who gave the song to rising star Billie Holiday. "Strange Fruit" became her signature show-closing number, raising public awareness of the anti-lynching movement. According to many historians, "Strange Fruit" was a seed for what would evolve into the civil rights movement of the 1960s.

U.S. parents average 38 minutes per week in "meaningful conversation" with their kids.

UNDERWEAR IN THE NEWS

It's not only fun to wear, it's fun to read about, too!

UNDERDRESSED

A local politician from southern Sweden was thrown out of a council meeting in May 2007 for showing up in his underpants. The politician, whose name was not released to the press, reportedly entered the meeting wearing a tank top, a military jacket, and "shorts." According to Moderate Party councilor Gerd Bernström, the shorts were actually "tricot underpants" (Americans would call them boxers). "I told him that I want appropriate dress at meetings of the municipality's elected representatives," said Bernström. The casual councilman quietly left the room without offering an explanation for his unusual attire.

THE PROLIFIC PANTY BANDIT

A 54-year-old Japanese construction worker named Shigeo Kodama was arrested in March 2007 for stealing a pair of woman's underwear from a house he was working on. When authorities searched his home a short time later, they found an unusual stash: a gigantic collection of stolen underwear, including 3,977 panties, 355 bras, and numerous pairs of stockings. It took Kodama more than six years to amass his collection. "He didn't steal any other kinds of clothing," explained a police spokesman. "But as long as it was underwear, apparently anything would do."

WHAT'S THE PUNCHLINE?

In 2006 Joe Heckel bought his son a TKO brand punching bag for Christmas. While they were setting it up in the basement of their Cincinnati, Ohio, home, they decided—out of curiosity—to unzip the bag and see what was inside. Bad idea. Instead of sand or styrofoam peanuts, the bag was filled with underwear. "There were thongs, women's underwear, men's underwear (some used), as well as bathing suits and bras," he told reporters, adding that the smell was "bad, real bad." When the Heckels contacted the store, the

---

A bar of gold the size of a matchbox can be flattened into a sheet the size of a tennis court.

owners said this was the first time they've ever heard of such a thing. The family tried contacting TKO to get an explanation, but the company's phone number was "unassigned." A few months later, company execs finally admitted their mistake and fired the "inventive" workers responsible. Heckel got his money back and said that the ordeal was "gross—but kind of funny in a way."

SHE'D PREFER FLOWERS

When New Zealand opera diva Dame Kiri Te Kanawa signed a deal to perform a concert with Australian rock star John Farnham in 2005, she thought it would be an excellent way to introduce opera to a rock audience. But after viewing a video of one of Farnham's concerts, Dame Kiri decided to pull out. Why? Because Farnham's female fans throw their underwear at him while he's on stage. Dame Kiri explained that the flinging of underwear is "disrespectful," and, even worse, Farnham collects the panties like they are "some sort of trophy." Farnham's reps tried suing Dame Kiri for breach of contract, but, like the underwear, the case was tossed.

"YOU'RE KIDDING, RIGHT?"

That's what the West Virginia convenience-store clerk asked the would-be robber who was wearing blue panties on his head and pointing a gun-shaped cigarette lighter at him. When the cashier refused to hand over any money, the thief ran out of the store and drove away. Police quickly caught up with 34-year-old Steven Stephenson and found the lighter in his pocket and the blue panties on the side of the road nearby. State Police Sgt. T. C. Kearns gave a statement to the press, ending it with, "I couldn't make this stuff up if I tried."

LADIES' FASHION

In 1992 Scott Teeselink, media spokesman for the Kansas Bureau of Investigation, received complaints from his fellow workers about a strange grooming habit: Teeselink wore a folded pair of women's panties in his jacket pocket in place of a handkerchief. When asked why, Teeselink explained that the color of the panties matched his collection of designer ties better than any handkerchief, stressing the importance of impeccable color coordination for television personalities. KBI supervisors disagreed; they ordered Teeselink to wear a handkerchief and leave the women's panties at home.

A dog's normal body temperature is 101.2°F.

DIANE ARBUS

Ever see the photo of smirking identical twin girls? Or the scrawny kid holding a toy grenade with a look of exasperation on his face? Or the portrait of the man covered in fur? They were taken by Diane Arbus (1923–1971). With simple but compelling images of Siamese twins, circus performers, and other people she called "freaks," Arbus's work found the beauty beneath the grotesque. Here's what she said about her art.

"Most people go through life dreading a traumatic experience. Freaks were born with their trauma. They've already passed their test in life. They're aristocrats."

"A photograph is a secret about a secret. The more it tells you, the less you know."

"What I'm trying to describe is that it's impossible to get out of your skin into somebody else's. Somebody else's tragedy is not the same as your own."

"I never have taken a picture I've intended. They're always better or worse."

"I work from awkwardness. I don't like to arrange things. If I stand in front of something, instead of arranging it, I arrange myself."

"You see someone on the street, and essentially what you notice about them is the flaw."

"The thing that's important to know is that you never know. You're always sort of feeling your way."

"It's important to take bad pictures. They make you recognize something you hadn't seen in a way that will make you recognize it when you see it again."

"I really believe there are things nobody would see if I didn't photograph them."

"Freaks were one of the first things I photographed and it had a terrific kind of excitement for me—a mixture of shame and awe."

"There's a quality of legend about freaks. Like a person in a fairy tale who stops you and demands that you answer a riddle.'"

"My favorite thing is to go where I've never been."

OLD-SCHOOL COMPUTERS

The next time your computer frustrates you, be thankful you live in
an age when computers are smaller than a two-story building.
Here are the stories of some early computers.

COMPUTER: The Atanasoff-Berry Computer
YEAR: 1939
STORY: The ABC ran on electricity and solved equations. That's what defines a computer, and the ABC was the very first. Built by physicist Dr. John Atanasoff and graduate student Clifford Berry in a basement at Iowa State College, it could do only one thing: simultaneously solve up to 29 linear equations. That's all. It could store only 60 numbers in its memory and perform 30 calculations per second (far less than the millions today's computers can handle). Still, technology pioneered by the ABC became the standard for computer operating systems. First, all data was represented by a series of 1s and 0s, called *binary code*. Second, it ran electronically and wasn't mechanically operated. Third, the computer's capacity for memory storage and computation were separate functions performed in different parts of the machine. The ABC was the size of a desk, used 280 vacuum tubes, contained a mile of wire, and weighed more than 700 pounds.

COMPUTER: MIT Whirlwind
YEAR: 1951
STORY: During World War II, the U.S. Navy commissioned the Massachusetts Institute of Technology to create a computer powerful enough to run a real-time flight simulator. Despite being some of the best scientific minds in the country, MIT scientists needed until 1947 just to invent the technology and complete the design. The navy had lost interest by that time, but the air force agreed to fund the $700,000 computer. It took 175 people and four years to build. The result: a monster. The processor—the element that makes a computer compute—required 18,000 vacuum tubes, each of which required 50 watts of electricity. When all tubes were firing, they generated so much heat that is was unsafe to walk past them. The "Whirlwind" filled both floors

---

Computer humor: 1001 01101, 10111 011001? 1010110101010101. (Ha ha!)

of a two-story building and needed a megawatt power substation in the basement and a rooftop air-conditioning system to pump out all the heat. The Whirlwind rate of calculation: about 2,000 equations per second.

COMPUTER: UNIVAC 1
YEAR: 1951
STORY: The "Universal Automatic Computer" is not only considered the first modern computer, but also the beginning of the modern computer industry. It pioneered another standard way computers operate to this day: Data is fetched from memory, worked on, then returned to memory. It was considered the best computer available for large-scale data processing. It weighed more than 13 tons, and a simple equation took 100 microseconds to solve—200,000 times slower than today's Pentium III microchip. The first to use the UNIVAC: the U.S. Census Bureau, which used it for 12 years. The manufacturer, Remington Rand, sold 45 of the computers to various government agencies and businesses at a cost of $750,000 each (plus $185,000 for a printer).
Random fact: In 1952 the UNIVAC analyzed election poll data and accurately predicted Dwight Eisenhower would win the presidency.

COMPUTER: Osborne 1
YEAR: 1981
STORY: This one's not as old (or gigantic) as the others, but it's definitely an important step in computer history. Made by the Osborne Computer Corporation, this was the first commercially available "portable" computer. But it was no laptop—it was the size of a very large dictionary, weighed 23 pounds, and had to be plugged into a wall outlet (no batteries yet). The keyboard folded out, and served as the computer's lid when it was folded in and closed. Its built-in, monochromatic screen was four inches wide (today's laptops are 15 inches or more). The Osborne was also the first computer to be sold with pre-installed software, in this case word-processing, spreadsheet, and mailing-list programs, all perfect for the businessperson on the go. The cost: $1,800. Osborne sold about 10,000 of them per month in early 1981.

In computer lingo, a *nybble* is half of a byte, or four bits.

THE BIRTH (AND DEATH) OF THE PHONE BOOTH

If the phone booth isn't on the endangered-species list, it probably should be. We decided we'd better celebrate its long history before the last ones disappear forever.

THE CHICKEN OR THE EGG

If you had to guess which came first, the phone or the phone booth, which would you pick? Believe it or not, they came into being at about the same time. The first person to build an enclosure for making telephone calls was Thomas Watson, the man who assisted Alexander Graham Bell as he invented the telephone in the mid-1870s.

Watson's first enclosure looked more like a kids' fort or living-room playhouse than like a real phone booth: He threw some blankets over the furniture in his room and crawled under them so that he could shout into his experimental telephone equipment (that was the only way he could be heard) without disturbing the neighbors or upsetting his landlady. Watson didn't build an actual booth until 1883, but when he did, he went all out: It was fine cabinetry, handmade from expensive woods, with large screened windows and a domed roof, and was large enough inside to contain a desk for him to work at.

GOING PUBLIC

By the time Watson built that first booth, hotels and other business that provided telephone service to their customers were already beginning to install privacy enclosures. Sometimes called "silence cabinets," they allowed people to make private calls without disturbing others or being disturbed by them. The phones inside these silence cabinets couldn't take money, so customers paid a fee to an attendant after they made their calls. Some silence cabinets had locking doors for security—the *phone company's* security: The attendants locked the customers in the booths and didn't let them out until they'd paid for their calls. It cost a lot of money to have attendants minding telephones, so the

---

Garlic is a member of the lily family. So are onions.

booths were limited to high-traffic areas that generated enough business to cover the cost of paying the attendant.

DROPPING A DIME

It didn't take long for someone to figure out that the easiest way to lower the price of a public telephone call would be to get rid of the attendant. An inventor named William Gray accomplished that task in 1889 when he invented the first telephone that was capable of accepting coins and installed it in a bank lobby in Hartford, Connecticut. Gray reportedly came up with the idea for the pay phone after neighbors refused to let him use their telephone to call for a doctor during a medical emergency.

Gray's phone was a "postpay" one: You deposited your coins *after* the call was placed. The first "prepay" phone, introduced by Western Electric, followed in 1898 and eventually became the standard for pay phones in the United States until 1966, when a "dial tone first" system was introduced to allow people to report emergencies even if they didn't have any coins to deposit.

Those first pay phones relied on the honor system for payment: The customer did have to deposit coins to use the phone, but there was no way to determine the coins' value. Had the caller inserted only a nickel to pay for a call that cost a dime? The operator couldn't tell. Gray stumbled onto the solution in 1890 when he happened to drop a coin on a bell and realized that the sound it made could be heard over the phone. That gave him the idea of fitting phones with bells and separate slots and chutes for each type of coin. Nickels hit a bell once as they slid down the nickel chute on the way to the coin box, dimes hit it twice, and quarters struck a special "cathedral gong" all their own. By listening to the sounds made by the bells, the operator could calculate the amount of money the caller deposited.

HERE, THERE, EVERYWHERE

Once the telephone attendants were out of the picture, it became possible to install pay phones just about anyplace where people might need to make a call. By 1902 there were more than 81,000 pay phones in the United States. Most of these were in phone booths, and virtually all of the phone booths were indoors. The Bell System, the company set up by Alexander Graham Bell and his partners, didn't get around to placing a phone booth outdoors until 1905, when it finally installed one on the sidewalk of a busy street in Cincinnati, Ohio.

OUTSIDE CHANCE

Outdoor phone booths took a while to catch on. People were not comfortable with the idea of making private phone calls out in public, even when they were protected inside a phone booth. The booths eventually did catch on, of course, and in the decades to come phone booths became an indispensable part of American life— they were installed on street corners, in train stations, restaurants, airports, drugstores, government buildings, just about every public place. By 1942 there were so many in New York City alone that, even at a nickel for most calls, the phone company was collecting $100,000 in revenues every *day*.

Early phone booths were pretty nice places to hang out in: Many 1940s models were constructed with fine hardwoods adorned with silk curtains, plush carpeting, and a bench to sit on while you scribbled phone numbers on the notepad that was provided for you. The nicest ones felt like tiny apartments, a far cry from the austere steel-and-glass boxes we know today.

LIFELINE SERVICE

In rural areas, a phone booth might be the only phone for miles around, the community's only lifeline to the outside world other than the telegraph office. Telephone service was a luxury, so why pay for your own telephone if there was a phone booth just down the street? In many urban neighborhoods, too, people made do with the phone booth on the corner; kids would hang out around it and wait for it to ring, in the hope of collecting a tip for taking a message and delivering it to the recipient. More than a few phone booths served as rent-free office space for cash-strapped businessmen who couldn't afford offices of their own.

Pay phones were so central to American life that when the Treasury Department redesigned American coins in 1964 and changed the types of metal they contained, it worked closely with the phone company to ensure that the new coins would still work in pay phones.

Ocean water contains traces of gold.

OFF THE HOOK

Inexpensive cell phone plans have driven pay phones to the brink of extinction in recent years, but the phone booth began disappearing long before that. The old, fully enclosed booths were great for privacy, but they were expensive to manufacture and easy to vandalize, and few were accessible to people in wheelchairs.

In the 1970s, enclosed phone booths began to give way to small, open-air kiosks or "acoustical shelves," as the phone company called them. They were cheaper to manufacture, less likely to be vandalized (though the phones themselves were still a target), and more accessible to disabled people, especially if the telephone was lowered to a level convenient for use by people in wheelchairs. The phone companies also discovered that kiosks generated more revenue than the old phone booths had—because they didn't offer much in the way of privacy, people kept their calls short, freeing up the phone for the next paying customer.

DEAD LINE

So are enclosed phone booths doomed to extinction? Maybe not, even if the pay phones inside of them are: A Massachusetts company has introduced what it calls the "Cell Zone," a phone booth *without* a pay phone in it, to give cell-phone users the privacy that pay-phone callers used to take for granted (and, presumably, to spare people within earshot of having to listen to them). And if you want to carry your own portable phone booth around with you, there's even a tentlike product called the Cell Atlantic Cell-Booth that you can carry around in a backpack.

*   *   *

THE WORLD'S DEADLIEST CITY, THEY WROTE

Cabot Cove, Maine, was the fictional setting of the 1984–1996 TV show *Murder, She Wrote.* An idyllic coastal village? More like the deadliest city on Earth. Under the watch of amateur detective Jessica Fletcher (played by Angela Lansbury), 286 people were murdered there during the show's 12-year run. That's a murder rate of 95 per 1,000 people. Real city with the world's highest murder rate: Caracas, Venezuela, at a relatively safe 1 per 1,000.

DUTCH TREATS AND JEW'S HARPS

It's not nice to call people names. But that never stopped anyone from making derogatory generalizations about entire cultures. Amazingly, some of those slurs have made their way into common English. Here are the origins of a few of the tamer examples.

GOING DUTCH

English sailors of the late 1500s mistook sailors from the Netherlands for Germans because their language sounded like German. They called the Netherlanders *Deutsche*, the German word for "German." Deutsche became *Dutch*, and the name stuck. By the 17th century, England and the Netherlands were imperial rivals and often at war with each other. The British trashed the name of the Dutch at every opportunity. Many phrases developed that suggested the Dutch were ill-tempered, immoral, cowardly, and stingy. They include: "Dutch auction" (where prices go down instead of up), "Dutch courage" (bravery induced by alcohol) and "Dutch widow" (a prostitute). The one expression from this era still in common use is "Dutch treat" or "going Dutch," meaning that everybody pays their own way. The English considered it rude to not pay for your guests' meals and transferred this trait onto their enemy.

INDIAN GIVER

This phrase may come from the difference between Native Americans' and white settlers' concepts of property ownership. Indians would allow settlers to live on their land during winter, but would want it back in the spring for growing crops. With the well-known history of the U.S. government breaking treaties and appropriating lands promised to Native Americans, the phrase may seem to be pinned on the wrong party. It's not: "Indian giver" was first used in the 1830s after President Andrew Jackson reclaimed land given to the Cherokee Nation. The phrase was actually derogatory to *Caucasians*, meaning someone who gave something to an Indian and then stole it back.

CHINESE FIRE DRILL

In the early 1900s, a British ship staffed by a Chinese crew came up with an elaborate procedure to deal with potential engine-room fires. The deck crew was supposed to get water from the port (left) side of the ship and take it to the engine room; the engine-room crew was supposed to scoop up the water from the floor of the engine room and toss it off the starboard (right) side of the ship. Something must have gotten lost in translation, because the whole thing became a frantic mess. During practice drills, neither group could remember which side to get water from or what to do with it once they got it. News of the drill quickly became folklore and the phrase "Chinese fire drill" came to mean any sort of hurried action in which people run around without accomplishing anything. Today the phrase refers to a car game: At a red light, everybody gets out of the car, runs around it, and gets back in.

UGLY AMERICAN

In Eugene Burdick and William J. Lederer's 1958 novel *The Ugly American*, a group of Americans attempt to "civilize" the fictional Asian nation of Sarkhan. They completely ignore the local anti-American sentiment and proceed with an unwanted construction plan. Use of the phrase spread with the 1963 film adaptation starring Marlon Brando. The fictional Americans' thickheaded inability to see things from anybody else's point of view came to be synonymous with any obnoxious American traveler who won't respect the customs of a foreign culture.

JEW'S HARP

It's a centuries-old instrument (a single reed played by placing it against the mouth and flicking it with a finger) common to many different world cultures, but only in English does the name refer to a specific group of people. Actually, the name has nothing to do with Judaism; etymologists believe it's an accident of bad pronunciation. The English once called it the *gewgaw*. That evolved to "jaws harp" and eventually to "Jew's harp." There's no evidence of the instrument originating with Jewish culture or of the term being deliberately derogatory—it's purely accidental. Nowadays, *juice harp* is the favored label. (And considering how much the player drools while playing it, that could be a much more fitting name.)

MYTH-CONCEPTIONS

*"Common knowledge" is frequently wrong. Here are some
examples of things that many people believe...but
that, according to our sources, just aren't true.*

Myth: Blues legend Robert Johnson sold his soul to the devil in exchange for superior guitar skills.

Fact: It was *Tommy* Johnson (no relation), one of Robert's blues contemporaries, who made the claim—about himself: "If you want to learn how to play anything you want to play...you take your guitar and you go to where the road crosses that way...A big black man will walk up there and take your guitar, and he'll tune it. And then he'll play a piece and hand it back to you. That's the way I learned to play." Robert wrote a song about Tommy's story called "Cross Road Blues." After Robert died in 1937 (at the age of 27), the legend became attributed to him.

Myth: Sushi is raw fish.

Fact: Technically, sushi isn't fish at all. The name of this Japanese dish refers to the vinegared rice, which often *is* topped with raw seafood. But many other foods can top the sushi, too—vegetables, eggs, or cooked meat of any variety—and it will still be called sushi.

Myth: Ninja warriors dressed all in black.

Fact: That's how the ninja—assassins and spies who relied on stealth—were first depicted on stage in Japanese plays; the black costumes were merely a symbol of their invisibility. That same black-clad ninja image was then transferred to the movies. In reality, the ninja donned dark *blue* outfits at night to blend in with the color of the night sky. In the daytime, preferring to blend in with the crowd, ninja would wear anything from peasant rags to noble gowns, depending on their mission.

Myth: As the old saying goes: "Beer before liquor—never sicker. Liquor before beer—you're in the clear."

Fact: There is no scientific basis to this aphorism. Besides, it's not the *order* in which you drink the alcoholic beverages that makes you sick; it's the *amount* you drink.

Scientists have no idea why dogs bury bones.

Myth: Every human is connected to every other human by "six degrees of separation."

Fact: The concept is based on a 1967 study by Yale psychologist Stanley Milgram. His subjects, found via newspaper ads in the Midwest, were asked to locate complete strangers by sending letters to their own friends, asking if *they* knew the stranger. If they didn't, the friends were asked to send the letters along to *their* friends, and so on, until one of the initial letters reached the stranger. It took an average of six steps, or "six degrees," leading to the pop-culture phrase. It turns out the research was flawed. A 2002 follow-up study by psychologist Judith Kleinfeld of the University of Alaska found that Milgram's original subjects were "particularly sociable" and, in truth, only about 30% of the strangers were found. Not only that, the average degrees of separation was nine, not six. Kleinfeld's conclusion: We don't live in a "small world," as Milgram suggested—it's more like a "lumpy oatmeal" world, in which a very few people are well connected, but most are not.

Myth: Urinating on a jellyfish sting will ease the pain.

Fact: While experts agree that running saltwater over a sting is better than freshwater (which will actually make it hurt more), just because urine contains salt doesn't mean it helps. Why not? The concentration isn't nearly high enough. The best cure: time. The pain from the sting will subside in about 24 hours.

Myth: People who are schizophrenic have multiple personalities.

Fact: Schizophrenia is a mental disorder that causes people to have delusions about reality or experience auditory hallucinations (hear voices). People who suffer from multiple personalities have what is called "dissociative identity disorder."

Myth: Goldfish only have a memory span of a few seconds.

Fact: We'll take partial responsibility for this misconception (we published the fact in *Uncle John's Absolutely Absorbing Bathroom Reader*). A recent study from Plymouth University in which goldfish were forced to press a lever for food showed that they not only have memory spans of up to *three months*, they also have built-in biological clocks that allow them to line up for food each day just before feeding time. Conclusion: Fish are smarter than we think.

REALLY BAD PUNS

Think these are bad? You should have seen the hundreds of bad puns we had to read through just to bring you these few "gems."

STOP CLONING AROUND. The mad scientist made a clone of himself, but something went wrong—all the clone wanted to do was stick his head out of the third-story window and shout dirty words at passersby. Embarrassed by the display, the scientist didn't know what to do. Seeing no other option, he pushed the clone out the window. He was arrested a short time later for making an obscene clone fall.

DREAM CAR. A man walks into his psychiatrist's office and says, "Doc, you've got to help me. Every night I dream that I'm a sports car. The other night I dreamed I was a Trans Am. Before that I was an Alfa Romeo. Last night I was a Porsche. What does it all mean?"

"Relax," says the doctor, "You're just having an auto-body experience."

KNIGHT MOVES. The fair young damsel was beautiful, but had no fashion sense. She wore a frilly green and purple dress with brown polka-dots and orange stripes. A dragon captured her, and she said, "You're in trouble, dragon! Any minute a brave knight will come to slay you and rescue me." The dragon just laughed. Many knights did come, but they took one look at her and rode off again.

"You see," said the dragon, "I knew no knight would ever try to rescue a damsel in this dress."

BEANTOWN. Mrs. O'Brien arrived in Boston from Ireland, and in no time at all her bean soup made her the talk of New England society. At a party celebrating the sale of her recipe to a fancy restaurant, an old matron went up to Mrs. O'Brien and said, "My dear girl, please tell me: What is the secret of your soup?"

"The secret to my soup is that I use but 239 beans to make it," said Mrs. O'Brien.

"Why only 239?" asked the matron.

"Because one more would make it too farty."

LAST MEALS OF THE RICH AND FAMOUS

Warning: These stories are morbid...but fascinating. By looking at their final meals, we catch an eerie glimpse into the everyday lives of these larger-than-life figures...whose worlds were about to end.

• **ELVIS PRESLEY.** The King stayed up most of the night of August 15, 1977. He was restless. Between midnight and 6:00 a.m., he went to his dentist to have a cavity filled (he did this at night to avoid mobs), then he returned to Graceland and played racquetball with friends, talked about marriage plans with his 20-year-old fiancee, Ginger Alden, and belted out some gospel songs at the piano. Around sunrise Alden went to bed, but Presley, still unable to sleep, ate one of his usual early-morning snacks: four scoops of ice cream and six chocolate-chip cookies. After that he went to bed, then got up a few hours later to go the bathroom, where he suffered a heart attack and died.

• **MAHATMA GANDHI.** On the evening of January 30, 1948, Gandhi enjoyed one of his standard healthy dinners of goat's milk, cooked vegetables, oranges, and a concoction of ginger, sour lemons, and strained butter mixed with aloe juice. He then took his nightly walk at Birla Bhavan in New Delhi, where followers often greeted him. Among the followers was an assassin, who shot the spiritual leader at point-blank range.

• **ERNEST HEMINGWAY.** By the time he reached his 60s, author Hemingway was suffering from severe depression. Several electroshock therapy treatments had left him frazzled. After a failed suicide attempt in the spring of 1961 at his home in Idaho, Hemingway tried again on July 2 by putting a shotgun to his head. But first, he ate his favorite meal: New York strip steak, baked potato, Caesar salad, and a glass of Bordeaux.

• **JOHN F. KENNEDY.** On the morning of November 22, 1963, JFK ate breakfast in his room at the Hotel Texas in Fort Worth. According to the hotel's executive chef, Otto Druhe, he served

---

Q: Which presidential daughter appeared in the 1964 Elvis film *Kissin' Cousins?*...

the president "coffee, orange juice, two eggs boiled five minutes, some toast, and marmalade on the side." The president's entourage then left for downtown Dallas, where they were scheduled for a 1:00 p.m. luncheon directly after Kennedy's motorcade made its way through town. Kennedy was shot at 12:30 p.m.

• **SADDAM HUSSEIN.** The former Iraqi dictator was allowed to eat his favorite meal before he was executed: boiled chicken and rice, along with several cups of hot water laced with honey.

• **JOHN BELUSHI.** The Rainbow Bar & Grill in Los Angeles was well known for its lentil soup. A very inebriated Belushi stopped in there on the night of March 5, 1982, after being told by concerned friends to "get your act together, or at least eat something." Belushi scarfed down a bowl of the soup in the Rainbow's kitchen, then returned to his bungalow at the Chateau Marmont. (Robin Williams and Robert DeNiro were there, too, but they left because of the "extremely" heavy drug use.) Belushi's girlfriend injected the 33-year-old comedian with what turned out to be a fatal dose of heroin and cocaine. When doctors examined the contents of Belushi's stomach the next day, the only food was the lentil soup.

• **PRINCESS DIANA.** By the evening of August 31, 1997, the day of her fatal car crash in Paris, Diana and her wealthy boyfriend, Dodi al Fayed, were so fed up with being stalked by photographers that they decided to end their vacation early and return to England the next day. Their plan: eat dinner at the Espadon, a restaurant in the Ritz hotel, and then take a half-hour drive to the Duke of Windsor's former mansion in the Bois de Boulogne, where they would spend the night. Diana ate a mushroom and asparagus omelette, Dover sole, and vegetable tempura. Around midnight, after sending out two decoy cars to fool the paparazzi, Diana and Fayed climbed into a black Mercedes S600, but they never made it to the mansion.

• **ADOLF HITLER.** The German dictator's last meal came on April 30, 1945, the day that he finally realized he had lost the war. Holed up at the "Führerbunker" in Berlin, Hitler ate lunch with his secretaries. According to most accounts, Hitler, a vegetarian,

...A: Maureen Reagan.

ate spaghetti with "light sauce" (although some biographies say he had lasagna). Either way, Hitler wanted a simple meal without any mention of the fall of Berlin, so the conversation consisted of dog breeding methods and "how lipstick was made from sewer grease." Shortly after the meal, Hitler and Eva Braun, whom he'd married less then 40 hours earlier, went into a private room and took their own lives.

• **JAMES DEAN.** The "rebel without a cause" was known for living life on the edge. It's ironic, then, that the last thing he ate during a stop at a roadside diner on September 30, 1955, a few hours before he crashed his Porsche Spyder, was a slice of apple pie and a glass of milk.

• **JOHN LENNON.** Sometime during the afternoon of December 8, 1980, Lennon ate a corned-beef sandwich before going to a New York recording studio to work on one of Yoko Ono's new singles. At around 10:30 p.m., having just received the happy news that their album *Double Fantasy* had gone Platinum, they decided to quit working for the night. Ono suggested stopping for dinner, but Lennon wanted to go straight back to their apartment at the Dakota to see their five-year-old son, Sean. Who knows what would have happened had Lennon gone out to eat? Instead, he went home, where a deranged fan was waiting for him.

*   *   *

SOLDIERS OF LOVE

In 1994 scientists at the Wright-Patterson Air Force Base were assigned the task of creating non-lethal weapons that would affect enemy combatants but leave civilians unharmed. Among their ideas: a "gay bomb." A strong aphrodisiac would be sprayed on the enemy, who would become so overwhelmed with desire that they would drop their weapons and start kissing each other. The project died when the scientists couldn't find any hormones or chemicals that did the trick. (They also proposed spraying the enemy with bee pheromones, then hiding beehives in combat areas, resulting in attacks from amorous bees.)

Saliva has no flavor.

HEY, THAT'S A FAKE...

Fakes, frauds, flim-flams, and phonies that fabulously flopped.

...BIG SPENDER. One night in 2007, Damon Armagost visited Deja Vu, a "gentlemen's club" in Nashville, Tennessee, where he lavishly tipped the dancers more than $600. The manager grew suspicious and called police, who discovered the money was fake— Armagost had simply downloaded an image of a $100 bill from a government Web site and printed out a stack on his home printer.

...TSAR. Russian tsar Ivan the Terrible died in 1584 (historians believe he was the victim of poisoning). His youngest son, Dmitriy Ivanovich, disappeared. Three men came forward in 1605, all claiming to be Dmitriy and also claiming a right to the throne. Grigory Otrepyev was determined to be the real one and ruled as tsar from July 1605 until he was murdered in May 1606—not because he was a fraud (which wasn't discovered until much later) but because he was believed to be the son of Ivan the Terrible. Otrepyev is remembered in history books as "False Dmitriy."

...BASEBALL PLAYER. In 2006 a Florida chiropractor named Rhonda Schroeder began dating New York Mets pitcher Pedro Martinez. They met through a patient of Schroeder's named Shirley Gordon. When Martinez kept encouraging his new girl-friend to give Gordon gifts of hundreds of thousands of dollars, Schroeder realized that her boyfriend probably wasn't the real Pedro Martinez and called the cops. He wasn't. And Gordon was already wanted by police on identity-theft charges.

...ARM WRESTLER. In 2007 a professional arm wrestler named Arsen Liliev tried to qualify for a lower (and easier) weight class at a European tournament by sending a look-alike to the pregame weigh-in. Liliev was caught when officials noticed that his look-alike didn't look anything like him.

...1950s SINGING GROUP. In July 2007, the state of Florida passed a law that made it a crime to be a fake band. Singing groups from the 1950s and 1960s were touring the casino-and-elderly-heavy state, but people who paid to see "The Drifters" were really watching a band with one or two replacement members and a bunch of hired singers. The legislation was introduced by Jon "Bowzer" Bauman, of the group Sha Na Na (which made a career of singing other people's hits).

...NUN. Mollie Brusstar, a secretary at the Catholic Diocese of Arlington, Virginia, put fake names on her employer's payroll and issued checks to herself. Then she used the money to fly to another state (Utah), where she charged dental work and cosmetic surgery to the diocese. Why would doctors allow Brusstar to charge their services to the church? She was dressed as a nun.

...REFEREE. A man named Christopher Norling was arrested in 1996 for running up a huge bill at Milwaukee's Pfister Hotel. Norling told the hotel to bill the National Football League, for whom he worked as a referee. (He was lying.)

...PRISON OFFICIAL. Michael Ewers, facing extradition to Alaska from a Florida prison, called officials at the Florida prison and pretended to be an Alaskan official. He told them that the extradition had been cancelled because it was too expensive. It worked: Ewers served the remainder of his time in sunny Florida.

*   *   *

A RANDOM ORIGIN

By 2000 Apple had lost most of its market share in the home computer industry to the PC, so CEO Steve Jobs decided to focus on MP3 players. Jobs didn't like the MP3 players on the market—he thought they were too big (the size of a Walkman) and fairly unimpressive (most held fewer than 100 songs). Jobs decided Apple should make its own, so he hired three engineers to work on the device in complete secrecy. A freelance ad copywriter came up with the name "iPod" after the sleek, white space pods in the movie *2001: A Space Odyssey*. Just one year after work began, Apple unveiled the iPod in October 2001. It was a vast improvement over other MP3 players—it fit in the palm of the user's hand, stored 1,000 songs, and cost only $399. Newer iPods can hold as many as 20,000 songs (cost: $349). More than 100 million iPods have been sold...and counting.

Q: Why wouldn't the oyster give up his pearl? A: Because he was shellfish.

DIM STARS

It's so entertaining when beautiful people appear shallow.

"I'm not anorexic. I'm from Texas. Are there people from Texas that are anorexic? I've never heard of one. And that includes me."
—**Jessica Simpson**

"I'm sounding worse than Jessica Simpson right now. She's looking like a rock scientist."
—**Tara Reid**

"It's kind of boring for me to have to eat."
—**Kate Moss**

"I tried on 250 bathing suits in one afternoon and ended up having little scabs up and down my thighs, probably from the ones with sequins all over them."
—**Cindy Crawford**

"If I didn't have some kind of education, I wouldn't be able to count my money."
—**Missy Elliott**

"I like Jennifer Aniston 'cause she's, like, homely. She must have something else going on 'cause it's not like she's gorgeous or anything."
—**Kimberly Stewart**

"Sundance is weird. The movies are weird. You actually have to think about them when you watch them."
—**Britney Spears**

"I dress sexily, but not in an obvious way. Sexy in a virginal way."
—**Victoria Beckham**

"I know I can be diva-ish, but the nature of my life, the nature of what I do, is divadom. It really is."
—**Mariah Carey**

"I love the confidence that makeup gives me."
—**Tyra Banks**

"A million pounds is not a lot of money."
—**Catherine Zeta-Jones**

"I think most people are curious about what it would be like to be able to meet yourself. It's eerie."
—**Christy Turlington**

"Every minute was more exciting than the next!"
—**Linda Evans**

First Lady Pat Nixon was a bit player in 1930s Hollywood movies.

IF YOU CAN READ THIS, I'VE LOST MY TRAILER

Just when we think we've seen every clever bumper sticker that exists, readers send us new ones. Have you seen the one that says...

99 PERCENT OF LAWYERS GIVE THE REST A BAD NAME

I feel like I'm diagonally parked in a parallel universe

The early bird may get the worm, but the second mouse gets the cheese

REMEMBER: HALF THE PEOPLE YOU KNOW ARE BELOW AVERAGE

PLAN TO BE SPONTANEOUS TOMORROW

Always try to be modest, and be proud of it!

Wrinkled was *not* one of the things I wanted to be when I grew up

If you can read this, I've lost my trailer

WHEN EVERYTHING IS COMING YOUR WAY, YOU'RE IN THE WRONG LANE

I used to have an open mind but my brains kept falling out

My dog can lick anyone

A journey of a thousand miles begins with a cash advance

My wild oats have turned to shredded wheat

IF WE QUIT VOTING, WILL THEY ALL GO AWAY?

It *is* as bad as you think and they *are* out to get you

You! Out of the gene pool!

I need somebody bad. Are you bad?

Earth is the insane asylum of the universe

Man cannot live on bread alone...unless he's in a cage and that's all you feed him

A committee's just a mob without the passion

TV IS GOODER THAN BOOKS

Come to the dark side: we have cookies

Shortest place name in the United States: Y, Alaska.

SECRET INGREDIENTS

A doctor friend of ours pooh-poohs fears about chemicals in our food. "Everything is made up of chemicals," he says. He's right, of course, and in that spirit we offer this article, with a warning that if the idea of weird stuff being in your food bothers you, you might not want to read on.

CHICKEN McNUGGETS
Good news: a McDonald's Chicken McNugget does contain chicken. But it's not the main ingredient—not even close. According to Michael Pollan, author of *The Omnivore's Dilemma*, a McNugget is made up of 38 ingredients, mostly chemicals and corn derivatives. In total, a McNugget is 56 percent corn products. But 0.02 percent is *tertiary butylhydroquinone*, a petroleum byproduct used as a preservative. TBHQ is actually butane, also known as lighter fluid.

COOL WHIP

Though it's often used as a substitute for whipped cream, Cool Whip contains no cream and no milk. The only dairy in the product is a milk protein called *sodium caseinate*. Instead of milk, Cool Whip uses a combination of ingredients, including water, corn syrup, coconut oil, and palm kernel oil, which have a much longer shelf life.

RED BULL

The main ingredient in energy drinks like Red Bull and RockStar that revs you up isn't caffeine. In fact, an 8.5-ounce can has only about as much caffeine as a cup of coffee. The "energy" actually comes from *taurine*, a stimulant much more potent than caffeine. Today taurine is synthesized in laboratories, but it was first discovered by German scientists in 1827, as a naturally occurring substance in the bile of oxen.

VELVEETA

As milk hardens into cheese, it leaves behind a liquid byproduct called whey. Many cheese manufacturers just threw the whey in the garbage, until Kraft found a use for it. With an added stabiliz-

---

In a year, an average elevator travels the equivalent of nearly halfway around the equator.

ing agent called *carrageenin*—a derivative of Irish moss—the whey can be processed into a soft, spongy cheesy brick, better known as Velveeta.

TWINKIES

Polysorbate 60 is one of many chemical compounds in a Twinkie. One of the ingredients in polysorbate 60 is *ethylene oxide*, a highly flammable material that's toxic if consumed in extremely high amounts. It was used in grenades during the Vietnam War.

SMOOTHIES

Jamba Juice, one the country's biggest fruit-smoothie chains, offers a non-dairy option for customers who are allergic to milk. Amazingly, the second most prevalent ingredient in the non-dairy blend: nonfat dried milk.

MAGIC SHELL

A chocolate-flavored ice cream topping similar to chocolate syrup or fudge sauce, Magic Shell hardens into a thick candy shell when it's poured over ice cream. (Similar to the chocolate coating on Dairy Queen's chocolate-dipped cones.) How does the chocolate liquid harden? The effect comes from a mixture of soybean oil and paraffin wax, a petroleum product also commonly used in candles and skin cream.

DEODORANT

Deodorant isn't a food, but you do consume it every day. (Don't you?) Secret, advertised as "strong enough for a man, but made for a woman," actually contains the exact same ingredients in the exact same proportions as the popular men's deodorant Sure.

*   *   *

BUT DO THEY SELL OUT EVERY NIGHT?

Only five NBA arenas have not sold their naming rights to a corporation. They are: the Rose Garden in Portland, Madison Square Garden in New York, Bobcats Arena in Charlotte, The Palace at Auburn Hills in Detroit, and the Bradley Center in Milwaukee.

Meatheads? Kobe Bryant's parents named him after a steak they saw on a menu.

MORE-SUPIALS

*Maruspials are a relatively small and, to most of us, odd group of mammals.
They are found mostly in Australia, on some islands near Australia, and
in South America. This ancient and primitive group is distinguished from
other mammals by the fact that the females don't develop a placenta,
so they must nourish their young outside their bodies, in a pouch.
From the kangaroo to the koala to the Tasmanian devil,
they are a fascinating bunch of critters.*

TIGER QUOLL

Australia's largest existing carnivorous marsupial, growing
up to 30 inches in length and 17 pounds in weight. They
look sort of like cats (quolls of several species are known as
"native cats"), with slightly elongated noses and thick, soft, dark-
brown fur spotted white on the flanks and lighter on the belly.
They eat birds (they can climb trees), smaller marsupials, lizards,
and insects. Tiger quolls have developed pouches that, as with
many burrowing marsupials, open toward the rear so dirt doesn't
get in it during digging.

MARSUPIAL LION

Australia's largest *extinct* species of carnivorous marsupial, living
from 1.6 million to about 50,000 years ago. They stood 30 inches
tall at the shoulder, were more than six feet from the nose to the
base of the tail, and weighed up to 350 pounds. Fossilized skeletons of the beasts have been found all over Australia. They had
extremely powerful jaws (some say the most powerful ever in a
mammal), elongated thumbs for grasping prey, long retractable
claws (no other marsupial known has had them), and probably
preyed mostly on giant kangaroos and diprotodons.

DIPROTODONS

Also extinct, they were the largest marsupial known to exist. They
were furry, with short tails, and could reach 6 feet tall at the
shoulder and 10 feet in length, and weighed more than two tons.
They lived on leaves and shrubs. Fossil remains have been found
all over the continent (one female was even found with a baby in
her pouch). Diprotodons went extinct about 40,000 years ago, and

Historical accounts say that Julius Caesar was a great swimmer.

some scientists believe that the first humans in Australia could have helped bring about their demise.

MULGARA

A light-brown, mouselike, burrowing creature, five to nine inches long, that inhabits Australia's central and western deserts. There are two species, Brush-tailed and Crested-tailed, distinguished by their different tails and the number of nipples in the females' pouches—the Crested has eight; the Brush, six. They don't have true pouches; they have two folds of skin that close around their young. Mulgaras are carnivores, living on insects, lizards, and young snakes, and they have specialized kidneys that excrete highly concentrated urine to conserve moisture...since they never drink water. (They get their liquids from their food.)

PIG-FOOTED BANDICOOT

This now-extinct herbivore lived in Australia's central deserts. The pig-footed bandicoots were slightly larger than guinea pigs, had orange-brown fur, long slender legs, long tails, long pointy noses, and ears like rabbits. And they had some of the oddest feet in the marsupial world: Their front feet had only two functional toes, both of them with hardened, hooflike nails...like a pig's. Each hind foot had a huge fourth toe with a hoof-shaped nail, all of the other toes being useless. They were once numerous in western and southern Australia; unfortunately, the introduction of carnivores like the red fox, and competing species like the rabbit, saw them disappear completely. The last ones were seen in the early 1900s.

THE YAPOK

Also known as the water opossum, these are the only known aquatic marsupials. They live in South America, Central America, and parts of Mexico. Yapoks reach about 12 inches in length, have long noses, and long, mostly hairless tails. They are black and white with webbed hind feet. They live in burrows on the shores of streams and lakes and are excellent swimmers, hunting at night for crustaceans, fish, and other small aquatic animals. The females' pouches can be pulled closed (using a specialized muscle) for waterproof protection of the babies. Oh...and the males have pouches too, into which they can pull their genitals (for safer swimming).

Hot dogs originated in China.

STRANGE CELEBRITY LAWSUITS

Even the rich and famous have to deal with lawyers. Ha ha!

THE PLAINTIFF: Vanna White
THE DEFENDANT: Samsung Electronics
THE LAWSUIT: In 1983 *Wheel of Fortune* was the hottest game show on television and Vanna White, who turned the letters, was an international celebrity. Capitalizing on the fad, Samsung ran a magazine ad that featured a robot wearing a blond wig turning a letter on a futuristic game show that bore a strong resemblance to *Wheel of Fortune*. White was not flattered by the notion that a robot could perform her job and sued the electronics giant for defamation. Samsung's lawyers argued for the case to be dropped since the company didn't use White's name or likeness— it was just a robot.
THE VERDICT: The court ruled that even though the robot wasn't a "true likeness" of the TV star, it did appropriate her identity to capitalize on her fame. White was awarded $403,000.

THE PLAINTIFF: Keith Urban
THE DEFENDANT: Keith Urban
THE LAWSUIT: In May 1999, Keith D. Urban, a pop-art painter from Wayne, New Jersey, registered for the Web site domain name *www.keithurban.com*. Four months later, up-and-coming Australian country singer Keith Urban registered for the same URL, but was told it was already in use, so he chose *www.keithurban.net* instead. Everything was fine until Urban the country singer hit superstardom. Then, in 2007, he wanted the .com site for himself and sued Urban the painter on the grounds that his Web site was misleading the singer's fans into thinking the painter was the singer, too. "It has become apparent that he (the painter) is attempting to capitalize on Keith's (the singer's) success," said the singer's publicist. As evidence, he pointed to the ads for Keith Urban concert tickets that appear at the top of the

painter's site, which the painter insists are placed there randomly by Google—he has no control over their content. The painter's strongest piece of evidence: his birth certificate. His name is—and always has been—Keith Urban. Now, instead of simply defending himself, the painter is countersuing. "The Musician is misusing the judicial process to intimidate the Painter…and is using his celebrity to threaten the Painter to give up intellectual property in which he has legitimate interests." All the painter wants, he says, is to continue to use the domain name he legally owns to promote his artwork.

VERDICT: Pending. But if you want to be kept up to date on the proceedings, they can be found on Keith Urban (the painter's) Web site.

THE PLAINTIFF: McDonald's restaurants
THE DEFENDANT: Burger King's ad agency J. Walter Thompson, and Sarah Michelle Gellar
THE LAWSUIT: In 1982 the four-year-old Gellar starred in a historic commercial for Burger King: It was the first time a direct competitor was named in a nationally televised ad. The commercial claimed, among other things, that McDonald's burgers were 20% smaller than Burger King's. At the end, Gellar stated, "I only eat at Burger King!" McDonald's sued not only Burger King's ad agency for defamation, they also sued Gellar for false advertising. (On cross-examination by a McDonald's lawyer, the little girl shakily admitted that she really didn't "only eat at Burger King.")
THE VERDICT: The case was settled out of court. Ironically, 17 years later, McDonald's became one of the main sponsors for *Buffy the Vampire Slayer*, which starred Gellar.

THE PLAINTIFF: Nancy Koeper
THE DEFENDANT: Charles Bronson
THE LAWSUIT: In 1996 Audrey Jean Knauer, a 55-year-old retired chemist from Louisville, Kentucky, scribbled out her last will and testament on the back of a grocery list. Completely ignoring her family, Knauer promised everything (around $300,000) to her favorite movie star, Charles Bronson, whom she had never even met. (Whatever Bronson didn't want was to be given to the Louisville Public Library.) After Knauer's death, her sister, Nancy

Koeper, was livid—she had thought Knauer's estate was worth only about $20,000. Koeper sued Bronson for the entire sum on the grounds that her sister was mentally unfit when she wrote the will. "Audrey saw Bronson as this avenging person who was generous and kind. Kind of a father figure," Koeper said about her sister's infatuation with the star of the *Death Wish* movies. Bronson, meanwhile, pledged to donate the money to charity. But Koeper was adamant: "I really believe this money needs to go to me," she said. "I think charity begins at home."

THE VERDICT: The case was settled out of court. Bronson gave Koeper an "undisclosed sum" and promised to give $10,000 to the Louisville Public Library on the condition that they stop publicly "dragging his name through the press." The library refused, saying that they're a public institution...and got nothing. (After Bronson died in 2003, his own family went to court in a bitter dispute over who should get how much of the fortune he left behind.)

THE PLAINTIFF: Russian President Vladimir Putin
THE DEFENDANTS: Dobby the House Elf and Warner Bros.
THE LAWSUIT: After the movie *Harry Potter and the Chamber of Secrets* was released in 2003, some viewers noticed an uncanny resemblance between the computer-generated Dobby and the Russian president. When Putin was shown an image of Dobby, he was reportedly upset that Warner Bros. had stolen his likeness. The filmmakers deny that they ever thought of Putin when designing the elf. There is a resemblance, especially in the eyes and the mouths of the two, but that's where the similarity ends—Dobby is a diminutive, bald, slightly gray, floppy-eared elf who wears only rags whereas Putin is a full-sized, brown-haired man who dresses well. The BBC posted pictures of the two characters on its Web site and asked readers to decide if the two looked alike (with a caption that read "Putin is the one on the right"). After more than 75% of the BBC readers agreed that the two do indeed look very similar, a group of Russian lawyers threatened to sue Warner Bros.

THE VERDICT: After much posturing, the Russian lawyers decided to drop the suit before it was ever brought to court.

First female police chief in America: Dolly Spencer of Milford, Ohio, in 1914.

UPSKILL YOUR LINGO

Every year Merriam-Webster's *and* The Oxford English Dictionary *add new words. If they weren't already commonly used, they couldn't make it into the dictionary, but it's kind of funny to think of these words as "official."*

Crunk. A type of hip-hop music that came out of Southern cities such as Memphis and New Orleans in the 1990s

Ginormous. Extremely large (from *gigantic* + *enormous*)

Yogalates. Exercise regime combining yoga and pilates

Mouse potato. Like a "couch potato," only someone who sits at the computer all day, not a TV

Perfect storm. A disastrous situation brought about by several concurrent factors (as in the film *The Perfect Storm*)

Bahookie. Scottish slang for a person's butt

Upskill. To learn more skills

Hardscape. Manmade features in a landscape, such as gazebos and fountains

IED. Abbreviation for "improvised explosive device"

Snowboardcross. A snow-board race featuring several turns and jumps (from "motocross")

Sandwich generation. People who are "sandwiched" between the parents they're taking care of and the kids they're raising

Soul patch. Small growth of hair below a man's lower lip

Smackdown. A decisive defeat of an opponent

Viewshed. Everything visible from one or more points (from "watershed")

Supersize. To increase in size (from a former McDonald's menu feature)

Big-box. Relating to large chain stores (like Wal-Mart or Home Depot)

Blowback. Unintended and undesirable results from the actions of politicians

Hoody. A hooded sweatshirt or other hooded top

Def. Cool

Drama queen. A person given to excessive emotional displays

Unibrow. When a person's eyebrows meet in the middle to form one long eyebrow

---

Did you make a *zugswang*? That's what it's called when you have to make a bad move in chess.

PILLOW TALK

Random facts about the pillow.

HEAD REST. The word "pillow" dates back to the 12th century. It comes from the Latin *pulvinus*, which means "cushion." But archaeologists say that pillows of various kinds, from plant-filled skins to "comfortable" rocks, have probably been used far back into human prehistory.

OLD SOFTIES. The oldest *known* pillows date back to the oldest known civilizations on Earth, with references to pillows in ancient Sumerian cuneiform texts. Ancient Egyptians placed feather-filled pillows in the tombs of their mummified dead.

BOOK 'EM, PILL-O. One of Japan's oldest narrative writings is *The Pillow Book* by Sei Shonagon, a lady-in-waiting in the court of Empress Sadako. It is more than 1,000 years old and hundreds of pages long, with personal lists, descriptions of the Japanese court, poetry, observations, and more. *The Pillow Book* is considered one of Japan's great masterpieces, and schoolchildren still must memorize the opening lines. (One list, of "Things That Make Me Happy," contains the item "When bad things happen to people I can't stand.")

HOLD YOUR HEAD UP. Pillows are mentioned in the Bible, but they're not mentioned favorably: "Woe to those who apply pillows unto their elbows," says the book of *Ezekiel*. Scholars believe the text refers to "false prophets," who Ezekiel thought were insufficiently austere.

KEEP A COOL HEAD. You know how your pillow sometimes feels too warm and you have to keep turning it over to get the "cool" side? Well, now a company called "Sooth-Soft" has come out with the "Chillow," a "fluid-filled, eco-friendly cushioning device" that "keeps you cool without electricity." It's actually gotten rave reviews. And they make one for dogs, too. Cost: $39.95. ($69.95 for dogs.)

IT'S A WAKE-UP CALL.

Are you the laziest person on Earth? (Why else would you be reading an article about pillows?) The PerCushion Pillow Phone could be made just for you. It's a combination pillow/cell phone, with a microphone, loudspeaker, and Bluetooth wireless connection built in. So when the pillow rings, just lie there and answer it. Beautiful!

DOING DOUBLE DUTY.

For anyone whose spouse farts in their sleep, Jim and Sharron Huza have invented the *GasBGon* anti-flatulence pillow. It applies "cutting-edge carbon filter technology to absorb the sound and odor that accompany flatulence." The filters have to be changed, they say, every six months...for women. And every three months for men.

BOY, I'M STUFFED. In

2005 Jeannette Hall, a taxidermist in Nevada, started offering to transform deceased cats or dogs into pillows for $75–$100. Unfortunately the offer led to "hundreds of hate e-mails from all over the globe." The outrage baffled the taxidermist, who claimed she had many happy customers. "Most people were happy that Fluffy was still on the couch," she said.

THE FIGHT CLUB. If

you're especially talented at pillow fighting, the Pillow Fight League (PFL) just might be looking for you. Founded in Toronto on New Year's Eve 2004, it was called "the most exciting and innovative new wave in sports entertainment" (by the league's founders). The sport, which features "strong female combatants," has regularly sold-out events around Canada and the United States. And please don't imagine that the PFL is some kind of tawdry sex act: Rule Number Six in the PFL Rule Book (it has seven rules) is "Pillow fighters must practice good sportswomanship. No rude, lewd, or suggestive behavior."

*   *   *

ZZZZZOOM: Sleep researchers have discovered that when clocks are set back an hour at the end of Daylight Saving Time, car accident rates plummet, probably because of the extra hour of sleep.

"Fatigue is the best pillow." —Benjamin Franklin

LINCOLNSPIRACY?

Abraham Lincoln was assassinated immediately after the Civil War.
But was it really John Wilkes Booth who did it?

BACKGROUND
On April 14, 1865, President Lincoln was shot while watching a play at Ford's Theater in Washington, D.C. The country was thrown for a loop: No American president had ever been assassinated. John Wilkes Booth, a young actor with Confederate sympathies, was witnessed pulling the trigger, but as with many sudden, tragic events, the facts couldn't prevent minds from wandering to thoughts of conspiracy. Here are some real conspiracy theories that circulated in the weeks and months after Lincoln's death.

CONSPIRACY THEORY: Vice President Andrew Johnson, next in line to the presidency and a Southerner, hired John Wilkes Booth to assassinate Lincoln.

THE STORY: On the afternoon of April 14, 1865, Booth stopped by the Kirkwood House, a Washington hotel where Johnson kept an office. Johnson was out, so Booth left a note (later found by Johnson's secretary William Browning). Why would an assassin want to meet with the vice president? To coordinate final details, such as Lincoln's whereabouts for that night. While Johnson was military governor of Tennessee in 1862, he and Booth had mistresses who happened to be sisters, and were often seen together. The relationship grew over their mutual hatred of Lincoln, whose death fulfilled both men's ambitions: fame for Booth, the presidency for Johnson.

THE TRUTH: Browning really did find a note, and Booth and Johnson really did know each other in Tennessee. The theory spread because northern congressmen hated Johnson. Booth may have been just stopping by to see a friend, albeit a curiously well-connected friend…but no one knows for sure.

CONSPIRACY THEORY: Mrs. Lincoln shot Mr. Lincoln.

THE STORY: The Rothschilds, a European banking family, wanted Lincoln dead for two reasons: 1) he was going to shut down their money-printing bank in favor of a federally backed currency, and

---

Q: If you fill a 3-cubic-foot container with water, how much will it weigh? A: About 187 lbs.

2) he'd sired an illegitimate child with a Rothschild. They planned to kidnap Lincoln from Ford's Theater and leave him drugged on a ship at sea for days. When he returned, the baby scandal would force him to resign and abandon his currency plan. The hired kidnapper: Mary Todd Lincoln's opium dealer, who also happened to be John Wilkes Booth's theatrical stand-in. But as "Booth" arrived, Todd, who was high on opium, shot Lincoln because she'd just found out about the illegitimate child. The fake Booth panicked and escaped. The real Booth changed his name and went into hiding.

TRUTH: Rumors about Mrs. Lincoln's involvement began when she didn't show up at her husband's funeral. But it's not because she was a murderer: She was simply overwrought. The Rothschilds were a very powerful banking family in Europe, but they never had any money-printing operations in the United States (although at the time, individual banks often did print their own money). There is no doubt that Booth pulled the trigger. Witnesses saw him enter the box, and since Mrs. Lincoln was sitting next to the president, she couldn't have shot him in the back of the head.

CONSPIRACY THEORY: The Catholic Church killed Lincoln.

THE STORY: In 1856 Lincoln, then a lawyer in Illinois, represented an ex-priest in a slander case over a claim that the Vatican planned to take over the United States. The Vatican was livid that their plot had been exposed. They decided to kill Lincoln, which would throw the country, still fragile after the Civil War, into chaos and allow for an easy takeover. The Church also planned to stack the odds by importing millions of Catholic immigrants from Ireland, Germany, and France. Former Confederate president (and secret Vatican puppet) Jefferson Davis offered a $1 million reward to anyone willing to pull the trigger on Lincoln. The man who stepped up: John Wilkes Booth, who had spent three years in Rome learning assassination techniques from the Jesuits.

THE TRUTH: The theory was spread by Charles Chiniquy— the ex-priest Lincoln defended in 1856. The Church had excommunicated Chiniquy because he'd had an affair with a teenage girl. After Lincoln died, Chiniquy published a book outlining the Catholic Church's "plan" to take over the United States and fill it with Catholic immigrants—indicative of both the anti-immigration and anti-Catholic sentiments of the time.

PEANUTS, PART II

On page 159 we told you about the beginning of Charles Schulz's comic-strip career. Now watch as his creation takes the nation by storm.

AN UNDIGNIFIED NAME

Schulz wanted to keep the name *Li'l Folks*, but because there was already a comic called *Li'l Abner* and another called *Little Folks*, the syndicate chose a new name: *Peanuts*. Schulz hated it. "It's totally ridiculous," he said. "It has no meaning, is simply confusing, and has no dignity. And I think my humor has dignity." Nevertheless, on October 2, 1950, the first *Peanuts* strip appeared in seven newspapers. Originally, there were four main characters: Charlie Brown, his dog Snoopy, a girl named Patty, and a boy named Shermy. Back then, Charlie Brown was more of a wisecracker than a loser, and he wasn't intended to be the star of the strip. But because Shermy didn't have much of a personality and Patty was just plain mean, Charlie Brown got the best lines, becoming the protagonist by default.

Over the next three years, Shermy and Patty's roles got smaller, and two new characters—Linus and Lucy—were added to the strip. Within a year, Linus became Charlie Brown's friend and Lucy became his foil. This really opened up ideas for Schulz, especially with the addition of a Sunday strip in 1952. The now-familiar themes of the baseball team always losing and Lucy pulling the football away really struck a chord with readers...*and* newspaper editors. By 1953 *Peanuts* had expanded to over 40 newspapers, and Schulz's original salary of $90 per week had grown to $30,000 per year.

BREAKING OUT

Interestingly, it was the limitations of the format that led Schulz to focus on more character-oriented storylines. Bill Watterson, creator of *Calvin & Hobbes*, explained what Schulz was up against:

> Back when the comics were printed large enough that they could accommodate detailed, elaborate drawings, *Peanuts* was launched with a tiny format, designed so the panels could be stacked vertically if an editor wanted to run it in a single column. Schulz somehow turned this oppressive space restriction to his advantage, and

developed a brilliant graphic shorthand and stylistic economy, innovations unrecognizable now that all comics are tiny and Schulz's solutions have been universally imitated.

Schulz distilled each subject to its barest essence, and drew it straight-on or in side view, in simple outlines. But while the simplicity of Schulz's drawings made the strip stand out from the rest, it was the expressiveness within the simplicity that made Schulz's artwork so forceful.

That "expressiveness within the simplicity" made Schulz a huge hit not only with readers, but with his contemporaries as well. In 1955 the National Cartoonists Society gave Schulz the Reuben Award for "Outstanding Cartoonist of the Year." And that was only the first of many: He won the Yale Humor Award in 1956 and the School Bell Award from the National Education Association in 1960. In 1962 *Peanuts* was named "Best Humor Strip of the Year" by the National Cartoonists Society. Two years later, Schulz became the first comic-strip artist in history to win two Reuben Awards. In 1978 more than 700 cartoonists from around the world cast their votes and named Schulz "International Cartoonist of the Year."

FAMILY MAN

Meanwhile, as *Peanuts* grew in popularity, Schulz maintained a low-key lifestyle, not flaunting his riches. In 1958, at the urging of his wife, Schulz moved his family to Sebastopol, California, where he built his first studio. He made it a goal to only work from about 9 a.m. to 4 p.m. on weekdays so he could have enough time to raise his five children. That alone provided most of the "research" that he'd need to add new characters and storylines to the strip; what Schulz didn't mine from his own childhood, he mined from his children—and later from his grandchildren.

But when it was time to work, he worked. Unlike other comic-strip artists who hired a consortium to letter, color, or even draw their strips, Schulz insisted on doing every aspect of the work himself. And his process was always the same: He began with a script idea, then drew rough sketches of the scenes. Then he worked painstakingly on the wording—getting it to flow perfectly before he finalized the characters and the background.

This attention to detail in such a "simply drawn" strip added to

Odd fact: The average female opossum has 13 nipples.

the realism—readers felt they *knew* Charlie Brown and Snoopy. It soon became obvious that they couldn't remain confined to the borders of a newspaper comic strip for long.

PEANUTS NATION

Books were the first crossover *Peanuts* products, starting in 1952 with a hardcover collection of cartoons called *Peanuts*. Books of comic strips were still relatively rare, but it sold well enough for a second collection, called *More Peanuts*, in 1954. After that came *Good Grief, More Peanuts!* (1956), *Good Ol' Charlie Brown* (1957), and so on. Over the years, there have been hundreds of *Peanuts* collections. In fact, the abundant comic-strip books we see today owes their origins to Schulz, who almost single-handedly launched this publishing phenomenon.

For the strip's first seven years, Schulz was reluctant to give in to the many marketing opportunities presented to him. "I never even thought about licensing; all I thought about was just trying to draw the strip. But I realized this is a business, and I knew it was possible to make a lot of money at it." In 1958 Schulz finally agreed to a request from Hungerford Plastics to release a set of *Peanuts* dolls. They created six plastic characters depicting Charlie Brown and his friends, which sold very well. Over the next 15 years, fans could buy everything from Snoopy plush dolls to Charlie Brown lunch boxes to Linus wristwatches to bedsheets, T-shirts, and hundreds of other items. By 1999, there were 20,000 *Peanuts*-related products per year. While Schulz had no problem with the saturation of his characters in popular culture, he did maintain the final say over what *couldn't* be produced. Among the products he rejected: *Peanuts* ashtrays, vitamins, sugary breakfast cereals, tennis rackets, and baby wipes (for "aesthetic" reasons).

AND NOW FOR A WORD FROM OUR SPONSOR

Advertisers also understood the appeal, and many approached United Features, but Schulz relented only on a few. Kodak was the first to use *Peanuts*, placing the popular characters in their 1955 camera instruction books. In 1961 the Ford Motor Company ran a huge promotion that featured the *Peanuts* gang boasting about how economical and safe the new line of Ford Falcons were. "We got criticized quite a bit for that," Schulz recalled years later,

---

Wow! In 1986 the city of Hamilton, Ohio, changed its name to Hamilton!, Ohio.

"which is something that always puzzled me." After Ford, the *Peanuts* kids spent 15 years selling Metropolitan Life Insurance. "We also received criticism for that. A lot of people apparently hate insurance companies. Maybe they're justified."

THE BEAGLE HAS LANDED

The 1960s belonged to *Peanuts*. The optimism of the 1950s had been diminished by the looming threat of a nuclear war with the USSR, and people were scared. That may explain the appeal of *Happiness Is a Warm Puppy*, the first in a series of little square-shaped books that featured each of the *Peanuts* characters celebrating the simple things in life. In 1963 *Happiness Is a Warm Puppy* became the first book based on a comic strip to reach the *New York Times* bestseller list. And as the public mood grew even darker following the assassination of President Kennedy and the escalation of the Vietnam War, *Peanuts* became more popular, treading a thin line between innocence (the kids still play ball in the sandlot) and rebellion (a bird complains to Snoopy that no one understands his generation). Basically, *Peanuts* was *everywhere*.

• In 1965 the *Peanuts* gang made the cover of *Time* magazine.

• That same year, a Presbyterian minister named Robert Short received Schulz's permission to write *The Gospel According to Peanuts*, which presented strips from the comic as modern-day Christian parables. The book sold more than 10 million copies.

• In 1966 a rock group called the Royal Guardsmen sold three million copies of their song "Snoopy and the Red Baron."

• In 1967 *Peanuts* made their off-Broadway debut with the musical *You're a Good Man, Charlie Brown* (starring as Charlie Brown: 22-year-old Gary Burghoff, who later played Radar on M*A*S*H). The musical ran for 1,597 performances and was revived on Broadway in 1998, when it won two Tony Awards.

But perhaps the *Peanuts* kids' greatest achievement in the 1960s was when they accompanied the *Apollo 10* astronauts to the Moon in May 1969. The crew chose Snoopy as its official mascot and named the lunar module after him. The command module was called *Charlie Brown*.

For part III of the Peanuts *story, turn to page 435.*

COMIC PHRASES

Many common words and phrases were invented by cartoonists and first used in comic strips.

PHRASE: Security blanket
ORIGIN: Pioneering child psychologist Richard Passman is given credit for identifying the phenomenon of children habitually clutching or carrying a favorite toy for comfort and security. Charles Schulz first used the concept in the June 1, 1954, *Peanuts* comic strip by giving Linus a blanket to carry everywhere he went. Linus called it his "security blanket." The term is now used by psychologists to define a child's (or anyone's) excessive attachment to a particular object.

PHRASE: "We have met the enemy and he is us."
ORIGIN: After winning the Battle of Lake Erie in the War of 1812, Commodore Oliver Perry wrote in a dispatch to General William Henry Harrison, "We have met the enemy, and he is ours." Walt Kelly, author of the comic strip *Pogo*, reworded the phrase as "We have met the enemy and he is us," in the foreword to his 1953 *Pogo* collection *The Pogo Papers*. The meaning: Mankind's greatest threat is...mankind. The quote became better known when Kelly used it on a poster he was hired to illustrate for the first Earth Day in 1970.

WORD: The heebie-jeebies
ORIGIN: Billy DeBeck coined the term in his hugely popular 1920s comic strip, *Barney Google and Snuffy Smith*, about a community of backwoods hillbillies and moonshiners. It first appeared in a 1923 strip where Barney tells someone to "get that stupid look offa your pan. You gimme the heeby jeebys!" It meant "a feeling of discomfort." Other phrases coined by DeBeck: "horsefeathers," "hotsie-totsie," and "googly-eyed" (after Barney Google, who had huge, bulbous eyes). The strip also gave us the nickname "Sparky," from the name of Barney's horse, Sparkplug. (Many young comic-strip fans were given the nickname "Sparky," among them, *Peanuts* creator Charles Schulz.)

Who's the "king" in chicken à la king? Edward VII of England.

WORD: Palooka

ORIGIN: It came from the main character of the 1920s strip *Joe Palooka*. Joe Palooka was a boxer—likable but dumb, a trait that probably came from repeated blows to his head in the ring. Soon after the strip's debut, any big, dumb guy might be called a palooka.

WORD: Milquetoast

ORIGIN: "Milk toast" was a simple dish (toast served in milk) frequently served at soup kitchens in the 1920s. Harold Webster named the main character in his late 1920s strip, *The Timid Soul*, Caspar Milquetoast. Thanks to the comic strip, by the 1930s the word "milquetoast" had become common slang to describe anybody who, like Milquetoast, was weak and timid.

PHRASE: Sadie Hawkins Day

ORIGIN: It's from Al Capp's *L'il Abner*. One day a year in the comic strip's rural setting of Dogpatch, single women would chase the single men around. If they caught one, they got to keep—er, *marry* him. The day got its name from Sadie Hawkins, the first woman in Dogpatch who caught a husband that way. High schools in the United States still hold "Sadie Hawkins Dances," to which the girls invite the boys.

PHRASE: Foo fighter

ORIGIN: In Bill Holman's 1930s strip *Smokey Stover*, the title character rode around in a bizarre-looking two-wheeled fire engine (with a fire hydrant attached to it) that Smokey called a "foo fighter." The term was used by World War II pilots for any unidentified aircraft (including UFOs). The phrase became popular again in the 1990s when it was used as the name of the rock band Foo Fighters.

*　　*　　*

THREE THINGS YOU DIDN'T KNOW HAD NAMES

- *Obdormition:* the scientific term for a limb that's "asleep"
- *Ophryon:* the space between your eyebrows
- *Purlicue:* that tight bridge of skin between the thumb and an extended forefinger

Q: What do you call a newly formed nerve cell? A: A *neuroblast*.

GOSH, BATMAN...

The 1960s Batman TV series is well known for its campiness. But we've always liked the lessons on civics and citizenship Batman/Bruce Wayne gave to his ward, Robin/Dick Grayson. Here's some of Batman's choicest advice.

Robin: You can't get away from Batman that easy!
Batman: *Easily.*
Robin: *Easily.*
Batman: Good grammar is essential, Robin.

Batman: Better put five cents in the meter.
Robin: No policeman's going to give the Batmobile a ticket.
Batman: This money goes to building better roads. We all must do our part.

Dick: Gosh, economics is sure a dull subject.
Bruce: Oh, you must be jesting, Dick. Economics dull? The glamour, the romance of commerce. It's the very lifeblood of our society.

Dick: What's the use of learning French, anyway?
Bruce: Language is the key to world peace. If we all spoke each other's tongues, perhaps the scourge of war would be ended forever.
Dick: Gosh, Bruce, yes. I'll get these darn verbs if they kill me!

Batman: When you get a little older, you'll see how easy it is to become lured by the female of the species.
Robin: I guess you can never trust a woman.
Batman: You've made a hasty generalization, Robin. It's a bad habit to get into.

Robin: Gosh, Batman, those look like honest eyes.
Batman: Never trust the old chestnut, "Crooks have beady little eyes." It's false.

Bruce: Most Americans don't realize what we owe to the ancient Incas. Very few appreciate they gave us the white potato and many varieties of Indian corn.
Dick: Now whenever I eat mashed potatoes, I for one will think of the Incas.

Robin: We'd better hurry, Batman.
Batman: Not too fast, Robin. In good bat-climbing as in good driving, one must never sacrifice safety for speed.
Robin: Right again, Batman.

It takes a combine harvester 9 seconds to harvest enough wheat to make 70 loaves of bread.

NAME THAT BASEBALL PLAYER

The stories behind some of baseball's most colorful nicknames.

TOMATO FACE

Nick Cullop got the nickname "Tomato Face" because his face turned bright red whenever he got angry, usually after striking out. His face turned red a lot in 1931—he led the league in strikeouts that season. Bonus: That year, Tomato Face played for the Cincinnati Reds.

THE HUMAN RAIN DELAY

Before *every* pitch of *every* at-bat, Mike Hargrove (the 1974 Rookie of the Year) attempted to psych out pitchers with an annoyingly long ritual: He'd step out of the batter's box, adjust his helmet, adjust his batting glove, pull each of his sleeves up, adjust his gloves again, wipe his hands on his pants, adjust his helmet again, etc., and then finally get back in the batter's box. The process took up so much time that sportscasters started equating Hargrove's at-bats with a rain delay.

LADY

Pro sports is a tough, macho world. Unlike many of his Detroit teammates, Charles Baldwin (who played in the 1880s) didn't drink alcohol or smoke cigarettes, and made it a point never to curse. His teammates thought that made him rather ladylike.

PUTT-PUTT

Richie Ashburn ran around the bases so fast that Ted Williams nicknamed him "Putt-Putt," commenting to a reporter that Ashburn "ran as if he had twin motors in his pants."

THE GROUNDED BLIMP

Ernest Phelps was a heavyset guy, which earned him the nicknames "Babe" (like Babe Ruth) and "the Blimp." In the 1940s, his team, the Brooklyn Dodgers, began to fly to road games, but Phelps opted to take the train because he was afraid of flying, which made him "the Grounded Blimp."

OIL CAN

Dennis Boyd, who pitched for the Red Sox in the 1980s, grew up playing baseball in the hot summers of Mississippi. Every time he'd drink a beverage to cool down, he supposedly remarked that it was so smooth, it was "just like drinking oil."

OLD ACHES AND PAINS

Luke Appling drove his White Sox teammates crazy during the 1930s and '40s because he constantly complained about minor medical discomforts, like a sore back or a sprained finger.

DUCKY WUCKY

Joe Medwick waddled when he walked, so fans in the 1930s nick-named him "Ducky Wucky," or just "Ducky." But Medwick wasn't chubby—he was actually very muscular, so his St. Louis Cardinals teammates (probably too scared to call the tough Medwick "Ducky Wucky") called him "Muscles."

THE GAY RELIEVER

This nickname would mean something entirely different today, but in the 1940s, "gay" meant "happy," and Joe Page, a top relief pitch-er with the Yankees, was well known for his sunny disposition.

CATFISH

In 1965 Kansas City Athletics owner Charlie Finley signed pitch-er Jim Hunter and decided Hunter needed a flashy nickname. Off the top of his head, Finley created a story that Hunter had earned the nickname "Catfish" as a little boy after he'd caught a giant catfish. The name stuck, and over his entire major league career, Hunter was rarely referred to as Jim.

*   *   *

"Baseball is like church. Many attend; few understand."

—Leo Durocher

LOONEY LAWS

Believe it or not, these laws are real.

Playing with Silly String is against the law in Lodi, California.

In Tennessee, it's illegal to sell bologna on Sundays.

In Seattle, a dog must pay full bus fare if it weighs more than 25 pounds.

In Michigan, it is against the law for a lady to lift her skirt more than six inches while walking through a mud puddle.

It's illegal to hunt moths under streetlights in Los Angeles.

No liquor may be served in Utah on Arbor Day.

Geese may not walk down Main Street in McDonald, Ohio.

In Chaseville, New York, it's against the law to drive a goat cart past a church in a "ridiculous fashion."

A Tylertown, Mississippi, ordinance prohibits shaving in the middle of Main Street.

In Louisiana, a barber may not charge a bald man more than 25¢ for a haircut.

It's against the law in Virginia to call someone on the telephone and not say anything.

In Alaska, it's illegal to push a live moose out of a moving airplane.

It's the law in French Lick Springs, Indiana, for all black cats to wear bells on Friday the 13th.

Women in Carrizozo, New Mexico, may not legally be seen in public with hairy legs.

In West Virginia, only babies may ride in baby carriages.

In Georgia, it's against the law to spread a rumor, but only if it isn't true.

In Corpus Christi, Texas, it's illegal to raise alligators in your home.

It's illegal in Indiana to open a can of food with a gun.

It's against the law in Arkansas to blindfold cows on public highways.

In Minnesota, you may be jailed for standing in front of a moving train.

How about you? The average adult American male receives six Christmas presents.

RETURN TO THE MOON, PART II

NASA's last Apollo moon mission: 1972. And we haven't been back since. But plans are underway for Project Constellation, a new lunar excursion to blast off in 2019. Here's Part II of America's next manned voyage into space. (Part I begins on page 122.)

DEJA VIEW

NASA's budget for a return to the Moon is tight, so the next generation of spacecraft are expected to look a lot like the Apollo craft, only larger and bristling with modern computers and other technology that didn't exist in the early 1970s. The Command Module has been renamed the Crew Exploration Vehicle (CEV), and will be large enough to carry four astronauts to the Moon instead of three. The Service Module will keep its name, but the Lunar Excursion Module will be renamed Lunar Surface Access Module (LSAM). During the Apollo missions, each crew got to name their spacecraft—the *Apollo 11* command module, for example, was named *Columbia*, and the lunar module was *Eagle*. This time, however, NASA is naming them. The new CSM has already been named *Orion*, and the LSAM will be *Artemis*.

UP AND AWAY

The biggest difference between the Apollo program and the new lunar program will be the rockets that lift the astronauts and their spacecraft into space. The days of sending everything up on a single, giant Saturn rocket are over—NASA doesn't have any rockets large enough to carry the bigger, heavier craft into space, and has no plans to develop one. Instead, it plans to launch two rockets for each Moon mission. The first, called the Ares V, will carry the LSAM lunar lander and a rocket called the Earth Departure Stage (EDS) into orbit. Ares V launches will be unmanned (one reason for dividing the mission is to reduce the risk to the astronauts).

Once the Ares V has safely entered Earth orbit, the astronauts will ride the Crew Exploration Vehicle into space atop a much

---

Bonjour, **Pardner: Quebec is twice the size of Texas.**

smaller Ares I rocket and dock with the LSAM, then the EDS will fire and launch everything on a course toward the Moon.

The rest of the mission will unfold in much the same way that the Apollo missions did, with one notable exception: Because the CEV and its attached Service Module are now fully automated, *everybody* gets to travel down to the lunar surface aboard the LSAM.

DEJA VIEW ALL OVER AGAIN

There's a good chance that the Ares I and V will look familiar to you too, especially if you're familiar with the Space Shuttle:

The Ares V. Picture the Space Shuttle sitting on the launchpad, attached to the giant orange external fuel tank and the two slender, white, solid rocket boosters. Now take away the Space Shuttle—the Ares V won't be much more than that. The Earth Departure Stage and the LSAM will be stacked *on top* of the fuel tank instead of attached to the side like the Space Shuttle. Putting the cargo on top is less risky because it can't be struck by insulating foam or other debris that falls off the fuel tank or the solid rocket boosters during launch. Falling foam is what doomed the Space Shuttle *Columbia* in February 2003.

The Ares I. Now picture a single solid rocket booster sitting on the launchpad. Stack a small external fuel tank on top of it, and put the Crew Exploration Vehicle and Service Module on top of that. That, in a nutshell, will be the Ares I.

READY WHEN YOU ARE

Because Project Constellation's long-term vision extends beyond simple Moon landings, the Crew Exploration Vehicle will be designed to stay in orbit for as long as six months at a time, so that if NASA ever realizes its long term goal of building a permanent base on the Moon, the astronauts will be able to spend months there before returning home.

Are you old enough to remember the Apollo Command Modules splashing down in the middle of the ocean? Water landings had a lot to offer, because 1) water is softer than hard ground, and 2) even if the capsules re-entered the atmosphere off course, the oceans are so large that it was still likely to land *somewhere* in the

The *Apollo 11* astronaut who *didn't* walk on the Moon: Michael Collins.

ocean, and rescue ships could be stationed over hundreds of square miles to recover the capsule wherever it did land.

This time, however, NASA hopes to design a space capsule that can touch down on land. NASA is still evaluating different methods of softening the impact of a dry landing. Parachutes will still do much of the work, but something more will be needed to slow the capsule to less than 18 mph so that it can land on hard ground. One possibility is small retro-rockets that will fire just before touchdown; another possibility is a set of airbags, similar to the ones used in automobiles, that will deploy when the capsule is less than 1,000 feet above the ground.

WHERE TO STAY

In the 1970s, budget cuts forced NASA to scrap *Apollo 18*, *Apollo 19*, and *Apollo 20*, and abandon Moon exploration altogether to free up money for the development of the Space Shuttle. This time NASA hopes to return to the Moon for good: The first manned mission to the Moon is scheduled for 2019, and NASA hopes to have a permanent base on the Moon as early as 2024. The Apollo missions explored areas around the lunar equator, but a base would probably be established near the Moon's north or south pole—the poles receive ample sunlight, which solar panels can use to provide energy to the base.

The south pole is the most likely candidate, because of its proximity to the Shackleton crater, parts of which are in permanent shadow. Because these areas are never heated by the Sun, they may contain frozen water that the astronauts could convert to hydrogen and oxygen, which can be used to make rocket fuel. The oxygen, of course, could also be used to provide breathable air for the Moon base. It may even be possible to convert lunar soil into rocket fuel, which is one of the things that makes NASA so interested in returning to the Moon—it may one day serve as both a fuel depot and a launching ground for a mission to Mars.

Mars? Yes, Mars. Have we whetted your appetite for a futuristic trip to the Red Planet? NASA's thinking about it, too.
For Part III of the story, turn to page 457.

SHOT HIMSELF IN THE...

How can someone accidentally getting shot be funny? Well, according to Mel Brooks, "Tragedy is when I cut my finger. Comedy is when you fall into a sewer and die."

L EG
Anna Herrera-Gomez of Oklahoma City was at a shooting range in 2006 when a hot shell casing from the 9-millimeter pistol she was shooting fell down the front of her shirt. She jumped, grabbed her shirt, and accidentally shot herself in the leg. According to the police report, she suffered only a minor wound.

...GROIN

In 2004 a man in Vancouver, British Columbia, was waving a .357 Magnum revolver around during an argument regarding, according to news reports, a "love triangle." At some point the man shoved the gun into his pants and accidentally shot himself in the groin. The two other members of the triangle brought the man to the hospital, where he was treated, released, and arrested.

...STOMACH

A 16-year-old boy in Lake Worth, Florida, found a live .45-caliber cartridge in his back yard in December 2005. For reasons unknown —perhaps he was just curious about how a shell fires—he decided to pound on it with a hammer. He found out: The pounding triggered it to fire, and the bullet ended up in the boy's abdomen. He was treated at a local medical center and, fortunately, wasn't badly injured.

...BUTT

In August 2004, a man on trial for assaulting a police officer escaped from the Bristow, Oklahoma, courthouse. A huge manhunt ensued, prompting local resident Drew Patterson to decide he'd better protect himself. So he grabbed his .22-caliber pistol, stuck it in his waistband...and shot himself in the buttocks. Then, he later told reporters, he went to his parents' home and said, "Mom, I did something bad." He was treated at a local hospital and released, saying it was "the most embarrassing moment of my life."

The 21 smallest U.S. states, combined, are still smaller than Alaska.

...ARM

In 2006 a Wellington, New Zealand, police officer was called to the scene of a domestic dispute. When the man of the house started making threatening statements, the officer pulled out a stun gun...and accidentally shot himself in the arm with the 50,000-volt weapon. The officer went on to accidentally shoot the man's 16-year-old son and then his 21-year-old daughter, after which the suspect, who hadn't been shot, surrendered.

...KEYS

A 50-year-old Iranian man accidentally shot himself in the leg in 1988. He recovered and hadn't thought about it for years...until the leg suddenly started to hurt in 2004. When the pain became excruciating he went to the hospital, where X-rays showed that he had a set of keys imbedded in his leg. Doctors who treated the man told reporters that the bullet from the 1988 accident had apparently struck keys in the man's pocket and propelled them into his thigh. The bullet had been removed—but the keys were left behind. The man's pain went away when the keys were finally removed.

...CALF (AND GROIN)

In 2006 a 23-year-old Wichita, Kansas, man attempted to kidnap a teenager in what the police report identified as a dispute over stereo speakers. When the kidnapping started going badly, the 23-year-old fired a shot at the teen but missed. He then shoved the gun into his waistband, where it went off and hit him in the testicles. Then, according to police reports, he "cringed"...which caused the gun to go off again, hitting him in the left calf. The injured man walked (or hobbled) to a medical center, where he was treated and released into police custody.

...FINGER

A 21-year-old man in North Vancouver, British Columbia, was playing with a loaded gun—in his bathroom—on New Year's Day 2006. The gun went off, hitting him in the fingers. (Whew!) "Perhaps our mothers never explained to us that it was not a good idea to play with handguns whilst using the restroom," the Royal Canadian Mounted Police said in a press release. "But then again, maybe that was supposed to be a given."

Don't let the movies fool you: An Old West stagecoach traveled at an average speed of 4 mph.

CAN WE PICK YOUR NOSE?

In past Bathroom Readers, we've printed lots of inadvertently funny signs. The following real signs were supposed to be funny.

At a maternity store:
We're open for Labor Day.

At a gynecologist's office:
Dr. Jones, at your cervix.

On a garbage truck:
Yesterday's meals on wheels.

On a septic tank truck:
We're #1 in the #2 business.

At a handyman's office:
We repair what your husband fixed.

At a plumber's office:
Don't sleep with a drip. Call your plumber.

At a pizza parlor:
7 days without pizza makes one weak.

At an optometrist's:
If you don't see what you're looking for, you've come to the right place.

At a plastic surgeon's office:
Can we pick your nose?

At a tire shop:
Invite us to your next blowout.

On a tow truck:
We don't charge an arm and a leg. We want tows.

At an electrician's office:
Let us remove your shorts.

In a non-smoking area:
If we see smoke, we will assume you are on fire and take appropriate action.

On a maternity ward door:
Push, push, push.

At a veterinarian:
Be back in 5 minutes. Sit! Stay!

At a car dealership:
The best way to get back on your feet: miss a car payment.

At a used car lot:
Second-hand cars in first-crash condition.

The only popcorn museum in the world is located in Marion, Ohio.

NAME YOUR AWARD

*Many of the top honors in the arts, sports, and
the sciences are named after people. Here are
the stories of the names behind the awards.*

JOHN HEISMAN

Heisman coached football at Auburn, Clemson, and Georgia
Tech in the 1890s and early 20th century. In the 1930s, he
worked as athletic director at the Downtown Athletic Club in
New York City. Since 1935, the club has issued the Heisman Trophy—for the year's best college football player (voted on by sports
reporters)—in his honor. Past winners include Reggie Bush, Barry
Sanders, Tony Dorsett, Roger Staubach, and O. J. Simpson.

ANTOINETTE PERRY

Perry was a stage actress and director in the early 20th century.
She also founded the American Theatre Wing in the 1940s,
which, among other theatrical-promoting activities, hands out the
Antoinette Perry, or "Tony," Awards honoring the best Broadway
plays, musicals, and performances of each year. All-time Tony
leader: Actress Julie Harris was nominated 10 times and won 5.

JOHN NEWBERY

John Newbery was an 18th-century publisher who specialized in
children's books, and is believed to be the first publisher ever to
do so. Since 1922, the American Library Association has annually
presented the Newbery Award to the author of the best new children's novel. Some Newbery winners: Hugh Lofting (for *The Voy-
ages of Doctor Dolittle*), Esther Forbes (*Johnny Tremain*), and
Katherine Paterson (*Bridge to Terabithia*).

RANDOLPH CALDECOTT

Caldecott was an illustrator in 19th-century England. He drew the
pictures for books including *The Babes in the Wood* and *The House
that Jack Built*. Like the Newbery Award, the Caldecott Medal is a
prize for children's literature presented by the American Library
Association, but this one awards only the illustrators. Caldecott-

---

Fame has its ups and downs: The world record for pogo stick jumping is 41 hours.

winning titles include *The Snowy Day* (Ezra Jack Keats), *The Polar Express* (Chris Van Allsburg), and *Where the Wild Things Are* (Maurice Sendak).

GEORGE FOSTER PEABODY

Peabody was a businessman who switched to public service in 1906 at age 54, working for various universities as well as the Democratic National Committee. After Peabody died in 1938, the University of Georgia, where he'd served on the board, established the Peabody Award. Officially presented by the college's journalism school, the award honors excellent radio and TV reporting and socially redeeming programming. Winners in 2006 included *60 Minutes*, *American Masters*, *The Office*, and *Scrubs*.

IRVING G. THALBERG

Thalberg was head of the Production Division at MGM Studios in the 1920s and 1930s. He sought to make film more respectable—not just profitable. He was the man behind *Mutiny on the Bounty* (1935) and the Marx Brothers' *A Night at the Opera* (1935), but he never allowed his name to be credited in the films he produced. He died of pneumonia in 1936 at age 37. Since 1938, the Academy of Motion Picture Arts and Sciences has presented the Irving G. Thalberg Memorial Award. It's a lifetime achievement award presented at the Oscars to a well-established director or producer. Past winners include Alfred Hitchcock, Steven Spielberg, and Billy Wilder.

WILL EISNER

Eisner was a writer and illustrator who pioneered the long-form comic, or "graphic novel," with his 1940s comic series *The Spirit*. Eisner Awards, established in 1988 in his honor, are given out each year to artists, writers, and publishers for excellence in comic books. Categories include Best Short Story, Best Writer, Best Cover Artist, Best Colorist, and more than 20 others. Past winners include Stan Lee for *The Silver Surfer: Parable*; Bill Watterson's *Calvin and Hobbes*; and Frank Miller for *Sin City*.

JOHN D. AND CATHERINE T. MACARTHUR

MacArthur made millions as the owner of several insurance com-

Bob Hope's autobiography is titled *Confessions of a Hooker*. (It was about golf.)

panies in the 1930s and 1940s. His wife, Catherine, held board positions at many of her husband's firms. When John MacArthur died in 1978, most of his fortune was used to start the John D. and Catherine T. MacArthur Foundation (Catherine died three years later). The major work of the charity is the awarding of the MacArthur Fellowship, or "genius grant." Between 20 and 40 Americans each year—nominated by a small selection committee —receive $500,000 dispensed over five years as an "investment in a person's originality, insight, and potential." Among the more than 700 "geniuses" are historians, writers, scientists, artists, musicians, and inventors. Some well-known MacArthur fellows: writer Thomas Pynchon, paleontologist Stephen Jay Gould, and critic Henry Louis Gates.

JOHN CHARLES FIELDS

Canadian mathematician John Charles Fields died in 1932 and stipulated in his will that a prize be awarded every four years to two, three, or four groundbreaking mathematicians who are under the age of 40. Presented by the International Mathematical Union, the Fields Medal is the highest honor in math. Andrei Okounkov won a Fields Medal in 2006 for "his contributions to bridging probability, representation theory, and algebraic geometry." (Don't worry—we don't know what that means, either.)

*   *   *

RIDERS IN THE SKY

Headlining musicians' contracts usually include "riders" requiring that certain items be provided backstage at each concert. Here are some bizarre rider requests.

P. Diddy: napkins with his name printed on all of them

Nine Inch Nails: cornstarch

Modest Mouse: new socks

Hank Williams III: a great white shark

Aerosmith: fresh corn on the cob

Mariah Carey: puppies and kittens to keep her company

Iggy Pop: "seven dwarves"

What do Sandra Bullock, Bill Cosby & Bruce Willis have in common? They're all ex-bartenders.

THE BIG APPLE

Some thoughts on America's largest and most famous city.

"One belongs to New York instantly. One belongs to it as much in five minutes as in five years."
—**Thomas Wolfe**

"Every great wave of popular passion that rolls up on the prairies is dashed to spray when it strikes the hard rocks of Manhattan."
—**H. L. Mencken**

"I moved to New York City for my health. I'm paranoid, and it was the only place where my fears were justified."
—**Anita Weiss**

"New York is nothing like Paris; it is nothing like London; and it is not Spokane multiplied by sixty, or Detroit multiplied by four. It is by all odds the loftiest of cities. It even managed to reach the highest point in the sky at the lowest moment of the Depression."
—**E. B. White**

"I don't need bodyguards. I'm from the South Bronx."
—**Al Pacino**

"In New York, you are constantly faced with this very urgent decision that you have to make, about every 20 minutes: You have to decide, immediately, 'Do I look at the most beautiful woman in the world or the craziest guy in the world?'"
—**David Cross**

"It is ridiculous to set a detective story in New York City. New York City is itself a detective story."
—**Agatha Christie**

"No matter how many times I visit this great city, I'm always struck by the same thing: a yellow taxi cab."
—**Scott Adams**

"The last time anybody made a list of the top hundred character attributes of New Yorkers, common sense snuck in at Number 79."
—**Douglas Adams**

"New York is the only city in the world where you can get deliberately run down on the sidewalk by a pedestrian."
—**Russell Baker**

When told that General Grant drank too much whiskey, President Lincoln reportedly replied...

"Someone did a study of the three most-often-heard phrases in New York City. One is, 'Hey, taxi!' Two is, 'What train do I take to get to Bloomingdales?' And three is, 'Don't worry, it's only a flesh wound.'"

—David Letterman

"I can't wait to get back to New York City, where at least when I walk down the street, no one ever hesitates to tell me exactly what they think of me."

— Ani DiFranco

"New York is a granite beehive, where people jostle and whir like molecules in an overheated jar."

—Nigel Goslin

"This is New York, and there's no law against being annoying."

—William Kunstler

Major Strasser: Are you one of those people who cannot imagine the Germans in their beloved Paris?

Rick: It's not particularly *my* beloved Paris.

Heinz: Can you imagine us in London?

Rick: When you get there, ask me!

Major Strasser: How about New York?

Rick: Well, there are certain sections of New York, Major, that I wouldn't advise you to try to invade.

—*Casablanca*

*   *   *

DOMESTIC DISPUTE

In May 2007, drivers in Braunschweig, Germany, noticed a sign in the window of a house that said, "Help! Please call the police!" Next to the sign were a little girl and a little boy. The police were alerted to a possible kidnapping and swarmed the house. The woman who answered the door (the mother of the two children) had no clue what that sign was doing there. It turned out that the mother had told her daughter to clean her bedroom. The daughter refused, which led to a big fight, after which the disgruntled daughter put up the sign. The cops sided with the mother. "That room looked like a battlefield," said a police spokesman.

HOW DO YOUR TASTE BUDS WORK?

Why do different foods taste different? How do we differentiate between those tastes? How many different tastes can we taste? And why do we taste in the first place? If questions like that have been bothering you for years, then have a taste of this article.

HERE COME DE BUDS

Stick out your tongue and look in the mirror. See those tiny bumps on your tongue, near the tip and along the sides and in the back? Those are called *papillae* (puh-pih'-lee), and many of those mounds house cavities, each containing 30 to 100 clusters of long, narrow *neuroepithelial* cells. The hairlike tips of those cells reach out of openings—called *taste pores*—on the papillae and interact with molecules of the food we eat. Those clusters are our taste buds, and each of us has about 10,000 of them.

There are four different types of papillae on your tongue:

• *Filiform:* These are the most numerous of the papillae—and are the only kind that contain no taste buds. Shaped like cones, they're arranged in rows on top of the tongue parallel to the center groove. They give the tongue the abrasive texture that aids in the breakdown of food.

• *Fungiform:* Fungiform means "mushroom-shaped" in Latin. These are located on the top of the tongue, mostly near the tip.

• *Foliate:* These form the ridges and grooves on the side and toward the back of the tongue.

• *Circumvallate:* There are only between 3 and 14 of these (usually). They look like large bumps in a curving line on the back and top of the tongue.

A TASTE OF DANGER

When you put a piece of food in your mouth, your saliva immediately starts dissolving it, and some of the food molecules come into contact with *chemoreceptors* on the taste bud cells. Those molecules are known as *tastants* (the equivalent of the nose's *odors*). The chemoreceptors are connected via *synapses* to sensory neurons that lead directly to the brain, and they carry information to the brain about that food. This works for obvious and practical reasons: It allows us to differentiate between food that is beneficial to us and food that is not. Remember: You didn't get your sense of taste at the hardware store—it's been evolving in animals for hundreds of millions of years, and your ancestors did a lot of the dirty work for you.

Much of what our bodies "know" automatically today we actually learned through that process. Poisonous foods often taste very bitter—and it's no accident that we don't like bitter foods. Protein-rich foods often taste "savory," and we tend to like that taste. So what we like and dislike has largely been programmed by the needs of our body. And remember also that you've likely already used your other senses (smell, vision, touch) to test the food—so taste is the last checkpoint before the food goes down the gullet.

A MATTER OF TASTE

Each taste bud is a cluster of cells equipped to sense different chemicals. Those chemicals are then translated as "tastes" by our brains. They do this in complex biochemical and bioelectrical processes, but the basics are pretty simple. According to biologists, for all the thousands of different foods out there, there are just five different fundamental tastes that we are able to detect: salty, sour, sweet, bitter, and *umami* (or savory). And they are all defined by the chemicals that result in them.

The Channelers

• *Salty* foods taste that way because they contain positively charged *sodium* ions. Those ions pass into special channels on some taste buds, triggering a bioelectrical interaction that results in the "salty" signal being sent to the brain.

• *Sour* foods get that quality from the acids they contain ("acid" comes from the Latin *acidus*—which means "sour"). Acids are defined by the presence of positively charged *hydrogen* atoms. Like sodium ions, they pass into special channels in the taste buds, initiating the "sour" signal. (Examples: Vinegar contains *acetic acid*, and citrus fruits like limes and lemons contain *citric acid*.)

So what if it's fake? Loch Ness Monster tourism adds $40 million a year to Scotland's economy.

The Receptors

Sweet, bitter, and umami foods are different. Each of them contains substances that don't pass into channels on the taste buds—they bond to specialized receptors on the surface of the buds, which trigger a cascade of biochemical events that result in these specific taste signals.

• *Sweet* foods contain *carbohydrates*, otherwise known as sugars (like *sucrose* and *fructose*), as well as some other substances that result in the "sweet" signal.

• *Bitter* foods can contain a great variety of substances, such as *quinine* (found in the bark of the South American *cinchona* tree), *caffeine*, and *naringin*, which is found in grapefruit.

• *Umami*, or *savory*, foods contain certain *amino acids*, the building blocks of proteins. One example is *glutamates*, found in the once-popular flavoring agent monosodium glutamate (frequently used in Chinese food), but also in fish, aged cheeses, mushrooms, processed meats, and fermented foods like soy sauce. (Umami means "deliciousness" in Japanese.).

Salty, sweet, and umami foods are generally translated as "good" or "safe" tastes by our brains, because they contain substances we need to survive. Sour and bitter foods, evolutionary biologists say, have been to some degree hardwired in our brains as "bad" tastes as a defense mechanism, since they are so often the tastes associated with toxic substances.

TASTY TREATS

That's how taste buds work—but it's not the whole story. We can detect many different chemicals with our taste buds, but they only register as five different tastes (though they can overlap to create many different taste sensations). Your nose—or *olfactory gland*, to be precise—on the other hand can distinguish between thousands of different chemicals. And when you eat it's working overtime, sending information to your brain about the food, gathered through the nostrils and the back of the mouth. Biologists say this accounts for as much as 80% of what we know as "flavor." (A well known test of this is to hold your nose and eat something.)

• Newborns and children have additional taste buds on their

palate, on the inside of their cheeks, and in the back of the throat. They are usually all gone by the time we are adults.

• People have differing taste preferences, of course, but recent research shows that different peoples around the world differ *genetically* as to how they taste substances. A "geography of taste" map published by Cornell University shows, for example, the difference in sensitivity to the bitter chemical *phenylthiocarbamide*. Native South Americans are very sensitive to it, but Native Alaskans are not. And Aboriginal Australians can barely detect it at all.

• *Dysguesia* is a condition displaying an altered sense of taste. It can have many causes, including side effects of medications and increased hormone production during pregnancy. (Women often show an enhanced sensitivity to bitterness in early pregnancy.)

• Studies show that about 35% of women and 15% of men are "super-tasters." They have extra—and extra-sensitive—taste buds. (Wine tasters are usually super-tasters.)

• Want to know if you're a super-taster? Yale University developed a simple test that you can do at home: You'll need some blue food coloring, a piece of paper with a seven-millimeter hole cut in it, and a magnifying glass. Put enough food coloring on the tip of your tongue to turn the top blue. The papillae will not be affected and will stand out as pink dots. Put the paper on your tongue with the hole on top of the tip. Using a mirror, look at the hole through the magnifying glass and count the pink dots: If you have fewer than 15, you're a "non-taster"; between 15 and 35 and you're an "average taster"; more than 35 and you're a "super-taster." (Cheers!)

*　　*　　*

WIENER ON THE ROAD

Walter Reckling, a 46-year-old truck driver from Germany, decided to cook some sausages in his cab...while he was driving. But when Reckling rounded a corner, his portable stove tipped over and the cab caught fire. He was able to pull over safely, but had to be taken to the hospital where he was treated for smoke inhalation. (The sausages were a complete loss.)

1987: THE PRICE WAS RIGHT

It's always fascinating to see what things used to cost. Here's a look at the prices of a few common items from 20 years ago, back when Uncle John was just starting to make Bathroom Readers.

- The average cost of a new home: $127,200

- A VCR (no DVDs yet): $270

- Ground beef: $3 a pound

- An 11-ounce can of ground coffee (Folgers): $2

- A six-pack of Coke: $1.89

- A box of frozen waffles: $1.50

- A 10-disc CD changer: $400

- A camcorder: $1,100

- A first-class stamp: 22¢

- Gas: 96¢ per gallon

- A candy bar: 40¢

- A Sony Walkman: $45

- A bottle of Advil: $6

- A dozen eggs: about $1

- A gallon of milk: $1.80

- A loaf of bread: about $1.25

- A pound of bacon: $1.80

- The average price of a new car: $10,500

- A cup of coffee at 7-Eleven: 49¢

- An LP (vinyl): $10

- A 25-inch color TV: $280

- A microwave: $200

- A pack of cigarettes: $1.25

- Film developing: $3 per roll of film (digital cameras weren't available yet)

- A McDonald's hamburger: 59¢

- A box of cereal: $1.90

- A copy of USA Today: 50¢

- A pair of Nikes: $45

- One share of Microsoft stock: about $100

- A basic haircut at Supercuts: $6

- A car phone: $1,400

Minimum wage in 1987: $3.35 an hour.

ANIMAL FART NEWS

Porter the Wonder Dog said to Uncle John one day: "Why do you always make such a big deal when I fart? Every animal does it." After Uncle John recovered from the shock of hearing his dog talk, he asked us to verify Porter's claims.

REDUCING EMOOSIONS. The world's grazing cattle are thought to emit as much as four percent of the Earth's harmful greenhouse gas emissions. The culprit: the methane gas from their flatulent eruptions (as well as from their burps). Scientists at Germany's University of Hohenheim are developing a "bovine Beano" pill that will help counter the gaseous effects. Instead of just passing the methane, cows who take the pill will convert the methane to glucose. In addition to reducing farts, the increased glucose will help the cows produce more milk. The reason the pill is still in development is that it's currently larger than a human fist, which, even for a cow, would make it a tough pill to swallow.

GAS BOMBS. Soldier termites tend to build up a lot of gas (and feces) inside them. That's not only nasty—it can be deadly. The buildup can lead to what is called *autothysis* which, in layman's terms, means the termite actually explodes. But it's not all for nothing: The explosion, which releases a sticky substance, is triggered by an attack on the termite colony, usually by invading ants. The foul secretion helps fight off the ants, but the exploding termites sacrifice themselves in the process.

CALL OF THE WILD. The female southern pine beetle attracts potential mates by emitting a pheromone when she farts. But interested males have to act quickly—the smell is so strong that it can also attract potential predators.

SPROUTING FEARS OF A CATASTROPHE. We reported this story in our *Uncle John's Slimy Sea Bathroom Reader For Kids Only*, but it was too good to leave out of this article, too. Sarah Leaney, a marine biologist from England, rushed to the Sea Life Aquarium in Weymouth, Dorset, the day after Christmas in 2006 after finding out the fire alarm had sounded. She expected the worst: Either it was a fire…or the giant tank had overflowed. But what she found actually made her laugh. "When I got there, I looked at the tube containing the sensor and saw a sea turtle beneath it. As I watched, a few large bubbles emerged from beneath him and rose to the surface next to the tube." The cause, it turned out, was the Brussels sprouts that had been fed to the turtle as a Christmas treat. "Brussels sprouts are a healthy treat for sea turtles," Leaney told reporters. "But they do give similar side effects to those experienced by humans who eat too many of them."

SOMETHING SMELLS FISHY. Not every animal gets to experience the satisfaction of passing gas. Jellyfish break down their food in their baglike mouths. What can't be absorbed through their mouths is then burped back out. Since they have no intestines, they cannot fart.

TOY STORY. In 2003 Dave Rogerson was passing through the security checkpoint at Norfolk International Airport in Virginia on his way home to England. Accompanying Rogerson was a life-sized toy terrier he had recently bought. The toy had a special feature: It could "fart" on command—sound, smell, and all. Unfortunately, the dog toy farted while traveling on the conveyer belt, going through the bomb-screening device. Federal agents immediately rushed in and detained Rogerson; a bomb squad was quickly called in to defuse the dog. "There's no humor at American check-ins," complained Rogerson. "They were very jumpy and were convinced there was something explosive in the dog." After the authorities determined that the toy was harmless, they explained to Rogerson that the "wind-breaking mechanism registered as a high explosive on the sensitive monitoring equipment." The toy was returned to Rogerson, which he now calls "Norfolk" in honor of their ordeal.

SQUELCHING PUPPY POWER. A company called Flat-D Innovations has created a device called the "Dogone," a thong for dogs that filters farts, trapping in the offending odors. The doggy thong is fully adjustable and machine washable. It also has a quick-release that allows for easy takeoff when the dog has to… do more than fart.

The Sonoran coral snake and the western hook-nosed snake both fart to scare off predators.

THE URGE TO MERGE

When companies merge, they often end up with boring names. But here are some funny combinations that our readers have sent us.

If **Hale Business Systems, Mary Kay Cosmetics, Fuller Brush,** and the **W. R. Grace Company** merged, the new company would be called *Hale-Mary-Fuller-Grace.*

If **PolyGram Records, Warner Bros.,** and **Cracker Barrel** merged, they would become *Poly-Warner-Cracker.*

If **3M** and **Goodyear Tire** merged, the new company would be MMMG*ood.*

If **John Deere** and **Abbey Party Rents** merged, they would become *Deere-Abbey.*

If **Zippo Manufacturing, Audi, Dofasco,** and **Dakota Mining** merged, the new company would be *Zip-Audi-Do-Da.*

If **HoneyBaked Ham, Imasco,** and **Home Service Oil** merged, they would become *Honey-Im-Home.*

If **Denison Mines, Alliance Semiconductor,** and **Metal Mining** merged, the new company would be *Mine-All-Mine.*

If **FedEx** and **UPS** merged, they would be *Fed-UP.*

If **3M, JCPenney,** and the **Metropolitan Opera** merged, the new company would be *The 3-Penny-Opera.*

If **Knott's Berry Farm** and the **National Organization for Women** merged, they would become *Knott-NOW.*

If **Yahoo!** and **Sirius Radio** merged, the new company would be *Yahoo-Sirius.*

If **Grey Poupon** and **Dockers Pants** merged, they would be called *Poupon Pants.*

If **Luvs Diapers** and **Hertz Rent A Car** merged, the new company would be *Luv Hertz.*

THE VOTER'S "LITERACY" TEST

On page 112 we mentioned that until 1965, Alabama had a literacy test for voters—a holdover from the era of Jim Crow laws designed to suppress the voting rights of minorities. Alabama wasn't the only state to have such a test, just the last. Could you have passed? Here are some of the questions from the original 1965 test. Good luck!

1. Which of the following is a right guaranteed by the Bill of Rights?
   a) Public education
   b) Employment
   c) Trial by jury
   d) Voting

2. True or False: The federal census of population is taken every five years.

3. If a person is indicted for a crime, name two rights which he has.

4. A U.S. senator elected at the general election in November takes office the following year on what date?

5. A U.S. senator is elected for a term of how many years?

6. Does enumeration affect the income tax levied on citizens in various states?

7. A person opposed to swearing in an oath may instead say (solemnly) what?

8. What words are required by law to be on all coins and paper currency of the U.S.?

9. True or False: The Supreme Court is the chief lawmaking body of the state.

10. If a law passed by a state is contrary to provisions of the U.S. Constitution, which law —state or federal—prevails?

11. Appropriation of money for the armed services can be only for a period limited to how many years?

12. If no candidate for president receives a majority of the electoral vote, who decides who will become president?

13. Cases tried before a court of law are two types, *civil* and what?

14. Of the original 13 states, the one with the largest representation in the first Congress was which?

15. Who passes laws dealing with piracy?

16. Complete the sentence: The only laws which can be passed to apply to an area in a federal arsenal are those passed by _____, provided consent for the purchase of the land is given by the _____.

17. True or False: "Involuntary servitude" is permitted in the U.S. upon conviction of a crime.

18. If a state is a party to a case, the Constitution provides that original jurisdiction shall be where?

19. The vice president presides over what?

20. Complete the sentence: The Constitution limits the size of the District of Columbia to _____.

21. Name two things that the states are forbidden to do by the U.S. Constitution.

22. How many states were required to approve the original Constitution in order for it to be in effect?

23. If election of the president becomes the duty of the U.S. House of Representatives and it fails to act, who becomes president, and for how long?

24. In which document is the Bill of Rights found?

25. Name two of the purposes of the U.S. Constitution.

26. If an effort to impeach the president of the U.S. is made, who presides at the trial?

27. If a person flees from justice into another state, who has authority to ask for his return?

28. If the two houses of Congress cannot agree on adjournment, who sets the time?

29. Money is coined by order of:
   a) the U.S. Congress
   b) the president's Cabinet
   c) State Legislatures

30. Any power and rights not given to the U.S. or prohibited to the states by the U.S. Constitution are specified as belonging to whom?

Did you get enough right to pass? Maybe…but you'd never know for sure—completed tests were often judged by a secret panel. You could have answered all the questions correctly—and still be found "unqualified" to vote. (*The answers are on page 595 anyway.*)

Country with the most kidney donors per capita: Iran. (The U.S. is #2.)

ALPHABET SOUP

Random facts about our favorite subject—food—from A to Z.

AVOCADO. Avocados (from the Nahuatl word *ahuacatl*, meaning "testicle") were first cultivated in Mexico as early as 500 B.C., but today about 90% of all sold in the U.S. come from 7,000 California groves. Myth: Shoving an avocado pit into guacamole will keep it from discoloring. Fact: A few drops of lime juice will do the trick much better.

BABY FOOD. Until the mid-19th century, all baby food was made at home. In 1873 Nestle's created a market for baby formula, pitching it as safer than milk, which could spoil and be fatal to infants. Convenience was Daniel Gerber's selling point when his canned, strained, unsalted peas first hit grocery stores in 1928. In 1931 he added salt at the insistence of taste-testing moms. (Babies actually prefer bland food, but they don't buy the family groceries.)

CAVIAR. Real caviar is the salted roe (eggs) of various species of sturgeon. The three main types are *beluga*, *sevruga*, and *osetra*. Caviar wasn't always a delicacy; in 19th-century America it was routinely served at free lunches in saloons. Most caviar came from Delaware River sturgeon, and it was so popular that by 1900 the supply was totally depleted. Today the best caviar is said to come from the Caspian Sea, where overfishing has endangered the sturgeon.

DEVIL'S FOOD CAKE. The recipe for this dense chocolate layer cake is said to have first appeared in 1902, in *Mrs. Rorer's New Cook Book.* Early versions of the cake were made with beets and cocoa; later cooks used red food coloring to reproduce the reddish-brown color of the original.

ESCARGOT. This dish of snails (yes, snails) boiled in their shells, served in a pool of garlic butter, is common on French bistro menus. Ancient Romans loved snails so much that they dedicated special vineyards to feeding and fat-

---

Will other veggies ever ketchup? There are more than 10,000 varieties of tomatoes.

tening the little creatures on grape leaves. In addition to leaves, snails eat soil and decayed matter. To become fit for consumption they must either be fed clean water for about a week or made to fast for several days.

FIGS. They've been cultivated since about 2900 B.C. and were brought to California by Spanish missionaries in 1759. Today California produces 30 million pounds per year, most of which goes straight into the filling for...Fig Newtons. One fig contains no fat or cholesterol, negligible sodium, and roughly 30 to 50 calories.

GUMBO. A Creole stew of seafood, meat, vegetables, broth, and rice. Gumbo is thickened with either okra (a vegetable with a naturally gummy property), filé powder (ground sassafras leaves, introduced by the Choctaw Indians), or roux (a mix of flour and oil or pork fat cooked very slowly to a dark brown). "Gumbo Ya-Ya" is a Creole term meaning lots of people all talking at once.

HONEY. Bees travel thousands of miles and visit thousands of flowers, collecting the nectar they need to make this high-energy bee (and human) food. One ounce of it would provide enough fuel for a bee to fly around the world.

IRISH COFFEE. Hot coffee, Irish whiskey, and sugar, with whipped cream on top. Invented in the 1940s by the head chef of a restaurant in the Irish port of Foynes to warm arriving travelers. Brought to San Francisco in 1952 by *Chronicle* writer Stan Delaplane, who convinced the Buena Vista Bar to serve it. Within weeks, 4 out of every 10 drink orders at the Buena Vista were for Irish coffee.

JELLY BEANS. First advertised in 1905, at a mere 9¢ per pound. President Ronald Reagan reportedly kept a jar of jelly beans on his desk, which boosted their waning popularity. Older flavors: cherry, orange, lemon, lime, grape, licorice. Newer (and weirder) flavors: buttered popcorn, cappuccino, cotton candy, kiwi, jalapeño, strawberry cheesecake, and toasted marshmallow.

KIMCHEE. This pungent relish is included at almost every Korean meal. The main ingredient is usually cabbage, though it can be made with turnips or radishes, plus ginger, garlic, hot pepper, and sometimes salted fish. The mixture is pickled and stored in sealed jars to ferment, and then the jars are buried in the ground to keep cold over the winter. American soldiers got sick from eating it when they fought in the Korean War.

LENTILS. Lentils pack a nutritional punch—a whopping 25% of their composition is protein. They're part of the legume family, which also includes lima beans and peanuts. Perhaps because they're a staple for poor people worldwide, lentils have had a humble reputation. In the Bible, Jacob offers Esau a "mess of pottage" in exchange for his birthright: The pottage was made of red lentils, and the implication was that Esau wasn't getting a very good deal.

MARASCHINO CHERRIES. Once upon a time, these garish additions to fruitcakes or cocktails were ordinary cherries soaked in cherry-flavored Maraschino liqueur. Today the cherries are soaked in almond- or mint-flavored sugar syrup and then dyed bright red or green. (They may look radioactive, but the FDA banned the harmful dyes once used.)

NAPOLEON. The Emperor Napoleon Bonaparte had nothing to do with the invention of this classic dessert of vanilla cream spread between layers of puff pastry, topped with a chocolate and vanilla "combed" icing. Its origin is probably Italian, and the name probably comes from the French *napolitain*, meaning "from Naples."

OLIVES. Olives, the fruit of a small evergreen tree, have been used since prehistoric times and cultivated since at least 3000 B.C. In Greek mythology, the goddess Athena gave the gift of olives to mankind, and for this the city of Athens was named in her honor. Olives are still grown in Greece, but also in many other countries, including Italy, Portugal, and Turkey. The world's largest olive producer: Spain.

PEKING DUCK. A Chinese delicacy dating back to the

Yuan Dynasty (1206–1368). Air is forced between the duck's skin and meat; then the whole bird is coated with honey or molasses, hung until the skin is dry, and roasted until the skin is crisp. The duck is cut into small pieces, but the skin is the real treat, served with thin pancakes, scallions, and hoisin sauce.

QUINOA. Pronounced "keen-wah," this ancient South American "grain" (actually, it's related to leafy greens) has many virtues: complete protein (with *all* the amino acids), high in unsaturated fat and low in carbs, fiber-rich, easy to digest, cooks fairly quickly, and expands to four times its original size. It's been called the "supergrain of the future."

REDEYE GRAVY. Sauce made from the pan drippings of ham mixed with black coffee or water, sometimes thickened with flour. The name may come from President Andrew Jackson's request for gravy "as red as his drunken cook's eyes," but more likely derives from the oily "red eye" that appears in the center of the reduced sauce.

SCHMALTZ. If you gently fry the chunks of fat and the fatty skin from a chicken or goose, what you get is *schmaltz* (the melted fat) and *gribenes* (crispy bits of skin, or cracklings). Schmaltz is a common ingredient in Eastern European Jewish cooking—a stand-in for the butter or olive oil of other European cuisines. After it's strained, schmaltz is used for frying foods or for spreading on bread.

TEMPEH. A firm, chewy cake related to tofu, made by fermenting partially cooked soybeans. Tempeh hails from Indonesia, but is common throughout Southeast Asia. High in protein, fiber, and vitamins, it's become a sort of meat substitute—some vegetarians like dark tempeh and light tofu as alternatives to the dark and light meat of Thanksgiving turkey.

UGLI FRUIT. This wrinkled, pockmarked citrus fruit, named for its unattractive appearance, grows only in Jamaica, where it was discovered growing wild in 1924. The original fruit is thought to have been an accidental hybrid of tangerine, grapefruit, and the Seville orange.

According to English legend, bread baked on Christmas Eve will never get moldy.

VINEGAR. Before the invention of corks that kept out air, wine (or any alcoholic drink) soured naturally and turned to vinegar. In fact, the word comes from the French *vin aigre*, meaning "sour wine." Today's vinegar is no accidental occurrence—it's made under carefully controlled conditions and from many sources besides wine, including apple cider, rice, sorghum, dates, white grapes, malted barley, and sugarcane.

WASABI. You may think wasabi is that green paste you find in sushi or in a little mound beside your Japanese food. It's probably not: That stuff is usually fake, a mix of horseradish, mustard seed, and green food coloring. The real (much more expensive) thing, which will also blow your sinuses inside out, is made from a plant called *wasabi*, a horseradish-like root full of *isothiocyanates*, chemicals that produce potent vapors that attack your nasal passages.

XANTHAN GUM. You can thank Dr. Allene Jeanes (1906–1995) for xanthan gum, the fermented corn-sugar polysaccharide that makes Creamy Italian salad dressing thick and smooth, keeps ice crystals from forming in Fudge Swirl ice cream, and gives a "fat feel" to low-fat and no-fat dairy products. Dr. Jeanes was the first woman to receive the Distinguished Service Award from the USDA.

YUCA. Also called *cassava* or *manioc*, this starchy tuberous root is native to South America and a staple food in Africa, where it's either cooked or dried and ground for flour. Cooked yuca is kind of like potatoes; yuca flour is used to make tapioca for pudding. All varieties contain cyanide, so yuca should never be eaten raw.

ZOMBIE. Drink a couple of these cocktails, and you'll be wandering around like a zombie. Invented in California in the 1930s at the Don the Beachcomber restaurant, the original recipe was a paralyzing combination of five or six kinds of rum, a couple of liqueurs, fruit juices, and a dash of grenadine, served over crushed ice. There are dozens of variations on the Zombie, but they're all based on the original recipe.

THE STELLA AWARDS

When Stella Liebeck's "hot coffee" suit against McDonald's made the news in 1994, many people mistakenly thought it was frivolous. It wasn't (see page 37). But it inspired Randy Cassingham's True Stella Awards, "honoring" ridiculous lawsuits. Here are some recent winners.

When Marcy Meckler left Chicago's Old Orchard Mall in 2004, a squirrel jumped out of a bush and attacked her leg. As she tried to shake the rodent loose, she fell onto the pavement, suffering cuts, scrapes, and bruises. Meckler sued the mall for $50,000, claiming the mall should have warned her that squirrels lived outside.

• Allen Heckard of Portland, Oregon, sued former NBA star Michael Jordan and Nike, for whom Jordan was an endorser, for a total of $832 million for emotional pain and suffering. Reason: Heckard says people mistake him for Jordan, causing him stress.

• In 2005 Robert Clymer of Las Vegas crashed his pickup truck while driving drunk. He sued the manufacturer of the truck and the used-car dealer from whom he bought it because he "somehow lost consciousness."

• In 2005 Barnard Lorence of Stuart, Florida, overdrew his bank account and incurred an overdraft charge. He then sued his bank for $2 million over the stress and lack of sleep he endured over the fee. (The fee was $32.)

• In 2004 Shawn Perkins got struck by lightning in the parking lot of Kings Island amusement park near Cincinnati, Ohio. Did he sue God for this "act of God?" No. Perkins sued Kings Island, claiming the park failed to warn him not to go outside during a thunderstorm.

• Michelle Knepper of Vancouver, Washington, called a dermatologist she found in the phone book about performing liposuction. After a consultation, she agreed to let him do the surgery. Sadly, he botched the job. Oddly, Knepper sued the telephone company. Why? Because the phone book ad didn't say that her doctor wasn't a board-certified plastic surgeon.

Hey! Get your own! Four Canadians have been featured on U.S. postage stamps.

Q & A: ASK THE EXPERTS

More random questions, with answers from the nation's top trivia experts.

NAME THAT DUNE

Q: *How are mountains officially named? Can I name a peak near my house "Bob"?*

A: "If you want to see your name on a government map, be prepared to scale the Everest-like federal bureaucracy. First, visit the U.S. Board on Geographic Names's Web site at *geonames.usgs.gov* and fill out—surprise—a long, involved form. Provide a description of the hill, its longitude and latitude, your reason for wanting to name it, the meaning of the name, evidence that the peak isn't already named, and the name you propose. (Bear in mind, they won't name a natural feature after a living person.) The Board will render its decision three to six months later, accepting approximately 90% of the proposals. Of course, even then there's no guarantee your name will be popular. People still call Alaska's highest peak Denali, despite its official name, Mount McKinley." (From *The Wild File*, by Brad Wetzler)

ENLIGHTENED SELF-INTEREST

Q: *Why is there a United States naval base at Guantanamo Bay in Cuba?*

A: "Cuba was still a Spanish colony in 1898, when the United States won the Spanish-American War. After the war, a convention was set up to frame a constitution for Cuba. The U.S. attached a proviso, known as the Platt Amendment, requiring the U.S. to maintain a military presence on the island. The convention initially refused, but the United States made it clear that they would not withdraw from Cuba until the proviso was accepted, and so the convention backed down. In 1903 the United States 'leased' bases at Guantanamo Bay and Bahia Honda at an annual rent of $2,000; in 1912 they surrendered Bahia Honda in return for a larger base at Guantanamo Bay for a rate of $5,000 annually." (From *The Best Ever Notes & Queries*, by Joseph Harker)

Farmers in England are required by law to provide their pigs with toys.

THE ONLY PRESIDENT TO...

You may know that Richard Nixon was the only U.S. president to resign or that Grover Cleveland was the only president to serve two non-consecutive terms. But there are many more presidential anomalies than that.

The president: Jimmy Carter
Notable achievement: Only president to write a children's book. Carter wrote *The Little Baby Snoogle-Fleejer*, which was illustrated by his daughter Amy, and published in 1995. The plot: A crippled boy named Jeremy meets a repulsive sea monster, who turns out to be quite friendly.

The president: Abraham Lincoln
Notable achievement: Only president to earn a patent. In 1849, Lincoln invented a type of buoy. Lincoln is also the only U.S. president to have worked as a bartender.

The president: Theodore Roosevelt
Notable achievement: Only president to be blind in one eye. Roosevelt took a hard punch to his left eye in a boxing match. It detached the retina, leaving Roosevelt blind in his left eye for the rest of his life. The boxing match occurred in 1908, while Roosevelt was president.

The president: Richard Nixon
Notable achievement: Only president to have been a carny. When he was a teenager, Richard Nixon was a midway barker at the Slippery Gulch Rodeo in Arizona.

The president: Gerald Ford
Notable achievement: Only president to survive two assassination attempts in the same month. In September 1975, former Charles Manson follower Lynette "Squeaky" Fromme tried to shoot Ford when he reached out to shake her hand in a public meet-and-greet. She pulled the trigger, but the gun's chamber was empty. Just three weeks later another woman, Sara Jane Moore, fired on Ford in a similar crowd situation, but a bystander knocked her arm away.

Justice denied: One in three murderers are never convicted.

NICE STORIES

In 2006 we put out a book called Tales to Inspire. *It was a nice break from all the cynicism we run across. Here are a few stories we've found since then that would have fit in well. Have a nice day!*

SOMETIMES, ALL YOU HAVE TO DO IS ASK
In the province of Shandong, China, in 2007, a teacher named Pan Aiying was robbed by a man on a motorcycle. As he passed her, he grabbed her purse and sped away with her mobile phone, bank card, and 4,900 yuan ($630). But instead of calling the police, Pan first decided to try to appeal to the man's good side by text messaging him on her phone. "I am Pan Aiying, a teacher from Wutou Middle School," she wrote. "You must be going through a difficult time. If so, I will not blame you. Keep the 4,900 yuan if you really need it, but please return the other things to me." She received no reply, so she sent another message: "You are still young. To err is human. Correcting your mistakes is more important than anything." No reply. She sent another message, then another, then another...after 21 text pleas, Pan was losing hope. But then, a few days later, she found her purse sitting in front of her home. Everything (including the money) was still inside it, along with a note: "Dear Pan, I'm sorry. I made a mistake. Please forgive me. You are so tolerant even though I stole from you. I will correct my ways and be an upright person."

JUAN MANN CAN MAKE A DIFFERENCE

He's been featured in news stories all over the world. His clip on YouTube racked up more than 15 million hits. He was even featured in a hit music video. What does he do? He hugs people. It all started in 2004 when "Juan Mann" decided that a simple way to make people feel better was to give them a hug. So he made a sandwich board sign painted with the words "FREE HUGS," and went to the Pitt Street Mall in Sydney, Australia, to distribute them. He gave away hugs in relative anonymity for a couple of years—until he was videotaped by Shimon Moore, another sandwich board sign wearer (for half-price shoes). A short time later, Moore hit the big time with his band Sick Puppies. Footage of Mann and his hugs was incorporated into the video for the song

---

Isaac Newton, considered one of the most important scientists in history,...

"All the Same," while the original clip became a YouTube sensation. Now copycat serial huggers have been spotted from New York City to Tokyo. That doesn't bother Mann because he doesn't do it for personal gain, he says. "It's a way to make people smile."

THE UN-MILLIONAIRE

Hal Taussig is worth millions, but he lives like a pauper. Why? Because he's given just about every dime he's ever made to charity, except for what it takes to eat, live in a modest home, and care for his sick wife. The 82-year-old from Media, Pennsylvania, still rides his bike to work every day (he hasn't owned a car since the 1970s). He earned his fortune by starting a unique travel service called Untours, which caters to travelers who want to explore foreign lands by staying with locals. In 1992 Taussig founded the Untours Foundation, which donates money to low-income housing projects and finds employment for people in need. Quoting his hero, Henry David Thoreau, Taussig says, "'Let your capital be simplicity and contentment.' Those are my sentiments precisely. If capitalism is good, it should be good for the poor. I invest in entrepreneurial efforts to help poor people leverage themselves out of poverty."

CLEANUP IN THE MUSIC ROOM

When the students at Mangum Elementary School in Durham, North Carolina, were looking at staff bios in the school newsletter in early 2007, they learned that their favorite custodian, 71-year-old Joe Venable, had a lifelong dream to see the Golden Gate Bridge in San Francisco. They decided to help him. With the superintendent's help, they organized a fundraising campaign. Teachers, parents, churches, and local clubs all pitched in until the kids had raised $2,000—enough to send Venable and his wife on a three-day vacation to the City by the Bay. And they had a little fun when they broke the news. Venable was told that there was a big spill in the music room. When he walked through the door, he saw his wife, 60 students, and the superintendent...all with big smiles on their faces. "What's all this?" he asked. The students answered with a special song they'd written for the occasion, "Mr. V., you're on your way / to the San Francisco Bay!" With tears in his eyes, Venable said, "This sure is something beautiful you all have done for me. Thank you so much!"

ARRGH!

Every profession has its own set of jargon that's incomprehensible to outsiders. But now you can use this guide to converse freely if you ever encounter any 18th-century high-seas pirates.

Avast. Dutch for "hold fast." It means "stop and pay attention."

Dance the hempen jig. To hang a man. Rope was made from hemp; the hangman's noose was called the "hempen halter."

Dungbie. Your rear end. Named, reportedly, because that's where "the dung be."

Cackle fruit. Chicken eggs

Shiver me timbers. An expression of shock or disbelief. When a wooden ship gets hit by a cannonball or unexpectedly runs aground, the whole ship shakes, or "shivers."

Barker. A pistol

Duffle. Everything a sailor owned and the bag used to carry it. This one made its way to the shore, giving its name to the "duffel bag."

Holystone. Bars of sandstone used to scrub the decks. Sailors kneeling to clean looked like they were praying.

Landlubber. It's an insult. *Lubber* is an Old English word for a clumsy oaf. If a pirate called another pirate a landlubber, it meant that he was ill suited to work on a ship, but was so dumb he wouldn't do much better on land.

Gulley. A knife

Powder monkey. A gunner's assistant in charge of filling the cannons with powder

Drivelswigger. A new pirate who reads about nautical terms too much. He's taking in, or "swigging," too much irrelevant nonsense, or "drivel."

Bluejackets. Navy sailors

Scuppered. Crippled or broken, applied to both people and ships

Swallowing the anchor. Retiring from the pirate's life

Tip yer daddle. Shake hands

Dead men. Empty liquor bottles—their "spirits" have left them

---

Plus a lot of dryer lint: A single bale of cotton will yield 215 pairs of jeans.

WHY ARE THEY SPYING ON US?

Careful: They may be spying on you right now!

SPYING ON THE GAYS

In 2007 a secret police report was leaked to the Canadian Broadcasting Corporation confirming what many people had believed for years: The Toronto Police Department had spied on the city's gay community during the 1970s and '80s. At least one officer, Detective Garry Carter, went undercover, attending gay men's clubs and conventions. They even spied on gay candidates for the Toronto City Council. Kyle Rae, the city's first openly gay councilor, told the CBC he wasn't surprised by the report. "We were seen as a subversive minority, worthy of ridicule and violence by the police," he said. Exactly why the police thought gay men needed to be spied on was not revealed in the report. The Toronto Police Services Board, a civilian agency that oversees the police force, said it would investigate the spying operations. (Another target of police spying, according to the report: the head of the Toronto Police Services Board.)

SPYING ON THE PROTESTERS

In 2005 the *New York Times* reported that the New York Police Department had spent a year spying on political groups prior to the August 2004 Republican National Convention held in New York City. Undercover officers traveled the world posing as activists, joining groups, and sending daily reports back to New York. The explanation given for the spy program was to disrupt any "criminal or terrorist activity." Lawyers for individuals and groups spied upon say their clients were engaged in perfectly legal activities, and that spying on them was an illegal activity. The NYPD tried to block access to their records, but in 2007 a judge ordered the police to release them. Some of the groups that were infiltrated by undercover NYPD officers:

• **"Bands Against Bush."** The San Francisco-based protest group got the department's attention because they were planning concerts with a "mixing of music and political rhetoric."

• **"Billionaires for Bush."** This theater troupe planned performances around New York, dressed in tuxedos, top hats, evening gowns, and tiaras, satirically "supporting" President Bush. Some of their performances: the "Billionaire Croquet Party," "Vigils for Corporate Welfare," and the "Taunting of the Unemployed." A secret FBI report said the group was "forged as a mockery of the current presidency and political policies," which may be illegal in some countries—but not in the United States.

• **"The Man-in-Black Bloc."** This was the idea of Erin Siegal, a 22-year-old Brooklyn resident and Johnny Cash fan who asked people "to peacefully protest in front of Sotheby's, wearing black clothing and pompadours, with real or cardboard guitars, and hair grease." The NYPD made more than 1,800 arrests during the RNC, many as a result of the spy operations. Of that number, more than 90% had their charges dropped or were acquitted. Of those found guilty, most were of charges equal to a traffic ticket. The NYPD and New York City face lawsuits totaling more than $1 billion for their actions at the RNC.

SPYING ON THE PUPPET MAKERS

In 2001 the *Ottawa Citizen* ran a series of articles on the widespread undercover surveillance of Canadian peace organizations, including the infiltration of a peace group on Vancouver Island. Police spies reported that the group planned: 1) to write letters to newspapers critical of the Canadian government; and 2) to build a giant puppet caricature of cabinet member David Anderson.

SPYING ON THE QUAKERS

In 2002 the American Civil Liberties Union obtained documents through the Freedom of Information Act and discovered that the Denver, Colorado, police department had been keeping "spy files" on individuals and groups since 1999. The department admitted it: They had secret files on 3,200 people and 208 organizations. One of the organizations was the American Friends Service Committee (AFSC), a national organization of Quakers founded in 1917. As part of their religious beliefs, Quakers refuse to use violence under any circumstances, and the group often holds peaceful anti-war protests. The Denver police had labeled them "criminal extremists," and secretly tracked their activities.

• In 2004 AFSC member Sarah Bardwell was fixing bicycles in the garage of her Denver home when two FBI agents in SWAT gear and two members of the Denver Police Department showed up. They questioned her about the upcoming Republican and Democratic conventions—which she had no plans to attend. "It definitely left a residue of fear," Bardwell later told reporters.

• In 2004 it was learned that undercover police officers had infiltrated AFSC meetings in Chicago. The Chicago PD, it turned out, was monitoring the group...and had been for years.

• It wasn't just the police: The Pentagon spied on the Quakers, too. A 400-page report, leaked to MSNBC in 2005, showed that the Pentagon had a file on an AFCS group in Florida (among many other groups), labeling them a "threat." (Another "threat" targeted by the Pentagon: "Raging Grannies," a group of senior citizen activists...who sing songs at protests.)

SPYING ON THE COMEDIAN JOURNALIST

In November 2003, freelance journalist David Lippman was in Miami to cover protests planned at a Free Trade Area of the Americas convention in the city. He had been contacted by Free Speech Radio to write about the events. He parked his pickup in a public garage and walked to the protests, and upon returning some hours later—saw his truck go by, being towed. He asked a garage employee what had happened and was told that the FBI had searched the vehicle for a bomb. He also learned that they had smashed one of his windows to get inside. Lippman was unable to get the truck back for two days. It turned out that Lippman had been under surveillance by the FBI, the Broward County Sheriff's Office, and the Miami Police Department since he left his home in North Carolina to cover the protest. The three agencies also cooperated on taking his car. The reason: An FBI report called Lippman a "known protester with history." What was his protest history? He had been singing satirical anti-war songs since the late 1960s, and since the 1980s he has performed a musical comedy act as "George Shrub, the Singing CIA agent."

The *Titanic* was running at 22 knots (about 25 mph) when it hit the iceberg.

ABOUT ANTARCTICA

Cold, hard facts about the cold, hard continent.

• Antarctica isn't completely covered in ice—98% of the continent is. The ice averages 1.34 miles thick, and is 3 miles at its thickest.

• At 5.5 million square miles, Antarctica is the fifth largest continent (only Europe and Australia are smaller).

• Antarctica is the driest continent. One region has received no precipitation for the last two million years.

• The Bentley Subglacial Trench is 8,383 feet below sea level—the lowest dry location on Earth.

• If Antarctica's ice sheets melted, the world's oceans would rise about 200 feet.

• There are 145 liquid lakes (and counting) beneath the Antarctic ice. One, Lake Vostok, is under 2.5 miles of ice and is about the size of Lake Ontario.

• The lowest temperature ever recorded on Earth was in 1983 at Russia's Vostok Station: –128.6°F.

• Cold, dense air being pulled by gravity down Antarctic mountains create the most extreme *katabatic* (Greek for "go down") winds on the planet. They have been clocked at 200 mph.

• Antarctic ice accounts for 70% of the world's fresh water.

• The largest non-migratory land animal in Antarctica is the *belgica*, a wingless midge (gnat) less than half an inch long. They don't fly (the winds would blow them away); they hop like fleas and live in penguin colonies.

• The Antarctic Treaty, drawn up in 1959, reserves the continent for exploration and scientific research and prohibits its use for military purposes. To date, 45 countries have signed the charter, technically the first arms-reduction treaty of the Cold War.

• Seven countries claim to own parts of the continent: Argentina, Australia, Chile, France, New Zealand, Norway, and the United Kingdom.

The mineral content and structure of human bone is nearly identical to some species of coral.

AUNT LENNA THE MAGNIFICENT

Aunt Lenna would like everyone to believe she has magical powers, but what Uncle John discovered on a recent visit is that her "powers" are more showmanship than magic. Can you figure out how Aunt Lenna does her tricks? (Answers are on page 595.)

TIME OUT

"My psychic abilities are frighteningly powerful," Aunt Lenna boasted. "They work like a vacuum cleaner. Why, with the flick of a mental switch, I can pull your thoughts right out of your head."

"No you can't!" I said. "Not if I don't want you to."

"Try me!" she challenged. She went to her writing desk, pulled out a piece of paper and drew the face of a clock with no hands—just the numbers 1 through 12 arranged in a circle. "I want you to think of an hour between 1 and 12 o'clock," she instructed. "Don't tell me what you pick, and try as hard as you can to keep me from reading your mind."

I picked 4:00, and I didn't tell Aunt Lenna. "I'm ready," I said.

"Now," Aunt Lenna replied, "I'm going to tap on the numbers of the clock with my pencil. Each time I do, mentally add 1 to the hour you picked. When you reach 20, say, "Stop.""

"Okay," I said. Lenna began tapping on her clock. "Five," I thought to myself when she tapped the first number, "6," when she tapped the second one, and so on, until I reached 20. Then I said, "Stop!"

When I did, Aunt Lenna's pencil was pointing at 4:00.

"That's the hour I picked!" I exclaimed. "How'd you do that?"

THE NUMBERS RACKET

"In a lot of ways, psychic powers are really just a numbers game," Aunt Lenna explained. "Here's an example," she said as she handed me a pencil and a piece of paper. "Write down the number of the month you were born." I was born in July, so I wrote down a 7.

"Multiply that by 2," she said. I did and got 14.

"Add 5, then multiply by 50, then add your age," she said.

I added 5 to get 19, then multiplied it by 50 to get 950, and added my age of 39 to get 989.

"Subtract 365," she said. I subtracted 365 to get 624. "And finally, add 115." I added 115 to get 739.

Lenna looked at the piece of paper. She smiled and said, "You're 39, and you were born in July."

How did she know that?

MAKING HER POINT

"Psychic powers are like muscles," Aunt Lenna told me. "If you want to keep them in shape, you need to take them to the gym. I do mental exercises all the time—crosswords, sudoku, word games, you name it. That keeps my psychic powers strong—so strong that I can actually project knowledge into other peoples' heads."

"Oh really?" I asked. "I don't believe it. Prove it to me."

"No problem," she said. "Uncle Gideon, will you please assist us?" Uncle Gid picked up his head (he's a dozer), and Aunt Lenna asked him to step out of the room for a minute.

As he closed the door behind him, Aunt Lenna whispered, "Point to an object in the room. Don't say what it is! I don't want Gideon to hear." I pointed to the brass spittoon next to Uncle Gideon's easy chair. (He's a spitter.)

"Okay," Aunt Lenna replied. "Gideon," she called, "please come back into the room." Uncle Gideon entered. "I'm going to point at different objects in the room," Aunt Lenna explained, "and I'll use my mind to tell Gideon the object you picked. Gideon, when I point to the object John picked, I want you to say, 'Stop!'"

"Sure thing," Uncle Gideon replied. (He's a pushover.)

Aunt Lenna pointed to objects all over the room—the couch, the picture over the fireplace, the rug, the piano, the spittoon... and as soon as she pointed to the spittoon, Uncle Gideon shouted, "Stop!" How did she do that?

For anyone who isn't psychic: The answers are on page 595.

The force of one billion people jumping at the same time is equal to 500 tons of TNT.

THE ALOHA SHIRT

It seems like almost everyone owns a Hawaiian shirt or two—Uncle John
owns seven that he wears in regular rotation. It turns out that their
history is every bit as colorful as the materials they're made from.

HOMEWARD BOUND
Not long after he graduated from Yale in 1931 with an
economics degree, 22-year-old Ellery J. Chun was summoned to Honolulu by his father, Chun Kam Chow. The family
owned a dry goods store in the city, and business was way off—the
entire United States was mired in the Great Depression, and the
store was in trouble. He needed his son's help to keep the business
afloat.

Chun must have been paying attention in his economics classes, because he came up with some ideas that helped to put the
store on sounder footing. In the past the store had catered to the
Chinese community—much of the store's inventory was imported
directly from China. But Chun thought the business would be
more profitable if it expanded its selection to appeal to a broader
market. But what kinds of goods should they offer?

TAILOR MADE
Chun got the idea for one of his most successful products just by
looking out the store's front window. There was a tailor shop next
door, and it was common to see local kids in colorful shirts leading
sailors, tourists, and other visitors from the mainland into the
shop. But what were they shopping for?

Chun inquired next door and learned that the visitors were
there to order colorful shirts just like the homemade ones the kids
were wearing. In the 1930s, Hawaii still had a largely agrarian
economy, and tens of thousands of immigrants from China, Japan,
the Philippines, and other countries had come to Hawaii to work
on the sugarcane and pineapple plantations. Wages were low, so
many laborers who had tailoring skills supplemented their income
by sewing clothing at night, often using colorful printed fabrics
sent to them by relatives back home in China or Japan. Most of
the work clothes, kimonos, and other garments were made for sale,

but the leftover scraps were used to make clothing for the family.
A lot of kids ended up with colorful shirts made from scraps of
kimono fabric, sparking a local fad among teenagers that was now
spreading to tourists.

IN STOCK

Chun hired the tailor to sew some ready-to-wear shirts that he
could stock in his store for people who didn't want to go to the
time and expense of having them custom made. The earliest
shirts had a distinctly *Japanese* appearance, Chun told the *Atlanta
Journal Constitution* in 1976: "There was no authentic Hawaiian
material in those days, so I bought the most brilliant and gaudy
Japanese kimono material, designed the shirts, and had a tailor
make a few dozen colorful shortsleeved shirts, which I displayed
in the window with the sign, 'Hawaiian Shirts.' And they sold
remarkably well."

It didn't take long for Chun's Japanese Hawaiian shirt to
take on a more distinctly Hawaiian feel. His sister, Ethel Lum,
started designing shirts with pineapples, palm trees, tropical
flowers, exotic birds, ukuleles, and other motifs associated with
the islands.

RIGHT PLACE, RIGHT TIME

The new shirts, priced at as little as 95¢ apiece, sold even better
than the Japanese-style shirts had, and in the years that followed
sales increased dramatically as Hawaii became an ever more popular and accessible tourist destination. In 1935 Pan American
World Airways began offering China Clipper service to Hawaii,
linking it to the U.S. mainland by air for the first time. Now the
islands were only an 18-hour flight away from the West Coast,
instead of six days by ocean liner.

It's probably not a stretch to say that as tourism helped spur
sales of Hawaiian shirts, so too did Hawaiian shirts help to spur
the tourist trade. When people came home from vacationing in
Hawaii, their loud shirts attracted a lot of attention and curiosity
about the islands. The shirts must have pulled more than a few
people out to Hawaii to experience the place and—of course—buy
some of the shirts—for themselves. What did Guam, Samoa, or
the Gilbert Islands have to compare with that?

It cost $560,000 to build Fort Knox in 1936.

THE BARE FACTS

By 1940 it was clear that Hawaiian shirts were much more than just a passing fad. The Hawaiian garment industry, which in the past had been geared toward providing clothing for plantation workers, was evolving into a tourist-oriented export business and growing very rapidly.

Hawaiian shirts could be seen just about everywhere on the islands—except on the backs of Hawaiians themselves. Their kids still wore them, of course, but everyone else saw the loud shirts as being strictly for the tourist trade, something not really authentically Hawaiian at all. You were about as likely to see a real Hawaiian wearing one as you were to see a New Yorker wearing an I ♥ NY shirt.

THE REAL DEAL

So how did made-up Hawaiian shirts finally come to be seen as a genuine Hawaiian article? It was a process that took more than a decade…and one that began on the morning of December 7, 1941, when Japan bombed Pearl Harbor, pulling the U.S. into World War II.

The war disrupted trade between the islands and the rest of the world, forcing Hawaiians to buy products manufactured locally, including the lowly Hawaiian shirt. It also helped to set the stage for Hawaii becoming an even bigger tourist destination after the war than it had been before. Many GIs passed through Hawaii on their way to or from the war in the Pacific, and their brief exposure to the islands made them eager to return once the war ended.

The soldiers and sailors bought a lot of Hawaiian shirts as they passed through, of course—years of wearing dull khaki and olive-drab uniforms made them hungry for all the color they could get while on shore leave. As a result, demand for Hawaiian shirts was even greater after the war than it had been during the war. The garment industry was beginning to emerge as a major segment of the Hawaiian economy.

DRESS CODE

Whether the traditionalists liked it or not, by the late 1940s Hawaiian shirts had become synonymous with the Hawaiian Islands. Even Hawaiians were wearing them…but still only in their free time. When people in Hawaii went to the office or met socially, they continued to wear business suits, ordinary dresses, and sport coats and slacks. People still took their fashion cues from the mainland, so business meetings and cocktail parties in Honolulu didn't look all that different from ones in Portland, Oregon, or Madison, Wisconsin.

SWEAT EQUITY

Have you ever tried to wear a business suit in the humid, tropical heat of the Hawaiian Islands? It's not easy, and if you spend more than a few minutes outside of an air-conditioned office it isn't very pretty, either. Even before World War II, various community and business leaders had lobbied to relax workplace dress codes to bring them in line with the climate, but the efforts were unsuccessful.

Things didn't begin to change until 1947, when the desire to sweat less at work merged with two other goals: celebrating Hawaiian spirit and supporting local industry. That was the year that the Honolulu Chamber of Commerce and other civic organizations established "Aloha Week," a celebration of authentic and faux Hawaiian traditions. Aloha Week began in late October and, despite its name, lasted nearly a month. Office workers, including even bankers and lawyers, were given permission and indeed were strongly encouraged to wear their Hawaiian shirts and muumuus to work. And 1947 was also the year that city and county employees were granted the right to wear Hawaiian shirts any time they wanted, even "with tails worn outside the trousers."

The door to full fashion acceptance had opened a crack, and further progress came quickly. Aloha Week was followed by Aloha Wednesdays, Aloha Fridays (the inspiration for "casual Fridays" on the mainland), and Aloha Summers. Which begged the question—now that people were wearing their Hawaiian shirts on Wednesdays and Fridays and during Aloha Week and Aloha Summer, why not just allow them all the time? Today the Hawaiian shirt *is* the business suit of the Hawaiian Islands.

THE SHIRTMAKER

...So whatever happened to Ellery J. Chun, the guy who helped turn a homegrown fad into Hawaii's third largest export? Did he

---

The word *millionaire* was first used by Benjamin Disraeli, in his 1826 novel *Vivian Grey*.

become the Bill Gates of Hawaiian shirts? Not even close—if you're used to thinking of Hawaiian shirts as "aloha shirts," you have him to thank for that: Chun trademarked that name in 1937. But he got out of the business not too long afterward and went into banking instead, rising to the rank of vice president before retiring in 1966. He died in 2000. His descendants probably wish they had saved more of his and his sister's early shirts: Today the rarest, most prized examples of his 95¢ shirts are framed like artwork and sell at auction for more than $10,000 apiece.

*　　*　　*

BERMANISMS

ESPN sportscaster Chris Berman is well known for making nicknames for athletes by crafting puns out of their names. Here are some of them.

- Bert "Be Home" Blyleven (baseball player)
- Curtis "My Favorite" Martin (football player)
- Jake "Daylight Come And Me Wan'" Delhomme (football player)
- David "Green" Akers (football player)
- Josh "Tears Of" McCown (football player)
- "Hey, You, Get Off Of" Mike Cloud (football player)
- Mark "Strawberry" Fields (football player)
- Scott "Supercalifragillisticexpialo" Brosius (baseball player)
- Jeff "Dream" Weaver (baseball player)
- Albert "Winnie the" Pujols (baseball player)
- John "I am not a" Kruk (baseball player)
- Samari "Shake, Rattle, and" Rolle (football player)
- Alexander "If Loving You Is Wrong, I Don't Wanna Be" Wright (football player)
- "Werewolves Of" London Fletcher-Baker (football player)
- Joseph "Live and Let" Addai (football player)
- Eric "Sleeping With" Bienemy (football player)

Power steering: One steer yields enough ground beef for nearly 1,000 Quarter Pounders.

DUMB CROOKS

Even more proof that crime doesn't pay.

LOVE AT FIRST SLICE

"Police in New Castle County, Delaware, say three young men ordered two pepperoni pizzas from Domino's Pizza, and when the 18-year-old delivery woman arrived they stole the pizzas (along with $20). A few minutes later one of them called the woman to ask her out on a date. 'He said, "I'm sorry I robbed you. You're pretty,"' said police chief David McAllister. She politely declined his offer, then turned his cell phone number over to the cops, who charged him with second-degree robbery. 'I suppose he hopes she doesn't believe in first impressions,' said McAllister."

—**CNN**

PAINTING HIMSELF INTO A CORNER

"In the category of dumbest criminals, consider the fugitive who took the job painting the Jacksonville Beach Police Department's headquarters in March. While wanted for a probation violation in South Carolina, the 25-year-old Jacksonville man showed up to paint both the outside and inside of headquarters. A background check landed him a little farther inside than he'd intended: behind bars."

—**Jacksonville.com (Florida)**

WHERE'S THE "EASY" BUTTON?

"Two car thieves failed to make their getaway in a car they had just stolen because they couldn't figure out how to use its manual transmission. The teenagers, armed with a gun, approached a man outside a pizza restaurant in Marietta, Georgia. They proceeded to steal his wallet and the keys to his Honda Accord, got into the car but couldn't make it start because it had a stick shift, according to a restaurant employee. 'The kid was just sitting in the car trying to start it but he had no idea what to do. The only thing he had going was the radio.' Restaurant employees called the police, who arrived and arrested the teenagers."

—*Atlanta Journal-Constitution*

The study of the Moon is called *selenology,* after the Greek goddess of the Moon, Selene.

TECH-NO

*For every new electronic gadget that flies off the shelves, a dozen
more sit there and gather dust. Here are some techno-flops.*

MINIDISCS
To compete with the compact disc in 1992, Sony introduced the MiniDisc: a three-inch CD housed in a clear plastic case. It combined the sound quality of a CD with the compactness and portability of a cassette. Despite Sony's huge marketing push on MTV, American consumers didn't bite—the MiniDisc was perceived as just a miniature CD. Minis also cost $5 more than CDs, and the new player they required cost more than $500. Sony slowly discontinued prerecorded MiniDiscs in the United States, but blank ones are still a popular format for musicians recording demo tapes.

HIWAY HI-FI
In 1955 Peter Goldmark of CBS Research (part of Columbia Records) came up with a novel way for his company to sell more records: install record players in cars. One obvious problem was how to keep the needle on the record while a car rides along. CBS solved that with a spring-loaded tonearm. Goldmark also devised a disc that had very thin grooves very close together, and played at 16⅔ rpm. It was as small as a 45 rpm record, but played as much music as an LP. The disc was also twice as thick and heavy as a regular record, which helped keep it from bouncing off the turntable. The whole thing was housed in a small, enclosed cabinet mounted under the dash. Columbia talked Chrysler into making the "Hiway Hi-Fi" an option on all new 1956 models, and produced 42 "Hiway" records (mostly classical and Broadway cast albums). But consumers were never convinced that the records would play without skipping. Few buyers selected the Hiway Hi-Fi option, so Chrysler abandoned the concept after just one year.

DIGITAL COMPACT CASSETTES
In 1992 Philips and Matsushita co-developed and introduced Digital Compact Cassettes. The new tapes looked exactly like

---

Q: How do you say Merry Christmas in Japanese? A: *Merii Kurisumasu.*

regular cassette tapes, but the sound quality was far superior—as clear and crisp as a compact disc. Another selling point: DCC players could play regular, older cassettes, so consumers wouldn't have to replace their music collections. The digital cassettes went nearly completely unnoticed in the United States, where cassette tapes were already considered clunky and obsolete. The format was extremely popular in the Netherlands, but that wasn't enough to sustain the product. Philips and Matsushita discontinued the DCC in 1996.

DIVX

In November 1998, Circuit City introduced this new DVD-rental concept. DIVX discs looked like and used the same technology as DVDs, except that the movies erased themselves 48 hours after they were first viewed. Customers bought a disc (available only at Circuit City) for about $5 and threw it away after they watched it. But customers weren't interested in buying special DIVX players (also available only at Circuit City) for $300. And Circuit City was heavily criticized for the potential environmental impact of landfills full of useless, erased discs. Circuit City discontinued DIVX in June 1999, only seven months after the launch, destroyed all unsold movies, and gave $100 refunds on DIVX players.

AUDREY

The Internet went mainstream in the late 1990s. But what if you didn't have a computer or didn't know how to use one? For those people, 3Com (a computer-modem manufacturer) came up with an "Internet appliance" called the Audrey. Even though it could only browse the Web and receive e-mail, technology experts believed Internet appliances would be the next big thing in computers—a way for the computer illiterate to communicate on the Internet. The Audrey hit stores in October 2000 for $499, which, at the time, was not much cheaper (or easier to use) than a basic, fully functional home computer. 3Com discontinued the Audrey a few months later, and in the wake of its failure, Gateway, Compaq, Virgin, Honeywell, AOL, and other companies quickly abandoned plans to develop their own Internet appliances.

THE "SUE ME, SUE YOU BLUES," PART II

Here's Part II of the story of George Harrison's battle over who owned the legal rights to his song, "My Sweet Lord." (Part I is on page 140.)

MY SWEET LAWSUIT

Most of the trial was spent on testimony from musicologists (hired by both Bright Tunes and Harrison) who broke down and analyzed the basic musical elements of the two songs, "He's So Fine" and "My Sweet Lord." According to Bright Tunes' experts, "He's So Fine" used two musical *motifs*. Motif A is the notes G-E-D repeated four times. Motif B repeats the notes G-A-C-A-C four times, with an extra "grace note" the fourth time. "My Sweet Lord," they further argued, used the same Motif A the same four times, then Motif B three times instead of four. In place of the fourth repetition, "My Sweet Lord" used a passage of the same length with the same grace note in the same place. Each motif is fairly common, they said, but for both songs to use the two motifs together and for the same number of times was no accident.

HEAR YE

In August 1976, U.S. District Court judge Richard Owen delivered his verdict. "It's perfectly obvious," said Owen. "The two songs are virtually identical." Owen went on to say, however, that he didn't think Harrison intentionally stole "He's So Fine." He noted that there are only eight notes in the scale, and that "accidents do happen." Though Harrison acknowledged being familiar with "He's So Fine" (it was a massive hit), Owen said that while Harrison didn't steal the song, he did infringe on the copyright. The difference: Harrison's theft was unintentional or "subconscious."

Nevertheless, Judge Owen ruled that a copyright had still been violated, a decision upheld on appeal with the court noting that United States copyright law does not require the showing of intent to infringe.

2nd-highest album sales in the U.S. after the Beatles (106 million): Garth Brooks (92 million).

Monetary damages were decided three months later, in November 1976. The royalties for "My Sweet Lord"—based on the sales of singles, albums, and sheet music—totaled $2.1 million. But Bright wasn't awarded the entire amount. Judge Owen determined that only 75 percent of the song's merit and success was due to "He's So Fine," with the other 25 percent owing to Harrison's lyrics and arrangement. So Owen recommended Bright get 75 percent of the royalties, about $1.6 million. Had Harrison been found to have *intentionally* stolen the song, Bright Tunes would probably have gotten the full amount.

After five years, the case was finally decided, but no money would change hands…yet.

HALLELUJAH

Shortly after the trial, Bright Tunes entered into an agreement to sell its entire catalog of songs—and their subsequent litigation rights—for $587,000 to music publisher ABKCO, a company owned by…Allen Klein. Still stinging from the Concert for Bangladesh scandal, Harrison refused to pay Klein the $1.6 million he owed Bright. By now, Harrison had become aware of Klein's secret double-cross with Bright, and filed a motion with the court arguing that Klein was ineligible to get any money from "My Sweet Lord" because the plagiarism trial was the result of Klein's illegal dealings.

It took another five years for that decision to be handed down. In February 1981, the U.S. District Court ruled that Klein had indeed illegally betrayed Harrison back in 1976, thereby compromising the integrity of the findings of the plagiarism suit. As a result, the financial terms from the case were ruled invalid, meaning Harrison didn't have to pay anybody the $1.6 million in royalties.

WILL IT GO ROUND IN CIRCLES

The court also ruled that Harrison reimburse Klein $587,000. That's what Klein paid for the Bright Tunes catalog. With Harrison paying that amount, Klein would break even—but not profit —from his purchase of the Bright Tunes catalog.

But there was yet another twist. The judge ruled that because of Klein's machinations, and because Harrison would, in essence, end up paying for the Bright Tunes catalog, Harrison would be the sole owner of the copyright to "He's So Fine." After a decade-long legal battle, Harrison would own the song he'd inadvertently plagiarized years earlier.

AFTERMATH

Harrison channeled his anger and frustration over the suit into two hit songs, "This Song" and "Sue Me, Sue You Blues." But the impact of the "My Sweet Lord" debacle was felt for years to come, in an explosion of pop-music plagiarism cases:

• The publishing company that owned the rights to the standard "Makin' Whoopee" sued Yoko Ono for her song "Yes, I'm Your Angel." She later admitted in court that she'd taken the melody and structure of the song, added new lyrics, and taken full credit.

• Jazz pianist Keith Jarrett sued Steely Dan for plagiarism on the title track of their album *Gaucho,* citing similarities to his composition "Long As You Know You're Living Yours." Future pressings of *Gaucho* credited Jarrett as a songwriter.

• The producers of *Ghostbusters* asked Huey Lewis to write the movie's theme song. When he declined, Ray Parker Jr. was enlisted. Lewis later sued Parker for plagiarism because his song "Ghostbusters" sounded strikingly similar to Lewis's "I Want a New Drug." Parker paid Lewis an undisclosed amount, but alleged that the producers told him to write a song that sounded "like Huey Lewis."

• Saul Zaentz of Fantasy Records owned the rights to all of Creedence Clearwater Revival's songs. In 1985 he sued former CCR singer John Fogerty, claiming Fogerty's song "The Old Man Down the Road" plagiarized CCR's "Run Through the Jungle." In other words, Zaentz sued Fogerty for sounding too much like himself. Fogerty won the case when the court ruled that an artist cannot plagiarize himself.

*   *   *

"Justice should remove the bandage from her eyes long enough to distinguish between the vicious and the unfortunate."
—**Robert G. Ingersoll**

Eeew! A U.S. ton is 2,000 pounds. A British ton is 2,240 pounds (also known as a *gross* ton).

IT'S A WEIRD, WEIRD WORLD

It's true: Truth is stranger than fiction.

GOING GREEN THE HARD WAY

"Villagers in southwestern China are scratching their heads over the local government's decision to paint a barren mountainside green. Workers who began spraying the Laoshou mountain told nearby residents they were doing so on the orders of the area authorities, but had not been told why. Some villagers believed county officials were attempting to change the area's *feng shui*. Others suggested it was an attempt to 'green' the area in keeping with calls for more attention to the environment. China's official Xinhua News Agency estimated the cost of the paint job at 470,000 yuan ($60,000) and quoted villagers as saying that, if spent on plants and trees, the money could have restored a far greater area of barren mountain."

—*The Guardian* (U.K.)

FOUR-WHEELIN'

"A Michigan man says it was 'quite a ride.' Police say they've never seen anything like it. Witnesses just watched in shock as a 21-year-old Kalamazoo man's wheelchair got lodged in the grille of a semi truck in June 2007 as the man was crossing the street. The truckdriver, a 52-year-old Kalamazoo man, says he did not see the wheelchair as he proceeded through the intersection when the light turned green. 9-1-1 dispatchers were flooded with callers who saw the semi pushing the wheelchair for about two miles. It then pulled into its destination, which is where the driver says he first saw that the wheelchair was attached to the vehicle. Police say the man in the wheelchair was not injured."

—**WWMT News (Grand Rapids, Michigan)**

WAR OF THE WORLDS?

"In March 2007, a baffling device which resembles a satellite or UFO landed in a rural area north of Somalia's capital, Mogadishu, eyewitnesses told Shabelle radio. Villagers reported that the device fell in a remote jungle area, killing one camel. The unknown object now sits on an area of 100 square meters as people grow more concerned that the device might explode or contaminate the area. The device is said to be intact as it gives alarming signals. 'In the evening of last Wednesday, a large device flew over us and some time later, we heard a big sound, BAM!' said Ilyas Ali, a villager who lives nearby. Ilyas said in the daylight it glitters—but in the nighttime it turns its lights on and speaks a strange language which can't be understood by the villagers."

—SomaliNet

THE TOOTING GODDESS

"An unemployed man from Tooting, England, has found work at last—as an Indian goddess who thousands of Hindus believe can cure infertility. Steve Cooper, 32, was living in a tiny flat until deciding on his new career after Indian friends told him he looked and moved just like the ancient goddess. When Cooper arrived at the temple in the state of Gujarat, he was immediately surrounded by followers. 'Everyone crowded around me and I naturally started blessing people.' said Cooper. He is now regarded as a reincarnation of Bahucharaji, the patron saint of Indian eunuchs. He calls himself Pamela, but his devotees have dubbed him Prema, Hindi for 'Divine Love.' Cooper said with a smile: 'All my life I just didn't fit. Now I've found my life. I plan to stay for good. I don't miss anything about Tooting!'"

—Ananova

*   *   *

DOUBLE BYPASS

Pizza Hut Japan recently introduced the "Double Roll" pizza. Building on their stuffed crust pizza (in which a ring of mozzarella cheese is baked into the outer crust), the Double Roll has a crust stuffed with cheese, pepperoni, and mini-sausages. Half the pizza is topped with Italian sausage, ham, two different kinds of bacon, onions, peppers, tomatoes, and garlic cloves. The other half is topped with soybeans, corn, and miniature hamburger patties.

The green ink used for U.S currency was invented by a Canadian, Thomas Sterry Hunt.

FOUND ON ROAD DEAD

No matter how much you love your car, when it breaks down, you hate it. Fortunately for bathroom readers, some people have channeled their hatred for their cars into these awesome automotive acronyms.

DODGE
Drips Oil & Drops Grease Everywhere
Dead On Day Guarantee Expires
Dear Old Dad's Garage Experiment

PINTO
Put In Nickel To Operate

HONDA
Had One, Never Did Again
Hang On, Not Done Accelerating
Hallmark Of Non-Descript Automobiles

SAAB
Swedish Abstract Art Backfire
Something Almost Automobilish, Broken
Shape Appears Ass-Backwards
Still Ain't A Beemer

AUDI
Accelerates Under Demonic Influence
Another Ugly Deutsche Invention

VOLVO
Very Odd-Looking Vehicular Object

FORD
Fix Or Repair Daily
Fast Only Rolling Downhill
First On Road to Dump
Found On Road Dead
Fix Or Recycle Dilemma
Follow Our Rusty Dogsled
Forlorn, Old, Rotten Dustbin
Frequent Overhaul, Rapid Deterioration
Fraternal Order of Restored DeSotos

BUICK
Butt-Ugly Imitation Chrome King

FIAT
Feeble Italian Attempt at Transportation
Fix It Again, Tony!

JEEP
Junk Engineering Executed Poorly
Just Empty Every Pocket

Electric cars were introduced in 1896. By 1900 almost 50% of cars worldwide were electric...

BMW
Break My Window
Born Moderately Wealthy
Bring More Wrenches
Brings Me Women
Bought My Wife

ACURA
Asia's Curse Upon
Rural America
Another Crummy, Useless,
Rotten Automobile

OLDSMOBILE
Overpriced, Leisurely Driven
Sedan Made Of Buick's
Irregular Leftover
Equipment
Old Ladies Driving Slowly
Making Others Behind
Insanely Late Everyday

EDSEL
Every Day Something Else
Leaks

GM
General Maintenance
Great Mistake
Generally Miserable

PORSCHE
Proof Of Rich, Spoiled
Children Having Everything

PLYMOUTH
Please Leave Your Money
Out Under The Hood

CHEVROLET
Can Hear Every Valve Rap
On Long Extended Trips
Cheap, Hardly Efficient,
Virtually Runs On Luck
Every Time
Constantly Having Every
Vehicle Recalled Over
Lousy Engineering
Techniques

AMC
All Makes Combined
A Moron Car
Another Major Catastrophe

HYUNDAI
Helps You Understand
Nothing's Drivable *And*
Inexpensive

GEO
Good Engineering Overlooked

MGB
Might Go Backwards

TOYOTA
Too Often Yankees Overprice
This Auto
The One You Ought To
Avoid
Tripling Our Yen. Oh,
Thanks, America!

TRIUMPH
This Really Is Unreliable,
Man. Please Help!

...Yet by 1905, 80% of cars were fuel-driven and by 1920 the electric car had disappeared.

BAD DOG

Man's best friend strikes back!

THE BARKER OF SEVILLE

North Carolina's Kenan Auditorium doesn't allow dogs inside unless they're assistance dogs. In 2001 a woman (unnamed) brought her "helper dog" into a performance of the opera *The Barber of Seville*, but they were both thrown out when the dog started barking during Act I. The staff told manager Don Hawley they'd let the dog in because the woman said it was a "hearing ear dog." "In retrospect," said Hawley, "that was silly."

WINNING THE ~~DRUG~~ LEG WAR

Bangkok's Chiang Rai Airport employed two drug-sniffing dogs named Mok and Lai, who were lauded by police for finding thousands of pounds of drugs smuggled in from Laos. But in 2007, the dogs were abruptly fired. Reason: They got caught urinating on luggage and latching onto female passengers' legs. Their handler blamed the lack of "manners" on the fact that both dogs were formerly strays. Mok and Lai were reassigned to farm work, herding chickens and pigs.

A JUMPY BREED

Jack Russell Terriers are compact dogs that love to hunt small animals. In 2007 a Terrier named Nell spotted a rabbit in a field outside Douglas, England. The rabbit took off and Nell gave chase. Then the rabbit unknowingly ran over the edge of a cliff. Nell kept following, and both animals flew over the edge, hitting the ground 150 feet below. The rabbit was never found, but Nell was completely unharmed. Her owners describe her as "bouncy."

IN-CAR-CERATED

A Bull Terrier named Chevy terrorized a Melbourne, Australia, neighborhood for an entire evening when he escaped from his home (without his owner's knowledge), ran to a local shopping center, and jumped into a customer's car and refused to leave, uncoerced by either yelling or food. Chevy was jailed in a pound for a week for what animal control officials jokingly called "carjacking."

Annually, about 60 million people visit France, a country with a population of 60 million.

RED CLOUD'S FAREWELL

Red Cloud (1822–1909) was chief of the Oglala Lakota (Sioux) people and one of the most successful Native American military leaders in history. This is the farewell speech he gave to his people on July 4, 1903.

My sun is set. My day is done. Darkness is stealing over me. Before I lie down to rise no more, I will speak to my people. Hear me, my friends, for it is not the time for me to tell you a lie. The Great Spirit made us, the Indians, and gave us this land we live in. He gave us the buffalo, the antelope, and the deer for food and clothing. We moved our hunting grounds from the Minnesota to the Platte and from the Mississippi to the great mountains. No one put bounds on us. We were free as the winds, and like the eagle, heard no man's commands.

"**I was born a Lakota and I shall die a Lakota.** Before the white man came to our country, the Lakotas were a free people. They made their own laws and governed themselves as it seemed good to them. The priests and ministers tell us that we lived wickedly when we lived before the white man came among us. Whose fault was this? We lived right as we were taught it was right. Shall we be pun- ished for this? I am not sure that what these people tell me is true.

"**As a child I was taught the *Taku Wakan*** [supernatural ways] were powerful and could do strange things. This was taught me by the wise men and the shamans. They taught me that I could gain their favor by being kind to my people and brave before my ene- mies; by telling the truth and living straight; by fighting for my people and their hunting grounds. When the Lakotas believed these things they were happy and they died satisfied. What more than this can that which the white man offers us give?

"***Taku Shanskan* knows my spirit** and when I die I will go with him. Then I will be with my forefathers. If this is not in the heaven of the white man I shall be satisfied. *Wi* is my father. The *Wakan Tanka* of the white man has overcome him. But I shall remain true to him. Shadows are long and dark before me. I shall soon lie down to rise no more. While my spirit is with my body the smoke of my breath shall be towards the Sun, for he knows all things and knows that I am still true to him."

TILTING AT WINDMILLS

Many common phrases actually come from books and poetry. Once they enter our language, we tend to forget their lofty origins.

SWEETNESS AND LIGHT

Meaning: Originally, a state of beauty, intelligence, and enlightenment seen as the hallmark of a people and their culture. Today it is also used to refer to a beautiful, intelligent, enlightened person: "She is all sweetness and light."

Coined by: Jonathan Swift, in his satirical *The Battle of the Books*, written in 1704: "The Difference is, that instead of Dirt and Poison, we have rather chose to till our Hives with Honey and Wax, thus furnishing Mankind with the two Noblest of Things, which are Sweetness and Light." It wasn't popularized as a phrase until the 1860s, when English poet Matthew Arnold used it in his treatise *Culture and Anarchy*, writing that culture seeks to "make all men live in an atmosphere of sweetness and light."

SHOT HEARD 'ROUND THE WORLD

Meaning: A brief, localized act or event that achieves broad attention and causes major influence. Examples: the gunshot that killed Archduke Ferdinand of Austria, seen as the immediate cause of World War I; or New York Giant Bobby Thompson's 9th-inning home run against the Brooklyn Dodgers in the final game of the 1951 baseball season.

Coined by: Ralph Waldo Emerson in "The Concord Hymn" (1837), which he wrote for the dedication of a monument commemorating the Battles of Lexington and Concord in 1775, the first military engagements of the American Revolution.

SEE THROUGH A GLASS, DARKLY

Meaning: To have an incomplete view of a thing or a concept due to one's own limitations. It's the title of a film by Ingmar Bergman, and the title of a short story by Isaac Asimov.

Coined by: Paul in the New Testament, *1 Corinthians* 13:12: "Now we see through a glass, darkly; but then face to face: now I

James Joyce coined the word "Klikkaklakkaklaskaklopatzklatschabattacreppycrottygraddaghsem-...

know in part; but then I shall know even as also I am known."
"Now" in the phrase refers to man's time on Earth, "then" is when
we can see clearly, and "face to face" is in heaven. (The "glass" in
the phrase is often translated as a mirror.)

DEATH BY A THOUSAND CUTS

Meaning: The metaphorical death of something not by one fatal
blow, but by the cumulative effect of many small "wounds," none
fatal in and of themselves. Example: "His political career was
doomed by the many minor scandals that plagued him over the
years—it was death by a thousand cuts."

Coined by: A Chinese proverb, "He who fears not the death of a
thousand cuts will dare to unhorse the emperor," a reference to a
form or torture used in ancient China: a person would have small
pieces of flesh cut from their skin over a period of days, resulting
in an un-metaphorical death.

TILTING AT WINDMILLS

Meaning: Used to describe an act of futility, or a ridiculous,
unwinnable battle against an imaginary enemy

Coined by: The phrase was inspired by the 1605 Miguel Cervantes novel *The Ingenious Don Quixote of La Mancha*. Cervantes'
hero, Don Quixote, is a crazed old man who believes he is a
knight errant. In the novel's most famous scene, Quixote jousts
("tilting" is another name for jousting) with a windmill, which he
thinks is a monster. The story first inspired a phrase in 1644, when
English poet John Cleveland wrote, "The Quixotes of this Age
fight with the Wind-mills of their owne Heads." The full phrase
"tilting at windmills" wasn't actually coined until the late 1800s.

THE MOTHER OF ALL...

Meaning: The ultimate

Coined by: No, it's not Saddam Hussein. He did use it in a speech
on the eve of the first Persian Gulf War in 1991, saying the fight
for Kuwait would be the "mother of all battles." But he was actually
borrowing from an ancient reference to the battle of Qadisiya in
Iraq in 637 A.D., when an army of Muslim Arabs defeated a massive Persian force. That began the Muslim conquest of the Middle
East—just five years after the death of Islam's founder, Mohammed.

...mihsammihnouithappluddyappladdypkonpkot" in *Finnegan's Wake*. It means "an act of God."

"I SPY"...AT THE MOVIES

You probably remember the kids' game "I Spy, With My Little Eye..."
Filmmakers have been playing it for years. Here are some in-jokes
and gags you can look for the next time you see these movies.

CASINO ROYALE (2006)
I Spy... A real "Octopussy"
Where to Find It: In the original *Casino Royale* (1967),
the high-stakes game was baccarat; in the updated version, it's
Texas Hold 'Em. One of the hands in that game, a pair of eights, is
called an "octopussy." The producers added this hand to the film
to pay tribute to the 1983 Bond film of the same name.

SIDEWAYS (2004)
I Spy... A character from another movie by director Alexander
Payne
Where to Find Him: The high-school principal in Payne's 1999
film *Election* is called Walt Hendricks. The actor who played him,
Phil Reeves, reprises the character in *Sideways*—he's the man who
tells Jack to watch his language as Jack passes by him and his
grandson. To explain what the character is doing in California
(he's from Nebraska), his name in the credits is listed as "Vacationing Dr. Walt Hendricks."

DONNIE DARKO (2001)
I Spy... References to other movies
Where to Find Them: The opening scene uses imagery from Martin Scorsese's *The Last Temptation of Christ*. The wolf howl heard
at the beginning of the Halloween party is a sound effect from *An
American Werewolf in London*. Donnie's skeleton costume is the
same one that the bully wore in *The Karate Kid*. Donnie's sister is
wearing a Lolita costume (writer/director Richard Kelly is a huge
fan of director Stanley Kubrick's *Lolita*). And the kids riding their
bikes on Halloween is Kelly's homage to Steven Spielberg's *E.T.
the Extra-Terrestrial*.

E.T. THE EXTRA-TERRESTRIAL (1982)

I Spy... Debra Winger

Where to Find Her: It's common knowledge among trivia buffs that Debra Winger was one of the actors who voiced the little alien. But few know that she also had a cameo in the film. During the trick-or-treating scene, she can be seen wearing a monster mask and carrying a poodle.

Bonus: When the aliens' botany collection is seen on the spaceship, one of the plants is a "triffid," a reference to the 1962 film *Day of the Triffids.*

FROM HERE TO ETERNITY (1953)

I Spy... The author of the book that inspired the film

Where to Find Him: While Ernest Borgnine is playing the piano at the New Congress Club, a man can be seen over his shoulder talking with the hostess. That's James Jones, the author of the book (although he probably regretted it, as he was later reported to be unhappy with the Hollywood "sanitization" of his novel).

TITANIC (1997)

I Spy... A depiction of a famous photograph

Where to Find It: While Jack is looking for Rose in first class, he passes a man watching a boy playing jacks. That scene matches an actual photograph taken aboard the *Titanic* just before the ill-fated ship left the dock for the last time and headed for the open sea.

ANCHORMAN: THE LEGEND OF RON BURGUNDY (2004)

I Spy... References to the *Mary Tyler Moore* show

Where to Find Them: In the names of the characters—Baxter the dog is named after the snide anchorman Ted Baxter; and the head of Burgundy's newsroom, Ed Harkin, is named after Ed Asner, who played Lou Grant, the head of Mary Tyler Moore's newsroom.

HAPPY FEET (2006)

I Spy... Ewan McGregor

Where to Find Him: In the scene where Mumble is dancing for what the penguins think are aliens (they're actually humans), one of the "aliens" is based on McGregor's likeness.

Bonus: The other "aliens" are modeled after the real-life researchers who spent a year in Antarctica filming *March of the Penguins*, the hit documentary that inspired *Happy Feet*.

LOVE, ACTUALLY (2003)

I Spy... An intentional blooper

Where to Find It: In the prime minister's neckties. The story goes that Hugh Grant took a nap between takes of the scene in which his character first meets Natalie at 10 Downing Street. He accidentally put on a different tie when he returned to the set and director Richard Curtis didn't notice it at first. When he did, he decided to have a little fun, and gave Grant a new tie in each take. Total number of ties: 11.

*　　*　　*

TWO LUCKY FINDS

• In May 2001, a man spotted a pair of jeans in a pile of mud in an abandoned Nevada mining town. Thinking they might be valuable, he contacted Levi's and found out that they had been made sometime in the 1880s. A spokesperson for the company said they were probably the oldest pair known to exist. The man decided to put them up for sale on eBay. They sold for $46,532—to the Levi Strauss Company.

• A Missouri soybean farmer named Gary Wennihan, 60, was clearing a field when he found a strange, shiny stone. He showed it to friends, but nobody was interested. Then he showed it to Ben Rogers, a geology student who attended his church, who offered to bring it to his professor at Northwest Missouri State University. In 2003, two years later, Wennihan got an answer: the rock was a meteorite from a previously unknown asteroid. Estimated value: more than $1 million. "Someone offered $10,000 for half of it," he later said. "I'm really glad we waited."

HOW TO RIG A COIN TOSS

A long-held secret of carnies and hucksters.
With a little practice, it really works.

WHAT YOU NEED
A large coin. The bigger and heavier, the better. When you get really good at it, you can use a quarter, but until then, a fifty-cent piece or silver dollar is best. The trick is nearly impossible with a nickel, dime, or penny.

HOW TO DO IT:

1. Place the coin in the middle of your palm with the side you want to win face down. For example, if you want "heads" to win the toss, put the heads side of the coin face down in your palm.

2. Hold your arm straight out and clench all the muscles in your arm so it's as stiff as possible.

3. While holding that arm out tight, toss the coin into the air.

4. Here's the tricky part: As you keep your arm clenched and toss the coin up, jerk your hand slightly back. In other words, very subtly pull your hand ever so closer to your body. The move may be somewhat noticeable, but don't worry. Nobody will be watching your hand—all eyes will be on the coin in the air.

5. Catch the coin in your palm. Result: The coin will turn over in the air exactly one whole time. It will land exactly the same as it was before the toss—with the predetermined winning side face down in your hand.

6. Slap the coin onto your forearm to reverse the coin and reveal the winning side—which is what was face down in your palm when you started and what you rigged it to be.

It takes some practice to learn when and how hard to jerk back your hand to spin the coin only once. The heavier the coin, the easier it is—a small coin weighs so little that it tends to spin too many times. With a heavier coin, you've got more control. Now get out there and cheat...er, uh...amaze your friends.

No *@#%! Two thirds of Americans say they regularly use the "f-word."

FUTURAMA II

Once again we look back to the past (1964) to see what the future was supposed to be like. (To look back even further into the past— 1939—to see what the future looked like then, turn to page 131.)

At the 1939 World's Fair, General Motors' "Futurama" exhibit gave visitors a glimpse of what the company predicted the year 1960 would be like. Their projections of domed fruit orchards and 14-lane, 100 mph freeways where cars electronically kept each other from crashing never came to pass. So at the 1964 New York World's Fair, GM presented a new, revised glimpse of life in the future. The setup was virtually the same as the first "Futurama." Riders sat in easy chairs with personal speakers in the headrests providing narration as they toured through dioramas and models of cities, homes, people, and landscapes of the future.

Here's what the future (no specific year was given) looked like in 1964:

• The need for lumber is greater than ever. No problem: The rain forests have plenty of trees. A machine that's five stories high and 1,000 feet long uses a laser beam to chop them down. Then the machine collects the trees and paves a multi-lane freeway behind itself as it transports the timber to the nearest city.

• All that deforestation will lead to an increase of desert lands. No problem: Scientists of the future have learned how to desalinate ocean water to turn it into fresh water, which is then spread across the desert to turn it into lush, habitable land. Machines operated by remote control thousands of miles away plant and harvest all the crops.

• Resorts have moved away from the beaches. Now they're underwater. Giant domed resorts on the ocean floor, such as the Hotel Atlantis, are the craze of the future. For recreation, vacationers (with oxygen helmets) ride aqua-scooters alongside dolphins and sea turtles. The resorts also have domesticated sea lions that children can ride like ponies.

• Not everybody is down there for fun. Giant industrial submarine/trucks called aqua-copters bore into the ocean floor to drill for iron ore, mineral deposits, and vast stores of oil. Atomic-powered submarine trains transport the oil and ore to coastal processing plants.

• The ocean, Earth's last frontier, is fully conquered, so scientists and explorers have left the Earth to exploit the Moon. (This was 1964—landing on the Moon was still a few years off.) Commuter spaceships leave from Earth every day to visit the Moon (travel time: three hours), the entire surface of which is colonized in domed cities.

• All worldwide weather is accurately predicted from Antarctica. An international team of scientists is stationed there to study the polar winds, ice, and surrounding sea to determine how the rest of the world will be affected. The information is then beamed via computer around the world in microseconds.

• City life is speedy and efficient. Cars are used almost exclusively on the freeway, so high-speed trains, moving sidewalks, and underground freight conveyor belts move people and cargo, eliminating traffic congestion. (This is almost an exact repeat of the 1939 Futurama's city of the future.)

• This was a GM exhibit, so of course cars were a big part of the future. Although a human driver will have to negotiate the car through suburban streets, once the round, bubble-topped automobile is on the freeway, it drives itself at 100 mph, with the destination preprogrammed. This leaves the family free to roam around the car to play cards, prepare and eat meals, listen to the radio on hi-fi stereo-quality speakers, or watch a program on their high-definition, flat-screen television.

• When the Futurama II ride ended, passengers exited onto another GM-sponsored exhibit called "The Avenue of Progress." It showcased GM concept cars as well as the ready-to-buy models from the far-off year of...1965.

*   *   *

"Never let the future disturb you. You will meet it with the same weapons of reason which today arm you against the present."

—**Marcus Aurelius**

It's legal in two states to fish with a semiautomatic rifle.

THE LOST NETWORK

You may not remember when TV was black and white. You may not remember when there were no remotes and you had to get up to change channels or adjust the volume. Even if you do, you still probably don't remember the DuMont Network.

PIONEER
Like a lot of people involved with the early development of television, Allen B. DuMont started in radio. In 1924 he was in charge of tube production at Westinghouse, the country's largest radio manufacturer. But by 1928, after his innovations had increased daily tube production tenfold, DuMont got bored and wanted to try something new.

Companies like RCA and the radio networks (CBS and NBC) were already experimenting with television. DuMont proposed to his bosses at Westinghouse that they do the same. They weren't interested, so DuMont quit and set up his own TV lab in the basement of his house. Just two years later, he had perfected the *cathode ray tube*, the component that allows a TV set to receive the broadcast signal from the air and convert it to an image. In other words, the most vital part of a television. And unlike previous cathode ray prototypes, DuMont's lasted indefinitely, rather than burning out after a few days.

DuMont sold the patent to RCA and used the money to start a TV manufacturing business. In need of more cash, he sold 40% of the company to Paramount Pictures in 1939, giving him plenty of money to make TVs. One problem: In 1939 few people were buying TV sets—there weren't any TV shows to watch. CBS and NBC aired a few experimental broadcasts in the New York area in the early 1940s and were rapidly moving toward regular commercial broadcasts, but when World War II broke out, they halted all TV work. DuMont felt that to sell TVs, there'd have to be programming. And now it looked like he'd have to do it himself.

ON THE AIR
In 1944 DuMont got a broadcasting license and opened his first station in New York: WABD (for "Allen B. DuMont"). He opened

a second station, WTTG (after DuMont's vice president Thomas T. Goldsmith) in Washington, D.C., in 1945. Then, using more than 200 miles of coaxial cable, DuMont connected his lab in Passaic, New Jersey, to the two stations. On August 9, 1945, DuMont aired an announcement that the U.S. had just dropped an atomic bomb on Nagasaki, Japan. That brief message was seen on TV sets in New York, New Jersey, and Washington. The DuMont Network—and commercial TV—was born. The network began regular broadcasts a year later with its first show, *Serving Through Science*.

IT'S THE PITTS

The television industry was about to take off. NBC was on the air in several cities in late 1946, including New York City, Philadelphia, and Schenectady, New York. CBS and ABC, a new network, followed in 1948. That year, more than a million TV sets were sold in the United States, most of them made by DuMont Labs.

The third DuMont station went on the air in 1949—WDTV (for "DuMont Television") in Pittsburgh. It was a smart move: CBS and NBC weren't broadcasting in Pittsburgh yet, even though Pittsburgh was America's sixth largest city at the time. In cities where it competed with NBC and CBS, DuMont was a distant third in the ratings; advertising profits suffered. But the profits from the monopoly in Pittsburgh offset the losses and kept the network afloat.

STANDARD VIEWING

CBS and NBC moved a lot of talent from radio to TV (Jack Benny, Edward R. Murrow, Lucille Ball). But DuMont didn't have a built-in pool of entertainers from which to draw. So for onscreen talent, the network hired New York theater actors and comedians. (Jackie Gleason hosted a variety show called *Cavalcade of Stars*; *The Honeymooners* originated as a sketch on that show.) And unlike CBS and NBC's shows, which were produced in state-of-the-art TV studios, DuMont shows were produced in unused rooms at Wanamaker's, a department store on Broadway.

DuMont made up for its lack of funds by innovating and taking risks. The result: groundbreaking ideas that defined the standards of television, even to this day. Among DuMont's contributions:

• **The First Sitcom:** *Mary Kay and Johnny* (1947). Mary Kay and

---

Johnny Stearns, married in real life, played "themselves." Most of the action took place in the couple's apartment.

• **The First TV Soap Opera:** *Faraway Hill* (1946). Widow moves to small town and falls in love with a man who's already engaged.

• **The First Religious TV Show:** *Life is Worth Living* (1952). Hosted by Catholic bishop Fulton J. Sheen, who delivered lectures on moral issues. It was DuMont's top show.

• **The First Kids' Show:** *Your Television Babysitter* (1948)

• **Home Shopping:** On *Your Television Shopper*, a host presented items (cheap jewelry, small appliances) and viewers called in to have them shipped to their home (they paid for them COD).

• **Televised Sports:** DuMont was the first network to regularly air football and basketball games (and boxing and wrestling matches).

• **The First Science Fiction Show:** *Captain Video and His Video Rangers* (1949). A group of interstellar police keep Earth and its space colonies safe.

• **TV Advertising:** The other networks did with TV what they had done on radio: One company sponsored an entire show. But DuMont sold individual blocks of commercial time—thirty seconds to a minute each—to multiple sponsors. That's how TV advertising works today.

DuMont's low-budget try-anything style produced a lot of really weird TV, too.

• *The Plainclothesman*: A private-eye filmed from the point of view of the main character, who's never seen.

• *Monodrama Theater*: One actor performs an entire play by himself in front of a curtain.

• *Night Editor*: A newspaper editor acts out news stories.

• *Inside Detective*: A cop solves crimes without ever leaving his office.

THE SIGNAL FADES

DuMont finished in third or fourth place in the ratings every week (always behind CBS and NBC, and always jockeying with ABC for third). He had affiliates in just three cities—New York, Washington, and Pittsburgh—but independent TV stations around the country paid DuMont and ABC for the rights to broadcast their shows. Allen DuMont wanted to buy more stations in more cities to increase viewers. But he couldn't—an FCC rule allowed a company to own a maximum of five stations. DuMont already owned three; his partner, Paramount, owned two.

Then in 1953, United Paramount Theaters, a movie theater chain (not owned by Paramount Pictures), bought ABC and funnelled millions of dollars into the network to make it more competitive. It worked: By the end of 1954, ABC had pulled ahead of DuMont into a solid third place. Most of the independent stations that had been splitting their schedules between ABC and DuMont shows switched to ABC programming exclusively.

SIGNING OFF

As a last-ditch effort to save the company, DuMont sold his most profitable asset, WDTV in Pittsburgh, for $10 million. But the money wasn't enough—the network was still losing viewers and stations to ABC. In early 1955, he decided to pull the plug. *Life Is Worth Living* broadcast on DuMont for the last time on April 26 (the show moved to ABC). The network feed remained intact for occasional sports broadcasts until August 6, 1956. That night, after a boxing match, the DuMont Network went off the air for good.

DuMont sold the New York and Washington stations to media mogul John Kluge for $7 million, who used them as the basis of a consortium of TV stations called Metromedia. Allen DuMont became a philanthropist and donated much of his fortune to help fund National Educational Television, a nonprofit TV network that evolved into PBS. He died in 1965.

A NEW BROADCAST DAY

The DuMont Network still exists today...sort of. Australian businessman Rupert Murdoch, owner of the 20th Century Fox film studio, set out to start a fourth major network in 1986. To do it, he put together a loose affiliation of independent stations around the country—many of which were the same stations that ran DuMont programming in the 1950s. But his first step: He created the basic elements for a new network by acquiring Metromedia, including the two original DuMont Network stations in New York and Washington, D.C., and created the Fox Network.

THE ENGLISH LANGUAGE

*If English is your first language, thank your lucky stars
that you didn't have to learn it as a second language.*

"Any language where the unassuming word 'fly' signifies an annoying insect, a means of travel, and a critical part of a gentleman's apparel is clearly asking to be mangled."

—**Bill Bryson**

"It's a strange language in which skating on thin ice can get you into hot water."

—**Franklin P. Jones**

"English has created the word 'loneliness' to express the pain of being alone. And it has created the word 'solitude' to express the glory of being alone."

—**Paul Tillich**

"Not only does the English language borrow words from other languages, it sometimes chases them down dark alleys, hits them over the head, and goes through their pockets."

—**Eddy Peters**

"Introducing 'Lite'—the new way to spell 'Light', but with twenty percent fewer letters."

—**Jerry Seinfeld**

"When I read some of the rules for writing the English language correctly, I think any fool can make a rule, and every fool will mind it."

—**Henry David Thoreau**

"If the English language made any sense, 'lackadaisical' would have something to do with a shortage of flowers."

—**Doug Larson**

"The English language is like a broad river on whose bank a few patient anglers are sitting, while, higher up, the stream is being polluted by a string of refuse-barges tipping out their muck."

—**Cyril Connolly**

"Even if you do learn to speak correct English, whom are you going to speak it to?"

—**Clarence Darrow**

"Do not compute the totality of your poultry population until all the manifestations of incubation have been entirely completed."

—**William Jennings Bryan**

THE MISSING MOM

Here's a nightmare: You set off on a simple trip, only to end up more than 1,000 miles away from everyone you've ever known, with no way to get home. It happened to a woman who became known as "Auntie Mon."

LANGUAGE BARRIER

In 1982 Jaeyaena Beuraheng left her home in the Narathiwat Province of southern Thailand to take one of her regular shopping trips across the border in Malaysia. After she was done at the markets, Beuraheng, 51 years old and a mother of seven, accidentally boarded the wrong bus. She fell asleep. When she woke up, she found herself in Bangkok...700 miles north of her home. Unfortunately for Beuraheng, she couldn't speak Thai, and her Malay dialect, Yawi, is spoken by very few people in Bangkok. In fact, to the people in Bangkok whom she asked for directions, it sounded like the woman was speaking gibberish. Without the ability to read signs or ask directions, Beuraheng boarded another bus—one that she thought was headed south. Instead, it took her another 430 miles north and she ended up in the city of Chiang Mai. Beuraheng was now more than 1,100 miles from home, she didn't know where she was, and she'd run out of money.

Meanwhile, back in her hometown, Beuraheng's family told the authorities that their mother was missing and were informed that a woman matching her description had been hit by a train and killed. Beuraheng's son went to identify the body—which was difficult—but he said that it could have been her. So, believing their mother was dead, they stopped searching for her. Beuraheng was on her own. With no other options, she resorted to begging in the street to survive.

A SHELTERED LIFE

Five years later, Beuraheng, now 56, was arrested in a section of the city where begging was not allowed. The police couldn't understand the woman's words, so they took her to a homeless shelter in nearby Phitsanulok. The staff at the shelter had deduced that the woman was crazy. Still, she seemed nice, so there she stayed. Mostly, Beuraheng sat in a chair and sang a song that no one could understand. They called her "Auntie Mon" because the song reminded them of the language spoken by the ethnic Mon people, who live on the Burma-Thailand border. They even brought in someone who could speak Mon to try and discern if that's what it was, but it wasn't. Everyone who tried to understand Auntie Mon only heard gibberish.

Twenty years passed.

THE POWER OF SONG

In 2007 three university students from Narathiwat were studying the homeless problem in Phitsanulok. As they were touring the shelter, one of the students asked about the old woman singing the song. "That's Auntie Mon. We can't understand her words, but we like the song," said one of the staff workers. The student replied that he could—it was Yawi, a dialect spoken near his hometown. He approached her, smiled, and asked her for her name. It was the first time Beuraheng had understood anything that anyone had said in 25 years. Overjoyed, she told the students about her ordeal—how she took the wrong bus, how she ended up at the shelter, how much she missed being able to speak to anyone, and how much she missed her family.

HOME AT LAST

Beuraheng's family was shocked to receive the news that their mother was alive. Her youngest son and eldest daughter traveled to the shelter to bring her home. She recognized her daughter, but not her son, who was just a small child when she last saw him. They flew back to Narathiwat…and took the *correct* bus home to their village. A two-day celebration ensued, during which Beuraheng— often crying tears of joy—told her amazing story to the press. "I didn't tell anybody where I was going on that day, because I went there quite often. I thought I would die in Phitsanulok. I thought about running away many times, but then I worried I would not be able to make it home. I really missed my children."

Beuraheng, now 76 years old, has a much larger family than when she left (there are many grandchildren). As in the shelter, she still spends much of her time sitting in her chair and singing her song. Only now, those around her can understand the words.

A year after quitting smoking, a person's risk of having a heart attack drops by half.

BATHROOM NEWS

Here are a few choice bits of
bathroom trivia we've flushed out.

HEAD TO HEAD

"British firefighters said in April 2007 that they had come to a boy's rescue after he got a toilet seat stuck on his head. The toddler, aged two-and-a-half, and his mother walked into a fire station in Braintree, Essex, saying the boy had put his head through a small trainer seat for the toilet and now could not remove it. 'His mum couldn't budge it so she asked us to have a look. We immediately went to work and managed to get it off in no time,' firefighter Chris Cox said. 'We simply put some dish-washing liquid on his head and ears and it slid off nice as pie.'"

—Reuters

ANCIENT PRUDES

"An international team of biblical scholars learned recently that the sect thought to have been responsible for the Dead Sea Scrolls (the Essenes) became extinct because they were too modest about their toilet habits. According to a report in London's *Independent*, the researchers found evidence of heavy fecal bacteria in a secluded area (which was also a graveyard) and deduced from the scrolls that the Essenes rejected defecating in the open, which would have allowed sunlight to kill the bacteria."

—News of the Weird

RING OF FIRE

"Toto Ltd., Japan's leading toilet maker, is offering free repairs for 180,000 bidet toilets after wiring problems caused several to catch fire. The electric bidet accessory of Toto's Z series caught fire in three separate incidents between March 2006 and March 2007, according to company spokeswoman Emi Tanaka, and sent up smoke in 26 other incidents. 'Fortunately, nobody was using the toilets when the fires broke out,' Tanaka said. 'The fire would have been just under your buttocks.'"

—Yahoo! News

A Colombian company makes a stab-proof T-shirt. Price: $500.

THE REAL ZORRO?

*Every cultural legend has to start someplace, even if it's from just a kernel
of truth, expanded and embellished until it bears no resemblance
to the original. Here's the possible origin of Zorro, the
"bold renegade" who "carved a Z with his blade."*

BACKGROUND

Pulp fiction writer Johnston McCulley created the swash-buckling character Zorro for a tale called "The Curse of Capistrano" that appeared in *All-Story Weekly* magazine in 1919. Literary historians believe McCulley based him on a number of characters, most of them fictional…and at least one real human being. It turns out that the story of the real man's life was just as unusual—and probably every bit as embellished—as Zorro's.

THE MAN

Not long after gold was discovered at Sutter's Mill in California in 1848, a young Mexican man named Joaquin Murrieta came to California with his wife, Rosa Feliz, and her brothers Claudio, Reyes, and Jesus. They hoped to strike it rich in the gold fields, but none of them did; the closest any of them got was when Claudio was arrested for stealing another miner's gold.

In 1850 Claudio escaped from jail and led his brothers and Murrieta in what became one of the most violent bandit gangs ever to terrorize the California gold country. The group was known to raid isolated ranches, but they preferred to rob lone travelers and Chinese miners (they thought the Chinese were less likely to be armed than whites or Mexicans). The gang murdered most of its victims after robbing them, to ensure that there were no witnesses.

The law began to catch up with the gang in September 1851, when Claudio was killed in a shootout following a robbery in Monterey County. Murrieta happened to be in Los Angeles at the time, and when Claudio died he assumed control of the gang. Not long afterward the bandits made the mistake of killing Joshua Bean, a major general in the militia. Murrieta then compounded the error by abandoning Reyes to his fate—Reyes was arrested for Bean's murder and hanged.

Don't tell St. Patrick! There are about 2,000 snakes living in captivity in Ireland.

THE END

Jesus, the youngest of the Feliz brothers, apparently never forgave Murrieta for Reyes's death, because when the posse of state rangers caught up with him he willingly gave them the location of Murrieta's hideout. On July 25, 1853, Murrieta died in a gun battle not far from where Interstate 5 now intersects Highway 33 outside of Coalinga, California. After Murrieta died, Jesus gave up his life of crime, moved to Bakersfield, and started a family. He lived to a ripe old age and died in 1910.

Murrieta was not as lucky. After he died in the shootout, the posse cut off his head and preserved it in a giant glass jar filled with brandy—there was a bounty on his head (so to speak), and in the days before fingerprinting and DNA evidence, posses had to be a little more creative in documenting that they'd gotten their man.

Murrieta's brandied head made the rounds of the "$1-a-peek, crime-doesn't-pay" lecture circuit for a few years; then it ended up as a feature attraction behind the bar of San Francisco's Golden Nugget Saloon, where for the price of a drink you could sit at the bar and stare at the head for as long as you could stand the sight of it staring back at you. The head was still floating there in its jar on the morning of April 18, 1906, when it, the jar, and the saloon were all destroyed in the San Francisco earthquake and fire.

THE LEGEND BEGINS

By then Murrieta's image had already been completely remade into a Robin Hood-like figure who robbed from the rich, killed them, and gave to the poor. (His infamy as a killer was so well-established that a complete whitewash would not have been believable.) The makeover had begun less than a year after his death, when a newspaperman named John Rollin Ridge wrote *The Life and Adventures of Joaquin Murrieta, the Celebrated California Bandit*. Ridge himself was on the lam for a murder he'd committed in Arkansas, which must have given him sympathy for his subject. He painted a picture of Murrieta as a good man at heart who embarked on his life of crime only after seeing his brother lynched and his wife gang-raped by a band of vicious gringos. Murrieta then got his revenge by killing every white man he met until he was finally hunted down and killed by a drunken, sadistic ranger who was only in it for a $5,000 bounty.

The human body's total daily requirement of vitamins and minerals is less than a thimbleful.

Ridge's book sold so well that five years later the *California Police Gazette* published an even more exaggerated version of the tale. That in turn led to new versions being published in France, Spain, and Chile, where a statue was erected in honor of Murrieta, who—in that version of the story, at least—was a native of Chile. These fictionalized accounts of Murrieta's life gained even more credibility when a historian named Herbert Howe Bancroft fell for them and passed them along uncritically in one of his volumes on the American West. Now that a prominent historian had signed off on them as true, the tales were accepted as unvarnished fact by just about everyone. Joaquin Murrieta became a folk hero, one whose fame continues to this day. He has been the subject of a play by the Nobel Prize-winning author Pablo Neruda, and in 1976 he even became the inspiration for the Soviet Union's first-ever rock opera, *The Star and Death of Joaquin Murietta, a Chilean Bandit Foully Murdered in California on 25 July 1853.*

NOW YOU SEE HIM...

So was Joaquin Murrieta ever really captured and killed? Was that really his head floating in the jar behind the bar in the Golden Nugget Saloon? Even that detail has been called into question. According to one version of the story, the posse on Murrieta's trail had only 90 days to catch the bandit and collect the reward. When the time was nearly up and they still hadn't captured their man, the party murdered the first Mexican they came upon and put *his* head in the jar so that they could claim the reward. "It is well known that Joaquin Murrieta was not the person killed," the editor of the San Francisco newspaper *Alta* wrote in August 1853. "The head recently exhibited in Stockton bears no resemblance to that individual, and this is positively asserted by those who have seen the real Murrieta and the spurious head."

EPILOGUE: Z MARKS THE SPOT

Seventy-five years after Murietta's death, writer Johnston McCulley was working as a crime reporter for the *Police Gazette*. After World War I, he switched to pulp-fiction writing. An amateur history buff, he based many of his stories in old California, and was undoubtedly familiar with the legend of Murrieta. But in addition to Joaquin Murrieta, McCulley is believed to have drawn inspiration from *The Count of Monte Cristo*, by Alexandre Dumas (1844–45), and *The Scarlet Pimpernel*, by Baroness Orczy (1905), both of which feature wealthy gentlemen who don disguises to fight evil.

McCulley created dozens of characters over the course of his career, and as was the case with so many of the others it is doubtful that he intended for Zorro to be more than a just one-story character. That all changed when United Artists, the film studio founded by Charlie Chaplin, Douglas Fairbanks, Mary Pickford, and D. W. Griffith, decided to base their first film, *The Mark of Zorro* (1920), on "The Curse of Capistrano." Why mess with success? McCulley happily went on to write more than 60 stories featuring Zorro, the most popular character he'd ever create.

Zorro, in turn, was one of the major inspirations for another character: Batman, who appeared in comics beginning in 1939. In the original version of the Batman story, Bruce Wayne's parents are murdered after leaving a movie theater. The movie they'd just seen: *The Mark of Zorro*.

*   *   *

GO, BALLOONS!

Don Mischer, the producer of the 2004 Democratic Convention in Boston, really wanted the balloons to drop on cue. When they didn't, here's what a live microphone caught him saying.

"Go, balloons. I don't see anything happening. Go, balloons. Go, balloons. Go, balloons. Stand by, confetti. Keep coming, balloons. More balloons. Bring them. Balloons, balloons, balloons! More balloons. Tons of them. Bring them down. Let them all come. No confetti. No confetti yet. All right. Go, balloons. Go, balloons. We're getting more balloons. All balloons. All balloons should be going. Come on, guys! Let's move it! We need more balloons. I want all balloons to go. Go, confetti. Go, confetti. Go, confetti. I want more balloons. What's happening to the balloons? We need more balloons. We need all of them coming down. Go, balloons. Balloons! What's happening, balloons? There's not enough coming down! All balloons! Why the hell is nothing falling? What the (censored) are you guys doing up there? We want more balloons coming down! More balloons! More balloons!"

Longest cells in your body: the motor neurons running from your spinal cord to your big toes.

WORD ORIGINS

Ever wonder where these words came from?
Here are the interesting stories behind them.

GLAMOUR

Meaning: A fascinating or alluring quality, especially when combined with charm and good looks

Origin: "Unlikely as it may seem, *glamour* is ultimately the same word as *grammar*. It was used in the Middle Ages for 'learning' in general, and by superstitious association, for 'magic.' The Scottish used the form *glamour* (l is phonetically close to r, and the two are liable to change places), used for 'enchantment,' or a 'spell.' The literal sense 'enchanted' has now slipped into disuse, gradually replaced by 'elusive charm,' and later 'fashionable attractiveness.'" (From *Dictionary of Word Origins*, by John Ayto)

MINION

Meaning: A docile follower or subordinate of a person in power

Origin: "Because the connotation of *minion* is 'small and insignificant,' a connection with *mini-* might be imagined. But the word actually comes from French *mignon*, which means 'darling' or 'delicately small person.' The word came to mean ladylove, loved one, favorite, and eventually fawning servant or servile attendant." (From *NTC's Dictionary of Word Origins*, by Adrian Room)

TALENT

Meaning: Natural skills or endowments

Origin: "From the Greek word *talanton*, for 'an amount of money.' The meaning 'ability' come from the parable in *Matthew 25:14-30*, which tells how a master entrusted money to each of his three servants. The servant with five 'talents' and the one with two 'talents' both doubled their money and were rewarded. The servant who had been given one 'talent' buried the money and returned only the original amount, and for this he was punished. The parable has been interpreted to mean that everyone has a duty to improve the natural gifts that God has given

---

How do they say "Godfather"? *Mafia* comes from the Old Arabic word for "swagger."

them." (From *Word Mysteries & Histories*, by the editors of The American Heritage Dictionaries)

LUSCIOUS

Meaning: Sweet and pleasant to taste or smell; richly appealing to the senses of the mind; richly adorned, luxurious

Origin: "This word has grown roundabout. There was a Middle English *licious*, a shortened form of *delicious*. But there was also English *lush*, juicy, succulent. The sense and sound of the other word—*licious*—moved along to *luscious*." (From *Dictionary of Word Origins*, by Joseph T. Shipley)

ACTOR

Meaning: A theatrical performer, or someone who takes part—a participant

Origin: "The original sense of the word in the 14th century was 'agent,' referring to a person who takes action in order to manage something. Later, an *actor* was simply a 'doer,' 'one who acts,' as recorded in Shakespeare's *Measure for Measure* (1603): 'Condemn the fault and not the actor of it.' The modern sense, 'stage player,' occurs about the same time." (From *Dunces, Gourmands & Petticoats*, by Adrian Room)

KILL

Meaning: To cause the death of a person or animal; to abruptly end something

Origin: "The word may seem age-old, but it evolved in its present sense in the 14th century out of the Old English *cyllan*, meaning 'strike' or 'beat.' A 14th-century poem in the West Midland dialect has the gruesome word in this sense: 'We kylle of thyn heued' (we strike off your head), and it is easy to see how this could develop in the modern sense, with *kill* first meaning 'put to death with a weapon,' then 'put to death' in general." (From *Words About Words*, by David Grambs)

*   *   *

"Words are but crumbs that fall from the feast of the mind."

—**Khalil Gibran**

FOR WHAT ALES YOU

It's not just for breakfast anymore! We've discovered that beer has many inventive and unlikely uses around the home and beyond. (Uncle John's never had so much fun researching an article.)

• Beer is slightly acidic, making it useful for cleaning copper pots. Throw a small amount of beer in the pot, let it sit for a few minutes, and then wipe it out.

• Beer adds shine and luster to hair. Boil one cup of beer until it's reduced down to ¼ cup. Let it cool and mix with your regular shampoo.

• After a beer shampoo, try a beer conditioner. Mix three tablespoons of beer with half a cup of warm water. After washing your hair, rub in the beer solution, leave it in for a couple minutes, then rinse. The beer reportedly makes flat hair bouncier.

• Beer kills pesky garden slugs. Fill some wide-mouthed jars a third of the way full with beer. Bury them about 15–20 feet from your garden, with the rims level to the soil. Slugs love beer. They'll smell it, try to drink it, then fall into the jars and drown.

• A bath of ice-cold, extra-bubbly beer soothes tired feet.

• If drinking too much beer got you lost, beer can also help you find your way back home. Put some in a bowl and let it go flat. Magnetize a needle by stroking it against a piece of silk, then put it in the bowl of beer and it will point north/south.

• Spray organic beer on the brown patches in your lawn. The grass will absorb the fermented sugars, which stimulate growth.

• Flat beer cleans wooden furniture. Wipe some on a soft cloth, clean the furniture, then wipe dry with another cloth.

• Try this only at your own risk, but beer can shine gold. Pour the beer onto a cloth, rub it gently over the gold (but *not* any gemstones) and wipe clean with a towel.

• Beer even removes coffee stains from rugs. Pour the beer directly over the stain, then rub it into the fibers. (Disclaimer: Try this one only at your own risk, too.)

The alcohol content of a can of beer and a shot of whisky are virtually identical.

THE FLEHMEN RESPONSE

No, that's not the name of Uncle John's latest punk rock band, it's an article about "Fixed Action Patterns." (Which, by coincidence, is the name of Uncle John's latest punk rock band.)

B ACKGROUND
In "Getting Organ-ized" (page 555) we mention the *flehmen response*, an instinctual behavior seen in many animal species, most notably in horses. Ethologists—scientists who study animal behavior—call this kind of instinct a "fixed action pattern" (FAP), meaning that it is an *inherited*, as opposed to a *learned*, behavior. FAPs are performed even by animals raised in complete isolation, and they are acted out in the same way by every animal within a species. The name also underlines the fact that once triggered, the behavior pattern—whatever it may be—is fixed; the sequence of movements is almost always completed in full, even if it's a very long sequence. Another characteristic is that the pattern is triggered by some kind of external stimulus, known as a *releaser*.

THE GOOSE AND THE EGG
In the 1930s, Konrad Lorenz and Niko Tinbergen, considered the fathers of modern ethology, studied instinctual behavior in Grey-lag geese, a species native to Europe and Asia. Through those studies, they were the ones who came up with the idea of *releasers*, or *innate releasing mechanisms*, and the idea that the encoded behaviors, once triggered, must follow through to completion—even if it is unnecessary or inappropriate. (The science of animal instinct has progressed since then, but the basics of Lorenz's and Tinbergen's findings are still widely accepted.)

Lorenz kept a flock of about 100 Greylag geese at his home. In 1937 he and Tinbergen studied a curious activity that the Greylags performed whenever they saw an egg outside of their nests. The mother would use a very particular sequence of movements to get the egg back: She would stretch her neck out and hook the egg with the underside of her bill; then move her head side to side, pushing the egg toward her until it was against her; then thrust her head down, pushing the egg under her belly and back into the nest.

A sloth can move twice as fast in water as on land (but it's still really slow).

All nesting Greylags do it in almost exactly the same way. Lorenz and Tinbergen surmised that this was an innately known behavior triggered by the sight of an egg outside the nest. They came up with a simple experiment to prove it: When a goose was roosting, they placed an egg outside of her nest. She would immediately go into the side-to-side head movement to get the egg back—but before she finished, they'd take the egg away. What did mother goose do? She kept moving her head side to side and toward her, then thrust her head under her belly and into the nest—all with no egg. When she raised her head up again, if she saw another egg outside the nest (placed there again by the researchers), she'd immediately go into the motions again—always to completion, no matter how many times the egg was taken away. The same results occurred with different geese, prompting Lorenz and Tinbergen to conclude that instinctual behavior must be performed in full once triggered.

HORSING AROUND

You've probably seen it in action or on TV: When a horse sticks its nose in the air and curls back its upper lip, exposing its teeth in a "grimace," that's the flehmen response. And they're not the only animals who display the behavior; many hooved animals do it, and so do housecats. In the horse's case, the releaser for this behavior is an odor, usually a stallion smelling traces of pheromones in the urine of a nearby mare. The stallion will curl back its upper lip and lift its nose, which, say ethologists, helps concentrate the pheromone molecules near the *vomeronasal organ* in the horse's nasal cavity, an organ especially sensitive to the pheromones of a mare in heat. In the presence of such a mare, a stallion will perform the flehmen response several times an hour, and, if things go right, will mate with her. Geldings—neutered males—perform the flehmen response, too. Even though they cannot mate, they are still set off by the odor of a female.

STICKLEBACK DADDY

No, that's not the name of Uncle John's new bluegrass band, it's an animal often used to demonstrate FAPs. Three-spined sticklebacks are a species of small European freshwater fish. Every spring, mature males of the species go through a very specific series of activities:

• They stake out a territory and, with a similar set of motions, gather debris to make a nest on the creek (or aquarium) floor. The culminating act: a wiggling dance through the nest to create a hollow for a female's eggs. The releaser for this activity is believed to be water temperature, or perhaps the change in hours of sunlight.

• At the same time, adult males undergo a drastic color change: Their belly and throat areas turn from gray to bright red.

• If a nesting male sees another sexually mature male (with a red belly) near its nest, it will immediately attack it in a very specific way: The fish takes a nose-down, vertical stance, displays the three spines on its back, and makes thrusting motions toward the intruder (they rarely do actual harm). All males do this in almost the exact same way when another male approaches its nest.

• Not only that, they'll attack anything that looks even *remotely* like a male stickleback. Researchers have put plastic fish into tanks with nesting sticklebacks. All were ignored…except ones with red bellies painted on them. (Niko Tinbergen even reported a stickleback attacking the side of its tank—when it saw a red postal truck drive by outside a window.)

OTHER "MUST-FINISH-THE-SEQUENCE" INSTINCTS

• The females of many spider species construct web cocoons when they're ready to lay eggs. First they build a base, then walls, lay their eggs inside the opening, then close up the top. It is an FAP that all females of the species perform in *exactly* the same way— which, for some, involves up to 6,000 movements. And once triggered, the sequence *must* be run to completion. If you remove a spider from her cocoon after she has built just the base, she'll build walls in her new location, then lay her eggs in the baseless cocoon—losing them out the bottom—then still put the lid on.

• It has been long known that the sight of nestlings' wide-open and upturned mouths triggers bird parents to feed their young. In 1966 Niko Tinbergen witnessed just how strong that instinct is. In a pond not far from where a mother cardinal lost her eggs were some minnows that would often surface at the water's edge, looking for food. Tinbergen documented the mother cardinal's amazing behavior: She saw the open, gaping mouths of the small fish at the edge of the pond—and started feeding them worms. The cardinal dutifully fetched worms and fed her "baby" fish like that for weeks.

Garden tip: Hydrangeas produce pink and white flowers in alkaline soil; blue ones in acidic soil.

CELEBRITY GOSSIP

*Here's the latest edition of the BRI's cheesy tabloid
section—a bunch of gossip about famous people.*

GEORGE CLOONEY

When Clooney was in middle school, he developed a medical condition called Bell's palsy, which partially paralyzed his face for nearly a year. Clooney's left eye stayed closed and he had trouble eating and drinking. This condition led to a lot of taunting in school, including the nickname "Frankenstein."

ICE-T

In 1984 Ice-T had just released the rap single "Killers," one of the first "gangsta rap" records. At the time, he was also a member of the notorious gang the Crips, as well as an occasional pimp and jewel thief. Somehow Ice-T also got the job of ghostwriting rap lyrics for Mr. T's motivational video for kids, *Be Somebody...or Be Somebody's Fool.* Sample lyrics from the song "Treat Your Mother Right": "'M' is for the moan and the miserable groan / From the pain that she felt when I was born."

ELVIS PRESLEY

Could you imagine Elvis—with a British accent—saying, "I fart in your general direction"? According to former girlfriend Linda Thompson, the King was a huge fan of the British comedy troupe Monty Python. "He'd be doing all the voices," she said, "which is mind-boggling. He'd even do the ladies' voices."

CORETTA SCOTT KING

Walter and Betty Roberts, a young couple in Atlanta, Georgia, gave drama lessons to the children of Coretta Scott and Martin Luther King Jr. in the 1960s. Even though the Robertses were white, they welcomed black children into their home during those racially charged times. In October 1967, upon hearing the news that Betty Roberts had to go to the hospital to deliver her third child, Mrs. King paid all of the Robertses' hospital bills as a gesture of thanks. That child: Julia Roberts.

DENNIS HOPPER

In the mid-1960s, the up-and-coming actor bought a painting called *Sinking Sun* by pop artist Roy Lichtenstein—which he then lost to his first wife in their 1969 divorce. What did it cost him? "I paid $1,100 for *Sinking Sun*," he explained in an interview. "My ex-wife sold it for $3,000, thinking *she'd* made a good deal." After changing hands one more time, the painting was auctioned off in 2006 for $15,780,000.

QUENTIN TARANTINO

"I've always thought that I might have been Shakespeare in another life," Tarantino told *GQ* magazine. "I don't really believe that 100 percent, and I don't really care about Shakespeare, but people are constantly bringing up all of these qualities in my work that mirror Shakespearean tragedies. I remember in the case of *Reservoir Dogs*, writing this scene where the undercover cop is teaching Tim Roth how to be an undercover cop. When Harvey Keitel read it, he thought I had just taken Hamlet's speech to the players and broke it down into modern words." Here's the spooky part: "I'd never read *Hamlet!*"

HILARY SWANK

The two-time Oscar winner was studying a script in a busy Los Angeles bakery when she noticed an older woman—who was obviously in a hurry—asking for help at the counter. All the sales-people were busy with other customers, so Swank got up, walked behind the counter, and put together the woman's order. (Swank was a regular there, so the staff welcomed her help.) Later that week, Swank was pulled over for speeding on the Pacific Coast Highway. The cop let her off with just a warning. Why? He had been in the bakery that day and witnessed Swank's good deed. And the woman she helped, he told her, was actually a high-ranking judge in Malibu.

*   *   *

"The nice thing about being a celebrity is that when you bore people, they think it's their fault."

—Henry Kissinger

The range of a medieval longbow was about 220 yards—more than two football fields.

THE NAME GAME

"Our names can say a lot about us"...says Uncle JOHN.

BOTTOMS UP

A woman in Marshalltown, Iowa, was arrested in June 2007 after she was spotted stealing three rolls of toilet paper from a storeroom at the Marshall County Courthouse. Her name: Suzanne Marie Butts.

FOR HEAVEN'S SAKE

A Catholic school in Melbourne, Australia, refused to allow a five-year-old boy to enroll in the school in 2007. Why? Because his name is Chris Hell. When the Hell family took their story to newspapers, school officials finally allowed the young Hell in. "We are the victims of our name," said Mrs. Hell.

TOY STORY

On July 2, 2007, Jason Michael Burrows of Seattle went to the King Country District Court Building and had his name legally changed...to Jason Megatron Burrows. He changed the name to honor his childhood hero, the Transformers character Megatron. (Jason Megatron Burrows, by the way, is 30 years old.)

BOTTLE-FED

In 1995 Shannon Cooper of Des Moines, Iowa, was arrested after leaving her three young children home and going out bar-hopping. Her children's names: Champaigne, 2; Chardonay, 1; and Chablea, 3 months.

THAT'S WHAT FRIENDS ARE FOR

Syvette Wimberly, 25, of Houston is an adult-film star. That's not her real name, though—it's really Lara Madden. She borrowed her screen name from a high school friend with whom she'd had a falling out. When the real Syvette Wimberly found out that her name was being used for less-than-wholesome purposes, she sued Madden for "humiliation, embarrassment, mental anguish, and anxiety." Madden's lawyer said his client never meant to bring harm to Wimberly; she just liked the sound of the name.

For six months in 1777, Vermont was called New Connecticut.

TAKE THE POLITICALLY CORRECT QUIZ

So you think you have a deep understanding of what offends other people?
Then try your luck at figuring out what the following politically correct
folks got so upset about. (Answers are on page 596.)

1. In the summer of 2005, the Belgian government tried to stop
the Belgian Boy Scouts from engaging in which of the following
practices at summer camp?
a) Sleeping in teepees. (It's "racially insensitive.")
b) Teaching the scouts to slaughter chickens and small game as
part of a lesson in wilderness survival. (It's "cruel to the animals.")
c) Dressing up as girls to play the female roles in the theater
pieces they perform at the end of summer. (It's "insensitive to
women and to persons of ambiguous gender identity.")

2. In the spring of 2006, Australian brothel owners asked the
government for an exemption from which of the following laws?
a) Sales tax. "The tax treats human sexuality as just another salable
commodity," said a spokesperson for the "Adult Entertainment
Industry," as the country's 87 legal brothels refer to themselves.
b) Gender discrimination laws. "Yes, we hire more women than
men," the spokesperson complained, "but we have to—most of our
customers are men who want to be with women."
c) Anti-smoking laws. "People smoke when they drink, and smoke
when they fornicate," said the spokesperson.

3. In the fall of 2005, the Ronald Reagan Presidential Library
made headlines when it abruptly "fired" nearly 30 volunteers after
many years of loyal service. The volunteers were let go on what
grounds?
a) Too liberal—a check of voting records found that many of
them voted for Jimmy Carter when Reagan first ran for president
in 1980.
b) Too fiscally conservative—security cameras caught them com-

---

It's probably jammed: In Belgium, there is a strawberry museum.

plaining to visitors about the huge growth in the federal deficit during the Reagan years.

c) Too old—even though many of them were younger than Reagan was during his presidency. (Reagan was 77 when he left office.)

4. The owner of Hotel Ostfriesland in Norden, Germany, charges customers on a sliding scale based on what?

a) Whether or not the hotel's owner, Juergen Heckrodt, finds them attractive. "I have to look at them while they're here," he explains. "If they're pretty, I give them a discount. If they're not so pretty they can pay extra for my trouble or stay someplace else."

b) Weight. Heckrodt charges his customers half a euro per kilogram. Maximum—for people weighing 148 kg (326 lb.) or more: 74 euros (about $100).

c) Skin color—if their skin is darker than the paper bag Heckrodt keeps behind the front counter, he gives them 15% off on their room. "This is the 21st century," Heckrodt explains. "We need more color in Germany."

5. In the summer of 2005, protesters wrote letters to the Aquarium of the Pacific in Long Beach, California, in protest of one of the aquarium's business practices. Which practice?

a) The disabled parking spaces are next to the killer whale tank, and Jamu the killer whale has taken to splashing customers if they get too close to the tank. "They either need to move the parking spaces or move Jamu," an advocate for the disabled told reporters.

b) The cafeteria serves fish. "Serving fish at an aquarium is like serving poodle burgers at a dog show," a spokesperson for the Fish Empathy Project of People for the Ethical Treatment of Animals told reporters.

c) The revealing "Little Mermaid" costumes that some female employees must wear are "sexist, demeaning, and limit mobility," says the National Organization for Women (NOW).

6. Which of the following groups staged a protest in front of the British Parliament to get an offensive term banned from the *Oxford English Dictionary*?

a) Potato farmers—they wanted "couch potato" replaced with the potato-neutral term "couch slouch."

b) Junk dealers—they wanted "junk in the trunk" replaced with "ample bottom."

c) Lawyers—they threatened to sue for emotional and punitive damages if "shyster" wasn't removed from the upcoming edition of the dictionary. "Friend of the court" would be allowed to stay.

7. In June 2005, a German court struck down which of the following clauses in Wal-Mart's code of conduct?

a) The prohibition against consuming alcohol during lunch breaks. "We Germans like our beer," an attorney for the state explained.

b) The prohibition against flirting on the job. (It also struck down a requirement that staff report violations of the flirting code to the company's ethics hotline.)

c) The prohibition against bringing pets to work. "German law protects the rights of workers and their animal companions," a lawyer told reporters.

*　　　*　　　*

ACCORDING TO...

...Bankrate, a consumer watchdog group, many American homes still rent their phone from the telephone company. It was a common practice as recently as 50 years ago, but a phone can be purchased for as little as $10 today. Bankrate estimates that 580,000 people still pay anywhere from $4 to $20 each month.

...a study by a publishing consultant, the average number of weeks a book remains on the bestseller list has greatly diminished since the 1960s. In that decade, the average number-one novel sat at the top for 22 weeks. In 2006 it was about two weeks.

...Canadian scientists, the reason for the *Mona Lisa*'s distinctive smile is that she's just given birth. Using an infrared scan, they found a "draft" beneath the painting that shows she's wearing a *guarnello*, a gauzy robe typically worn by new mothers in the 1500s.

Pilgrims didn't eat with forks. They used spoons, knives, and their fingers.

PROJECT GREEK ISLAND, PART II

*It's still one of the best-kept secrets of the Cold War—a bomb
shelter large enough to house the entire U.S. Congress.
Here's Part II of our story of your tax dollars
at work. (Part I starts on page 201.)*

TRY NOT TO THINK ABOUT IT

For all its amenities, the bomb shelter was still a *bomb
shelter*, after all, one designed to be used at what would
probably have been the end of the world. The designers put a lot
of thought into managing the psychological stresses the shelter
occupants would undoubtedly be under if nuclear war ever came.
Each of the 18 dormitory rooms had its own lounge stocked with
books, magazines, an exercise bicycle, and a TV to provide dis-
tractions (though it's unclear what people would have watched
on postapocalyptic TV). To make the shelter seem less like an
underground tomb, the walls of the cafeteria had fake "windows"
that looked out onto painted landscapes. The pharmacy was
stocked with plenty of antidepressants, and there was an isolation chamber to contain anyone who went completely nuts
under the strain.

OPEN FOR BUSINESS

In all the shelter cost more than $10 million to build, and the
hotel wing on top of it cost another $4 million. Both projects were
completed in October 1962—just in time for the shelter to be
activated during the Cuban missile crisis, the only time in the
shelter's 30-year history that it went on full alert. At one point
during the crisis the Senate and House of Representatives (and
numerous crates of top-secret documents) came within 12 hours of
relocating to the Greenbrier. That was as close as Project Greek
Island ever came to actually being put to use.

But just because the shelter was never *put* to use doesn't mean
that it wasn't kept *ready* for use. For the next 30 years, 12 to 15
retired military personnel with high security clearances were

---

World's oldest restaurant: Ma Yo Ching's Bucket Chicken House. It opened in China in 1153.

always stationed at the Greenbrier, where they posed as TV repairmen working for a shell company called "Forsythe Associates." To make their cover story believable, the "repairmen" really did spend as much as 20 percent of their time repairing TVs at the resort.

KEEPING IT FRESH

The rest of the time, they and a few dozen trusted Greenbrier employees who had been sworn to secrecy were down in the bunker maintaining equipment, replacing burned-out lightbulbs, changing bedsheets, restocking expired food and other supplies, and cleaning the 110 showers, 187 sinks, 167 toilets, and 74 urinals that were never used. They rotated the magazines and books in the lounges to keep the reading material fresh, and they kept the pharmacy stocked with the prescription medications of all 435 members of the House and Senate.

Once a year, they replaced outdated medical equipment so that the hospital kept up with advances in medicine. Because bed space in the dormitories was assigned by seniority, after each election the workers changed the name tags on the bunk beds as older politicians left office (or died) and younger ones moved up the ranks. They even turned the pages on the daily calendars scattered throughout the facility so that they would always show the correct date. If at any time in those 30 years the House and Senate had been forced to evacuate to the Greenbrier, it would have seemed as if the bomb shelter had just opened for business that morning.

SHHH!

So how secret was the bomb shelter? It depends on what you mean by secret. As far as anyone can tell, the people who signed secrecy pledges did honor their commitment. Not that they had much choice—they faced stiff fines and prison time if they talked. But you just can't build a facility that big without it attracting *some* attention, if from no one else then at least from the construction workers who watched as 4,000 loads of concrete, more than 50,000 *tons* in all, were hauled up to the site and poured to make five-foot-thick walls and ceilings in a "basement" that was 65 feet underground. How many hotel basements are 65 feet underground?

Jesse James's nickname was "Dingus."

How many have five-foot-thick walls and ceilings? Even if the workers didn't know *what* they were building, they knew it was *something* unusual, and by the time the project was finished the entire valley buzzed with gossip and speculation.

At one point the government became so concerned about how much the locals might have pieced together about the site that they sent two agents who knew nothing about it to the area posing as hunters to see how much information they could pry out of the locals. According to one version of the story, they returned with so much information about the bomb shelter that the government had to give them top-secret security clearances.

One thing that helped to keep the secret from traveling outside of the area was the fact that with more than 1,500 employees, the Greenbrier wasn't just the largest employer in the valley, it was pretty much the only one of any significance in the entire county. Even if you didn't work there you knew someone or were related to someone who did. People gossiped about the facility with each other (and with the occasional nosy hunter), but somehow the story never got much farther than that. The world outside Greenbrier County remained almost completely in the dark.

BLAME IT ON THE MEDIA

Project Greek Island remained a secret (if you can call it that) until May 1992, when the *Washington Post* revealed its existence in an exposé. By then the Cold War had been over for several months—the Soviet Union passed into history on Christmas Day 1991—and the bomb shelter had fulfilled its purpose. Rather than deny the *Post* story, the Pentagon acknowledged the shelter's existence...and then promptly shut it down. Ownership of the facility reverted to the Greenbrier, which converted half of it into a data-storage facility and opened the rest to public tours...for now, anyway: At last report the resort was thinking about turning it into a casino with a James Bond theme.

DOWN UNDER

The United States isn't the only country that sank a lot of time and money into holes in the ground for top government officials: The British government built an entire underground city, complete with two train stations, 60 miles of road, and one pub in a rock quarry 70 miles outside of London. Canada built a network of seven "Diefenbunkers" (nicknamed in honor of Prime Minister John Diefenbaker, who had them built) outside of major cities around Canada.

WHITE ELEPHANT

When the Cold War ended, these countries learned the same lesson that the U.S. did: It's a lot easier to build giant underground facilities with five-foot concrete walls than it is to figure out what to do with them when you're done with them. The British site has been for sale since 2005 (so far, no takers); the Canadians did manage to sell off one Diefenbunker in Alberta, but when rumors spread that the new owner was thinking about reselling it to a biker gang, the government bought it back and demolished it.

And even though the Cold War has long been over, the threat of a nuclear attack on Washington, D.C., remains. Chances are there's another hi-tech, high-luxury bunker located somewhere on the outskirts of the nation's capitol…that hopefully will never have to be put to use.

*   *   *

FAMOUS PEOPLE AND
WHAT THEY COLLECT(ED)

Brad Pitt: chairs

Richard Simmons: dolls

Dustin Hoffman: antique toys

Janet Jackson: porcelain pigs

Winston Churchill: hats

Penelope Cruz: coat hangers

Tom Hanks: antique typewriters

Claudia Schiffer: dried insects

Quentin Tarantino: board games based on TV shows

Marilyn Manson: Kiss dolls and prosthetic limbs

Kim Basinger: inflatable ducks

The cost of a cellular phone in 1984: $4,195.

CELEBRITY RESTAURANTS

For decades, celebrities have invested their millions in opening restaurant chains, hoping their names will pull in business. With the occasional exception (Roy Rogers, Kenny Rogers Roasters), they usually flop.

MICKEY ROONEY'S WEENIE WHIRL. In 1980 the former child actor started a hot dog-centered fast-food chain. Its signature dish: O-shaped hot dogs served on hamburger buns. A few opened on the East Coast but closed by the end of the year. Undeterred, Rooney tried—and failed—with several other fast-food concepts in the 1980s, including Rooney's Star-B-Que, Rooney Shortribs, and Mickey Rooney Macaroni.

MINNIE PEARL'S FRIED CHICKEN. Cashing in on the popularity of Kentucky Fried Chicken in the 1960s, Nashville businessman John Jay Hooker convinced Pearl (the *Grand Ole Opry* and *Hee Haw* comedienne who wore a hat with the price tag on it) and gospel singer Mahalia Jackson to lend their names to fast-food chains. Until an accounting scandal put them out of business, Tennessee was plastered with Minnie Pearl Fried Chicken (slogan: "Howww-deeee-licious!") and Mahalia Jackson's Glori-Fried Chicken.

PAT BOONE'S DINE-O-MATS. Boone, best known for his sanitized remakes of raunchy 1950s R&B songs, started a chain of 96 self-service cafeterias in 1961. Customers got food out of vending machines and heated it themselves in microwave ovens. Boone wanted to revive the automats popular in New York City during the Great Depression. The chain flopped, largely because microwaves were a new—and still feared—technology.

JACK KLUGMAN'S CORN CRIBS. In the early 1980s, there was a brief "flavored-popcorn" fad. Klugman (*The Odd Couple*; *Quincy, M.E.*) had lost a lot of weight on a popcorn diet and thought he could make money off popcorn. In 1983 he opened a chain of 100 popcorn parlors. The fad was pretty much over by the end of 1983; Jack's Corn Cribs were defunct by 1985.

SMUGGLERS' BLUES

Lots of people try to bring home contraband. Some get away with it (probably more than we'd like to think) and others get caught. And sometimes the stories can be pretty entertaining.

The Contraband: Chameleons

The Story: Dragos Radovic, 25, was arrested in April 2007 after flying from Bangkok, Thailand, to Zagreb, Croatia, when customs guards noticed his carry-on bag was "moving." A search turned up 175 chameleons stuffed into the parcel. Radovic told officials that the man who sold him the lizards told him they would change color and camouflage themselves...and would be invisible to border guards.

The Contraband: $1 billion bills

The Story: Customs agents in Los Angeles got a tip in early 2006 that Tekle Zigetta, a 45-year-old naturalized American citizen, was involved in some kind of currency smuggling. They got a warrant to search his West Hollywood apartment, where they were surprised to find $250,000,037,000 in cash. The $37,000 was real; the $250 billion was in the form of 250 billion-dollar notes. The bills were dated 1934, bore the likeness of President Grover Cleveland, and were stained yellowish to make them appear old. Zigetta said he found them in a cave in the Philippines. (There is, of course, no such thing as a billion-dollar bill.)

The Contraband: Human bones

The Story: In June 2007, Indian police announced that the discovery of a "bone warehouse" near the Bhutanese border had led to the uncovering of an extensive international bone-smuggling operation. The smugglers claimed that the bones had come from bodies meant for cremation in the Indian city of Varanasi. "During questioning they confessed that there is great demand for femurs that are hollow, to be used as musical instruments," officer Ravinder Nalwa told Reuters, "and skulls as bowls for drinking during religious ceremonies." He said the bones were headed to Buddhist monasteries in Bhutan and Japan.

Lost generation: 33% of American 4th-graders can't find their own state on an unmarked map.

The Contraband: Critters

The Story: The smuggling of wildlife isn't uncommon, but in March 2007, a woman attempting to travel from Egypt to Gaza was caught taking it to bizarre heights. "The woman looked strangely fat," border spokeswoman Maria Telleria said, prompting guards to call for a strip search. According to Telleria, the female guard who performed the search "screamed and ran out of the room." The woman had three 20-inch-long crocodiles taped to her torso. She said she planned to sell the crocs to a zoo.

The Contraband: Cows

The Story: In India the majority Hindu population considers the cow a sacred animal. In bordering Bangladesh, the majority Muslim population considers the cow a food source. That may explain the huge cow-smuggling trade between the two nations: In 2006 more than 400,000 cows made their way from Indian villages to Bangladeshi dinner tables. In 2007 the Indian government came up with a plan to stop the trade: All cows living in villages near the border are now required to get photo IDs. "A bit strange it may sound," said Somesh Goyal, a top Indian Border Security Force officer, "but the photo identity cards of cows and their owners is helping."

The Contraband: Tobacco

The Story: In 2001 Indiana State Police arrested John Hester, 51, for smuggling tobacco into Pendleton Correctional Facility. The operation was troubling for two reasons: 1) Hester worked at the prison slaughterhouse, where he was in charge of acquiring cattle to be consumed by inmates; 2) he smuggled the tobacco into the facility in plastic bags…in the cows' rectums. "It was stuffed into the cow," said Indiana State Police Detective Gregory Belt, "and then the cow was brought onto the floor and it was removed."

*   *   *

LOUIS LOUIS

World's most counterfeited items: Louis Vitton purses. The company estimates that only 1% of "Louis Vitton" purses are authentic.

LIFE IMITATES BART

The Simpsons is loaded with references to cultural moments, historical people, and current events. But occasionally things happen on The Simpsons *first...and then they happen in real life.*

ON THE SIMPSONS: In the 2001 episode "Hungry Hungry Homer," the local minor-league baseball team—the Springfield Isotopes—want to move to New Mexico and become the Albuquerque Isotopes.

IN REAL LIFE: When the Calgary Cannons announced a move to Albuquerque in 2003, they held a contest for Albuquerque citizens to name the new team. The winning entry: the Isotopes. "Isotope" is a term used in nuclear energy, something the fictional Springfield (with its nuclear power plant) has in common with New Mexico, which is home to many of the nation's nuclear research facilities, including the Los Alamos National Laboratory.

ON THE SIMPSONS: In a 1992 episode, Homer's brother Herb—with the help of baby Maggie—invents, markets, and gets rich off of a device that understands an infant's gurgles, whines, and shrieks, and translates them into plain English.

IN REAL LIFE: In 2004 the Japanese company Takara announced that it had developed a successful prototype for a baby translator. In addition to analyzing a baby's coos and cries, it also examines facial expressions and body temperature to tell parents what their baby wants or needs. (No word on whether the product was successfully marketed...or turned to poo-poo.)

ON THE SIMPSONS: School superintendent Chalmers remarks to school principal Skinner in a 1993 episode: "We're dropping the geography requirement. The children weren't testing well. It's proving to be an embarrassment."

IN REAL LIFE: In 2007 Washington-state lawmakers dropped the math and science sections of the state's 10th-grade assessment test. Reason: Too few students passed those sections, severely driving down statewide scores.

Bestselling Christmas album of all time: *Elvis' Christmas Album* (1957).

ON *THE SIMPSONS*: Marge leads a group that wants to censor cartoons. She abandons the group and the cause when the other members go too far, trying to cover up the private parts of Michelangelo's statue of David when it is put on display at the Springfield Museum.

IN REAL LIFE: In 2001 a store in Lake Alfred, Florida, put a replica of Michelangelo's David on the grounds outside its front door. A handful of citizens fiercely protested the "indecent" statue and successfully led a drive to cover up David's private parts with a white cloth. (The store's manager later replaced the cloth with a leopard-print bandanna.)

ON *THE SIMPSONS*: While juggling groceries, a dog, and baby Maggie, Homer sees a newspaper inside a paper vending box with the headline "Senator Helms Proposes Donut Tax." Frantically wanting to read the article, he shuffles his bag of groceries, the dog, the baby, and his coins from arm to arm until he gets the paper while, he thinks, keeping all his stuff safely in his arms. He's wrong: Somehow, his juggling results in Maggie getting stuck inside the newspaper box.

IN REAL LIFE: In 2006 three-year-old Robert Moore of Antigo, Wisconsin, spotted a SpongeBob SquarePants doll in a grocery store's "claw"-style toy vending machine. While his grandmother went to get a dollar to feed the machine, impatient Robert crawled through the dispenser at the bottom of the machine and got stuck inside. (The store didn't have a key to the machine, so they had to call firefighters, who safely rescued the toddler.)

ON *THE SIMPSONS*: In the 1996 episode "Hurricane Neddy," a hurricane hits Springfield. Most of the town is spared. In fact, only Ned Flanders's house is destroyed. Rebuilding his house and his life is an expensive test of faith for the extremely religious Ned, who doesn't have homeowners' insurance because, as his wife says, he believes "insurance is a form of gambling."

IN REAL LIFE: In 2007 Darul Uloom Seminary of Deoband, a politically influential Islamic school for Sunni Muslims in India, issued an edict, or *fatwa*, declaring life insurance illegal under Muslim law. Reason: "Insurance is nothing less than gambling."

ODD ANIMAL NEWS

Step right up, folks, and read about vigilante sheep, gay penguins, spiders that cuddle, and other strange animal tales.

WARNING: GUARD SHEEP ON PREMISES

A group of sheep is usually referred to as a "flock" or a "mob." This group is a mob. Shattering the "gentle as a lamb" myth, there's a group of sheep in the village of Leighterton, England, that's always on the ready to attack invaders. Retired farmer named Keith Clifford says that his 24 sheep have been "highly trained" since birth to do whatever it takes to protect the town. "Normally sheep run away if they are frightened, but these don't. They are quite capable of handling themselves." So far, though, no attackers or burglars have tried to mess with the mob. According to Lester Haines, who reported the story for England's *The Register*, it wouldn't be a pretty sight: "The thought of a couple of behoodied ne'er-do-wells being torn limb from limb in a lanolin-lubricated killing frenzy is too horrible to contemplate."

TURTLE-ECTOMY

When Dabao was acting lethargic (even for a turtle), her keepers at the Chengdu City Zoo in China took her to a human hospital for an X-ray. "We were amazed to see that there were 14 eggs inside her," said a zoo spokesman. They determined that the larger-than-usual concentration was preventing Dabao from laying them —and also causing her great pain. Because none of the area veterinarians had ever treated turtles, the human doctors at the hospital decided to perform a cesarean section. Their first task: waiting for Dabao to emerge from her shell so they could administer the anesthesia. Once she did, the tortoise was fully sedated. "We decided to open the shell covering on her stomach with a skull opener since the shell is about as hard as a human skull," said Dr. Liu Wei. After two hours, the eggs were removed and the shell was resealed with epoxy resin. The eggs were buried in an undisclosed location where they will (hopefully) hatch, and Dabao has returned to her former chipper self.

Average number of lights on an American Christmas tree: 200.

GAYNGUINS

Zookeepers at the Bremerhaven Zoo in Germany have been attempting to pair up adult penguins so they can produce babies. But as the birds paired up, the keepers became concerned when some of the couples turned out to be all-male. They tried to introduce a few females from another zoo in hopes of wooing some of the "wayward" males. The plan, however, was scrapped when gay-rights advocates protested the intervention, calling it "organized and forced harassment through female seductresses." Heike Kueck, the zoo's director, bowed to the advocates' wishes and let the penguins choose their own partners. "Everyone can live here as they please," she said.

THREE'S A CROWD

Mitch Walter was just doing his job when he was driving a golf cart through Cape Rock Water Treatment plant in Cape Girardeau, Missouri, inspecting the grounds. That's when a rabbit jumped up into the seat next to him. Before Walter could react, a 25-pound bobcat leaped into the golf cart, too. The rabbit then escaped, and the bobcat freaked out. "That cat went from a sleek predator after fast food to a ball of fur trying to jump through the windshield of the golf cart," Walter told reporters, showing off the scratches he received on his neck while trying to push the bobcat out of the cart. But it turned out that the worst part of Walter's ordeal wasn't the brush with bobcat—it was the series of rabies shots he had to endure afterwards.

SUCK IT UP

A hamster named Henry escaped from his cage in his Staffordshire, England, home and ended up getting stuck in the pipe of a kitchen sink. A rescue operation ensued. First came the RSPCA (Royal Society for the Prevention of Cruelty to Animals)—they tried to coax Henry out by lowering kitchen utensils into the pipe for the hamster to climb onto, but he couldn't. Then came the council wardens from the local Borough Council. They attached several little hamster ladders together with twist ties and lowered them down for Henry. The little guy clawed and clawed, but there wasn't enough space in the tiny pipe for both Henry and the ladders. That's when they brought in the vacuum cleaner. After a narrow attachment was lowered into the pipe, the vacuum was switched on, and FWOOP!—Henry emerged from the pipe firmly attached to the end of the hose...unharmed.

WEB OF LOVE

Biologists recently discovered two species of arachnids that have maternal attributes more commonly seen in humans. They found the odd behavior in whip spiders, about the size of a dime and native to Florida, as well as a much larger species from Africa. Instead of laying their eggs and then never seeing them again (the method used by most female spiders), these furry spiders stick together. Mama spiders were observed "snuggling" with their young and stroking them gently with their legs. According to Linda Rayor, the lead researcher from Cornell University, "This was the best example I had ever seen of friendly behavior in an arachnid. They are in constant tactile contact with one another."

BAD LUCK DUCK

A man and a woman (unnamed in press reports) drove up to a strip mall in Lynwood, Washington, in 2007 and parked in a parking space. The woman got out of the car, carrying a duck, and walked into a pet supply store. The man then exited the car and went into a nearby electronics store. A moment later, he ran out of the store carrying a stolen iPod accessory. Security guards ran out after the shoplifter and chased him to his car, just as the woman with the duck was exiting the pet supply store. The man reached the car first and started to drive away. The woman yelled at the man to stop and ran up to the moving car. He didn't stop. She attempted to open the passenger door but was knocked to the ground, dropping the duck. Just then, another woman (she worked at the pet supply store) ran out to try to save the duck but instead got hit by the shoplifter's car, which he then crashed into a parked car, which put an end to the incident. A few minutes later, the police arrived to sort things out. The man was arrested. The first woman was treated at the scene and released. The second woman was taken to the hospital with a sprained ankle. (The duck waddled away, injury free.)

REDUCE, REUSE, RESIDE

Have you ever wondered what happens to your old tires when you buy new ones for your car? Say hello to the "Earthship."

OFF TO SEE THE WIZARD

Mike Reynolds was an environmentalist and architect living in Taos, New Mexico, in 1970. One evening he saw a couple of news items on television. One was about the growing garbage crisis in the United States: As Americans generated more and more trash, landfills were straining to cope with it. The other was a story about a shortage of lumber available for new housing.

The two stories stuck in his mind. One day while meditating in the pyramid he'd built in his backyard (Reynolds was a bit of a hippie), he had a vision in which some wizards came to him and told him that the solution to both problems was to tackle them at the same time—if he could find a way to build housing out of items that people threw away, he'd save trees and keep trash out of landfills while creating places for people to live.

Reynolds set out to invent a new method of homebuilding so simple and affordable that anyone could use it to build their own home. He also wanted the house to be self-sufficient—to heat itself, cool itself, generate its own electricity, provide its own water on site, and even dispose of its own sewage and wastewater without being hooked up to normal utilities. After experimenting with tin cans and "rammed earth," a building process similar to adobe, he hit on the idea of pounding dirt into old tires using a sledgehammer, then stacking them to build the walls of a home. He completed his first "Earthship," as he called it, in the early 1970s and he's been building them ever since. Today there are more than 1,000 Earthships all over the world.

FREEWHEELING

The first thing to know about an Earthship is that the tires are well concealed beneath plaster, stucco, or other surfacing materials. If you visited an Earthship without knowing how it was built, you'd probably never suspect it was made out of tires. Other materials like cinderblocks work just as well, but the tires are popular

---

Don't say it! The term "superhero" was jointly trademarked by DC Comics and Marvel Comics.

because they're easy to come by, and cheap or even free. The United States generates an estimated 253 million scrap tires every year, and they're such a burden to dispose of that some Earthshippers even get *paid* to haul them away. Dirt's free, too, and a sledgehammer to pound the dirt into the tires will run you about $17.

HOW AN EARTHSHIP WORKS

The dirt-filled tires are arranged in a giant U shape to create the north-, west- and east-facing walls, and a bank of windows serves as the south wall that faces the sun. The roofline is angled to let in the low winter sun, filling the house with light and warmth during cold months, but block out the high summer sun, which keeps the house cool and shady in the summer. The high thermal mass of the tire walls absorbs heat all day, then radiates it back out at night, keeping the house at a comfortable temperature 24 hours a day, year-round. Interior walls are made with aluminum cans held together with cement and covered with thick layers of plaster to create an adobe effect. Glass bottles, with the round bottoms left exposed, are used where a more artistic look is desired.

Solar panels and windmills on the roof generate enough electricity to meet all of the Earthship's electrical needs; the excess is stored in batteries for use when the sun isn't shining. Rainwater collected on the roof is filtered and channeled into a cistern, where it is stored until it is used not once, but twice: the first time for cooking and bathing, and then (after it's refiltered) it's cycled through again to flush the toilets in the house. Afterward, the water is piped outside to a septic system.

READY TO COME ABOARD

Earthships aren't for everyone—even the name itself turns off a lot of homebuyers. But they're affordable: Construction costs range from $50,000 to $150,000 if you hire someone to build it, and as little as $10,000 if you pound all that dirt into all those tires yourself. With no utility costs, they're also cheap to operate. Some Earthship owners who do hook up to utilities report electric bills as low as $61 per year. Interested? Reynolds is developing an entire subdivision of Earthships outside Taos, New Mexico, and at last report, many building lots are still available. Give it some thought—it might be great place for an old hippie to re-tire.

THE HARVEY HOUSE

The story of America's first restaurant chain.

GO WEST, YOUNG CHEF

In 1850 a 15-year-old boy named Frederick Henry Harvey emigrated from London to New York City, where he found a job washing dishes in a restaurant for $2 a day. From there he moved to New Orleans and worked his way up in the restaurant industry until 1860, when he and a partner opened their own restaurant in St. Louis. But when the Civil War broke out, the partner went to fight (for the Confederacy). Harvey soon ran out of money and went through a succession of jobs—one of them for the Chicago, Burlington & Quincy Railroad in Kansas. That would prove to be a fortuitous move.

In the early 1870s, Harvey saw what people had to put up with when they traveled by train: dingy, dirty restaurants with lousy food. He knew he could do better. He pitched the idea to open restaurants in train stations to his bosses at the CB&Q...and they told him to take a hike. So he approached the Atchison, Topeka & Santa Fe Railway. Fortunately for Harvey the company superintendent, Charles Morse, was a bit of a food snob—and in 1876 he hired Harvey to manage the Topeka depot lunchroom.

WESTWARD, HO-NGRY!

Harvey's standards were cleanliness, friendly service, quality food, and reasonable prices. Not surprisingly, the Harvey House, as it was called, was a hit, and the Sante Fe Railway entered into a partnership with "The Harvey Company." Harvey Houses started popping up every hundred miles on the Santa Fe line as it went farther and farther into the New Mexico and Arizona Territories. And they even had what would later be called fast food.

As the system developed, passengers filled out menus on the trains as they approached a station, and the orders were sent by telegraph to the restaurant. That way a Harvey House could feed large numbers of people in the short amount of time allotted for a train stop. It was a dynamic change in the travel experience, but Harvey didn't know he was about to change the Western landscape, too.

HARVEY GIRLS

In 1883 Harvey had another idea for getting people to come to his restaurants: He started recruiting young women to work as waitresses. He advertised, "Wanted: Young Women between 18 and 30 with high moral standards. Salary $17.50 plus room and board and very generous tips." The advertisement attracted thousands of applicants...and a storm of protest. "A woman's place is in the home!" preachers shouted. Harvey responded by requiring the women to take a pledge, promising not to marry for at least the first six months after being hired. Then he set up a training program to teach his female employees strict rules of behavior. Anyone violating the rules was dismissed. It worked. Protest died down (probably because people liked the restaurants so much), and over the next decade "Harvey Girls" would change the Western landscape.

The Harvey Company became a regular feature for the growing number of travelers to the Southwest. And Harvey expanded the operation into hotels, barbershops, department stores, cocktail lounges, and gift shops, where he sold "Harvey" postcards, mugs, hats, playing cards, and even a Harvey's Special Scotch whiskey. The press dubbed Fred Harvey "Civilizer of the West," saying that "he made the desert blossom with beefsteak and pretty girls."

END OF THE LINE

By the time of Harvey's death in 1901, the company owned 47 restaurants, 30 dining cars, and 15 luxury hotels. Fred's two sons grew it to 84 restaurants by 1917, stretching the empire from Cleveland to Los Angeles. America's first restaurant chain lasted until 1968, when it was sold to a large hotel conglomerate. But the legacy of the Harvey Houses lives on. At least two Harvey hotels are still in operation: La Fonda, in Santa Fe, New Mexico, and El Tovar, near the Grand Canyon in Arizona.

Will Rogers wrote of Harvey: "In the early days, the traveler fed on the buffalo. For doing so, the buffalo got his picture on the nickel. Well, Fred Harvey's picture should be on one side of the dime and one of his waitresses with her arms full of delicious ham and eggs on the other side, 'cause they have kept the West supplied with food and wives."

Q: Who holds the record for most career Super Bowl fumbles? A: Roger Staubach, with 5.

HOME MOVIES

Today it's common to watch a movie in the comfort of your own home. But only a few years ago, it was revolutionary.

REEL-Y UNUSUAL

Until the late 1970s, if you wanted to see a movie, you had to catch it in a movie theater right when it came out. Unless it proved so popular that it had a long run or was re-released a couple of years later, you were out of luck. A few years later, you might catch it on TV. Otherwise, once a movie was gone, it was gone forever. Until the VCR.

Videocassette recorders hit the market in the late 1970s, but home video machines had actually been around since the early 1960s. The electronics company Ampex offered a reel-to-reel video recording machine in 1963. The cost: $30,000 (the equivalent today: about $200,000). Not surprisingly, few of the Ampex units sold, and neither did similar models from Sony in 1969 and 1972.

AVCO's Cartrivision—a combination TV/video player—was released in June 1972 at a price of $1,350. That marked the first time prerecorded movies were available for home viewing. Cartrivisions were sold only at Sears, Macy's, and Montgomery Ward, which is also where a Cartrivision owner rented the movies. Customers could pick from a catalog of 200 movies (mostly from the 1940s and 1950s, including *The Bridge on the River Kwai, High Noon,* and *Casablanca*). The tape was shipped to the customer's home; the customer returned it to the store when they were done. Despite the allure of being able to watch films at home, it was considered an expensive novelty. Cartrivision bombed and was discontinued in 1973.

THIS MEANS WAR

But electronics companies in Japan and Europe kept trying to create *the* machine that would make home video accessible and affordable. Two contenders emerged in the mid-1970s almost simultaneously—Sony's *Betamax* in 1975 and JVC's *VHS* ("video home system") in 1976. Both used plastic cassettes that housed miniature reel-to-reel systems (although VHS tapes were slightly larger than Betamax). But JVC licensed other companies, such as Zenith, RCA, and Matsushita, to make VHS players; Sony didn't allow anybody else to use the Betamax format. Result: Stores carried more VHS players than Betamax. And because customers were buying more VHS players, that's what the movie studios favored. VHS won the format war and became the video standard.

Among the earliest groups to adopt VHS were the studios that made X-rated films. Before the 1970s, adult films could be seen only in seedy theaters. Videos made it possible to view such films in private, fueling the purchase of VCRs. Even when more mainstream films became available in the late 1970s, adult films still made up a whopping 50% of all video sales.

WHAT DO YOU WANT TO WATCH?

By the end of 1977, more than 200,000 Americans had plunked down $1,000 to $2,000 for a VCR. One problem: There wasn't much to watch on it. TV shows and home movies could be taped, but few Hollywood movies were available. Paramount Pictures had licensed about 20 of its movies for Betamax, but that was it.

Andre Blay, who ran a Detroit video production company called Magnetic Video, recognized the demand, and in November 1977, started a mail-order service called Video Club of America. He paid 20th Century Fox $300,000 for the right to put 50 of its movies on tape, and then ran a two-page ad in *TV Guide* promising popular movies on both Betamax and VHS formats, including *Butch Cassidy and the Sundance Kid, M*A*S*H, and The Sound of Music.* Video Club membership was $10; the videos were $50 each. The response was so huge that within just two months, Blay had recouped his entire investment. His business grew even more in December 1978, when a Christmas-season price war between RCA (the biggest VHS manufacturer) and Sony drove VCR prices below $1,000. By the end of 1978, Blay had sold a quarter of a million videos and sold his company to 20th Century Fox, which made Blay president of their new home-video division. A new industry was born.

In the early days of home video, film buffs were the ones buying VCRs. Only 200,000 people had bought the machines—but there are hundreds of millions of people in the United States.

Snails kiss before mating (by rubbing their antennae together).

Why wasn't *everyone* buying a VCR? Because it was still too expensive. The cost had fallen to below $1,000, but movies that you could watch on your VCR cost $50, and most consumers didn't want to shell out that kind of cash for an old movie they'd probably already seen.

The average customer was much more likely to pay a few bucks to watch a new movie…just once. So while Blay made a fortune *selling* videos, George Atkinson of Los Angeles got rich *renting* them out. In late 1977, Atkinson opened Video Station, the country's first video rental store. He bought two copies of all 50 Video Club movies—one each on Betamax and VHS—and then rented them to customers. Cost of a rental: $10 per day. Two years later, Atkinson owned 42 Video Stations. By that time, Paramount, Columbia, Fox, and Warner Bros. had released hundreds of movies on video.

JUST AROUND THE CORNER

As the selection of available movies exploded between 1977 and 1980, so did the number of places to rent them. Seemingly every street corner, strip mall, and small town had a video store at the time. In 1979 there were 700 in the United States; by the end of 1981, there were 5,500. (And that's not counting convenience stores, supermarkets, and photo labs that added videos to their inventory.) During the economic recession of the early 1980s, video stores were one of the few growth industries in America.

Most stores were small mom-and-pop operations with a selection of around 2,000 videos. A rental cost about $7 in 1979, but went down to $3 by 1982 (plus fees for returning a tape late or for not rewinding it). Some of the small stores of the time developed into regional chains, including Erols Video in the Virginia-Maryland area, Family Video in the Midwest, Universal Video in the Northwest, and Movie Gallery in the Southeast.

The novelty of home video was gone by 1985—over 30% of all American homes had a VCR by then. And that year over a *billion* movies were rented.

BUSTING BLOCKS

In October 1985, David Cook opened a neighborhood video store in Dallas, Texas, called Blockbuster Video. Unlike other inde-

---

The doors that cover U.S. nuclear silos weigh 748 tons and open in 19 seconds.

pendently owned video outlets, Blockbuster was a "superstore." Cook offered twice as many movies as most mom-and-pops (more than 6,500, but no pornos—Blockbuster was and remains "family friendly") and he used bar codes and scanners to check movies in and out in order to speed up transactions. It was immediately—and wildly—successful. Just four years after opening, Blockbuster had grown to an international chain of 1,500 stores. On the way up, it bought out numerous independent and chain video stores and drove many others out of business. And it kept growing. By 1993, Blockbuster had 3,600 locations in the United States alone. Communications giant Viacom bought Blockbuster for $8.4 billion in 1994.

THE DIGITAL AGE

By 1997 VCRs—and tapes—were over 20 years old. While music had gone digital in the 1980s with the compact disc, it took a while for video to catch up. That year the DVD (digital video disc) was introduced. The difference between DVD and VHS was vast: A CD-size disc could hold about six hours of material; film studios could pack DVDs with "bonus features" such as behind-the-scenes footage, documentaries, previews, games, deleted scenes, and the option to watch the movie in foreign languages; and all of it was presented with a crystal-clear image and stereo sound. In contrast to the slow victory of VHS over Betamax in the original format war, DVD blew VHS out of the market. Americans bought DVD players at a faster rate than any electronic device in history—more than 85% of all American homes now have a DVD player.

CASTING A NET

Reed Hastings, the owner of a San Francisco computer company, went to rent a movie one night in 1998 at a large video superstore (he won't name the company). He was told that he owed $40 in late fees for returning *Apollo 13* a few days late. Hastings was livid. Even though he was a multimillionaire, he still hated late fees (and he knew he wasn't the only one). So in 1998, Hastings opened up his own video rental business. He called it Netflix.

Hasting's Netflix model: Customers went to the company's Web site to select a movie, Netflix sent them the DVD in the

---

Food for thought: Pill bugs are more closely related to crabs and shrimp than to insects.

mail, and the customer kept it for as long as they wanted. When the customer sent one back, Netflix sent another movie. Rather than charge rental and late fees, Netflix users paid a single monthly fee of $20, which covered as many movies as they cared to watch and return in 30 days.

Netflix quickly became Blockbuster's top competitor. But in 2000, it almost went bankrupt. Hastings had spent millions of dollars opening up DVD mailing centers around the country to speed up the movie turnaround time, but unfortunately, Netflix wasn't generating revenue quickly enough to keep up with expansion plans. So Hastings sought a buyout...from Blockbuster. But the video chain wasn't interested in Netflix's low-tech movies-by-mail concept. It had recently invested $600 million in a movie-downloading service. Unfortunately, Blockbuster picked the wrong partner to back the project: Enron. And when Enron spectacularly went out of business in 2001, Blockbuster lost every penny. Since then, Blockbuster has lost around $1 billion per year and has closed over 600 stores. Netflix, meanwhile, has grown to more than six million customers (and long since became profitable).

ROLL CREDITS

What's next? It might be high-definition DVD, which has even better picture and sound quality than regular DVD. Or it might be movie downloads: Netflix has a service where customers can watch movies on their computers and Amazon.com can beam movies to cable boxes—meaning that you can now "rent" a movie without having to go out and actually "rent" a movie.

But there are still *lots* of video stores in the United States—more than 27,000. And the switch from VHS to DVDs (which are cheaper and take up less room) has actually brought the industry full circle. Despite the proliferation of big chains, 50% of all video stores today are locally owned mom-and-pop businesses.

*   *   *

"Video won't be able to hold on to any market it captures after the first six months. People will soon get tired of staring at a plywood box every night."
—**Daryl F. Zanuck, 1946**

SOUND SMARTER

Experts say the path to success is built on a good vocabulary. Here are a few words, with examples of their use, that might make you sound smart enough to be president. (Hmm...maybe that was a bad example.)

NEW WORD: Endemic (en-DEM-ik)
MEANING: Belonging to a particular region or people
INSTEAD OF... "Them Tasmanian Devils are only found in Tazakistan, I'm pretty sure. And zoos."
SOUND SMARTER: "The Tasmanian Devil is *endemic* only to the Australian island of Tasmania."

NEW WORD: Cavil (KAV-uhl)
MEANING: To quibble or nitpick
INSTEAD OF... "Well, I guess that's for the jury to decide."
SOUND SMARTER: "I hate to *cavil*, darling, but I'm fairly sure that man you just hit was riding a Segway, not a scooter."

NEW WORD: Parlous (PAHR-lous)
MEANING: Dangerous
INSTEAD OF... "This won't hurt a bit!"
SOUND SMARTER: "I assure you there is nothing *parlous* about the intracranial demulsification procedure."

NEW WORD: Imbibe (im-BAHYB)
MEANING: Drink; absorb
INSTEAD OF... "Let's go sit on the porch, down a few cold ones and take in the scenery."
SOUND SMARTER: "Please join me on the veranda to *imbibe* some refreshing beverages and enjoy the spectacular ocean view."

NEW WORD: Soporific (soh-puh-RIF-ik)
MEANING: Sleep-inducing
INSTEAD OF... "I could eat a whole 'nuther helping of pie— but I'm just too pooped."
SOUND SMARTER: "Unfortunately, the *soporific* effects of the

---

Ancient Roman wrestling matches had only one rule: No eye gouging.

turkey, not to mention all the wine I've imbibed, prevent me from staying awake long enough to partake of dessert."

NEW WORD: Alacrity (uh-LAK-ri-tee)
MEANING: Quick, cheerful enthusiasm
INSTEAD OF... "Brian's a go-getter, isn't he? I like him. But he kind of bugs me, too."
SOUND SMARTER: "Brian's tendency to approach every task with *alacrity* made him not only one of the office's favorite employees, but also one of the most annoying."

NEW WORD: Circumspect (SUR-kuhm-spekt)
MEANING: Cautious
INSTEAD OF... "Uh, Fred, you might not want to look down that tube."
SOUND SMARTER: "Frederick, a more *circumspect* approach to that fireworks cannon you just lit might be advisable."

NEW WORD: Phlegmatic (fleg-MAT-ik)
MEANING: Apathetic; sluggish
INSTEAD OF... "Get your lazy butt up off the sofa and answer the phone yourself."
SOUND SMARTER: "*Guinness World Records* just called to let you know you've been named Most *Phlegmatic* Couch Potato."

NEW WORD: Enmity (EN-mi-tee)
MEANING: Ill will, hostility, or outright hatred
INSTEAD OF... "I hate you! I hate, hate, hate you!"
SOUND SMARTER: "Be assured, my charming friend, that my *enmity* for you is outmatched only by my resistance to having my tonsils extracted through my nasal passages."

NEW WORD: Temerity (teh-MEHR-eh-tee)
MEANING: Foolhardiness; reckless courage
INSTEAD OF... "I don't know if that was brave or just stupid, what you just did. Did it really eat your cell phone?"
SOUND SMARTER: "It takes extreme *temerity* to jump into the grizzly bear enclosure, Jethro. Shall I call an ambulance?"

During the Arctic's winter solstice, the Sun is below the horizon for at least 24 hours straight.

THE HISTORY OF BREAD, PART II

Since its prehistoric origins, bread has been closely linked to civilization's rise. But the mass-produced bread we know today didn't appear until the 1900s. Here's another slice of bread history. (Part I is on page 251.)

BREAD LINES
In turn-of-the-20th-century America, bread was an assembly-line business, with conveyor belts moving loaves through the ovens and into the hands of workers who wrapped them in waxed paper. In 1928 American Otto Frederick Rohwedder perfected a machine that both sliced *and* wrapped loaves of bread. Streamlined machinery, consistent products, and constant availability were the pluses—but there were minuses to the new technology, too. The most significant one was that the grain's nutrients got stripped away during the exhaustive process of milling the flour.

• Even in the late 19th century, it was clear that for people who depended on bread for good nutrition, bread made with nutrient-poor flour wouldn't give them what they needed, so European governments began to require manufacturers to enrich the flour. (America followed suit...eventually. In 1941 Congress passed a law requiring the addition of niacin, thiamine, riboflavin, and iron to white flour and bread.) Ironically, at the same time that bread manufacturers were investing in the technology that made white bread affordable, other technological advances made it possible for farmers and distributors to supply other important foods—meat, dairy products, and potatoes—that threatened bread's status as the number-one staple food.

WHERE HAVE ALL THE FLOURS GONE?
• The middle of the 20th century saw the flourishing of corporate bakeries—Continental Baking (Wonder Bread), Pepperidge Farm, and Oroweat, for example. As the century progressed and people became intrigued with "health" foods, corporate bakeries respond-

---

Shoplifters? Florida's beaches lose 20 million cubic yards of sand annually.

ed with whole-wheat and other breads containing "healthful" ingredients like honey and molasses. Homemade bread made a comeback, too, as consumers wanted to make "somethin' lovin' from the oven" at home. So the corporations came up with packaged mixes, frozen breads, and "heat-and-serve" products that simulated home baking without too much fuss and bother.

• Americans now eat 51 one-pound loaves of bread per person annually—about one per week. There's no question that we still consider it to be a vital part of our diets. Packaged bread from a supermarket may supply some of your dietary needs because it *is* enriched, but commercial breads are routinely treated with preservatives, emulsifiers, stabilizers, and dozens more chemicals in order to provide loaves that are cheap, shippable, and have a long shelf life. Small wonder that contemporary bread-lovers seek out neighborhood bakeries that make their own fresh, delicious baguettes, *ciabattas*, and other varieties of old-fashioned "artisan" bread.

BREAD FACTS

• In 1987 the kids at Eisenhower Junior High in Taylorsville, Utah, baked the world's largest loaf of bread, weighing 307 pounds. Where do you bake a 307-pound loaf of bread? In a Hercules oven usually used for hardening missile casings.

• Bread was once so prized that it was used as currency, which is why money is sometimes called "bread."

• A family of four could live for 10 years on the bread produced by one acre of wheat in one growing season.

• Pillsbury Doughboy facts: In 1965 more than 50 actors competed to become the Pillsbury Doughboy voice; the winner was Paul Frees, who also did the voice for Boris Badenov in *The Adventures of Rocky and Bullwinkle*. When Frees died in 1986, Jeff Bergman (Charlie the Tuna) became the new Doughboy voice. The Doughboy still gets about 200 fan letters each week.

• Sales of fresh bread in the United States in 2006: Over $6 billion.

• Got a few tons of Bisquick in the pantry? In 1981 the world's largest peach shortcake was made at the South Carolina Peach

Festival. The five-layer shortcake was 25 ½ feet in diameter and used nine tons of peaches...and more than four tons of Bisquick.

• The five bestselling brands of bread are Wonder, Pepperidge Farm, Oroweat, Nature's Own, and Sunbeam.

• Grains used for baking bread must be rich in *gluten*—the protein that gives dough its elasticity, which allows it to rise. Grains with the most gluten: wheat, rye, and barley.

• Subway was the first sandwich chain to bake its bread on-site. (In downtown locations they leave the door open so passersby will smell the bread baking and come in for a sandwich. It works.)

• In 1997 Kansas farmers produced more than 490 million bushels of wheat, enough to make about 36 billion loaves of bread—six loaves for every person on Earth.

• An average slice of packaged bread contains one gram of fat and 75 to 80 calories.

• Store-bought bread will stay fresh longer if you don't refrigerate it. Keep it at room temperature in a dark, dry place (bread box, kitchen drawer, cupboard) for up to a week. If you're not going to eat it within a week, freeze the loaf in its original packaging.

• It takes nine seconds for a combine to harvest a bushel of wheat, which is enough to produce about 70 one-pound loaves of bread.

• During the Civil War, one wing of the Senate in Washington was converted into a huge oven that baked 16,000 loaves of bread a day for Union soldiers.

• According to legend, the cross cut into the top of an Irish soda bread is there to ward off the devil.

• In 1937 Margaret Rudkin was determined to nurse her asthmatic son back to health with whole-wheat bread. She put a big oven in an empty stable on the family property in Connecticut—Pepperidge Farm—and began baking, despite never having done it before in her life. Customers paid a 25¢ for a one-pound loaf, 15¢ more than the average loaf. By 1940 she was selling 4,000 loaves per week.

Before you run to the refrigerator for a slice of white bread, check out our Encyclopedia of Bread (page 573).

HOWDY, COUSIN!

A few years ago, Grandma Uncle John decided to take up one of the country's fastest-growing hobbies: genealogy. In drawing up the Uncle John family tree, Grandma discovered dozens of "cousins" she never knew she had (including a few who lived just down the street). That made Uncle John wonder what "cousin" exactly means. Our bathroom genealogist, John Dollison, did the research and came up with these answers.

SAY HELLO TO YOUR COUSIN HARRY

It's an experience that a lot of us have had, especially those of us who come from large families: Distant relatives meet for the first time at a family gathering and try to figure out just exactly how they're related to each other. Your mom says you and her cousin's kids are second cousins to each other, but Uncle Dave thinks you're first cousins once removed—who's right? It's enough to make you envy the orphans. Here's a little refresher course to get you in shape for your next big family reunion.

FIRST COUSINS

The first step in finding out exactly how you're related to your distant relatives is to find the closest blood ancestor that the two of you have in common. To keep things simple, let's start with your "first" cousins—the children of your aunts and uncles.

• If you trace your finger up your family tree, and your first cousin does the same with their family tree, how far do the two of you have to go to find the first ancestors that appear in *both* of your family trees—the first ancestors that you and your first cousins have in common?

Answer: You and your first cousin are both descended from the same grandparents, or one generation beyond your parents and your cousin's parents. You're called "first cousins" because you're as close as cousins can be—only one generation, that of your parents, separates you from your common ancestors.

• What about a more distant cousin? Again, trace your finger up your family tree to find the first ancestor that you share with your distant cousin. If you have the same great-grandparents, you are second cousins. If you have the same great-great grandparents, you are third cousins, and so on.

FIRST COUSINS ONCE REMOVED

• Here's a trickier question: How are you related to the *children* of your first cousin? Your grandparents are their great-grandparents. This is where the expression "once removed" comes in. You're still first cousins, because there's only one generation between the person most closely descended from the common ancestor—you—and that ancestor. (When you're comparing family members of different generations, the cousin who is closest to the common ancestor is the one that counts.)

Then, because there's also one generation separating you from your cousin's children, you are considered first cousins *once removed*. There's one generation separating you from your common ancestor, and one generation separating you from your cousin's children. Likewise, you and your cousin's *grand*children are first cousins *twice* removed.

IS YOUR HEAD SPINNING YET?

Do you think you have the system figured out? Here's a question to test your knowledge. If you have children and your first cousin has children, how are your children related to your cousin's children?

• Again, you start by working up the family tree until you find the first common ancestor. Your children have to go *two* generations beyond their parent—you—to get to the common ancestors that they share with your cousin's children: their great-grandparents. That means your children and your first cousin's children are *second* cousins to each other.

• Here's your final question: When you have grandchildren and your first cousin has grandchildren, how will they be related to each other? Answer: The common ancestor again is your grandparents. Your grandchildren have to count three generations past *their* parents—*your* children—to get to the ancestors that they share with your cousin's grandchildren. That makes them 1) the third cousins of your cousin's grandchildren, 2) the second cousins once removed of your cousin's children, and 3) the first cousins twice removed of your cousins.

"TWENTY YEARS"

As part of our celebration of bringing you Bathroom Readers *for two decades, here are some quotations we recently found that ponder what can (or cannot) happen in a mere 20 years.*

"Live as long as you may—the first 20 years are the longest half of your life."
—**Robert Southey**

"Instead of thinking about where you are, think about where you want to be. It takes 20 years of hard work to become an overnight success."
—**Diana Rankin**

"Youth is something new: 20 years ago no one mentioned it."
—**Coco Chanel**

"I say, play your own way. Don't play what the public wants—you play what you want and let the public pick up on what you're doing— even if it takes them 20 years."
—**Thelonious Monk**

"It only takes 20 years for a liberal to become a conservative without changing a single idea."
—**Robert Anton Wilson**

"We know that the nature of genius is to provide idiots with ideas 20 years later."
—**Louis Aragon**

"I've been on a constant diet for the last two decades. I've lost a total of 789 pounds. By all accounts, I should be hanging from a charm bracelet."
—**Erma Bombeck**

"A mother takes 20 years to make a man of her boy, and another woman makes a fool of him in 20 minutes."
—**Robert Frost**

"It takes 20 years to build a reputation and five minutes to ruin it. If you think about that, you'll do things differently."
—**Warren Buffett**

"My wife and I were happy for 20 years. Then we met."
—**Rodney Dangerfield**

"I prayed for 20 years but received no answer until I prayed with my legs."
—**Frederick Douglass**

"The best time to plant a tree is 20 years ago. The second best time is today."
—**Chinese proverb**

GREEN GRAVEYARDS

When it comes to burying our dead, it may be time to think outside the box.

UN-SANITARY LANDFILL

Here's a typical scenario: Old Uncle Fester has finally kicked the bucket, and it's up to you to plan his funeral. But before you run to call your local undertaker, consider these facts: The average cost of a funeral in the United States ranges between $8,000 and $10,000. The casket alone could set you back $10,000. A typical coffin is made of select hardwood, finished with brass fittings, lined with copper, and set in a concrete vault. Your uncle may have a fine send-off to the next world, but his funeral—and millions like it—carries some nasty baggage. Here's what a typical 10-acre cemetery has buried in it: 562,500 board feet of lumber (enough to build 40 homes), 1,000 tons of steel, 20,000 tons of concrete, and 1,000 gallons of embalming fluid (mostly highly toxic formaldehyde).

Extend that to include all of America's 22,500 cemeteries, and the numbers get really big: 30 million feet of hardwoods, 104,000 tons of steel, and 2,700 tons of copper and bronze (enough metal to build the Golden Gate Bridge), 1,636,000 tons of reinforced concrete (enough to build a six-lane highway from Boston to Philadelphia), and 827,000 gallons of embalming fluid.

BURN, BABY, BURN

Okay, you say—just have the old boy cremated. If that's your decision, you'll have lots of company: Cremations are becoming more and more popular. They accounted for 30% of burials in North America last year, and are expected to rise to 50% by 2025. But you may want to rethink that strategy, too. Crematoria are major polluters, spewing carbon monoxide, sulphur dioxide, and other toxic gases into the atmosphere. The most toxic element released from crematoria: mercury, around 7,800 pounds a year. But only 75% stays airborne; the rest settles back into the soil, where it can contaminate the groundwater. One more thing: It takes a lot of fossil fuel to operate all those crematoria—the annual equivalent of driving a car to the moon and back 84 times.

The average homeowner spends three days per year waiting for repairmen to arrive.

But now there's an alternative: eco-cemeteries. When ministers at eco-funerals say the words, "Ashes to ashes, dust to dust," they mean it literally. Bodies are (reverently) placed in the ground in either biodegradable coffins of pine, wicker, or cardboard...or no casket at all—some people want to be buried in cloth shrouds. No embalming fluid is used; graves are simple mounds of earth covered in wildflowers and shrubs, which act as living memorials to the deceased. Sometimes an indigenous flat stone engraved with the name of the loved one marks the burial place, but the body itself quickly returns to the earth.

ECO-ANSWERS

• According to experts, the law doesn't require that bodies be embalmed, nor that they be buried in coffins.

• Worried about possible water contamination? Eco-cemeteries use no pesticides or irrigation, so there's no toxic run-off. When a person dies, the bacteria in their body eventually dies, too. But to be safe, eco-cemeteries don't bury bodies near springs or creeks, and they recommend that any untreated water within 75 feet of the cemetery be considered non-potable.

• Without headstones or statues, some people worry they won't know where their loved ones are buried. Greensprings Natural Cemetery, located in upstate New York, uses a GPS tracking system and magnetized nails to chart the location of each interment.

HAPPY ENDINGS

The goal of a natural burial preserve is to protect and restore the land, thus allowing it to become a living memorial. "We put death in its rightful place," says Dr. Billy Campbell, owner of the nation's first eco-cemetery, the Ramsey Creek Preserve of South Carolina. "It's part of the cycle of life." If green graveyards get just 10% of the $20 billion mortuary-cemetery business, Campbell says, "we'd have $2 billion a year going toward land conservation on memorial preserves." At Greensprings, a 15' x 15' burial plot goes for only $500, about 6% of the cost of a conventional casket extravaganza. Plus you can rest in peace knowing developers will never build a mall on top of you at some future date. Cemetery legislation protects natural burial preserves in perpetuity.

HARE'S TO YOU

*If we find a news story that's got rabbits
in it, we hop right on it.*

WABBIT SEASON. Thirty-one inmates were working in a garden outside a Ugandan prison in 2002 when a rabbit jumped out of the bushes. All five guards watching the inmates took off after it...and all 31 of the inmates, including one murderer, took the opportunity to escape. None of them were captured. And neither was the rabbit.

A HARE-RAISING TALE. In 2006 *New Scientist* magazine reported that researchers at Wake Forest University had successfully grafted artificial penises onto rabbits with damaged genitals. According to the report, after the operations the rabbits went on to breed (like rabbits).

HARDY HARE HARE. In 2007 two planes were forced to abort landings at a major airport in the United States when coyotes suddenly appeared on the runway, directly in their path. The coyotes, officials said later, were chasing rabbits. The airport: Chicago's O'Hare (get it?) International Airport.

EGGHEAD. In April 2003, Montell Howard, 21, of Wausau, Wisconsin, walked into a local mall and approached a man dressed in a pink bunny costume (it was Easter). As the children looked on in horror, Howard put the Easter Bunny in a headlock and punched him several times in the face. The Easter Bunny (whom Howard didn't know) was treated at a local hospital, and Howard was arrested for assault.

LOOK! A RABBIT! In March 2007, *Metro* newspaper (U.K.) ran a story about an Australian man who had his groin badly injured in an accident at a local sawmill. (Owwwwwww!) Luckily, the man survived. *Metro* paired the story with a picture of a white rabbit, captioned with, "Here is a picture of a nice fluffy rabbit to take your mind off this story."

Hair is 70% easier to cut when soaked in warm water for 2 minutes. (Downside: You drown.)

I'M GONNA WALLACE!

Cockney rhyming slang is a 150-year-old British tradition. It may be old, but it's still going strong. Here are some Cockney terms from the modern age. (For some classic examples, see page 129.)

Al Capone: telephone

Barney: to be in trouble (short for "Barney Rubble")

Bill: curry, meaning any kind of Indian food (short for "Bill Murray")

Brad: physically fit (short for "Brad Pitt")

Bradys: lunch (short for *The Brady Bunch*)

Judi: a horrible stench (short for "Judi Dench")

Davy: a pocket (short for "Davy Crockett")

Fawlty: a shower (short for *Fawlty Towers*, a TV show)

Babe Ruth: the truth

Green eggs: exams (short for "green eggs and ham")

Vincent: ice (short for Vincent Price)

Wallace: to vomit (short for "Wallace and Grommit")

Winnie: a shoe (short for "Winnie the Pooh")

Winona: a pint of hard cider (short for "Winona Ryder")

An Uncle Toby: a cellular phone, which the English call a *moby* (short for "mobile")

Thomas Edison: medicine

Donald: Well, it's short for "Donald Trump" and it rhymes something you "take" in the bathroom

Ace of Spades: AIDS

Gary: an "all-dayer"—a daylong drinking session (short for "Gary Player")

Roller coaster: a toaster

Britneys: a couple of beers (short for "Britney Spears")

Kermit: a bog—English slang for toilet (short for "Kermit the Frog")

Tom Cruise: booze

Arthur: cash (short for "Arthur Ashe")

Jim Rockfords: piles, the English term for hemorrhoids (short for *The Rockford Files*)

Because fruits ferment, virtually all fruit juices contain minute amounts of alcohol.

THE HIT MAN

Even if you've never heard of Otis Blackwell, you've almost certainly heard his music—he was one of the most influential songwriters of the 20th century. Here's the story of the most famous songwriter most people have never heard of.

TIGHT CHRISTMAS

In the mid 1950s, Otis Blackwell was a struggling songwriter who pressed pants in a New York City tailor's shop during the day to make ends meet. He'd been selling songs since he was a teenager and had made a few contacts, but he just wasn't making it in the business. On Christmas Eve 1955, he was so broke that he went and stood on the sidewalk in front of the famous Brill Building (then the unofficial headquarters of the American recording industry), in the hope of spotting someone he knew and cajoling them into buying a song or two so that he'd have some money for Christmas.

"I was standing outside the building with no hat and holes in my shoes. And it was snowing," Blackwell told an interviewer in 1979. When Leroy Kirkland, an arranger for a popular rhythm and blues artist named Screamin' Jay Hawkins, walked up, Blackwell asked if he could sing him a few of the songs he'd written.

COME ON IN

It was Christmas Eve, after all, so Kirkland gave Blackwell a quick listen...and was impressed enough that he invited Blackwell into the building and introduced him to Al Stanton, who worked for a company called Shalimar Music. Stanton not only bought six songs on the spot for $25 apiece (an advance against future royalties), he signed Blackwell to a publishing contract and gave him some space to work in the office. Not a bad day's work, but the really big news came two weeks later when the president of Shalimar, Aaron "Goldie" Goldmark, called Blackwell and told him that RCA was interested in one of the $25 songs, the one titled "Don't Be Cruel." They wanted it for one of their rising young stars—a 20-year-old singer named Elvis Presley.

"I said, 'Who is Elvis Presley?'" Blackwell remembered years later. "But Goldie said not to worry, because the kid was hot."

ELVIS, IMPERSONATOR

It was a common practice in the music industry for writers to create quickie "demo" records of their songs to make it easier for the recording artists to pick the ones they wanted. Unlike many songwriters, Blackwell was also a talented pianist and singer, so he recorded his own demo of "Don't Be Cruel" instead of having studio musicians do it, which was how demos were usually recorded. He played the piano, sang, and beat on a cardboard box to simulate the sound of drumming.

If you were a recording star and didn't know how to read music, how would you learn a new song? Elvis couldn't read music, so he listened to the demo tape of "Don't Be Cruel" over and over again until he'd committed the notes, the lyrics, and all of the subtleties of Blackwell's performance to memory. It took him 28 takes to do it, but when he finished, Elvis had recorded a single that was for all intents and purposes an exact imitation of Blackwell's performance on the demo tape.

But Blackwell didn't just pen a song for the impressionable artist who would soon become the king of rock 'n' roll, he was also instrumental in helping him develop the singing style that would put him on top.

B IS FOR BLOCKBUSTER

"Don't Be Cruel" was released on the B-side of another Elvis song titled "Hound Dog." In those days B-side songs were like B movies: RCA saw "Don't be Cruel" as second-rate compared to "Hound Dog," and unlikely to get a lot of airplay or become a hit. That was why they didn't release it as a single on its own. RCA couldn't have been more wrong—"Don't Be Cruel" not only went to #1 on *Billboard* magazine's pop singles chart just like "Hound Dog" did, it spent nine weeks in the top slot, compared to four for "Hound Dog." "Hound Dog/Don't Be Cruel" went on to become the most successful double-sided single in pop-music history. Blackwell didn't do too badly, either—by the time the next Christmas Eve rolled around, he'd earned more than $80,000 in royalties from his $25 song.

Blackwell must have felt that he was the one who'd gotten a big break that day when Leroy Kirkland brought him in from the snow, but in truth it was Shalimar Music that had really scored, because Blackwell soon revealed himself as one the most talented and prolific songwriters the industry had ever seen. He became known within the Brill Building as a guy who could write a song about anything.

Anything? One day Al Stanton put that claim to the test after he dropped a bottle of Pepsi he'd bought from the vending machine. Now it was too fizzy to open—if he popped the top he would have sent soda spraying everywhere—so he set the bottle down next to Blackwell and told him, "Write about this!" Legend has it that Blackwell finished writing "All Shook Up" before the soda even reached room temperature. It, too, became a #1 hit and one of the biggest songs of Elvis's career. Even the Post Office could serve as a source of inspiration for a song—in 1962 Blackwell co-wrote another one of Elvis's big hits after seeing the message "Return to Sender" stamped on a piece of mail that had been sent to the wrong address.

HOWDY, PARDNER

So how did Blackwell become such a prolific songwriter? An African American who grew up in a home that played and sang gospel music, he also developed an interest in rhythm and blues as a young man and was a huge fan of the singing cowboys in the movies, people like Gene Autry and especially Tex Ritter (father of John Ritter, who played Jack Tripper in the 1970s sitcom *Three's Company*). Blackwell liked the singing cowboys so much, in fact, that when he was a teenager he got a job sweeping up the local movie theater just so he could hang around and listen to them all day. "Like the blues, cowboy songs told a story, but it didn't have the same restrictive construction," he explained many years later. "A cowboy song could do anything."

BY THE BOOK

Blackwell's wide-ranging musical interests were fertile ground for the types of stories he wanted to tell with his own songs, and believe it or not *comic books* were what gave him the titles for many of his songs. He'd flip through stacks of romance comic books looking for catchy phrases that would make good song titles, and as soon as he found one he liked, he'd sit down and write a song to go with it. As for the lyrics, Blackwell believed that less was more: He figured that if the lyrics to a song were clear enough and simple enough for a five-year-old child to sing them, the song had a good shot at becoming a hit.

MUSIC MAN

Blackwell wrote or co-wrote "Great Balls of Fire" and "Breathless" for Jerry Lee Lewis (who copied Blackwell's demos just as closely as Elvis had), "Handy Man" for a singer named Jimmy Jones (James Taylor covered it in 1977), and more than 1,000 other songs that have been recorded by artists as diverse as Carl Perkins, Ray Charles, The Who, The Judds, Cheap Trick, Neil Diamond, Tanya Tucker, Otis Redding, Billy Joel, Frankie Valli, Mahalia Jackson, Pat Boone, and Dolly Parton.

Did Blackwell even write "Karma Chameleon" for Boy George and Culture Club? He certainly thought so—the chorus to "Karma Chameleon" was so similar to the chorus in "Handy Man" that he sued Culture Club in the mid-1980s for copyright infringement and reportedly won a small settlement. "We gave them 10 pence and an apple," Boy George joked in an interview.

DO IT YOURSELF

In all, Blackwell has been credited with selling more than 200 million records over the years, and he might have sold a lot more than that had the Beatles not turned the music industry on its ear in the early 1960s by writing their own songs instead of hiring songwriters to do it for them. Their success emboldened a lot of other recording artists to start recording their own songs, too. Even Blackwell tried to get in on the act in the late 1970s when he recorded an album titled *These Are My Songs* and went out on tour. But the man who created so many hits for other artists never did have a hit record of his own. Not that that really bothered him—Blackwell had made an indelible mark on popular music, made a lot of money in the process, and had a lot of fun as well. Or as he once put it in an interview, "I wrote my songs, I got my money, and I boogied!"

The reddish colors magenta, sienna, and Venetian red are all named after Italian cities.

ON A ROLL

Uncle John's grandpa used to say that the key to success is the ability to turn a negative situation into a positive one. And it's fascinating how many successful products came out of a goof that everybody thought was garbage... except the one guy who figured out a way to turn it into gold.

PAPER TRAINED

In 1879 E. Irvin and Clarence Scott founded the Scott Paper Company in Philadelphia and began selling what many historians believe are the Western world's first rolls of toilet paper. In 1907 E. Irvin's son, Arthur Scott, by that time the president of the company, tried to improve on their design by using thicker paper. Ready to change the TP world, Scott had a train car full of the thicker paper delivered to his factory. Unfortunately it turned out to be *too* thick for toilet paper (ouch), and it looked like they were going to end up having to flush the idea and take a loss on the shipment. But Scott came up with an interesting idea.

Earlier that year, during a Philadelphia cold epidemic, a local schoolteacher had made the news when she noted that all the kids in her class used the same cloth hand towel that was hanging from a hook in the bathroom. She believed that by sharing the same dirty towel, the kids were spreading germs to each other. So she gave her students squares of heavy paper to dry their hands with instead.

Arthur Scott had heard about the teacher's experiment, so he had his trainload of too-thick paper cut into 13-inch-wide rolls, and then perforated into tear-off 18-inch sheets. He marketed them as "Sani-Towels," using the slogan "For use once by one user." The product was a success: Businesses such as factories, hospitals, and hotels, which were becoming increasingly sanitation-minded, used Sani-Towels in their public washrooms. But Scott was determined to get the product into homes, too.

PAPER CHASE

In 1931 Scott introduced the American public to ScotTowels—complete with a ScotTowel holder to put on the wall—at grocery stores around the country. It worked...obviously.

The "real" name of the Comic Book Guy on *The Simpsons*: Jeff Albertson.

ABSORBING FACTS

• Today paper towels are found in an estimated 94% of American households. Overall PT sales add up to more than $2 billion per year.

• If you took two billion average-size paper towels and laid them end to end, the paper-towel highway would be about 380,000 miles long. (380,000 miles, just by coincidence, is how many miles of road the U.S. Forest Service estimated it maintained in U.S. national forests in 2007.)

• Paper towels are more than just paper—bleach is added to make them whiter so they appear "cleaner." Resin is added to make them more durable.

• Why are paper towels "quilted"? The little designs provide pockets for moisture to go into, making the towels more absorbent.

• Paper towels are made of softwood trees, usually pine and spruce.

• The average family spends $188 each year on paper towels.

• The paper towels used by Americans in three years would stretch about 100 million miles—about the distance from the Earth to the Sun.

• Most paper towels are made from fresh wood pulp, not recycled material. If every household in the United States replaced one roll of regular towels with a roll of recycled, it would save 553,000 trees, 1.4 million cubic feet of landfill, and 197 million gallons of water.

* * *

BRAIN IN A BOX

Ian Pearson, head of British Telecom's "futurology unit" predicts that by the year 2050 humans will be able to download the entire contents of their brains onto a supercomputer. He said the research was linked to BT's studies into making "conscious computers." Pearson said the technology being worked on today could one day build emotional machines, such as airplanes that are afraid of crashing.

The South Korean government has promised to put a robot in every home by 2013.

CAR NAME ORIGINS

What's a Kia? Or a Fiat? Here are the
stories of how your car got its name.

ALFA ROMEO: The company began in Italy in 1910 as *Anonima Lombarda Fabbrica Automobil*, or ALFA. Nicola Romeo bought the company in 1915 and added his name.

KIA: In Korean, the name means "rising from Asia."

TOYOTA: Originally called *Toyoda*, after founder Sakichi Toyoda, the company held a contest to come up with a better name. The winner: *Toyota*.

ASTON MARTIN: Lionel Martin started the company in England, near Aston Hill.

HUM-VEE: It's an approximate pronuncitation of HMMWV—an acronym for "**H**igh **M**obility **M**ultipurpose **W**heeled **V**ehicle."

HYUNDAI: "Modern" in Korean.

VOLVO: The Latin word for "I roll" is *volvo*. But that's not a reference to the company's cars: Volvo's first product was a ball bearing.

SAAB: The Swedish company started in 1937 as *Svenska Aeroplan Aktiebolaget*, or SAAB for short.

DAIHATSU: Was a cheap, compact Daihatsu your first car? In Japanese, *dai* means "first"; *hatsu* means "engine."

AUDI: In 1899 August Horch started a car company—he called it Horch ("hark" in German)—but left it in 1909 to start another car company, which he called *Audi*, Latin for "hark."

FIAT: It's an acronym for *Fabbrica Italiana Automobil Torino* ("Italian Factory of Cars of Turin").

ROLLS ROYCE: Engineer Frederick Royce built his first car, the Royce, in 1904. In 1906 he partnered with auto dealer Charles Rolls—Royce made the cars, and Rolls was the exclusive sales agent. In 1998 the company was sold to Volkswagen.

VOLKSWAGEN: German for "peoples' car."

Most common symbol of romantic love worldwide: the heart.

POP CAUSES

Do you wear a yellow bracelet or have a ribbon magnet on your car? Here are the origins of some charitable fads.

RIBBONS

Inspired by the 1973 multimillion-selling Tony Orlando and Dawn song "Tie a Yellow Ribbon 'Round the Ole Oak Tree," many families tied large yellow ribbons around trees as a show of support for American hostages during the Iranian Hostage Crisis in 1980, and again to support American troops at the height of the Persian Gulf War in 1991. The early 1990s were also a period of high public concern about HIV and AIDS. *Outweek* magazine columnist Michael Goff wrote an article questioning why there was a ribbon for troops, but none for AIDS victims. A New York artist collective that raised awareness of the disease thought Goff was on to something and created the Red Ribbon Project. Like the yellow ribbons for troops, the red ribbons were meant to raise AIDS awareness. The ribbons were publicly unveiled at the 1991 Tony Awards (Jeremy Irons was the first person seen on TV wearing one). Throughout the 1990s, red ribbons worn on dresses or lapels became more and more common on televised award shows. Today the ribbons are used to promote awareness for a variety of causes—pink for breast cancer, blue for child abuse (baby blue is for prostate cancer), and green for organ donation (also for Lyme disease).

BRACELETS

In 2004 cancer survivor and professional cyclist Lance Armstrong teamed up with Nike in a massive fundraising drive for his Lance Armstrong Foundation. Nike's ad agency came up with the idea of selling inexpensive rubber wristbands for $1.00 each, with the proceeds going entirely to cancer research. They decided to make the bracelets yellow because of the color's importance in professional cycling (the Tour de France leader wears a yellow jersey). By the summer of 2004, numerous celebrities and Olympic athletes were wearing yellow bracelets emblazoned with the Foundation's slogan, "Wear Yellow, Live Strong." The results of the drive far exceeded

Armstrong's goal. He'd hoped to raise $5 million by selling the bracelets. To date, more than $70 million worth of "Live Strong" bracelets have been sold. They've also inspired other causes to sell bracelets to raise money. There are bracelets for breast cancer (pink), wounded veterans (camouflage), and epilepsy awareness (half blue and half red). It's even a fashion statement—knockoff yellow wristbands can be found in discount and dollar stores all over the country, but the money doesn't go to any charity.

HANDS ACROSS AMERICA

In 1985 rock music manager Ken Kragen introduced his client Lionel Richie to Michael Jackson. A few months later the duo wrote "We Are the World" together, then recorded it with an all-star ensemble and raised $50 million for Ethiopian famine relief. Inspired, Kragen decided to start a charity to raise $50 million for soup kitchens in the United States. His plan? A coast-to-coast chain of people holding hands (everyone in the chain had to pay $10 to participate). In September 1985, he announced that "Hands Across America" was scheduled for May 25, 1986. For the next nine months celebrities including Oprah Winfrey, Prince, Jane Fonda, and even President Reagan gave speeches and appeared on talk shows pledging support and promising to join in the chain. The Hands Across America staff worked tirelessly, making thousands of phone calls to get people to sign up. A theme song called "Hands Across America" was played regularly on radio and MTV. Finally, on Sunday, May 25, 1986, at 3:00 p.m. Eastern time, Hands Across America began at Battery Park in New York City, passing through New Jersey and Pennsylvania, dipping down to Washington, D.C., winding through Memphis, Cleveland, Chicago, St. Louis, Dallas, and Phoenix, and ending in Long Beach, California. Five million people held hands over 4,125 miles and 17 states for 15 minutes and sang "We Are the World" and "America the Beautiful." Unfortunately, over half of the day's participants never paid the $10 entry fee. On top of that, miles-long gaps in the chain were reported in Maryland, Illinois, and the Arizona desert. Even worse, it had cost $17 million to stage the event, and only $20 million was raised. In the end, only $3 million was raised for soup kitchens, far short of the $50 million goal. Despite the noble cause and the monumental effort, "Hands Across America" was a flop.

Switzerland hasn't gone to war with another country since 1515.

MODERN WISDOM

Contemporary thoughts on timeless subjects.

"Sometimes the road less traveled is less traveled for a reason."
—**Jerry Seinfeld**

"A depressing number of people seem to process everything literally. They are to wit as a blind man is to a forest, able to find every tree, but each one coming as a surprise."
—**Roger Ebert**

"The most erroneous stories are those we think we know best—and therefore never scrutinize or question."
—**Stephen Jay Gould**

"You never really learn much from hearing yourself talk."
—**George Clooney**

"There are no shortcuts to any place worth going."
—**Beverly Sills**

"The truth will set you free. But first, it will piss you off."
—**Gloria Steinem**

"The first step to getting the things you want out of life is this: Decide what you want."
—**Ben Stein**

"It is useless to put on your brakes when you're upside down."
—**Paul Newman**

"People who talk the most about morality are the people who possess the least amount of it."
—**James Carville**

"When one's expectations are reduced to zero, one really appreciates everything one does have."
—**Stephen Hawking**

"In the practice of tolerance, one's enemy is the best teacher."
—**Dalai Lama**

"When you confront a problem you begin to solve it."
—**Rudy Giuliani**

"In a free society the biggest danger is that you'll become afraid to the point where you censor yourself."
—**Tim Robbins**

"We're our own dragons as well as our own heroes, and we have to rescue ourselves from ourselves."
—**Tom Robbins**

Pig in a basket: Marshmallow Peeps contain pork.

PEANUTS, PART III

Our story of Charles Schulz continues with the tale of a low-budget holiday special that became a classic. (Part II is on page 295.)

READY FOR PRIMETIME

In 1964 a San Francisco television producer named Lee Mendelson made a documentary about baseball legend Willie Mays that garnered some pretty good reviews. Having honored the world's greatest baseball player, he later recalled, "now I should do the world's worst baseball player, Charlie Brown." So Mendelson approached Schulz with the idea of making a documentary about *Peanuts*. Schulz had seen the Willie Mays show and was very interested. The two had just started work on the documentary *Charlie Brown & Charles Schulz*, which focused on Schulz's troubled childhood, when the Coca-Cola company approached Mendelson about making a *Peanuts* Christmas special for 1965. "I said, 'Absolutely!'" recalled Mendelson. "I phoned Sparky and told him that I had just sold a Charlie Brown Christmas show. He asked which show and I told him, 'The one we're going to make an outline for tomorrow.' And we literally did the outline in one day."

With the story worked out, Schulz hired Bill Melendez, the animator that Ford had used on the *Peanuts* commercials. (Melendez's impressive resume included such Disney films as *Bambi* and *Fantasia*, and many classic Bugs Bunny and Daffy Duck cartoons for Warner Bros.) The three men would end up working together on dozens of *Peanuts* specials and films over the next 30 years.

ON A SHOESTRING

But their first project turned out to be the most difficult. For one thing, they had a tiny budget to work with, which resulted in very choppy animation, even by 1960s standards. There were other problems, too: CBS wanted to hire adult actors to voice the children, *and* they wanted a laugh track. By this time, Schulz was powerful enough to get what he wanted, and he wanted actual children's voices with no laugh track. (He cringed at the idea of telling people when they should be laughing.) CBS gave in, but had another demand—they didn't want Linus reciting a Bible verse. "The whole thing is about the true meaning of Christmas!" Schulz argued. "Take that out and there's no show!" After some hard-fought negotiations, the network finally relented, as they also did about using jazz music in the soundtrack. CBS executives didn't understand it; they were expecting the special to flop.

A TRADITION IS BORN

Airing on Thursday, December 9, 1965 (in *Gilligan's Island*'s regular time slot), *A Charlie Brown Christmas* became an overnight sensation. More than half of the televisions in the United States tuned in. While Schulz, Mendelson, and Melendez cringed at some of the low-budget technical aspects of *A Charlie Brown Christmas*—the static speaking style of the kids (especially Sally, who was voiced by a little girl too young to read, so she had to be fed her lines phonetically)—they felt that they had created something unique. The critics agreed. They lauded its simple message that Christmas means more than crass commercialism (even though the special *was* sponsored by Coca-Cola). The public agreed, too. *A Charlie Brown Christmas* won an Emmy and a Peabody Award and became a Christmas tradition.

More animation followed, most notably *A Boy Named Charlie Brown* in 1969 (the first *Peanuts* feature film) and two more well-received holiday specials: *It's the Great Pumpkin, Charlie Brown* in 1966 and *A Charlie Brown Thanksgiving* in 1973. In all, the team of Schulz, Mendelson, and Melendez produced more than 40 primetime specials over the next three decades. (Melendez also provided the squeaky voices of Snoopy and Woodstock.)

HEAVY BURDENS

But as the years went on, Schulz devoted less and less of his time to these outside projects, leaving most of the screen work to Mendelson and Melendez. In the early 1970s, Schulz's home life started to deteriorate, leading to a divorce in 1972. "I didn't think she liked me anymore," he said, "and I just got up and left one day." A year later, while skating at a local ice rink, Schulz met Jeannie Clyde. The two hit it off and were married in 1973. They remained together for the rest of Schulz's life.

With a renewed spirit and more time to work on the strip, Schulz spent the rest of the 1970s perfecting the characters he'd been fleshing out over the previous 20 years. Only a few new characters were added; instead, he focused more on extended story lines such as Peppermint Patty's troubles at school, Snoopy's campus adventures as "Joe Cool," and Charlie Brown's first-ever win at a baseball game (he walked with the bases loaded). But even though *Peanuts* remained popular, it was obvious that it had peaked in the 1960s. That was fine with Schulz—the fewer promotional appearances and outside projects he had to deal with, the better.

LOSING ITS EDGE

By the 1980s, Schulz found himself in the odd position of being the "old timer." Suddenly it was no longer "*Peanuts* and everything else." A new crop of humor cartoonists, all inspired in some way by *Peanuts*, were making their own marks on the daily comics page—Lynn Johnston's *For Better or For Worse*, which Schulz loved, Jim Davis's *Garfield*, which Schulz loathed, and Gary Larson's *The Far Side*, which Schulz never said much about... although he probably wasn't too pleased to see Larson's depiction of Charlie Brown buried up to his neck in the sand (by Indians) awaiting an army of oncoming ants. Yet that's the kind of cutting-edge humor that was catching people's attention in the early 1980s. Charlie Brown and Snoopy's antics seemed passé next to, say, the political volatility of Garry Trudeau's *Doonesbury*. For the first time, *Peanuts* was no longer leading the way.

To compete with the new strips, Schulz was urged by his syndicate to modernize the look of *Peanuts*—or at least make the kids start commenting on current events. Schulz refused both requests and stubbornly kept *Peanuts* locked in the same innocent setting where it began. "I could never be a political cartoonist," he said in 1988, "because I refuse to blast people I don't know. I suppose that's why they say *Peanuts* is no longer on the cutting edge. That's absurd. What's 'cutting edge,' anyway? Insulting the president? Delighting in meanness? If that's cutting edge, then I don't want it." One of Schulz's strongest advocates was up-and-coming comic strip artist Bill Watterson, creator of *Calvin & Hobbes*. In 1987 he came to Schulz's defense:

> Every now and then I hear that *Peanuts* isn't as funny as it was or it's gotten old. I think that what's really happened is that it

---

Take your kid to work day? Columbus took his son Diego along on his 4th trip to the New World.

changed the entire face of comic strips and everybody has now caught up to him. I don't think he's five years ahead of everybody else like he used to be, so that's taken some of the edge off it. I think it's still a wonderful strip in terms of solid construction, character development, and the fantasy element. Things that we now take for granted—reading the thoughts of an animal, for example—there's not a cartoonist who's done anything since 1960 that doesn't owe Schulz a tremendous debt.

HEART PROBLEMS AND INTO THE WOODS

Schulz's struggles with keeping the strip timely only increased when his health started to deteriorate in the early 1980s. For one, it made the demands of a daily strip more difficult to keep up with. Normally, Schulz had a three-month lead time, meaning the comic he drew today would run in the newspapers 90 days later. That gave him ample time to develop new stories. But in 1981, the 59-year-old cartoonist suffered a heart attack, prompting an emergency quadruple-bypass. As he recovered, he saw his lead times shrink down to a few weeks. And he hated working under pressure. Worse yet, he developed Parkinson's disease, which caused his hands to shake. "It's just annoying," Schulz said in 1988. "It slows me down, and I have to letter very carefully. After my heart surgery, it was intolerable, and then I wracked up my knee playing hockey. That was worse than the heart surgery; it just took all the life out of me. I remember one day I came back, and I was so weak I finally had to quit. I just couldn't hold that pen still. Am I supposed to sit here the rest of my life drawing these things while all my friends are dying or retiring?"

Rather than pack it in, however, Schulz invented new story lines in the 1990s to help him cope. He focused heavily on Snoopy's adventure as a Beagle Scout—following the dog and his bird friends into the forest. "Hiking, camping, and roasting marshmallows over an open fire can revive a writer's dampened spirit," Schulz said.

THE END OF AN ERA

Schulz had planned to draw the strip well into his 80s...until he suffered a stroke and was diagnosed with colon cancer in November 1999. Yet he still refused his syndicate's insistence that he bring in ghostwriters. "Everything has to end," he said. "This strip is my excuse for existence. No one else will touch it." (Schulz was always saddened to see one of his cartoonist friends retire or die, only to have their syndicate hire other artists to keep the strip going.) But with his health failing, on December 14, 1999, Schulz, now 77, reluctantly announced his retirement. He died on February 12, 2000, the same day the last original Sunday *Peanuts* strip ran. It was a montage of classic scenes, along with a note that came straight from Snoopy's (and Sparky's) typewriter:

> Dear Friends, I have been fortunate to draw Charlie Brown and his friends for almost 50 years. It has been the fulfillment of my childhood ambition. Unfortunately, I am no longer able to maintain the schedule demanded by a daily comic strip. My family does not wish *Peanuts* to be continued by anyone else, therefore I am announcing my retirement. I have been grateful over the years for the loyalty of our editors and the wonderful support and love expressed to me by fans of the comic strip. Charlie Brown, Linus, Lucy...how can I ever forget them...

YOU'RE A GOOD MAN, CHARLIE SCHULZ

Schulz was buried in Sebastopol, California, with full military honors. Fittingly, four Sopwith Camel biplanes (Snoopy's plane from his battles with the Red Baron) performed a flyover. A few months later, nearly 100 of Schulz's fellow cartoonists showed their appreciation with *Peanuts*-themed comic strips.

According to Robert Thompson, a professor of popular culture at Syracuse University, *Peanuts* may be the "longest story ever told by one human being." He pointed out that the 50-year journey of the *Peanuts* gang is longer than that of any epic poem ever written, and dwarfs any Tolstoy novel or Wagnerian opera. One of Schulz's heroes and best friends, a World War II cartoonist named Bill Mauldin, summed up Sparky's impact: "I rank Schulz with Gandhi in the scope and influence on people in the 20th century. Sure, Gandhi spoke to multitudes, but has anybody counted Schulz's circulation? And the same message is conveyed: Love thy neighbor even when it hurts. Love even Lucy."

If you're like us, you can never get enough of the Peanuts characters. For their individual stories, check out the Peanuts Gallery on page 545.

A common housefly carries some 1,941,000 bacteria on its body.

MORE APRIL FOOLS!

Don't look now, but your fly is open. Made you look again!
Here's a look at a few other classic April Fools' jokes.

FISH TALE

On April 1, 2000, the animal-rights organization People for the Ethical Treatment of Animals sent a fake press release announcing plans to dump tranquilizers into Lake Palestine in Texas during the annual Red Man Cowboy Division Fishing Tournament. "This year, the fish will be napping, not nibbling," the group said in its press release. Lake officials fell for the prank and announced plans to patrol for people dumping drugs into the lake. "There will be game wardens and deputy sheriffs involved, but I won't go any further at this point," a spokesman told reporters.

PAPER TRAIL

On April 1, 2007, Google announced that it was introducing a new option called "Gmail Paper" as part of its popular e-mail service. Customers could choose to have Google send them printed copies of each and every e-mail that landed in their in-boxes. Bonus: The service was free of charge. "The cost of postage is offset with the help of relevant, targeted unobtrusive advertisements, which will appear on the back of your Gmail Paper prints in red, bold, 36-point Helvetica.... You can make us print one, one thousand, or one hundred thousand of your e-mails. It's whatever seems reasonable to you."

THE LIBERAL MEDIA

In 1982 the *Connecticut Gazette* and its sister weekly the *Connecticut Compass* announced they'd both been purchased by TASS, the official news agency of the Soviet government, as part of its plan to expand beyond the USSR. The article also reported that the editors of both papers had been killed in freak "simultaneous hunting accidents" after shooting each other in the back of the head with Soviet rifles. The publishers eventually admitted the article was a joke...but not everyone bought it. "You expect me to believe a bunch of commies?" one caller asked the *Gazette*.

About a million Americans have named their dog the primary beneficiary in their wills.

DÈJÁ VIEW

In 2001 England's Southern FM radio station told listeners that a life-size replica of the *Titanic* would sail past Beachy Head, a famous local lookout. So many people made their way to the edge of the cliff at Beachy Head that a huge crack opened in the cliff and officials made them evacuate. Fortunately, the only injuries were to the pride of the people who fell for the joke. "I felt like such an idiot," one angry listener told reporters.

LIFE IMITATES FOOLS

At the height of the dot-com craze in 2000, *Esquire* magazine ran an April Fools' story about FreeWheelz.com, a startup company that would cover new cars with a giant, bumper-to-bumper, shrink-wrapped advertisement and give them away free to people who agreed to drive them at least 300 miles per week. The online application form was 600 questions long and took seven hours to complete. If you wanted to keep the car for a second year, the magazine said, you had to provide a stool sample. The article was intended as a satire on stupid dot-com ideas…but an entrepreneur for a company with a similar idea paid the article's author $25,000 for the rights to the FreeWheelz.com Web site. The *Esquire* article "validated our business model," the entrepreneur told reporters.

*   *   *

DEATH EUPHEMISMS

Some professions have their own slang term for "kicked the bucket."

- **Writers:** made the big deadline
- **Baseball players:** got traded to the Angels
- **Bartenders:** answered the last call
- **Computer programmers:** cached in his chips
- **Chefs:** cooking for the Kennedys
- **Editors:** got red-lined
- **Equestrians:** jumped the last hurdle
- **Clothing designers:** went permanently out of fashion

The average American household wastes 14% of the food it buys.

LOONEY (CANADIAN) LAWS

Weird laws that were never taken off the books is one of our favorite
Bathroom Reader *features. Here's a batch from Canada.*

Living in a streetcar is illegal in Thompson, Manitoba.

In Quesnel, British Columbia, one may not exercise in a manner frightening to a horse.

Wildlife may not be hunted with flashlights in Alberta.

It's illegal for a teenager to walk down the street in Fort Qu'Appelle, Saskatchewan, with his shoes untied.

In Montreal, it's illegal to swear in French. (Swearing in English is okay.)

Playing craps is legal in Alberta, but using dice to do so is not.

In Wawa, Ontario, it's against the law to paint a ladder.

If you catch an edible fish in Canadian national park waters, according to federal law, you must eat it.

In Alberta, it's illegal to set fire to a man's wooden leg.

In Winnipeg, it's illegal to goad an alligator into a fight. (There are no alligators in Winnipeg.)

Taxi drivers in Halifax, Nova Scotia, are legally required to wear socks.

Possessing a chipped bathtub is against the law in Dartmouth, Nova Scotia.

Dartmouth also prohibits citizens from throwing chickens across the road.

In Ontario, it's illegal to drive and watch television at the same time.

It's against the law in Nova Scotia to do cartwheels and somersaults on the street.

Street musicians in Victoria, British Columbia, are breaking the law if they hand out balloon animals to children.

In Ontario, it's against the law to drive a hovercraft on the highway.

IRONIC, ISN'T IT?

There's nothing like a good dose of irony to put the problems of day-to-day life into proper perspective.

I'M STUMPED

For three years, a Canadian man tried to convince city officials in Belle River, Ontario, to remove a tree stump from the often-frozen Lake St. Clair, claiming the stump posed a danger to people riding snowmobiles on the lake at night. One night in early 2007, the same man was killed when his snowmobile struck the stump.

POWER TO THE PEOPLE

In 2005 Toronto Hydro-Electric began conservation measures to help its customers save money by offering a credit on their fall bill if they cut their summer electric use by 10 percent. So many people took advantage of the offer that in 2007 the power company had to announce a rate hike to offset the $10.4 million they lost in the conservation program.

THEY SHOULD HAVE CALLED IT "THE SHOOSHER"

An amusement park ride at the Scandia Family Fun Center in Sacramento, California, lifts customers 160 feet in the air and then spins them around at 60 mph. Nearby residents finally got fed up with the thrill seekers' bloodcurdling screams and filed a class action suit against the park. But park manager Steve Baddley is already taking steps to limit the noise on the ride (which he originally purchased because of its relatively quiet motor). Baddley's first step: No screaming allowed. "If we can hear a noise, we're required to take you off the ride," he says. The name of the ride: The Screamer.

ACID REFLEX

In the chilly waters off Antarctica in 2007, two animal activists were preparing to attack a Japanese whaling ship with a bottle of acid. But the attack had to be postponed when their ship got lost in the fog. They sent out a call for help, and a few minutes later the very whaling ship they were targeting came to their rescue.

White wine gets darker as it ages. Red wine gets lighter.

Once the activists were out of danger, they thanked the crew of the whaling ship. After a long, awkward silence, one of the activists said, "I guess we're back on schedule," and threw the acid onto the whalers' deck (two crewmen were injured). Then they jumped back on their boat and raced away.

WHEN FAKE BECOMES MORE REAL THAN REAL

During a 2007 reenactment of the Battle of Anderson County (South Carolina), Stewart Lambert, one of the "Confederate soldiers" was wounded when his gun accidentally fired (it was loaded with blanks) as he tried to remove it from its holster. The shot burned and cut Lambert's leg, resulting in stitches. Ironically, in the original Battle of Anderson County, no Confederate soldiers were wounded at all.

ANTI-SPAM SPAMMER

An anti-spam software company called SpamArrest had to issue this apology to its customers. "Recently we have received some inquiries regarding a mailing we delivered to users of SpamArrest. Because of this, SpamArrest will not send unsolicited bulk e-mail again."

AN IRONY OF ORWELLIAN MAGNITUDE

In his 1949 novel *1984*, George Orwell predicted that in the future, England would be ruled by "Big Brother," a government which constantly spies on its citizens to keep them in line. In England today, there are a reported 4.2 million closed-circuit cameras watching the people. But one neighborhood in London is leading all of the others: On a single block in Canonbury Square in Islington, North London, there are 32 cameras trained on the streets, alleys, even on peoples' properties. One of Canonbury Square's biggest claims to fame: George Orwell lived there while he was writing *1984*.

*   *   *

"I wish people who have trouble communicating would just shut up."

—Tom Lehrer

DO-IT-YOURSELF JELLO

In previous editions of Uncle John's Bathroom Reader, *we told you how to make shrunken heads and atomic bombs. Those are pretty tough acts to follow...but we think this comes close.*

WHAT YOU'LL NEED
A few pounds of animal remnants (see Step 1), a sharp knife, a surgical-grade bone saw, a colander or strainer, a power washer, an aluminum cauldron, a roasting pan, two huge plastic vats, 20 gallons of lime, 20 gallons of a 4% hydrochloric-acid solution, distilled water, a microwave, cheese-cloth, a food dehydrator, a food processor, Kool-Aid mix...and about a week.

1. Gather up any cow, sheep, or horse bones, hooves, skin, or any random body tissue you might have lying around. Don't have any? Don't worry: Call a local slaughterhouse and ask for "raw pre-processing waste." But make *sure* that the bones and skin they give you are fresh—no more than a day old.

2. Carefully inspect the body parts. Discard any pieces that smell foul or look rotten. Overly decayed bits of bone and flesh produce stringy and inconsistent gelatin. (And besides, they're gross.)

3. Cut the parts into small, five-inch-wide pieces. Use a sharp paring or serrated knife on the skin and tissue. For the bones, you're probably going to have to use a top-of-the-line electric carving knife, power saw, or surgical bone saw.

4. Place the small pieces in a large colander or strainer. Take it all into the backyard and thoroughly wash all of them off with a high-pressure hose or power washer. This will free them of any unwanted animal debris, such as leftover blood or gristle.

5. Throw the clean pieces of bone, hoof, and tissue into a big pot and soak them in boiling water for about five hours. (The power-washing got rid of the blood and gristle, but a boiling bath gets rid of almost all of the fat.) After five hours of boiling, the fat will be floating at the top of the pot. Skim it off and throw it away.

6. Preheat your oven to 200°F. Place the clean, fat-free bones, skin, and other tissue in a roasting pan and bake them for 30 minutes.

7. Back to the backyard. Get a huge plastic vat, fill it with lime, and toss in the animal chunks. This semi-decomposes the materials, removing unwanted minerals and organic body chemicals from the cow parts. Let it all soak in the lime for about two days.

8. Get another plastic vat and fill it up with a mixture of 96% water and 4% hydrochloric acid (available in any scientific-supply store or on the Internet). This facilitates the release of collagen from the animal material, which is the bouncy, "gelatinous" element of gelatin. Leave the pieces in the vat for three days.

9. After removing them from the acid bath (wear gloves!), take the pieces back inside and throw them into an aluminum cauldron and boil them in *distilled*—not tap—water. Using a slotted spoon, carefully skim off any gooey chunks that rise to the surface. This is waterlogged gelatin, and it's what you've been after for the past week.

10. Next, the liquidy gelatin chunks have to be sterilized. In gelatin-processing plants, they go into a high-heat flash heater for four seconds. If you don't have an industrial flash heater, put the goopy bits in the microwave on a ceramic plate (it's soak-proof) for about 10 seconds.

11. Strain the chunks through fine cheesecloth to filter out any tiny remnants of bone, skin, or meat that remain attached to the gelatin.

12. Separate the semi-solid gelatin from the liquid by drying it out. Processing plants use the industrial flash heater for this, too, but you can substitute a home food dehydrator or beef-jerky maker lined with wax paper. Let it sit for about 24 hours.

13. You're almost done! Scrape the dry (but slightly sticky) gelatin out of the dehydrator and put it all in a food processor. Grind it into a powder. Mix in some powdered flavorings—Kool-Aid mix works pretty well. Add in the hot water and let it stand in the fridge for a few hours. Alternative: Go to the store and buy a box of gelatin dessert mix for 59 cents. Follow the directions on the box.

SUPERMAN RETURNS
...EVENTUALLY (PART I)

*Superman Returns was one of 2006's biggest box-office hits, earning
$400 million worldwide. It was also the first Superman film since
1987. In the two decades in between, Warner Bros. tried—
and failed—to make a Superman movie seven times.
Here's the story of how Superman finally returned.*

SUPERMAN V

Even before the 1987 release of *Superman IV: The Quest for Peace*, Cannon Films was planning *Superman V*. An entire subplot was cut from *Superman IV*, giving filmmakers about two-thirds of a movie that was already paid for. They'd need to film a few more scenes with star Christopher Reeve, but that was it. Beyond that, plans were made for *Superman VI*, too—it was going to be directed by Reeve (who'd co-written *Superman IV*).

But then *Superman IV* actually came out. Critics loathed it and it flopped at the box office, earning just $15 million (a fraction of the $134 million that *Superman: The Movie* had made in 1978). Reeve was so stung by the failure that he not only backed out of his deal to direct *Superman VI*, he decided it was time to quit Superman altogether and refused to film the additional scenes needed to complete *Superman V*. Suddenly all Superman movie plans had to be put on hold. Then, because of a string of box-office flops in 1987 (including *Superman IV*), Cannon went out of business.

SUPERMAN: THE NEW MOVIE

Cannon Films's deal to make Superman movies had a clause that stipulated that if it passed on making *Superman V* for any reason (including going out of business), the rights passed to father-and-son producers Alexander and Ilya Salkind, who had made *Superman, Superman II,* and *Superman III,* and had sold the rights to *Superman IV* to Cannon. At the time they got the rights back in 1988, the Salkinds were producing *Superboy,* a syndicated TV series about Superman as a teenager.

If you divide the world's Legos among the human race, every man, woman, and child gets 75.

The Salkinds decided to make *Superman V* a continuation of *Superman II* and ignore the events of *Superman III* and *IV*, which had largely ignored the conventional Superman mythos. In *Superman: The New Movie* (the working title), the villain Brainiac comes to Earth, shrinks Metropolis, and adds it to the zoo of specimens he's gathered from planets he destroyed. Superman escapes from the bubble, defeats Brainiac, saves Metropolis, and learns that Lois Lane is pregnant with his child.

To write the script, the Salkinds hired Cary Bates, a 20-year veteran writer for the Superman comic books. Then they asked Reeve to star. He declined, so they approached Gerard Christopher, the star of *Superboy*. He agreed…but the Salkinds didn't make the movie. They couldn't—by the time production was ready to begin in 1992, their movie rights had expired. The rights reverted to DC Comics, which, at the time, was a division of Warner Bros. Pictures.

SUPERMAN REBORN, TAKE ONE

In order to revive interest in Superman—comics and movies— DC decided to take a daring step in 1992: Superman was going to die. And so, in *Superman #75* in January 1993, a villain named Doomsday killed Superman. (For more on that story, see *Uncle John's Fast-Acting Long-Lasting Bathroom Reader*.) His death in the comics would lead into a movie about Superman's resurrection, to be titled *Superman Reborn*. Warner Bros. assigned producer Jon Peters to lead the project because of his successful work on 1992's *Batman Returns*. In early 1994, Peters hired Jonathan Lemkin to write the script. Lemkin was fairly inexperienced: He'd written for several TV shows (*21 Jump Street* and *Beverly Hills, 90210*), but only one movie—a *Lord of the Flies* knockoff called *Exile*.

Warner Bros.' board of directors feared risking their lucrative movie franchise on an unproven writer, so they made Lemkin pitch his plot outline before the entire Warner board. Here's the script Lemkin wanted to write: Superman plans to tell Lois that he loves her, but before he can, Doomsday kills him. Superman's ghost enters Lois's body and impregnates her with Superman Jr. The child is born and grows to adult size in a few weeks. The new Superman saves the world and Lois dies. The board thought it sounded completely ridiculous. They told Peters to fire Lemkin and get another screenwriter.

SUPERMAN REBORN, TAKE TWO

Peters hired another unproven talent, Greg Poirier, screenwriter of a handful of B-movies like *The Adventures of Dynamo Duck* and *Danger Zone III: Steel Horse War*. Poirier's plot: Brainiac (revived from 1992's failed *Superman: The New Movie*) comes to Earth, falls in love with Lois Lane, and keeps her as a specimen of the planet before he destroys it. Superman, meanwhile, is dealing with severe depression over his dual identity, questioning his place in the world. Brainiac sets Doomsday on Superman. Doomsday and Superman kill each other. Then an alien named Cadmus revives Superman and gives him a special suit that makes him powerful again. Superman kills Brainiac and regains his natural powers. Finally, Lois finds out that Clark Kent and Superman are the same guy (despite the fact that she already found out in *Superman II*).

Warner Bros. executives weren't thrilled with the story, but they thought it was better than Lemkin's. The movie went into production in late 1996.

SUPERMAN LIVES, TAKE ONE

In early 1997, writer/director Kevin Smith was in the Warner offices doing some promotion work for his upcoming film, *Chasing Amy*. Warner executive Lorenzo di Bonaventura invited Smith, a comic-book fan who peppers his movie scripts with lots of superhero references, to rewrite *Superman Reborn*. Smith enthusiastically agreed, but then he actually read Poirier's script...and hated it. "The thing that bothered me was that they were trying to give Superman angst," Smith later wrote. "Superman's angst is not that he doesn't want to be Superman. If he has any angst, it's that he can't do it all. He can't do enough and save everyone." Di Bonaventura agreed with Smith and offered him the chance to write a completely new script.

Smith wrote an outline and gave it to Jon Peters, still the producer. Peters liked it, but gave Smith this list of "suggestions."

• Superman can't be shown flying.

Onions contain a mild antibiotic. (It doesn't kill bad breath.)

- Superman has to have a modern costume with lots of black body armor.
- There should be as little dialogue as possible.
- The final battle must include a fight with a giant spider.
- Instead of fighting bodyguards when he finds the Fortress of Solitude (Superman's secret Antarctic hideout), Brainiac should fight angry polar bears.
- Brainiac should have a funny dog sidekick "like Chewbacca."
- Brainiac should also have a sassy, black, gay robot sidekick.

Why did Peters suggest these changes? Merchandising. Warner Bros. had made more money on products with the Batman logo on them than it had from the box office receipts of any of the Batman movies. Peters's suggestions—an armored Superman, giant spiders, polar bears, dogs, and robots—could easily be turned into toys.

Smith did incorporate some of Peters's ideas into the script and in 1997 turned in *Superman Lives*. In it, Superman and Doomsday kill each other. Lex Luthor convinces the world that Brainiac is Superman's successor. Then a cyborg from Krypton brings Superman back from the dead and together they defeat all the villains.

Warner Bros. put the movie into production, hoping to have it in movie theaters the weekend of July 4, 1998—the biggest movie attendance weekend of the year, as well as the 20th anniversary of the first Superman movie and the 60th anniversary of the very first Superman comic book. When director Tim Burton was hired, it looked like the fifth Superman movie might finally happen, and it would probably be a pretty good movie. After all, Burton had directed the first two *Batman* movies, which were critically well received and commercial smashes.

But that movie never got made, either.

Look, up in the sky! It's a bird! It's a plane! It's Part II of our story on the 20-year process of getting Superman V *made. To see how the Man of Steel came back to the screen, turn to page 560.*

Q: What's an *atluk*? A: A hole in the ice where seals come up to breathe.

FINAL THOUGHTS

Some unusual epitaphs and tombstones from the United States and Europe, sent in by our crew of wandering BRI tombstonologists.

In England:
Here lies Stephen
   Rumbold
He lived to the age
   of a hundred
   and one
Sanguine & strong,
A hundred to one
   you don't live
   so long

In Virginia:
Here lies Vera
   Bemish—
For twenty years she
   preserved her
   virginity—
A very good record
   for this here
   vicinity.

In Michigan:
Bill, a horse
Here lies
My horse Bill
If he hadn't died
He'd be living still

In Washington:
Anonymous
Here I am.
How do you do?
I am dead
And so are you.

In England:
Here lies the body
   of William Dent,
Death turned up his
   heels
and away we went.

In Connecticut:
Mary Buel
Here lies the body
   of Mrs. Mary, wife
   of Deacon John
   Buel. She died
   aged 90, having
   had 13 children,
   101 grandchildren,
   147 great-grand-
   children, and 40
   great-great grand-
   children; total of
   410. May she rest
   in peace.

In Minnesota:
John Sargent
Accidentally shot
As a mark of
affection
by his brother

In Illinois:
Here lies Samuel
   Wells
The victim of a
   dishonest woman

In Jersey:
A brewer
Here lies poor
   Burton
He was both hale
   and stout;
Death laid him
   on his bitter bier,
Now in another
   world he hops
   about.

In Ireland:
Here lies John
   Higley,
Whose father and
   mother were
   drowned in their
   passage from
   America. Had
   they both lived,
   they would have
   been buried here.

In Scotland:
Here lies I, Martin
   Elmrod;
Have mercy on
   my soul,
   good God,
As I would have
   on thine if I
   were God,
And thou wer't
   Martin Elmrod

Hydrofluoric acid will dissolve glass...but can be safely stored in plastic containers.

AMAZING ANIMAL ACTS

*It's no big deal when humans say their names out loud, feed
their pets, or scrub out the toilet. But when an animal
does it, it makes for great bathroom reading.*

HERE, FISHY FISHY

Submarine is the name of a carp who lives in a pond in Guizhou Province, China. Why would someone name a wild fish? Because they wanted to train it to respond to its name. According to a local fisherman named Fang Peng, that's just what his father did with Submarine many years ago. Now all Fang has to do is walk up to the shore, yell, "Submarine!" and wait for the fish to surface to get his treat. "Submarine is very smart," says Fang. "He never takes the bait of anglers."

TIDY BOWL CHIMP

Zoo workers were stunned to watch Judy the chimpanzee's exploits after she escaped from her enclosure at the Little Rock (Arkansas) Zoo in 2007. The first thing the 37-year-old, 120-pound chimp did was go into one of the bathrooms in the staff area, grab a scrub brush, and clean the toilet. Then Judy went into a kitchen and raided the cupboard for snacks. Afterward, she wrung out a sponge and cleaned off the front of the refrigerator. (Zookeepers attribute Judy's domestic behavior to the fact that she spent some time as a house pet before living at the zoo.)

THE CAT'S MEOW

Agui, a two-year-old cat in Beijing, China, meows his own name when he gets scared. His owner, referred to only as Mr. Sun, says he first learned of Agui's talent when trying to give him a bath. "He was scared of the water. After couple of 'meow's, I heard a clear 'Agui.' At first I doubted what I was hearing, but he kept calling his name, very clearly, and sounding like a child." To prove his claim, Mr. Sun took Agui to a local vet, where they pretended to prepare Agui for a bath. When the cat saw the water, it yelped out, "Agui!" A vet spokesman said, "If Mr. Sun can give him systematic training, the cat should be able to speak more Chinese."

Studies show: Most mall Santas prefer chocolate-chip cookies and the Green Bay Packers.

SO A DOG WALKS INTO AN EMERGENCY ROOM...

In October 2006, Buddy the German Shepherd ran away from his home in Bellflower, California, and was hit by a car. Hurt but able to limp, the six-year-old dog stumbled into the emergency room at a nearby hospital. Hospital staffers tried to remove the dog, but Buddy wouldn't budge. He held his ground until a doctor came out to inspect him, and found that one of Buddy's hind legs was broken. The dog had been implanted with a microchip, so his owner, Fabian Ortega, was called and showed up at the hospital with a veterinarian. Only then would Buddy allow himself to be moved, so the vet could set his broken leg.

THE HEIM-LICK MANEUVER

When Toby the two-year-old Golden Retriever saw his owner, 45-year-old Debbie Parkhurst, punching her own chest at the dinner table in their Calvert, Maryland, home, he somehow knew exactly what to do. "The next thing I know," said Parkhurst, "Toby's up on his hind feet and he's got his front paws on my shoulders. He pushed me to the ground, and once I was on my back, he began jumping up and down on my chest." Good thing, too—Parkhurst had been choking on an apple, which Toby successfully dislodged. "I'm still a little hoarse, but otherwise, I'm okay," she told reporters. "I literally have pawprint-shaped bruises on my chest."

HERE, FISHY FISHY, PT. 2

A swan at the Safari Park in Shenzhen City, China, likes to feed the fish. Every day he flies in, picks up the feed, and deposits some into the open mouths of the waiting fish. "They became close friends after three years of playing together," explains a keeper at the park. "When everyone has eaten enough, the swan goes back onto the water and plays with his fish friends again."

*　　*　　*

"Lots of people talk to animals. Not very many listen, though. That's the problem."

—**Benjamin Hoff,** *The Tao of Pooh*

A FEW FACTS FROM '42

BRI stalwart Amy Miller brought us The 1942 World Almanac. *Uncle John immediately took it into the, er, "research lab" and emerged with this conclusion: The world sure has changed a lot since 1942.*

• A new army recruit received a base pay of $21 a month. (Today, a new private makes about $1,200 per month.)

• In 1940 candy consumption in the United States hit the then all-time high of 16.9 pounds per person. (In 2005 it reached 26 pounds.)

• From the *World Almanac's* section on ethnology: "All mankind, according to Professor A. C. Haddon, Cambridge University, can be divided into three kinds—woolly hair, wavy hair, and straight hair. According to Dr. Ales Hrdlicka, U.S. National Museum, Washington, three main human races are recognized today, which are: the whites, the yellow-browns, and the blacks."

• According to the U.S. Census Bureau, the average American father was 44 years old, lived with his wife and 1.5 children in a medium-sized city, worked in the private sector, was born in the United States, was white, and paid $480 in taxes per year.

• The birth rate in 1940: 17.3 babies born per every 1,000 people. The death rate: 10.6 deaths per 1,000. (Both have gone down. The birth rate in 2005 was 14.1 babies per 1,000 people; the death rate was 8.26 deaths per 1,000.)

• Federal gas tax, per gallon: 1.5 cents. (Today: 18.4 cents.)

• In 1942 the total area of the British Empire was 13.6 million square miles. Today, the Empire comprises only 250,000 square miles. (India, Australia, and parts of Africa are no longer British territory.)

• Unofficial, but recognized, holidays celebrated in the 1940s: Susan B. Anthony Day (February 15), Army Day (April 6), Navy Day (October 27), Pan American Day (April 14), and Forefathers' Day (December 21).

• In 1940 there were 221 million "Mohammedans" worldwide. Today, there are about 900 million, and they're called *Muslims*.

You have to process 88,000 pounds of liquefied air to get 1 pound of neon gas.

LUCKY TO BE ALIVE

Amazing luck...sometimes we're blessed with it. These folks, for instance, survived close brushes with death and are thanking their lucky stars.

DIDN'T HEAR THAT TRAIN A-COMIN'

After a night of heavy drinking in 2007, a Russian man named Vladimir Rasimov passed out on some train tracks on his way home from the local bar. Some time later, train driver Vladimir Slabiy saw his worst fears come true. "There was a man lying between the tracks and I tried to stop, but it was too late," he said. "The train went right over him and I thought he must have been killed." When the huge cargo train finally stopped, Rasimov was found underneath one of the cars, still sleeping. Rescuers tried to pull him out, but they couldn't reach him and couldn't wake him. Their only choice: have Slabiy restart the train and continue on. After Rasimov was clear of the train, he was finally woken up and taken to the hospital for observation. Other than a hangover, he didn't have a scratch. "It was lucky he was so drunk," said Slabiy.

THE PINNED-TAR INCIDENT

In early 2007, a 91-year-old German man was tarring the roof of his garden house. At some point during the afternoon, the old man (who was not identified) slipped and began to tumble down the roof...only to be stopped cold by the still-sticky tar he had just laid down. The man laid there on his back for nearly an hour, completely stuck to his roof, until passersby saw him and called the fire department. It took rescuers a long time to free the man—they had to cut him out of his clothes because the tar had dried.

LOOK BEFORE YOU LEAP

"We've only been in the new apartment for a week, but we thought TJ would have gotten used to it after climbing up all the stairs. We never thought he'd try his usual trick of jumping from the window to get into the garden," said Angela Baecker, TJ's owner. But that's just what the dog did. Unlike the ground-level house he used to live in, TJ's new apartment was on the sixth floor. Amazingly, the dog landed on a balcony three floors down (still a long drop) and had to be rescued by firefighters because the tenants were away on vacation. TJ was bruised a bit, but okay.

LEAVING AN IMPRESSION

Yong Jin Kim, a five-year-old boy who lives in Hamilton, Ontario, was playing on the balcony of his mom's ninth-floor apartment in 2007. Somehow he managed to climb over the railing...and fell all the way down to the ground, landing flat on his back. Luckily for the boy, the grassy spot he landed on had been softened by spring rains. Yong Jin left an eight-inch-deep depression in the grass that looks just like a little boy (picture the crater left by a cartoon character after a long fall). When his mother found him, she was hysterical and carried him to a nearby convenience store where they called paramedics. Yong Jin was crying but awake, lucid, and complaining that he'd hurt his leg (both of his legs turned out to be broken). He is expected to make a full recovery.

WAKE-UP CALL

On the night of March 19, 2007, a Roanoke, Virginia, auto mechanic named Dean Blevins woke up underneath a car...on his bed. It happened at 2:30 a.m. when 34-year-old Wesley Dewayne Smith lost control of his Jeep and crashed through the wall of Blevin's two-story apartment building. While hot antifreeze dripped onto Blevins's face, firefighters worked for more than an hour to free him. When they did, everyone realized just how lucky Blevins was: The Jeep's windshield had gotten snagged in the ceiling, pinning Blevins but not crushing him. He attributes his survival to the sturdy construction of the apartment building, which—he bragged to reporters—Blevins himself helped build in the 1980s. And while the Vietnam vet was pinned underneath the Jeep, he admits that he was getting angrier and angrier, recalling, "If I had my gun, I would have probably shot that guy." But later Blevins cooled down and told reporters, "Hell, I guess I'm just lucky to be alive." He received only a few nicks and bruises.

MISSION TO MARS

*On page 122 we told you about NASA's plans to return astronauts
to the Moon. Here's a look at how we may one day step foot
on the Red Planet...if NASA can be convinced to do it.*

RED SCARE

In July 1989, President George H. W. Bush announced an
ambitious new spacefaring program for NASA: the Space
Exploration Initiative. SEI called for tripling the size of Space Station *Freedom* proposed by Ronald Reagan in 1984, and using it to
build a giant *Battlestar Galactica*-type craft to go to the Moon and
then to Mars, with permanent outposts being built in both places.
SEI was the most ambitious program ever proposed for NASA,
and at an estimated cost of $450-$500 billion, it would have been
the most expensive government project since World War II.

Presidents are free to cook up new ways to spend the public's
money, but it's the Congress that gets to decide whether it will
actually be spent. When SEI got to Congress it was dead on
arrival, the victim of its enormous price tag. Space Station *Freedom* eventually became the International Space Station, but only
after several other countries chipped in to help pay for the cost of
a stripped-down station.

But what about the mission to Mars? Could that be saved, too?

MARS...ON A SHOESTRING

Two aerospace engineers named Robert Zubrin and David Baker
thought so. And they thought it would be possible to get to the
Red Planet for a lot less money than NASA did. They got permission from their company, Martin Marietta, to develop their own
plan for going to Mars, which came to be known as "Mars Direct."

A *conventional* manned mission to Mars, one similar to the
Apollo missions to the Moon, would be a very expensive proposi-
tion. Even when it's closest to the Earth, Mars is still more than
34 million miles away, about 142 times as far as the Moon. It would
take six months to get there and another six to get back. All the
fuel and all the food, water, and oxygen that the astronauts would
consume on the trip would have to be carried with them.

GAS GUZZLER

The rocket fuel was one of the most expensive factors. It takes a lot of fuel just to get to Mars, and if you have to carry the fuel for the return trip, too, the total amount needed climbs dramatically. Just launching all of that fuel into Earth orbit would cost more than $10,000 *a pound*—sending it on to Mars would cost even more—and it's estimated that returning a spacecraft from Mars back to Earth would require about 100 *tons* of fuel. You would save a fortune if you could somehow figure out a way to leave all that fuel at home...and that's just what Zubrin and Baker managed to do.

Why go to the trouble and expense of sending all that rocket fuel to Mars, the two engineers reasoned, when you can send a fuel *factory* instead? The Martian atmosphere is more than 95% carbon dioxide (CO_2), and chemists have known how to combine CO_2 with hydrogen to create methane and oxygen since the 1800s. Methane and oxygen can in turn be combined to make rocket fuel.

RUNNING ON EMPTY

Here's the plan Zubrin and Baker came up with:

• More than a year before the astronauts are scheduled to blast off to Mars, another craft, which they called an "Earth Return Vehicle" (ERV), would leave for the Red Planet. It would have enough fuel to get to Mars, but no fuel for a return trip. The ERV would contain a small robotic chemical plant powered by a nuclear reactor, and six tons of hydrogen that would serve as feedstock for the chemical plant. The trip to Mars would take about 11 months. (Since there are no astronauts on board being exposed to deadly cosmic rays and solar radiation during the flight, there's no need to expend extra fuel getting there more quickly.)

• As soon as the ERV lands on Mars, the chemical plant would deploy itself and begin combining the hydrogen with the CO_2 in the Martian atmosphere to make methane and oxygen. It would take the chemical plant about eight months to produce the 100 tons of rocket fuel needed for the ERV to get back to Earth.

• Only when the ERV was fully fueled would the astronauts depart Earth. A "habitation module" would serve as their home during the six-month flight and on the Martian surface.

• When you make a trip to Mars, you have two choices about when to return to Earth: You can return immediately, while the two planets are still fairly close together in their solar orbits, or wait another 500 days until the orbits line up again. The ERV would produce enough extra oxygen to allow the astronauts to remain on Mars for the 500 days, and enough extra methane for them to explore the Martian surface in methane-powered rovers.

• When the 500 days are up, the astronauts would transfer over to the Earth Return Vehicle and blast off on their six-month trip back to Earth. The habitation module that served as their home would remain on the surface of Mars, where it could be linked to the habitation modules of future Mars missions to form the first permanent human outpost on another planet.

SAFETY FIRST

Sending an Earth Return Vehicle to Mars without fuel for the trip home may sound risky, but it might actually be *safer* than a conventional mission. Remember, the ERV goes to Mars more than a year before the manned flight is scheduled to leave Earth—which won't leave at all unless the ERV is confirmed to be fully fueled and in good working order. If anything goes wrong, NASA learns about it while the astronauts are still safe on Earth. On a conventional mission, the astronauts might not learn of a malfunction until they were stuck on the Martian surface, 34 million miles from home.

Still not safe enough for you? It's possible to add an extra margin of safety by launching a *second* ERV—intended for use by a second mission some time in the future—at about the same time that the astronauts leave for Mars. If everything goes well with the first ERV, the second ERV would remain on standby on the surface of Mars until it was needed by astronauts at the end of the second mission. But if something did go wrong with the first ERV, the second one would be fully fueled by the time the astronauts were ready to return home. By launching a new ERV every time a new group of astronauts left for Mars, there would always be a backup ERV on Mars ready to be used in an emergency.

THANKS, BUT...

In 1990 Zubrin and Baker finalized their plan and presented it to their superiors at Martin Marietta. The company was so impressed

---

The phrase *a cappella* literally means "in chapel style."

that it arranged for the duo to travel to NASA facilities nationwide to present their plan in person. Mars Direct withstood the scrutiny of the scientists and aerospace engineers who studied it, and received rave reviews just about everywhere. Then they presented it to NASA's administrators…who rejected it. Zubrin and Baker were stuck. They'd spent more than a year trying to convince the space agency to at least consider the plan…and got nowhere.

SECOND ORBIT

Mars Direct languished until 1992, when Bill Clinton was elected president and the new administration took another look at the plan. This time NASA agreed to consider it…*if* Zubrin could prove its validity by building a prototype machine capable of combining CO_2 and hydrogen to make methane and oxygen as he'd claimed he could. It took him about a month.

NASA finally started taking Mars Direct seriously. The agency spent a year considering it and then responded with its own plan, the Design Reference Mission, a study that serves as a sort of educated guess as to how NASA will get to Mars when the time comes.

The Design Reference Mission drew heavily on Zubrin and Baker's ideas, but it wasn't a carbon copy of Mars Direct. Perhaps because NASA has lost astronauts in earlier mishaps, the agency wants to go to the Moon first, even though Zubrin thinks that's a waste of time and money. The space agency believes that it still has a lot to learn about interplanetary travel, and if it's going to make mistakes, it would rather make them on a celestial body that's three days away from Earth, not six months away.

The Design Reference Mission also rejects the idea of sending an unfueled Earth Return Vehicle to the Martian surface. Instead, it will put a fully fueled ERV in orbit around Mars. NASA will still manufacture methane and oxygen, but it will be used to fuel rovers and the launch vehicle that the astronauts will take from the Martian surface up to the ERV. That's where the Design Reference Mission stands as of 2007, but it's been revised three times already, and there are probably more changes to come. Who knows? We may end up taking Mars Direct to the Red Planet after all.

LONG, STRANGE TRIP

What will a trip to Mars be like? In some ways, manned missions to Mars won't be much different from lunar trips, but in other ways they'll be unlike any that astronauts have ever been on before. Spending six months in deep space carries much greater risks than short hops to the Moon. Here's how Mars Direct addresses them:

- **Zero Gravity.** Humans lose bone density and muscle mass at a rate of about 1% per month during extended stays in zero gravity, and Mars Direct plans to minimize this by using centrifugal force to simulate gravity on the way to and from Mars. In the past, after a multi-stage rocket has lifted astronauts into Earth orbit, the burned-out stages are jettisoned and allowed to fall back to Earth—that's why most rockets are launched over the sea. On a Mars trip, however, the upper stage might not be discarded; it could be connected to the habitation module by a mile-long tether. The two would then rotate around a common axis at a rate of about one revolution per minute, all the way to Mars. The resulting centrifugal force would provide artificial gravity. On the return trip to Earth, the launch vehicle that lifts the astronauts off of the Martian surface would serve as the counterweight to the Earth Return Vehicle, again providing artificial gravity.

- **Solar Flares.** With little warning, the sun can emit *solar flares*— bursts of radiation that are strong enough to kill astronauts in space. It turns out that water makes an excellent shelter against this solar radiation, so the solution to this problem may be as simple as designing the water tanks or even the food pantry—food contains plenty of water—to create a protective "storm shelter" surrounded by the water or food. The astronauts can retreat there for brief periods during solar flares.

- **Radiation.** Cosmic rays are another form of radiation in space, and they are much more difficult to protect against. Exposure to large doses can lead to cataracts and various forms of cancer in later years. One solution may be genetic screening to exclude any astronaut candidates with an elevated risk for developing cancer; another may be to send older astronauts—if it takes 30–40 years for cancer caused by radiation to develop, it may make sense to send astronauts who are in their 50s or even their 60s. Then, even if they are unfortunate enough to develop cancer, it will come at or near the end of their lives. (So if you've always dreamed of traveling to Mars but thought you were too old, there may yet be hope.)

COMING OF AGE

All over the world and for thousands of years, humans have been engaging in rituals built around the universal transition of a child becoming an adult.

THE POY SANG LONG
By: The Shan people of Myanmar (Burma) and Thailand
For: Boys between 7 and 14 years old
The Ritual: The Poy Sang Lang marks the time when many Shan boys are ordained as novices into the Buddhist monastic order. The three-day festival is said to mimic the transformation of the Buddha from royal prince to austere monk. The boys are shaved (head and eyebrows), dressed in brightly colored "princely" attire and gaudy jewelry (usually fake), made up with rouge and powders, and carried—over the three days—on the shoulders of their "attendants" through their towns and to feasts held in their honor. The end of the festival sees the boys being carried to the temple and ordained, their worldly clothes being exchanged for simple robes. They will then stay in the temple for anywhere from a week to as long as many years.

QUINCEAÑERA
By: Latin Americans
For: Girls aged 15
The Ritual: This ceremony is performed in different ways throughout Mexico, Central and South America, and in Latin American communities in the Caribbean and the United States. It is believed to be a combination of Catholic and native "Indio" traditions. It usually begins with a *Misa de Acción de Gracias*, a "Mass of Thanksgiving," followed by a banquet, which the Quinceañera ("15-year-old girl") attends in a formal ball gown. Over the course of several hours, she dances choreographed waltzes with her father and the male members of her "court." Her court is comprised of 14 young people, usually the Quinceañera's friends, one for each of her passed years. Normally she will receive as gifts (at least) a tiara, a bracelet, a ring, earrings, and

---

Bad call: Mark Twain decided not to invest in Alexander Graham Bell's telephone company.

a necklace, a Bible, and a "Quinceañera doll," which can be bought at Quinceañera supply stores.

SEIJIN SHIKI

By: Japanese

For: Men and women aged 20

The Ritual: The second Monday in January is a national holiday in Japan. The streets of towns and cities fill up with young men in traditional men's kimonos, called *hakama* (though many men today wear dark business suits), and young women in formal kimonos known as *furisode*. The ceremony is held for all Japanese students who have turned (or will turn) 20 during that school year and marks their entrance into adulthood. Morning ceremonies are carried out at local government offices, where speeches are made and gifts handed out, and are commonly followed by day-long parties involving "adult" activities (which often result in hangovers the following day).

BAR MITZVAH

By: Jews

For: Boys aged 13

The Ritual: When a Jewish boy reaches 13 years of age, he is no longer, in terms of his religion, the responsibility of his parents. He is *bar mitzvah*, or "he to whom the commandments apply." The passage is marked by a service on the Sabbath on or after his birthday, during which the boy will, for the first time, be called to read from the Torah at the synagogue. It's usually followed by a celebratory meal, which in most places in the world has become a full-blown party. The bar mitzvah tradition is believed to have begun in Europe in about the 13th century. The female version of the ritual is called a *bat mitzvah*. The "bat" makes the phrase read "*she* to whom the commandments apply," and it's for girls upon reaching 12 or 13 years of age, depending on the denomination. It's similar in most aspects to the bar mitzvah but is not a part of Orthodox Jewish tradition, which doesn't allow women to read the Torah. But it became a part of less-orthodox Jewish movements in the 20th century. The first bat mitzvah performed in the U.S. was in 1922, for the 12-year-old daughter of Rabbi Mordecai M. Kaplan, considered one of the most influential rabbis of America's non-Orthodox Jewish tradition.

Legal exemptions from "Peeping Tom" charges in Texas? Men over 50 and men with only one eye.

STYLE NAME CEREMONY

By: Chinese

For: 20-year-olds

The Ritual: This naming ritual began in China more than 3,000 years ago. When someone turned 20, they were considered an adult, and it was no longer polite for people of the same generation to call them by their given names, an honor only reserved for elders. Therefore they chose a "style name," also known as a *zi*, or "courtesy name." Example: The Chinese philosopher Confucius's real name was Kong Qiu (Kong being the family name and Qiu his given name). At the age of 20, he took the courtesy name Zhòng Ní (*Zhòng* meaning "second son" and *Ní* being the name of a hill, where, according to legend, his parents had prayed for his birth). Twenty-year-olds could also choose a *hao*, or an alternate style name, which could be longer and more personal. During the modernization of the 20th century, use of style names disappeared almost completely...but they're starting to make a comeback.

INITIATION BY THE SPIRIT OF THE FOREST

By: The Baka Pygmy people of Central Africa

For: Adolescent boys

The Ritual: The details of this ritual have been kept secret by the Baka for thousands of years. What is known about it comes primarily from Italian anthropologist Mauro Campagnoli, who in 2000 lived with the Baka and was invited to take part in the ceremony (though under strict agreement that he keep certain parts secret). The boys are shaved, undressed, and rubbed with palm oil, then led to a secret place in the rain forest, where they perform ritualistic dances and other secret rites for a week. During that time they eat, drink, and sleep very little. Some of the secret rites, Campagnoli says, are very dangerous. Upon completion the boys are led to the Spirit of the Forest, who "kills them," then brings them back to life—now not only as men, but possessing "special powers."

*   *   *

"Feasts must be solemn and rare, or else they cease to be feasts."

—**Aldous Huxley**

The term Generation X was coined in MCMLXIV.

WHAT AM I?

Flex your brain muscles with these classic riddles.
(Answers are on page 597.)

1. There are no other words like me. I have three letters and one syllable. But add one letter to my end (the same as the first letter)...and now I have three syllables.
What am I?

2. First comes my thunder, then comes my lightning, then come my clouds, then comes my rain.
What am I?

3. My hands quickly wave at you, though I never say goodbye. But you'd be cool to hang with me, especially when I say HI.
What am I?

4. Try to raise only one of my legs. It's impossible. Two, three, or four? Not so hard.
What am I?

5. Head and tail are equal; my middle is barely here. Right side up or upside down, the same I do appear. But if you cut my head off, nothing would be there.
What am I?

6. I am very small, but I help to carry a great weight, even though I walk on my head.
What am I?

7. I am a five-letter word and I am very capable... of murder if you remove my first letter. If you then take away my new first letter, it'll make me sick.
What am I?

8. I surround you, but you rarely ever notice me. Even though I weigh almost nothing, if you move me I'll come right back. And if you bite me, your life you will lack.
What am I?

9. When I am young I am sweet in the Sun. When I am middle-aged I make people happy. When I am old I am valued more than ever.
What am I?

10. My visionary name is both present and past. When I sink, I also rise. But I'll never move until you sit down.
What am I?

80% of American husbands, and 50% of wives, say they'd marry the same partner again.

YOU (DON'T) GET WHAT YOU PAY FOR

When you receive a bill, do you just blindly pay it? You may want to read it over to see exactly what you're paying for.

E-Z MONEY.
Like many drivers, Shari Johnston of Niagara Falls, New York, uses E-ZPass—an automatic collection service that several states offer for their toll roads. Drivers pay a monthly fee and get a transponder to put in their cars, allowing them to drive through the fast lane without having to stop at tollbooths. In 2006 Johnston, who uses the service for her regular trips over the Grand Island bridge to her job in Buffalo, found some extra charges on her E-ZPass bill. The odd thing about the charges: Johnston had undergone surgery several weeks earlier and wasn't using her car while she recuperated—exactly when the charges were made. She called the State Thruway Authority and was told that if you're not going to be driving for more than one week, you have to call E-ZPass and tell them to suspend your pass—or you'll be charged extra. "That's pretty bad," Ms. Johnson told *WGRZ News*, "when New York State needs to know my personal business to get over the bridge." (Thirty states in the U.S. have toll roads, and most of them now have some kind of electronic toll collection...and fees for "insufficient toll use.")

LONG DISTANCE RUNAROUND

Daniel Bius, a retiree from Durham, North Carolina, looked at his April Verizon telephone bill and noticed an unexplained $2 charge on it. What was it for? For *not* making long-distance phone calls. (He's not even signed up for Verizon's long-distance plan.) The *Raleigh News & Observer* reported that Bius, like many people, has home-based local service, but uses his cell phone for long-distance calls. Verizon spokesman Jim Smith defended the practice, saying, "What they're helping to do is supporting the network they would use if their cousin Tillie is critically ill in California and they need to arrange a critical-care nurse." (No word on whether Bius

---

In Ancient Egypt celibate priests abstained from salt because it was thought to be too exciting.

has a cousin Tillie.) Verizon offers to drop the $2.00 fee if the long-distance service is blocked…but that carries a $6.75 fee. "It's infuriating," says Consumers Union spokesman Bob Williams, "because they take advantage of grandmothers. It's really cynical, but they count on that." (According to industry experts, Verizon isn't the only company to charge such fees—the practice is common around the country.)

WHAT USED TO BE IN YOUR WALLET?

In 2006 British banks were ordered by the Office of Fair Trading to stop charging what the government deemed to be unfair penalty fees for customers who missed credit card payments. To make up for the lost revenue, one of the UK's most prominent banks, Lloyd's TSB, instituted a new annual fee to customers who didn't use their cards often enough. They notified the customers by mail, saying, "So that we can offer you an attractive product now and in the future, we will be charging you an annual fee of £35 ($70)." They gave customers a 10-day notice of the new charge. (Lloyd's was the first of Britain's largest banks to begin charging the fees, but industry analysts said the others are likely to follow suit.)

THE GIFT THAT STOPS GIVING

In April 2007, the Federal Trade Commission reached a settlement with Darden Restaurants, which runs the Olive Garden, Red Lobster, Bahama Breeze, and Smokey Bones chains, for its gift card scam. For years the company had been selling credit card-like gift cards, which often ended up unused. After a period of time— 15 months for cards purchased before February 2004—the recipients started being charged a $1.50 monthly "dormancy fee," which was deducted from the value of the cards. Darden stopped charging the fees in October 2006 and agreed to refund all previous fees. They also promised to disclose all future fees on cards "clearly and prominently." In December 2006, *E-Commerce Times* reported that an estimated $80 billion worth of gift cards were sold in the U.S. that year. The estimated returns for dormancy fees: about $8 billion. (According to the report, Home Depot and Best Buy raked in more than $40 million each—just from unused gift cards.) Many states are now working to make "dormancy fees" illegal.

Duh! More than 10 hrs. a week of TV has been shown to negatively affect academic achievement.

UNCLE JOHN HELPS OUT AROUND THE HOUSE

Uncle John has been collecting strange household hints and bizarre cleaning tips for years. He can't promise that all of them actually work, only that they're weird...and fun to read.

• Having a copper-polish emergency? Look in the fridge: Ketchup eliminates tarnish from copper.

• It's really gross to find mealworms in your cereal bowl. Keep them out of the cupboard with a few sticks of wrapped spearmint gum on the shelf. They hate the smell.

• To repel ants, find where they're coming into the house and spray the area with a mixture of equal parts water and vinegar. They hate the smell. Bonus: It's non-toxic.

• Besides being great on steak, Worcestershire sauce makes an excellent brass polish. It also repairs scratched wood.

• If you've got a dirty toilet bowl and you're all out of cleanser...try Tang.

• Emergency shaving cream substitutes: whipped cream (*not* Cool Whip) or peanut butter (*not* the chunky kind).

• Over time, a thermos will absorb the stains and odors of whatever you put in it. To undo the damage, pour in a tablespoon of uncooked rice and a cup of warm water. Then shake it up and rinse it out.

• Need to paint a room, but hate the noxious fumes? Add two teaspoons of pure vanilla extract to a gallon of (water-based) paint. It neutralizes the odor.

• Been pruning branches or chopping down trees and now your hands are covered in sap that won't wash off? Try rubbing half a jar of Miracle Whip (*not* mayonnaise) on them—it makes the sap rinse right off.

• If you have stains on your golf balls or piano keys, erase them—with an old fashioned pink eraser.

• Did you spill coffee on the carpet? Sop it up with a baby wipe. It won't even stain.

• Fill stinky sneakers with kitty litter (*unused* kitty litter) and leave them overnight. They'll smell fresh the next morning.

• To prevent tools from rusting, keep a charcoal briquette inside the toolbox. It absorbs moisture.

• Don't use paper towels or rags to clean windows and mirrors. They've got lint on them. Instead, use coffee filters. They're lint-free.

• Attention cheaters: Lipstick stains on a collar go away with a dab of petroleum jelly.

• Ink is one of the hardest substances to get off of skin. If a pen leaks on your hand, rub shortening on it to help remove the stain.

• If you've got a nasty sunburn on most of your body, soothe it with a bath…in iced tea. Dissolve a jar of iced tea mix in a tub of warm water.

• Hard-to-remove price stickers can be taken off with a dollop of corn oil.

• Denture-cleaning tablets don't clean just fake teeth. Dissolve one in water to polish diamonds…or hubcaps.

• Toothache? Apply a dab of Tabasco sauce to the gum.

• If there are holes in your car's radiator, try adding pepper. It sinks to the bottom, lodges in holes, and expands to fill them.

• When a metal shaving-cream can gets wet and rusts on the bottom, it can stain a shelf or countertop. To prevent this, apply a coat of nail polish to the bottom of the can and let dry.

• If static cling is making your pants stick to your legs, rub a dab of lotion into your hands until it's absorbed, then rub your hands on the clingy clothes.

*   *   *

A DIRTY NEWSFLASH

"A dump truck rolled over yesterday afternoon and all the dirt came out. The truck rolled onto more dirt. It was hard to tell all the dirt apart. There were no injuries."

—**Fox 7-TV, Austin, Texas**

Top-selling toys of 1929: American Flyer model trains and the Popeye Paddle & Ball.

THE CHICAGO FAIR

World's Fairs aren't that big a deal today, but until fairly recently, they were huge. To give you an idea of what it was like to be at a fair, we've dissected one of the best: the World's Columbian Exposition, held in Chicago in 1893.

BACKGROUND
The second half of the 19th century was the golden age of world's fairs. From 1860 to 1880, they celebrated countless cultural milestones and unveiled amazing and never-before-seen examples of human ingenuity. By the mid-1880s, as the 400th anniversary of Columbus's landing in the New World approached, many American cities, including New York, Washington, and St. Louis, were vying for the opportunity to host the 1892 fair, which would celebrate that milestone. After intense negotiations, Chicago was awarded the honor. It would be the city's chance to prove to the nation—and the world—that it had fully rebounded from the Great Fire of 1871.

The decision was made in 1890, which meant that city officials had only two years to pull the fair together. It was to be called the World's Columbian Exposition (WCE)—the biggest and grandest of all the fairs to date. The event actually wouldn't be ready until May 1, 1893, but as millions of people would find out over the following months, it was worth the wait. The WCE had everything a successful fair should have. It had...

• **A THEME.** With the Columbus journey as its backdrop, the WCE honored:

> ...the highest and best achievements of modern civilization; all that is strange, beautiful, artistic, and inspiring; a vast and wonderful university of the arts and sciences, teaching a noble lesson in history, art, science, and invention, designed to stimulate the youth of this and future generations to greater and more heroic endeavor.

That was the main theme, but Chicago officials took it a step further, giving each day its own specific sub-theme. For example: May 17 was "Norway Day," August 25 was "Colored People's Day"

Average amount of time per day spent on travel: 1.1 hours per person, worldwide.

(remember—it was still the 19th century), and August 30 was "Butchers' and Grocers' Day."

• **A TEMPORARY CITY.** Expositions were immense and grand by design. Usually spread out over hundreds of acres, they had all the basic components of a city: shops, restaurants, banks, museums, public transportation, and hotels. They employed thousands of people and ran for months at a time. Workers could remain inside the grounds for the duration of the fair if they wanted to.

The 1893 Exposition in Chicago created an entire city within its boundaries. Called the "White City," it was designed to be a modern Utopia—a place where everything good about humanity coexisted in harmony. Featuring neoclassical domes, fountains, and arches, the White City was located on a 1.3-mile strip in Jackson Park. By the fair's end, 27 million fairgoers had visited it—nearly a quarter of the nation's population. One patron, L. Frank Baum, was so inspired by the White City that he used it as a model for the Emerald City in his book *The Wonderful Wizard of Oz*.

• **NEW TECHNOLOGY.** This was perhaps the biggest draw of any world's fair: People came to see new inventions.

✔ The automobile made its U.S. debut at the Exposition. Karl Benz brought his car from Germany and drove it around the White City.

✔ Nikola Tesla introduced the public to alternating-current electricity. His new technology was used to illuminate the fair.

✔ Attendees also encountered the brand-new handheld camera, moving sidewalk, and automatic washing machine.

✔ Standard time had been adopted in the United States less than a decade before, and many rural people had not yet become accustomed to it. So Western Union built 200 precision clocks for the fair and provided kiosks with information about the new system.

✔ The new science of statistics was featured as well. Based on the average measurements of thousands of college students, sculptures of "the ideal man" and "ideal woman" were displayed at the fair.

• **NEW PRODUCTS.** World's fairs were a shopper's paradise: Thousands of merchants from all over the world set up booths to peddle their new products. The 1893 Chicago fair was one of the largest trade shows ever, featuring 65,000 separate exhibits. Crack-

The first recorded mention of soap was on Sumerian clay tablets from about 2500 B.C.

er Jack, Aunt Jemima Syrup, Cream of Wheat, Pabst Beer, and Juicy Fruit gum all made their first appearances at the fair. Another novelty was picture postcards, which fairgoers sent to family and friends as souvenirs. And two foods that would come to define the United States in the 20th century made their debut: carbonated soda and an early version of the hamburger (it was perfected 11 years later at the 1904 World's Fair in St. Louis).

• **INTERNATIONAL FLAIR.** Putting the "world" in world's fair, dozens of nations contributed exhibitions and demonstrations of the foods, customs, and music unique to their homelands. The Chicago fair boasted booths from "every inhabited land." Fairgoers could stroll through Little Egypt, sample ales at a German beer garden, and watch authentic Samoan wrestling.

• **AN ART SHOW.** Painters, sculptors, architects, and photographers all clamored for a chance to exhibit their work at a world's fair. The WCE came at a time in history when women were finally gaining real headway in their struggle for equality. And as any good fair should look to the future, the WCE gave female artists—the most famous being painter Mary Cassatt—an unprecedented opportunity to participate. In all, there were more than 10,000 separate pieces of artwork on display, including Thomas Eakins's *The Gross Clinic*, Eastman Johnson's *The Cranberry Harvest*, and Winslow Homer's *Eight Bells*.

• **CELEBRITIES.** Before the rise of mass media, world's fairs were a great way for the rich and famous to get exposure. The presence of celebrities, in turn, added prestige to the events. Everyone from presidents and entertainers to business moguls and inventors were invited to participate. President Grover Cleveland opened the fair on May 1, 1893. Other celebrities who attended: Scott Joplin, who wrote ragtime compositions especially for the WCE (classical composer Antonín Dvořák wrote his *New World Symphony* for it too); Frederick Douglass, who gave a stirring speech condemning racism; and Susan B. Anthony, who attended the fair's "International Council of Women," which fought for women's suffrage.

• **ARCHITECTURE.** Every world's fair featured at least one new building or structure that the designers hoped would be

The investing term "blue chip" comes from the color of the highest value of poker chip, blue.

unlike anything that people had ever seen. And the best ones survived long after the fairs ended. Many internationally known landmarks—such as the Eiffel Tower in Paris and the Space Needle in Seattle—were built specifically for expositions. Unfortunately, most of the White City—including structures designed by world renowned architects Charles McKim, Louis Sullivan, and Richard Morris Hunt—was destroyed in a fire after the WCE was over, but a few structures were left standing, including the Palace of Fine Arts, a massive Roman-style building with columns in front and a domed roof. Today it houses Chicago's Museum of Science and Industry.

• **AN AMUSEMENT PARK.** In keeping with the spirit of new technology, the fairs tried to introduce new forms of amusement. The WCE's contribution was huge: They allowed a bridge designer from Pennsylvania named George Ferris to unveil his new "Ferris Wheel." At 264 feet tall, it dominated the White City skyline.

The Ferris Wheel was located in the Midway Plaisance, 80 acres devoted to entertainment. It featured carny games, a German beer hall, and for adults, exotic dancers. The Midway was extremely popular...and highly profitable. The take from general admission tickets wasn't enough to cover the high cost of building the fair—it was the revenue from the Midway that put the WCE in the black.

A FAIR TO REMEMBER

Though the WCE is long gone, its influence lives on. The White City, still deemed one of the largest artistic collaborations ever, inspired scores of architects. To get a feel of what the White City was like, take a walk through the buildings of the Smithsonian Institution in Washington, D.C. They were designed and built with the White City in mind. And the next time you're at a carnival, take a ride on the Ferris Wheel and then treat yourself to a burger and a soda...and maybe a box of Cracker Jack.

*   *   *

Fair fact: After the World's Columbian Expo refused to include Buffalo Bill Cody as an attraction, Cody set up his entire Wild West Show just outside the fairgrounds.

GHOSTVILLE, U.S.A.

*Everyone says they don't believe in ghosts. If that's so, then
we'd like know why so many people go to see haunted
houses like these ones...but we're afraid to ask.*

Alcatraz, the island prison near San Francisco, is no longer a working penitentiary. It's a tourist attraction. On the "night tour," guides say, you can hear the screams of long-dead prisoners, footsteps of jackbooted guards, and the slamming of jail doors that remain motionless before your eyes.

Big Bay Point Lighthouse in Michigan is haunted by the ghost of its first keeper, Will Prior. If you go—he's the red-haired ghost—they say he's harmless.

The old high school in Brunswick, Maine, is said to be haunted by a student who died there. She was rehearsing a play on a balcony when she fell to her death. The building is now used for school board meetings...which are sometimes interrupted by slamming doors and flying books.

Kemper Arena in Kansas City, Missouri, is the haunt of former WWF wrestler Owen Hart. During a 1999 match, Hart was being lowered from the ceiling to the ring when the cable holding his harness snapped. He fell to the floor and died instantly. In his wrestling trunks, mask, and harness, Hart has been seen floating near the ceiling.

Huntress Hall at Keene State College in New Hampshire is a freshman class dorm. Who else lives there? The college's benefactress (and the building's namesake), Harriet Huntress. Her wheelchair is stored in the attic, and students say it can be heard rolling around in the middle of the night.

Belcourt Castle, in Newport, Rhode Island, is famous for its ghosts, the spookiest of which is a spectral monk who appears in front of a lion statue, walks away from it, then disappears. Then he comes back and repeats the whole process over again.

The Lizzie Borden House in Fall River, Massachusetts, where Borden notoriously murdered her parents with an axe in 1892, is according to locals, home to a ghost. One of Borden's parents? No—it's the ghost of Lizzie's cat. The invisible feline is friendly: It likes to rub up against tourists' legs and sit in their laps.

At the **Vanderlip Mansion in Palos Verdes, California,** legend says Mrs. Vanderlip killed her entire family (including the dogs) and then committed suicide. At night, the faces of the family stare out of the windows. The dogs run around and bark at squirrels in the woods behind the house.

The **Hardee's in West Union, Iowa,** was built on top of a 19th-century cemetery—and ghosts now hang out at the restaurant. Employees find objects moved and hear their names being called when nobody's there, and the building has spots that stay icy cold year round.

At the **Radisson Suite Hotel in Ogden, Utah,** a ghost named Mrs. Eccles lives in the elevator. She died on the fifth floor, the story goes, so the elevator always stops there, whether anybody has pressed the button or not. You can't see Mrs. Eccles, but when she walks past, you can feel her brush against you and you can smell her perfume.

In **the desert outside Anthem, Arizona,** the ghosts of Native American warriors on horseback have been seen riding at night. And if they see anybody...they shoot (ghost) arrows at them.

At the **Gregory Graveyard in Lancaster, South Carolina,** you can hear the children laughing and a minister giving a eulogy over a grave. As you leave the graveyard, you may see a path to the left that wasn't there when you came in. If you walk down that path, you'll see several ghostly human figures. On Halloween night, the path is said to glow green.

*   *   *

"The artist alone sees spirits. But after he has told of their appearing to him, everybody sees them." —**Goethe**

GIMME SHELTER

In the 1950s, nuclear war with the Soviet Union seemed inevitable. But survival was possible. All you had to do was retreat into a super-fortified hole in the ground. Here's the story of the bomb shelter.

COLD COMFORT

In August 1949, the USSR detonated its first atomic bomb test. Suddenly, the United States wasn't the only superpower on Earth. It had a rival—one that could blow America to smithereens.

In 1950 President Harry Truman created the Federal Civil Defense Administration to prepare the populace for possible nuclear war. In addition to assigning "spotters" to watch the sky for enemy aircraft and making schools hold "duck-and-cover" drills, the FCDA made plans for a series of massive underground bomb shelters in major metropolitan areas—enough to house 50 million Americans (a third of the population) in the event of an attack. But after many scientists publicly doubted the effectiveness of the shelters' ability to protect against explosion, Congress rejected the FCDA's $3 billion shelter budget, allocating just $32 million. So instead of building giant bomb shelters, the FCDA simply encouraged people to build their own.

DIG YOUR OWN GRAVE

The FCDA distributed pamphlets containing bomb-shelter plans, and dozens of companies sprang up to build and install them for you. The most popular shelter choice: about 10-by-10 feet, big enough to hold a single family. Inside, it was stocked with rations—canned water and powdered food—as well as a Geiger counter and a battery-operated radio. The shelters were buried completely underground, usually in the backyard, and topped with a one-foot-thick concrete door that was in turn covered with a lead plank. Once safely inside, families would have to stay put for two weeks after an attack, which is how the long the government said it would take for radiation and fallout to disperse. The cost: anywhere from $100 for a bare-bones version to $5,000 for a prefabricated luxury model (with a telephone and working toilet).

If you couldn't afford to install a bunker in the backyard, the FCDA recommended walling off a section of your home's basement or improvising a shelter out of a septic tank. But an in-ground shelter was best: Based on murky data (because bomb shelters had never been tested in a nuclear attack), the FCDA estimated that underground shelters were 500 times more effective than above-ground protection.

The FCDA oversaw the conversion of thousands of base-ments, locker rooms, and boiler rooms in apartment complexes, public buildings, libraries, and schools into concrete-lined shel-ters that could hold hundreds of people. They were advertised on the outside of buildings with bright yellow "fallout shelter" signs. Inside were FCDA-issued rations, including things like 14-pound tins of "survival biscuits" and the SK IV—a chemical toilet sup-posedly able to service 50 people for two weeks.

BOMBING OUT

Just as they had backed the war effort during World War II, Americans got behind civil defense...and the "bomb culture" exploded.

• The FCDA predicted that larger, eastern cities such as Boston, New York, Washington, and Philadelphia were the most likely to be targeted by the Soviets. In those cities especially, "survival stores" opened, selling first-aid kits, canned water, fallout-protection suits, air filters, do-it-yourself shelter kits, and "underground rations" of dry goods made by General Foods and General Mills.

• *Popular Mechanics* and *Life* magazines printed shelter blueprints.

• People threw cocktail parties in their new backyard shelters to show them off.

• A farmer in Elkhorn, Iowa, built a shelter for his 200 cows.

• In Glendo, Wyoming, a potato cellar was turned into a shelter to house all of the town's 294 residents.

• In 1951 the *Wall Street Journal* predicted shelter sales could gross $20 billion in the next five years (if there was a next five years).

By 1958 tens of thousands of shelters of all kinds were built and ready to go. But the long-predicted nuclear war with the

Soviets never occurred. The hysteria cooled and the "fad" died (although there was a brief shelter-building revival during and immediately after the 1962 Cuban Missile Crisis). By the 1960s, there were over 200,000 bomb shelters across the country, capable of protecting 60 million Americans. But as the decade progressed, public and governmental anxiety shifted from a possible nuclear war with the Soviet Union to the spread of Communism in southeast Asia, a fear that culminated in the Vietnam War. Bomb shelters were quickly forgotten.

HOW RETRO

Interest in shelters was renewed briefly in 1983. President Ronald Reagan announced a plan to revamp, restock, and prepare existing shelters for use in case of nuclear war, and to build new shelters to protect every American. That was something the FCDA couldn't do at the peak of the 1950s scare. But the plan died when relations between the USSR and the U.S. began to warm in 1985. That left more than 100,000 backyard shelters all over the country. What happened to them?

• A large one in Dallas was converted into a theater.

• A shelter for city officials in Oklahoma City was converted into the area's 911-dispatch center.

• A fallout shelter built under the University of Nebraska at Lincoln was converted into a state-of-the-art emergency preparedness center in 1999, just in time for the Y2K crisis (the possibility that the nation's computer-based infrastructure would collapse when the calendar turned over to the year 2000). But that crisis never materialized either.

• Some were converted into wine cellars or fruit cellars; most were forgotten and filled up with groundwater over the years. (If you live in a house that's old enough, you might have a "lost" bomb shelter in your yard.)

The Soviet Union collapsed in 1991, ending the Communist era in Europe. But the U.S. still had food rations left over from the 1950s. They were still showing up at food banks and soup kitchens as late as 1993—the supplies meant to help save Americans from the Soviets had actually outlasted the Soviet Union.

ELECTION FOLLIES

*Since presidential campaigns all seem to have their own official
"campaign songs," we thought it would be fun to assign
some song lyrics to these strange election stories.*

HE'S A REAL NOWHERE MAN

Randy Wooten, a karaoke bar owner and mayoral candidate from Waldenburg, Arkansas (pop. 80), cried foul when he was told that he didn't receive a single vote in the 2006 election. He knew that he got at least one—his own. Wooten also claimed that "about eight or nine" of his friends voted for him, too, which would have made it a close election, as only 36 votes were cast. Wooten's wife said that she voted for him, too, and she blames the city's brand-new touch-screen voting machines for the screwup. "When you touched one name, it would jump to the next. If you didn't touch it just right, exactly where you were supposed to, it would jump. It makes you wonder about all of them." After a recount—which he lost—Wooten said he's done with politics, adding, "After a while, it just gets tiresome."

GROUND CONTROL TO MAJOR TOM

Online visitors to the reelection Web site of Jyrki Kasvi, a member of parliament in Finland, can read about his platform in Finnish, Swedish, English…and Klingon. "Some people say that combining *Star Trek* and politics is blasphemy," Kasvi said, but he did it to show that "politicians can laugh at themselves." He wasn't able to post a direct translation, however, as there are no Klingon words for "tolerance" or "green" (Kasvi is a member of the Green League). He won.

SIGN, SIGN, EVERYWHERE A SIGN

On the morning of the Fitchburg, Wisconsin, mayoral election in 2007, incumbent Tom Clauder was driving past city hall in his pickup truck when he saw a woman pulling one of his campaign signs out of the ground. Angry, he made a U-turn and chased the woman as she drove away. Clauder got right on the sign puller's tail and followed her through an adjoining parking lot. Both drivers called the police. It turned out that the woman was Jessica Nytes, the wife of Jeff Nytes, the other mayoral candidate. Nytes claimed that his wife yanked the sign because, according to campaign rules, signs are supposed to be at least 33 feet from the center of the highway, and this one wasn't. She was simply performing a "public service," Nytes said. Clauder told reporters that the sign-pulling incident was "low, really low," while Nytes countered that as many as 50 of *his* roadside campaign signs had been stolen in the week leading up to the election. Most experts say that yard signs have little effect effect on local elections. Either way, Clauder won by a significant margin.

WE ARE THE WORLD

While traveling across the United States in May 2004, President Bush's campaign bus proudly displayed a large sign that read: "Yes, America can!" The statement—which reaffirmed Bush's pledge to keep jobs in the United States—was called into question when reporters discovered that the bus was actually manufactured by Prevost Car, an auto company based in Canada, which is jointly owned by Volvo (based in Sweden) and Henley's Group PLC (from England). When asked at a press conference for an explanation, a Bush campaign spokesman assured reporters that "many of the bus's components are American-made."

SATURDAY NIGHT'S ALRIGHT FOR FIGHTING

While debating an election reform bill in Taiwan's parliament in May 2007, dozens of lawmakers from opposing parties started brawling. They sprayed each other with water, threw punches, and even hurled their shoes at each other. And this was not an isolated incident—there have been many brawls since the 1980s. It turned out, though, that the brawls are staged for media coverage. Lawmakers will call each other the night before and ask that they wear soft running shoes to work. Opposing party members have even been spotted having drinks together after the melees. Why do they do it? To prove to their constituents that they will fight for them. "They just want to steal the spotlight going into the primaries," said People First Party member Lee Hung-chun, who is ashamed of the tactic. "Parliament," he argues, "should be a sacred and noble place."

It takes about 600 grapes to make a bottle of wine. (And a bottle.)

HISTORICAL BLUNDERS

*Here are some critical decisions in history that came
back to bite the decision-makers on the butt.*

BAD KITTY

When the Black Plague devastated Europe in the 14th
century, many people assumed it was caused by witchcraft.
And cats, with their glowing eyes and night-prowling habits, were
thought to be tools of witches. Thousands of cats (and a lot of
women thought to be witches) were slaughtered. Scientists later
determined that the plague was transmitted by fleas that lived on
rats. Had all those cats not been slaughtered, they might have
been alive to kill all those rats, which could have vastly reduced
the death toll of approximately 30 million.

THE UNTALENTED MR. RIPLEY

Colonel James Ripley, chief of U.S. Army Ordnance in the
Civil War, outfitted Union troops with short-range "smoothbore"
rifles that dated to the War of 1812. He declined to buy the
more modern, long-range Enfield rifles on the grounds that they
were too expensive and made in England, whom Ripley still
hated fiercely, even 50 years after the War of 1812. But Enfield
found a buyer: the Confederate army. At the First Battle of Bull
Run in July 1861, the Confederacy devastated the Union troops
and suffered a third fewer casualties because their Enfield rifles
could hit targets at 800 yards, compared to the Ripley's 500-
yard guns.

URBAN WARFARE

In the 1450s, the gunsmith Urban of Hungary crafted "the Basilic," the largest cannon ever built. The 19-ton behemoth required
100 men to move and could shoot a 1,200-pound cannonball over
a mile. Urban tried to sell the Basilic to Byzantine emperor Constantine XI, but Constantine turned it down on grounds that the
cannon was too expensive. So Urban sold it to Ottoman Turk
leader Sultan Mehmed II, who used the cannon to blow down the
walls of Constantinople in 1453 and take over the city.

In 1961 the U.S. launched a male chimpanzee called Ham into space. He made it back safely.

CLARKE'S BARBS

Choice observations from Arthur C. Clarke, author of 2001: A Space Odyssey *and one of the most influential science-fiction writers of all time.*

"At the present rate of progress, it is almost impossible to imagine any technical feat that cannot be achieved within the next few hundred years."

"It may be that the old astrologers had the truth exactly reversed: The time may come when men control the destinies of stars."

"If we have learned one thing from the history of invention and discovery, it is that, in the long run—and often in the short one—the most daring prophecies seem laughably conservative."

"The only way to discover the limits of the possible is to go beyond them into the impossible."

"New ideas pass through three periods: It can't be done; It probably can be done, but it's not worth doing; I knew it was a good idea all along."

"As our own species is in the process of proving, one cannot have superior science and inferior morals. The combination is unstable and self-destroying."

"The truth, as always, will be far stranger."

"The greatest tragedy in mankind's entire history may be the hijacking of morality by religion."

"I don't pretend we have all the answers. But the questions are certainly worth thinking about."

"If there are any gods whose chief concern is man, they can't be very important gods."

"Information is not knowledge, knowledge is not wisdom, and wisdom is not foresight. But information is the first essential step to all of these."

"The intelligence of the planet is constant, and the population is growing."

"We seldom stop to think that we are still creatures of the sea, able to leave it only because, from birth to death, we wear the water-filled space suits of our skins."

"I'm sure the universe is full of intelligent life. It's just been too intelligent to come here."

The entire area of Japan (pop. 127 million) is slightly smaller than California (pop. 34 million).

IMPOSTORS!

Because for some folks, being yourself just isn't quite enough.

MODEL IMPOSTOR

When a last-minute photo spread of a handsome male model—dressed only in his underwear and lying next to a bottle of Gucci perfume—arrived at the offices of the Swiss news magazine *SonntagsZeitung*, the advertising department looked it over, liked it, and turned it into a two-page spread. As per instructions from the model (via a phone call), the magazine then billed Gucci 60,000 Swiss francs ($50,000) to run the ad in the February 20, 2007 issue. The next day, the Gucci people saw the ad—and then the invoice—and refused to pay. Why? They had no idea who the model was or where the photos came from. The magazine explained that the ad came in too close to deadline to be verified, then apologized to Gucci and ate the cost. "We're going to try and get the money back from this guy, but we don't rate our chances," said a magazine spokesman. Even months later, no one knows who the mystery man is, but they do know he's struck before. He once tried to book a concert for himself in Switzerland, claiming to be the popular Puerto Rican singer Chayanne. He almost made it, too, until the real Chayanne found out he was booked to play in Switzerland. Yet even though thousands of people have seen his face (thanks to the Gucci ad), the anonymous model remains... anonymous.

MILITARY IMPOSTOR

In 1972 Peter Bennett tried to join Australia's army but was denied for medical reasons. Over the next few decades he tried his hand at truck driving and bank robbing (for which he was caught and jailed), but never gave up his military dreams. In May 2005, the 54-year-old civilian purchased a tailor-made Air Force uniform along with real medals and badges, then posed as a warrant officer at the RAAF Base at Point Cook, Australia. After smooth-talking a clerk, Bennett was issued a temporary Department of Defense ID. Thus begun his 10-month fantasy military career. In September he waltzed into a formal dress function at the base, proudly displaying

---

The Homer? The U.S. Mint once considered producing doughnut-shaped coins.

a Vietnam Medal, a National Medal, a South Vietnamese Star, and an Infantry Combat Badge. He stayed long into the night, telling made-up war stories, even sharing a few laughs with Air Vice Marshal Geoffrey Shepherd, the chief of Australia's air force. Bennett acted so comfortable in his role that no one questioned it when he later applied to become a member of the Australian Defense Force security team. Bennett's house of cards began to tumble the following March, when a guard ran a routine background check and found no record of a Peter Bennett prior to May 2005. When confronted and asked to give proof of his identity, Bennett said he would go and fetch the proper documents...and then vanished. Six months later, Australian federal police caught up with him and found his uniform and medals, but no documents. At his "court-martial," Bennett pled guilty to impersonating a public official and was sentenced to 18 months of community service.

CONSTABLE IMPOSTOR

Lee MacInnes, a 19-year-old from Edinburgh, Scotland, really wanted to impress a teenage girl he had a crush on. Knowing that women are often drawn to men in uniform, MacInnes dressed up as a constable (police officer) and drove his Alfa Romeo around town—he even attached flashing blue lights to his roof and pulled a driver over (letting him off with a warning). There aren't too many Alfa Romeos with flashing blue lights on the road, so it wasn't hard for the *real* constables to catch up with MacInnes. The lovelorn teen was sentenced to 160 hours of community service...working as an "acting coach" at the police department. (No word on whether the girl was impressed.)

COLLEGIATE IMPOSTOR

On September 18, 2006, a tall, dark-haired teenager named Azia Kim showed up at the Kimball dormitory on the campus of Stanford University. She introduced herself to two girls, telling them there had been a technical mix-up and she hadn't been assigned a room yet—could she stay with them? Kim seemed nice enough, so the girls let her sleep on their floor. A few days later, Kim told them that she really didn't like her assigned roommate, so they said she could stay there for the rest of the term. Kim bought textbooks, ate lunch in the cafeteria, and studied for her exams in the

In 1933 Syria banned yo-yos, blaming their up-and-down action...

Student Union. But she never *took* any exams, because the 18-year-old wasn't really enrolled at Stanford. And when she thought her first set of roommates had started to get suspicious, Kim went across campus and talked her way into another dorm—the Okada dorm for Asian-Americans. "She came to my room and asked if anyone wanted a roommate," said Jennifer Lee, a resident advisor. "She seemed like a typical Stanford student, dressed in jeans and a T-shirt, so I just told her which rooms were available." Because Kim didn't have a student ID or a key, she had to sneak into the cafeteria to get her meals and climb through the window of her dorm room when it was locked. She even joined the ROTC at nearby Santa Clara University, providing military instructors with forged transcripts that showed she'd made the Dean's list.

In May 2007, some resident advisors were discussing Kim when they realized that no one had ever seen her in a classroom. Within hours, police escorted her off campus. Her friends still don't know why she did it (Kim refused to talk to the press), but they speculate that she was under immense parental pressure to attend a top-tier college. No charges were filed by Stanford or the ROTC, which simply called it a "harmless prank."

BEAUTY QUEEN IMPOSTOR

Miss Virtual Yakutia is an online beauty contest that has taken place in Russia each year since 1999. Contestants send in pictures and bios, online users vote for their favorites, and the top 10 then compete for the crown. In the 2007 contest, a beautiful woman named "Angela Adamova" received more votes than hundreds of other contestants—enough to reach the finals. When the organizers looked for more information about the top 10, they discovered something odd about Adamova: She didn't exist. A little more digging revealed the truth: "She" was actually a 25-year-old man named Oleg Goncharov. As a lark, he'd gone to a beauty parlor to get made up as a woman and hired a photographer to take some glamour shots. The stylist and photographer did such a good job that online voters were fooled. They also liked the comment from "Angela" in which she said, "I'm just trying to make every step in life brighter and more remarkable for myself and for people who surround me. Give me your vote and I won't disappoint you!" Voters were probably disappointed when "Angela" was disqualified.

BATHROOM GRAFFITI

Want to find the meaning of life? Just check out these real examples of bathroom graffiti collected from the hallowed walls of the world's stalls.

"Just when I was getting used to yesterday, along came today."

"Help! The paranoids are after me!"

"If life is a waste of time, and time is a waste of life, then let's all get wasted together and have the time of our lives."

(Written on the left wall): "TOILET TENNIS Look right." *(Written on the right wall):* "Look left."

"Make love, not war...Hell, do both—get married!"

"This ~~is~~ was the cleanest bathroom wall I've ever seen!"

"Everything you know is wrong...even this."

"Friends don't let friends take home ugly men."

"I feel more like I did when I got in here than I do now."

"Cakes: 66 cents Upside down cakes: 99 cents"

"All's FEAR in love and war."

"Wash your hands thoroughly—you don't know where the soap has been."

"Department of Redundancy Department"

"I used to be a werewolf, but I'm alright nowwwwwwwhh!"

"Toilet camera for researching purposes only, go about your business."

"To do is to be. —Socrates To be is to do. —Sartre Do be do be doo. —Sinatra"

"Don't wait for your ship to come in... Swim out to it."

"Every time you flush, an angel gets its wings."

"Proofread carefully to see if you any words out."

"Don't beam me up now, Scottie, I'm taking a sh…"

"Happiness can't buy money."

"The Mona Lisa was framed!"

"Deja Moo: The feeling you've heard this bull before."

Q: **What's a *swallet*?** A: The place where a stream disappears underground.

THE SWEET SINGER OF MICHIGAN

Who is the woman widely considered to be the worst poet in American history? Julia A. Moore (1847–1920).

DIAMOND IN THE ROUGH

In 1877 a Cleveland, Ohio, publisher named James F. Ryder happened to get ahold of a pamphlet titled *The Sentimental Songbook*, a collection of 37 poems composed by Julia A. Moore, a farmer's wife and mother of several children living in Edgerton, Michigan. The pamphlet's first two editions had been sold only locally, but as Ryder flipped through his copy he immediately saw the commercial potential and ordered a new printing. He mailed copies to every major newspaper in the country, along with a letter that hyped Moore's work with a sales pitch worthy of a health tonic. *The Sentimental Songbook* "will prove a lift to the overtaxed brain," he wrote. "It may divert the despondent from suicide. It should enable the reader to forget the 'stringency,' and guide the thoughts into pleasanter channels. It is productive of good to humanity."

READ ALL ABOUT IT

Many critics who received the letter saw the same thing that Ryder saw and praised *The Sentimental Songbook* effusively in their pages. "We believe in the Sweet Singer of Michigan," wrote *The Hartford Daily Times*. "To this author, manifestly all things are possible."

Even Mark Twain was a fan. He is believed to have based Emmeline Grangerford, a poet character in *Huckleberry Finn,* on Moore, and 20 years after *The Sentimental Songbook* hit bookshop shelves he was still singing Moore's praises. "*The Sentimental Songbook* has long been out of print, and has been forgotten by the world in general, but not by me. I carry it with me always," Twain wrote in 1897.

So what was it that Ryder, Twain, and the critics saw in Moore's work? "It is a well-known fact among critics that two kinds of poetry, and only two, go [well] in the public estimation and are worth anything in the market," Ryder explained in his memoirs in 1902. "One kind is very good and the other kind is very bad."

Moore's poetry was *terrible*. Her grammar was self-taught, many of her words didn't rhyme, and she was so obsessed with morbid topics—deadly epidemics, train wrecks, children choking on their dinners, people perishing in fires or being crushed to death by crowds, you name it—that her work was funny in ways that she never intended. "Julia is worse than a Gatling gun," another reporter wrote in the *Laramie Boomerang*. "I have counted 21 killed and nine wounded in the small volume she has given to the public."

TWO THUMBS UP

It's difficult to say whether a poet as bad as Julia A. Moore could achieve cult-figure status today. The critics would probably just say she was bad, readers would stay away, and that would be the end of it. And to be sure, Moore got plenty of scathing reviews. The *Connecticut Post* called *The Sentimental Songbook* "rare food for the lunatic," and the *Rochester Democrat* wrote that "Shakespeare, could he read it, would be glad that he was dead."

But many other newspapers around the country adopted a tongue-in-cheek attitude and praised the book instead of condemning it, in the hope that readers might pick up a copy and join in the fun. The *Worcester Daily Press* wrote that Moore's work "clutches the tendrils of the soul as a garden rake clutches a hop vine, and hauls the reader into a closer sympathy than that which exists between a man and his undershirt."

Was it the negative reviews that did it? Was it the "good" ones? Or was it just the astonishing power of Moore's eccentric verse? Whatever it was, *The Sentimental Songbook* caught on with the public, selling thousands of copies and becoming one of the bestselling poetry books of its day.

OF COURSE I'M FAMOUS

Moore's fame came as no surprise to her. She had always believed that she had talent, and though she understood that her writing was popular, it took her several months for her to figure out *why* it was popular.

It was probably the few public readings she gave that did it— her audiences laughed so hard at verses that weren't supposed to be funny that she eventually realized that they were there to make fun of her, not to celebrate her genius. Not that she let her audiences see her humiliation. "You have come here and paid twenty-five cents to see a fool," she shouted back to the audience in December 1878. "I receive seventy-five dollars, and see a whole houseful of fools!"

TIME'S UP

In 1878 Moore published two more books of verse: *The Sweet Singer of Michigan: Later Poems of Julia A. Moore* (which she prefaced with 74 pages of seemingly positive reviews of the first book) and *A Few Choice Words to the Public With New and Original Poems*. But they didn't sell nearly as well as *The Sentimental Songbook* did, and by now both she and her husband Fred were becoming embarrassed at being the butt of so many jokes. Moore continued to write occasionally when she felt inspired, but other than a few pieces that appeared in small journals and newspapers, she never published again.

By the time Moore died in August 1920 at the age of 72, the public had largely forgotten her...but the newspapers hadn't. When they learned of her passing, many sang the Sweet Singer's praises one last time. "In absolute good faith she had given the world her poem creations," the *Boston Evening Transcript* wrote, "and little did she realize that many poets of greater worth have done the same and fared far worse."

IN HER OWN WORDS

A few choice excerpts from some of Julia's finest works:

...Those little girls will not forget
The day little Hattie died,
For she was with them when she fell in a fit,
While playing by their side....

—*Hattie House*

To see the people run for life;
Up and down the blazing streets,
To find then, their escape cut off
By the fiery flaming sheets.

—*The Great Chicago Fire*

Quick! Convert –40°C into Fahrenheit! Answer: –40°F. (It's the one temp that's the same in both.)

'Tis said that Brigham Young is dead,
The man with nineteen wives;
The greatest Mormon of the West
Is dead, no more to rise;
He left behind his nineteen wives
Forsaken and forlorn;
The papers state his death was caused
By eating too much green corn.
—*Brigham Young's Wives*

It was the eleventh of December,
On a cold and windy day,
Just at the close of evening,
When the sunlight fades away;
Little Henry he was dying,
In his little crib he lay.
—*Little Henry*

This prison was a horrid place,
Many brave boys died there,
In rags and filth and wretchedness,
They died for want of care.
Many a brave and noble man,
As he lay sick and sore,
Was thinking of his friends and home
He never would see more.
—*Libby Prison*

…One morning in April, a short time ago,
Libbie was active and gay;
Her Saviour called her, she had to go,
E're the close of that pleasant day.
While eating dinner, this dear little child
Was choked on a piece of beef.…
—*Little Libbie*

And now kind friends, what I have wrote,
I hope you will pass o'er
And not criticise, as some have done,
Hitherto herebefore.
—*To My Friends and Critics*

Family fireworks? 80% of Americans spend the 4th of July with their relatives.

WHO SPEAKS LATIN?

Latin was the language of the ancient Romans and is the root of several modern languages, including French, Italian, and Spanish. Because Latin itself is no longer commonly used, it's considered a "dead" language, but that's not exactly true. In fact, you probably speak Latin every day without even knowing it. And if you do know these Latin words and phrases, do you know what they really mean?

BONA FIDE
Translation: "in good faith"
Everyday meaning: Genuine or well-intentioned

PRO BONO
Translation: Short for *pro bono publico*—"for the public good"
Everyday meaning: Work done for free

AD NAUSEAM
Translation: "to the point of nausea"
Everyday meaning: Doing something until people are sick of it

MEA CULPA
Translation: "my fault"
Everyday meaning: An admission of guilt

NON SEQUITUR
Translation: "does not follow"
Everyday meaning: A phrase that seems absurd because it doesn't make sense within the context

DE FACTO
Translation: "from the fact"
Everyday meaning: In reality, or in fact

ALTER EGO
Translation: "other I"
Everyday meaning: One's second self or alternate personality

IN VITRO
Translation: "in glass"
Everyday meaning: A non-natural, laboratory setting

MODUS OPERANDI (M.O.)
Translation: "method of operating"
Everyday meaning: A pattern of procedure (often criminal)

MAGNA CUM LAUDE
Translation: "with great praise"
Everyday meaning: A high honor given to college students who graduate with a superior academic record

AD HOC
Translation: "to this"
Everyday meaning: Quickly thrown together or improvised

MAGNUM OPUS
Translation: "great work"
Everyday meaning: A masterpiece

STATUS QUO
Translation: "fixed place or thing"
Everyday meaning: Things as they are

ET CETERA (ETC.)
Translation: "and the rest"
Everyday meaning: And others (especially of the same kind)

PERSONA NON GRATA
Translation: "person not pleasing"
Everyday meaning: An unwelcome person

RIGOR MORTIS
Translation: "stiffness of death"
Everyday meaning: Temporary stiffness of muscles after a person dies

AD INFINITUM
Translation: "to infinity"
Everyday meaning: Going on forever

SEMPER FIDELIS
Translation: "always faithful"
Everyday meaning: Extreme loyalty—the motto of the U.S. Marine Corps

CAVEAT EMPTOR
Translation: "let the buyer beware"
Everyday meaning: Be careful before you buy—you bear the final responsibility for any purchases you make

ALMA MATER
Translation: "nourishing mother"
Everyday meaning: An affectionate name for the school you once attended

PATER FAMILIAS
Translation: "father of the family"
Everyday meaning: Master of the house

ET AL
Translation: Short for *et alia*, "and other things"
Everyday meaning: The rest

SIC
Translation: "thus"
Everyday meaning: A publishing term meaning "printed as it was found," even if it was misspelled

Last word in Kurt Vonnegut's book *Breakfast of Champions*: "ETC."

RANDOM ORIGINS

Yet again the BRI asks—and answers—the question:
Where does all this stuff come from?

TIKI BARS

The very first was Don the Beachcomber, opened in Hollywood in 1933 by Ernest Gantt, a bohemian who had traveled the South Seas and brought back all kinds of idols, masks, and other relics. He used them to decorate his restaurant/bar, which created a singular ambience that attracted a movie-star clientele. In 1944 Victor Bergeron, owner of a generic Oakland, California, bar called Hinky Dinks, visited Don the Beachcomber, fell in love with the format, and immediately redid his bar as a Polynesian restaurant, adding to the walls thatch, tiki statues, masks, idols, and torches. He renamed the establishment Trader Vic's. Both restaurants became chains (Gantt even legally changed his name to Donn Beach) with locations all over the country. The food: Chinese cuisine, still exotic to most Americans in the 1950s. Added flourishes like colorful fruit and serving food aflame made it even more exciting.

ICE CAPADES

In 1940 John H. Harris, owner of a minor-league hockey team in Pittsburgh, began booking former Olympic figure skaters to perform during game intermissions as a way to increase attendance. It worked: Families (not just hockey-loving men) packed the arena. As Harris added comedians, jugglers, clowns, and barrel jumpers, other arenas became interested, so Harris decided to take the show on tour (Boston Garden owner Walter Brown combined "ice" with "escapades" to come up with the name "Ice Capades"). On November 5, 1940, a 21-city tour began. For the next 50 years, the Ice Capades toured the world with an evolving format that included everything from movie-themed shows to Olympic-skater showcases. But in the 1980s, the popularity of the Ice Capades dropped sharply, facing new competition. Fans of Olympic-level skating could see Scott Hamilton's Stars on Ice, while families had Disney on Ice. The Ice Capades died in 1991.

"HE SLUD INTO THIRD"

Verbal gems actually uttered on the air by sports announcers.

"Can you felt the electricity?"
—**Michael Irvin,
NFL analyst**

"This evening is a very different evening from the morning that we had this morning."
—**David Coleman,
BBC Sports announcer**

"Last night I neglected to mention something that bears repeating."
—**Ron Fairly, Seattle
Mariners announcer**

"These American horses know the fences like the back of their hands."
—**Harvey Smith,
British horse-racing analyst**

"Well, I see in the game in Minnesota that Terry Felton has relieved himself on the mound in the second inning."
—**Fred White, Kansas
City Royals announcer**

"Watch Darren Daulton use his mitt like a glove."
—**Tim McCarver**

"He hit him like a two hundred pound ton of bricks."
—**Joe Theismann**

"Those two are very much alike in a lot of similarities."
—**Casey Stengel**

"One good bit of news for England is that Ian Botham's groin is back to full strength."
—**Eleanor Oldroyd,
British sports analyst**

"Enos Cabell started out here with the Astros and before that he was with the Orioles."
—**Jerry Coleman,
San Diego Padres announcer**

"The Dallas Cowboys have two kinds of plays in their offense: running plays and passing plays."
—**John Madden**

"Nolan Ryan is pitching much better now that he has his curveball straightened out."
—**Joe Garagiola**

"Other than being castrated, things have gone quite well for Funny Cide."
—**Kenny Mayne,
ESPN analyst**

"At the finish, it was all over."
—**Jim Watt, boxing
announcer**

On average, a person can hold their breath for 1 minute. (World record: 9 min., 8 sec.)

THE MOST POPULAR BABY NAMES IN...

In the United States, it's Emily and Jacob. But in...

Afghanistan: Gzifa for girls; Adjani for boys

Australia: Olivia and Jack

Brazil: Maria and Sterling

Chile: Costanza and Benjamin

Denmark: Mathilde and Magnus

Finland: Emma and Veeti

France: Camille and Lucas

Germany: Marie and Max

Hungary: Anna and Bence

Iceland: Anna and Sigurour

Ireland: Emma and Sean

Italy: Maria and Giuseppe

Japan: Misaki and Shun

Lithuania: Gabija and Jonas

The Netherlands: Sanne and Daan

Norway: Emma and Markus

Portugal: Maria and João

Quebec: Mégane and William

Scotland: Sophie and Lewis

Slovenia: Nika and Luka

Spain: Lucia and Alejandro

Turkey: Zeynep and Mehmet

Above-average Joe: Superman's full Earth name is Clark *Joseph* Kent.

DUMB CROOKS

Even more proof that crime doesn't pay.

NEXT TIME, TAKE OFF THE BLINDERS

"In November 2006, Derek Pierson tried to rob a Shreveport, Louisiana, convenience store. He walked in, looked directly at the clerk and told her to 'give (the money) up.' What he didn't notice was that a member of an armed robbery task force—wearing a shirt marked 'Shreveport Police' on the front and back as well as 'Police' on the sleeves—was standing in an aisle 10 feet away. The agent, who had stopped by on a routine check, pulled his gun and arrested Pierson without incident. The officer described him as looking 'like a deer caught in the headlights.' 'I guess I picked the wrong place,' Pierson told police. He faces up to 10 years in prison."

—*Shreveport Times*

TALKING TRASH

"Minutes after getting a report of two men trying to break into a parking meter, police began looking for suspects. It wasn't hard. Witnesses say one of the suspects wore an all-black outfit, while the other was dressed in a bathrobe. Police located one likely suspect near the scene of the crime. They began searching the neighborhood for a second suspect when they were attracted to a garbage dumpster by the sound of a ringing cell phone. When officers lifted the lid of the bin, they found the second man inside. Both suspects were taken into custody without incident."

—*Halifax Daily News*

IGNORING THE RULE OF THUMB

"A robbery at a Git-N-Go Convenience Store on the south side of Des Moines was called off for lack of convincing theatrics. 'Well, I could tell he didn't have a gun,' said Terry Cook, a clerk at the store. 'I knew it was his finger. I could see his thumb sticking out of his coat pocket.' The would-be robber, who acted tough and even inserted a harsh expletive in his demand for cash, wanted to argue. 'It is a gun,' he told Cook. 'No it isn't,' Cook replied. The frustrated suspect left the store but paused a moment in the parking lot, perhaps to go over in his mind the argument he'd just lost. He left the scene just before police arrived."

—DribbleGlass.com

THIEF-TRACKING MADE EASIER

"Kurt Husfeldt, 46, and two others were arrested in Lindenhurst, New York, in January 2007 in possession of 14 stolen electronic devices that they apparently assumed were cell phones. However, they were global positioning devices from a nearby municipal facility, and police had followed their signals to Husfeldt's home."

—News of the Weird

GOOGLED

"Kevin Fitzpatrick, 32, was arrested in connection with a 2005 bank robbery after leaving a trail of cyberclues. Police said Fitzpatrick was staying with a woman at the time of the Norwich robbery and spent a great deal of time on her computer. He borrowed her car the day of the robbery and returned with a lot of cash, claiming he won it at a casino. Police say Fitzpatrick walked into a Liberty Bank branch and handed a teller a note demanding money. A week later, the woman friend contacted police, saying she recognized Fitzpatrick from a surveillance photo on a newspaper Web site. A police search of the computer revealed numerous searches concerning bank robberies, including one for 'Norwich bank robbery' and another for 'how to rob a bank.'"

—Associated Press

BANKS FOR TELLING ME

"A would-be robber was arrested after he tried to hold up his local town hall, mistaking it for a bank, Austrian police said. Wearing a mask and waving a toy pistol, the unemployed man burst into the town hall in the village of Poggersdorf and shouted, 'Hold-up, hold-up!' The building has a sign indicating there is an ATM on the outside wall, police said. He realized his mistake when an employee explained to him where he was, and then fled to a nearby woods. The 34-year-old man was arrested when he came back later to pick up his motorbike, which he had parked outside the town hall."

—Reuters

The straight dope: For 3,000 years, hemp was the world's largest agricultural crop.

THE NOBEL PRIZE SPERM BANK

*In 1979 a man who thought humanity was being overrun by idiots
sought to even the score by breeding super-babies. Here's
the amazing story of Robert Graham.*

WHO'S YOUR DADDY?

Hermann J. Muller, an American scientist who worked in the Soviet Union during the 1930s, was a pioneer in the science of *eugenics*: selective breeding designed to create a pure, superior race of people. (Another supporter of eugenics: Hitler.)

Muller wanted to create his master race by impregnating Russian women from a sperm bank stocked with samples from the Soviet Union's top scientists. The hoped-for result: ultra-smart babies. Unfortunately for Muller, the technology required for storing specimens had not yet been invented.

GRAHAM: QUACKERS?

American scientist and businessman Robert K. Graham was an admirer of Muller. In the mid-1960s, Graham became convinced that dumb people were corrupting the gene pool and taking over the world. Graham, the father of eight, believed that intelligent people had an *obligation* to breed in order to offset all the stupidity. The answer, he thought, was sperm banks, which were brand new at the time (the first two opened in 1965—one in Tokyo, Japan, and the other in Iowa City, Iowa). But Graham didn't have the money to start one, so instead he started a charity to finance the rearing expenses of children born to cash-strapped college professors and scientists.

In 1978 Graham sold his company, Armorlite (through which he'd invented plastic eyeglass lenses), to the 3M Company for $70 million. That was more than enough to start a sperm bank. So in 1979 Graham, now 74 years old, placed a half dozen liquid nitrogen freezer tanks in a storage shed on his San Diego, California, estate and named it "The Hermann J. Muller Repository for Germinal Choice." Later that year, he dropped Muller's name and moved his sperm freezers to an office in nearby Escondido.

It was time for Graham to start recruiting world-class "daddies." And the only sperm he'd accept would be from Nobel Prize-winning scientists. Graham solicited the 30 Nobel laureates who lived in California. Most were appalled by the idea, but three actually agreed to participate...on the condition of anonymity.

LIQUID ASSETS

Graham didn't publicly announce the existence of the Repository until a 1980 interview with the *Los Angeles Times*. There was instant backlash —Graham was compared to Hitler, and the media nicknamed the Repository "the Nobel Prize Sperm Bank." Graham was forced to hire armed guards to protect the bank. It didn't get any better when physicist William Shockley revealed himself to be one of the three donors. Shockley was a brilliant physicist, but was better known for his racist sociological theories—he once told a reporter that because African-Americans were reproducing faster than whites, America's collective IQ was dropping.

The media furor died down by late 1980, but Graham suddenly found himself with no donors. Not wanting to be associated with Shockley, the other two of Graham's three donors pulled out of the project. Then Shockley did, too, considering himself too old (70) to produce viable sperm. Graham was forced to abandon the Nobel-only concept and opened the bank up to athletes, businessmen, and lesser scientists, provided they had a genius-level IQ.

Graham and his assistant, Paul Smith, approached candidates at scientific conventions, contacted professors and doctoral students at the UC Berkeley, and wrote to men they found in *Who's Who of Science*. They had some success—about 19 donors had signed up by 1983. But they had to be even more selective when female applicants—answering an ad in a Mensa magazine—told Graham and Smith that they wanted their genius-donors to be, if at all possible, tall, athletic, and handsome.

SOMETHING FOR THE LADIES

Graham required female applicants to be married (to infertile men), well educated, and financially stable. (One other requirement: Graham's wife asked him to exclude lesbians.) Soon he had a

---

The average bee can travel up to 11 mph...about 4 times as fast as the average human.

waiting list. Several hundred women applied; only two were rejected: a woman with depression and a diabetic.

Potential mothers chose donors from a typed, mimeographed catalog that listed donors' personal details, including general health facts, eye color, ancestry, height, and weight. Each donor was assigned a color and a number and given a summary:

• "Mr. Fuchsia No. 1 is an Olympic gold medalist. Tall, dark, handsome, bright, a successful businessman and author."

• "Mr. White No. 6 is ruggedly handsome and outgoing, a university professor and expert marksman who enjoys the classics."

Once a woman was accepted, vials of frozen sperm were mailed to her doctor, who would then thaw out the sperm and implant it during ovulation. Fertilization would often take several tries; 75% of applicants never got pregnant at all. At least it was free—Graham personally paid all Repository expenses at a cost of more than $500,000 per year. He considered it charity work. (Sperm donors weren't paid.)

FROZEN IN TIME

In total, the Repository for Germinal Choice resulted in 218 children. Did they all turn out to be geniuses? It's impossible to say. Only one child conceived via the Repository has identified himself. Doron Blake, born in August 1982, was a child math and music prodigy and attended prestigious Reed University. No other mothers or children have ever come forward. And other than Shockley, no donor has come forward, either.

Robert K. Graham died in 1997 at the age of 92. He considered leaving a trust to continue to fund the sperm bank, but left the choice to his wife and children. Having never liked the project, they closed down the Repository for Germinal Choice for good in 1999. All the sperm left behind in freezer tanks—along with all of the bank's records about the identities of its donors, the mothers, and the offspring—was destroyed.

Today's sperm banks are open to to the general population (no IQ test required). Potential parents still choose from boastful anonymous donor "catalogs." But modern sperm banks exist to help people who would otherwise be unable to have children—a far cry from Graham's goal of intellectually dominant super kids.

Sad fact: Since 1495, the world has never seen 25 consecutive years without at least one war.

WORD ORIGINS

Language changes over time, as old words morph into new ones. But where do they all come from? Here are some more interesting origins.

LEPRECHAUN

Meaning: A small, mischievous sprite who can reveal hidden treasure to those who catch him

Origin: "The *leprechauns* are a race of Irish elves, usually portrayed as cobblers. One theory of the origin of the name holds that, since they are often depicted as working upon a single shoe, the name comes from the Celtic words *leith*, meaning 'half,' and *brog*, meaning 'brogue or shoe.' However, more recent research indicates that the word comes from the Old Irish *luchorpan*, which in turn comes from *lu*, 'small' and *corp*, 'body' (from the Latin *corpus*)." (From *Dictionary of Word and Phrase Origins*, by William and Mary Morris)

MAUDLIN

Meaning: Effusively or tearfully sentimental

Origin: "Favorite among the subjects of English Miracle plays in the Middle Ages were those that presented the life of Christ. In all of these one of the chief characters was Mary Magdalene. Thanks to the pronunciation of the French name, *Madelaine*, the English 'Magdalene' was always pronounced and frequently spelled *Maudlin*. So bearing in mind that in almost every pageant in which Mary Magdalene appeared she was in tears, it is not at all amazing that, during the course of many years, *maudlin* was taken into the language to signify a state of sentimental and tearful affection." (From *Thereby Hangs a Tale: Stories of Curious Word Origins*, by Charles Earle Funk)

DWEEB

Meaning: A boring or contemptible person, especially one who is studious, puny, or unfashionable; a nerd

Origin: "The term has been in printed use since the early 1980s and may have originated in U.S. prep school slang, probably influenced by the words *dwarf*, *weed*, and *creep*." (From *The Oxford Dictionary of New Words*, edited by Elizabeth Knowles)

A bottle of champagne has three times as much air pressure as the tires on a car.

CRACKING *KRYPTOS*

*It sits just steps away from some of the most brilliant cryptographers
in the country, and yet after nearly 20 years of trying,
no one has been able to unlock its secrets.*

OBJET D'ART

In the late 1980s, the General Services Administration, the federal agency responsible for building and operating government buildings, started accepting proposals for artwork to decorate a courtyard outside the cafeteria of the CIA's new headquarters building in Langley, Virginia. One artist who submitted an idea was James Sanborn, a sculptor from the Washington, D.C. area. Sanborn was struck by how CIA agents spend their entire lives keeping secrets from even their closest loved ones. He decided to put himself in their shoes: His sculpture, if accepted, would contain an encoded message—the CIA's stock-in-trade—and only he would know the solution. If no one ever managed to crack it, he'd take the secret with him to the grave, just like a CIA agent.

OFF TO SEE THE WIZARD

Sanborn pitched his concept to the GSA and won the commission. But he's an artist, not a code expert, so he asked the CIA for assistance in coming up with a code that would be difficult for even the agency's own cryptographers to crack. They put him in touch with Ed Scheidt, chairman of the CIA's Cryptographic Center, and known within the agency as the "Wizard of Codes."

Scheidt coached Sanborn for four months—he was free to teach any technique that did not compromise the agency's security—and then Sanborn spent two and a half years cutting 865 individual letters, plus some question marks, in rows onto a giant sheet of copper that was to be the main part of the sculpture. He named it *Kryptos*, after the Greek word for "hidden." The work was unveiled in November 1990; it consisted of a standing petrified log with the sheet of copper flowing out from it, almost like a sheet of paper rolling out of a computer printer. The work also featured several smaller elements: carved stones, smaller sheets of copper, and even a duck pond, located around the CIA campus.

GOING PUBLIC

Few people would have guessed that *Kryptos* would attract much public interest. The CIA headquarters is off-limits to anyone who doesn't have business there, so the public never gets a chance to see the sculpture in person. Nevertheless, as CIA employees began to talk about it with outsiders—the sculpture is apparently one of the few things around the CIA that *isn't* top secret—it wasn't long before photographs, detailed descriptions, and transcriptions of the inscribed letters began circulating outside the agency. All over the country, aspiring code breakers set to work trying to unlock *Kryptos'* secrets.

The first person outside the intelligence community to make significant progress was James Gillogly, a computer scientist from Los Angeles. In 1999 he announced that the information on the copper scroll was actually *four* different encrypted passages, not just one, and that he had succeeded in cracking three of them (768 of the 865 characters) using software he had written.

Gillogly's announcement prompted the CIA to admit publicly what had already become well known within the intelligence community: A team of four National Security Agency employees had cracked the same three sections of the code in 1992 using NSA computers, and in 1998 a CIA analyst named David Stein had accomplished the same feat using only pencil and paper.

But no one—not Gillogly, not the NSA team, and not Stein— had been able to crack the last section of the code.

AS EASY AS ONE, TWO, THREE

As the code breakers discovered, Sanborn encrypted the first two sections, known as K1 and K2 to code buffs, using *substitution*, a classic technique in which each letter of the alphabet is switched with another. For example, if X substitutes for the letter D, R substitutes for O, and B substitutes for G, then the word DOG is encrypted as XRB.

K3, the third passage, was encrypted using another classic technique called *transposition*. Instead of substituting one letter for another, the existing letters are rearranged according to some systematic pattern. Using transcription, DOG could be encrypted as DGO, OGD, ODG, GOD or GDO. That may sound pretty simple

---

1 in 10 Canadians say they'd support a law encouraging people in major cities to wear nametags.

to crack, but if DOG appeared in a larger body of text, the hundreds or thousands of letters that made up all of the words would be transposed together, making the code very difficult to solve.

ADD 'EM UP

How do cryptographers identify these codes? One interesting feature of many languages—including English—is that no matter what the text, letters always appear in roughly the same frequency. For example, the letter E is likely to appear about 12% of the time in any passage, more often than any other letter of the alphabet. The letter Q appears least often—only 0.2% of the time.

• So if the letter X appears in a body of encrypted text about 12% of the time, there's a good chance that the letter X is substituting for the letter E, and the encryption method used is substitution.

• But if the letters in the encrypted text appear about as often as you'd expect them to in an *un*encrypted text—E still appears about 12% of the time—then the encryption method used is likely to be transposition.

ENCRYPTION REVEALED

The first passage of *Kryptos*, **K1**, was decoded to read as follows:

BETWEEN SUBTLE SHADING AND THE ABSENCE OF LIGHT LIES THE NUANCE OF IQLUSION.

(Sanborn deliberately misspelled illusion to make it more difficult to crack; he did the same thing with other words in K2 and K3.)

The second passage, **K2**, was decoded to read:

IT WAS TOTALLY INVISIBLE HOWS THAT POSSIBLE ? THEY USED THE EARTHS MAGNETIC FIELD X THE INFORMATION WAS GATHERED AND TRANSMITTED UNDERGRUUND TO AN UNKNOWN LOCATION DOES LANGLEY KNOW ABOUT THIS ? THEY SHOULD ITS BURIED OUT THERE SOMEWHERE X WHO KNOWS THE EXACT LOCATION ? ONLY WW THIS WAS HIS LAST MESSAGE X THIRTY EIGHT DEGREES FIFTY SEVEN MINUTES SIX POINT FIVE SECONDS NORTH SEVENTY SEVEN DEGREES EIGHT MINUTES FORTY FOUR SECONDS WEST X LAYER TWO

The geographic coordinates indicate a point on the CIA campus about 200 feet south of the sculpture. Why that point is mentioned in the text, or what the rest of the text is supposed to mean, is anyone's guess. Sanborn hasn't given up many clues. He has revealed, however, that WW stands for William Webster, who was CIA Director when *Kryptos* was dedicated. (According to CIA legend, Webster refused to pay for the sculpture unless Sanborn handed over a copy of the solution... which is how "WW" came to know the "exact location" of whatever it is that is "buried out there somewhere"...if there really is something buried "out there." The CIA's copy of the solution—if it really does exist—is believed to remain in the CIA director's safe to this day.)

The third passage, **K3**, decoded:

SLOWLY DESPARATLY SLOWLY THE REMAINS OF PASSAGE DEBRIS THAT ENCUMBERED THE LOWER PART OF THE DOORWAY WAS REMOVED WITH TREMBLING HANDS I MAD A TINY BREACH IN THE UPPER LEFT HAND CORNER AND THEN WIDENING THE HOLE A LITTLE I INSERTED THE CANDLE AND PEERED IN THE HOT AIR ESCAPING FROM THE CHAMBER CAUSED THE FLAME TO FLICKER BUT PRESENTLY DETAILS OF THE ROOM WITHIN EMERGED FROM THE MIST X CAN YOU SEE ANYTHING Q(?)

Sanborn created this passage by paraphrasing archaeologist Howard Carter's description of his opening of King Tut's tomb in his 1923 book, *The Tomb of Tutankhamun*. The passage deals with discovery, which fits in with the sculpture's theme of decoding encrypted texts. Sanborn included the text because it was one of his favorite passages since childhood.

So how is **K4**, the fourth section of the sculpture, encrypted? No one but Sanborn knows. Here's the encoded text as it appears on the sculpture. Let us know if you get anywhere with it:

?OBKRUOXOGHULBSOLIFBBWFLRVQQPRNGKSSOTWTQSJQSSEKZZ-WATJK LUDIAWINFBNYPVTTMZFPKWGDKZXTJCDIGKUHUAUEKCAR

CONCEALED IN PLAIN SIGHT

Why is the K4 passage so much more difficult to crack than the other three? It could be that it's not written in English—Sanborn has used Russian-language codes in other works of art—which would make statistical analysis of the characters much more difficult. He could also have used any number of "concealment" techniques to mask the text. Removing all the vowels before encoding the message is one method of concealment; another is spelling words out phonetically: If a word like "people" is spelled "peepuhl," for example, the correct solution may appear to be meaningless gibberish at first glance, causing code breakers and computer software to discard the correct solution without realizing what it is.

The number of people attempting to crack the final *Kryptos* code grew dramatically after two references to the sculpture appeared on the dust jacket of the bestseller *The Da Vinci Code*. One Web site dedicated to solving *Kryptos* saw its traffic increase from a few hundred hits per month to more than 30,000…but no one has been able to crack the final code yet. There have been hints that *Kryptos* will be featured in the plot of the sequel to *The Da Vinci Code*; if so, the sculpture's fame is just beginning.

QUESTIONS, QUESTIONS, QUESTIONS

There may be other clues that will aid in decoding the fourth passage. Some of the letters cut into the copper are slightly higher than others in the same row. Why? And because all 865 letters are cut all the way through the copper, sunlight flows through the sculpture to create interesting patterns of light and shadow on the ground. Do these patterns provide some clue to cracking the code? It's a big possibility—remember, the first decoded passage reads, "Between subtle shading and the absence of light lies the nuance of Iqlusion." If the light and shadows around the sculpture do provide a clue, that will make cracking the code very difficult, at least for outsiders, since none of them have been allowed into CIA headquarters to study the sculpture in person. Adding insult to mystery, Sanborn placed a number of large stones around the base of the sculpture. This, and the fact that the copper sheet curves around to form an S shape, makes it virtually impossible to capture all of the encoded text in a single photograph.

BUT WAIT, THERE'S MORE

Remember, the copper scroll is only the *main* part of Sanborn's work—there are several other mysterious objects scattered around the CIA campus, including stone-and-copper slabs with mysterious messages like "virtually invisible" and "t is your position" engraved into the copper in Morse code. There's also a magnetic

---

Bar-ter: The Hershey bar was used overseas as "currency" during World War II.

lodestone set on the grounds that appears to be pulling a compass needle carved into a nearby rock away from due North. What does it all mean...and what about the duck pond? Are there clues hidden there, or does Sanborn just like ducks?

Denied access to the genuine article, many aspiring cryptographers have visited other code sculptures Sanborn has created since *Kryptos*. *Antipodes,* one he created for the Hirshhorn Museum in Washington, D.C., contains a copy of the same encrypted text that appears on *Kryptos*. Other code crunchers use 3D modeling software to create elaborate models of *Kryptos* and the CIA grounds and study those for clues. A few pesky diehards have even stooped to calling Sanborn on the phone to beg for hints...but he refuses to play ball.

Which of the sculpture's features provide clues to decoding the fourth passage...and which ones hint at the solution to the final riddle within a riddle that Sanborn says can be solved only after all four passages have been decoded? Is there really something buried somewhere on the CIA campus, perhaps a prize of some kind, waiting to be discovered by the person who finally cracks the rest of the code?

Only Sanborn and (perhaps) the CIA director know for sure, and they aren't talking.

*　　　*　　　*

NOSEWURST

"A motorist is nursing a broken nose after being hit in the face by a frozen sausage. The unsuspecting driver was hit by the flying banger as he approached the junction of Inchbonnie Road and Broughton Road, in South Woodham Ferrers. The 46-year-old man was taking advantage of the warm April sunshine and had his window rolled down. However, as a car passed in the opposite direction, he suddenly became aware of a sharp pain in his face. Essex Ambulance Service paramedic Dave Hilton said he had not come across an incident like it in 30 years on the job."

—*The Chelmsford Weekly News* (U.K.)

There are more of George Washington's handwritten letters in existence than there are of JFK's.

MEET THE BEETLES

A magical mystery tour to the world of Coleoptera.

HERE, THERE, AND EVERYWHERE

What are the most numerous of all the animal species on the planet? If you said "beetles," you were cheating (it's in the title of the article). But you were right. Of the approximately 1.2 million known animal species on Earth, about a million are insects—and about 350,000 are beetles, compared to 5,000 species of mammals and 9,000 species of birds. Beetles are a very successful animal: They can be found everywhere on Earth except in the polar regions and the seas, and come in an enormous variety of sizes, shapes, colors, diets, and habits. They inhabit a vitally important place in the world's ecosystems, breaking down plant and animal debris, and of course serving as food for countless species of other animals.

ME SHELL

All insects have *exoskeletons* ("outer skeletons") that, like our *endoskeletons* ("inner skeletons"), maintain the body's structural integrity and protect the internal organs from harm. But on beetles they're especially thick and hard, and often ornate and colorful. And that plays a large part in the success of these insects. Aside from the obvious physical protection, a beetle's "cuticle," as it's known, can also regulate the beetle's body temperature and even house sensory organs.

The exoskeleton is a series of plates made of a plasticlike material called *chitin* that bonds with proteins in different ways from species to species, making them either very flexible or very rigid. It's also covered with a waxy substance that holds in moisture in dry climates and keeps out moisture (or harmful chemicals) in damp climates. The fact that beetles' muscles are anchored to this strong "suit of armor" gives these tiny creatures their enormous strength, enabling them to lift objects hundreds of times their own weight. And some cuticles hold miniscule, layered, light-reflecting structures that give off a bright iridescent sheen, such as that of the beautiful *scarab* beetles.

In Cuba, you can be jailed for three days if your house burns down.

A HARD WING'S FLIGHT

All beetles are placed in the taxonomical order *Coleoptera* (co-lee-OP-ter-a), Latin for "sheathed wing." This refers to the hardened pair of wings, known as *elytra*, that are characteristic of the order. The elytra are beetles' *fore*wings: They are not used for flying; they serve to protect the abdomen and the fragile, membraneous *hind*-wings—the ones that *are* used for flying, and are folded beneath the elytra when not in use. You've probably seen a beetle—like a junebug or ladybug—open its elytra, expose its hindwings, and fly away. (On some species, the elytra are fused along the back and don't open; these species have no hindwings and cannot fly.)

Another characteristic of all beetles is that the elytra meet in a straight line down the center of the back. That's also where the word "beetle" comes from: Its roots are in the Indo-European word *bheid*, which means "to split"—and that line does make beetles look "split." (Some etymologists say *bheid* also meant "to bite," and that the name comes from the fact that beetles bite.)

IN THEIR LIVES

A beetle's life cycle has four stages: egg, larva, pupa, and adult. Several to thousands of eggs are laid in that particular species' larval food source, such as on specific plants, inside fruit, or in wood. The wormlike larvae, some soft and whitish, others dark and already having armor-like plates, emerge after a few days and start eating—and some are already predators at this stage, eating other insects. (You've probably seen some of these larvae as "grubs.") They have well-developed heads, often already hardened and with mouthparts for chewing, and legs. They molt several times, each time emerging larger and more developed. The larval stage can last from weeks to, in some species, more than 10 years.

At the end of this stage the larvae secrete a silky substance that will form a cocoon. This pupal "resting" stage can last from days to months, and upon completion the completely transformed adult beetle emerges. The wings, both the fore and hind, are still inside the body at this point and will now slowly emerge. And the cuticle, which is pale and soft, will harden over the next several hours. The adult stage is often shorter than the larval stage, but in some adult beetle species they have been observed to last for, again, up to 10 years.

ALL YOU NEED IS BUGS

Beetles are everywhere! Some live in rain forests, some in deserts, some in trees, some in crops, some in buildings, some in streams, creeks, ponds, and lakes. Some examples:

The Dung Beetle: Dung beetles search for dung with their antennae, which serve as smelling and tasting sensors (some like cow dung, some like sheep dung, some like camel dung, etc.). They shape it into nearly perfectly round balls with their legs and roll them into their nests. There the females lay eggs in the dung and then cover the nest with more dung. When the eggs hatch, the larvae survive by eating the dung balls, eventually growing into adult dung beetles...and the cycle starts all over again.

Dung beetles are a type of *scarab* beetle, and one species, *Scarabaeus sacer*, was worshiped in ancient Egypt. This dung-rolling beetle became associated with the Egyptian sun god, Ra, in the form of *Kephri*, a winged god who rolled the sun like a giant dung ball across the sky every day. The fact that baby beetles emerged from dung balls also inspired the Egyptians to associate them with rebirth and immortality. Thousands of examples of *Scarabaeus sacer* represented in amulets, jewelry, sculpture, and paintings have been found in the archeological ruins of ancient Egypt.

The Hercules Beetle: This family of beetle is found mostly in the rain forests of Central and South America. They have thick plates on their heads from which a single horn or a pair of horns protrudes. The largest of the Hercules beetles can grow to more than six inches long, including the three-inch horn. And they're strong: They can lift objects 850 times their own weight.

The Goliath Beetle: This is the largest scarab, the largest beetle, and the largest (by weight) insect in the world, weighing in at a whopping 3.5 ounces. They're found in tropical forests in Africa.

The Feather-Winged Beetle: These are the *smallest* known insect in the world, with one species, *Nanosella fungi*, measuring only one-third of a millimeter in length. They're found in the eastern United States and, like many species of beetle, live on fungi.

The Firefly: More than 2,000 species of fireflies, or "lightning bugs," are found around the world, and they use their *biolumines-*

---

cence organs on their lower abdomens to attract mates. Some species have been known, in spread-out groups numbering in the hundreds, to flash their lighted behinds on and off simultaneously— a breathtaking sight. And in some species males flash to males of other species, as their female partners would, and then eat the unlucky would-be suitors when they approach.

The Short-Necked Oil Beetle: This beetle was thought to be extinct in England for decades: No sighting had been recorded since 1948. Then in 2007, an amateur entomologist found several on the country's south coast. The short-necked beetle is known for its peculiar life cycle: Females lay thousands of eggs in a burrow. The larvae emerge, crawl into a flower, and wait for bees to come by. They latch on to the unsuspecting bees and get a ride back to the beehive, where they molt into maggotlike creatures and live off bee eggs and pollen. The following spring they emerge as sluggish, flightless green beetles, known for the oily, highly toxic substance they secrete when threatened.

The Blister Beetle: Have you ever heard of an aphrodisiac known as "Spanish Fly"? Well, it doesn't come from flies—it's made from the ground-up bodies of blister beetles, in particular the *Lytta vesicatoria*, a member of the Meloidae family, all of which produce an extremely toxic substance called *cantharidin*. The substance has been used in tiny quantities by people around the world for thousands of years, but is it really an aphrodisiac? The chemical has never been proven to have that quality. (But it has proved fatal in many cases.)

The Ladybug: There are about 5,000 known species in the genus *Coccinella*, and they all have colorful elytra, usually reddish, though they can be orange, pink, or yellow, with black spots. Nearly all species are considered beneficial, as their food consists of aphids and other plant-destroying insects. A single ladybug may eat as many as 5,000 aphids in its lifetime. Most cultures consider the ladybug an omen of good luck.

The Whirligig Beetle: These are several hundred types of aquatic beetles, some of which you've probably seen swimming on the surface of a pond or creek. They gather in groups and swim in circular patterns, their flattened back legs serving as "oars" that propel

Why? The word "monosyllable" has five syllables in it.

them over the water, and their antennae alerting them to the movements of injured insects, which they grasp with their elongated forelegs and eat. Their divided compound eyes allow them to see below and above water at the same time: If they see a fish, they scurry for the shore; if they see a bird coming to get them, they can dive underwater. Whirligigs can trap air bubbles beneath their abdomens and hold them as they go underwater, breathing the air as they stay under…for as long as six hours. And they can fly, too.

The Leadcable Borer: Found on the Pacific Northwest coast, this is a type of wood-eating beetle that gets its name from the fact that it can, will, and does bore through the lead sheathing on telephone cables. (Beetle experts believe they're just trying to get warm.)

The Dermestids: These are flesh-eating beetles that help break animal corpses down into organic matter. The U.S. Fish and Wildlife Services National Forensics Lab in Ashland, Oregon, has a colony of dermestids on their list of "volunteers." The lab uses them to "skeletonize" bird and animal corpses brought in for law-enforcement purposes. They have to keep the voracious beetles carefully contained: They also like to eat books and carpets.

*　　　*　　　*

THE SUN IS WATCHING YOU

When actress Courteney Cox needed to research a role as a tabloid magazine editor, she visited the offices of *The Sun* in London. While there, an editor asked her, "Courteney, do you want to see what you've been doing for the past couple of weeks while you've been in Europe?" His description freaked her out: "Then he showed me pictures from the week before, when I had been in Sardinia, pictures of when I left the London hotel I was staying in half an hour before, pictures of me in my car, pictures of me arriving at *The Sun*. Even a shot of me opening the door to *The Sun* five minutes earlier."

Pres. Eisenhower's interstate highway plan required 1 mile in 5 to be straight (for use as a runway).

FUNNY ANIMALS

We've scoured our vast archive of stand-up comedian quotes to bring you these witty (and weird) takes on the animal world.

"What's the deal with 'Chicken of the Sea' tuna? There's no chicken in the sea! Are they afraid to tell us it's fish?"

—**Jerry Seinfeld**

"What are the two things they tell you are healthiest to eat? Chicken and fish. You know what you should do? Combine the two: Eat a penguin!"

—**Dave Attell**

"When I was a kid my old man took me to the zoo. He told me to go over to the leopard and play connect the dots."

—**Rodney Dangerfield**

"You learn a lot in your teenage years. For instance, I learned that if you're ever being chased by a police dog, try not to go through a little tunnel, then onto a mini see-saw, and then jump through a ring of fire—they've trained for that, you see."

—**Danny McCrossan**

"Sometimes I'm afraid of bears. Sometimes I'm not. I must be bipolar."

—**Peter Sasso**

"I don't kill flies, but I like to mess with their minds. I hold them above globes. They freak out and yell, 'Whoa, I'm *way* too high!'"

—**Bruce Baum**

"You can catch more flies with honey than you can with vinegar, but either way you've got flies."

—**Richard Lewis**

"Watching a baby being born is a little like watching a wet St. Bernard coming in through the cat door."

—**Jeff Foxworthy**

"I was sleeping the other night, alone…thanks to the exterminator."

—**Emo Philips**

"I once tried to commit suicide by jumping off a building. I changed my mind at the last minute, so I just flipped over and landed on my feet. Two little kittens nearby saw it happen. One turned to the other and said, 'See, *that's* how it's done.'"

—**Steven Wright**

It takes about 20 minutes to milk a dairy cow by hand. They need to be milked 2–3 times a day.

THE WORLD'S FIRST HOME COMPUTER

Today it's hard to imagine a time when computers weren't a part of everyday life. Thirty years ago, it was hard to picture a time when they would be.

LOGIC MACHINES

When the first computers were built in the 1940s, no one ever imagined that one day they would be commonplace. They were such enormous technological undertakings, and were so expensive, that the head of IBM predicted "a world market for maybe five." The idea that individuals might own their own *personal* computers was the stuff of science fiction.

At first the new "electronic logic machines" were the exclusive domain of the government, the military, and a handful of the world's richest corporations—the only groups capable of maintaining the army of technicians required to keep the machines running. But as the technology improved, computers got smaller. The big breakthrough that allowed computers to become manageably sized and affordable: the transistor.

Transistors were small slices of crystal—in the early days usually silicon—that acted as electrical relays. Because they made use of the conductive properties of *solid* materials, transistors became known as *solid-state* technology. And because of a classification issue over whether transistors were insulators or conductors, they were called *semiconductors*. Finally, because they were thin slices of crystal, scientists began referring to them as *chips*.

In 1955 William Shockley, one of the inventors of the transistor and co-winner of the 1956 Nobel Prize in physics for his efforts, founded Shockley Semiconductor in Palo Alto, California. Other companies soon split off from his and drew the best electronic engineering minds from around the country to the region. Because of this, the area became known as *Silicon Valley*.

THE MINI

Silicon chips allowed computers to become smaller and cheaper. This new generation of technology, called *minicomputers*, helped

---

Yuck! There are about 650 different species of leeches in the world.

computer use spread to smaller companies and to universities. Throughout the 1960s, more and more people were able to gain access to computers, and interest in learning about them grew. The problem, however, was that even minicomputers were too big and expensive for any individual to own one. Anyone who wanted to learn computer programming had to enroll in classes at a large university and sign up for terminal time in a computer lab. A hierarchy of technicians charged with making sure the system ran smoothly further limited what sorts of tasks individuals could use computer labs for. The idea that someone could spend hours on end leisurely learning computer programming through trial and error was still a far-off dream.

THE MICRO

The next big step toward home computing came in the late 1960s, when a Silicon Valley company called Intel was commissioned to design a chip that would serve as the brain of an expensive desktop calculator. The Intel engineers were familiar with minicomputer design and soon realized that the sophisticated chip they were building could easily be made to run a more complex machine than a calculator. Basically, they were designing a programmable chip that combined the functions of several thousand individual transistors. It was *almost* a simple computer on a chip. Called a *microprocessor,* the Intel 4004 heralded the dawn of *microcomputers*—machines small enough and cheap enough to make home computers a real possibility.

"IT'LL NEVER WORK"

The advent of the microprocessor may have made home computers possible, but that didn't mean the big companies were interested in developing such a product. This was a time when office work was done on typewriters, engineers carried slide rules, and school teachers still stained their fingers purple operating the mimeograph machine. IBM and the other technology giants simply couldn't imagine a market for personal computers. No one had ever heard of a word processor or a spreadsheet program. Why would people spend money on something they had no use for? The experts were wrong, of course, but it would take a grassroots computing movement to show them their error.

Strike two! 60% of second marriages end in divorce.

HOMEGROWN

By the early 1970s, so many people were aware of computers and interested in learning programming that computer clubs were springing up across the country. They held meetings and published newsletters devoted to sharing information about the latest in computer design and technology. The hope of computer enthusiasts everywhere was that some day soon they might own their own computers. When Intel followed up their 4004 microprocessor with the more advanced 8080 chip in 1972, computer nuts believed that their dream was finally at hand.

The editors of *Popular Electronics* magazine saw what IBM and the other big companies did not: There were an awful lot of people out there who would buy home computers—if only such a product existed. In 1974 the editors began casting about for a company willing to design a computer kit that they could promote in their magazine.

Meanwhile, in Albuquerque, New Mexico, a retired air force officer and electrical engineer named Ed Roberts was losing his shirt in The Great Calculator Crash of '74. His company, Micro Instrumentation Telemetry Systems (MITS), had started out selling radio-control circuitry for model airplanes by mail order. From there he had moved into build-your-own calculator kits—also mail order—through ads in hobby magazines like *Popular Electronics*. It was a great little business...until the big electronics firms decided to get into it, too. All at once, companies like Texas Instruments realized they could make more money selling their own calculators than by supplying the components to outfits like MITS. The results were dramatic: The average price of a calculator fell from $150 in 1973 to $26.25 a year later. Roberts couldn't get his price under $100 and he was getting desperate. Already $400,000 in debt, he decided to borrow *more* money and stake everything on the *Popular Electronics* gimmick: With a single technical assistant, he set out to design a microcomputer.

THE ALTAIR

Back in New York, the *Popular Electronics* editorial staff was receiving a lot of messy computer designs—"rat's nests of wires," according to one editor. Roberts came to them with a clean, professional design, and something even more important: a deal with

Intel to buy 8080 chips in bulk at a fraction of their market price. The machine would be affordable.

Roberts was in; a deadline was set and MITS went to work. They decided to call it the Altair—supposedly after an imaginary planet visited by the USS *Enterprise* on an episode of *Star Trek*. Working nonstop, Roberts' team finished the prototype just in time to ship it off to New York for its cover story photo shoot.

Unfortunately, the shipping company lost the package. With no time to build a replacement, Roberts threw together a fake. The January 1975 issue of *Popular Electronics* featured an empty Altair casing on the cover and an article announcing the computer's arrival on the home-electronics market.

DO IT YOURSELF

Buying an Altair in 1975 was nothing like purchasing a new PC today. To start with, the Altair was a computer *kit*. This meant that customers had to break out a soldering iron and physically assemble their new computers. Once they'd managed to put the thing together, the Altair didn't actually do anything.

It had no monitor, no keyboard, and no preexisting software. It was simply a metal box with a motherboard and 18 empty slots designed to hold circuit boards. MITS shipped the first orders with just two boards available to plug into those slots: a central processing unit, or CPU, built around the Intel 8080 chip, and a 256-byte memory board.

Not only did the Altair come without a programming language, there wasn't even enough memory to hold one. All that the machine had in the way of a user interface was a handful of lights and a few toggle switches. Programming it amounted to entering binary machine code by flipping the switches on and off.

THE LATEST THING

It would be a hard sell today, but in 1975 electronics nuts were so eager to own their own computers that they gladly shelled out the $397 that Roberts was asking for a new Altair. So many orders poured in that MITS was initially unable to keep up with demand. They were nearly sunk by their own success.

They had promised delivery within 60 days. To keep pace with the flood of orders, all extra hardware was shelved until the basic

---

Tube nation: There are 3 times as many TV sets in the U.S. as there are people in the U.K.

machine could be shipped to everyone who had sent in money. The computer itself had been rushed through production, and now there was no time to finish developing extra features like expanded memory boards or any sort of user interface.

MITS was selling Altairs as fast as they could make them, but they were falling behind in further development. Eventually, their success would be their undoing: They were never able to catch up.

DESKTOP REVOLUTION

Because there was no software or expanded hardware available from MITS, the computer enthusiasts who were their customers began creating their own. Two young programmers named Paul Allen and Bill Gates went so far as to call Roberts on the phone claiming they had written a BASIC programming language that would run on the Altair.

They hadn't actually written the language yet, but they didn't let that stop them. They set up an appointment with Roberts and got busy. When the language was finished they licensed it to MITS and used the proceeds to found Microsoft—one of the first companies to sell *soft*ware for *micro*computers.

Other enthusiasts were building expanded memory boards and finding ways to connect their Altairs to teletype machines and paper tape readers. These efforts would soon become real competition for MITS.

THE BOTTOM LINE

Business was booming, but trouble was on the way. In creating the home-computer market, Roberts had inadvertently created a whole new set of problems to deal with. For one, the new Microsoft programming language required four times more memory than the Altair came with.

In 1975 MITS finally designed a 4K memory board that would plug into one of those empty circuit board slots. Unfortunately, the design was rushed into production before the bugs were worked out, and the thing simply didn't work. Small companies soon sprang up out of people's garages to sell memory boards that *did* work.

In an effort to force customers to buy his inferior board,

Roberts tied the price of the programming language to the purchase of the MITS board. He charged $150 for the language with the board, and $500 for the language alone, but the plan backfired. Outraged Altair users now felt justified in pirating the programming language. They simply made paper-tape copies of it and passed it out free to their friends.

Roberts made a similar mistake when retail home-computer stores began to emerge. He insisted that licensed Altair dealers sell only MITS equipment. As new companies emerged selling their own computers and hardware, dealers dropped the Altair in favor of carrying a wider variety of products.

UNPLANNED OBSOLESCENCE

By 1977 MITS was facing direct competition from many emerging companies. Rival microcomputers with names like the IMSAI 8080, the Poly-88, the Processor Technology Sol, the Commodore PET, and the Apple II were eating into the Altair's share of the new market.

Roberts had introduced the world's first commercial home computer, but he proved unable to keep up with the monster he had created. In May of 1977, he sold MITS to a company called Pertec, a manufacturer of mainframe hardware. With no real understanding of the emerging home-computer market, Pertec ran MITS into the ground in less than a year.

All told, the Altair existed for just a little over three years. During that time, the personal computer went from a science-fiction fantasy to the most lucrative new technology of its era. By 1981 industry giants like IBM would enter the market, proving that the personal computer was here to stay. The Altair showed the big companies that the microcomputer was a viable product and, in so doing, kicked off the desktop revolution.

*   *   *

"A computer lets you make more mistakes faster than any invention in human history—with the possible exceptions of handguns and tequila."

—**Mitch Ratcliffe**

Gary Cooper's real name was *Frank* Cooper. His agent (from Gary, Indiana) made him change it.

TWENTY

Fascinating facts about a fascinating number—and one more tribute to the 20th anniversary of Uncle John's Bathroom Reader.

TWENTY is the number of *deciduous* or "baby" teeth in humans. They emerge at around six months and last until about age six years, when they're replaced by permanent teeth.

TWENTY, in many languages around the world, is a base number used in counting. For example, in French the numbers from 80 to 99 are based on 20—80 is *quatre-vingts* ("four twenties"), 86 is *quatre-vingt-six* ("four-twenty-six"), and 92 is *quatre-vingt-douze* ("four-twenty-twelve"). This is also true of the Danish, Breton, Basque, Gaelic, Albanian, and Georgian languages.

TWENTY is the number of possible first moves in a game of chess.

TWENTY is an *integer*, which is any whole number, positive or negative, and 0 (...-2, -1, 0, 1, 2...). It's also a *composite number*, meaning it is not a prime number—it has divisors other then 1 and itself. For example: 19 is prime because it can be divided only by 1 and 19. Since 20 can be divided by 2, 4, 5, and 10, as well as by 1 and 20, it is composite.

TWENTY is the age of majority, the age at which one becomes a legal adult, in Japan, South Korea, Taiwan, and Thailand.

TWENTY is used as a base counting number by the Japanese ethnic group known as the *Ainu*. The word *hotnep* in the Ainu language means 20. *Wanpe etu hotnep* means "ten more until two twenties," or 30. *Tu hotnep*, or "two twenties," is 40 and *ashikne hotnep*, or "five twenties," is 100.

TWENTY is the number of digits on the (typical) human body.

TWENTY has a nickname: "score." (The word comes from the ancient practice of counting sheep in twenties and keeping tally by cutting, or "scoring," notches on a stick.) It was most famously used by Abraham Lincoln—"Four score and seven years ago...", meaning 87 years ago—in his Gettysburg Address.

MOVIE OF THE WEEK

Remember the "made-for-network-TV" movie? In the 1970s, it was one of the schlockiest—and most popular—things on TV.

CHEAP AND EASY

One of the most popular TV genres of the 1950s was the anthology. Over one to two hours, shows like *Playhouse 90* and *GE Theater* showed a complete dramatic presentation each week. Episodes weren't connected; each played like a mini-movie. But by the mid-1960s, audience tastes had evolved to favor series with regular characters and continuing storylines.

Old movies were often shown on TV in those days, mostly during the day and late at night. When the anthology died, the networks didn't drop the concept—they started showing Hollywood movies in primetime instead. One problem: Movies were expensive—the studios charged the networks about $700,000 for the rights to air a single movie.

NBC was broadcasting in color full-time by 1964 and didn't want to pay a fortune for black-and-white movies, even recent ones. So they decided to make their own: They could control the costs, and there'd be no hefty rights fees to cut into profits. *World Premiere Movies*, an anthology of stand-alone, two-hour films, premiered on October 7, 1964, with a crime thriller called *See How They Run* (starring John Forsythe and Leslie Nielsen). The plot: Hired killers follow three children who are unknowingly carrying evidence that could sink an international crime ring, which also just murdered the kids' father. It was a hit, landing in TV's top-20 shows of the week. Apparently audiences liked the novelty of seeing a brand-new movie, at home, for free.

UNIVERSAL THEMES

In 1966 NBC contracted with Universal Pictures to make movies for television. Universal had traditionally made B movies for drive-in theaters, but drive-ins were rapidly closing down all across the country. In NBC, Universal found a profitable outlet for its films, and made-for-TV movies could have higher production values. The first NBC/Universal project (today they're actually the

In his lifetime, Elvis Presley played only 5 concerts outside the US. They were all in Canada.

same company) aired on Thanksgiving weekend in 1966. Titled *Fame Is the Name of the Game*, it was about a magazine reporter using clues in a murdered prostitute's diary to find her killer. The movie was so popular that in 1968 it was turned into a regular TV series called *The Name of the Game*.

EASY AS ABC

Barry Diller, the 27-year-old head of primetime programming at ABC, noticed NBC's success and decided to make movies at his network. The difference: NBC aired only 6 to 10 movies a year; Diller wanted a new movie every week of the TV season—about 25 per year. So he hired independent film producers (including future superstar producer Aaron Spelling), set a $500,000 budget per 67-minute movie (90 minutes with commercials), and set out to make each and every movie feel like a television event. To make that happen, he told the producers to make the movies over-the-top: as titillating, violent—or sappy—as possible. In fall 1969, ABC's *Movie of the Week* premiered with *Seven in Darkness*, a plane-crash drama starring Milton Berle. It was a smash hit. For the 1970 TV season, *The Movie of the Week* was the #6 show on television.

SCHLOCK IT TO ME

The majority of TV movies were exactly what Diller had ordered: exploitative and sensationalistic.

Sarah T–Portrait of a Teenage Alcoholic (1975) Linda Blair (*The Exorcist*) plays a 15-year-old alcoholic who hits rock bottom, learns her lesson, and straightens up.

Dawn: Portrait of a Teenage Runaway (1976) A teenage girl (Eve Plumb—Jan from *The Brady Bunch*) runs away from home and turns to prostitution to support herself.

Alexander: The Other Side of Dawn (1977) In this sequel to *Dawn*, Dawn's friend Alexander runs away from home to become a movie star but turns to prostitution to support himself.

Trilogy of Terror (1975) Three horror vignettes, all starring Karen Black: "Julie" (a college student blackmails his teacher into dating him, until she kills him), "Millicent and Therese" (a disturbed woman claims to have killed her sister, but the two sisters turn out to be the same person), and "Amelia" (an African doll stalks and kills a woman).

Killdozer (1974) Construction workers uncover a magical meteorite that takes "possession" of their bulldozer. The bulldozer goes on a killing spree.

The People (1972) A teacher (Kim Darby) is sent to a school in an isolated rural community. But her students aren't hillbillies—they're aliens!

Bad Ronald (1974) A teenager accidentally kills a neighbor, so his panicked mother hides him in a secret room of their house. His mother dies a few years later and a new family moves in. Ronald's still there and he's gone crazy from the isolation.

The Desperate Miles (1975) A crippled Vietnam War vet makes an inspiring, 180-mile journey in a wheelchair. Heartwarming? No—along the way, a crazy truck driver keeps trying to kill him.

Someone I Touched (1975) Cloris Leachman plays a woman who contemplates divorce when she finds out her husband has been unfaithful and contracted a venereal disease. She also finds out that she's pregnant, especially surprising because she's 50 years old.

HEY, THAT WAS ACTUALLY PRETTY GOOD

The Movie of the Week also aired many well-regarded, critically acclaimed movies.

Brian's Song (1971) In this fact-based drama, NFL stars Gale Sayers (Billy Dee Williams) and Brian Piccolo (James Caan) are the best of friends having the time of their lives. Then Piccolo dies of cancer. *Brian's Song* won an Emmy for Outstanding Single Program (Caan and Williams were also both nominated but didn't win) and a Peabody Award.

The Boy in the Plastic Bubble (1976) John Travolta plays a teenager trying to explore the world and exert his independence, which is tough because he's confined to a plastic bubble because of an immune deficiency.

Duel (1971) A businessman (Dennis Weaver) driving on desolate backroads is pursued by an evil, possessed semi truck. It was one of

---

Bad boy! One in four British veterinarians say they've treated a drunk dog.

the first movies ever directed by Steven Spielberg. It was so well regarded that it played in movie theaters in Europe.

The Morning After (1974) Dick Van Dyke plays a man who's a successful public relations agent by day and an uncontrollable alcoholic at night. One of Van Dyke's first dramatic roles, it made headlines because around the same time, Van Dyke announced that he was also an alcoholic and had begun to seek treatment.

That Certain Summer (1972) A teenage boy (Scott Jacoby) tries to cope with his parents' divorce, as well as with the reason for it: his father (Hal Holbrook) is gay. This movie was one of TV's first-ever depictions of homosexuals. Jacoby won an Emmy and the movie won the Golden Globe for Best TV Movie.

MOVING ON

All the networks (broadcast and cable) still air made-for-TV movies, but the ABC *Movie of the Week* showcase ended in 1976. Many of them were so popular that they lived on as regular ABC series, including *Wonder Woman, Fantasy Island, Kolchak: The Night Stalker, The Six Million Dollar Man, The Bionic Woman, The Young Lawyers, Starsky and Hutch,* and *Marcus Welby, M.D.* But there were also a few wannabes that didn't make it, such as the 1971 flop *The Feminist and the Fuzz,* in which a radical feminist (Barbara Eden) ends up sharing a house with a male-chauvinist cop (David Hartman).

*   *   *

THE SOUND OF SCIENCE

Stephen Hawking is as proud of his British heritage as he is of being the world's most renowned physicist. So why does his voice synthesizer have an American accent? "It's a very old hardware speech synthesizer made in 1986," he explains. "I keep it because I have not heard a voice I like better." In early 2006, Hawking joked that if he ever got a new synthesizer, it should have a French accent. "But if I do," he said, "my wife would divorce me." Later that year, one of those predictions came true: the divorce. However, Hawking plans to keep the "voice" he has because it is the one that people associate with him.

MARCH ON

One of the greatest moments of the 1963 March on Washington for Jobs and Freedom was Dr. Martin Luther King, Jr.'s "I Have a Dream" speech (see page 528). But it wasn't planned that way.

THE MARCH THAT WASN'T

In 1941 A. Philip Randolph, founder and president of the Brotherhood of Sleeping Car Porters, one of the first African-American civil rights organizations, called for a march on Washington, D.C., in order to pressure President Franklin D. Roosevelt into providing wartime job opportunities for black men and women. When Roosevelt finally gave in and issued an executive order desegregating defense industries, the march was called off.

Twenty years later, Randolph felt the time had come again for a protest march in Washington. On July 2, 1962, he met with the nation's most influential civil rights leaders, including Roy Wilkins, president of the National Association for the Advancement of Colored People (NAACP); James Farmer of the Congress of Racial Equality (CORE); Whitney Young Jr. of the National Urban League; John Lewis of the Student Nonviolent Coordinating Committee (SNCC); veteran civil rights organizer Bayard Rustin; and Martin Luther King, Jr., chairman of the Southern Christian Leadership Conference (SCLC).

The group decided a March on Washington would be held the following August. Rustin, chief coordinator, produced a flyer to announce it, demanding "meaningful civil rights legislation; a massive federal works program; full and fair employment; decent housing; the right to vote; and adequate integrated education."

AGAINST IT

Opposition to the March on Washington was widespread. Not only did Southern senators and congressman have negative opinions—many others who were allies of the Civil Rights movement also objected to the event.

• President John F. Kennedy worried that a mass gathering could undermine legislative efforts to pass his recently introduced Civil

---

Adolf Hitler was a teetotaler. His adversary, Winston Churchill, was a heavy drinker.

Rights Bill. He told the organizers: "We want success in Congress, not just a big show at the Capitol."

• Malcolm X, representing the Nation of Islam, referred to it as "the farce on Washington" and threatened members who attended with suspension from the Nation.

• Stokely Carmichael of SNCC called it a "sanitized, middle-class version of the real black movement."

• The United States' largest labor organization, the AFL-CIO, declined to participate in the March, claiming neutrality.

There were also concerns from the law enforcement community, and even from some of the organizers, that there would be violence, either from the participants or from anti-civil rights groups. All District of Columbia police leave was canceled. The National Guard and Army paratroopers were put on emergency alert. Nearby towns gave their police forces special riot-control training. The sale of liquor was banned for the day; even the Washington Senators baseball games were postponed. The federal Justice Department and the police worked with the march committee to develop a high-tech public address system, which the police then secretly rigged so they could take control of it if they saw fit. Perhaps the most cynical view of the meaning of the rally was over the site itself. A hundred years after the Emancipation Proclamation, the Lincoln Memorial represented all the collective hopes and dreams of the marchers. For the police, their dream was a site in which all those people could be contained on three sides by water.

NEWS COVERAGE

The heavy police presence turned out to be unwarranted—the March was passionate but peaceful. An estimated quarter of a million people marched from the Washington Monument to the Lincoln Memorial, about 25% white, 75% black, and many of the black participants were from middle-class neighborhoods in Northern cities. It was the largest political demonstration in the United States to date. Media coverage was extensive, carried live on all three broadcast networks and internationally. There were more cameras than at the 1960 presidential inauguration. One television camera—positioned atop the Washington Monument—provided the dramatic shot of the March most people remember today: a sea of demonstrators a third of a mile long filling the narrow swath of land surrounding the reflecting pool.

THE SPEECH

The all-day event included hundreds of speakers: civil rights leaders, labor leaders, politicians, celebrities such as James Baldwin, Charlton Heston, Sidney Poitier, Paul Newman, Harry Belafonte, and Marlon Brando, with singing performances from Josephine Baker, Eartha Kitt, Marian Anderson, Joan Baez, Sammy Davis Jr., folk trio Peter, Paul and Mary, and Bob Dylan. There had been a lot of wrangling among March organizers about who would speak and for how long. Dr. King agreed to be the last speaker. Rivals thought that tired marchers would be gone by then, and live TV coverage would have ended. But the network cameras and the crowd waited to hear him.

Most of King's speech had been written the night before; much of its content and phrases he'd used many times. As he wrote in his autobiography, "The night of the 27th, I got into Washington about ten o'clock and went to the hotel. I thought through what I would say, and that took an hour or so. Then I put the outline together. I did not finish the complete text of my speech until 4:00 A.M. on the morning of August 28."

Following a powerful performance from gospel singer Mahalia Jackson, King stepped up to the podium to read his speech, delivered in intentionally short phrases to meet the four-minute time limit. And then something happened: "I started out reading the speech, and read it down to a point. All of a sudden this thing came to me. The previous June, I had delivered a speech in Cobo Hall, in which I used the phrase 'I have a dream.' I had used it many times before, and I just felt that I wanted to use it here. I don't know why. I hadn't thought about it before the speech. I used the phrase, and at that point I just turned aside from the manuscript altogether."

He may have used the phrase before, but the inspiration he received from that huge crowd, calling out to him, repeating his words back; the power of the moment, standing in front of the Lincoln Memorial, allowed him to improvise for over 10 minutes, turning four minutes of remarks into a 16-minute oratory that will never be forgotten.

Harassment in the workplace? 12% of Canadians have kicked a photocopier in frustration.

LET FREEDOM RING

*The words "I have a dream" have become a part of American culture.
On August 28, 1963, Dr. Martin Luther King, Jr. gave this legendary
speech to an audience of more than 200,000 people in front of
the Lincoln Memorial in Washington, D.C. (For more
on the March on Washington, see page 525.)*

Five score years ago, a great American, in whose symbolic shadow we stand today, signed the Emancipation Proclamation. This momentous decree came as a great beacon light of hope to millions of Negro slaves who had been seared in the flames of withering injustice. It came as a joyous daybreak to end the long night of their captivity.

But one hundred years later, the Negro still is not free. One hundred years later, the life of the Negro is still sadly crippled by the manacles of segregation and the chains of discrimination. One hundred years later, the Negro lives on a lonely island of poverty in the midst of a vast ocean of material prosperity. One hundred years later, the Negro is still languished in the corners of American society and finds himself an exile in his own land. And so we've come here today to dramatize a shameful condition.

In a sense we've come to our nation's capital to cash a check. When the architects of our republic wrote the magnificent words of the Constitution and the Declaration of Independence, they were signing a promissory note to which every American was to fall heir. This note was a promise that all men, yes, black men as well as white men, would be guaranteed the "unalienable Rights of Life, Liberty and the pursuit of Happiness." It is obvious today that America has defaulted on this promissory note, insofar as her citizens of color are concerned. Instead of honoring this sacred obligation, America has given the Negro people a bad check, a check which has come back marked "insufficient funds."

But we refuse to believe that the bank of justice is bankrupt. We refuse to believe that there are insufficient funds in the great vaults of opportunity of this nation. So we've come to cash this check, a check that will give us upon demand the riches of freedom and the security of justice.

Male emperor penguins incubate their eggs on top of their feet.

We have also come to this hallowed spot to remind America of the fierce urgency of *Now.* This is no time to engage in the luxury of cooling off or to take the tranquilizing drug of gradualism. *Now* is the time to make real the promises of democracy. *Now* is the time to rise from the dark and desolate valley of segregation to the sunlit path of racial justice. *Now* is the time to open the doors of opportunity to all of God's children.

It would be fatal for the nation to overlook the urgency of the moment. This sweltering summer of the Negro's legitimate discontent will not pass until there is an invigorating autumn of freedom and equality. Nineteen sixty-three is not an end, but a beginning. Those who hope that the Negro needed to blow off steam and will now be content will have a rude awakening if the nation returns to business as usual. There will be neither rest nor tranquility in America until the Negro is granted his citizenship rights. The whirlwinds of revolt will continue to shake the foundations of our nation until the bright day of justice emerges.

But there is something that I must say to my people, who stand on the warm threshold which leads into the palace of justice. In the process of gaining our rightful place, we must not be guilty of wrongful deeds. Let us not seek to satisfy our thirst for freedom by drinking from the cup of bitterness and hatred. We must forever conduct our struggle on the high plane of dignity and discipline. We must not allow our creative protest to degenerate into physical violence. Again and again, we must rise to the majestic heights of meeting physical force with soul force. The marvelous new militancy which has engulfed the Negro community must not lead us to a distrust of all white people, for many of our white brothers, as evidenced by their presence here today, have come to realize that their destiny is tied up with our destiny. And they have come to realize that their freedom is inextricably bound to our freedom. We cannot walk alone.

And as we walk, we must make the pledge that we shall always march ahead. We cannot turn back. There are those who are asking the devotees of civil rights, "When will you be satisfied?"

We can never be satisfied as long as the Negro is the victim of the unspeakable horrors of police brutality. We can never be satisfied as long as our bodies, heavy with the fatigue of travel, cannot gain lodging in the motels of the highways and the hotels of the cities. We cannot be satisfied as long as the Negro's basic mobility is from a smaller ghetto to a larger one. We can never be

Bargain? A brand new Model T Ford cost $850 in 1908. (About $17,500 today.)

satisfied as long as our children are stripped of their self-hood and robbed of their dignity by signs stating: "for whites only." We cannot be satisfied as long as a Negro in Mississippi cannot vote and a Negro in New York believes he has nothing for which to vote. No, no, we are not satisfied and we will not be satisfied until "justice rolls down like waters and righteousness like a mighty stream."

I am not unmindful that some of you have come here out of great trials and tribulations. Some of you have come fresh from narrow jail cells. And some of you have come from areas where your quest for freedom left you battered by the storms of persecution and staggered by the winds of police brutality. You have been the veterans of creative suffering. Continue to work with the faith that unearned suffering is redemptive. Go back to Mississippi, go back to Alabama, go back to South Carolina, go back to Georgia, go back to Louisiana, go back to the slums and ghettos of our northern cities, knowing that somehow this situation can and will be changed. Let us not wallow in the valley of despair.

I say to you today, my friends, so even though we face the difficulties of today and tomorrow, I still have a dream. It is a dream deeply rooted in the American dream.

I have a dream that one day this nation will rise up and live out the true meaning of its creed: "We hold these truths to be self-evident, that all men are created equal."

I have a dream that one day on the red hills of Georgia, the sons of former slaves and the sons of former slave owners will be able to sit down together at the table of brotherhood.

I have a dream that one day even the state of Mississippi, a state sweltering with the heat of injustice, sweltering with the heat of oppression, will be transformed into an oasis of freedom and justice.

I have a dream that my four little children will one day live in a nation where they will not be judged by the color of their skin but by the content of their character. I have a dream today.

I have a dream that one day, down in Alabama, with its vicious racists, one day right there in Alabama, little black boys and girls will be able to join hands with little white boys and girls and walk together as sisters and brothers. I have a dream today.

If you're average, your lifetime will last about 2,475,576,000 seconds.

I have a dream that one day "every valley shall be exalted, and every hill and mountain shall be made low; the rough places will be made plain, and the crooked places will be made straight; and the glory of the Lord shall be revealed and all flesh shall see it together."

This is our hope. This is the faith that I go back to the South with. With this faith, we will be able to hew out of the mountain of despair a stone of hope. With this faith, we will be able to transform the jangling discords of our nation into a beautiful symphony of brotherhood. With this faith, we will be able to work together, to pray together, to struggle together, to go to jail together, to stand up for freedom together, knowing that we will be free one day. This will be the day, this will be the day when all of God's children will be able to sing with new meaning: "My country 'tis of thee, sweet land of liberty, of thee I sing. Land where my fathers died, land of the Pilgrim's pride, From every mountainside, let freedom ring!"

And if America is to be a great nation, this must become true.

So let freedom ring from the prodigious hilltops of New Hampshire.

Let freedom ring from the mighty mountains of New York.

Let freedom ring from the heightening Alleghenies of Pennsylvania.

Let freedom ring from the snow-capped Rockies of Colorado.

Let freedom ring from the curvaceous slopes of California.

But not only that:

Let freedom ring from Stone Mountain of Georgia.

Let freedom ring from Lookout Mountain of Tennessee.

Let freedom ring from every hill and molehill of Mississippi.

From every mountainside, let freedom ring.

And when this happens, when we allow freedom to ring, when we let it ring from every village and every hamlet, from every state and every city, we will be able to speed up that day when all of God's children, black men and white men, Jews and Gentiles, Protestants and Catholics, will be able to join hands and sing in the words of the old Negro spiritual: "Free at last! Free at last! Thank God Almighty, we are free at last!"

ON POLITICS

We tried to find a bunch of quotes about politics that weren't cynical, but that was too hard...and these are more fun.

"Under every stone lurks a politician."
—**Aristophanes**

"Whenever a man has cast a longing eye on office, a rottenness begins in his conduct."
—**Thomas Jefferson**

"In order to become the master, the politician poses as the servant."
—**Charles de Gaulle**

"I don't know much about Americanism, but it's a damn good word with which to carry an election."
—**Warren G. Harding**

"We may not imagine how our lives could be more frustrating and complex, but Congress can."
—**Cullen Hightower**

"Today's public figures can no longer write their own speeches or books, and there is some evidence that they can't read them, either."
—**Gore Vidal**

"Get all the fools on your side and you can be elected to anything."
—**Frank Dane**

"We live in a world in which politics has replaced philosophy."
—**Martin L. Gross**

"Politics is the gentle art of getting votes from the poor and campaign funds from the rich, by promising to protect each from the other."
—**Oscar Ameringer**

"Just because you do not take an interest in politics doesn't mean politicians won't take an interest in you."
—**Pericles**

"Good thing we've still got politics—the finest form of free entertainment ever invented."
—**Molly Ivins**

"Our elections are free—it's in the results where eventually we pay."
—**Bill Stern**

Last president who did not graduate from college: Harry Truman.

THE GREAT WALL(S)

Can you really see the Great Wall of China from outer space? No, that's a myth. (Next time you're in outer space, see for yourself.) But it has a fascinating history that you can read...right here on Earth.

WALL-TO-WALL WARFARE

Back in the 7th century B.C., the Far East was a wild and dangerous place. Seven separate warring states were spread out over the vast, mountainous terrain. Nearly constantly at war with each other, the feudal kings constructed walls to defend their borders.

At the same time, smaller walls were built around villages that dotted the landscape in order to keep out another threat: the dreaded Hsiung Nu tribes, known today as the Huns. They roamed the land and ransacked the villages for food. But these walls—crumbly packed earth and rocks—were a poor defense against well-armed attackers. As the feudal wars and Huns' pillaging dragged on, new walls were built, torn down, and replaced with slightly stronger walls. That's the way it went for 500 years.

WALL #1: THE CH'IN DYNASTY

In 221 B.C., Ch'eng, king of the Qin state, conquered the others and declared himself Ch'in Shi Huangdi, "The First Exalted Emperor of the Ch'in." Naming the new empire China, he dissolved the feudal system and built a capital city called Xian. In just 11 years, Ch'in's new government standardized weights, measures, money, writing, and laws. Even with all of his improvements, however, Ch'in was a brutal tyrant. Those with ideas contrary to his were publicly executed. In his quest to wipe out Confucianism, scholars were buried alive. And the heavy taxes Ch'in levied to complete his ambitious projects—including a life-size army made out of terra-cotta—left millions impoverished.

But one group that Ch'in couldn't control was the Huns, who continued to invade from the northern lands, now called Mongolia. Just keeping them out of the villages wasn't good enough—Ch'in wanted to banish them to the frozen lands forever. His solution: connect the existing walls in northern China into one

---

Average lifespan of a human taste bud: 7–10 days.

long barrier. Rounding up what was perhaps the largest workforce in history—soldiers, dissidents, forced laborers, even convicts—Ch'in employed over one million people, nearly three-quarters of China's entire population. For every worker who was building the wall, six more scoured the surrounding areas for building supplies.

ULTERIOR MOTIVE?

After a decade of nonstop construction, 3,000 miles of the Great Wall were completed. The cost to the Chinese people was devastating: More than a million workers died—an average of about 300 deaths per mile. Because the walls were built along the ridges of mountains in order to give the sentries the best possible line of sight, weak building materials and nasty weather led many workers to either freeze or fall to their deaths. As if that wasn't bad enough, they were still being attacked by the Huns, who took advantage of the many missing sections by simply traveling around them. And newer sections—where the stones and earth hadn't yet fully settled—were broken through.

As it turned out (to the dismay of Chinese citizens) the Great Wall did a better job keeping them in than keeping the Huns out. When the people realized that this was probably Ch'in's main goal from the outset, whispers of revolution traveled along the Great Wall, but before anyone actually rebelled, Ch'in died. In 210 B.C., while on an inspection tour in eastern China, he took pills laden with mercury, believing that the heavy metal would give him immortality. Instead, it killed him. Soon after, the Chinese people rose up against the oppressive regime he had left behind. Ch'in's dynasty crumbled, but the Great Wall remained.

WALL #2: THE HAN DYNASTY

From the ruins of Ch'in's reign rose the Han dynasty, and with it came a new period of enlightenment that saw the return of Confucianism, the invention of paper and steel, lower taxes, and a less-centralized government. After a brief quiet period, attacks from the north resumed...and grew more intense. In 127 B.C., the Han Emperor Wudi began a campaign to fortify and extend the barrier, creating China's second Great Wall, which extended Ch'in's wall hundreds of miles west into the Gobi Desert.

Building a massive wall through a desert presented a unique chal-

---

Green Bay, Wisconsin, calls itself the "Toilet Paper Capital of the World."

lenge. With few building supplies available, workers collected red willow seeds and twigs, then mixed them with sand and a little water to make a gravel-like mixture. A layer was laid down, then tamped down with feet or rocks—then another layer was added, then another, until the wall reached the desired height. Again, watchtowers were built at regular intervals to house soldiers and store supplies.

As the second Great Wall took shape, it became a major thoroughfare for travelers along the Silk Road, which carried Chinese goods to the rest of the Western Hemisphere. It couldn't keep new groups of invading nomads out, but even with the constant threat of attack, millions of citizens would successfully travel the Wall and the Silk Road during the 400-year rule of the Han Dynasty, during which China's population grew to more than 55 million.

By the end of the first millennium, most of the remains of the first and second Great Walls had been washed away by nature or stolen by villagers in need of building materials. Very few pieces of them remain today.

WALL #3: THE MING DYNASTY

The 12th century brought a new threat to China: the Mongols, a group of disparate northern clans united by Ghengis Khan. In 1449, after 200 years of attacks, the Ming Dynasty began work on a new Great Wall, this one much farther south, in yet another attempt to banish the invaders to northern China.

Reaching nearly 4,000 miles long, a workforce that rivaled Ch'in's worked continuously while the Chinese army fought off the Mongols—and later the Manchus—in skirmishes over the next 200 years. The strongest and most elaborate sections were constructed around Beiping (now called Beijing), the capital of the Ming Dynasty. This new wall, built of large granite blocks overlaid with marble, dwarfed the previous two.

In these nearly constant times of war, the Ming Great Wall was an imposing structure. Looming over the steep terrain—sometimes at a pitch of 75 degrees—the ornate structure was manned by more than one million soldiers, who kept constant watch on the lands to the north. Watchtowers were placed at strategic intervals, some less than half a mile apart, others much farther, depending on the line of sight. Climbing two stories high, the lower sections were used as barracks. By design, the corridors within

Cher refuses to wear the color orange.

were narrow and confusing to any attackers who made it inside. The defenders knew the layout, so they could hide and then trap the invaders in labyrinthine passages that often led to dead ends.

Sentries were stationed on top of the towers to communicate impending dangers up and down the Wall. Burning straw and dung, they sent signals to the soldiers by fire at night and smoke by day: A single fire or smoke plume meant 100 enemies were coming; two signals denoted 500; three warned of over 1,000 (which was not uncommon). Even more elaborate signals—flags, clappers, drums, bells, and later, gunpowder—could communicate exactly where along the Great Wall the danger was coming from. In only a matter of hours, every single general along the 4,000 miles of the Wall could be alerted to an invasion and know whether—and where—they would need to send reinforcements.

CORRODING FROM WITHIN

This defense, though impressive, wasn't enough to keep the Ming Dynasty's enemies at bay. But it wasn't the Wall's fault—it was because of the growing disillusionment of the Chinese people, both civilian and military, who believed the government was putting far too much of the nation's resources into the Great Wall. What would happen if, instead of constantly fighting off the Manchus, the Ming Dynasty just accepted them into the country?

That question was answered in 1644, when a border general named Wu SanGui opened up the gates of the Wall at an important outpost near Beiping. The city was currently being attacked by a small army of angry rebels who wanted to end the Ming's reign. So Wu—accepting a promise of a leadership position from a Manchurian general—allowed thousands of troops to march into Beiping, where they seized the rebels and also quickly wiped out the last vestiges of the Ming Dynasty. In its place rose the Qing Dynasty, which finally accepted the northern states into China, extending its borders all the way north of Mongolia.

And with that, modern China began to take its present shape, and the Great Wall was no longer a necessity. As had happened so many times in the past, the Wall began to fall into ruin as sections were ransacked for building materials. It would be another 500 years before the Chinese government would return its attention to the Great Wall: In 1937 the Japanese army attacked four sections

---

Wall-eyed: A chameleon can look in two directions at the same time.

of the Wall, leaving it in further ruins. The Wall languished after the war, as the Communists consolidated their grip on the country. Then, when China began to re-open its doors to the West in the early 1970s, the Wall was saved by an invasion of another kind.

THE GREAT WALL TODAY

Where the Great Walls of China's past were designed primarily to keep people out, today's Wall has the opposite goal: to draw in tourists. Hundreds of thousands of visitors a year marvel at the dragon-like beauty of the world's largest manmade structure. The Chinese people refer to it as *Wan-Li Qang-Qeng*, or "10,000-Li Long Wall" (a *li* is about a third of a mile).

The years haven't been kind to the Great Wall, though. Entire sections have been turned into roads or housing developments, others have eroded off steep mountainsides, and much of what does remain has been vandalized. It wasn't until 1961 that the Chinese government took steps to protect the Great Wall, declaring it a historic site and outlawing any vandalism or graffiti. In 1987 it was given another boost when the United Nations included it in the List of World Heritage sites. In the years since, a massive tourist industry has sprung up, bringing much-needed revenue to the nation. For the first time in five centuries, many of the crumbling sections are being rebuilt, keeping alive one of humanity's most enduring and important achievements.

GREAT WALL OF FACTS

• How much would the Wall cost to build today? $260 billion—about half the cost of all annual construction in the U.S.

• Only an estimated 30% of the Great Wall is still intact.

• The Wall averages 25 feet high; it's 15–30 feet thick at the base.

• If the Great Wall began in Florida and ran due north, it's so long that it would end at the North Pole.

• There are enough bricks in the Great Wall to build a wall five feet high and three feet thick around the Earth at the equator.

• Participants in the annual Great Wall Marathon run 26 miles on top of and alongside the Wall, traveling, ascending and descending more than 3,700 steps (some four feet high) and then running on top of uneven stone next to sheer cliffs.

"You're not a real man until you've climbed the Great Wall." —Chinese proverb

THE WORLD'S OLDEST CALCULATOR

You've probably seen an abacus—a rectangular wooden frame with columns of beads strung on wires or rods attached to the frame. And if you're like Uncle John, you've always wondered how it works. Well, here's how.

MATH PROBLEM

If you didn't know anything about mathematics, how would you count things or subtract one number from another? The question doesn't come up very often in a country with a public-education system, but for much of human history, most human beings were completely uneducated.

It's easy to assume that if illiterate people couldn't read or write, then people with no knowledge of arithmetic probably couldn't add, subtract, multiply, or divide. It may seem logical, but it isn't true: Three thousand years ago when a goatherder on a hillside in Syria went to sleep at night, if he had 37 goats in his herd, his well-being depended on his being able to figure out if all the goats were there when he woke up the following morning. This very basic, very important human need existed independently of whether the goatherder knew that the number 37 had its own name, or that it could be expressed by writing a 3 next to a 7, or whether these abstract mathematical concepts had even been invented yet.

STICKS AND STONES

So how did people count things without using arithmetic? One way was by using a stick to draw lines in the dirt on the ground.

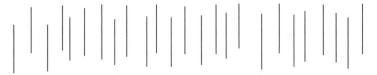

Before the goatherder went to bed, he might have made a mark on

---

the ground for every goat he saw in the field. Then when he got up in the morning, he could rub out one line for each goat that was still there. If he ran out of goats before he ran out of marks, he knew some of his animals were missing.

Another common method for keeping count was to gather up a handful of small stones or pebbles and lay one out on the ground for each of his goats. The following morning he would remove one stone for every goat that was still in the field. How widespread was the practice of using small stones as counting tools? Consider this: The word "calculate" comes from *calculus*, the Latin word for "pebble."

EVERYTHING IN ITS PLACE

These simple counting techniques worked well with small numbers, but as societies grew larger and more complex, more sophisticated systems for counting things were needed. A goatherder might never need to count higher than 40 or 50, but a merchant in a market stall might deal with hundreds of transactions every day, and counting out handfuls of stones every time someone visited his stall would have been impractical. At some point more than 2,500 years ago, perhaps in Mesopotamia or maybe in China, some clever person devised a *positional* counting system, where the positions of the stones, not just the quantity, determined the values they represented.

The written number system that we use today is also a positional system. Take the number 11, for example: We know that the 1 on the left, by virtue of its position, is worth ten times as much as the 1 on the right. This what's known as a "base-10" number system—moving left from the decimal point, each column increases in value by a factor of 10. Take the number 482: We know that the leftmost column is for hundreds, the middle column measures tens, and the rightmost column represents ones. There are 4 hundreds, 8 tens, and 2 ones in the number 482.

LAYING IT ON THE LINE

How did the earliest positional system work? Lines were drawn in the dirt to represent columns of increasing value, then marks or stones were placed on top of them. If the goatherder had used a base-10 positional system similar to ours, he might have laid out his pebbles like this:

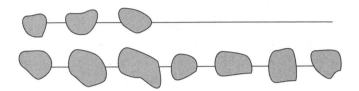

Instead of laying out one stone for each of his 37 goats, the goatherder only had to place three on the line that represented tens, and seven on the line that represented ones.

Many different positional systems were tried over the centuries, including ones where the columns increased in value by a factor of two, three, or five. But the one that caught on in the most places—perhaps because we have ten fingers and toes—was the base-10 system that we still use today.

ON THE GO

Once this system was devised, it was just a matter of time before people found a way to make it portable so that they could do their calculations anywhere. Carrying around a flat piece of wood or a slate was one way to do it: When the user was ready to start counting he sprinkled dirt or sand over the board, drew columns in the sand, and then started making marks or laying the pebbles in place. These portable surfaces were the first abacuses—the word "abacus" comes from the Greek *abax,* which can mean either "calculating table" or "table sprinkled with sand."

In time people came to prefer the convenience of having the "stones" permanently attached to the board, so that they didn't have to go looking for them every time they wanted to make a calculation. This was accomplished by replacing the stones with beads, and stringing them on dowels or strings that represented the different columns.

Abacus styles varied from one region to another: Some designs are simple and have just a single set of columns of beads. Others,

---

Last U.S. president with a mustache: William Howard Taft (1909–1913).

like the abacuses still in use today in China and Japan, have added a crossbar to divide the beads even further. The Chinese abacus, perhaps the most common type of abacus looks something like this:

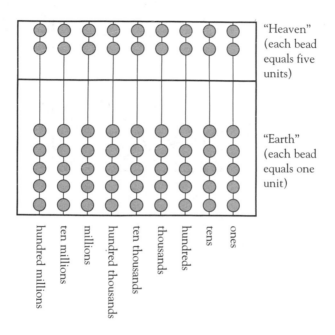

"Heaven"
(each bead
equals five
units)

"Earth"
(each bead
equals one
unit)

hundred millions · ten millions · millions · hundred thousands · ten thousands · thousands · hundreds · tens · ones

HOW IT WORKS

The crossbar divides the abacus into two separate areas: "Heaven," the upper area with two beads per column; and "Earth," the lower area with five beads per column. The beads in Heaven represent five units each, and the beads in Earth represent one unit each. The units represented in each column increase by a factor of 10 as the columns move from right to left. The abacus shown above is in the "cleared," or zero, position: All of the Heaven beads are pushed to the top of the frame, and the Earth beads are pushed to the bottom. The abacus is ready for calculations to begin.

• **Adding.** If the goatherder has an abacus with him, he can count

his goats by moving beads. He counts to 5 by moving the five
Earth beads in the ones column up to the crossbar, like this:

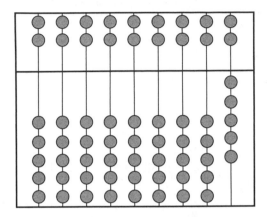

Remember, the beads in Heaven are worth five units, which in
the ones column means they are worth five ones, or five. The
goatherder counts to six by replacing the five Earth beads with
one Heaven bead and then adding the sixth Earth bead, like this:

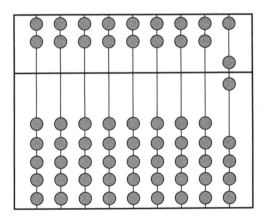

Now the goatherder can continue counting to 10 using the beads
in the ones column. When he gets to 10 and wants to continue on
to 11, he does so by replacing the five one beads in Earth with the
second Heaven bead in the ones column.

Remember, though, that those two five beads together are worth one of the "ten" beads in the second column. The goat herder can replace them by sliding back up and then moving up one of the ten beads in the second column, like this:

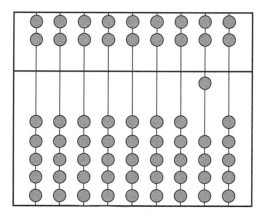

The abacus above shows a value of 10. By continuing to move the beads in this fashion, the goatherder can easily count to 37. When he's finished, the abacus will show three tens, one five, and two ones, like this:

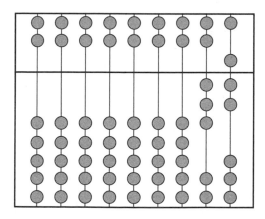

Subtraction and beyond: From here, moving on to subtraction, multiplication, and even division is a snap. If the goatherder wants to know how many goats he would have if he sold five of

---

A Swiss doctor claims to have invented a camera that can identify aliens posing as humans.

them to a neighbor, all he has to do is set up the abacus to read 37 and then subtract five beads. If he wants to know what 37 times 4 is, all he has to do is count out 37 beads four times. He can keep track of how many times he's counted out 37 by moving the beads in the leftmost column. (Since they're worth 100 million apiece, they're not going to get much use.) When he's finished, the abacus will look like this:

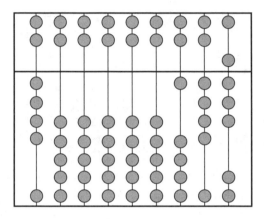

Can you figure out what 37 x 4 equals, just by looking at the abacus? Take it step by step—ignore the leftmost column; those beads just tell you how many times you counted to 37. There's one bead in the hundreds column, four beads in the tens column, one five bead up in the Heaven section of the ones column, and three ones in the Earth section of the one column. One hundred plus four tens plus one five plus three ones equals 148.

Division is the same process in reverse. If you want to know how many times 37 goes into 148, you set the abacus up to display 148 and then start removing one set of 37 after another. In this example, of course, 37 goes into 148 an even four times. If a number can't be divided evenly, say if you're dividing 150 by 37, then beads will be left over after you've subtracted the last set of 37 beads. These extra beads are the remainder: 150 is divisible by 37 four times, with a remainder of two.

THE *PEANUTS* GALLERY

Over 50 years, Charles Schulz created more than 60 different characters for Peanuts. He consistently added new ones, wrote others out, and allowed the ones he kept to grow. On page 159 we told you about the Peanuts story. Now here's a look at the cast.

CHARLIE BROWN

• First appearance: October 2, 1950. Charlie Brown started out around four years old, but aged to six in 1957, and later to eight years old.

• While Charles Schulz was teaching at the Art Instruction School in the late 1940s, he fell for a "red-haired girl"—an accountant named Donna Johnson. His heart was broken when she chose another man shortly before he was going to propose to her. As he did with so many other aspects of his life, Schulz used it in the comic strip. Over the course of the strip's run, an unseen "red-haired girl" is the object of Charlie Brown's unrequited love. Another of Johnson's characteristics showed up in *Peanuts*, too: Like Charlie Brown, she often wore a pale yellow shirt with a black, horizontal zigzag going across it.

• Schulz was often asked if Charlie Brown was bald. "He's got hair," he responded. "It's just so light you don't notice it."

"I wonder what would happen if I walked over and asked the little red-haired girl to have lunch with me. She'd probably laugh right in my face. It's hard on a face when it gets laughed in."

—**Charlie Brown**

SNOOPY

• First appearance: October 4, 1950. "Originally he was to be called Sniffy," recalled Schulz, "but I was walking uptown one day and saw a comic magazine about a dog named Sniffy. On my way back to my job, I remembered that my mother had said, 'If you ever have another dog, you should name him Snoopy.' I thought, hey, why didn't I think of that before?"

• Snoopy communicated (via a thought balloon) for the first time in 1952 and walked on two legs for the first time in 1956.

• On December 12, 1958, Snoopy first attempted to sleep on the

---

Leaping mammals! There are twice as many kangaroos as people in Australia.

top of his doghouse, but he fell off, and thought to himself, "Life is full of rude awakenings." That awakening was great for Schulz, who made Snoopy's doghouse a *Peanuts* character in its own right. He never showed it from any other angle but the side, and never showed the inside. (It's said to be very roomy.)

• Over the decades, Snoopy's various fantasy characters included Joe Cool, the World War I Flying Ace, Foreign Legionnaire, Beagle Scout, and the Literary Ace, whose first written words were: "It was a dark and stormy night." In all of *Peanuts* history, Snoopy has taken on more than 150 different personas.

"My life has no purpose, no direction, no aim, no meaning, and yet I'm happy. I can't figure it out. What am I doing right?"
                                                                    —**Snoopy**

LINUS VAN PELT

• One day while Schulz was still teaching at the Art Instruction School in the early 1950s, he drew a little baby with wild hair and showed it to a friend named Linus Maurer. Maurer thought the kid looked funny, so Schulz decided to work him into the *Peanuts* strip, and call the boy Linus. He first appeared on September 19, 1952, as Lucy's happy baby brother, but aged quickly as Schulz realized Charlie Brown needed a friendly ear.

• Seeing his own kids drag their blankets around the house, in 1956 Schulz gave one to Linus. Even though Linus "grew up" to school age, he never lost the need for it. Schulz was always proud of having introduced the term "security blanket" into the lexicon.

• Linus represented Schulz's spiritual side, as the boy often quoted the Bible. As a young man in Minneapolis, Schulz was involved in the Church of God, but grew disillusioned with organized religion. Late in life he described himself as a "secular humanist."

• Linus's infatuation with the Great Pumpkin first played out around Halloween of 1959. "Linus, who is bright but very innocent," explained Schulz, "got one holiday ahead of himself and confused Halloween with Christmas."

"Dear Great Pumpkin, I am looking forward to your arrival on Halloween night. I hope you will bring me lots of presents. Everyone tells me you are a fake, but I believe in you. Sincerely, Linus van Pelt. P.S. If you really are a fake, don't tell me. I don't want to know."
                                                                    —**Linus**

Nothing to sneeze at: A cough travels at 600 mph.

LUCY VAN PELT

• First appearance: March 3, 1952. Lucy was originally a baby, but her self-centered streak was there from the beginning. "Lucy comes from the part of me that's capable of saying mean and sarcastic things," Schulz said. She was originally modeled on Schulz's daughter Meredith, whom he once described as a "fussbudget."

• Nearly every autumn, Schulz would dedicate a Sunday strip to Charlie Brown's attempt to kick a football held by Lucy, who invariably pulls it away at the last second—something that Schulz's friends often did to him when he was a kid.

"I'm worried about a little boy who sits in front of me at school. He cries every day. This afternoon I tried to help him. I whacked him one on the arm. There's nothing like a little physical pain to take your mind off emotional problems."
—**Lucy**

SCHROEDER

• First appearance: May 30, 1951. Early in the strip, as a lark, Schulz wanted to show Charlie Brown singing the melody to Beethoven's Ninth Symphony, so he copied the actual notes—clef and all—into the strip. He loved the way it looked, and searched for a way to keep using the musical staff. He thought of the toy piano that his young daughter liked to play and decided that one of the *Peanuts* cast should play one, too. So he chose his newest character, a baby he called Schroeder, who was named after a boy Schulz used to caddy with at a golf course in St. Paul.

• Although Schulz's favorite composer was Brahms, he chose Beethoven to be Schroeder's hero because the name "Beethoven" is intrinsically funnier than "Brahms." (It also explains why Schroeder is so adamant about turning down Lucy's advances: Beethoven was a lifelong bachelor, so Schroeder has to be one, too.)

Lucy: *Schroeder, do you think a pretty girl is like a melody?*
Schroeder: *I can't say…I've never known any pretty girls.*

SALLY BROWN

• Charlie Brown's little sister first appeared on August 23, 1959, as a baby, but quickly grew up to kindergarten age. Over the years, her main role has been to offer her (and Schulz's) cynical opinions on the state of modern education, most notably the "new math."

Movie director John Waters is a crime junkie; he had seats at the Watergate and Manson trials.

- Another victim of unrequited love in the *Peanuts* world, Sally is infatuated with her big brother's best friend, Linus. In Sally's eyes, Linus can do no wrong (she calls him her "sweet babboo").

"I worry about getting old...who wants to be nine?"   **—Sally**

PATRICIA "PEPPERMINT PATTY" REICHARDT

- Peppermint Patty debuted on August 22, 1966. It started when Schulz looked at a bowl of candy in his kitchen and was intrigued by the name "Peppermint Patty." He decided to use the name for a character before another cartoonist did.

- Schulz liked Peppermint Patty—the way she didn't understand that Snoopy was a dog (she called him "that funny-looking kid with the big nose," and his dog house is "Chuck's guest cottage"). He worked her into numerous story lines, giving her an outsider's perspective, and believed she could "carry a strip all by herself."

- Because of Peppermint Patty's penchant for sleeping through school, in the 1980s researchers at Stanford University asked Schulz to send her to a narcolepsy clinic to help raise people's awareness of the disorder. (She did go, but it was determined she was falling asleep in class because she stayed up too late at night.)

- Peppermint Patty's troubles with schoolwork echoed Schulz's. Both would rather draw, look out the window, sleep—anything that didn't involve studying. She got a "D-minus" on just about every school project she attempted.

"That was a hard test, Marcie. I didn't know if it was an essay test, true or false, or multiple choice. I just put down 'Not Guilty.'"

—Peppermint Patty (she got a D-minus)

MARCIE

- Named after Schulz's friend Marcie Carlin, Marcie joined the gang at summer camp in 1971, where she met Peppermint Patty.

- Some readers wondered if Marcie was gay, not only because of her boyish appearance, but because she also called her friend, Peppermint Patty, "Sir." So is she? Schulz never commented on it, but did say that "if Marcie and Peppermint Patty ever have a falling out, it's likely to be over Charlie Brown, who they both secretly love."

The latrine at a Roman fort near Hadrian's Wall in Britain had room for 20 to sit side-by-side.

Peppermint Patty: *How come you're always calling me "Sir" when I keep asking you not to? Don't you realize how annoying that can be?*
Marcie: *No, Ma'am.*

WOODSTOCK

• On April 4, 1967, a bird that resembled Woodstock haphazardly flew up to Snoopy's doghouse and landed on his nose. Over the next four years, a series of birds regularly visited Snoopy and complained about various things, including the state of affairs for young people, Schulz's nod to the growing Hippie movement. He was finally named in 1970 in honor of the Woodstock music festival.

• "I've held fast with Woodstock's means of communication," said Schulz, "though it has been tempting at times to have him talk. I feel it would be a mistake to give in on this point."

"iii iiii iii ii ii iii!" 　　　　　　　　　　　　　　　　　　—**Woodstock**

FRANKLIN

• The first African-American kid in the *Peanuts* neighborhood, Franklin first appeared on July 31, 1968. It was the height of the Civil Rights movement, leading many fans to see it as a statement on desegregation. But Schulz said he never meant it that way. "I simply introduced Franklin as another character, not a political statement." Schulz recalled an editor from the South who said, "I don't mind you having a black character, but please don't show them in school together." Schulz ignored the request.

• Often playing the straight man, most of Franklin's humor comes from his deadpan reactions to Peppermint Patty, who sits behind him at school, and to the other kids in Charlie Brown's neighborhood, who are a bit too weird for his tastes.

"My grandfather says that once you're over the hill, you begin to pick up speed."

　　　　　　　　　　　　　　　　　　　　　　　　　—**Franklin**

PIG-PEN

• First appearance: July 13, 1954. Pig-Pen never really evolved beyond just being a complete mess, and Schulz, never wanting to force anything, gradually worked him out of the strip. The character did, however, have one lasting influence on society: When

---

What's *fulgerite?* "Fossilized lightning," occurring when a bolt melts soil into glass.

scientists discovered that every kid really does have their own individual "pollution cloud," they termed that cloud the "Pigpen effect."

"I have affixed to me the dirt and dust of countless ages. Who am I to disturb history?"   **—Pig-Pen**

PATTY AND VIOLET

• Patty, not to be confused with Peppermint Patty, was there from the beginning; Violet first appeared as her best friend on February 7, 1951.

• Although the two girls shared Lucy's snobbery and her disdain for Charlie Brown, Schulz never really fleshed them out. "Some characters just don't seem to have enough personality to carry out ideas," he said.

• Interestingly, it was Violet who first pulled the football away from Charlie Brown in 1950. Lucy took over the following year.

Violet: *"Charlie Brown, it simply goes without saying that you are an inferior human being!"*
Charlie Brown: *"If it goes without saying, then why did you say it?"*

RERUN VAN PELT

• Linus and Lucy's younger brother first appeared as a baby in 1972, and Schulz really didn't know what to do with him...until he put Rerun on the back of his mother's bicycle in 1974.

• When Schulz became a grandfather, he had a new crop of young ones to mine for character traits, so he applied them to Rerun.

• Like the kids of the 1970s, Rerun was more cynical than Linus, and therefore easier for Lucy to identify with. It allowed Schulz to show Lucy's softer side as she sort of became Rerun's protector.

Lucy: *Okay Rerun, let's work on our counting again. Now, how many fingers do you see?*
Rerun: *All but the thumb.*

GROWN-UPS

Why are there no adults shown in the *Peanuts* comic strips? "Well," answers Schulz, "there just isn't any room for them. They'd have to bend over to fit in the panels. If you added adults, you'd have to back off and it would change the whole perspective."

Longest recorded flight of a champagne cork: 177 feet, 9 inches.

WHAT IS FAME?

Uncle John has always been fascinated by the fact that a few people out of millions can achieve a level of fame that the rest of us will never know. What makes them so special? How does it affect them? Why do we even care so much? Enquiring minds want to know.

"If you come to fame not understanding who you are, it will define who you are."
—**Oprah Winfrey**

"It would be churlish to say there's nothing good about being famous; to have a total stranger walk up to you as you're walking around Safeway, and say nice things about your work. I mean, of course you walk on with a bit more spring in your step. That's a very, very nice thing to happen. I just wish they wouldn't approach me when I'm buying items of a questionable nature."
—**J. K. Rowling**

"It takes a very strange person to enjoy fame, with all the byproducts that come with it. It's not necessarily a thrill."
—**Kelsey Grammer**

"I don't think I realized that the cost of fame is that it's open season on every moment of your life."
—**Julia Roberts**

"I'm not into the celebrity culture aspect of being an artist. To me it represents extinction. The more people know about you, the less they want to try to figure out what you have to say in your movies, and the less credibility you have. To me it seems: Go do your thing, then get out."
—**John Cusack**

"Fame is like a VIP pass for wherever you want to go."
—**Leonardo DiCaprio**

"The cult of individuals is always, in my view, unjustified. To be sure, nature distributes her gifts unevenly among her children. But there are plenty of the well-endowed, thank God, and I am firmly convinced that most of them live quiet, unobtrusive lives. It strikes me as unfair, and even in bad taste, to select a few of them for boundless admiration, attributing superhuman powers of mind and character to them."
—**Albert Einstein**

60% of all chicken soup sold in the U.S. is bought during cold and flu season.

"I find celebrity status difficult to bear when I am in the company of my mother."

—**Phil Donahue**

"Fame will go by and, so long, I've had you, Fame. If it goes by, I've always known it was fickle. So at least it's something I experience, but that's not where I live."

—**Marilyn Monroe**

"Being a public figure can keep you tremendously shallow. There's a life of ease that's offered to you, where you never have to make plane reservations or know how much a quart of milk costs, and you can exist with a new friend every day and a different party every night. Or it can turn you into just the opposite, which is somebody who is fiercely grounded and responsible because that feels real to you. I guess I fall into that category."

—**Jodie Foster**

"Fame is a bee.
It has a song
It has a sting
Ah, too, it has a wing."

—**Emily Dickinson**

*   *   *

CONGRESSIONAL FOUL

OFFENSE: In 2007 Rep. Louie Gohmert (R-Tex.) was walking through a congressional office building on the way to a spending meeting when he passed a sign on an easel in front of the office of Rep. Heath Shuler (D-N.C.). The sign tracked the daily changes to the federal deficit. Gohmert thought it would make a good prop for his speech, so he took it. During the meeting, Gohmert held up the sign and mocked Shuler's fiscal policies.

PENALTY: When Shuler, a former NFL quarterback, found out the next day, he was livid, and he confronted Gohmert on the House floor. Towering over the seated congressman, Shuler called him a "gutless chickensh*t thief." Gohmert apologized, then later recalled his harrowing incident: "Congressman Shuler is such a great guy, I feel sure he did not mean anything too personal. I know I did not go into his office; I know I did not steal anything, but I am still trying to discern if he might be right about my being chicken excrement."

Hippocrates, the "father of medicine," had a cure for baldness. (Pigeon poop.)

MASCOTS GONE WILD

There's an old adage in Hollywood: "Never work with kids or animals."
These sports teams didn't heed this message (well, the animal part), and
found out what happens when a beast decides to act on its own.

THE ATLANTA FALCON

On September 11, 1966, the Atlanta Falcons took the field for the first time as the NFL's newest expansion team. The first game in franchise history was a major event for a city on the rise. In front of a sellout crowd that included a who's who of local politicians and dignitaries, the Atlanta squad was supposed to be led out onto the field by a real-live falcon—who was trained to make two majestic laps of the stadium before settling onto a high-profile perch from which he would then lend moral support to his team.

Right on cue, the bird of prey gracefully winged out over the field...and kept on going, soaring up over the 54,000 screaming fans and out of the stadium, never to be seen again. Undeterred, the team's owners went out and got a new falcon and tried again—three more times, only to watch their prized falcon fly out of the stadium each time. Atlanta's football Falcons may have wanted to do the same after losing their first nine games in a row.

TEXAS A&M'S REVEILLE

Since 1931 Texas A&M University has had seven different dogs named Reveille serve as the college's official mascot. The latest incarnation is a purebred collie that took over mascot duties in 2001. And Reveille VII has been the most troublesome by far. Her nearly nonstop high-pitched yelping has actually been heard over the school band in a stadium full of 82,000 screaming fans. Worse yet, Reveille bites people. On the field before a football game in 2004, she ran around and tore off a piece of a "yell leader's" pants. She's also snipped at a number of students (fortunately, none seriously). But because Reveille is "the most revered dog on campus," the university has repeatedly refused to replace her. Why? She is, quite simply, Top Dog.

• As the highest ranking member in the Corps of Cadets, a student military organization, Reveille (she is the Cadet General) wears a ceremonial blanket studded with five diamonds

- She's the only non-service dog allowed to roam campus buildings
- Military cadets must address her as "Miss Reveille, ma'am!"
- If she feels like sleeping on a cadet's bed, the cadet must sleep on the floor.
- She even has her own cell phone (which is carried around by the Mascot Corporal, who acts as her caretaker and secretary).

But some students aren't so sure Reveille is the best dog for the job. They've stopped short of asking for her replacement, but do request that she stay in obedience school until she can handle her duties better. (She's been through several stints already.) "Even though Rev is held in high regard," student columnist Jim Foreman wrote in 2004, "she is certainly outranked by A&M President Robert M. Gates, and God knows what would happen if he were to bite one of the yell leaders."

Update: As Reveille VII has matured out of puppyhood, she's calmed down and seems to be performing her mascot duties honorably…and obediently.

THE AUBURN WAR EAGLE

Animal trainers at Auburn University in Alabama have gone through five eagle mascots since 1930. While they've had a nearly perfect track record of not flying away (only one has escaped), one particular War Eagle (IV) seemed to take an opposing team's touchdown rather personally. It happened in a 1976 game against rival University of Florida, when late in the game Florida receiver Wes Chandler caught a pass and ran the ball 80 yards for a touchdown to put the visiting Gators ahead. Apparently unable to stand by and watch his team go down in defeat, the War Eagle flew onto the field and attacked the startled receiver. "The last Auburn defender who had a shot at me dove and missed," recalled Chandler. "Just about that time, I heard a loud squawk and the bird bit me. It probably would have hurt if I didn't have the pads on." Not quite sure what to do, the referees ended up charging War Eagle with a 15-yard personal foul (fowl?) on the ensuing kickoff. Auburn went on to lose the game.

GETTING ORGAN-IZED

*A look at a handful of amazing organs in animals
from all over the Earth. Even humans!*

Unique Body Part: Ampullae of Lorenzini
Found in: Sharks
What It Does: These specialized sense organs give sharks a "sixth sense." Named after Italian scientist Stephano Lorenzini, who first described them in 1678, ampullae are dozens of specialized cells located in a shark's head that enable *electroperception*—the ability to sense electrical fields. Here's how they work: The cells contain a thick, electrically conductive fluid; specialized hairs in the fluid respond to changes in the electrical charge. That in turn results in a signal being sent to the brain. (It's similar to the way we hear using the tiny hairs in our ears, but that's called *mechanoperception*, because the hairs respond not to electrical fields but mechanically to vibrations caused by sound waves.)

What causes a change in electrical charge in the fluid and the movement of the specialized hairs? The incredibly tiny fields of energy created by cellular activity in other living creatures traveling through the seawater. The ampullae of Lorenzini allow sharks to "see" prey behind an obstacle...even if it's buried under sand. Biologists believe the organs are also used to sense electromagnetic fields generated by the Earth, and that sharks use them to navigate to predetermined feeding or breeding grounds.

Unique Body Part: Eimer's Organ
Found in: Star-nosed moles
What It Does: Ever seen a star-nosed mole? If not, do yourself a favor and find a photo of one. They're one of the most bizarre-looking animals in the world. On the end of the star-nosed mole's nose is what looks like a tiny, pink octopus-like flower. The "flower" is actually made up of 22 small appendages covered in tiny goosebump-like nodes called *Eimer's organs*, named after German zoologist Theodor Eimer, who wrote about them in 1871. All moles have them, but no others have nearly as many—and no others have the star.

Long-distance call: An inch-long cricket has a chirp that's audible for nearly a mile.

Star-nosed moles live almost exclusively in burrows, where the darkness makes their eyes almost useless (which is why they're virtually blind). But the appendages on their noses, which can move independently of each other, are constantly touching the world around them, sensing changes in terrain and temperature, and the presence of prey, such as insects and grubs. It gives the moles one of the most sensitive senses of touch in the entire animal kingdom. The organs are so sensitive and highly developed that the moles can detect prey, figure out what it is, and eat it...all in about a quarter of a second. That's what researchers at Vanderbilt University, using extremely high-speed cameras, determined in 2005. It is by far the fastest feeding activity known in the animal world. They also found that star-nosed moles have about 100,000 nerve fibers running from the star to their brain—about six times as many as from touch receptors in the human hand to the human brain.

Extra Organ Fun: Star-nosed moles live near wetlands, and they're the only species of mole that can swim. While swimming they use their Eimer's organs to find and catch small fish.

Unique Body Part: Jacobson's Organ

Found in: Snakes

What It Does: Named after Danish anatomist Ludvig Jacobson, who studied snakes in the 1800s, the *Jacobson's organ* is located in two pits on the roof of a snake's mouth. A snake flicks its forked tongue to catch scent molecules in the air, then transfers them to the Jacobson's organ, which "smells" them. Each fork of the snake's tongue dips into one of the organ's two pits to transfer molecular information. That information may include chemicals that tell the snake there is suitable prey nearby, or that something is about to prey on it. Take the garter snake, for example. One of its primary foods, earthworms, produce a collagen-like substance containing a chemical that the garter snake's Jacobson's organ is particularly sensitive to. The Jacobson's organ allows the garter snake—which, like many snakes, has poor eyesight—to smell the presence of its prey...and get a meal.

Extra Organ Fun: Snakes aren't the only animals that smell with their mouths and tongues. Other reptiles, amphibians, and even mammals—possibly including humans—have a Jacobson's organ.

• Mice have it, and biologists believe they use it to detect certain pheromones from other mice, inducing them to mate (or fight).

• A male elephant wets the tip of his trunk with a female elephant's urine and touches it to the roof of his mouth. If the Jacobson's organ detects chemicals given off by a female in heat, stand back—the male could become a bit...er...excited.

• Ever see a horse lift up its nose and curl back its lips, seeming to "smile" for no apparent reason? That's known as the *flehmen response*—and it's used by horses and other animals, such as llamas, tapirs, and lions, to expose their Jacobson's organ to scent molecules in the air. (More on page 383.)

• Scientists have long known that humans have vestigial remains of Jacobson's organs—that's why we have that small pit on the roof of our mouths. But most believe that, like our tails, they disappear during fetal development and serve no purpose. Other biologists disagree. They say that humans do indeed use them—to detect pheromones from the opposite sex.

Unique Body Part: Neuromasts
Found in: Blind cave fish
What It Does: "Blind cave fish" is the designation given to several species of freshwater fish found all over the world that live in underwater caves and have adapted remarkably to their environment. They are albino, with translucent white skin almost completely lacking in pigment, and they have no eyes. None. But they still manage to avoid bumping into things and to easily sense prey and food. How do they do it? They use *neuromasts*.

All fish have neuromasts—special cells that make up what is known as the *lateral line system* because it runs in a distinct line along the length of both sides of fish's bodies. Like the sharks' *electroreceptors*, the cells are filled with fluid-surrounded hairs. Unlike the sharks' *receptors* (and also like our ears), neuromasts are *mechanoreceptors*, the movement of water being the mechanical signal that activates them. But in no fish are they as sensitive as they are in blind cave fish.

Dr. Theresa Burt de Perera, an animal behavior specialist, studied the most common blind cave fish, the Mexican tetra, in 2004. She found that when new obstacles were added to their tank, the completely blind fish would actually swim up to it *faster* than normal. That, she said, is because the fish were stimulating stronger signals to bounce off the object so it could "read" its contours with its neuromasts. The fish would rush a brand new obstacle, stop just short of it, and then very quickly circle it—only millimeters away from it. The study also showed evidence that cave fish make mental maps of their habitat, and when it's altered, they compare the old maps with the new information gathered via their lateral lines.

Extra Organ Fun: Along with having no eyes, blind cave fish also have highly developed taste buds—they can actually taste prey in the water before they catch it. Recent evidence revealed that the gene that causes the loss of eye development also causes the more highly developed taste buds.

Unique Body Part: "Eyes"

Found in: Tuatara

What It Does: What's so strange about having eyes? Nothing, unless you're talking about an extra eye in the middle of your forehead, covered with skin. That's what *tuatara*, primitive reptiles found only in New Zealand, have. Those third eyes are actually *pineal glands*, primitive glands that are also found in the brains of nearly all animals—fish, birds, reptiles, even humans. In most animals it produces the hormone *melatonin*, which, among other things, helps the body regulate sleep patterns. Release of the hormone is triggered by information it receives from the eyes: When it gets dark, the pineal gland releases melatonin and sleep is induced; when it's light, the opposite occurs.

In the tuatara, which looks like an iguana but is actually more closely related to dinosaurs than to modern reptiles, something altogether different occurs. The pineal gland *is* an eye, with a lens, a cornea, a retina, and a nerve connected to the brain. And it's not at the center of the tuatara's brain, as the gland is in humans—it's in the tuatara's forehead. It's visible in very young tuatara, but gets covered over by skin as the animal matures. Exactly what purpose the skin-covered "pineal eye" serves is unknown.

Extra Organ Fun: The concept of a "third eye" in humans, located in the middle of the forehead, has long been a part of Eastern mysticism. Ancient Hindus and Buddhists saw it as an "eye" to hidden knowledge and a key to enlightenment. Some say the pineal gland, only recently discovered in humans, is that third eye—it's simply dormant.

The Jesse James gang's disastrous final Northfield First National Bank robbery netted them $26.70.

THE PRODUCERS

Some companies and products have been around for so long that they're household names. But what these companies are known for today is often very different from what they did when they started.

HASBRO. Hasbro began in 1923 as the Hassenfield Brothers Company, a wholesaler and reseller of textile remnants. It then moved into pencils and school supplies. It contracted its name to Hasbro in the 1940s when it started making toys. The first Hasbro toy: Mr. Potato Head.

TOPPS. In 1890 Morris Shorin founded the American Leaf Tobacco Company, an importer and wholesaler of Turkish tobacco. When World War I cut off his supply, Shorin switched to selling gum and renamed the company "Topps." In 1951 the company made a lucrative move when it started producing baseball cards. Every pack included a stick of bubblegum. Topps was the #1 baseball card producer until the 1980s and it still makes candy and gum (including Bazooka). The cards no longer come with gum, though—the company discontinued that in 1992.

TANDY/RADIO SHACK. In 1919 Norton Hinckley and Dave Tandy started the Hinckley-Tandy Leather Company. They sold leather that they'd tanned and cut themselves to shoe repair stores in Fort Worth, Texas. During World War II, Tandy's son Charles turned it into a leather goods store. In 1963 Tandy bought a small chain of electronics hobby stores called Radio Shack and sold off the leathercrafts business. Tandy grew Radio Shack into a massive electronics retailer and also sold a line of personal computers (called TRS-80s) in the 1980s under the Tandy brand name.

MITSUBISHI. Founded in 1870 as a shipping company, the Japanese firm moved into coal mining in 1881 to fuel its fleet of steamships. Over the years it diversified into ship building, banking, insurance, paper, steel, glass, and oil, and started producing cars in 1960 (first car: the Mitsubishi 500) and electronics in the 1980s.

Cold feet? Fewer than 5% of U.S. weddings take place in January.

SUPERMAN RETURNS ...EVENTUALLY (PART II)

In Part I of this story, we saw how 10 years and a revolving cast of producers, directors, and screenwriters failed to revive the Superman movie series. It would take yet another 10 years. (Part I is on page 447.)

SUPERMAN LIVES, TAKE TWO

Tim Burton's first move as director: he refused to use Kevin Smith's script, calling it "unwieldy." Despite not having a script, Burton cast the film anyway: Sandra Bullock as Lois Lane, Kevin Spacey as Lex Luthor, Chris Rock as Jimmy Olsen, and Nicolas Cage as Superman.

In 1997 Burton hired Wesley Strick (he wrote *Batman Returns* for Burton in 1992) to write a new *Superman Lives*. In this version, Braniac and Lex Luthor fuse into a single supervillain named "Luthiac" while Superman deals with his emotional pain over his dual alien/earthling life. Warner Bros. gave Burton a budget of $140 million—at the time, the biggest movie budget ever.

But in early 1998, after six weeks of set construction and pre-production, Warner Bros. chairman Terry Semel suspended work on the film. Reasons: 1) the script wasn't good enough, and 2) he got skittish about the huge budget after his studio's two big-budget flops in 1997–98, *The Postman* and *Sphere*. So Semel fired Strick and threw out the script. The movie, once again without a script, was now rescheduled for release in July 1999.

SUPERMAN LIVES, TAKE THREE

Semel hired Dan Gilroy to write a new draft. Gilroy's biggest movie to date was *Freejack*, a 1992 sci-fi movie starring Mick Jagger. Gilroy didn't write a new script—he just made Strick's script longer, but not much different. Gilroy submitted his draft of *Superman Lives* to Warner Bros. in July 1998, right about the time the movie was originally supposed to have arrived in theaters. But then Burton, still annoyed that his movie had been canceled, quit because the endless delays were preventing him from pursuing other projects. Nicolas Cage dropped out for the same reason.

The plane truth: There are fewer deaths annually from skydiving than from bee stings.

Warner Bros. execs negotiated with a few other high-profile directors, including Oliver Stone, Robert Rodriguez, and John Woo, but nothing panned out, so they cancelled *Superman Lives*.

SUPERMAN: THE MAN OF STEEL

By 1999 the Internet had emerged as a major forum for movie buffs. Chat rooms, message boards, and fan sites sprouted up, with thousands of readers giving their opinions and discussing rumors about upcoming movies. One reader of film-forum sites was a Superman comic book fan named Alex Ford who was fed up with the *Superman V* delays. Despite never having written a screenplay before, Ford decided to write his own *Superman V* script, one faithful to the original comic book. Titled *Superman: The Man of Steel*, Ford abandoned the death of Superman storyline, which was old news in 1999. His plot: In order to destroy Superman, Lex Luthor creates Metallo, a robot made out of kryptonite. (Superman wins.)

Ford wrote the script for fun and to satisfy his own Superman fixation. But his wife thought the script was pretty good and insisted he send it to Warner Bros. Lots of amateur screenwriters without agents or experience send scripts to movie studios. Most of them go in the trash. But somehow Ford's script made its way to Peters and di Bonaventura, still interested in a Superman movie. Amazingly, they loved Ford's script and flew him to Los Angeles.

Ford came prepared with not just the script, but with an elaborate seven-film outline. In each movie, Superman would fight a different classic villain from the comics. Peters and di Bonaventura were impressed. They had no intention of making Ford's seven movies, but they liked some of his ideas. They bought his script and his seven-film outline so they could use the parts they liked. Ford was very disappointed. "I can tell you they don't know much about comics," he said later. "Their audience isn't the people who pay admission. It's the parents who pay $60 for toys and lunchboxes."

SUPERMAN LIVES, TAKE FOUR

Warner Bros. kept going with Superman, asking several major screenwriters to take a turn at writing a script. In 2000 William Wisher, co-writer of the first two *Terminator* movies, turned in a death-of-Superman version with lots of special effects inspired by

The Matrix. It brought back the story arc Warner execs had wanted for years, was written by a proven screenwriter, and cashed in on one of the most popular movies of the past year. Can't miss, right? Wrong. Negotiations stalled and Wisher's script was rejected.

The following year, Peters brought in two-time Oscar-nominated screenwriter Paul Attanasio (*Quiz Show, Donnie Brasco*). For $1.7 million, he wrote a death-of-Superman script that also included, according to Attanasio, Superman's "spiritual journey as he battles the darkness." Peters loved it. Warner Bros. executives didn't, although the fact that Attanasio had written the box-office bomb *Sphere*—which led to the cancellation of Tim Burton's *Superman Lives*—was probably a factor. This one died, too.

BATMAN/SUPERMAN

By 2002, 15 years had passed and every attempt to make a fifth Superman movie had failed. Deciding to focus on its other super-hero franchise, Warner announced plans to make multiple Batman movies, including *Batman Beyond* (set 60 years in the future), and *Batman: Year One* (about the origin of Batman, eventually retitled *Batman Begins*). But Warner had another project in the works, too, which could revive the dormant Batman *and* Superman movie series: *Batman/Superman*. The world's two biggest super-heroes in the same movie, fighting side by side.

Wolfgang Peterson (*Das Boot, The Perfect Storm*) signed on to direct in May 2002. Andrew Kevin Walker (*Se7en, Sleepy Hollow*) was hired to write a script, but first he turned in an outline. The plot: Lex Luthor builds a line of what he says are industrial, humanoid robots and exhibits them at the Gotham City World's Fair. Clark Kent and Lois Lane come to Gotham (Batman's turf) to cover the event for *The Daily Planet*. But Luthor's top business rival, Bruce Wayne (Batman's alter ego), suspects Luthor may have evil plans, so he starts to spy on him. Luthor realizes Batman is on to him, clones the Joker (who died in the 1989 *Batman* movie), and together they use the robots to terrorize Gotham City. Batman and Superman show up and beat the bad guys.

BATMAN VS. SUPERMAN

But Peterson didn't like the plot. He wanted to make a much darker movie, specifically one in which Batman and Superman didn't fight together—they fought each other. Why would Batman and Superman fight each other? Here's Walker's plot: Lex Luthor murders Bruce Wayne's new wife and Wayne wants to kill him in revenge. Superman, a pacifist, tries to stop him, so Bruce Wayne wants to kill Superman, too. When Luthor starts terrorizing Metropolis, Batman and Superman come to their senses, team up against Luthor, and win. Warner planned to get the new movie, *Batman vs. Superman*, into theaters for the summer of 2004.

SUPERMAN I

In mid-2002, J.J. Abrams (writer of *Armageddon* and creator of the TV series *Alias* and *Lost*) came on as a producer and immediately nixed *Batman vs. Superman*. Reason: He didn't think a character as iconic as Superman should be a second banana. Instead, in just a few weeks, he handed Warner execs the script for a brand new Superman trilogy. The first movie was titled *Superman I*.

Abrams completely rewrote the Superman mythology. A villain named Kata-Zor on the planet Krypton stages a coup to take over the government, headed by Superman's father, Jor-El. Hoping to invoke an old prophecy that says a "son of Krypton" will help another planet, then return home to save Krypton, Jor-El puts baby Superman on a rocket and sends him to Earth. (In the comics, Superman was sent away because Krypton was about to explode.) The baby grows up on a farm in Smallville and eventually realizes he has special powers, but avoids the role of Superman because of the tremendous burden. Twenty years later, Kata-Zor's son Ty-Zor invades Earth, and he and Superman fight. (Superman wins.)

McG, the young director who'd made the *Charlie's Angels* movie, was hired to direct in order to appeal to a young audience. Every young actor and actress in Hollywood was interested in playing Superman or Lois Lane. Josh Hartnett and Kate Hudson were the frontrunners, but by early 2003 no casting choices had been made, and McG left the project to make the sequel to *Charlie's Angels*. Warner Bros. replaced him with Brett Ratner, whose biggest movie at the time was the *Silence of the Lambs* prequel *Red Dragon*.

SUPERMAN RETURNS

After being announced as director, Ratner announced that his *Red Dragon* star, Anthony Hopkins, would play Jor-El in a movie now being called *Superman Returns*. Then, from 2003 until 2004, there was almost no news. Fans weren't sure if the movie was on or not. But in 2004, budget problems and casting disagreements with Peters led Ratner to quit. This actually moved the movie forward—McG returned as director, shooting locations in Australia (it's cheaper to film there) were selected, and crew members were hired. Then McG quit *again*—he had a severe fear of flying and refused to go to Australia to work on the movie. Warner Bros. was on the verge of cancelling the movie once more, until Bryan Singer (*The Usual Suspects*, *X-Men*) signed up to direct. Yet another script was commissioned, this time by Michael Dougherty (*X-Men 2*) and Dan Harris (*Imaginary Heroes*).

Superman Returns, the 14th try at a 5th Superman movie, finally went into production in late 2004. And, amazingly, it *stayed* in production. Singer decided that Superman had to be played by an unknown actor, and cast *One Life to Live* star Brandon Routh. Singer picked Kate Bosworth to play Lois Lane and Kevin Spacey for Lex Luthor (he'd been Tim Burton's choice for the role in 1997, too). The plot, a continuation from *Superman II*, showed Superman returning to Earth after a five-year absence spent searching for a remnant of the planet Krypton. Lois is married and has a son, who seems to possess some familiar powers.

UP, UP, AND AWAY

Superman Returns was one of the most anticipated movies of 2006. In the United States, it earned decent reviews and took in $200 million, roughly its budget (at the time, it was the third most expensive movie ever made). Overseas, it made another $191 million, which surprised Warner Bros. because Superman is an *American* icon and has never been all that popular outside of the United States. But *Superman Returns* performed well enough that Warner Bros. and Singer discussed a sequel. It's scheduled to hit movie theaters in 2009…so they say.

*   *   *

"The words 'Kiss Kiss Bang Bang,' which I saw on an Italian movie poster, are perhaps the briefest statement imaginable on the basic appeal of the movies."

—**Pauline Kael**

Yak, yak, yak: At any one time, there are 100 million phone conversations going on in the US.

SAY WHAT?

Here are some random quotations that don't have much in common except that they're strange, confusing, strange, esoteric...and strange.

"I'm now at the age where I've got to prove that I'm just as good as I never was."
—**Rex Harrison**

"When I'm talking about myself, and when he's talking about myself, all of us are talking about me."
—**George W. Bush**

"I think we all have a need to know what we do not need to know."
—**William Safire**

"My brothers and sisters all hated me because I was an only child."
—**"Weird" Al Yankovic**

"The best cure for insomnia is to get a lot of sleep."
—**W. C. Fields**

"Indecision may or may not be my problem."
—**Jimmy Buffett**

"Reality is that which, when you stop believing in it, doesn't go away."
—**Philip K. Dick**

"I am not a demon. I am a lizard, a shark, a heat-seeking panther. I want to be Bob Denver on acid playing the accordion."
—**Nicolas Cage**

"I distinctly remember forgetting that."
—**Clara Barton**

"If I ever saw myself saying I'm excited going to Cleveland, I'd punch myself in the face, because I am lying."
—**Ichiro Suzuki, baseball player**

"I suddenly realized that anyone doing anything weird really wasn't that weird at all and it was the people saying they were weird that were weird."
—**Paul McCartney**

"I don't have no fear of death. My only fear is coming back reincarnated."
—**Tupac Shakur**

"I hate dead people."
—**Paris Hilton**

Q: Who was Hanson Gregory? A: The inventor of the doughnut (1847).

THE GOLDEN RULE

"Do unto others as you would have them do unto you" is a principle so basic to morality that nearly all of the world's cultures express it in one way or another. In an earlier Bathroom Reader, *we presented versions from the world's major religions. Here are some lesser-known examples.*

ANCIENT EGYPT

"Do for one who may do for you, that you may cause him thus to do."

—*Tale of the Eloquent Peasant*, 1970–1640 B.C., (oldest version of the Golden Rule discovered to date.)

SHINTO

"The heart of the person before you is a mirror. See there your own form."

SIKHISM

"As you see yourself, see others as well; only then will you become a partner in heaven."

—*Bhagat Kabir Guru Granth Sahib* (c. 1600)

TRANSCENDENTALISM

"Each man takes care that his neighbor shall not cheat him. But a day comes when he begins to care that he does not cheat his neighbor. Then all goes well—he has changed his market-cart into a chariot of the sun."

—**Ralph Waldo Emerson** (1803–1882)

EXISTENTIALISM

"You should always ask yourself what would happen if everyone did what you are doing."

—Jean-Paul Sartre (1905–1980)

YORUBA (NIGERIAN)

"One going to take a pointed stick to pinch a baby bird should first try it on himself to feel how it hurts."

SCIENTOLOGY

"Try to treat others as you would want them to treat you."

—*The Way to Happiness*, L. Ron Hubbard (1980)

BRITISH HUMANIST SOCIETY

"Don't do things you wouldn't want to have done to you."

LAKOTA SIOUX

"All things are our relatives; what we do to everything, we do to ourselves. All is really One."

—*Black Elk Speaks*

Caribbean natives invented the hammock.

MEMORY PALACES

How did people in ancient times remember things when they had no computers, books, or even paper? The only way they could: in their heads, where they created a special place for information to reside.

BACKGROUND

Mnemonics is any system of mental touchstones that helps you to retain larger amounts of information. (The word comes from Mnemosyne, the Greek goddess of memory.) A *mnemonic device* can be as simple as a word, such as "HOMES," to remember the names of the Great Lakes: Huron, Ontario, Michigan, Erie, and Superior. Or a song, such as Rodgers and Hammerstein's "Do Re Mi" ("Doe, a deer, a female deer / Ray, a drop of golden sun / Me, a name I call myself...."), through which many people learned Do Re Mi Fa So La Ti Do, the notes of the musical scale. One of the most elaborate mnemonic devices ever devised was the *memory palace*, an intricate, often beautiful way to store information in "rooms" of the mind.

HIS HEAD WAS HERE...

The person credited with inventing the concept of mnemonics was the ancient Greek poet Simonides of Ceos. Some time in the 5th century B.C., Simonides' incredible abilities regarding memory were revealed when he was a witness to a great catastrophe: He had just left a banquet where he had recited a poem for the crowd when the building collapsed. According to legend, the corpses were so badly mangled that no one could be recognized. Yet Simonides remembered the exact location and specific details about every guest at the banquet and was able to identify them to their relatives for burial.

From this experience, Simonides devised a system in which he memorized *images*—or mental pictures—as if he could see them in a particular *place*, in a specific sequence, so that they could be recalled later, exactly as they had appeared in real life. At a time before pen and paper were readily available, he had to rely on his visual sense, improving his memory by "storing" things in his mind as if he were writing them down. This system of mnemonics came

---

The world's earliest known plank-built ship, made from cedar and sycamore...

to be called *memoria loci* (literally, "memory locations"), or "memory palaces."

PALACE REVOLUTION

To build a memory palace, you need mental *places* and *images*.

• The *place* should be one that you're very familiar with—your house, a library, a school. It can be as ornate as a palace or as simple as one four-cornered room, like a bedroom.

• *Images* are representations of whatever it is that you want to remember. They can be living beings, inanimate objects, or symbols—and the more vivid the better. If you want to remember something concrete, such as a lion or a tree, you might simply picture a lion or a tree. If you wanted to remember a more abstract concept, you might create a representation to stand in for that concept. For example, an image of your sister to represent motherhood, or a five-pointed star to represent the solar system. It's like using a special system of writing. Once you learn the "alphabet," you can use it to "write down" information.

If there's more you want to remember, you can create more *places* in your mind. If a room becomes cluttered, knock out a back wall, and build another room. Add a staircase or furniture. The *place* is essentially a blank page in a notebook, and each new idea you want to write down takes the form of an image. You can use any combination of rooms and objects as long as you commit the details to memory. And you do this by observing specific rules, like following the same order every time you "walk" through the memory palace.

EXAMPLES

Simonides and his contemporaries used memory palaces for very high-minded concepts, but to get the idea of how they work, we'll use a more common example. Say you have an acquaintance whose name and birthday you can never remember. Her name: Ginger Weinhardt. Her birthday: March 17.

Walk into your memory palace, and then walk down the hall and into the room you have reserved for remembering people's names. (Yes, you *do* have one.) You have the walls in the room divided into 26 sections—one for each letter of the alphabet. When you get to the room, turn to the right (that's one of the "rules" that will help you next time you use the memory palace) and walk to the section marked "G." Now put a picture of your friend Ginger on the wall—and below that, imagine a gingerbread man. Really look at the picture. See her face and all the details of her face…and do the same with the gingerbread man. Keep them in that room, and you'll be able to go back to it any time and say, "Ginger! That's her name!"

Put a shelf on the wall next the picture, and put a glass of wine on it—right next to an actual beating, bloody heart. (Remember: Vivid images work the best.) Wine…heart…Weinhardt! That's her name! Now put a calendar and some "marching" toy soldiers on a shelf next to the beating, bloody heart. Put 17 marching toy soldiers on it for "March 17." Now you'll remember her birthday, too.

The trick, as you might have noticed, is repetition. If you picture the scenario we just created only once, you might remember it, but then after a while you'll probably forget it. If you really want to develop the skill, you have to walk through your memory palace and look at all the things you've placed in it on a regular basis. After repeated use you'll be surprised at how simple and natural it is to walk through the palace to remember things.

THROUGH THE AGES

Memory palaces aren't commonly used today, but in ancient times they were, and by some of history's greatest scholars. Greek philosophers like Aristotle and Plato believed it was as important to strengthen the memory as it was to strengthen the body. Memory was a significant part of *rhetoric*—the classical art of speaking and writing effectively. Nowadays we have books, CDs, and other recording media, but in ancient Greece and Rome the study of language was an almost completely oral exercise. To be able to persuade and influence an audience took a great deal of skill. It was an art for which one needed talent, discipline, and practice. Here's how the memory palace was used through history.

• **The Romans.** As they did with all great Greek ideas, the Romans also adopted the memory palace concept. The great senator and philosopher Cicero wrote about Simonides and memory palaces in *De Oratore* (c.55 B.C.), saying that using what he called the *art of memory* allowed one to retain volumes of knowledge,

---

Leave some for us! Cacao, chocolate's main ingredient, is the most pest-ridden tree in the jungle.

much of it lying dormant until brought to the forefront by "medi-tation of the eyes." Another ancient book, *Ad Herenium* (c. 85 B.C.) promoted the idea that using vivid images made them easier to remember. Example: Picturing human figures dressed in purple cloaks or wearing jeweled crowns; or to make them even more memorable, the book said, one could "disfigure them, as by introducing one stained with blood or soiled with mud or smeared with red paint."

• **The Christians.** Most European scholars and teachers in the Middle Ages (400–1500) were Christian monks and priests. In their fervor to "bring the Bible to life," they expanded the use of memory palaces. Many religious students meditated on the Bible by mentally placing images of people they knew into scenes from the Old or New Testament, so that they could "feel" the same things as the saints and angels, or the disciples…or Jesus himself. Some even made religious paintings from the scenes they'd imag-ined in memory palaces, and then used the paintings to meditate on. These were among the first paintings to give Jesus or his disci-ples physical form as opposed to symbolic representation, like the sign of the fish.

• **Occultists.** During the Renaissance (1300–1700), memory palaces were used in occult practices. An Italian monk, Giordano Bruno (1548–1600), devised intricate memory palaces that he claimed actually tapped into the powers of the cosmos. Using the 12 houses of the zodiac as the foundation for a memory palace, Bruno fashioned detailed "wheels of memory" in which each spoke held thousands of ideas full of esoteric knowledge based on ancient teachings. By invoking the power held in the images placed on the wheels, he believed he could harness the forces of the universe, including planets and stars, wind and water, even the thoughts of all the great men in history whose collective knowledge was now part of the cosmos. The objective was not just to exhibit mastery over magic, but to draw himself closer to God by being like God—omniscient and all-powerful. Not surprisingly, such ideas were viewed as blasphemous by the Catholic church. The Inquisi-tion wasn't a good time to equate oneself with God, or to suggest that you could have the same cosmic powers as God. In 1600 Giordano Bruno was put on trial for heresy and burned at the stake.

If you're driving 50 mph, half the gas your car consumes is used to overcome wind resistance.

BAD SPELLLING

Wunce in a grate wyle, eiven wee at the BRI maik spelllnig mistooks.

A road sign in Hagerstown, Maryland, directing traffic to Municipal Stadium, misspells the word as "**Municpal.**" (They left out an "i.") It's been there since the 1980s.

• The West Virginia Mountaineers beat the Clemson Tigers in the 2007 NIT college basketball tournament. The traditional championship T-shirts had their state spelled as "West **Virgina.**" (They left out an "i.")

• On the 1999 first-issue Millennium Beanie Baby, both her tush tag and her ear tag said "**Millenium.**" (They left out one "n.") The spelling was corrected on the second run, but for some reason, only on the tush tag.

• On the road through Midland Beach on New York's Staten Island, drivers noticed a big sign that said, "**YEILD** TO PEDS.**" Then they saw another, then another… In fact, *all* of the new signs on the thoroughfare. (They forgot the old "i before e" rule.)

• At Jim Backus's grave site (he played Mr. Howell on *Gilligan's Island*), there is a plaque donated by fellow cast member Dawn Wells, who played Mary Ann, that reads: "REMEMBERED WITH LOVE AND LAUGHTER, JIM BACKUS (Mr. Howell of **Gillian's** Island)."

• The annual Einstein's Challenge math contest took place at Ohio University in 2007. One of the sponsors, WKKJ, a country music radio station from Chillicothe, Ohio, ran a story on their Web site detailing the events, and repeatedly referred to the contest as "Einstein's **Challange.**" (Hopefully, nobody told Einstein.)

• The city of Tampa, Florida, made headlines in 2007 when commuters noticed a new road sign for Kennedy Boulevard that misspelled the popular president's name as "**Kenndy.**" Tampa Public Works Director Irv Lee, trying to defend the mistake, gave this confusing explanation: "Sometimes when you're baking cakes, you break a few eggs."

"I don't see any point in spelling a word right, and never did." —Mark Twaine

NAME THAT HEIRESS

Proving once again that the rich get richer and the rest of us get jealous, this person will get two pots of gold at the end of the rainbow—one from her family, and one through her own talent and hard work. Guess who.

She was born in New York; her father was born in Paris.

• Her grandfather was a hero in the French Resistance during World War II.

• Her father's name is Gerard, but he uses "William" in the United States, where he runs a business, because he thought his real name sounded too French.

• He is worth an estimated $3.4 billion.

• She moved to Washington, D.C, when she was two, after her parents divorced.

• She studied acting at Northwestern University, class of 1982.

• She never graduated.

• She got her first break in 1982, getting a part on a late-night TV comedy.

• She stands to inherit in the neighborhood of $500 million from her father, who is 75.

• She doesn't really need it—she made (and, thanks to syndication, still makes) millions of dollars a year from a TV show in which she co-starred.

• Her role wasn't part of the show's original plan, but after the first episode the producers felt they needed a woman to offset the male characters.

• One of her cousins owned the Adidas shoe company.

• Another (distant) cousin starred in *The Goodbye Girl*.

• After two bombs, she landed a successful TV show all her own.

Who is she? (Answer on page 597.)

(Answer on page 597.)

Their beers had *two* heads: Vikings used the skulls of their enemies as drinking vessels.

AN ENCYCLOPEDIA OF BREAD

You're probably familiar with the basics: white, wheat, and sourdough. But next time you're rolling down the supermarket aisle, why not try a ciabatta or a poori? (For a History of Bread, see page 251.)

BAGEL. Traditionally handmade with only five ingredients: high-gluten wheat flour, water, yeast, salt, and malt syrup. Historically, long fermentation of the dough gave bagels a rich flavor, long kneading made them chewy, and brief boiling before baking ensured a good, hard crust. To meet the growing demand, automated commercial bagel-making machines were introduced in the early 1960s, and the self-defeating result was a bagel that was bland, fluffy, and thin-skinned.

BAGUETTE. Long, narrow white French bread (*baguette* means "little stick") with a crisp, golden crust and a light, chewy interior with large air pockets. Made its first appearance in the 19th century, in response to the Parisian love of crust: Longer, narrower bread = more crust. Eat it on the day you buy it—baguettes get stale quickly. Small ones are called *demi-baguettes*; thicker ones are *flûtes*; skinnier ones are *ficelles*.

BISCUITS. Tender little "quick breads," so called because the dough rises quickly with the aid of baking soda or baking powder instead of longer-rising yeast. Biscuits are also called "short" because, unlike ordinary breads, they include shortening (strawberry shortcake, for instance, is made with biscuits). Biscuit dough is usually rolled out, then cut in rounds or squares before baking, but "drop" biscuits skip the cutting process altogether: craggy spoonfuls of dough are simply dropped onto a cookie sheet and baked. Sweeten the drop biscuit dough and you've got scones.

BOSTON BROWN BREAD. True Boston brown bread is made with rye flour, wheat flour, cornmeal, molasses, and leavened with baking soda—and it's steamed like a Christmas pudding, in a mold (or a coffee can) sitting in a water bath in the oven. The method is akin to one used centuries ago by Native Americans and taught to the colonists who settled New England. Eaten with baked beans—in the time-honored way—it's an entire meal.

CIABATTA. The name means "slipper," and while the texture and ingredients vary from region to region in Italy, the American version is pretty consistent: a flat, round-edged rectangle with a light brown crust and large holes in the white crumb. There's nothing neat and perfect about the shape of a true ciabatta, thanks to the very wet dough from which it's made. The toasted sandwiches called *panini* are made with small loaves of ciabatta.

CORN BREAD. One of the simplest quick breads—a cornmeal batter poured into an iron skillet or a baking pan, and baked in a very hot oven. Corn bread can be thin and crisp, or thick and cakelike. It's a tradition both in the North (where it's made with sugar) and in the South (where it's unsweetened and often made with sour milk or buttermilk). Johnnycake, hoe cakes, corn sticks, and corn muffins are all forms of corn bread.

CRUMPETS. Quintessentially British, crumpets are similar to English muffins. They're made by pouring yeast-raised batter into four-inch-diameter ring molds on a hot griddle and cooking until the bottoms are barely light brown and the tops are riddled with little holes. This undercooking is deliberate: Crumpets are then toasted whole and buttered on top. Alternatives to butter: clotted cream (cooked, thickened cream, something like *crème fraîche*) and jam. The earliest published recipe for crumpets appeared in 1769.

ENGLISH MUFFINS. Not really muffins and not really English, except that they were first made in America by a Brit, Samuel Bath Thomas, who started selling them in his New York City bakery in 1880. English muffins are reminiscent of crumpets (see above) in that they're deliberately underbaked by the manufacturer: When you split them with a fork (and you must use a fork) and toast them, they'll be perfectly browned and full of "nooks and crannies" for butter and jam.

FOCACCIA. This round, flattish, yeast-leavened Italian white bread is brushed with olive oil, sprinkled with salt, and usually "dotted"—poked on top with a finger—before baking. Served with meals or used for sandwiches, focaccia is often topped with onions, herbs such as rosemary and sage, tomatoes, or other savory ingredients. The more ingredients on top, the more focaccia resembles thick-crust pizza. Focaccia derives from the Latin word meaning "fireplace," because it was traditionally baked on the family hearth.

PITA. Nicknamed "pocket bread," pita is a slightly leavened round or oval-shaped Middle Eastern flatbread made of white or whole-wheat flour. During baking, steam makes it puff up, which creates a space between the round top and the round bottom. Then it can be split across one end to form one big stuffable pocket, or across the equator to form two smaller ones. Pitas can also be wrapped around kebobs or cut into wedges and used for dipping, especially into baba ghanoush or hummus. One reason it's so popular today: no fat and only a very small amount of sugar.

POORI. There are many varieties of Indian bread, all flat (to start with) and most falling into one of five categories: poori (or *puri*), chapati, roti, paratha, and naan. They're all made of similar simple doughs, and they differ mainly in size and cooking method—some are cooked in an oven or on a griddle, and some, like poori, are deep-fried. Rolled out from a dough made of whole-wheat flour, water, and clarified butter (called *ghee*), pooris puff up dramatically when the flat rounds are dropped into hot oil.

PUMPERNICKEL. The original pumpernickel (also called Westphalian rye) was a dark-brown German sourdough bread made of coarse rye flour. The loaves were steam-baked at low temperatures for 16 to 24 hours, and came out dense and crustless. American pumpernickel uses both rye and wheat flours, is flavored (and colored) with molasses, coffee, cocoa, or other ingredients. We also add more yeast to give it a less dense texture, and bake it for a much shorter time, without the steam. In fact, it could logically be called "dark rye" instead of pumpernickel. (It's also one of our all-time favorite word origins: *Pumpernickel* is believed to mean "devil's fart" in German.)

Perfect games in bowling are seven times more common than they were 20 years ago.

RYE BREAD. You can't beat traditional New York rye (also called Jewish rye), piled high with corned beef or pastrami and slathered with mustard, with coleslaw on the side. What is usually meant by "rye bread" is the light-colored variety, with or without caraway seeds, that makes for a great sandwich. Like American pumpernickel (see above), American rye bread is made with both rye and wheat flours. Traditional ryes sometimes use sourdough starters for a tangier taste.

SEVEN-GRAIN BREAD. There are two kinds of seven-grain bread. One is made with flour from seven different grains; the other is made with seven-grain cereal. Either way, the grains are likely to be wheat, plus six of the following: rice, millet, barley, oats, rye, corn, triticale, spelt, or buckwheat. The exact combination is up to the baker. The other ingredients are the usual: yeast, milk or water, oil, sugar (or honey), and salt. Seven-grain bread has that health-food aura of good nutrition and high fiber content.

SODA BREAD. Soda refers to baking soda, a simple but effective leavening used in quick breads—and familiar also as sodium bicarbonate, an old-fashioned indigestion remedy. The trick here is that soda bread is made with buttermilk. When you make a dough that combines buttermilk (or any other acidic liquid, such as yogurt) and baking soda, bubbles of carbon dioxide form and—presto!— the dough rises. Irish soda bread, a tender-crumbed, unsweetened round loaf—often studded with raisins—is one of the most popular forms of this quick bread.

SOURDOUGH BREAD. Sourdough is made using one of two kinds of "starters": a *sponge*, a yeast-and-flour mixture often kept going for years, which is added to each new batch of bread dough, or a chunk of unbaked dough from a previous batch, which is incorporated into a new batch. In both cases the older starter yeast and its slightly sour taste (from the earliest fermentation of the ingredients) is passed along to grow in the new dough. Sourdough is associated with San Francisco, where it has been a mainstay of local cuisine since the California Gold Rush of the mid-1800s.

THE TOPIC
OF CANCER

Quick quiz: What's the most insidious disease known to humanity? You probably said "cancer." BRI writer Thom Little thought we all ought to know a little bit more about the enemy, so he came up with this basic introduction to shed a little light on an otherwise dark subject...and provide a little light at the end of the tunnel.

OFF THE RADAR

Can lizards get cancer? Can bananas? Do you even know what cancer is? Or where it came from? Odds are you can't answer those questions—most people can't. Cancer is a frightening subject, so much so that its common nickname is the "Big C"—people don't even want to speak its name. And our fear, say experts at the American Cancer Society, is a problem in itself: The more people know about cancer, the more they can do to prevent it, or detect it early if they do get it. And the more they can do to help increase public awareness and funding toward finding treatments and cures.

So what is cancer? Well, to begin with, it isn't just one disease. It's the name used for more than 200 different diseases that have one basic thing in common: cells with damaged, or *mutated*, DNA. Those damaged cells lose their ability to regulate their division process—and lose their ability to die naturally—which results in their multiplying uncontrollably. It's really that simple...and it's really, really complicated. But let's start at the beginning, or at least close to it.

THE HISTORY OF CANCER

Nobody can say for sure how long cancer has been around, but most researchers believe it goes back nearly as far as multicellular life itself—about 700 million years. The oldest examples of cancer are actually found in dinosaur fossils: The Carnegie Museum in Pittsburgh, for example, has a 150-million-year-old dinosaur bone with the remnants of a tumor preserved in it. The oldest evidence of cancer in a primate is a tumor in the bones of a four-million-

---

Lemons contain more sugar than strawberries do.

year-old specimen of *Australopithecus*, a long-extinct hominid closely related to humans, found by famed archaeologist Louis Leakey in 1932.

The earliest writings on the subject go back to *the* earliest known writings on medicine: several Egyptian papyri from the 16th century B.C. which describe different types of tumors along with treatments such as cauterization (burning or searing with a heated tool) and surgery.

Much of today's cancer terminology, including the word "cancer" itself, can be attributed to the Greek philosopher and scientist Hippocrates, who lived from 460 to 370 B.C. Hippocrates called benign (noncancerous) tumors *oncos*, which meant "swelling," giving us the root of today's *oncology*—the study of cancer. Malignant tumors he called *carcinos*, or "crab," which was later translated into Latin as *cancer*. It's believed he gave it that name because of the crablike appearance of tumors, which often have roundish, compact centers with radiating "arms" of blood vessels. Hippocrates believed that cancer was caused by an imbalance of the *humors*, the body's "four basic fluids" that were the basis of medicine at the time and for centuries afterward. In this case the imbalance was "excessive black bile," which in Greek was *melancholia*—from *melas* (black) and *kholé* (bile). Based on Hippocrates's mistaken theories, the prevailing theory in Western medicine for the next 2,000 years or so would be that cancer was caused by "melancholy"—what we now call depression.

IN THE DARK

From the start, and for most of recorded history, cancer treatments were almost completely ineffective. Doctors recognized the disease but didn't know enough about how it worked to do anything about it. Some of the more exotic, but usually unsuccessful, treatments employed through the centuries: ointments and oils, bloodletting, magic potions, arsenic pastes, magic spells, and prayers. In the 1500s, medical science in general began to improve noticeably. Scientific thinking, as opposed to superstition, was becoming more accepted; autopsies, long unthinkable for religious reasons, began to be performed in Europe on a regular basis; and in the early 1600s, the microscope was invented—cells, which lie at the heart of all cancers, could be seen for the first time. Some of the most important cancer research break-throughs since then:

• In 1775 British doctor Percival Pott noticed a high rate of scrotal cancer among chimney sweeps. He attributed it to the fact that their occupations (and their poor hygiene), led them to develop permanent deposits of soot in that seldom-inspected part of the body. The discovery made Potts the first person in history to identify a *carcinogen*, or a substance that causes cancer. It would lead to the discovery of scores more over the next century.

• In the 1800s, the microscope was greatly improved and its use became widespread. For the first time it was observed that cancer cells looked different than the cells around them.

• In 1858 German scientist Rudolf Virchow, now considered the "father of cellular pathology," came up with one of the most important theories in the history of cell biology: *Omnis cellula e cellula*, or "Every cell originates from another like it." He theorized, correctly, that all living tissue comes about via cell division rather than by "spontaneous generation," as had long been believed.

• In 1953 British doctors James Watson and Francis Crick ushered in the modern era of cancer research when they became the first to describe the structure of *deoxyribonucleic acid*, or DNA. The science of genetics, which we now know is crucial to the understanding of cancer (and of many other diseases as well), was born.

CORE BREACH

One of the things that makes cancer so insidious is its connection to cell division, a biological process essential to life. All living things, from single-cell amoebas to humans, come into being through cell division. Each and every one of us starts from a single cell: an egg cell from your mother that's been fertilized by sperm from your father. That single cell splits into 2 cells, they split into 4 cells, then 8, 16, 32—some becoming eye cells, some bone cells, some muscle cells, kidney cells, and on and on to the trillions of cells that make up a person. And it's still happening: Your body creates in the neighborhood of 300 million new cells every *minute*.

That process of cell division is something that all human cells do, and they do it in a controlled, orderly fashion. Different types of cells do it at different rates, and some even stop replication

---

Roughly half the world's newspapers are published in North America.

completely: Skin cells, for example, continue to divide and multiply almost constantly throughout our lives, while nerve cells almost never divide once we reach adulthood.

Most of our cells divide through a process called *mitosis*. Only our sex cells—males' sperm and females' eggs—divide differently, through a process known as *meiosis*. In both cases, division is regulated by what is known as the *cell cycle control system*. Cancer, simply put, is the breakdown of that system.

DIVISIONS

Biology teachers often compare the *cell cycle control system* to a timer on a washing machine. That's because cells have different cycles they must go through in order to complete their division processes. Washers have to fill up with water, agitate the clothes, drain out the water, rinse, and spin. The human cell-division cycle has four main phases that take between 12 and 24 hours to complete, depending on the type of cell.

The G1 (gap 1) phase: The cell increases in size, preparing for the duplication process.

The S (synthesis) phase: The cell's DNA is *synthesized*, or duplicated. At the end of this phase there will be two exact sets of DNA waiting to go to the two new cells.

The G2 (gap 2) phase: The cell increases in size again in preparation for the actual division (the two new cells will be roughly the same size as the original).

The M (mitotic) phase: Two new nuclei, or cell centers, are formed, each containing one of the DNA sets. The cell is then seemingly "pinched," and it divides into two separate—and genetically exact—*daughter* cells.

Just like with a washing machine, the cycles have to occur in the right order, and each step must be completed before the next begins. The control system is monitored by proteins that act as sensors, messengers, repairmen, and, if something goes wrong, cell killers.

BIG C & THE PROTEINS

The proteins that monitor cell division (and *all* proteins) are made inside cells by our genes. That's what genes do, and it's how they complete that seemingly magical task of making us from bits of Mom and Dad. Here are some gene basics to help you understand how they— and the proteins they make—are related to cancer:

• In its nucleus, every human cell contains 46 chromosomes arranged in 23 pairs. One of each pair comes from your mom, and one of each pair comes from your dad. (Sex cells, sperm and eggs, are different—each has 23 *single* chromosomes, which join up during fertilization.)

• Each chromosome pair is one long single molecule of DNA, which you've probably seen represented in its "double-helix" form: the long, "twisted-ladder" shape.

• Genes are simply sections of those chromosome molecules—the rungs on the ladder, so to speak. There are about 45,000 different genes in the human genome, and each one is structurally unique from all the others.

GAZILLION-COURSE MEALS

Every gene has, by nature of its unique chemical structure, biochemical instructions for making unique proteins. That's basically because genes make copies of themselves to make those proteins. Each protein has a specific job in the construction and then the maintenance of your body.

Think of your genes as recipes: Our complete package of DNA, known as our *genome*, is like a cookbook, and our genes are recipes in the book, the difference being that the final product isn't food—it's *you*. Examples: *Tyrosinase* is a protein that affects your hair and eye color, and it's produced by one specific gene. *Type II collagen* is a protein that helps produce your body's cartilage, and it's made by another specific gene. *P53* is a protein that stops cells from dividing if their DNA is damaged, and it's made by yet another gene.

Here's the kicker in regard to cancer: If a gene is malfunctioning, it can produce malfunctioning proteins, and that can lead to genetic disease. If the gene that produces *tyrosinase* is damaged, the result can be the milky skin and eyes of *albinism*. If the gene that produces *type II collagen* is damaged, the result can be

Q: What's a *piddlin*? A: A baby beluga whale.

dwarfism. If the gene that produces p53 is damaged—the result can be cancer. How significant is p53 to cancer researchers today? In more than 50% of all human cancers, the gene that produces the p53 protein—known as the p53 gene—is damaged.

THE GUARDIAN

P53 is just one of many genes now known to be related to cancer, and it is one of the most studied over the last 10 years. (It has been nicknamed the "Guardian of the Genome," and in 2000 the journal *Science* even named it the "Molecule of the Year.")

Every single cell in your body has the p53 gene (it's on chromosome 17 if you're planning on looking for it). Through its chemical wizardry, if the p53 gene senses damaged DNA in a dividing cell, it creates the p53 protein, which temporarily stops division from continuing. If the damage can't be repaired, p53 biochemically instructs the cell to perform *apoptosis*—programmed cell death. It actually instructs the cell to kill itself.

DANGER! DANGER! CELL DIVISION!

So imagine a cell with badly damaged DNA—including damaged p53—going through cell division. It goes into the G1 phase, grows to its appropriate size, and is then supposed to be checked by p53 for DNA damage. But the p53 isn't working, so the mutated cell goes on to the S phase and replicates the bad DNA. Then it goes to G2, where it grows again, and is supposed to be checked again by p53. But it isn't, and it goes on to divide into two new cells—exact copies of the original damaged cell. They divide into 4 damaged cells, then 8 cells, 16 cells, a million cells, and, finally, a tumor. And they all came from one single damaged cell. P53 is classified as a *tumor suppressor gene*, just one of three known types of "cancer genes." (The other two are *DNA repair genes* and *proto-oncogenes*.) Any one of them, if it becomes mutated, can produce cancer cells.

THE DAMAGE DONE

What exactly does it mean for a gene to be mutated, and how does it happen in the first place? A mutation in a gene simply means that its biochemical structure has been altered. Picture the "twisted ladder" of DNA mentioned earlier, of which a gene is a part. Break one rung, and you've just mutated the ladder. Or remove a rung and put it back in the wrong spot. Again, mutated. There are many ways that this can happen, only a few of which we know about. Here are a few that we do know:

Inheritance. If your parents had a mutated gene, you will have a mutation of that same gene in every single cell of your body (on the "mom" half, the "dad" half, or both, depending on who had the mutation). This could lead to an inherited genetic disease like cystic fibrosis or hemophilia. Cancer, on the other hand, is almost always the result of gene mutations that occur *later in life*. But some cancers, or at least susceptibility to them, are known to be the result of inherited gene mutations. These include some breast, ovarian, prostate, and stomach cancers.

Exposure to ultraviolet (UV) radiation from sunlight or artificial lamps. UV is part of the light spectrum that we cannot see, and it's the part that causes tanning, sunburn, and the aging effect on skin. It can also cause skin cancer. That's because the size of UV's wavelength allows it to penetrate skin cells (whereas visible light mostly just reflects off our skin) and change the structure of the genes inside. One of the genes *known* to be affected by exposure to UV radiation: p53.

Smoking. Tobacco smoke contains more than 40 carcinogenic agents. One of them, *benzo(a)pyrene* (also found in burnt toast and charred meat), biochemically interacts with DNA, changing its structure. Among the many genes it is known to alter: p53. Smoking is linked to 13 different cancers, including lung, stomach, and colon cancer.

Asbestos. *Mesothelioma* is a cancer that affects the protective tissue that covers most of our organs. It usually begins in the lining of the lungs, when asbestos fibers are inhaled. Exactly how it happens is unknown, but it is believed that asbestos fibers are so tiny that they can enter cells and actually do physical damage to genes, resulting in mutations that lead to this cancer.

Viruses. Viruses are so small that they can enter cells and interact with genes (it's how all viruses work, even the ones that cause the common cold). Some are known to cause mutations that can lead to cancer. Some kinds of HPV—*human papillomavirus*—for example, can lead to cervical cancer in women by interacting with cervical cells and damaging their DNA.

What city calls itself the "Polar Bear Capital of the World"? Churchill, Manitoba.

SERIAL KILLER

Don't freak out: One little gene mutation doesn't necessarily lead to cancer. Mutations happen all the time in our bodies, usually with no ill effects. Several factors must come together in order for a cancer to develop, and that actually makes it an unlikely event. For cancer—any cancer—to occur, cells must go through an unlucky *series* of mutations.

A cell might first be damaged, say by UV light, on a tumor suppressor gene, which would allow the damaged cell to divide. Several divisions later, one of those cells, during *its* division process, might acquire another mutation, say to a DNA repair gene. Normally it would be stopped from dividing—but it already has a bad p53 gene…so it goes on. Later a proto-oncogene might be mutated, turning it into an oncogene, spurring the cell on the path to becoming cancerous again. This process usually takes a long time, sometimes many years, and may never lead to full-blown cancer anyway. But in other cases, the road to cancer can be much quicker.

GRADES AND STAGES

Cancer progression is measured in two main ways: by *stage* and by *grade*. Stages, measured from I to IV (IV being the worst), reflect the physical presence of cancer in the body: how big the tumor is, whether it has spread to surrounding tissue or to other parts of the body, and so forth.

Grades are more involved: A biopsy of a tumor is taken and the cells are viewed under a microscope to determine their level of *differentiation*. This refers to how different the mutated cells are from the cells of origin (skin cells, in the case of skin cancer). Cells are graded from 1 to 4.

Grade 1: Well-differentiated (they look like the original cells)

Grade 2: Moderately well-differentiated

Grade 3: Poorly differentiated

Grade 4: Undifferentiated (they don't look anything like the original cells)

Some tumors stay in grade 1. These are *benign* tumors—they hardly grow at all and are not usually considered a threat (depending

---

Makes sense? The *offishal* state fish of Nevada is the Cutthroat Trout.

on their location). When you get to grades 3 and 4, the cells look nothing like the cells they originated from. These are *malignant*, or cancerous, cells. They don't have a uniform shape—they're just blobs, due to the fact that once they reach these stages they are dividing rapidly, before they can mature. Cancers at grade 4 are very aggressive and bring the worst prognoses. And they're often up to other bad things as well.

ON THE ROAD

When a collection of cancerous cells grows to just the size of a tiny BB, the cells at the center of it begin to die. They need what all cells need—nutrients from blood. In yet another insidious trick that our bodies can play on themselves, cancer cells are able to instruct the cells around them to build blood vessels. This is known as *pathological angiogenesis*. Oxygen-starved cancer cells, like those in a tumor, release molecules that attract our *endothelial cells*—the kind that form blood vessels. This results in blood vessels being constructed that go directly into the tumor. Now it can *really* grow.

This ability of tumors to create their own blood supply is another new area of cancer research. *Anti-angiogenic agents*, which inhibit tumors from getting blood vessels built for them, are often part of cancer treatment today.

The new network of blood vessels gives cancer yet another tool in its toolbox of horrors: It can now *metastasize*, or travel to other parts of the body. Just one single malignant cell traveling through a blood vessel from the original site, known as the *primary tumor*, can end up in another part of the body, where it will continue dividing and form a *metastatic tumor*. Different types of cancer tend to spread to certain other parts of the body—for example, lung cancer to the brain, and prostate cancer to the bones—but they can spread unpredictably as well. This makes metastatic cancers very hard to stop, and it's why early detection is so important in treatment.

THE FIVE MAIN TYPES OF CANCER

Cancers are generally named for their point of origin: skin, stomach, breast, lung, and so on. But whatever the origin, they all fall into five main categories:

Camel's milk has 10 times more iron than cow's milk does.

Carcinomas: These are cancers of the body's *epithelial cells*, the cells that line our bodies' organs, such as the skin and the lining of the intestines. The most common carcinomas are lung, breast, and bowel cancer. Carcinomas make up about 85% of all cancers.

Sarcomas: Sarcomas begin in supportive tissues of the body, such as muscle, bone, cartilage, fat, and other connective tissue. There are about 70 different varieties.

Leukemias: These are cancers of the bone marrow, the spongy substance inside bones that produces blood cells. The most common type sees the marrow producing many cancerous and immature white blood cells. Hence the name: *leukemia*, Greek for "white blood."

Lymphomas: These develop in the lymphatic system, which, as part of our immune system, carries lymph fluid and white blood cells throughout the body.

Adenomas: Adenomas are tumors that begin in glandular tissue, such as in the pituitary or thyroid gland. They're usually benign, but can be dangerous because of their effect on these important glands and the areas around them.

MODERN TREATMENT

Currently, cancer is treated in three main ways: surgery, chemotherapy, and radiation.

• **Surgery:** This, as we mentioned earlier, is actually an ancient treatment, but doctors do it much better now. Surgery works best when the cancer is contained, because leaving a single cancerous cell behind can result in another tumor. It is most often used in combination with chemotherapy and radiation.

• **Chemotherapy:** "Chemo" was first used in the 1940s. It involves using chemical substances designed to kill, halt the division process of, and/or inhibit blood supply to cancer cells. It may include side effects such as hair loss, nausea, and vomiting, but they're less severe with modern chemotherapy drugs, and the treatment of the side effects themselves has greatly improved.

• **Radiation:** This technique was first used in 1896 by Chicagoan Emil Grubbe, who treated two breast cancer patients with X-rays.

The results were negligible. But the technology has improved, and today more than 50% of all cancer patients receive radiotherapy. For some it is the only treatment they need. It involves sending high-energy radiation directly into malignant tumors to kill targeted cells. But it doesn't always involve a machine: Today radioactive pellets or capsules are often inserted directly into tumors, allowing them to kill the cancer cells from the inside out.

THE FUTURE

Nobody needs to be told that cancer is still a major problem: More than 500,000 people in the United States alone are killed by cancer-related diseases every year, making it the second-leading cause of death (after heart disease). But immense progress has been made in prevention and treatment, and today people with the disease are living much longer than was previously possible: Since 1975 mortality rates of childhood cancers have declined by more than 50%, and in 2005 (the latest year with available numbers), the number of cancer deaths per year in the United States declined for the first time since 1930. Thousands of clinical trials are constantly ongoing worldwide, with many of the experiments geared toward the field of gene therapy. Some of the work in that area, according to the National Cancer Institute: replacing missing genes or mutated genes in cancer cells with healthy genes, inserting genes into cancer cells that make them more sensitive to chemotherapy or radiation, and inserting "suicide genes" into the cells. One of the reasons gene therapy is so attractive to those studying it is that if it works out the way many researchers believe it may, it could be much more effective than chemotherapy and radiation—with none of their unpleasant side effects. One day it may even replace them altogether.

In July 2007, researchers at Penn State College of Medicine in Pennsylvania announced that a common virus, one that 80% of people carry in their bodies, was found to kill cancer cells. *Adeno-associated virus type 2*, or AAV-2, has no known ill effects on humans, but it "recognizes that the cancer cells are abnormal and destroys them," said Professor Craig Meyers. The virus is currently under intense study, and could be another possible "side-effect-free" cancer treatment.

EXTRAS

• Answers to the questions on page 577: Yes, lizards can get cancer—all animals can. Bananas and all plants can contract a condition similar to cancer, caused by viruses and bacteria that genetically alter plant cells and cause uncontrolled cell division. You may have seen this as *galls*—tumorlike growths on trees. They are rarely fatal, largely because plants lack a circulatory system, so their "cancers" can't metastasize.

• Scary fact: Some people have gotten cancer via organ transplant. Tiny tumors in the donor organs have gone undetected and continued to grow in the organ recipient. Fortunately, it is very rare.

• Thank goodness cancer isn't contagious. Oh, wait. Yes, it is. In 2006 scientists in London proved that tumor cells from *Sticker's sarcoma*, a cancer found only in dogs, could be passed from one dog to another during sex or by dogs simply licking or biting one another. Not only that: They studied sick dogs from five different continents and found that their cancers all came from a single dog, probably Asian, that lived hundreds of years ago, and whose cancer has since spread around the world. (Stricker's sarcoma is not usually fatal.)

• In 1950 a woman named Henrietta Lacks was diagnosed with cervical cancer. A biopsy was taken and the cells put in a tissue culture to be studied. Normal human cells put into cultures die after about 50 divisions, but, as we all now know, cancer cells just keep dividing. Henrietta Lacks died in 1951, but her cells are still dividing today—and they are still being studied in labs all over the world.

• The Pap smear, invented by Greek cell biologist George Papanicolaou, was the first early cancer detection test ever developed. Since its public introduction in 1939, it has reduced the death rate of women with cervical cancer by 75%. Literally millions of lives have been saved by the test.

• Other tests, like the PSA (prostate-specific antigen) test that the American Cancer Society recommends for men, have similarly saved lives, and new tests for "cancer markers," some of which may be able to detect cancer when it's only a few cells old, are currently in development.

• Cancer experts stress the importance of early detection. Craig

King, a 25-year-old in Orangeburg, South Carolina, who developed cancer when he was 17, agrees. That's why he didn't hold back on his experience in the third-grade class he teaches. "I let my students know I had cancer," he told the American Cancer Society's news center in 2007. "It's so important for young people to know about the symptoms and what to look for," he said. "I hope none of them experience it, but if it happens, they can look back and say, 'Mr. King did it and I can, too.'"

• In 2003 National Cancer Institute Director Andrew von Eschenbach announced a "Challenge to the Nation" and to cancer researchers all over the world: the "elimination of suffering and death from cancer by 2015." Let's hope we achieve it.

*   *   *

ACCIDENT REPORTS

After a car accident, the police require each party to fill out a report. Here are real excerpts from "Please describe what happened" sections.

"Coming home, I drove into the wrong house and collided with a tree I don't know."

"I had been driving my car for 40 years when I fell asleep at the wheel and had an accident."

"In an attempt to kill a fly, I drove into a telephone pole."

"An invisible car came out of nowhere, struck my vehicle, and vanished."

"The pedestrian had no idea which direction to go, so I ran over him."

"The guy was all over the road. I had to swerve a number of times before I hit him."

"I collided with a stationary truck coming the other way."

"My girlfriend kissed me. I lost control and woke up in the hospital."

"The indirect cause of this accident was a little guy in a small car with a big mouth."

Most-watched series finale of a TV drama: *Magnum, P.I.* in 1988.

HONORING THE TOILET

Now we conclude our 20th Anniversary Edition with our continuing quest to explore the complex relationship between humanity and its smallest room.

THE BATHROOM & THE NATURE OF YOUTH

"A new father quickly learns that his child invariably comes to the bathroom at precisely the times when the father's in there, as if he needed company."

—Bill Cosby

"When a child is locked in the bathroom with water running and he says he's doing nothing but the dog is barking, call 911."

—Erma Bombeck

"A child can go only so far in life without potty training. It is not mere coincidence that six of the last seven presidents were potty trained, not to mention nearly half of the nation's state legislators."

—Dave Barry

THE BATHROOM & THE BATTLE OF THE SEXES

"Men who consistently leave the toilet seat up secretly want women to get up to go the bathroom in the middle of the night and fall in."

—Rita Rudner

"How many times do you get away with this—to take a woman, grab her upside down, and bury her face in a toilet bowl? The thing is, you can do it, because I didn't do it to a woman—she's a machine! We could get away with it without being crucified by who-knows-what group."

—Arnold Schwarzenegger, on a scene in *Terminator 3*

"It is better to have a relationship with someone who cheats on you than with someone who does not flush the toilet."

—Uma Thurman

THE BATHROOM KEEPS LIFE IN PERSPECTIVE

"I'd rather be able to face myself in the bathroom mirror than be rich and famous."

—Ani DiFranco

Interviewer: Do you ever wake up in the middle of the night and find yourself amazed at what you've accomplished?

Tiger Woods: Usually when I wake up in the middle of the night, it's to do something else.

First basketball player to enter the NBA directly from high school: Moses Malone, 1974.

"I am sad because my people are in bondage. If I drink water I will have to go to the bathroom and how can I use the bathroom when my people are in bondage?"

—Saddam Hussein, to U.S. interrogators

THE BATHROOM AS A METAPHOR

"I don't want to abolish government. I simply want to reduce it to the size where I can drag it into the bathroom and drown it in the bathtub."

—Grover Norquist

"Acting is invigorating. But I don't analyze it too much. It's like a dog smelling where it's going to do its toilet in the morning."

—Liam Neeson

THE BATHROOM & COMIC RELIEF

"My roommate says, 'I'm going to take a shower and shave. Does anyone need to use the bathroom?' It's like some weird quiz in which he reveals the answer first."

—Mitch Hedberg

"You know what's an odd feeling? Sitting on the toilet eating a chocolate candy bar."

— George Carlin

THE BATHROOM & THE NATURE OF OUR STRANGE UNIVERSE

"How long a minute is depends on which side of the bathroom door you're on."

—Zall's Second Law

"Anything dropped in the bathroom falls in the toilet."

—Flucard's Corollary

"What if humans are just the pet alligators that God flushed down the toilet?"

—Chuck Palahniuk

THE BATHROOM: MORE THAN JUST A ROOM

"Today, the degradation of the inner life is symbolized by the fact that the only place sacred from interruption is the private toilet."

—Lewis Mumford

"Psychiatry's chief contribution to philosophy is the discovery that the toilet is the seat of the soul."

—Alexander Chase

"We have had women's liberation, the sexual revolution, the workers' revolution... the toilet is the last taboo which must be broken. We can finally talk about it now."

—Jack Sim, founder of the World Toilet Organization

1960s comic book hero (and villain): Eclipso, the "Genius Who Fought Himself."

ANSWER PAGES

AUNT LENNA THE GREAT
(Answers for page 105)

Seeing is Believing: Aunt Lenna has been shooting craps since the Eisenhower administration, and she's known for a long time that the opposite sides of a die always add up to seven. That gives her two ways to figure out the dice on the bottom: She can figure out herself that on the opposite side of the four, the two, and the five she sees on top of the dice are a three, a five, and a two, and then add them up to get 10. Or she can subtract the four, the two, and the five from 21 to get 10.

Dead To Rights: Aunt Lenna knew that the top third of the paper had one smooth edge (the top of the sheet of paper) and one rough edge where she made the tear. The bottom piece of paper had one smooth edge (the bottom of the sheet of paper) and one rough edge where it was torn, just like the top piece of paper. But the middle piece of paper had *two* rough edges, because it was torn on the top *and* the bottom. Aunt Lenna had me write the name of the dead person on the middle piece of paper—and then when she reached into the hat, she just felt around until she found the piece of paper with the two rough edges.

Ring Cycle: When she went to get her jewelry box, Aunt Lenna actually came back with two identical yellow bracelets—the one she showed me and one she was already wearing (she had it over her forearm and hidden up her sleeve). As soon as she had her back turned, she slipped the free bracelet into a pocket and slid the one up her sleeve down over the scarf.

"MADMAN" NEWMAN'S BRAINTEASERS
(Answers for page 170)

1. RAPID AGING?
Today is January 1; Johnny's birthday is on December 31. The day before yesterday, he was 9, yesterday he turned 10, this year he'll turn 11, and *next* year he'll turn 12.

2. TIME AFTER TIME
Amy gave Brian a watch.

3. A BAD FLIGHT PLAN
By telling Uncle John about

his dream, the watchman unwittingly admitted that he'd been sleeping on the job.

4. STORMY WEATHER

The four men were pallbearers carrying a body in a coffin.

5. A CLOWN-UNDRUM

Plungy juggled the bricks while walking across the bridge, keeping one in the air at all times.

6. PUZZLING BUS TRIP

They are all married.

7. COUNT DUCKULA

Julia has seven ducks; Viola has five.

8. MARITIME QUERY

Because of the curvature of the Earth, the mast, which is located at top of the sailboat, actually traveled the farthest.

9. BRIGHT THINKING

Thom waited until nighttime and then left through the magnifying-glass room.

10. RELATIVITY

Four—two adults and two children. The two adults are brother and sister, and each of them has one of their children with them, making them mother and father as well. They are also aunt and uncle to the two children (a boy and a girl), who are the cousins, as well as the nephew and niece to each of two the adults.

11. AND THEY'RE OFF!

Because the horse (not the rider) that finished last would win the race, Uncle John told Malcolm and Jahnna to get back up on *each other's* horses.

TEST YOUR MOVIE I.Q.
(Answers for page 257)

1. Oliver (Oliver Hardy), *Sons of the Desert* (1933)

2. Carl Denham (Robert Armstrong), *King Kong* (1933)

3. Mr. McGuire (Walter Brooke), *The Graduate* (1967)

4. Norma Desmond (Gloria Swanson), *Sunset Boulevard* (1950)

5. Travis Bickle (Robert De Niro), *Taxi Driver* (1976)

6. Howard Beale (Peter Finch), *Network* (1976)

7. Loretta Castorini (Cher), *Moonstruck* (1987)

8. Marie "Slim" Browning (Lauren Bacall), *To Have and Have Not* (1944)

9. Clyde Barrow (Warren Beatty), *Bonnie and Clyde* (1967)

There are 92 known cases of nuclear bombs being lost at sea.

10. Arthur "Cody" Jarrett (James Cagney), *White Heat* (1949)

11. Customer (Estelle Reiner), *When Harry Met Sally...* (1989)

12. Carol Anne Freeling (Heather O'Rourke), *Poltergeist* (1982)

13. President Merkin Muffley (Peter Sellers), *Dr. Strangelove* (1964)

14. Cole Sear (Haley Joel Osment), *The Sixth Sense* (1999)

15. Martin Brody (Roy Scheider), *Jaws* (1975)

16. Ted Striker (Robert Hays) and Dr. Rumack (Leslie Nielsen), *Airplane!* (1980)

17. George Taylor (Charlton Heston), *Planet of the Apes* (1968)

18. Jack Dawson (Leonardo DiCaprio), *Titanic* (1997)

19. Margo Channing (Bette Davis), *All About Eve* (1950)

20. Colonel Nathan Jessep (Jack Nicholson), *A Few Good Men* (1992)

21. Carl Spackler (Bill Murray), *Caddyshack* (1980)

22. Norman Bates (Anthony Perkins), *Psycho* (1960)

23. Lt. Colonel Bill Kilgore (Robert Duvall), *Apocalypse Now* (1979)

24. Joan Crawford (Faye Dunaway), *Mommie Dearest* (1981)

25. Jimmy Dugan (Tom Hanks), *A League of Their Own* (1992)

26. Captain (Strother Martin), *Cool Hand Luke* (1967)

27. Johnny Castle (Patrick Swayze), *Dirty Dancing* (1987)

28. Rod Tidwell (Cuba Gooding Jr.), *Jerry Maguire* (1996)

29. Oliver Barrett IV (Ryan O'Neal), *Love Story* (1970)

30. Gordon Gekko (Michael Douglas), *Wall Street* (1987)

31. Wicked Witch of the West (Margaret Hamilton), *The Wizard of Oz* (1939)

32. Henry Frankenstein (Colin Clive), *Frankenstein* (1931)

33. Caesar Enrico "Rico" Bandello (Edward G. Robinson), *Little Caesar* (1931)

34. Captain Jeffrey T. Spaulding (Groucho Marx), *Animal Crackers* (1930)

35. Michael Corleone (Al Pacino), *The Godfather: Part II* (1974)

36. John Keating (Robin Williams), *Dead Poets Society* (1989)

37. Count Dracula (Bela Lugosi), *Dracula* (1931)

38. "Ratso" Rizzo (Dustin Hoffman), *Midnight Cowboy* (1969)

39. Scarlett O'Hara (Vivien Leigh), *Gone With the Wind* (1939)

40. Jakie Rabinowitz/Jack Robin (Al Jolson), *The Jazz Singer* (1927)

THE VOTER'S "LITERACY" TEST
(Answers for page 324)

1. c) Trial by jury
2. False (every 10 years)
3. Habeas corpus (immediate presentation of charges); a lawyer; a speedy trial
4. January 3
5. Six
6. Yes
7. "Affirm"
8. "In God We Trust"
9. False
10. Federal
11. Two
12. House of Representatives
13. Criminal
14. Virginia
15. Congress
16. Congress; state legislatures
17. True
18. The Supreme Court
19. The Senate
20. 10 miles square
21. Coin money; make treaties
22. Nine
23. The vice president, until the House acts
24. The Constitution
25. From the Preamble: "to form a more perfect union, establish justice, insure domestic tranquility, provide for the common defense, promote the general welfare, and secure the blessings of liberty to ourselves and our posterity."
26. The chief justice of the Supreme Court
27. The governor of that state
28. The president
29. a) The U.S. Congress
30. The states; the people

AUNT LENNA THE MAGNIFICENT
(Answers for page 341)

Time Out: When Aunt Lenna started tapping on the numbers of the clock, she was keeping count, too. She picked the first seven numbers at random, but she made sure that the eighth number she tapped was 12:00. From there she counted down the hours in order: 11:00, 10:00, 9:00, 8:00, and so on. That way, no matter what hour

---

Takin' care of business: Elvis Presley collected police badges in nearly every city he performed in.

I picked, when I counted up to 20, Aunt Lenna's pencil would be pointing to it. Don't believe it? Try it and you'll see that it works.

The Numbers Racket: When I added 115 to 624, the total was 739. Aunt Lenna remembered the following formula from her college days (she was a math major): She knew that if I followed it to the letter, the last two digits of my answer would reveal my age (39), and the first digit (or first two digits) would reveal the month of my birth: the seventh month, July. (Aunt Lenna also knows that the formula doesn't work for people over 100 years of age—which is why she never tries this stunt in retirement homes.)

Making Her Point: Could you tell that Uncle Gideon was an accomplice in this trick? (He's not a psychic.) He and Aunt Lenna have pulled this stunt before, and they've agreed that every time they do it, Aunt Lenna will point to a black object—in this case, the piano—just before she points to the object that has been chosen. All Lenna has to remember to do is not to point to any black objects until she's ready.

TAKE THE POLITICALLY CORRECT QUIZ
(Answers for page 389)

1. b) The Belgian Ministry of Health took the action after receiving complaints from parents. Most Scout groups complied with the order, but at last report at least one of them was still slaughtering chickens. "These kids have to be taught how to kill an animal in order to feed themselves," one Scout leader told the ministry.

2. c) The spokesperson for the Adult Entertainment Industry worried that sending the sex workers and their clients out into the street to smoke might cause problems. "Having them standing outside, dressed in clothes not conventional for the street, would be a magnet for violent, anti-social behavior," the spokesperson told reporters.

3. c) The library claims that age has nothing to do with it—the senior citizens were let go because the "physical and intellectual" demands of the job increased after Air Force One was added to the exhibits and the library doubled in size. But the ex-volunteers aren't buying it. "As we went along, we figured out that all of us were over 70 or had gray hair," one of them told reporters. "Believe it or not, you can walk and talk in your 70s, as Mr. Reagan did."

4. b) Heckrodt insists he isn't being unfair to overweight people. "First of all, there's the upper limit on price," he explains. "And besides that, I don't force anyone onto the scale." Customers have fun with the promotion and some of them even strip down to their underwear to save money. He got the idea after a regular customer lost 77 lb. and joked that she wanted a discount on her room. "It seemed like a reasonable demand," he says.

5. b) "It's easy to think of fish as swimming vegetables," says PETA's Karin Robinson, "but if there's any place in the country where fish should get a fair shake it's an aquarium." Jerry Schubel, the aquarium's president, says all fish served in the cafeteria are caught using "sustainable and environmentally friendly" practices.

6. a) "The potato industry is fed up with the disservice that 'couch potato' does to our product when we have an inherently healthy product," a spokesperson told reporters. ("Couch potato" is still in the dictionary.)

7. b) The court struck down the ban on "any kind of communication that could be interpreted as sexual" as being too broad to comply with German labor law.

WHAT AM I?
(Answers for page 465)

1. ARE, AREA	5. The number 8	ILL
2. A volcano	6. A nail in a	8. Dust
3. A fan	horseshoe	9. Wine
4. A table	7. SKILL, KILL,	10. A seesaw

NAME THAT HEIRESS
(Answer for page 572)

Julia Louis-Dreyfus. Her father, Gerard (or "William") Louis-Dreyfus, runs the family business, the Louis-Dreyfus Group, a "diversified commodities, shipping, real estate, manufacturing, and communications conglomerate." (Her *Goodbye Girl* cousin is Richard Dreyfuss.) Julia dropped out of Northwestern University in 1982 when she was invited to join the cast of *Saturday Night Live*, where she appeared for three years. She was then in two short-lived sitcoms before being cast as "Elaine Benes" in one of the most successful sitcoms in history, *Seinfeld*, in 1990. In 2006 she got her own (very successful) show, *The New Adventures of Old Christine*.

UNCLE JOHN'S BATHROOM READER CLASSIC SERIES

Find these and other great titles from the *Uncle John's Bathroom Reader* Classic Series online at **www.bathroomreader.com**. Or contact us at:

Bathroom Readers' Institute
P.O. Box 1117
Ashland, OR 97520

Also available
from *Uncle John's
Bathroom Reader!*

THE LAST PAGE

FELLOW BATHROOM READERS:
The fight for good bathroom reading should never be taken loosely—we must do our duty and sit firmly for what we believe in, even while the rest of the world is taking potshots at us.

We'll be brief. Now that we've proven we're not simply a flush-in-the-pan, we invite you to take the plunge: Sit Down and Be Counted! Become a member of the Bathroom Readers' Institute. Log on to *www.bathroomreader.com*, or send a self-addressed, stamped, business-sized envelope to: BRI, PO Box 1117, Ashland, Oregon 97520. You'll receive your free membership card, get discounts when ordering directly through the BRI, and earn a permanent spot on the BRI honor roll!

If you like reading our books...
VISIT THE BRI'S WEB SITE!
www.bathroomreader.com

- Visit "The Throne Room"—a great place to read!
  - Receive our irregular newsletters via e-mail
    - Order additional *Bathroom Readers*
      - Become a BRI member

Go with the Flow...

Well, we're out of space, and when you've gotta go, you've gotta go. Tanks for all your support. Hope to hear from you soon. Meanwhile, remember...

Keep on flushin'!